I0210185

DOOMERISM

&

"Me first"

Baby Boomers

HOW ONE MISGUIDED GENERATION DESTABILIZED
OUR SOCIETY'S FOUNDATION
AND WHAT "WE THE [EVERYDAY] PEOPLE"
MUST DO ABOUT IT!

Doomerism & "Me first" Baby Boomers © 2021
Copyrighted by Jeffersonian Jeff

All rights reserved. No part of this publication may be reproduced, distributed, or transmitted in any form or by any means, including photocopying, recording, or other electronic or mechanical methods, without the prior written permission of the publisher, except in the case of brief quotations embodied in critical reviews and certain other noncommercial uses permitted by copyright law with proper citation attributions.

Although the author and publisher have made every effort to ensure that the information in this book was correct at press time, the author and publisher don't assume and hereby disclaim any liability to any party for any loss, damage, or disruption caused by errors or omissions, whether such errors or omissions result from negligence, accident, or any other cause.

Adherence to all applicable laws and regulations, including international, federal, state, and local governing professional licensing, business practices, advertising, and all other aspects of doing business in the US, Canada or any other jurisdiction is the sole responsibility of the reader and consumer.

Neither the author nor the publisher assumes any responsibility or liability whatsoever on behalf of the consumer or reader of this material. Any perceived slight of any individual or organization is purely unintentional.

The author wrote this book in his personal capacity. Ideas conveyed and opinions expressed in this book are his own unless where cited, and do not reflect an official view of any government. For more information, email Jeffersonianjeff@outlook.com

ISBN: 978-1-7357757-0-8 (digital)
ISBN: 978-1-7357757-1-5 (paperback)
ISBN: 978-1-7357757-2-2 (hardcover)

This is a **●Black Dot Books** Publication

Black Dot Books, LLC
P.O. Box 344
College Park, MD 20740

Hello! Thanks for looking into my book! To get the best experience, please check out my *Liberty Learning Resources* pamphlet. It will connect you to resources on liberty, virtue, democracy, and citizenship. These are our POWER TOOLS. They are being abandoned and getting damaged. We need to repair them with some critical thinking. With it, you will more quickly recognize when the BABY DOOMERS (power elite wannabe aristocracy) are LYING to you and feel competent in your assessments of "what's going on." With my book, you will be able to make sense of the nonsense on the evening news. This will prepare you for the necessary "next steps" we must take to defeat DOOMERISM. Get ready! Hold the POLITICIANS in our polity and the ELITES in our economy accountable. They SERVE US. We must help them BEHAVE as better CITIZENS. They cannot do it by themselves. We, the everyday people, work to make things amazing. We work together! We are the community that will make the USA a more perfect UNION with liberty and justice for all. In this book, I tell you how. For the sake of our liberty, please buy my book. Join me in this essential endeavor! Let's launch our country into a resurgence of honest-to-goodness citizenship. It will save our United States Enterprise from gloom and doom!

The year 2020 brought us CRISES. To press forward UNITEDLY, we must recreate neighborliness as a way of life. We can do this, one conversation at a time. We'll rebuild a more bonded, kind, and caring national community. It begins by us uniting to protect our liberty and democracy. We create. We can do this through a return to living by FIRST principles. We must rewrite our currently violated social contract. We are not now, but need to be, in accord with the ONE imagined by our CONSTITUTION (as amended), period—no ifs, ands, or buts. We are all born EQUAL! Egalitarian societies survive forever. Tyrannical ones die off. Let's commit to forever by reviving our democracy.

To sign up for my *Liberty Learning Resources* pamphlet go here: https://mailchi.mp/14792e36daf0/jeffersonianjeff-learning-liberty-resources-pamphlet. *(Alternatively, you could buy this book. It's in the appendix).* It has a bunch of great resources and a whole lot of COMMON SENSE!

Yours in the pursuit of Liberty,

JEFFERSONIAN JEFF

Check out my website: https://jeffersonianjeff.com/
Facebook: https://www.facebook.com/RealRocknRollPoetry
Twitter @RocknRoll_Poet: https://twitter.com/RocknRoll_Poet

BEFORE MATTERS

$P_{reamble}$

Join me in rediscovering the lost wisdom of the founders. They risked their lives to declare independence from the world's then-most-powerful kingdom. By great courage, with the help of the French, they pulled off an historical separation. They followed this spectacular feat by capturing into a constitution their revolutionary idea on how to frame a society. Novus ordo seclorum, a new order of the ages was born. A society for the everyday people, led by us, of us, and without need of an over lording ruler. Now, our self-government for, by, and of the people needs our courage and declaration of unity. Our radical constitutional concept has prospered through eight generations. As inheritors of this endowment, we must learn to live up to it and better exercise our responsibility to uphold it. If we fail in our vigilance to protect it, we'll lose it, and with it, our liberty. Let's not let that happen! Remember that the words of the first imagined seal of the United States were "Rebellion to Tyrants is Obedience to God."

Commit to the new order of the ages as a 21st-century patriot. Become to the utmost, a full-fledged thoroughgoing citizen exhibiting service above selfishness; saying yes! Dictate to those in authority that we, the everyday people, possess the rightful real power. Vote, vote, vote, and vote again! Keep voting until we convince our fellow citizens who seek to be our elected officials that we only want incorruptible officials. We only want honest brokers, those who can resist the temptation of absolute power and who oppose bribery by special interest groups. We only want officials who dissuade these groups that seek to exert undue influence upon their decision-making. We only want officials who will never forget that their job is to protect our liberty.

An over policed state is not liberty. An unsafe, insecure state is not liberty. Poverty is not liberty. Pollution is not liberty. Perversion is not liberty. Being perplexed in perpetuity is not liberty. Prostitution is not liberty. Perfectionism is not liberty. Paying for pensions with future generations' earnings is not liberty.

All persons in authority must come to understand the ideals of liberty and the proper and improper ways, means, and methods of power that affect it. They must improve the leadership, administration, and management of the business of our society (LAMBS). With improved knowledge, aptitude, acquisition, absorption, application, and skills advancement abilities (KA^{4}SA^2), we'll reinvigorate our project to establish a more perfect union. We must remix our powers to restore us to our former pole position as a positive force for this planet's inhabitants. We must lean forward into a risky, uncertain future and equip our population for the rough-and-tumble rapids ride ahead.

Exhibiting service above selfishness; saying yes to the utmost full-fledged, thoroughgoing constitutionally allied, united citizenship, understandingly synchronized, cultivates critical civility. Our unity as one people depends upon this new kind of civics. We must not only prepare for the future, but we must avert present-day assaults against our liberty. Please join me in getting the reins of control over the levers of power in our United States Enterprise (USE) back into the hands of the people. If we don't want to feel used, we must demand respect. We must rise to service above selfishness; saying yes to our first written principles: those found in the Declaration of Independence and the Constitution of the United States. We must serve these, reflexively, respectfully, and reflectively, everywhere in every way. We must learn to trust in them as our truth and prepare to *grow in obedience to them, with reasonable discipline, within our homes, neighborhoods, communities, states, regions, and nation. By self-governing, we create opportunities in ways far better for us than by allowing gigantic behemoths to control our lives. Why the fewest who profit the most assemble monopolies is obvious. But why are we tolerating it? It is creating instability in our society. It is a threat to our democracy-based culture.*

As citizens, are we not both the flock and its shepherd? It is our culture if we are one people. We need to act like one people! Is that not the great mystery revealed by the Constitution? Did it not set us up for self-government? Yes, it did. We are the United States of America, a cultural democracy. So let's get on with it! To keep us above all forms of tyranny, we must not sink into allowing an aristocracy to form a plutocracy over us! We need everybody of every stature to insist of themselves and of one another that we think more of and live better by our first principles, principal among them, liberty.

Yes, liberty, at that time was a radical idea. It meant dissent. Know that it has worked. After 245 years, our Constitution is the oldest one still in use. It is our endowment. We must protect it from the baby doomers who seek to steal it stealthily from us. We cannot be quiet. We must unleash liberty as it was in 1776.

Generationally inconsiderate, the baby boomers are nervous about dissent. As they lose the consent of the governed, they will placate. Their egregious cohort's idealism and rush to riches crippled their moral development. They know that many among them got to where they are illegitimately, by rigging the system. Putting on a partisan political drama, a theatrical act to fool us and distract us from the truth, they have been making out with the bags of money, leaving us stupefied. Are they laughing at us as if it were funny? We are not falling for it any longer. If the baby doomers fear we'll come for them with pitchforks to collect our commonwealth back, they will get authoritarian and aggressive. They simply never learned how to share. The lesser of them, the regular boomers, will want order and will go along with it. As a majority, by edict they will want to rule. Stacking the financial decks against the future, they will want to keep what they define as "mine, mine, all mine" and so will hoard while in charge. They will try to stop dissention, use division to justify law and order, and implement police control like the one we see on TV in dictatorships. They have forgotten their youthful dissent. Yet dissent is how this nation began: dissent against injustices. We the people, in order to form a more perfect union, began with, allowed, perpetrated, tolerated, and employed dissent! It is how liberty ensures that we exert checks and balances upon power. Dissent is our civic right. It countervails. It balances wrong. It holds power in check. It is our responsibility and duty as citizens of this republic, imbued with and born of democracy for liberty. It is our culture to control! It is our job to prevent power from concentrating into the hands of a few. We must resist complacency and control it.

Among its many other dangers to liberty, doomerism put consumerism above citizenship. It altered our power structure. It weakened democracy by putting at risk our society's foundation, constitutional obeisance. Under the cultural baggage of the boomer generation, our republic's footings cracked. Voters must act as colonists did in 1774 and shock the polity! Then we must continuously replace officials until we have a full generational change in authority! This is how we will prove our power. We cannot allow apathy. Voting in repeating record setting volumes is how we reclaim our society. United we'll stand, or divided we'll fall. Please hear my call! Read on.

*P*oem

Walk This Way

For LIBERTY every day
WE must by VIRTUE play
By rules of our DEMOCRACY
It's our ENDOWMENT to sustain
Courageously repeat its DECLARATION claim
In healthy REPUBLIC, we VOTE again & again to remain
Regenerating a nation takes good CIVICS educated CITIZENRY
Synchronously replacing REPRESENTATIVES with greater regularity
We OWE this much to the founded CONSTITUTION in every tiny way
DOOMERISM is destroying us, fleecing our rights, freedoms, & treasury
Let's RISE into a civilizing SOCIETY, a new age of ENLIGHTENMENT
DISSENT civilly, be CIVICALLY ENGAGED in NEIGHBORHOODS
PARTICIPATE in POLITICS fervently! We the People, UNITED States!

*D*edication

I dedicate this book to the memory of my ancestors, who fought for freedom of thought, speech, and action, regardless of the consequences. I write this to encourage my comrades in arms and the veterans who came before us. I thank Abraham Lincoln (my super-distant cousin), for his speeches and stalwart manner. I appreciate Teddy Roosevelt, who, too, overcame asthma without excuse or limitation. I am enamored of the ideas of the founders. Providence, the Almighty God, forgive our forebears their generations' sins. I pray that they rest in peace and not be irate over the cultural damage caused by the most dominant generation's performance in power. May this book's turn toward our first principles, proposed edifications, and alterations to a better way of being American, please them!

I devote this book to the everyday people who self-govern. Thank you for living virtuous lives, for daily pursuing truth and justice, and for teaching good ethics by the example of your character. Thank you for your purposeful American countenance and your moral convictions in citizenship. Continue upholding our ideals and protecting the Constitution. It is our reason for being free from tyranny.

I offer this book to our founding ideals, which mitigate the risks of failure, of us falling under the control of an autocratic kingdom's aristocracy. It's my honorific homage to the Constitution, the framers, and the country they created that put checks and balances on power to prevent its concentration in one horrific ruler. It deters abuses of power by those we elect to guide us, to whom we've granted authority only while they are in office. Forever we must guarantee that liberty is real by insuring, d'uring, ensuring, assuring, luring, and securing it into the hearts of our citizenry. It is our principal first principle, our inalienable right!

Last, to my family who raised me "properly" and to my extended relatives, with whom I wish we could have been closer, thanks for putting up with me. Mom and Dad, I love you! Semper fidelis says your Seabee son. Aunt Bobbie, Thomas Jefferson was a redhead too. Do you think he'd be happy with this? To my loving, supportive wife who cheered me on as I wrote this book, finally, after hearing all about it for ten years, may God bless you! To my siblings, and my boys who are my pride and joy, I hope that one day when you read this book you'll better understand my fervent, fomenting, feverish patriotism. I hope you might find a better society because of this book. In large measure, I wrote it for your younger generation. Thanks for hearing me out.

*B*efore You Begin

I plead that you be patient with me. Communication is difficult. I ask that you suspend emotional reactions (do not let the amygdala do your thinking) and seek to understand what I mean. Language is an imperfect medium. Words have several denotations as well as changing connotations, and their context influences their interpretation. Courteously trust me that I am writing to convey not harm but help. My intended patient is liberty. It is the spine of the government. It is our foundation for the nation. It is why the founders framed the Constitution. It is an idea that requires interpretation by the institutions that are to uphold it for us. If we are to be a society and culture offering democracy, we must continuously read it to understand its sentiments. We as persons and as a community, in concert with our institutions, which we staff, must dialogue more vigorously about it. Humans, albeit divinely oriented ones, set up our Constitution. It is amendable by design, but we must unite to adjust it, if we must, for just cause. But before we begin to doubt it, let's give it a round or two of new civics. Let's aspire to allow it to inspire us to gain its higher purpose. The quills that wrote it were feathers from an angel's wing. Let us recognize and reify it as a guide, seeking with all dispatch to make its ideals real, once and for all, and raise others to do the same. Please.

To benefit your reading experience, please flag the Figures and Acronyms pages so you may easily find them as you move through the book. Revisiting figures and continuous familiarizing with the acronyms respective impressions and definitions should assist you keep the messages of the book clearly in mind. Lastly, you'll need to employ the requisite determination and discipline to read the entire book. As you do so, contemplate and connect the content with its considerable purpose. If you love our country, please feel free to perform this scholarship like a duty of what you can do for your country. We the everyday people must do more to preserve it before we face dire consequences for being complacent. It will not take care of itself automatically. It needs our constancy to it. We must lead it.

*T*opics

"OUT OF MANY, ONE"

"PROVIDENCE FAVORS OUR UNDERTAKINGS"

1776

"NEW ORDER OF THE AGES"

Figure 0-1-1: The Great Seal of the United States. Obverse (current) & Reverse (circa 1786)

*F*igures

To save the Constitution, in pursuit of virtue we go...

Introduction

If you are between 18 and 56, worry about our future, and are struggling to understand what's wrong in our society, how we got into such a mess, and what you can do to help us get out of it, this book is for you. If you are between 56 and 76, I mean no offense. Please be ready to look deep within as you reflect upon our outward social discord. If you are 77+, you may find encouragement here to be a part of the repair. We could use your wisdom. If we are to keep posterity and ourselves free, then those who enjoy seniority, get priority, revel in affluence, and exert influence must give way to us. The time to pass the American torch has come. We need to change our authorities and replace older position holders with younger ones. We need new ideas, compassion, conscientiousness, empathy, respectful dissidence, love, and dignified commitment to one another. We must all be brave. As Woody Guthrie sang, "This land is your land, this land is my land . . . this land was made for you and me." We, the everyday people, must commit to honesty with integrity to get liberty and justice for all. This is everyone's birthright. Nevertheless, to keep it, we must practice a new, more responsible citizenship. We must practice greater civic engagement and informed political participation. We must better understand the nature and structure of power in our society.

In this book, I integrate scholarship from the social sciences*, history, insightful journalism, and community planning. I'll explain the many broken pieces in our society. You'll learn how you, your posterity, and our democracy are at risk from baby doomerism. I'll explain it, and how it violates our Constitution's sanctity. I'll outline how it destroys the promise of the social contract granted us at birth. We popped out with inalienable natural rights that need protected, not disrespected. You'll also find diagrams and analytical critical thinking tools. Use these to think about and make sense of "what's going on". Follow along as I explain what we must do to work together to solve the problems we face in our society.

With your help, we can save our society from an impending doom, which is certain to happen if we do nothing. By acting in unison, we'll avert the dangerous forces hiding behind curtains that seek to divide us. The baby doomers think we can't see them as they masquerade and lie to us. Pretentiously they parade before us, pretending to work for the people while actually fleecing our nation. Sadly, like most impostors faking it to make it, they have put democracy on all wrong. They've gotten it backward, inside out, and upside down. We the everyday people must correct them. Doomerism has perverted, distorted, twisted, and blistered democracy. The boomers have fallen from honor, and it's our duty to restore them as citizens once again. Unconsciously, they know not what they do. Consciously, they know exactly what they do, masterfully! But as irresponsible manipulators, they've forsaken the rest of us.

We'll benefit when we hold them accountable. This is in accord with our country's first principles. Allying ourselves with liberty, we'll restore wholesome community life. It's the first principle needed in a citizenry for democracy to survive. Accountability begins by blocking doomers from positions of authority. But first, we must begin their removal from office, delivered on each successive Election Day for a decade to come. The United States of America is a nation "of the people, by the people, and for the people." These are not worthless words. Only the shallow, hollow men and women suffering from doomerism think these are meaningless phrases for exploiting puppets.

We are not puppets! We know who works for whom under our Constitution, but many of our compatriots have failed to live by or uphold it. We have no choice but to remove the baby boomers to recover. By the common will of the people, we must restore our authority for the good of the commonweal. Our Constitution was ordained for the wealth of our nation, our country's states and territories. We are a free people. Being a charitable and forgiving people, we need to help the "me first" baby doomers. They don't yet realize their misguided actions. After a period of reflection, they'll be able to repent and return to us in new, vital roles. Their example of how they almost rubbed liberty off the face of the earth will become a lesson. Once they become elder teachers of civics, they'll have a worthy legacy. That is, if they want to gain a respectable dignity before they die. Otherwise, their bane will earn them scorn forever. Before they go, we'll encourage them to return to us what they've stolen. Peaceably we will remake the rules, unrig the systems, and carefully bring the doomers among them back into the fold of real Americanism.

Briefly allow me to address the boomers. Boomers, you may yet be respected in history books to come, if you change your ways and work to make the nation unite, and leave a legacy of a beneficial bequest, not the burdensome debt and doom getting passed down to America's children. It benefits you to renew our nation's prosperity. If you do this, you may yet be seen as heroes by your children, and not as participation trophy giving cowards. When you're elderly, they'll respect you, knowing you helped make the world heathier than the one inherited by you.

As the doomers recognize that they have misguided our ship, they'll come around, wanting a solid reputation. They'll find peace in admitting they set our country adrift as a "ship of fools." By telling them they nearly ran it aground on enemy territory, a land known as aristocracy, we'll help them heal. If we don't tell them, if we don't stop them, they'll crash us in a greedy search for buried treasure, thinking they've struck Fantasy Island. In reality, Shipwreck Island has no treasure but only tyranny. Aristocracy is the tempting land of delusions of grandeur and moral absolutes. It's full of fallacious, fraudulent felons, whose illogical and unconstitutional arguments distract from truth based on fact. Nevertheless, we'll save them, and in return, they'll awaken and help us get this nation through the rough seas ahead once they discover the joy of giving credence to the Constitution and forward thinking freedom from the pure place of devout selflessness.

But why should anyone listen to me? Well, because, doesn't everyone want to be able to love America? Don't we all want to believe that it is what it portends to be as described in the writings of the framers, particularly, Thomas Jefferson's? I get it. I'm a Jeff. I'm a patriot. I want to help. I want us, as a people, to stop giving up our power and to start behaving in ways that will make our wills match our Constitution's words. I invite everyone to join me. Moreover, as a "Twice the Citizen" Navy reservist, I'm sworn to defend our Constitution. Us sworn to an oath patriots cannot do it alone. We need everyone to pitch in to help the nation. After 10 years as an enlisted Seabee, an Utilitiesman Third Class Petty Officer, I commissioned Ensign in the Civil Engineer Corps. I've been an officer now for 24 years. At heart, I am "everyday people." I worked my way through college, taking many jobs to pay for it. Needing to borrow money, I kept declaring majors to remain enrolled full time. I ended up earning an Associate of Arts degree from a community college as well as two bachelor's degrees and two master's degrees from a university. I guess I'm a bit of an emblem of hard work, gritty determination, and Uncle Sam's kindness to give grants and deferred loans to a somewhat smart kid. In the Navy, I gained respect for tradesman doing manual construction labor. They trained me on how to use hand tools. This made me well rounded. I've done technical work in the field and creative work in the office. I've led teams in both areas and have helped manage programs of national importance and international reach. At night after work and on weekends, I made it my personal mission to search relentlessly for answers to the dilemmas plaguing our society. Every evening and in every place, I scoured for truth. From my scholarship, I finally found answers. I wrapped it into conceptual models and explanations. In this book, I tell of them. They combine professors and historians versions of what has gone wrong, why, and what we can do about it.

Because I want everyone to know what I've discovered, I wrote this book. I see a path through the darkening gloom. We must reignite the flame of liberty to brighten our future. We must resurrect the Constitution from our past and infuse it with the energy and vitality of our next generations. We need the rising young adults to want to become leaders. To make way for them, we need to intervene and block the baby doomers from remaining in control.

To the rising millennials and the generations entering adulthood that follow, you all are the most gifted and talented, the best educated, and the most civil, teamwork-oriented American generation. The likes of your kind, gregarious and ungrudging, graced us during World War II. These GIs freed most of Europe from tyranny. Long before them, a similarly great generation of generous geniuses founded our country. They pledged their lives for democracy and hoped to make a more perfect union. Obviously, it's still a work in progress, yet we're on the cusp of making it real. To advance onto it, we must stop the anti-democracy influences of doomerism, before it corrupts our core, taking us over, eating our souls, and ruining the great venture that is the once exceptional United States.

This book grew out of 47 Facebook posts to my friends. That medium became insufficient for me to express my discoveries of the real root causes of our societal problems. This book satisfies my desire to share them, my oath to the Constitution, and my moral commitment to the founders' vision. Because we are in crisis, I had to get this book published as soon as possible. I began writing it on July 4, 2020. America, we need better ideas than what we're hearing from the powerful if we are to save ourselves from their gloomy doom.

Please read this book. Please contemplate. Please commit. Please apply its recommendations in your everyday life. We'll make a difference, I promise. The benefits to humanity are huge. The world needs us to be a functioning society to prove democracy can work. The benefit of secured liberty is our legacy to our progeny. Our unborn children depend upon it.

Boomers, this is a "crucial conversation" (Patterson, Grenny, McMillan, & Switzler, 2012). If you're still reading, please don't be defensive, dismissive, shallow, or superficial. Your ideological absolutist thinking that scoring points is what counts isn't working. Life isn't a game, and others' lives aren't game pieces. Politics isn't an exercise in being witty or cunning. It's the exercise of the authorities to apply power given to the governors by the governed. Ours is a nation in pain. We need healing, not arguments. Please get over yourselves and get out of the way before your idealist strengths bring us down. Can't you see the dialectic at play? We need your energies applied in a different direction, toward unity in the light of day for liberty's sake.

Non-boomers, it will take time. It might mean long-suffering and severe perseverance, but time is on our side, we have the talent, and we aren't the ones soon to die. Millennials, our rising civic generation, prepare to take up the reins of leadership. If you want to live in a better world than the one you see devolving before your eyes, you must evolve the courage to take charge. I will be here for you. I can coach and mentor you. Let me give to you what my life of service has given to me. Please. We need you. You need to do this, not for you but for your children. Don't fall victim to doomerism. Avoid its traps. Read this book.

This is the real power of the United States. We transfer power with peaceful elections. This is democracy. Our brilliant, team working, civic-minded up-and-comers can clean up the mess made by doomerism. Plus they all will do it civilly, without the ugliness we've witnessed for the past forty years. Our national community is crying out to every one of us to "come to my aid." We cannot delay. We must grasp the fact that tyranny never sleeps. It's in the instincts of humans. We will continuously grab for power. Our Founding Fathers' generation defeated it. Our great GIs' generation defeated it. We can too. We, like them, are idealistic Americans. Now is the right time. History beckons. With civic minds and neighborly hearts, we must do our duty and pay homage to the best in our history, while avoiding our worst.

This book will help us believe in unity. Unity and liberty are our means to stop our own internal cultural tyranny: doomerism. If we don't stop it, it will destroy us. Let's begin reclaiming our future with lessons from the past, those of the origination, determination, and perpetuation of liberty. Liberty is freedom's elixir. It's the lifeblood of our great political experiment, our republic formed from a democracy-based culture. Freedom to be free makes it possible to feel at home in America.

To recap: our problem = doomerism; our solution = exhibiting service above selfishness; saying yes to the utmost full-fledged thoroughgoing constitutionally allied, unified "citizenshipping", understandingly synchronized by us simultaneously living committed, virtuous lives. We'll resuscitate liberty and remove doomerism. We'll rebalance power in our society.

If you want this, join my team to SCORE one for liberty. We have a mission together. We will succeed. We are Americans. We will:

Survive doomerism

Communicate its wrongfulness

Organize to retire the baby boomers currently in positions of authority

Resist the furtherance of misguided, undermining values

Escape from social, cultural, and societal doom, unvirtuous authority, arcane arguments, and dangerous decisions baby doomers' immoralities bring us.

We'll do it by reviving virtue and liberty as our American purpose.

If you don't want our civilization to collapse, join me today! Let's get to work. Let's create a new, civically engaged, politically active citizenship culture. Ready, set, go! Start the voyage. Read on.

(psychology, sociology, anthropology, political science, and economics)

SECTION 1: POWER

1. "Quicksilver Rising"

This chapter requests that we attend to society and recognize where we are. It asks we fathom the gift of the founders, seek to know better what is going on in our society, and prepare to get deeply involved in fixing it.

"We the People," "under God, indivisible, with liberty and justice for all"—these are not hollow words. These powerful words give birth to a culture of democracy. We make them meaningful when we pledge ourselves to them in our hearts, minds, bodies, and souls. If we are shallow, they will fail, and we will fail. Unless we rebalance the societal powers, we'll become a mere disenfranchised, miserable collection of individuated persons, living in the same territory and inhabiting the same lousy life of serfdom. Yes, it will get that bad, unless we act! To come out of crises, we need a better appreciation of one another as a loving family. We have a Constitution to guide us. Find it, dust it off, and let's get to work, shall we? But first, let's find out where we are today. This chapter begins in the yesteryear of our beginning, when the founders declared the new American age. It sets the stage for the rest of the book.

Prologue

When considering how many civilizations have come and gone, it began, not too long ago. In earlier eras, rulers justified the status quo hierarchy with edicts they claimed were divine. The founders of the United States desired to be free from such mysterious control. They contended the people could govern themselves. This was a radical idea in their age.

They Went Outside the Lines!

Like 1776, 2020 felt mystical, like a magical, divining moment. It is a time of calling, the calling of destiny to reflect upon our responsibility to govern ourselves. We carry the prescient flame. The ultimate promise in human relations is the light of liberty, found only in self-government and in a culture forged in democracy. We must strengthen the principles that are our lines of defense. These barricades, our core moral values, the cardinal virtues, if crossed, put us in jeopardy of losing our liberty.

The baby boomers went outside these lines. They pushed the boundaries of civility. They dealt with society by slinging "isms" around, never quite addressing real problems. The use of "isms" is an ambiguous language that is hard to comprehend. Many still linger, causing painful confusion. Newly invented isms disguise never fully understood old isms. Neologisms and euphemisms abound now, confusing our dialogues. The boomers created a new, sin-centered, wisdom-avoiding subculture, which has spread like a cancer taking over our country. Their counterculture, devoid of discipline, dedicates itself to serving their favorite ism, consumerism, which fed the ism exposed in this book, doomerism.

Exactly what did the baby boomers do that upset the balance of power and now threatens our liberty? They muddled around with isms, amplified existing disagreements, and pumped and trumped them up in a hyperbolic manner to sell. They always pressed to compete for more for themselves, one to the other, in their so-called "game of life." They reduced social responsibility as a purpose. But life is not a game! They treated it that way, though, and now we see the problems that such immaturity leaves unsolved. Perhaps we should call it "gamerism". Yet this does not point to the consequences of incompetence. In life, we need to be competent. Gamerism, like consumerism, is a characteristic of doomerism. Doomerism is a cancer causing a decline in civility. It is an overarching danger to democracy.

Some baby boomers are good, and a few are great. Most are normal folk trying to get by, do their thing, do good work, and do well. Some are just plain bad. The worst among these are the baby doomers. They hide their intentionally manipulative motives. It's maddening. Though they cannot see it, and they think we cannot see it, we can. We know when the egregious baby boomers play a game on us. To us it is obvious, pathetically so. But because their inflated egos, puffed up like a blowfish, convince them that they are great, they are completely oblivious. Worse, in their gamerism they see only two colors: winners and losers. By zero-sum, limited binary, insufficiently complex mental capacities, they think we must be dumb because we don't argue with them. More than that, we're dumbfounded by their callous self-centeredness. It's just as the king of England did to the colonies. In their hubris, they look down their noses at us, as if we were peons beneath them. But we hold allegiance to no crown, nor to cronies.

The ism-tossing baby boomers surfed rising waves of economic prosperity. Spawned by near-exponential growth in knowledge, careers were plentiful. Spectacular electronic, computational, and communications technologies led to ever-increasing economic opportunity. Greed for growth led to worship at the altars of financial markets. Wall Street replaced Main

Street as the national political priority. We, the everyday people, are being left behind. The seeking of flush retirement income is not wrong. A better financial future is good. However, the ends don't justify the means, which began to differ from past arrangements. A super celebrity subculture of hyper-high executive salaries was born. Their coming-of-age counter-culture became the abacus counter culture. All that mattered was counting their money.

Of course, with all this opportunity, growth, immorality, and disloyalty to the Constitution, society transformed for the worse. Social change caused by all this led to expanded efforts by political lobbyists. As incomes increased, a rising "gaming the game" competitiveness arose like a feeding frenzy on the raw meat of commerce floating in the ocean, a shark pack's attack. Boomers' work became more than a job. It became an identity. Competition over who could get the most consumed conspicuously as status symbols changed people's definitions of themselves. Expanding incomes led to enlarging egos, and greater materialism became the indicator of one's self-worth. This pursuit of luxury, materialism, consumerism, and gamerism metastasized into doomerism. The baby doomers' value set, wholly oriented toward satiation and the aggrandizement of "me first," solidified.

Driven by their competitiveness, boomers created more and more isms. But did these help the regular people? Or was a new class of know-it-alls manufacturing isms for their own delight? To keep pace, boomers in communications (public relations, journalism, news reporting, and broadcasting, i.e., the media) latched onto these isms. Racing to be first on the scene, first to speak, and first to produce "breaking news," their greed lusted for increasing information. Like gluttons, they cooked up and ate a twenty-four-hour cable news cycle. Information overload further increased the competition to become first, regardless of accuracy. The race was on here, there, and everywhere. To where, nobody knew, but they quickly pursued greenbacks with every inroad. Breaking news began to do exactly that, break the society as it became new. Their counterculture was shredding our democracy-based culture, shoving liberty aside and pressing us into impropriety. This brought about an adaptive problem for the society, which remains unsolved.

The constant flood of information gave rise to "information technology". Solutions created new problems. Increased computational complexity, software algorithms, data analytics, and artificial intelligence outpaced understanding. How do we trust these new machines? One glitch can bring the whole system to a sudden, raging halt. Not only is that a risk, but the volume of data is intimidating. Bad data inputs, near incomprehensible throughputs, and data outputs we think we can trust, lead to anxiety. This outcome is a new "dataism", an addictive fascination with data because of the scale of profitability made possible due to its use by money making centered technologies. Computers process massive amounts of data. Dataism, materialism, gamerism, and consumerism—the doomerism cancer grows. We have lost sight of the humane kindness that was once what we knew as everyday people, as human beings. Babies' futures became forgotten and irrelevant, posterity went unprotected, and the erosion of liberty began.

It's as if the boomers suffer from a syndrome they pass on to all of us. One where professing a new ism makes one a new thought leader rock star! It's innate. People flock to learn the latest thing, the newest development, especially if it's profitable. It's nearly insane how this consumer behavior driven by boomers' competitiveness has reshaped their whole outlook on life. It inanely removed wisdom from view, forgetting its lessons from the ages. Success comes from an ability to delay self-gratification. Civilized societies rest on this. Through the practice of good morals, good order, and good discipline, we move toward creating a more perfect union. A better world comes to us as persons when we as a society do "good" for goodness' sake. Good goodness is its own reward, doing good exhibiting service above selfishness, saying yes to the utmost full-fledged, thoroughgoing constitutionally allied united citizenshipping, understandingly synchronized, (E-SASSY-T-TUF-FT-CAUCUS), is the nutrient of our great liberty tree. It feeds our national community, our republic, our democracy.

Negative consequences materialized as the boomers, and those who imitated their ways, adopted new isms of behavior. Their "me first" mannerism was their adaptation to our economic prosperity. The growth of knowledge and computer technology move us quickly along. To keep from getting left behind we've learned herd behaviors that the marketplaces count upon. Counting profits from constituent consumers becomes our reason for being. We have followed the crowd while also racing to be at its head. We've sought out savior superstars and attended lectures for new insights. Companies have sprung up selling seats in large theaters to learn from lecturers, while colleges have gone online. The need to know is an adaptive result of the fast pace of change our creativity as a species now brings. Ironies abound. We chase our tails and go faster to bite at them, but then we fall down from instability. Ironies are making life laughable at times. But doomerism is not funny. It is deadly for our society and thus for us, the everyday people.

This accelerating pursuit of newness, whether to create a new ism, or invent a new technology like splicing a genome, matures work in cycles of increasing complexity. Our species' power of industry is amazing. Society organizes experts who've "been there and done that," who figure out the new patterns and then sell off their knowledge. Others crave to learn how to go about "making it." Whether it is the sought after thing, an innovation, an ism, or a genome, crowded competitive fields trade their wares in new marketplaces. Crafty creators clamor for cash and a chance to save the world with their inventions. We need such entrepreneurs, hustlers, and marketplaces to solve our problems. But we also need stability and a deeper commitment to social agreements of fair and reasonable conditions for all. As we enter an uncertain future, we cannot change everything and leave more than half of us out of the forward progress of our special project of a nation. That is just not humane. We need to recognize the unhealthy thinking in doomerism. Our society has evolved with our powers of industry and artistry. It has created buyer, seller, and labor markets full of helpers, merchants, miners, makers, movers, and marketers [HM^5]. These folk manage our powers of economy. They are always on the lookout to solve a problem that people have, which is the good aspect of entrepreneurship. Yet it can come with the blind ambition to make a fortune (or fame) at all costs, regardless of law. Such strong motivation raised a generation stuck in a competition mindset: the boomers. Add this "competitivism" to materialism, consumerism, and gamerism, and see how the risks in doomerism grow too. These mighty risks we'll discuss later. Boomers' cravings caused an increasing need for self-rewarding, attention-getting experiences. These gave rise to a new self-improvement way of life. This was an adaptation to the problem of staying aboard the accelerating escalator of progress!

The new HM^5 technology innovation hunters, among the boomers and those wanting to be like them, became the new economic elites. They expanded their participation in the body politic. They applied profits to pay for campaigns. They lobbied and persuaded the politicians to make decisions in their favor. They sought to create a field of play in which they, the newest economic elites, have the best advantages. For this, they took control of the rules and the rulemaking. This application of economic power to control the polity only added temptations to an already power-hungry vocation, the risks of which typically trend toward corruption. Politics arranges and controls the societal powers. Doomer changes show yet another societal adaptation to the third stage in knowledge creation. An ancient concept, corruption (no ism for it, but we add it to the list of components), gets amplified in the externalities of doomerism. The evidence is an exponential rise in legislative lobbying (Clawson, Neustadtl, & Scott, 1992) and the power of money in campaigns (Clawson, Neustadtl, & Weller, 1998).

We've seen how lobbying alters the orientation and purpose of politicians. It distracts them from serving the needs of their constituents and leads them toward serving themselves. It is uncivilizing when they ignore the needs of the people who elected them to represent them. On the flip side of this kind of lobbying is another kind of increased participation in demands upon the polity by special interest groups. The pressure to give out more benefits from many to one group or another is an externality of the "me first" mentality of baby boomers. While the welfare state arose to cope with the instability caused by the social upheavals during the second stage of knowledge evolution, its humane solutions are prone to manipulation by baby doomers seeking something for nothing. Boomers have a sense of entitlement like no generation before them. But the welfare state does not resolve the economic inconsistency we face with the ups and downs of occupations, gains and losses of wealth, and ebbs and flows in employment opportunities. The vicissitudes of globalizing markets still plague our comprehension and philosophies to cope with them. In our academy power, many isms contest one another, without any attempt at synthesis. The dialectic process is unpursued. We simply see the perpetuation of theses verses antitheses. Armies of true-believer boomers just keep clobbering at one another. Obsessed over being right, they continue to fight for control of the wheel and levers on the helm. Without any effort to find a new synthesized resolution, our society, like a ship, drifts dangerously off course. Thanks to the third stage of new knowledge and its production of new technologies, the making of isms becomes our way of communicating. In its enhanced symbolic sophistication, we talk past one another, our symbols ill matching our moment in time. We are arguing over the wrong matters. Our patterns of comprehension, sold for profit, influence us to think unreasonably. Even professionals begin to seek new conventions. More externalities launch at us in rapid-fire succession, as the baby boomers throw ill-adapted punches at the wrong problems. We begin to wonder if the simple answer is to find, brand, and market one's own identity as an "ism." Perhaps this thought underlies the rotten ideality of victimization. Many desire to be a victim to have an identity in the eyes of others. Such a thought is but another negative externality of doomerism.

Isms

Isms appear every day, everywhere and for everything. We the people get pushed out of the way to make room for them. Every explanation in our lives seems to get an ism. They increase as complexity expands. Isms have been around for a long time. The list keeps growing, which indicates that knowledge is growing. The isms become shortcuts to whole books of knowledge. The risk to a society running amuck with isms is that sound-bite summaries of vast amounts of information take over our thinking. We are in trouble. Our government officials make critical decisions. Our everyday lives are at stake if they debate issues using isms of confused details. "Ism-ism" will lead to our doom as a citizenry. It adds to the corruption, materialism, consumerism, and gamerism of doomerism. Do the baby doomers really know what they are saying, what they are doing, gun slinging around all these isms? Or are they miscommunicating with erroneous symbols past one another, or worse, playing a game on us? When they nod along, as if in agreement, to satiate the ego of another, is this not cowardly, and are they not creating real linguistic challenges? Understanding one another is essential for democracy. We cannot protect liberty with debates over isms. They do not lead to the necessary discussions. Isms distract our best thinkers from having real debates about what to do about the suffering on Main Street. We use an ism to get their attention, a device to free them from their entrapment within their ism-ism. Below is a list of some of the top isms of issues of organizing the powers in and of society. The boomers egregious cohort, the baby doomers, mostly those whereat the mean, median, and mode of their demographic bell curve align, but others acting like the doomers, who came before and after their generation, earn this label too. It is a label for those afflicted with, and inflicting upon others, that which this book names—"doomerism". The baby doomers lob isms about to keep us confused, so they might keep fleecing us. These get used in the landscapes of our politic, polarized by those who control the history power that daily now seeks profits over facts. We must be aware of the games they are playing on us, with us, and against us.

- ○ Traditionalism (the kind that focuses on maintaining structural hierarchy power; not the kind that seeks the retention of heritage celebrating customs)
- ○ Modernism (the scientific method is helpful but not the be-all and end-all problem-solving method for each and every piece of the whole)
- ○ Elitism (the snobbery to which democracy responds, "No, you are not better than me because you have more money; go read Thomas Paine for the American truth")

○ Capitalism	○ Communism	○ Socialism	○ Sexism
○ Totalitarianism	○ Feminism	○ Machoism	○ Racism
○ Jingoism	○ Classism	○ Expressionism	

Not that having these and discussing them is bad. But never defining them clearly, and using them with broad brushes to paint many in the same stripe, is just childish. This leads to those parts of "identity politics" that hurt citizens' souls. It is unhelpful and unhealthy. We need fewer aggravating aggregations. We need to stop forcing identities upon people. Our species is global; science proves we are one species. Our histories pitted us against one another, but now we are on the verge of planetary realities against which we cannot prevail if we don't stop the ancient ways of argument and power pursuits. We all need to wake up to the risks this foolishness presents, not just to us but also to the species. This group policy is how aggregated data can aggravate the people. Politicians and reporters are causing a decline in civic and political participation. Perhaps this is their goal, to turn us off, so they might create an oligarchy. They don't fully explain the parameters of the studies from which possibly erroneous assertions derive. Do they understand the reports, if they even actually read them? Or are they just parroting the talking points their staffs have prepared? This is the way of doomerism. Aggregated data diffuses truth. It buries the real experiences of a person's unique realities. It leads to the assumptions of system thinking. It leaves out the human story and often misses the point of need needing addressed. It too often results in a one-size-fits-all solution that benefits nobody well. The limitations, hypothesis, underlying theory, and science behind a study all matter in policy-making. The citizenry deserves to hear these parameters of reports used in decision-making. To deny them is an injustice, an insult to intelligence, and frankly, just plain disrespectful. Of course, we must also be more attentive, exercising our citizenship responsibilities. This will force better truth telling with less statistical manipulation to prove that one ism is better than another ism.

Rolling up data comes with challenges and risks. Statistics tells us about standard deviations and levels of confidence in findings. We need to hear about how. Politicians and reporters too often leave out these critical facts of analyses in their pronouncements. If they are pushing a narrative of their own, as the doomers are prone to do, we must insist they pull back the veils. Narrativism is another aspect of doomerism. See, the ism list grows. Add it to isms-ism corruption, materialism, consumerism, and gamerism. It evolved as their competitive need to harden their soft egos drove them to prove a point at all costs. Foolishly, as it relates to our survival, they believe that either to score points, or to win an argument, is more important than to tell the truth. No necessary solutions can emerge in such a pathetic storm. We need the norms of democracy restored, so we can save our nation. Baby doomers go about serving the people all wrong. Like the generation before them, they built upon the endowment they received. Doomerism emerged as they picked up where the previous generation left off, where a higher circle of the societal upper classes formed from a political directorate alongside a national marketplace dominated by corporate business elites (Mills, 1956). With the boomers, upper-class inner circles of power elites colluded like never before, and steadily forgotten were the notions of democracy. New rational, bureaucratic, hierarchical organizations began to rule the shapes of the national community. As we continue to lay the groundwork for the rest of this book, let's go backward to our country's founding for clues on how we must remake societal power arrangements to get better service of, by, and for the people toward achieving our constitutional objectives.

Human History

Remember what school's history textbooks told of ancient and modern civilizations? They were a string of power churning violence. Remember what made transitions of empires, dynasties, regimes, and kingdoms? They were hell-bent on conquering, battling, warring with, and raping one another. The founders of the United States, for reasons of both politics and economics, wanted such activity to stop. They stood up to tyranny and said "no," "no thank you," "no more," and we'll have "none of you." They wanted something different, creative, and imaginative. They invented a democracy in a republic with allegiance to no crown. This was a positively electric innovation. This occurred at a time when science was exploring electricity. Ben Franklin flew a kite in 1752, realizing static electricity from lighting. It was a slow evolution for electricity. In the 1880s, Thomas Edison and George Westinghouse learned how to harness it by alternating and direct currents, AC/DC. But invention by scientific exploration resided within our democracy-based culture. Providence seemed pleased by us. The founders, believing in the creativity of the people, kept government limited. This ensured that it would not get in the way of an industrious people. Liberty fused their framing. They divided government powers to protect it, protect us from it, and block corrupting concentrations of power. The separation of powers kept tyrannical politicians from getting away with "dirty deeds, done dirt cheap."

Mostly, we all are the better for it, though we have yet to achieve the goal and attain the objectives they set forth in the Constitution's Preamble. In homage to it, we must continue to work toward its completion. We ought to show some respect and gratitude for their great innovation in social organizing by doing a better job as stewards of the nation set up for the everyday people to be free from tyranny.

Let's look at our society as a ship, the US Enterprise (USE). It blends private and public into a unity of effort. Working together, a common end of making a better life and livelihood for its people is within its reach. Yet how has forty years of baby boomers at its helm panned out? We are a bit adrift because the baby doomers among us control all of the power structures in our society. They are not steering us with the winds of liberty toward our idealized destiny. Instead, they have parked us in dry dock for repairs they refuse to make. Our society is suffering from an overtly irrational bureaucratic malfeasance, which is not appropriate to what we need and it allows them to fleece our resources. Ill-focused, argumentative, and selfish, they did not preserve our ship nor keep it on its purposeful exemplary-minded mission. Now it needs significant repair. We must make it ready. It must stand upright and sail once again in the intended direction of our Constitution. But first, we need to revisit the reasons for and heroics of the creation of our USE in America. The best social innovation ever, and the greatest news in all human history is next.

*L*ove

Shared circumstances and similar conditions formed feelings of affection to the idea of creating a people by a creed. A people, a nation, e pluribus unum, hoped to be free from tyranny. This then launched a need for care and concern for a wider circle of others. A nation as community needed to extend kinship beyond historical animosities. With hope for a spreading a love for country and fellow citizens, ideas moved toward reality. A historic declaration occurred, and imperfect humans moved forward to establish a more perfect union.

What Happened in 1776?

The framers of the Constitution went outside the lines, bravely (and in a much more impressive manner than did the boomers). They reversed history and flipped power arrangements upside down (see Figure 1-2). They gave the people the power. This was unheard of! How could they do that? Our job now is not to lose what we got. Our job has always been not to lose it. Somehow, the instincts that have ruled history got into us, and we failed democracy. The boomers had the greatest opportunity, with all the wealth accumulation, to do something about advancing our constitutional objectives. But they did not focus on it or on us, the everyday people. They chose "me first" attitudes that guided their behaviors and shaped a "count the cash going into my pockets" narcissistic baby doomer culture. Posterity now knows the name of its traitor, treasonous to the vision of the republic and the ideals of justice and liberty.

The figure below shows what society was like for the everyday people before the American Revolution. Power was concentrated at the top of a pyramid. The ruler on top was far above the masses of people at the bottom. The few ruled the majority. Imperfect humans make imprecise polity. Rulers enforce power to create a more perfect pyramid. The hierarchy rises as the span of control broadens. But they have to divide their empires into levels to exert control. As empires expand, the pyramid's chances of reaching perfection decline. Reality does not match the ruler's ideality. Unable to obtain perfection, rulers become angry and brutal. The culture punishes the most imperfect within the empire. The ruler's representatives closest to the people, because exposed to real people, cannot be as cruel as instructed. The empire begins to get sloppy; it fails to achieve an ideal pyramidal form. The polity slumps downwardly. Like concrete made with too much water, it is not firm enough to hold its shape. Perfection is unmet. Imperfect humans cannot be completely cruel. The frustrated tyrant becomes worse, projecting his or her own inadequacies for not having achieved a perfect state. Absolute power turns to torture upon the subjects.

The ideal imperial pyramid, never achieved, crumbles under its own weight. Another tyrant, enslaved to the same types of crimes as the prior one, builds a new one on its rubble. This cycle of violence and hate perpetuates, and our species sees it repeatedly throughout our history. The pursuit of power may be an instinct, but a better society for the everyday people it does not make. There is no love for such regimes in the hearts of the people. They may love their place of birth but regret the dictators in charge. A coerced citizenry only feints loyalty to the kingdom. No human ever wants to give up his or her liberty. In tyranny, people who suffer to survive must take the pain to get along, day by day, without hope, with limited dreams for their children, in a way of hate not love. The brilliant social invention of our founders was to flip the power pyramid. This is democracy. It requires that diplomacy be first. Our first cabinet official, third in line in power succession, is the Secretary of State, our chief diplomat. If diplomacy is first in the cabinet, why do we give all our money to the Department of War (now called the less offensive-sounding "Defense")?

Convened on November 26, 1791, President George Washington held the first cabinet meeting. It included the Secretary of State, Thomas Jefferson; the Secretary of the Treasury, Alexander Hamilton; the Secretary of War, Henry Knox; and the Attorney General, Edmund Randolph. Notice the order, by missions: 1. Peace, 2. Money, 3. War, and 4. Justice. Is this the order of importance today? Should it be?

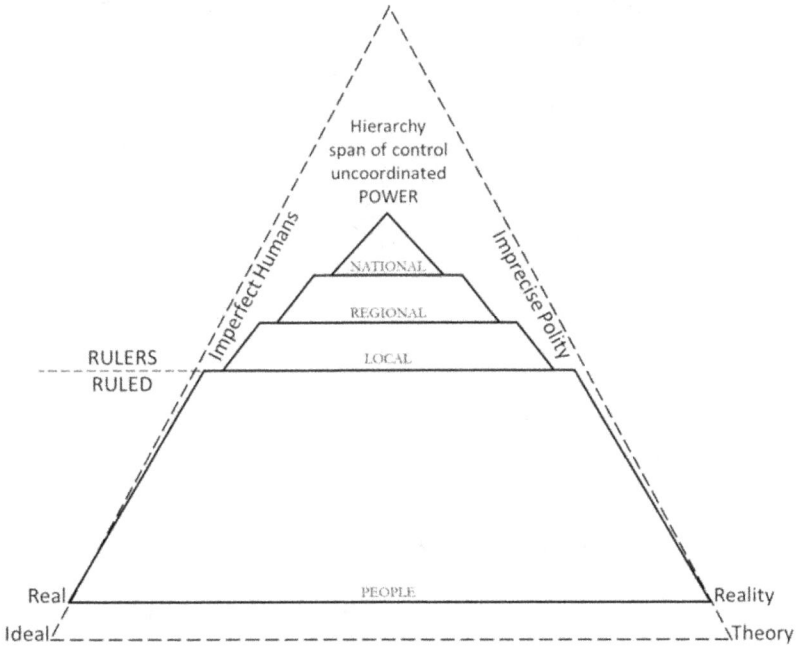

Figure 1-1: Dominant Polity Hierarchy—Rulers Use Power to Achieve the Ideal (for them)

Our diplomats need more support. Soft power averts the need to use hard power (i.e., controlled violence that makes more enemies if the enemies are not completely defeated. This is an expensive proposition). By the way, we won the Cold War by numbers one and two. We could because of the readiness for three and the great detective work of four. This model beat totalitarian tyranny. Maybe, just maybe, we ought to try it again. Especially since our world is now more codependent than ever.

Vote for Diplomacy

Doomers' absolutist ideology is failing us in this epoch of crises. They need to step aside. We need the more civic-minded in charge. We do not need the selfish-minded, the stubborn hardheads who won't talk to each other. Think of Congress. Are we not paying them to work together, to talk with each other on our behalf to improve society? If not, then for what are we paying their salaries? And how do they thank us? By committing insider dealmaking to enrich themselves, each other, and their campaign financing industry lobbyists. They go about like children, pointing at one another as if the other is to blame. Both the politicians and the industrialists are at fault for not being good citizens. Do they not realize that we see the real fleecing going on behind the scenes? We are the flock; we know what that feels like, and it has got to stop! Congress needs an enema. A complete washing out of its chambers is in due order. We must begin it again with brilliant young minds. The cantankerous old curmudgeons, arguing over old ideas, are not solving our problems. The fighting to protect positions instead of listening to our problems is not helping us. Meanwhile, they amass gains—many obtained near-illegally, certainly unethically, and definitely immorally. We need younger generations willing to help us reach our constitutional objectives.

Good governing takes real statecraft, which requires diplomatic sophistication to master, not an obnoxious blunt verbal club that only requires hatred to bludgeon another with it. Help us demand a reorganization of funding priorities to match the intents of the founders. Vote for diplomacy. Vote for those who have the necessary cognitive complexity and empathy to work toward achieving a more perfect union. We can no longer handle the baby doomers who seek only selfish recognition, like children, and reward them with our coins. The treasure is ours, not theirs.

The sons and daughters of liberty moderate between the extremes, apply reason, and use what makes rational sense for the majority. They use common sense, which exists only in the hearts and minds of the honest. The dishonest seek to destroy its existence and manipulate the reasonable. They want to get away with their theft and cheating to get ahead, though they are actually going nowhere. Life is not a race. It is a parade: people being able to do what they enjoy, sharing their talents, and appreciating one another for it. This is freedom. Some are marching, some applauding in the audience, but all are in it together, enjoying the parade. Parades include everyone celebrating the precious experience called life. If we see society differently, we can still have a parade together, enjoying the circumstances and conditions of freedom.

Our past is broken; it is full of shame. Its weight is upon us as a people. However, we can carry on by stopping blaming each other for it, by courage and by commitment to our Constitution's goal and objectives. If we can read aloud and hear clearly the words written down, we can achieve a more perfect union. We cannot get distracted, and there is much to distract us. The present is confusing. The power games played intentionally make it so. We cannot become jaded. We must be awake, learned, smart, and ready for greater complexity. We can untangle the portrayed complications. We can understand it. We must lean on knowledge, not ideology or ignorance. The future is not fearful to a brave citizen in the land of the free. If we commit to better constitutional living, we can restore for our progeny the opportunity to live in liberty. We do it by practicing constitutionally allied, united citizenshipping, understandingly synchronized.

*E*nlightenment

Great thinkers' studied past societies and philosophies. They declared opinions and debated with one another to find agreeable common conclusions. They sought out to reform the civilization. They wanted to improve the circumstances and conditions of humanity.

What Was That, Again?

The age of reason, an era of thinking about nature, people, and politics, brought forth the Enlightenment. Ideas arose that influenced how humans might organize societies. A belief in scientific inquiry and evidence assembled into facts, and facts into knowledge, and knowledge into truths would shape the future. Truths described the universe. Its study led to scientific discoveries, inventions, and engineering. It brought about all the things we take for granted today. Every gadget and computational device, all the conveniences of modern living, began in the Enlightenment. So why do so many pooh-pooh science? Think! Rulers rule by telling lies. They fear they will lose something. They fear the challenge by truth of evidence and facts. Remember this lesson from our history books. Tyrants tell fibs, and just like bullies, they beat us when we disagree or deny them dominance over our personal sovereignty. They dislike it when we exhibit integrity. They like to claim we are defective then blame us for our social circumstances and physical conditions. When they get away with it, they see themselves as god-like superior persons. How weak in spirit are they. Think! The most important organizing a society experiment came to us as an endowment of the Enlightenment: a republic born of democracy framed upon the idea that we all are created equal. Do we want to keep it? If we do, we must work for it. We must keep the Liberty Tree's lamps lighted. Let us not let darkened fear put out its light.

Maybe we need to remember our first principles. We ought to revive and recite lore for this greatest gift of polity: giving power to the people by the Constitution. Our Constitution, the revelation, the happening, the document, the embodiment of the diplomacy, negotiations, and rightful attempts to write it, needs us to rediscover it, uncover it, and commit truly to it. We reify it by living it out respectfully and honorifically. We ought to memorize it and inculcate it into our core. It induces us to be citizens first. We have an awesome opportunity in this responsibility. We are born to be free, but we must work to avoid the risks of tyranny. We are born to be leaders in American society—not to take from it until it fails, but to give of ourselves for its constant nurturing toward its destiny, which is enshrined in its words. We all must uphold and live up to them one day. That day is coming. The experiment became a project. It completion we the everyday people must labor toward accomplishing it. Misguided doomerism only temporarily delays its full realization. We the next generations are its hope. We must pick up its torch, push aside the baby doomers, and get back on the correct constitutional course. We can do it! We can again be its stewards. Go forward we must!

The world continues to turn. Generations come and go. Wrongs continue to be exposed. What is right for us now is a renewed, rejuvenated, revolutionarily active civic action, done civilly. We will call it an action of exhibiting service above selfishness, saying yes to the utmost full-fledged thoroughgoing constitutionally allied, united "citizenshipping", understandingly synchronized (E-SASSY-T-TUF-FT-CAUCUS). By it, we will once again be good examples, "rocking in the free world". When freedom of natural rights and citizenship responsibilities become our strengths, the genesis of a time of better living is upon us. Commitment to being citizens first will reinvigorate in us the will to work toward achieving the virtue required of us.

For us to be one people, a national community, not just a collection of persons, we must adopt better citizenshipping. When we do, we will become a truly united people with a common cause of making a more perfect union. We should not shy away from the difficulties. Look at what it gave to us, its posterity—a complete reversal of power in society. As shown in the figure below, we the people are on top, put in charge. We must lead! To lead, we must not be afraid of civic engagement or avoid politics. We must enter it with dignity, respect, and the understanding that it is better than any other way. We must do it politely to bring credit to democracy. We need it to restore the possibility of prosperity for our progeny. We cannot let liberty fail. I cannot afford for us to be "A Nation of Spectators" cheering on only our chosen team. "Democracy is neither a consumer good nor a spectator sport, but rather the work of free citizens, engaged in shared civic enterprises", (The National Commission on Civic Renewal, 1997).

The creation of the US was momentous! It changed the perspective of the entire world! We owe it. It must be our first cause and not our excuse to do whatever we want! If we are true to it and take our identity from it, we will know that our first self-definition is as citizens. As citizens, we will responsibly uphold the words of the Constitution by our deeds. If we do, we'll begin to escape the shark-toothed jaws that are tearing us apart. Doomerism puts us in a sea full of sharks; once they begin biting, we start peeling apart. Once we are bleeding, then more sharks will feed on us, predator upon prey. We the people are not prey; we cannot behave as predators in our land of democracy. It will shred if we do.

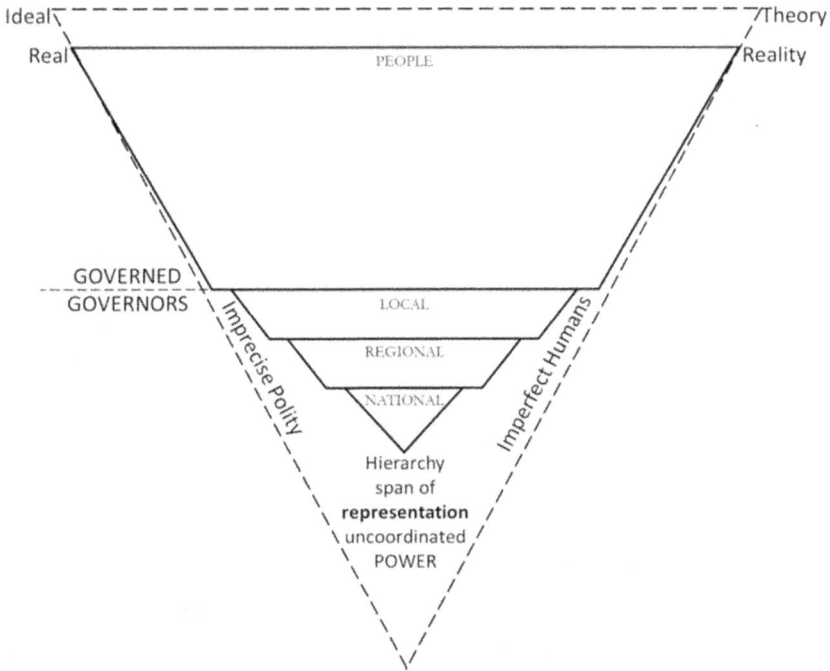

Figure 1-2: Representative Democracy in a Republic Puts the People in Charge, Designates Them the Object, Not the Subject

Our orientation toward one another will change when we begin again to walk forward with a belief in the Constitution as amended. It levels us to respect one another when we abide by its words. Attaining its objectives is our primary citizenship responsibility. We must work for it. As we achieve it in our daily lives, through mutually supportive behaviors that promote trust, neighborliness, honesty, and integrity, we will remake our society. We will rebuild and unify our many social communities into one people. We will restore our national community and put our nation back on course toward its destiny a victory of peace with justice and honor.

Twenty-Twenty, What a Prescient Number

The number 20/20 signifies good vision. We need clarity. Yet it seems we cannot see the same thing in the same way, as we used to be able to do when what we saw was our common good. Our hopes and dreams for the perfection of our union need reviving. They've suffered distortion. Misguided notions have watered them down. Dilution by beliefs in the false guides of consumerist materialism and governmental largess drowns them. Yet since our beginning, we the everyday people struggled. Since the ink was flowing into the parchment of the founders' Declaration of Independence, we have hid our hypocrisy. Each generation henceforth progressed toward remediating it, pushing us toward our Constitution's ideals. Each generation succeeded in getting a little bit closer, until the last one, which has held majority rule longer than any generation before it.

Forty years too long in majority did to them what our founders warned happens with power when held too long—corruption. Now here we are, a broken society, unaware of its true roots and missing the point of its true purpose. We need a massive revival of our society's first principles. We need everyone's personal commitment to aim at living by the virtues inspired by them. We particularly need it of those who've requested our permission to hold positions in the polity and govern. To govern is to administer the rules we put in place by our shared polity. To govern is not to rule. Nevertheless, if we do not lead the way in making our Constitution's objectives our focus, we will all find ourselves sailing on a ship of fools. This ship is full of risks we must mitigate, or we will sink or run aground, and our gift will have become lost forever.

We are floundering in our duty to shine the light of justice and hope for humanity in the power of democracy. We must restore ourselves as that city on a hill, whose temple to liberty and justice remains bright. Let us be seen in a better light. Let us be a better light. Let us, like a lighthouse, show the way to liberty. Let us be that beacon to the world. Let us proclaim that the everyday people, educated to the purpose of good citizenship, can self-govern their societies. By living virtuous lives, pursuing truth and justice with a deep moral and purposeful commitment to upholding our Constitution, we can illuminate humankind. Behaving correctly is our reason for being free from tyranny. Our Constitution and our being good citizens to uphold it, eliminates the risks of a kingdom, and daily subjugation. It establishes only the government we need. It puts checks and balances in place to prevent power concentration and abuse. We must honor it.

Throughout our history, there have been those who make life more miserable for the next generation. After forty years under the influence of baby doomers, our society has drifted off course, which dooms our progeny by reducing posterity's chance for prosperity. The most callous of them doom the entire society; destabilizing it is irrelevant to them. They want no accountability. These baby doomers hoard and chide. They hide and divide.

There would be no baby doomers if the majority of the baby boomer generation did not tolerate their egregious cohorts. They do not seem to know what liberty truly is. The result of their generation's time in power reveals they do not understand that their responsibility as citizens of the US is to protect our Constitution. They have failed to prevent it from disappearing from our daily lives. A majority of well-intentioned citizens would disallow such doomerism to prevail. Yet here we are in crises and chaos with them in charge, holding the top positions in the instruments of the societal powers, instruments they play mainly to please themselves, ignorant of the consequences to us. We've been the audience to their self-satisfaction. They offer no refunds for their poor performance. We are at risk of losing everything that we should be holding dear. Their superficiality is staring them in the face. But being shallow they like what they see. Yet we who are not them grow incensed by it. We ask ourselves, cannot they see that they are responsible for how superficial and failed our society has become under their tutelage? We need sensible stewardship. For forty years, fools afraid of catching the rats and throwing them overboard stood watch. Without pest control and good maintenance of the tenets of democracy, doomerism will continue to expose us to the risks of tyranny. Like a cancer tumor, it seeks dominance in our body polity. It seeks to rule all our societal powers and convert each of them into little tyrannies, exterminating liberty one organ at a time. Be warned. Beware a royalist's coat of arms. The bald eagle is in our heraldry. Proud and free, we are to be loyal to each other, constitutionally.

Constricting the bad to enjoy the good is the way democracy works to secure liberty. By encouraging the pursuit of virtue, society gets better and not worse. Happiness replaced the word property in a late draft of the Constitution's Preamble. Holding humans as property for labor, slavery, the means to wealth creation in the colonies was contrary to political humanistic idealism, but greed compromised a fear of economic impossibility, so it occurred. Yet we learned and turned away from it through civil war. Happiness grows from virtue. Virtue's pursuit in one's life course takes commitment. Pursuing higher standards through increasing levels of moral development takes work. Seeking to live toward being more honest and truthful takes effort. This is the truth. It is real. It is human. It is what makes democracy in a society possible. Democracy as the foundation of a society makes its governance by a republic workable. Be not confused! A Constitution writ from democracy, making a republic for the purpose of liberty, begins and ends in the behavior of the citizenry. Our collective commitment to the pursuit of virtue, period—no ifs, ands, or buts—is what is necessary to sustain it. If we want to be Americans, this is what we must do. The baby doomers have done the opposite. They need cast aside, reformed, and brought back into the fold in a different, subordinate role. Please read George Washington's Farewell Address to gain an appreciation for what an American people needs to be like to achieve the dream.

Continental Congress

Our Constitution's legal political construction gives us a voice in polity power's use. Its use by application, employment, implementation, operationalization, utilization, yoking, yielding, and keeping (AEIOUY^{2}K) is to serve the Constitution's fulfillment. We the citizenry believe in liberty and serve a purpose to defend it. The Constitution is our framework for freedom. Through our democratically elected representatives, we hire our officials. We periodically grant these officials positions in the pilothouse, on the bridge, and at the helm. We expect them to turn the wheel and pull the levers of our nation's steering mechanism to maneuver us toward our objectives. When our direction differs from the Constitution's, we end up in crisis. We the citizenry own the responsibility to ensure our officials pursue the objectives in the Constitution and no others. We're under constant distraction by doomerism. The officials are not using our polity power to act on our behalf. In a republican form of government that exists to uphold the agreed-upon common law, the citizenry, in majority rule, must lead society. We must work to keep in existence the believed foundational truth of the nation that all humans are as fact, created equal before the law of our society. Baby doomers couldn't care less about this higher-minded aim. It does not enrich them, and it requires sacrifices too deep for their superficial doomer selves to make.

Two hundred forty-five years ago, the Continental Congress of thirteen colonies declared their natural rights to be independent of the king of England's rule. Disrupting the pattern of power of rulers over the ruled, subjects of a king they wanted to be no more! Conceptually, liberty meant freedom to be dominant, not dominated. In reality, inequality persisted. Yet words written of an ideal condition, provided a guide to humanity and set a course to follow. These words indicated how to evolve a society of liberty. People no longer were to be subjects of tyranny but could own the responsibility to lead their societies.

Each generation must work toward the common goal of ensuring liberty for every citizen, no matter his or her origins. However, we've not yet normalized it to achieve the words' grand vision. We've not risen above the limited views of subjects. We've not followed perfectly the directions given to us. We are imperfect, but we can improve when we choose to work toward our common purpose to keep our liberty. Through the intentional disuse, abuse, misuse, and nonuse of power (DAMN), we've fallen off course. Various forms of trickery and pockets of deceit exist within our society. These retard our progress and divide us, so we resist moves to bring us together in pursuing the ideals of our country's founding. In fact, the wisdom in the founding, given to the citizenry, in general seems too often ignored. This is ignorant, because democracies are fragile and ever threatened by dark forces within. Without its full comprehension and complete commitment by the citizenry, liberty gets lost. Each successive generation's cohorts gain a majority of important societal positions. The combined consequences of its authorities' attitudes, behaviors, and actions shape society. With baby boomers in power, we've seen changes in social norms for the worse. Positions have roles, and the person in them is to play them professionally, living up to the position's importance to society. However, boomers have personalized role performance making it about their personal power and not the position's professional requirements of proper authority's application and administration. They act the way they personally want to because they think with ego only, imagining they were picked for the position because of their personal not professional qualities. They too often mistakenly conflate the two. This is one of their misguided presumptions.

Consequently, the majority of their cohort of elected officials, politicians, administrators, business managers, press executives, traders, commercial agents, advertising executives, etc. (name your occupation) have used their control over the decision-making to choose paths that enriched top position holders. This kind of choice is aristocratic in nature, creating super salaries and privileges for a few, which destabilizes trust in the society. If there are those who have more, simply because they can take extra for themselves, why would we trust them to make community consequential decisions? Why support such a system of society? When doomers adopt a purpose in life to find loopholes and widen them, so they may take more from others, it reshapes what is permissible. Action in this direction dooms everyone else's hope and destabilizes the whole society. It creates the policies that guide behavior and culture, resulting in the corrosion of society's mores. The future gets nothing but useless rust. It is immature to do as they have done. It's doomerism. We need to intervene with some adulthood wisdom from a slower time in history when great minds thought through the relations of human nature and human made society, creating a culture of democracy as an ideal posture for both.

Baby boomers' forty years of destructive (not instructive) mannerisms give us pause. We now must reform around our Constitution as amended. We must rid ourselves of doomerism caused corruption. We must rid our societal and social powers of it. As a citizenry we must revamp our purpose to serve one another through better behavior when we operate the functionaries, instruments, logistics, mechanisms, structures and systems (FILMS[2] [P7]) of our powers.

o The **Functionaries** are the functionary offices and their officials who hold the authority of the function of the power, like a priest in a church, a principal in a school, a governor in a state, a chief executive officer in a corporation, etc.

  • Example = Members of the governing body of the National Hot Rod Association

o The **Instruments** are the socially agreed upon legitimate forms of social groupings given specific authorities and status respect, typically known as organizations and institutions. Organizations can range from small clubs to professional associations, civic leagues, and corporations. Institutions are more behaviorally prescriptive organizations concerned with formal orders focused on meeting social and societal needs. People form institutions to last. Organizations more easily come and go.

- Example = National Hot Rod Association

o The **Logistics** are the methods by which the instruments AEIOUY²K power using culture. Logistics include the communications, customs, rites, actions, activities etc. performed by the functionaries, members, employees, fans, and believers of the instruments. Logistics, methods, are animate.

- Example = Racing series

o The **Mechanisms** are the means by which the instruments AEIOUY²K power. Mechanisms include the structures and systems of the instruments of power. Mechanisms, means, are inanimate. Logistics, methods, need mechanisms, means, to function.

- Example = Racetracks' governance, administration and operations

o The **Structures** & **Systems** created by the functionaries serve the mechanisms. Structures and systems shaped and sustained through shared Philosophies, Purposes, Processes, Precedents, Processes, Policies, Procedures, and Practices [P7] control powers by the force of these. These nine social inventions guide the work of people done for, in, and with the instruments, their logistics, and mechanisms. By using the structures and systems guided by the P7 to AEIOUY²K power, society happens. It comes into being as a thing we acknowledge. By cooperatively behaving to make a common interest happen, we reify the benefits of society and enjoy its expressive activities.

- Example = Race day race rules

We must regain control of society. We must pull out the roots of corruption in the micro level of society—ourselves, and our families, neighborhoods, and communities. We must pull out the roots of corruption in the meso level of society—our organizations and institutions. We must pull out the roots of corruption in the macro level of society—our structures of power that pervade all our lives. Our work is the work of gardening. Adults must develop and exhibit the patience and wisdom to do it properly. Baby doomers of seemingly perpetual pubescence do not.

As a generation, the boomers began adulthood waging a counterculture that in their middle ages became a culture war of righteous opinions. They amplified divisions by profiteering from the whole. Now they make irrelevant, distracting arguments as they pad their pockets. They commit a passive-aggressive crime against the citizenry. We let them. They, we, failed to lead properly. We cannot allow further thievery. We must grow up as a people, behave wisely, and get to work weeding our garden. We must free the roots of the Liberty Tree from the weeds of doomerism.

Adulthood

Human biology develops us as adults by the age of 24. However, our social-emotional-moral-spiritual-intellectual maturation can take a lifetime. Society does better when we strive to behave as adults, not remain as children. Supportive adulthood befits our American ideals. Maturity sustains our purpose as a people. This intention seems forgotten. As persons in positions at stations performing roles for the community, we must reclaim this wisdom, and live it.

Did They Ever Fully Grow Up?

It must have been nice to grow up in a time of amazing fortune and incredible opportunity. The world was devastated after World War II. The United States of America's military industrial base fully ramped up to produce consumer goods. The world needed supplies and financing to rebuild. The Marshall Plan in Europe and the reconstruction of Japan turned enemies into friends of democracy. This is the epitome of good adult behavior. Virtue in diplomacy is a hallmark of a democracy-loving people. Caring is sharing, and the dignity of others matters. Our commitment to help the vanquished restore civility and economy is a blessing of liberty shared. Liberty expands well; its contraction is the desire of tyrants, who are jealous of how loving it is since they crave to be adored. Allowing liberty means that it takes center stage and not them. A tyrant is like a spoiled child who becomes a bully when made to feel unloved. Our efforts to assist others recover from war's damage helped others live their lives free from starvation and death. We helped them live free from disease and regimes of tyranny. Our modern efforts prove that we were an adult leader for humanity. We gave hope to the world through our constancy, our aid, our strident belief in democracy, and our helping people be free to choose liberty. Liberty yields better circumstances and conditions for majorities than any other force of will. But we've been imperfect.

Boomers on the television (and all the other screens) tend to bicker. Like idealistic teens, they are unwilling to compromise to get something real done. Everything falls apart without the wisdom guided pragmatism and practicality of adult thinking. What has the majority baby boomer Congress done to keep our people from starvation and death by disease? Are they yielding a country where we can live our lives in dignity? What has happened to the riches of our victory in World War II? For what we've done as a people for the world, where is the benefit in living in this nation now?

We are less civilized than we think we are. Agitators, anarchists, and rebels always take advantage of chaos. Some try to get away with something wrongful, something they want to do that harms others. That is immature.

They create distractions (or leverage existing ones) to steal, as looters do. Those who disagree with movements do ruthless things to stop them, like rioting. We know all of this, but boomers seem incapable of stopping it. We are in a war of public opinion. The battleground is the media of the history power. Its instrument, the journalists, seems not to be reporting facts but choosing extreme sides. This is characteristic of non-truth-seeking baby doomers, who would rather exploit to profiteer than steer toward unity. In order to dominate market space and profit, they build echo chambers to perpetuate discord. They seek to shape opinions in line with what sells the most advertisements to a defined market segment. Advertisements by powerful corporations fund the division. How are these corporations helping society by doing this? They are not. They are only helping themselves by distracting the society from looking behind the dealmaking curtain for crooks. It's not transparent, as democracy requires. It's rather shameful. We must expose it to the light of day! It undermines the good that free markets can do when honorably led by ethical HM[5]. Our marketplaces are not perfect if they enable a plutocracy. An entitled class wants to be "in line for the crown" of American power. The plotting is brewing within our upper classes. This is what we must realize. This is something to fear, and we must fight against it as if it is 1774. The time is here for the next generations to engage in peaceable revolt at the polls.

Challenged by forgotten reasons for our success our survival as a species needs debated. The power of geography is changing. Our planet's climate is different than it was. We need to attend to this pending circumstance. Sadly, at a time of need for unified powers of academy, science, and polity with lawmaking and diplomacy, we suffer from baby doomers' contrarian arguments that do not guide us to face the facts. Are they in denial? Are they too selfish to sacrifice or share and care about our viability? Without a healthy geography, we are doomed. Our primate instincts drive us toward tribalism. Not controlling these instincts is immature. We need better adults aboard our ship's bridge. We need fewer intolerant self-righteous baby doomers in the pilothouse taking turns on the bridge at the helm of our society. They are not properly oriented to effectively deal with dangers up ahead. They spin the wheel riskily. They do not steer. They play around with our lives, whimsically pushing buttons and pulling the levers to please their selves. We need less careless, unserious, myopic thinking. Our lives depend on overcoming the small-mindedness controlled by instinctive fears, which allowed the baby doomers to drive us toward a jagged rocks culture of hoarding and hatred. These two kinds of human failure ruin our chances. We cannot afford to fail by falling for these tactics of doomerism. We must climb out of them. We must revive liberty and democracy. These must be our purpose. They will guide us to find solutions to save us from self-destruction—as a nation, as a people, and as a species.

Human Community Failures

The adjective "shortsighted" applies to both hoarding and hating behaviors. To engage in them is also uncivil and inhumanely selfish. Our capacity to cooperate defines our species. Yet thanks to doomerism, we forget this and think we must compete to win so all who are "other" will lose. Zero-sum is a false belief at the core of shortsighted, inhumane, selfish calculations. Game theory has proven this.

By the way, these mathematical estimations of selfish gain are capricious corruptions of the human spirit. That spirit being the inner voice telling us we are not alone and we cannot survive alone. Therefore, we must cooperate. The foundation of our democratic republic depends on the strength of this voice. It's our moral compass of right and wrong. Regrettably, because it is a countervailing power to the corruption that leads to hoarding and hatred, those tempted by the sense of power that hoarding and hatred give them suppress it. These feelings corrupt them. To help the species survive peaceably, we must divide and conquer power. This is the adage of American wisdom. The framers abided by it. As the parchment paper slowly absorbed the ink from their quills, our founding documents absorbed the greater meanings of it. Yet our generations since battle within, refuting and denying their wisdom. It was revolutionary. It placed new demands on humans to rise up and create a new order for the ages that was pleasing to Providence.

Getting people to agree upon and commit to the same voice of wisdom is the beginning of betterments and the problem solution behaviors we need. Wisdom enables us to become a self-sustaining, peaceful species on this planet. We can coexist without war. The amount of war among us is declining. We need to continue this trend. Deplorably, many power-hungry charlatans treat us as hordes of idiots and confuse us on purpose, incessantly stirring up the unnecessary emotions. It is an uphill battle to help people block the propaganda noise and be able to hear their inner voice of wisdom, which is the voice of humanity.

Humanity's Voice Cries Out for Love

Poets, prophets, and aphorists have tried for centuries to communicate important matters of being, becoming, and living in harmony. Consider this thought. It is a parent's innate love for their own creation, a baby, and not expectation of any reward the baby might bring them, which drives parental behaviors to assist babies. We need family to help the extended community survive. We need children for the species to survive. We reproduce by necessity of species survival. The economics of child rearing are, in part, an aspect of the survival of the whole society. People survive by helping society survive. The person thrives when the society thrives. The whole makes it possible for the "me." Survival is our primary value. Our species needs to survive. We must do what is good for us. Our culture is what helps us survive. Cultures evolve (Skinner, 1974). It is not a matter of scarcity, so that only a few thrive and the rest struggle to survive. Plenty exists. What are missing are distribution systems that justly reward the contributions that humans can make to the whole. The systems serving raw power hurt the ability of love to deliver. A few destroy the possibilities. Out of their weakness, we all suffer an ugly society. We war out of weakness, not strength (Schmookler, 1988). Love takes strength!

A **MEGALOMANIAC** Politician
wants to use **POWER** against
the **PEOPLE**

The "We the People" government delivered a Bill of Rights to us. Rights are a popular idea. Like on a coin, they are the obverse, and the reverse is responsibility. The edge that results from their joinery is democracy, which cannot exist without a good citizenry. The coin is worthless without a population that behaves as good citizens. Without citizenship as a common goal, bad, raw, gorilla-like primate power instincts corrupt. They shutter and sink the human humane spirit of wisdom and love. Bullies tend to take charge. Acting tough masks their weaknesses. We have too many complexities to act like a band of jungle primates. The herd of humans amassed does not organize well to fight back against the bully, but we must learn how. Predators are dangerous. Some among the herd must steel their spines and turn toward the hazard, motivate the herd, and advance in a holding action to stop the predator. The pack can then charge the predator and scare it off. This is the good from of power in numbers. But let this line of thought be a later discussion for us. Presently, out of 195 countries, (United States Central Intelligence Agency, 2020), there are only twenty fully functioning democracies (DeSilver, 2019). The tradition of the species is to be ruled. Any American calling their selves a "conservative" cannot hope in such tradition. It is anathema to democracy. A real conservative seeks to conserve the society of ideals framed by the Constitution. Any American calling their selves a "liberal" cannot hope in the government controlling everyone. It is anathema to democracy. A real liberal seeks to preserve the society of ideals framed by the Constitution, to advance the idea of America by leaving behind the hierarchical presumptions of monarchy. No one born is superior over others. This is the common sense of pamphleteer Thomas Paine.

The progression toward the Constitution's ideals is the progress of not giving the government more power. Progress is people improving ourselves to live up to the Constitution, so that we need less government. It is on the citizenry, our civil society and us. We are the ones who must repair our ways and save our nation from doom. We cannot love with doomerism in our hearts and heads. It blocks the whispering wisdom of the voices in our souls. We need to drop the argumentative labels with all their isms and re-build our society from the vision of a democracy-based culture in our founding documents as applicable to all human beings, without parsing by physical characteristics. Let's stop making excuses and get on with this work. We must figure out how to cope with the storming of the third stage in knowledge evolution (see Figure 5-1). Threats to our humanity exposed by technologies, whose profiteers use them to eliminate our necessity, need mitigation. There are many bleak visions of the future of our species and our society (Harari, 2019). We must avoid these dystopias by stopping the pathetic arguments over isms we cannot prove or disprove. The rhetorical polemics are jeopardizing our preparedness for the risky future of our en-terprise. We must get past them. To guide us fulfill our promise in the Con-stitution's Preamble, and do so better than previous generations, we need new words, new theorems, and new paradigms, based on originating prin-ciples. Or, we could face doom.

What we have in this country is unique and incredibly special. It comes with serious responsibilities. We must love it or lose it. It has inspired the rest of the world since it began. We must grow up, throw off doomerism, and assume a proper leadership role of adulthood guided by love. We can-not act only for material self-enrichment; we are not just economic pawns.

*S*ociety

Society is a human-made collection of social relationships organized like a system. An ideal one is a community propelled by a love for its endow-ments and agreements to honor it. If good, people live a good life. Society gives security, identity, and continuity of structure for progeny to perpetu-ate it.

Is It Yours, Mine, or Ours?

Society is a construction of everyone in it. We are all in it. We make it. It makes us. We can shape and reshape it when we have the liberty and framework that enables our work on it.

In the tyranny model, the polity has power over the people. The rulers and their court of butt-licking sycophants set the tone and determine its fate. The people are subjects, kept ignorant and without power. In the re-public model, the people have power over the polity. The culture comes from the folk; it is a culture of democracy. However, this is more difficult than being a subject. It takes work to be one's better self, commit to one's neighbors, and be a good citizen. But if that is what it takes to have democracy and a republic, then let's do it, without excuse and without fear!

These United States produced the generation that made this nation. We produced the generation that won World War II. These were our most civic-minded generations. We have another one, which is on the cusp of becoming our representatives. Blocked by a glass ceiling built by a generation that never grew up, we wait. They might yet mature fully as citizens. Until then they will continue to behave as spoiled brats, never knowing the strife and hardships that other generations survived. If only a few of them have, is this their fault? Not completely, but their idealism is off-center and a luxury we can no longer afford.

We need civic-minded energetics and a whole bunch of pragmatists to heal the wounds they have inflicted upon our society. We need to fix the ship and get it sailing in the correct direction. We need the next generations to sail it. We can join them in exhibiting service above selfishness, saying yes to the utmost full-fledged thoroughgoing constitutionally allied, united citizenshipping, understandingly synchronized (E-SASSY-T-TUF-FT-CAUCUS). This will get the job done. It will help the next generations prevent doom.

It is our society, not that of a ruling class. Why have we, the everyday people, been so foolish, giving away our power? By not behaving as good citizens, by making excuses and blaming others, and by being complacent and apathetic, we act as fools. It is time for the baby boomers' extended adolescence to end. It is time for them to grow up finally. It is time for us to love and behave lovingly. We need enlightened adult citizens guiding society for the sake of the newly born and unborn. Society needs future generations for our care and for our species' survival.

Being a citizen first is a rewarding investment of time, energy, and contribution. We can all contribute to society. It enriches our souls. Volunteerism enriches daily living. Charity, helping others through participation in associations and community-based groups, has been foundational in our society. Civic engagement of this kind helped make cities beautiful. We never waited around for someone else to come along and solve problematic situations. We, the everyday people, made a difference when it mattered. We did not seek to burden our government with aid provisioning. We knew that caused more taxation, and we dislike taxation. Can we remember the Stamp Act and the Liberty Tree in Boston? Taxation takes money away from our neighborhoods and redistributes it to other states. This has risks.

Central governmental policy drifts toward one-size-fits-all solutions. These do not quite solve anything locally, nor do they fit well the circumstances of the needy. By our local roots, we must find solutions in our regions that work best for our local social circumstances and particular environmental conditions. Local focus fixes frustrations, we get to know our neighbors, and we work together. Universal modernism had it wrong. We must recover from its failed beliefs in largesse operations to war on this and war on that and war, war, war until there is no longer any form of peace in society. All war does is make a few bastards too rich, and feeling powerful, they lust for more and more raw power, as if they rule the world. No one should rule over others.

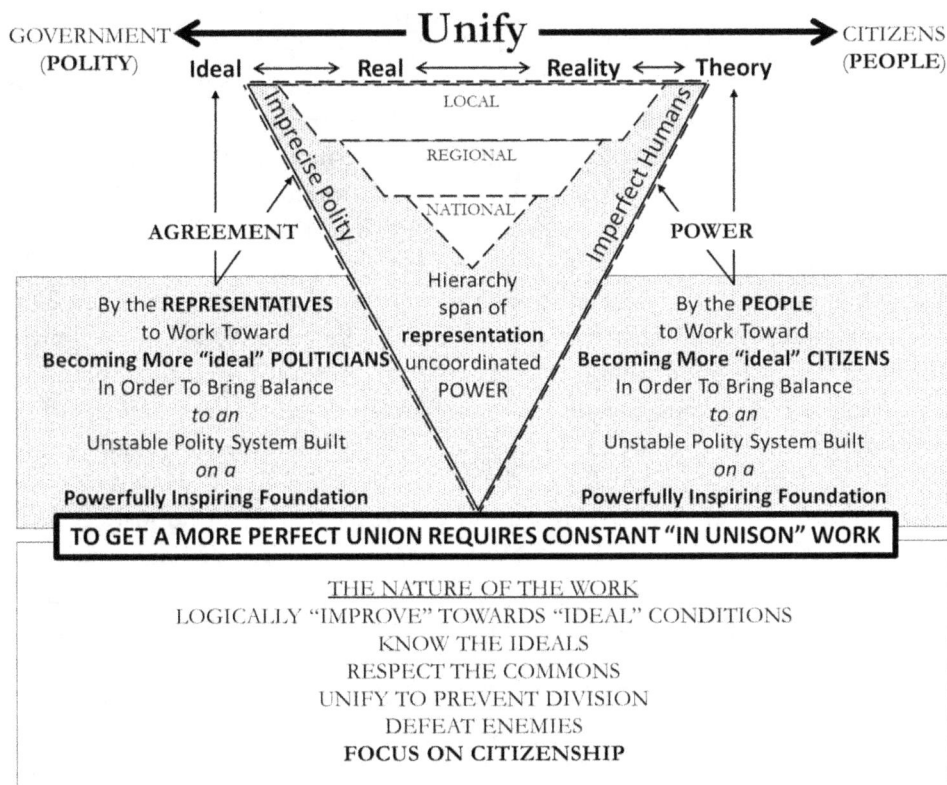

GOVERNMENT ←————— **Unify** —————→ CITIZENS
(POLITY)   Ideal ←——→ Real ←——→ Reality ←——→ Theory   **(PEOPLE)**

LOCAL

REGIONAL

NATIONAL

Imprecise Polity / *Imperfect Humans*

AGREEMENT   **POWER**

Hierarchy
span of

| By the **REPRESENTATIVES** to Work Toward **Becoming More "ideal" POLITICIANS** In Order To Bring Balance *to an* Unstable Polity System Built *on a* **Powerfully Inspiring Foundation** | **representation** uncoordinated POWER | By the **PEOPLE** to Work Toward **Becoming More "ideal" CITIZENS** In Order To Bring Balance *to an* Unstable Polity System Built *on a* **Powerfully Inspiring Foundation** |

TO GET A MORE PERFECT UNION REQUIRES CONSTANT "IN UNISON" WORK

THE NATURE OF THE WORK
LOGICALLY "IMPROVE" TOWARDS "IDEAL" CONDITIONS
KNOW THE IDEALS
RESPECT THE COMMONS
UNIFY TO PREVENT DIVISION
DEFEAT ENEMIES
FOCUS ON CITIZENSHIP

Figure 1-3: The Wisdom and Work of Citizenship to Stabilize Democracy
This image depicts the values of our republic's polity. It shows how to stabilize the power pyramid of our society. The theory that people can self-govern motivates us to apply personal biology, academy, and mythology powers to be more perfect persons. We aggregate to become a people when we recognize this common purpose and use our power to make our theory a reality. Furthermore, when our representatives seek to achieve our ideals by agreement through diplomatic deliberate discussions and debates using evidence and proven facts, they make our theory real. This is the work of E-SASSY-T-TUF-FT-CAUCUS. This is the work of democracy required for a republic to stay upright and not tip over. It is the essential duty of all of us to insure, d'ure, ensure, assure, lure, and secure (IDEALS) liberty.

We the people should govern. We the people consent to government. We the people staff it. Those who do must be the best examples of citizens among us. Not the worst, like the present-day baby doomers. They are a disgusting ilk of vile wannabe plutocrats who shamelessly shred the Constitution. They DAMN power. They must go, and we must rise to gain control of the way our societal powers, made by democracy-based culture, are fully ours to AEIOUY^{2}K in the service of our national ideals. We have the epic responsibility to complete the project begun 245 years ago. We need once again to take it seriously.

We must act now to stop the decay in our communities. We must unite as citizens to prevent any further destruction of the rule of law. Figure 1-3 shows a model of how we must work in unison to hold up our society. We can do it without depending upon a top down rule making hierarchy of control. The foundation of our community is following a few rules, and preventing the writing of more rules. We, the everyday people, must reclaim our leadership willpower and act together. These are our United States. It is our enterprise. We must steer it on the correct course of the Constitution's calling. Declaring our commitment to this momentous project, loud and proud, we will put it back on its path to liberty and justice for all, by truth.

Though we've departed from it from time to time, it originally was set up with inspiring words of wisdom. We need to quiet ourselves, reflect, think strategically, and hear the voices of wisdom again. We need to ignore the extremist noise and abide by the wisdom that all humans are equal in potential for good when created. We need to move in its direction, all of us, every day, in every way, in all we do and say. If we do, we will finally get to a promised land envisioned for us, by us, of all of us, a land we govern as a more perfect union. This is our union made for us. Continuously it calls upon us to steer constantly clear of emerging hazards like demagoguery and doomerism.

We must shepherd our society into the hands of the next generation and teach them how to steward it for the following one. This pattern must repeat for our posterity. We, the everyday people, must sustain this effort and stop being distracted by the false trappings of consumerist materialism that the baby boomers have used to enrich but a few of us. We, the citizens of the United States, must act like citizens first! This is how we right the course and get our enterprise back on the path toward a perfect union, in obeisance of its founding wisdom. This is within us as Americans. We have not forgotten how. We must not allow the fear of doom to overwhelm us. We must not lose our minds, our sense of decency, or our courage.

Wisdom is like a tree. It draws nutrients from the soil and spreads out to catch the sun. It lives proudly, giving away oxygen and taking in carbon dioxide. It breathes. It is true; it represents beauty in truth, a system of good. It is a symbol of truth. If truth symbolically is a tree, it is a tree of knowledge. Can we no longer see it for what it is? Do we only know it by an overly specialized catalog of its parts, a PhD for each identified element without vision to see it both as a whole and as a part of a larger ecosystem? Have we missed the ecology of its biology and symbiosis with its host—its earth, ground, climate, and atmosphere?

Figure 1-4: We Can See Society as a Forest Ecosystem, Aware of the Interplay of Its Parts

The Liberty Tree, symbol of the Revolution in Boston, needs replanted among others to form a Freedom Forest to save the ecosystem of earth and symbolize a resurgence of democracy for liberty in the US. Lanterns adorned the tree in March 1766 to celebrate the repeal of the Stamp Act. The tree was a rallying place to demonstrate opposition to British actions. In August 1775, British troops chopped down the tree. To Americans, General Marquis de Lafayette declared, "The world should never forget the spot where once stood Liberty Tree, so famous in your annals." The tree, while missing in reality, is metaphorically alive. As Thomas Jefferson wrote in 1787, "The tree of liberty must be refreshed from time to time with the blood of patriots & tyrants." As a sign of unity in reviving our first principles, we should all plant elms in our yards and parks. Liberty requires our vigilance. Until the elms are grown, on July 4th we should decorate a tree in each of our houses, yards, or neighborhood parks with replicas of the lanterns used in Boston in 1766. We'll take pictures and share them on social media to demonstrate we are making a comeback as the land of liberty. Everyone can also tell the world what liberty means to us by virtually hanging a statement lantern on the Liberty Tree found at the website: libertytree.historyisfun.org (an online exhibit of the Jamestown Settlement & American Revolution Museum at Yorktown, Virginia [historyisfun.org]).

Why does this matter? Well, conversely, if society metaphorically is the forest, (see Figure 1-4), a society built upon inalienable truths is sure to be in trouble when not one of its trees is visible for what it is and does to make the forest a living biosphere. Nor can we see what a disease upon one part of one tree is doing to the whole of the forest. If each tree is diseased and not behaving in accord with the needs of the ecosystem, we have a problem of colossal proportions, existentially threatening. We need to pull back from overspecialization and listen better, learning how to step back from the microscope and use our macro-scope. The one with a lens that helps us see the whole and attend to its needs, not just try to heal a bad part.

Our whole is society. We are its forest. Each of our families is a kind of tree. Each of us is a part of our tree: root, bark, branch, leaf, flower, trunk rings, etc. To learn who and what we are, what we feel is our identity, and our purpose for being alive, we search for answers inside and outside of ourselves. We have a whole forest to explore, but if we burn some of it down out of fear, we may ruin a part to which we belong.

Society presents itself to us at many levels in many ways, which trace back to the cultural powers we've created in it. We organize powers into social structures. Like a forest's ecosystem, we must be aware of how our society exists. We must each help it by finding and performing our role within it, and we must trust those who control its FILMS[2] [P7] to do so in a manner that favors our personal journeys toward becoming who we need to be to further everyone's self-fulfillment and societal sustainment. This is what "we the people" and "e pluribus unum" herald in stars and stripes.

Yet have we the people forgotten how to see the whole, while also seeing the parts and how they work sympathetically as a self-sustaining ecosystem? It is too easy to become complacent and confused by all the hyperbole of the media, the information overload, and the ease of finding data on the internet. We might now be so distracted that we don't recognize the metaphorical forest that is our republic and each tree (i.e., societal aspects like a family, a politic, or a generation) that makes it breathe with the livable lives of a free people.

It is not just a tree, a forest, or an ecosystem in which we exist. This is metaphor for a society: you, me, we, person, family member, neighbor, community member, state resident and national citizen. Forests are ecosystems. Ecosystems are incredibly complex. Society is complex. It is also complicated because it is made of us, imperfect humans, and we the people can be unpredictable. Thus, society can be unpredictable. People, one by one, can begin to understand society, like arborists and ecologists come to understand the behaviors of the forest: by tree, by parts of the tree, and by symbiosis of trees with one another and the climate. We must do this important work.

In addition, we need to remove the scales built up on our eyes. After eight generations of Americans since the founding, our eyes disguise the hurtfulness of the truth. To help envision how to remove obfuscatory blinders, this book singles out a societal disease that daily inflicts social damage that harms our Constitution. It diagnoses it and offers a cure that penetrates the crust caused by calloused hearts and closing minds. It uses stern language, tough-love talk, to get across its point. What is this conceptual disease, might we ask? It is an appraisal of the summation of the whole of a generation's way of being; its value set that differs from previous generations and how it has demonstrably demoralized and destabilized our constitutional democratic republic. Shall we hear more about it? Let's round out this introductory chapter and then move on to understand better human-made culture and societal powers.

*E*xperience

As we participate in living and development as a human in a community, we observe, sense, and apprehend in our mind, body, and spirit memories, knowledge, and skills that we come to as truth to ourselves. We experience our society, socially.

What Is Going on Here?

Not all in our citizenry share the experience of democracy as culture. We've had a rough history. However, we have a clear direction: the Constitution. Sadly, we've not lived up to its calling in totality. We've many marvelous pockets. But if we are to reach our heights, we need to climb out of our holes, and we need to be serious. The outside world is made frightening; this is how the rule of rulers, not the rule of law, operates. Persons who cannot behave as people create the problem. Persons who occupy extreme fantasies in their minds, devoid of comprehending the intent of democracy, are fringe elements that make better sound bites than regular folk doing good work. The bad persons got on the airwaves everywhere to everyone else. The mere fact of their fame causes a weakness to take over. Soon we start to emulate and worship them because they appear on the ubiquitous screens in our hands, houses, restaurants, and everywhere else. Images seen a thousand times reshape perceptions of reality. We tell stories. We idolize a few. Is this by mistake? Alternatively, is it a conspiracy to distract the people from being citizens, to fleece our riches?

Regular folk are going about living their lives without rule breaking or being nutcases, trying to earn enough to buy the necessities, enjoy holidays, and love their families. This everyday experience is real. It's cruel to portray it as lesser than to make us feel, or look, badly. It deserves respect and the dignity it preserves. So, who is responsible for the challenges we face, for the crises that we can never seem to stop seeing on the screens that are everywhere in our lives? Is evil making imagery irrevocably invading us?

When a society does not produce an experience of enlightened adulthood full of love, it devolves into an accumulation of a million selfish decisions made every day by self-centered, self-satisfying, self-aggrandizing, aggressive, greedy, lustful, vainglorious, and gluttonous persons. Such persons cannot be a people. They take and do not give. They just want it all, and they want it now, like a mad queen. Becoming one people requires that each person give. We cannot have a society of only those who take. The name for the condition when such persons get the majority and create in society an ugly culture is "baby doomerism", which amplifies and exaggerates the worst instincts in our species.

Baby doomerism began its dominance in our society during a single, materialistically fortunate generation that failed its moral tests due to insufficient integrity. Acting unethically, baby boomers worst practitioners made up the majority of the citizenry. They have dragged all of us off course, leading our democracy toward tyranny. Forgetting to be citizens first, they failed to thwart invasive traits from taking root in our soil. Now we have some serious gardening to do to remove the unwelcomed weeds, before they kill our homegrown democracy and extinguish its fragrant liberty.

Baby boomers quash the chances of posterity, which is an oppositional act against the Constitution. Strictly speaking, in the most conservative terms, as a patriot trying to conserve the Constitution: they have been treasonous. To enable the rise of tyranny as they have, so long as they got theirs, proves they do not care about our society. For them it was all about "me first," not being a citizen first. They lie to themselves. They rationalize. They will not listen. They will immaturely shout, "Screw you!" Under the rule of doomerism, we now live in a society full of doom for our babies, newly born and unborn.

Doomer society does not support our nation's founding values enshrined in our Constitution. We don't live as if we were Americans. Yet here we are in the year 2021. We must better educate ourselves on the nature and essence of power and society's FILMS[2] [P7] intentions with it. Those who use power wrongfully are playing games on us, with us, and against us as a people. We need to recognize power at play. It can be operant as:

- Political (government, voting, countervailing factions)
- Economic (money, markets, distribution, recognition)
- Social (organizational [charismatic, technical knowledge base, authority positional], change-demanding group movements, neighborly bonding, teamwork-inducing, empathetic, educational, and psychological resiliency)
- Knowledge (academic clout, manipulated values)
- Technology (weapons, information computation, communication, medical, engineering of all types [nano, bio])

We the everyday people need to converse more about what power is and why it is dangerous if dealt with improperly. We must keep it divided, conquered, and dispersed democratically throughout our society. We must recognize its proper uses and ensure its sharing is transparent. Power is a human tool. We invented many social forms of it in society. We are social organisms. We need to understand ourselves as a species better than we do. We must reconcile our behavior with the knowledge of how we behave. We behave in more predictable ways than we think. We have a way that is species-based (Skinner, 1974). Power is a behavioral component. We have an unchanging human nature, which we can nurture under control and use to make democracy work. But it is work: self-work and societal work. It is the work of power properly managed to prevent the risk of instincts taking over. Because our republic is a special social invention, a politic miracle that changed the world (Skousen, 1981), we must act differently than our instincts predict.

We must act as Americans! Our duty is to keep power in check and balanced. This is a patriotic calling—a purposeful legacy—we must pursue with every fiber of our being. We must generationally prove our mettle. Citizens of this country, this is our presiding responsibility! We must mature as a citizenry to be always E-SASSY-T-TUF-FT-CAUCUS. But before we begin to learn more about this, each of us needs to take inventory of our present attitudes. The above figure is an analytical tool with which we can do so. It will help each of us identify what we believe to be true about liberty. Our thinking about liberty is essential to our understanding of how we must control power to fulfill the promise of democracy. Our thinking about power arrangements influences the essence of society.

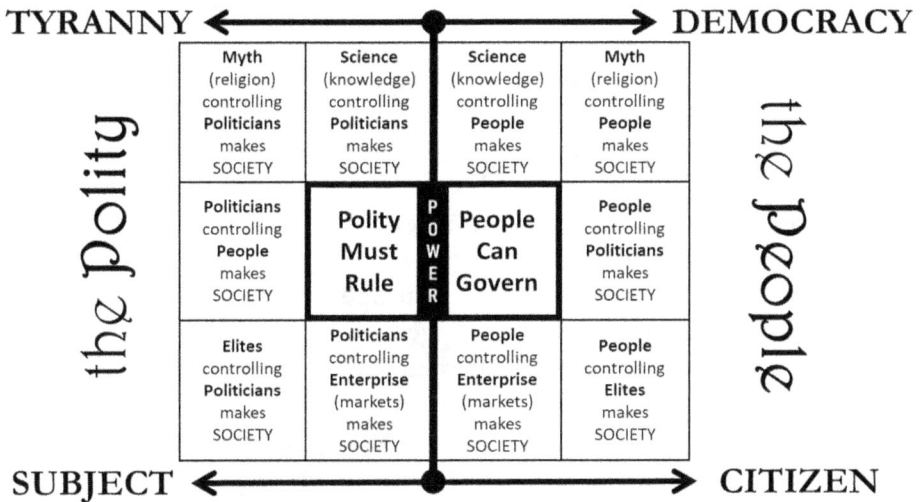

TYRANNY ⟵————————⟶ DEMOCRACY

Myth (religion) controlling **Politicians** makes SOCIETY	Science (knowledge) controlling **Politicians** makes SOCIETY	Science (knowledge) controlling **People** makes SOCIETY	Myth (religion) controlling **People** makes SOCIETY
Politicians controlling **People** makes SOCIETY	**Polity Must Rule**	**People Can Govern**	**People** controlling **Politicians** makes SOCIETY
Elites controlling **Politicians** makes SOCIETY	**Politicians** controlling **Enterprise** (markets) makes SOCIETY	**People** controlling **Enterprise** (markets) makes SOCIETY	**People** controlling **Elites** makes SOCIETY

the polity — POWER — *the people*

SUBJECT ⟵————————⟶ CITIZEN

Figure 1-5: Power in Tyranny and Democracy Assessment Card

The card divides vertically into two halves. On the left of the power-line is tyranny, and on the right is democracy. Each horizontal row includes a statement of who, or what, is controlling whom, or what. The top row shows the control of science and myth. The second row shows the control of the people and politicians. In the center, around the power core, find the essential liberty statement regarding the relationship of the people-power vs. the polity-power. The third row shows the control of the economy. The double-arrowed top line indicates the degree to which a society is creating the conditions of tyranny or democracy. The double-arrowed bottom line indicates the degree to which a society is creating the conditions of liberty for the people. In a tyranny, every person is a subject, while in a democracy every person is a citizen (with or without legal status, since citizen here refers to a proper attitude and behaviors).

To fill it out with your perspective, read each box. Each box represents a relationship of control. Fill in the boxes that you feel best represent your attitude. There is no right or wrong answer. There is only your answer. What is important is to think it through and record what you think. This will clarify for you your present perspective. When you complete this book, you will have a chance to complete this card again. At the end, enjoy comparing your cards. Reflect on them. Show them to your family, friends, coworkers, neighbors, and community associates. Invite them to get this book and do it. Then get together and talk about what changed, if anything changed, what it means, and why. Compare, contrast, and discuss everyone's results in a diplomatic and collegial manner, seeking to understand. Try to convince one another with reasons, not emotions, why one box is better for our society than another box. This is one exercise of enjoying democracy-based culture. It is a practice of power comprehension and civic awareness. We the everyday people must be more engaged or those in positions of authority will walk all over us because of (guess what) human nature and power's pull upon us.

Our requirement as citizens is to regulate power. To regulate it, we must know it. This book will helps us know it. Either we come to practice and enjoy democracy to control it, or we let ourselves by entertainment fall into numb, dumb fools by those who: want it, will do anything to get it, or do whatever they want with it. The latter is the path toward dependency and the return of the rule of tyranny over the descendants of the former European colonies in North America. European subjects we are no more, thanks to our forebears and following generations who advanced our project toward its stated ideals, in historic determination to be free.

Next, we will move on to a discussion of human-made powers, crafted of culture and shaped into structures of society. We will look at the good, the bad, and the ugly powers in the context of their relationship to democracy and liberty. We will realize how they form and stabilize society and how they are currently destabilizing society in the hands of the baby boomers at the helm of our society, in control of the FILMS[2] [P7] of our nationhood's good enterprising ship. We must recover the proper operant behavior of our powers for democracy to prevail over tyranny of every kind. In particular, doomerism's dangerous risks are explained later. We will also discuss the ideality of democracy and its life cycle in civilizations. Be warned: tyranny is a pressing, ever-present threat both within and outside our borders.

2. "Unity Calling"

This chapter theorizes that power expressed in many forms shapes culture. Combined, these "powers" make society.

It is in our genetic code that we are social beings. Called to unify are we. If we do not, we die. Our survival as a person depends on others, and others depend on us for the survival of society. In our American culture as one people, we fight our tribal voices to look past the obvious differences to see the character of others. We as a species do more cooperation than competition. How else could we have built a society governed by a republic polity using a culture of democracy? We did it through cooperation. Baby boomers opened up vulnerability in society, a hazard that threatens us. Call it doomerism. Doomerism's obsessive competitiveness is an immature challenger to democracy culture's drive toward harmony and unity. Yet if people are persons, and not a people, we'll lose it all. Prepare to be a citizen, a champion for the cause of liberty, or get ready to be a serf. This is the clear choice when we open our eyes to see what is happening today in our society. We, the everyday people, must restore a balance of societal powers that works in our favor—the propped up, upside-down pyramid, which is the right side up of power for our unique society (see Figure 1-2 and Figure 1-3), or it will come tumbling down. If that should happen, we'll be looking up and seeing a crown. Do we really want that? Is doomer society better for you, for me, for us? Is it full of harmony, love, and unity or iniquitous hatred, anger, and fear? Don't desert the cause of liberty in the name of a tribe. Don't tread on me. Unity is the key. It is calling. Let's listen to it. Hear the voice of wisdom whispering through the ages into our American ears and know that our true soul clamors for liberty. Power divided accordingly is a safer course of action for an American society, or else it will conquer us. Let's take a closer look at power and understand the basics of it. How does it operate in society? How is it "engine energy" for the business of society? Let's examine it: the good, the bad, and the ugly.

*G*ood Power Modes

Firstly, power is good. Without it, there would be no society, no humanity, and no personal, cultural, or societal growth and fulfillment. In the simplest sense, skeletal, muscular, and other tissues give us the ability to eat, walk, play, work, etc. Mind power gives us both the ability to think and the ability not to have to think about how to exist, that is, to breathe and make our organs function so we remain alive. It, with our nervous system, biologically keeps us going. This is biology power. Power is good when it works properly. It is proper in a society, when it works for good, for goodness' sake, which is when it serves the people, and we, the everyday people, regulate it to protect our liberty.

Secondly, power to serve the people in a democracy must insure, d'ure*, ensure, assure, lure, and secure (IDEALS) liberty in all its good uses in every realm. The realms and arenas of power and their FILMS[2] [P7] are all matters of social organization by human culture. Thus, all societal powers are human-made and are therefore malleable. As an American society, we must keep our eye on power in all the forms it presents to us. Questions about power are the most important questions we must ask ourselves in society, and of those, we authorize to AEIOUY[2]K them. This is the lesson of wisdom that we have forgotten. We must revive our regulatory spirit to control the societal powers, before those in positions of authority disavow us, forgetting that we by consent allow the powers to govern us. We the people came and come first; the powers come second, in all their permutations. Our preeminence is our inalienable, natural right from birth. Let us examine how we must IDEALS liberty. This is our job as citizens, as a citizenry in unity. We IDEALS liberty by putting it in place in our hearts, minds, bodies, and souls, and in our culture of, by, thru, with, and for, democracy.

- We must make the societal powers **insure** liberty.
  - What do we mean by "insure?"
    - It's democracy culture's **pledge** to make certain that no matter what we'll have it, worthily and affordably.
      - to **insure** its existence
        - we must protect it from possible loss to negative risks becoming realized
- We must make the societal powers **d'ure** liberty.
  - What do we mean by "d'ure?"
    - It's democracy culture's **practice** of it in all the ways we can, to accustom ourselves to it, to use it. Any

exercise of it we can in order to be with it and live in it.

- to **d'ure** it is used
  - o We must promote taking positive risks.
- We must make the societal powers **ensure** liberty.
  - o What do we mean by "ensure?"
    - ▪ It's democracy culture's **safeguard** to make liberty safe and certain to be there, and that we'll work to guarantee its availability.
      - to **ensure** it exists
        - o we must protect it from the consequences of negative risks
        - o we must promote it for its positive risk-taking opportunities
- We must make the societal powers **assure** liberty.
  - o What do we mean by "assure?"
    - ▪ It's democracy culture's **tale** that tells everyone "liberty is here to stay", and we may take comfort that it is available.
      - to **assure** it exists
        - o we must protect and promote it, regardless of the risks within it and outside of it
- We must make the societal powers **lure** liberty.
  - o What do we mean by "lure?"
    - ▪ It's democracy culture's **promise** of its rewards to draw everyone into its sphere and commit to making certain it is in them and others.
      - to **lure** people to it
        - o we must protect and promote it, regardless of the risks within it and outside of it
- We must make the societal powers **secure** liberty.
  - o What do we mean by "secure?"
    - ▪ It's democracy culture's **certification** that it will be available for everyone, at all times and everywhere.
      - to **secure** it exists
        - o we must protect and promote it, regardless of the risks within it and outside of it

Thus, to IDEALS liberty, we must pledge, practice, safeguard, communicate, promise, and certify that it is here to stay and it is not going away, over our dead bodies. As Virginian founder Patrick Henry said in his speech when revolutionary war was looming with Great Britain, "I know not what course others may take, but as for me, give me liberty or give me death!" This is the fervor we need in our rising generations. This patriotism will cast off doomerism and restore democracy to IDEALS liberty. What greater purpose in humankind's existence is there?

*(d'ure is a creative neologism borrowing from the French, remembering that our founders depended upon them during the Revolution. Linguistically, the French d' is an elision of the prepositional "de" that happens before words that start with vowels. It serves a prepositional function to deepen the meaning and understanding of the word it precedes. In this case, it means of, with, in, the noun liberty. This transitive verb, "ure", tells us we are "to use; to exercise; to accustom by practice our use of. Using d' before it deepens its meaning. Plus, it pays a bit of homage to General Marquis de Lafayette and the French, without whom General George Washington and the Comte de Rochambeau could not have defeated General Lord Charles Cornwallis and received his surrogate's surrender of the British army at Yorktown, Virginia on October 19, 1781.)

Thirdly, power helps us organize. Without sharing power in society, we would find ourselves in an anarchistic state of wildness, survival our only cause. This would hinder our creativity and ability to celebrate one another's gifts, modulating and adapting our culture to the events of life in every generation. Organizing allows all in our society to pursue harmony and to survive disharmony, conflict, and chaos. The best case for us is that the central purpose of liberty in all things should regulate. Understood as a core value of our society, liberty is the foundation of our culture, based in democracy that provides, produces, and preserves personal dignity. This requires thought and effort. Our ideal conception of liberty comes to fruition when we are unaware of and believe in inalienable natural rights as the foundation for a society of people who choose to be free. Our passions want to be free; freedom in mind, body, heart, and soul is natural and inalienable. We must nurture one another to IDEALS liberty. Given by citizenship we own a great honor to pledge allegiance to this task as citizens of the United States, with a serious responsibility to set examples for all human history and the rest of our species. Our best immigrants have honored this special calling. We must not be conceited or arrogant. We must live up to it to prove we deserve the label, American.

Homo sapiens have determined certain means to exert control over and to extract resources from the planet and in doing so have encultured power into various forms for particular purposes, both for survival and for creative expression and higher-minded pursuits, such as liberty and justice. Power has found its way into key areas of our lives and our society. Structured in social forms, organization by culture in society, we AEIOUY^{2}K power. Principal among the social forms of power is that which is within the people, the polity, and the economy. Let's take a closer look at these three societal powers, then examine subordinate and alternative forms of social power in society.

The Three Primary Powers

In organizing society, personal power provides a means for each person, and a people, to demonstrate leadership in their lives and for others. Assembled together, it is people power. We make this power into our polity power that best provides for administration of the rules by which we conduct the business of society. The business of society is to provide us what we need to survive, to live, and to thrive. This involves our people power making our economy power. This power best provides for management of the provision of necessities, first to survive, then to live, and ultimately to thrive. This power is extremely important. It makes the goods and services. It gives us work, the processes that makes such products we can exchange, buy, or sell in the marketplace. These three primary powers combine to form the essential triangle of powers in a society framed upon democracy as the principal culture for organizing people. The balancing of these three shapes the experiences people have in society. The best experiences happen when these societal powers are in a stable balance that supports liberty. People come first, then the rules, then the trading. This is the virtue of democracy. We should never allow either the rules or the trading to be more important than the people are. Such misbalancing destabilizes American society and dooms its success.

Let's Stabilize Society!

As a basis for society, why is democracy the best way of organizing people and the most radical social innovation of all time? Can we remember 1776? It began with a love for liberty. Liberty is the inalienable natural right of every human being. This love we must reignite. Liberty led to our Constitution, which as amended by social movements and majority consent of the governed, moves us closer to its ideals. When loved, the Constitution births a way of living and being that is wholesome, healthy, and happy because it elevates the spirit of love for liberty. Without this love of the concepts in our founding document, we cannot love one another as neighbors, as family, or as citizens. The Constitution is our touchstone. We must read and ruminate upon it regularly, and at least once in our lives make pilgrimage to see it and its harbinger, the Declaration of Independence, in the National Archives in Washington, DC. Visiting the magnificent originals is magnanimous. Being with them reflectively and reflexively, thinking upon their courageous miracle for humankind enlivens an honorable sense of our responsibility for unity with each other as the recipients of their endowment and our opportunities. When we see them for what they created, we can become inspired, and confident that we too can be creative and solve the problems we now face in our society. The Constitution as amended teaches us how to get along, how to solve intractable problems, and move past what feels like permanent argument. We need to adopt its advice.

When we do, when we walk with it within ourselves, when it gives us meaning and purpose, we need to sit with it because it needs us now. As our touchstone, it has gone cold. It needs the warmth of our hearts and our outstretched hands reaching to feel its magnitude's energy course through veins, give chills up spines, and honor its creation for us, the everyday people. It awaits this respectful grace of our hands and prayers as we close our eyes to imagine the awesome, risk-taking courage given for its creation and preservation and for the opportunities imagined by its begetters in colonial America.

Let's now reflect upon it for good luck, for Providence, good government, and a better civilization of better citizens to uphold it. Our fortune intertwines with the love we give to it, the love we give to others, and the love we have for our own selves. Selves we must own on our own by ourselves. This is what makes a people of liberty joyous. When we allow this kind of love, we'll again discover its power. From that moment on, we will not be able to stop talking about it, like grandparents of their grandchildren, parents of their kids, brothers and sisters of each other, and fans of their favorite sports team, artist, musician, scientist, or mathematician.

Built to love were we. Love is our bonding force. When we begin to love the Constitution to the point at which we commit to serve it by giving evidence of its wisdom, then we'll begin to see the unity it intends for us. This is in our hands. We must get this into our heads and possess it in our hearts if we want to be the Americans of liberty and justice for all. The Constitution meant to solve problems of its day (Rakove, 1996) and to provide a way for future generations to perfect its intended ideals. Indeed, we are at a timely hour once again in 2021, one year, two score, and a second millennium later. For us, this is a time meant for significant civic engagement and intelligent political activity, as it was for the revolutionaries in the colonies.

We are in turbulent trials of crises, as were they. We can find strength and resolve for liberty in their example. At this timely hour, the clock ticks for us, its tocks counting down to when we ignite a necessary and proper full-throttle, nationwide constitutional revival. The calling is rising in our ears, in our patriotism hidden deep within us. We feel it. We need to hear its yearning. We must begin relearning the lessons of love for liberty. We must know what it really means for us as persons and as a people. What it brought forth before was grand. What glory will it yield now with us? For us, the everyday people, we must regain our love of our country's purpose, its reason for being, and our awesome responsibility to serve the liberty of humankind, eliminating tyranny. We must sustain the dream of democracy. It is an honorable duty. No greater mission exists!

We must cease and desist from the drifting caused by virtueless misguiding values lived by the baby boomers. Have no misgivings. We are off course. It happened during their tenure in the pilothouse on the bridge at the helm, and it runs like the mutiny of cowards throughout the compartments of our good ship, an enterprising nation. We've an awesome responsibility to steward it, IDEALS liberty and fulfill its unresolved healing. We must stop reeling from the assaults of forty years of a pervasive, invasive doom in our culture. To do so, we need to behave as better citizens.

We, the everyday people, must rise up to be a heroic citizenry. We must desire to inspire. We must aspire to deserve the victory achieved in the name of liberty! Liberty ordained our republic with a culture of democracy. Our polity, unlike any other, formed us to make a more perfect union and build a legacy for freedom for all humankind to see, believe, and feel each day. The possibilities are immense. We must dispense with the defeatist mentality given us by doomerism. Its scare tactics of scarcity are the strategy of wannabe aristocrats to take back the power the framers and latter day prophets of liberty, Abraham Lincoln and Martin Luther King, Jr. ensured its sharing with us. To put it plainly, a few want power to feel superior. No one is superior in power in a democracy. Some have more of this or that capability or capacity to perform this or that activity. However, this inequality is natural (Will, 2019). We should not begrudge anyone the gifts they have been given. Liberty allows it. What liberty does not like is the DAMN of good power for bad or ugly purposes.

Watched are we being, but we are floundering in our duty. We seem lost. This is because we misplaced our unconditional affection for our Constitution, both the document and its occurrence. The promise it gives us is our core center of mass, liberty, which is our true stability and our unflappable confidence in what we are expected to be—true to it and good to our posterity. For "we the [everyday] people" to enjoy a society with justice, domestic tranquility, common defense, and to generally fare well in the course of our lives, we must pursue virtue to get to that which makes us happy. Virtue principally must precede any of our other ambitions because it creates the conditions by which we do not infringe upon one another's liberty. Without it, we degrade into tribal primates fighting over who is in power. We are now too technologically mature for that sort of puerility, as if being perfectly purely this or that kind of person is a purposeful possibility. Life simply is not that simple. It is complex. This fact we must accept. Then next, seek to understand the rest. Coming to know each other better as human beings is the progress made possible by the Constitution's Preamble. If purity were possible, we would not have so many schools of thought. Moreover, a purist's monoculture would be very boring, and vulnerable to risky hazards like boredom, which can lead to idlers doing credulously bad things in search of finding some meaningful spice. Vices like spite and villainous prejudice could disguise hatred of an "out" crowd by a purifying "in" crowd. We know the history on this lie. As technology increases the damage we can cause one another, such danger ought to push us together socially, not divide us. Think, could it be some power lusters intentionally aim to flog us with dogma to separate us from what is ideologically American? If we continue in this way, into the hands of evildoers the artificially intelligent machines we will build will go, and they will annihilate us (Harari, 2019).

Established governments by the people with democracy culture separate the polity power structures set up to protect the people from unruly power ploys. This is as it should be in a republic. Three polity power structures administer the rules of society—legislative, executive, and judicial. The US Constitution calls these roles "branches" of government. Trees have branches. The founders imbibed the famed symbolism of the protest Liberty Tree, whose branches held the lamps of dissent against tyranny. Most of us learned about these in school. Let's refresh our memories. These three branches must stay balanced for liberty.

Legislative powers

For making the rules, the laws assemble the foundation upon which structures of power build a frame for a society. To establish norms to guide behavior, we need legislatures. Laws benefit society as we travel through time into an uncertain future of increasing levels of knowledge and technology. Each new era finds us in a constellation of generations, together discovering new ideas or new materials. We make new discoveries, invent new technologies, or realize the wrongs in our past we must right. We write laws for society to adapt and keep a foundation in place for society to flourish. When we are under threat, we legislate to deal with it, such as a declaration of war or the borrowing of funds from future generations to pay for fixes in the present, which we feel makes their future possible. Through representatives to the legislature, we make our voice heard in society's rule making. If we are not engaged in regulating the legislative powers, we may get laws we disagree with, so it is incumbent upon us to participate in politics. This is actually a blessing of liberty. Representation protects us from tyranny. However, we must pay attention and participate regularly! We the everyday people must regulate by dissent and consent to protect our first principles—to IDEALS liberty, which leads us by the rule of law to justice for all.

The legislative power is the branch we must most closely regulate to ensure they do not DAMN their powers. They have "not-used" their power properly because they allowed the executive to amass too much power. Why is this? Did they not want watched? Were they deflecting and allowing the media to go hyperbolic with reporting the behaviors of the executive so they could get away with something? Where were we the people? This is a failure of the people power to seek to know what the legislatures are doing.

This is a failure of the history power to report facts of events correctly, which would support the people's need of truth. What is it about baby boomers that while they dominated the society, staffing the FILMS[2] [P7] of the history powers that they disproportionately misbalanced their reporting on the activities of the polity? They shaped public opinion too much on the importance of the executive, wrongfully apportioning their time to it, (likely, selfishly, because it was easier that way). Were they all in it together as a generation? How could they have been so off course for what the Constitution, the republic, democracy, we the people, and liberty needed?

Executive powers

For enforcing the rules made by the legislature, a coequal executive branch was established. The executive office, led by the president, meant to be weaker in dictating the nature of society is supposed to focus on foreign affairs, external threats to our common defense, more than on domestic matters of the states. The founders foresaw many problems with too much power vested in any one office or person, especially after their experiences under the king of England. They intentionally limited the basic roles of our government, particularly confining the president to foreign policy, the administration of cabinet offices, executing followership of the laws formed and funded in Congress. Key among these is a department of waging and preparing for war to aggress or defend. This contains the military services. A related department exists to support veterans of war. An important need in foreign policy is for a department of peace to engage in diplomacy and make, negotiate, monitor, and manage our agreements with other sovereign nations, including indigenous tribes. For both war and peace, we need information, or "intelligence," about other nations' interests and intentions regarding our relationship.

To benefit society, we establish government departments to put rules in place. Domestic policy that manifests the ideas in laws, to ensure domestic tranquility and promote the general welfare, is a key area in our government's administration of its assigned role in society. Also key are the departments that frame marketplace feasibility for the freedom of exchange that allows our economy power's best use of, by, and for the people. These include departments of natural resources, trade and commerce, and work security to support labor. We also have departments of financial security to help with pension management. Pensions are delayed compensation for lifelong laboring that enable society to increase in plenty as it thrives. In addition, to support human rights, the natural rights protected by the Constitution and valued in democracy, the executive branch manages many other departments. We have departments of humane humanness, like medicine (healthcare), which provide assistance to the infirm, disabled, and elderly, who need care from others to survive, live, and thrive. Lastly, governments fund and administer much of the discoveries of science. Private

funding is not sufficiently prevalent. Profits are more important than science to save the species. The people need help, the governments filled the void left by the greedy fleecing of private persons taking and not giving to aid the community. This gives the
executive more power over the shaping of society.

Why did the baby boomers allow the executive to gain in power? The Constitution requires a weak executive because the founders knew of the dangers of allowing too much power in one human being. Knowing human nature, and the imperfect aspects of it, the executive powers were limited. Did the baby boomers simply want to be superstars and worshippers of celebrities, so they turned the executive into a royal to gossip about? Is this a good social circumstance for American society? Were they all in it together as a generation? How could they have been so off course for what the Constitution, the republic, democracy, we the people, and liberty needed?

Judicial powers

To interpret the rules, a coequal judicial branch was established. To isolate the courts from political pressures, judges' appointments are for life. Thomas Jefferson and Abraham Lincoln viewed the judicial branch as the least democratic because elections do not select judges of the federal government (Rakove, 1996). This branch, with its courts, is integral to establish justice, ensure domestic tranquility, and protect our liberty by keeping the other two governmental branches inside their canals, while preventing cabals. The judiciary has courts for both criminal and civil disputes. It settles conflicts in the interpretation of the application of laws in appellate and the Supreme Court. In the US, citizens are innocent until proven guilty, viewed as trustworthy. This concept does not mean that one can do wrong and then say, "Prove it." That mentality undermines democracy. We must pursue honesty first, not dishonesty that then tries to hide behind the cultural value of presumed innocence. Interpretations of the Constitution provide further legal infrastructure on how the people are to follow the rules, which further sets the expectations of behavior. The best way for people to stay out of legal trouble and prevent too much treasure spent on courthouses is for them to see themselves as citizens first. Citizens uphold the law by obeisance, and police who keep the peace must abide by good citizenship to prevent biased enforcement. Wrongdoing and wrongful treatment are uncivilized and uncivilizing. Neither one is helpful or healthful for the citizenry as a whole.

Judicial powers also help ensure for the economy power a level playing field with fair rules and fair play. Yet despite the warning of the founders regarding the despotic risks in the judicial powers, the use of the powers drifted into legislative territory, and the legislative branch and executive branch allowed it, even seeking to put justices in place in hopes not of fair judgement, but wishing for biased judgements toward their political philosophical biases. Yet, the judiciary's deference to the other branches undermines their coequal branch status. They cannot become derelict in their duty in protecting people's liberty from the overreach of government or from a majority faction overtaking our lives. Majority may rule, but the judiciary must uphold our liberty, and not let the other electorate chosen branches take away any law-abiding citizens' liberty (Will, 2019). Why did the baby boomers perpetuate such political action related to selecting justices? Were they all in it together as a generation? How could they have been so off course for what the Constitution, the republic, democracy, we the people, and liberty needed?

Primary Powers' Proper Operant Behaviors

The primary powers—people, polity, economy—through the FILMS[2] [P7], perform operant behaviors in the business of society. In the United States Enterprise (USE), each power is best suited for an essential purpose to keep society going. The alignment of the powers with these purposes is a balancing of operant behaviors for society's survival. For the USE, the leadership, administration, and management of the business of society (LAMBS) model, demonstrates this. Our enterprise is a republic polity shaped to maximize its cultural base, democracy, which creates a will in the people to pursue freely open and honest exchanges of goods and services in the marketplaces we create. Freedom unleashes the most apt use of the economy power. By the process of freely permitted trade, the markets adjust to circumstances and conditions to keep provisions flowing and perpetuate the pursuit of prosperity.

We the people in the USE govern how we want to operationalize these principal powers. If we want to create livelihoods for ourselves, we need fair playing fields of opportunity without monopolies, money tyrants, or restrictive marketplaces. Remember, democracy seeks to maximize liberty. Freedom needs room to operate. The powers' operant behaviors can constrain or free society to benefit or suffer from them. This is essential for us to understand. If one form of power does another power's duty, we'll have confusing errors and omissions, failed performances, and a poorly functioning society—an enterprise off track. We will be off the course of our intended direction toward constitutional objectives. The risks of misbalanced powers and wrongly aligned purposes are serious. The following diagrams in Figures 2-1 thru 2-11 seek to illustrate the proper alignment of the three primary powers with the principal purposes, the operant behaviors necessary for the business of society to be maximally successful for all the citizenry.

Each diagram is a circle with a triangle in it. The powers arise in our species as it strives to survive in the geography in which we have settled. The operant behaviors and purposes of the powers arise from culture, the repeated group behaviors we invent to survive as a society. Culture is our great creation. It is a process, a precept power. Culture is all the ideas and things we make and reshape to carry on with the tasks of our daily lives. It helps us make life orderly and predictable. It has values, symbols, knowledge, beliefs, and norms that consist of folkways and mores (Kammeyer, Ritzer, & Yetman, 1992). Culture undergirds our behaviors. It is the transmitted and reinforced ideas, beliefs, values, knowledge, shared social action and activities, habits, traditions, mores, and customs of a group of people. Between the circles of geography and culture are the questions asked by us in our quest for understanding. We want to know how, what, why, who, where, and when. What power is, how it is used, why it is used, and who controls it are of vital concern to us. Democracy wants the people on top (see Figure 1-2). The people need a society that holds each person's liberty sacred by establishing control of power by agreed-upon laws. This is the rule of law. A commitment to it is fundamental to making our society successful.

Within the geography circle's triangle of the primary powers are the secondary and tertiary social powers. Within the culture circle's triangle of the principal purposes, the needed operant behaviors from the powers, is their ultimate reason: the business of society. If this business fails, civilization goes extinct. Our survival depends on each of us to properly AEIOUY^{2}K all of our powers. Our ability to survive, live (above mere survival), and thrive (in conditions of luxury we enjoy today) depends on the three primary powers used in reasonable balance, so all may prosper. Democracy leads to this. Tyranny destroys this. To prevent doom, we must ensure that all the powers' FILMS^2 [P7] serve the objectives of entrepreneurial enterprise. The objectives listed in the Constitution's Preamble must be at the core of all people in all positions for all decisions so that power pursues proper purposes. This applies to the micro, meso, and macro levels of actions and activities that have a societal benefit or consequence.

The two large circles representing the two forces (geography and culture) that shape our lives in society are like steering wheels. When turned to align the powers and operant behaviors properly, we do well, and when they turn against one another, or when one power dominates the turning wheel, we do not do well. Geography power is the planetary nature to which we must adapt to survive. Culture is the means by which we adapt to and understand ourselves. In the business of making a society, we must first respond to the power of geography, the natural world. We do so through creating culture. A society has to go about its business to provide the resources necessary to sustain it. It needs the three operant behaviors to do this. At the micro level, persons within the powers' FILMS^2 [P7] perform and conduct these behaviors. At the meso level, the behaviors are performed by regional and community-based FILMS^2 [P7] of society. At the macro level, national and international FILMS^2 [P7] that overarch all of society, influence the entire culture perform these behaviors. These operant behaviors in the

USE serve the business of our society, and across the planet, human civilization and its connected markets of human economy power cooperating globally. Leadership guiding administration that provides boundaries for management is the method for the business of society in the USE.

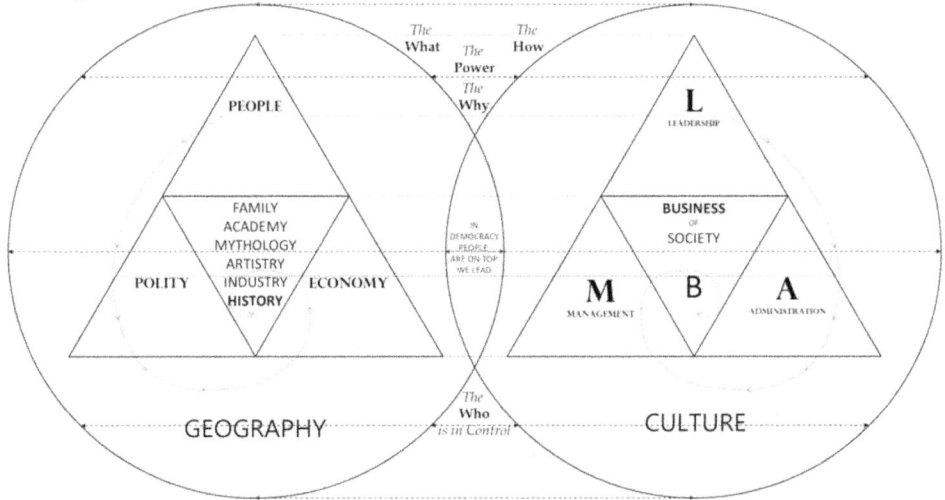

Figure 2-1: The Primary Powers in Society: The LAMBS Model
Each of the two triangles, the one bound by geography and the one bound by culture, has a line connecting to the other's equal and opposite corner. The spiral reads in the direction of the operations that make each work. Within the circle that represents geography power, people make the polity that makes the rules for economy, which enables life that, recorded, becomes the history of the society. Within the circle that represents culture power, leadership makes the administration that makes management possible. Leadership expresses the will of the people. It initiates the operant behaviors that serve the business of society, which keeps us alive, and in our enterprise enables us to thrive.

Geography determines the physical conditions and provides the natural resources that humans use to survive. The powers, organized into structures by culture, shape society. Culture is like a landscape in which the three primary powers mostly cooperate but also compete for more control. This is because the persons who act as their keepers have ambition. Some ambitions can be excessive, drawn to raw control of a power. This is the risk of too much power controlled by one person. It leads to the rule of men instead of the rule of law. Persons authorized to AEIOUY^{2}K power in a social organization must guard themselves against the corrosion of corruption. The ambition of the persons authorized to pull the levers, push the buttons, and turn the wheels of the powers requires controls to check and balance it, or it will control them. Persons controlled by excessive ambition enlarge the risks to society's balance. The structures, from which we get our livelihood, depend on all of us helping to keep the powers from getting out of balance. The negative consequences of misbalancing disrupt society quickly and create vulnerabilities in our enterprise. If we are all concerned with the loss of liberty by any one of us, we will regulate our ambitions, and we will respect the culture of democracy. If not, we will drift into periods of crises, overreaction, counteraction, and instability.

In Figure 2-1 notice that the geography circle's large triangle of the powers of society includes smaller triangles with the three primary powers: people, polity, and economy. In the middle of these are the other powers of society that relate to geographic adaptations. The center of the culture circle's large triangle of the purposes of the societal powers contains the business of society, which starts with our survival in geography. The other powers at the center of the geography's circle are the culturally made secondary and tertiary societal, or since closer to our everyday lives, "social powers". This power and purpose (operant behaviors) LAMBS model of society, represents the symbiotic relations between Homo sapiens and planet earth. Similar to this are two ideas of life and its courses, the yin-yang and the dialectic. Yin and yang is an ancient Chinese philosophical concept of how seemingly contrary dual forces are actually interconnected and complementary. The dialectic is a way of improving by relating opposites. The interrelatedness is such that neither changes without changes in the other. A mutation to one causes a change in both and in the total system, which is not only a dualism but includes the relationship too. It is three. It is three as one.

With a polity as government of the people, by the people, and for the people, democracy needs people to recognize that each person has a role to play in the success of the society. This is especially true in a republic. This is the foundational principle of personal responsibility. Being personally responsible to oneself as a person is to become conscious of one's responsibility for one's liberty. This requires an understanding of what liberty means. Each of us has it when the other knows what it is and respects our right to have it, and we theirs, while also realizing that we must protect it for one another. Truthfully, this is citizenshipping, which is our civic duty as fellow citizens to achieve a truly American society.

The geography power circle and the culture power circle intersect. This brings nature and nurture together at the center between them. Democracy is in the overlap of the two. The USE uses a culture made by its people who've adapted to varying geographic conditions. Influenced by their original land's cultures, the settlers and immigrants brought to the continent ideas that developed colonial society. It became a combination of brought and found, as settlers, servants, and slaves learned from the indigenous people certain survival techniques.

Above and below the space in between the circles is potential-power to turn the wheels, made kinetic by the questions we ask about power. The "what" of it, the "how" of it, the "why" of it, and the "who" controls it are outside the circles but also between them. As the wheels turn by the force of imagination and inquiry of human minds, the powers align to operant behaviors. Possible different alignments show what works to achieve the best success for people as we go about using it in the business of society. This mostly happens as the FILMS[2] [P7] for the LAMBS AEIOUY[2]K the powers.

Now, let's turn these wheels to orient the people power in the geography sphere to align with the leadership behaviors in the culture sphere (see Figure 2-2). This results in an alignment of democracy. Notice the lines connecting the corners of the triangles form a harmonious pattern of horizontal lines, which connect the other primary powers to their best-use operant behaviors.

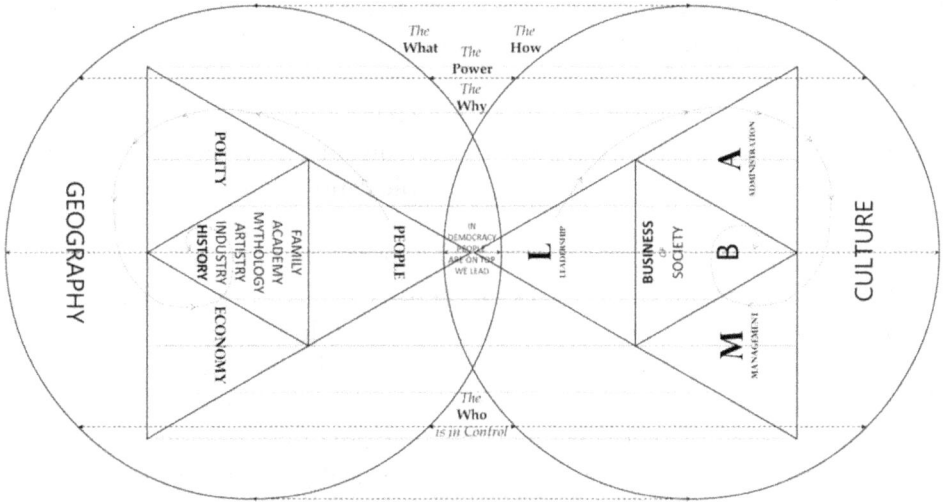

Figure 2-2: In a Democracy, People (Not One Person) Provide Leadership
Rotating the people to be the leadership, democracy, is how American society begins. The "what" power is people power, the "who" is in control is the people, and the "how" to use people power is for leadership in the conduct of the business of society. The why is to IDEALS liberty and justice for all. Note that the questions about power are contained within the top and bottom horizontal lines of the diagram.

This diagram above in Figure 2-2 demonstrates the revolutionary idea of our country. Note that the lines connecting the corners of the triangles to the best methods of powers' use remain aligned. This is a reflection of the founders' polity structure enabling the new American society, a society built upon the foundation of the Constitution's framework. We have not yet fully achieved the ideal they sought, which we ought, by what they wrought. What happens when people take full ownership of leadership? The people power controls leadership, and the people lead the business of society and benefit from it. Everyone benefits with liberty and freedom, provided the powers are used properly and behaviors are properly performed. When they are not, the people do not benefit, and such a social circumstance makes deplorable conditions for democracy and the people. This describes a misbalance in the societal powers, which creates negative risks for liberty and justice.

Shown in the next diagram in Figure 23 is a maximum success from people leading. This practice of fully positive beneficial self-control and doing a good job at work, when combined with civic engagement and fully informed political participation, is good citizenshipping. Good citizenshipping is essential to make democracy real. It is necessary for our society to maximize everyone's benefit by our enterprise. If not done fully, we won't realize the benefits. This diagram shows a complete immersion of the people in their leadership role by fully overlapping their triangles. This LAMBS model arrangement portrays a unified society aligned on its goal and objectives with an engaged and active citizenry E-SASSY-T-TUF-FT-CAUCUS. In this case, the leadership role performs at all levels within a society: micro, meso, and macro. Self, organizational, and institutional leadership of society by citizens is ideal for democracy. It influences and achieves better uses of the societal and social powers for the common good producing a commonwealth in concert with the core principles and virtues of democracy. At the micro level, we have immediate proximity to basic powers. When done well, leadership behaviors create harmony and domestic tranquility. Micro-level leadership produces positive influences for society. Families, neighborhood groups, community associations, and local governments living healthfully and happily in harmony add up. At the meso level, we have influential statewide, regional, and a few nationwide organizations, businesses, professional and trade associations, institutions, and governments. They create a context for opinions about one's vertical integration into the main aspects of life, learning and working. At the macro level, we have nationwide and internationally operating organizations, businesses, institutions, government, and by treaty, affiliations with international entities (like the United Nations) that support the needs of the species in full respect of sovereignty, liberty, and human dignity.

The scale and scope of impact of the use of power at these levels is part of the influence each level has on the others. Sadly, due to several factors in our settlement patterns, such as our localized and regionalized subcultures, we've not been living toward our enterprise's fulfillment of its objectives of prosperity and equality of opportunity. We have contradictions in our society and growing neuroses of distrust. In cities, suburbs, and rural areas, and in our North, South, East, middle, and West we find many challenges of inequality, destabilizing social circumstances, and uneven physical conditions. We are hardly one nation under God. The separation of us as a people directly relates to the people not providing the primary leadership at each level in our society. Not all people are engaged fully in performing their personal and societal duties in a positive leadership manner. Take voting in the national, macro level of our society: elections. Sixty percent perform this leadership role. This is not good. Sixty percent means a "D" on a high school history exam. We need to do better; we must to live up to our responsibilities as citizens of this country, or it will not be in our power to

lead. This is a simple fact. This is part of why our society is not in good
shape and has issues with injustice and unequal liberty. To get to a more
perfect union, once all are engaged in it, we'll be better able to deliberate,
discuss, and factually debate issues that we must address as a national
community, within normal participatory bounds of our democracy culture.
A culture of democracy—of people seeing other people as equals—intends
to be passive, not aggressive; peaceful, not violent. Our societal crises and
social chaos indicates we've been delinquent in our duties as citizens. We
are not living up to our responsibilities in sufficient mass to ensure our
primary power purposefully operates to lead the society toward the objectives of the Preamble. We've been seduced by doomerism to pursue other
things.

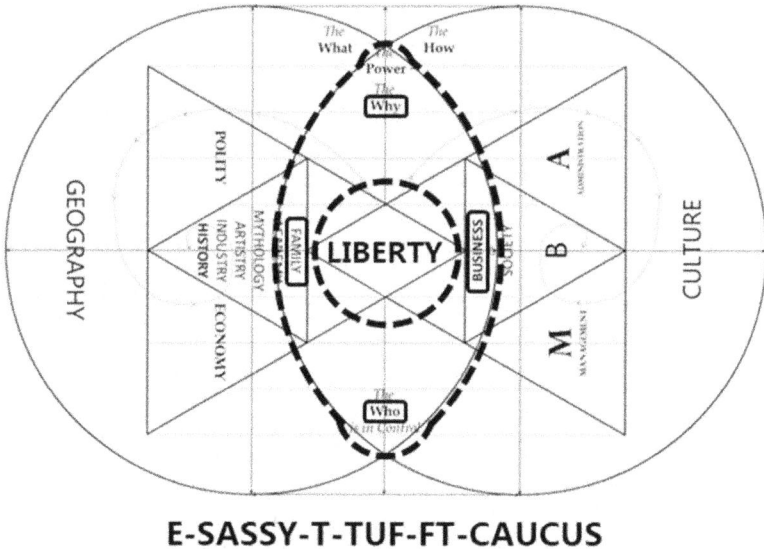

E-SASSY-T-TUF-FT-CAUCUS

**Figure 2-3: The People Power Overlapping Leadership Within the Business of Socie-
ty**

*When people power is fully in control over providing the leadership, the polity aligns to its
strength, administration, and the economy aligns to its strength, management. Further, the
"What" section is squarely above the family (for socialization benefit), academy (for [educa-
tional] skills formation benefit), and mythology (for morality and spirituality benefit). These
are all essential secondary and tertiary powers that help society survive, live peaceably, and
thrive in luxury. The "How" is squarely above the business of society. People are the "Who"
and the "Why" for this liberty benefiting overlap of people power with leadership.*

What this implies is that in these ideal conditions, people lead. Family
businesses are a why and who is in control. In this diagram, note the major
hemispheric horizontal line, which lines up the "business of society" with
the cultural powers of society: family, academy, mythology, artistry, industry, and history. Note that within the rectangle made by the vertical hemi-
spherical lines are secondary powers of society. These are family, academy,
mythology (home, school, religious building), and the business of society.

This is a society with common purpose and an understanding of the proper use of power for the common good.

What other arrangements might this LAMBS model's simple diagram of primary powers and their purposeful operant behaviors illustrate? Let's explore it by spinning the wheels to look at other possible alignment scenarios of the powers to operant behaviors and imagine what they might mean.

First, what happens if the polity power takes control of leadership in the business of society? In this, the wheels of fortune turn into a different primary power to operant behavior method of use, purpose, and societal arrangement. We'll call this next diagram in Figure 2-4: Scenario A.

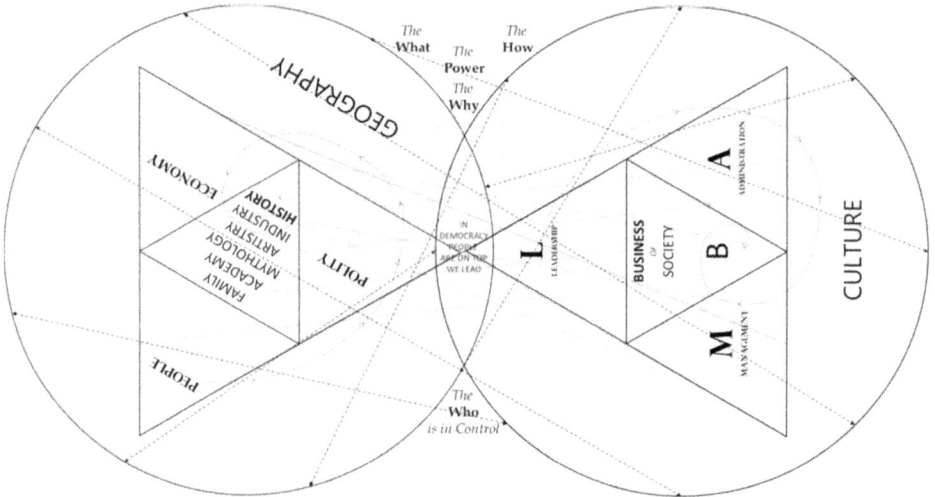

Figure 2-4: Scenario A—Alternate Scenario of Power Alignments—When the Polity Tries to Lead the Business of Society

Note that the questions about power are not neatly contained within top and bottom lines of the diagram. Leaving us to wonder, "Who really is in control?" Knowing full well, it is not us, the people. This then causes suspicions and numerous conspiracy theories those who are in charge welcome. Because such contemptuous story telling causes tempestuous distractions, they can use to their advantage to gain more power. For us, we miss-understand how we are being manipulated by propaganda built around the power hungry human's ambitions. We must awaken to how its use is intentional to divide us into warring camps of various isms worship. To fracture unity, power grabbers want us to fall like loyalists into tribalistic factions, because this social circumstance prevents us from communicating with one another over what really is best for all of us in common. Those in positions of authority, who want to rule with raw power by the threat of violent law enforcement, enjoy watching us make fools of ourselves. If their lies seduce us we'll get trapped, unable to escape the echoing chambers they have constructed around us. These media cones enslave us to irrationality, turning us against one another. We must be better on guard to preserve our dignity and unity so we might yet enjoy the full blessings of liberty.

Note the misalignment and confusion indicated by the crisscrossing of the lines connecting the triangles' corners. It is a messy, unattractive image. Metaphysically, if we find truth in elegant solutions, in pure beauty, then this ugly arrangement cannot be truth. Yet if beauty is in the eye of the beholder and the beholder of this is a tyrant, then such chaos looks wonderfully exciting because it appears as though only more control can fix it. Of course, this leads to a mistake. Thinking only one strong person can straighten it out is an endorsement for an autocrat. To such a tyrant, this despotic social circumstance is beautiful because it will produce a seemingly loyal cadre of flattering sycophants who, seemingly blind to truth, worship the tyrant and become eager self-serving greedy butt-lickers. The tyrant gains pleasure from accepting their adulation and from cruelly manipulating them. This is a dysfunctional arrangement. It cannot last. It will frustrate. It will cause mistakes and crimes. It will fail us. It will destroy democracy. It will eradicate liberty in all but the few underground patriots who will plot to restore the force of liberty as the mandate of the polity, by raising a majority to take back leadership and restore democracy. Examples of Scenario A's risks and consequences include what happens when a government invades another country without a declaration of war, or an uncoordinated response to a pandemic crisis. The everyday people in Scenario A's society suffer from a misbalance of powers that cause a poor quality of life.

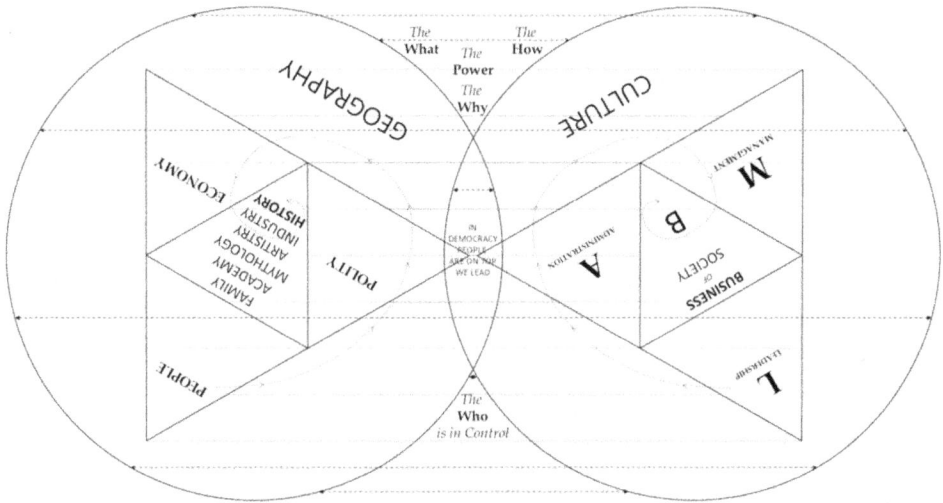

Figure 2-5: Scenario B—Alternate Scenario of Power Alignments—In a Democracy, the Polity Power Provides Administration of the Societal Context within the Business of Society
Note that the questions about power are neatly contained within the top and bottom lines of the diagram.

Second, what happens if the polity power is not in control of leadership but is focusing its power on its principal skill strength, administration? In this, the wheels of fortune turn into a different primary power to operant behavior, method of use, purpose, and societal arrangement. We'll call this next diagram in Figure 2-5: Scenario B,. In it, above, we see that the lines connecting the triangles' corners once again align horizontally, gracefully. We note that the main horizontal line travels across and joins the economy with management.

Third, what if the polity is not controlling leadership but is focusing its power to control management? In this, the wheels of fortune turn into a different primary power to operant behavior, method of use, purpose, and societal arrangement. We'll call this next diagram in Figure 2-6: Scenario C.

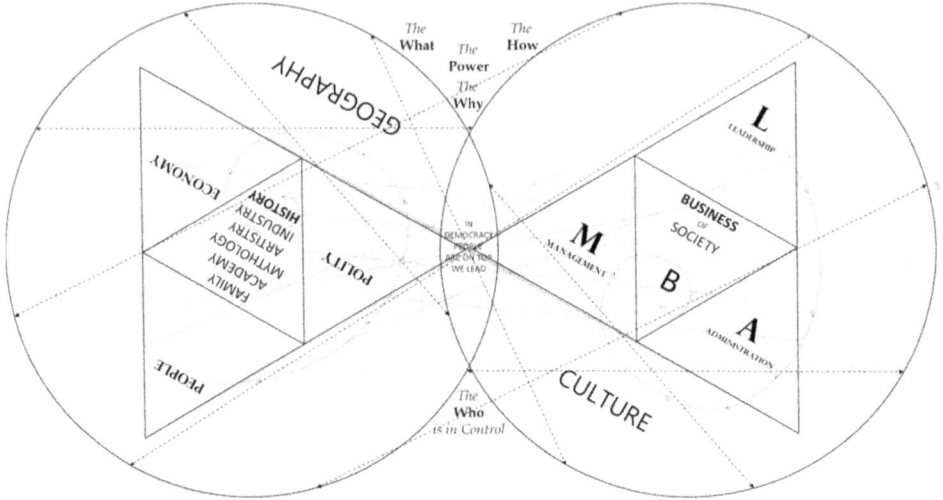

Figure 2-6: Scenario C—Alternate Scenario of Power Alignments—When the Polity Tries to Manage the Business of Society

Note that the questions about power are not neatly contained within the top and bottom lines of the diagram. Leaving us to wonder, "Who really is in control?" Knowing full well, it is not us, the people.

Note the misalignment and confusion indicated by the crisscrossing of the lines connecting the triangles' corners. It is a messy, unattractive image. Metaphysically, if we find truth in elegant solutions, in pure beauty, then this ugly arrangement cannot be truth. Yet if beauty is in the eye of the beholder and the beholder of this is a bureaucratic oligarchy, then such chaos looks wonderfully exciting because it appears as if only more law and orderly control of everything can fix it. Of course, to them this implies a committee of strategic planners, technocrats, and economists could be that group to be the controlling official nationalistic heroic central party. This social circumstance, to a party oligarchy, is beautiful because it will produce for their power-hungry ideological determinism a seemingly necessary construction of society in which the system's perfection will override human imperfection and market variability. They will demand near-worship of the system, which turns people into unquestioning "yes" persons, who go along to get along and hide their misery or join in and rat out their neighbors who complain about the system. This social control gives the oligarchs pleasure from adulation (albeit false-faced) and a raw sense of importance. This is a dysfunctional arrangement. It cannot last. It will frustrate. It will cause mistakes. It will fail us. It will destroy democracy. It will eradicate liberty in all but the few underground patriots, who will plot to restore the force of liberty as the mandate of the polity, by raising the majority to take back the leadership and restore democracy. An example of this is what happens when a government creates too many laws to control the economy power's operant behavior and restricts the free exercise of curiosity and exploration that leads to betterments from the marketplaces, where people negotiate the value of provisions for our own survival, living securely, and thriving conditions. Or, it causes the provisioning of goods and services diminishment or disruption. An extreme example of this is what happens when a polity dominates the economy power and the people power with an iron fist by way of a centrally planned command economy. The everyday people in Scenario C's society suffer from a misbalance of powers that cause a poor quality of life.

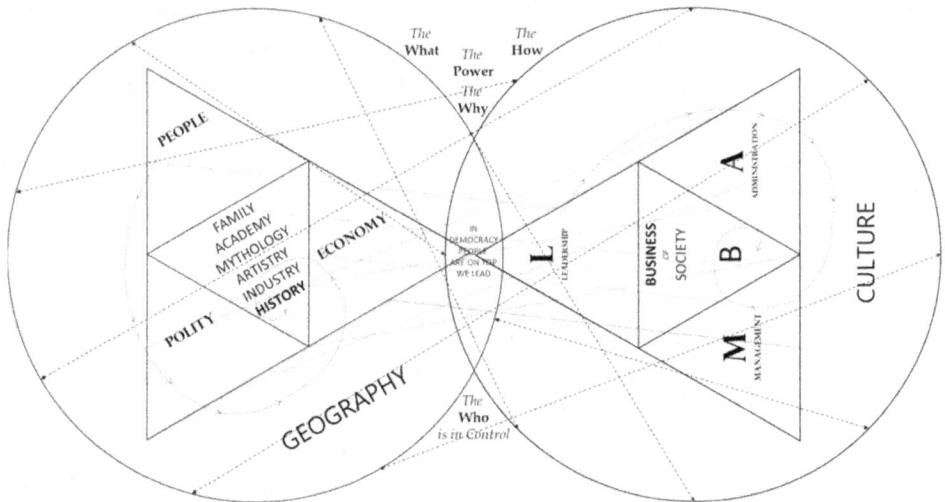

Figure 2-7: Scenario D—Alternate Scenario of Power Alignments—When the Economy Tries to Lead the Business of Society
Note that the questions about power are not neatly contained within the top and bottom lines of the diagram. Leaving us to wonder, "Who really is in control?" Knowing full well, it is not us, the people.

Fourth, what happens if the economy power controls leadership application in the business of society? In this, the wheels of fortune turn into a different primary power to operant behavior method of use, purpose, and societal arrangement. We'll call this next diagram in Figure 2-7: Scenario D. This occurs when the elites at the macro and meso levels use their FILMS[2] [P7] of the economy power to influence the behavior of the people and the polity at the micro, meso, and macro levels of society. A micro-level personal appeal to a politician in Congress, who is to represent and operate at the national level of concern but who for personal purposes takes a bribe from a meso-level lobbyist who represents an international scale, macro-level sector of the economy power, is an example of what happens in this scenario.

This arrangement correlates to the culture-altering conditions of doomerism. In Scenario D, the trains may run on time, but the people will feel disconnected. Unled and not well fed, the people become the exploiter and the exploited. The economy power is best at management methods. Management is not leadership. In such circumstances, we, the everyday people, must rely on the FILMS[2] [P7] of our own family, academy, mythology, and neighborhood-supporting community to explain why things are out of order and to support our survival in the times of inequality this arrangement can cause. When under this social circumstance we wonder whether how much money or purchasing power one has, determines ones worthiness. We wonder why so few seem to be able to get ahead. We cannot fathom why there is so much celebration of so few, rewarded so richly, especially for things that seem to be mostly a matter of luck or inherited advantages of high society, not earned by merit or talents. We wonder whether such excessive inequality is just, and how we will continue to believe in a society that makes surviving, living, and thriving into a caste-like system. We wonder if getting and keeping a job, planning a future, hoping for security and stability, or having and raising kids is worthwhile. The "only the top-tier earners benefit" competitiveness of such an arrangement is exhausting in its provoked anxiety and distrust. Because it encourages degrading cheating to get a larger slice of the pie, people begin to lie. Slowly, faith in one's neighbor and society erodes when honor is no longer a guarantee of a good life, and virtue forgotten. This is a rotten posture. Doom grows on everyone's minds. This doomerism corrupts our souls. Society falls below the worthy and prestigious goals it once pursued.

The polity's politicians and the economy's elites get the most benefits from the misaligned arrangement of primary powers in Scenario D. By it, they cause precarious social circumstances and physical conditions for the people. This dysfunctional society serves very few well. In it, the economy power serves solely to enrich the elites. It makes the focus of leadership to lead them to maximum gain. It destabilizes society. Parts of the government sever, cut out of the administration of the business of society. For example, financial regulators, IRS tax collectors and enforcers, or any other countervailing powers to the economic elite's massive accumulation gets intentionally rendered ineffective and unable to administer properly. The elites fund massive public relations propaganda campaigns to convince the people that the elites' way is the best and only way, which causes people to vote contrary to our own economic interests and puts more money in the personal pockets of the politicians whom the elites come to "own" by legal forms of immoral bribery. Because people are manipulated and do not vote in full engagement, the politicians receive rewards for their behavior and come to think that it is what the people want: for them to continue to serve the elites and not the voters, whom they are supposed to represent. Feeling and fearing no real consequences endorses corrupt behaviors and corruption as an approach to life as a perfectly acceptable method. It is not. Yet, this is how power works. Only democracy enables controls over this process by giving the people the leadership role in operating the business of society. The everyday people in Scenario D's society suffer from a misbalance of powers that cause a poor quality of life.

People, we possess the operant behavior of leadership. We must be willing to be responsible to perform it—to have the integrity to do it properly in accordance with the pursuit of virtue to obtain happiness, and in union—to prevent the misalignment of societal powers and ensure their best and highest uses for society. Our agency as virtuous citizens must take primacy over all else, or we cannot have a democracy.

With Scenario D's diagram, we also note misalignment and confusion indicated by the crisscrossing of the lines connecting the triangles' corners. It is a messy, unattractive image. Metaphysically, if we find truth in elegant solutions, in pure beauty, then this ugly arrangement cannot be truth. Yet if beauty is in the eye of the beholder and the beholder is a conceited, know-it-all, money-loving, merchant aristocratic wannabe plutocracy ruler, then such chaos looks wonderfully exciting because it appears as is only more control of everything by economic elites can fix it. Of course, only a few superrich (and therefore powerful) uppity classes of collegial vested-interest partners, business-strategic so-called friends, and smoking-lounge exclusivity country club resort members will benefit. This social circumstance, to an "upper class knows best" perpetuated self-lie, is beautiful because it produces for their high-society, high net worth luxury lifestyle competition. A seemingly necessary construction of society in which an aristocracy lifts them above human imperfection and shapes markets into gods, to which they declare loyalty in near-mythological worship of the economy system that they control by controlling the polity and the people. This turns people into mere units of production and consumption. To baby doomers, we are to be machine-like, working to buy to survive, until robots with no other purpose or responsibility but to feed their accumulation ambitions replace us. When discarded, living poverty, we provide them something to despise, filthy lowlifes, so they can feel superior to us. This doomerist culture creates "balance sheet humans" whose only value is to enrich the elites. This social control gives the plutocrats pleasure from (albeit false) security against calamity from geography's power and a raw sense of exceptionality and importance due to their money-based power. As another form of dysfunctional arrangement, it cannot last. It will frustrate. It will cause mistakes and crimes. It will fail us. It will destroy democracy. It will eradicate liberty in all but the few underground patriots, who will plot to restore the force of liberty as the mandate of the polity, by raising a majority to take back leadership and restore democracy.

Fifth, what happens if the economy power is not controlling leadership but focusing its power to control its principal skill strength, management? In this, the wheels of fortune turn into a different primary power to operant behavior method of use, purpose, and societal arrangement. We'll call this diagram above in Figure 2-8: Scenario E. In it we see that the lines align horizontally, gracefully. We note that the main horizontal line travels across and joins the polity with administration. We see that the five questions about power are contained and answers knowable.

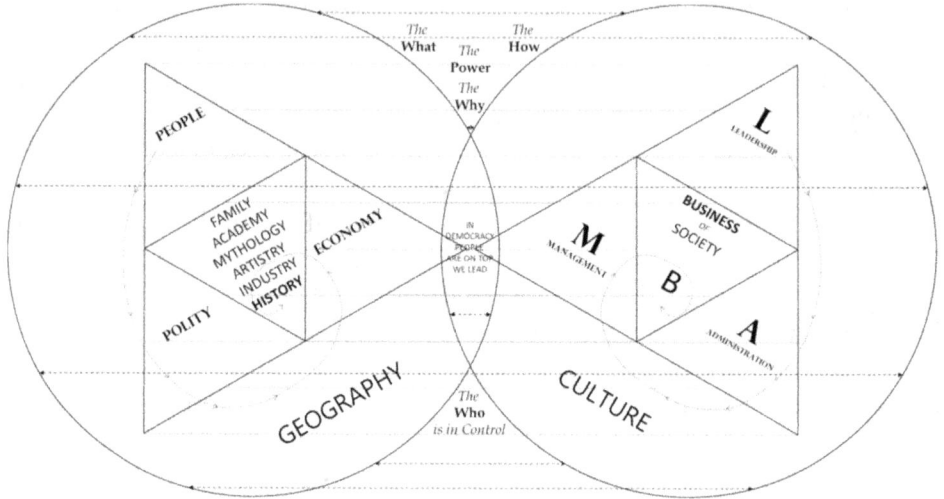

Figure 2-8: Scenario E—Alternate Scenario of Power Alignments—When the Economy Tries to Manage the Business of Society
Note the lines align nicely.

Sixth, what happens if the economy power is not controlling management but focusing its power to make dominant use of its weakest skill set, administration? In this, the wheels of fortune turn into a different primary power to operant behavior method of use, purpose, and societal arrangement. We'll call this next diagram in Figure 2-9: Scenario F. Administration is its weakest because it is the least profitable exertion of effort, and thus its functionaries are not motivated to do it well. They do it as a contracted service to assist the polity in meeting its administrative obligations. Note the misalignment and confusion indicated by the crisscrossing of the lines connecting the triangles' corners. It is a messy, unattractive image. Metaphysically, if we find truth in elegant solutions, in pure beauty, then this ugly arrangement cannot be truth. Yet if beauty is in the eye of the beholder, and the beholder is an overambitious, overzealous, and overconfident cluster of the HM[5] believing that the basic premises of economy power are best suited to run everything—that is to set the rules, be large and in charge, put all power in private hands, and completely deny that there is any need of public ownership or functioning of fairness controls by the polity—then to these no-government-is-necessary-just-business fantasizers, such chaos looks wonderfully exciting because it appears as if everything can be a scheme for profit. If a polity must have government, let it contract out all its services and have no employees. To such persons this social circumstance is beautiful because it produces private operators of public affairs, a seemingly maximally profitable construction of society, because privatization overrides bureaucratic inefficiencies through exploited temporary workforces with no social security future. This turns people into unrepresented desperate persons who "spend it all now because there may not be any tomorrow" and everyone must fend for himself or herself in a corporation-controlled governmental system.

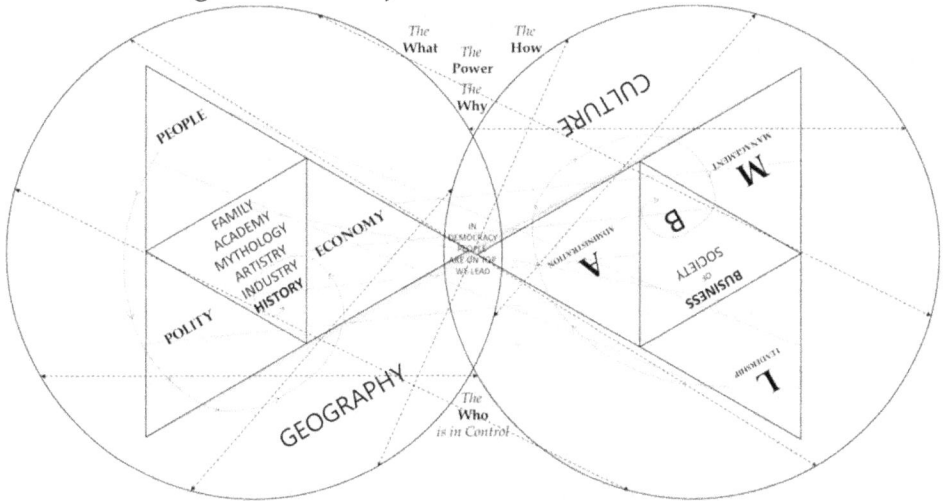

Figure 2-9: Scenario F—Alternate Scenario of Power Alignments—When the Economy Tries to Administer the Business of Society

Note that the questions about power are not neatly contained within the top and bottom lines of the diagram. Leaving us to wonder, "Who really is in control?" Knowing full well, it is not us, the people.

This social control gives the privatizers great pleasure from a raw (albeit false-faced) sense of importance in running the show, when in fact they risk replacement by the next low bidder to do low-paid administration. This is a most dysfunctional arrangement. It cannot last. It will frustrate. It will cause mistakes and crimes. It will fail us. It will destroy democracy. It will eradicate liberty in all but the few underground patriots, who will plot to restore the force of liberty as the mandate of the polity, by raising a majority to take back leadership and restore democracy. An example of this is what happens when a privatization plutocracy is established in which the polity becomes an oligarchy controlled by the international, globalizing, monopolistic corporations who buy politicians to do their bidding. It leads to the societies called "banana republics." Essentially, these dictatorships parade around and call themselves republics, but the polity officials only have power from the money paid to them by the businesses that extract their country's resources for a lower price than they are actually worth. Elections are not free, and the economy is typically dependent on one geographic resource. Payouts of the privatized industries to the polity turn into palaces for so-called presidents. A secret police contracted to silence truth-telling dissent-ers suppress liberty. The people are not free, only the inner circle at the top appears to thrive; the rest in the country barely survive. All the laws result in the enrichment of the politicians at the top of the polity. Ostensibly, it is totally an exploitative society. In it, we get less than one-half of one percent of the total population owning eighty percent or more of all the society's wealth. It is a kind of new feudalism. The powerful providers of provisions, the economy power elites, pay off politicians. Gross inequality in all aspects of society corrodes by corruption the civility in democracy culture, destabi-lizing the societal and social powers. It causes humanly unhealthful and an unhelpfully unharmonious disequilibrium in the primary powers' arrange-ment.

Seventh and eighth, what if the people power is not controlling leader-ship but is focusing its power to make dominant its weakest skills: admin-istration or management? In these, the wheels of fortune turn into a differ-ent primary power to operant behavior, method of use, purpose, and socie-tal arrangement. We'll call these two diagrams that follow in Figure 2-10, Scenarios G, and in Figure 2-11, Scenario H. Without agreed-upon FILMS^2 [P7] to AEIOUY^{2}K power, these arrangements are highly improbable and problematic. Yet they are possible in catastrophic circumstances with ca-lamitous conditions that devolve into chaotic anarchy, or mobocracy. It is a situation of no good powers, no real society. Out of it, often through dem-agoguery, a tyrant can arise, promising law and order upon obeisance to him or her to curb the disorderliness of the people's lives. Good power comes from majority rule in democracy-culture based society with a con-comitant respect for minorities. Goodness comes from the social powers when meso-level organizations coexist within a balanced healthy beneficial competitiveness. Because people power forms through its proper control of the polity, or intentional behaviors in the marketplaces, such control of administration and management are not typical, as they imply that either the polity or the economy has failed. The figures below show the misalignment and entanglement.

These two ill scenarios of the LAMBS model keep the people distant from leadership. Note the misalignments and confusion indicated by the crisscrossing of the lines connecting the triangles' corners. Both are messy, unattractive images. Metaphysically, if we find truth in elegant solutions, in pure beauty, then these two ugly arrangements cannot be truth. Yet if beau-ty is in the eye of the beholder and the beholder is a tyrant wannabe, then both are ripe for a law-and-order takeover to establish a dictatorship, those with weapons performing a kind of military coup d'état. These are the most dysfunctional arrangements. Neither can last. Both will frustrate. Both will cause mistakes and crimes. Both will fail us. Both will destroy democracy.

Both will eradicate liberty in all but the few underground patriots, who will plot to restore the force of liberty as the mandate of the polity, by raising a majority to take back leadership and restore democracy. The proper role of the people, if we want a good society that benefits each and all of us, is leadership. By E-SASSY-T-TUF-FT-CAUCUS, we do it best. A good society of democracy-based culture requires that we, the everyday people, assume leadership of it. We must be responsible to ourselves, being good and doing goodness, so we all may be and do well. We must develop good morals, ethics, character, and empathetic concern for our fellow humans and unite with our fellow citizens. We must recognize that this is our honorable duty to our country that enables our liberty to pursue our happiness. "Our country 'tis of thee" belongs equally to everybody in our citizenry. This is our part to play. It brings us honor to give dignity to one another, to trust, and to be trusting. To behave in a way that builds this trust, every day and in every way, makes us free. It puts us in control of society, so that power does not get DAMN by the FILMS[2] [P7] and the HM[5] of society.

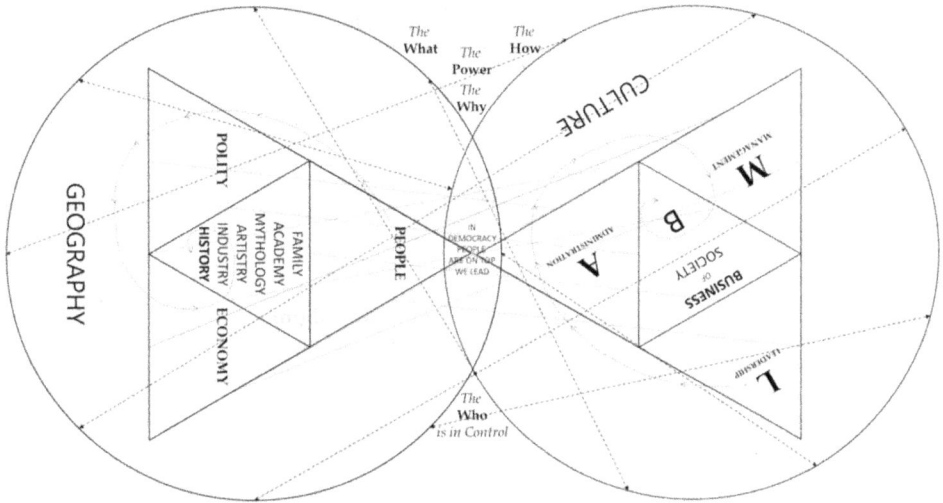

Figure 2-10: Scenarios G—Alternate Scenario of Power Alignments—When the People Power Tries to Administer the Business of Society

Note that the questions about power are not neatly contained within the top and bottom lines of the diagram. Leaving us to wonder, "Who really is in control?" Knowing full well, it is not us, the people.

Our full engagement in good citizenship behaviors will enable us to live up to standards that make our contributions in micro, meso, and macro positions within the polity and economy FILMS[2] [P7] in particular the HM[5], supportive of not destabilizing to American society, its opportunity platforms, and our liberty. This is very important to the successful functioning of our society and the integration of all of us into its benefits. We must do it in a manner that is best for the perpetuation of a (to be realized) ideal American society. We must do it by E-SASSY-T-TUF-FT-CAUCUS. For each one of us, this is actually the only acceptable form of selfishness, that is, unselfishness—to be unselfish is ultimately selfish—because we are social beings in need of others to survive peaceably and securely, live in comfort and dignity, and thrive in luxury. This self-helping-unselfishness benefits us socially, and because we are mostly social, it benefits us personally. This is a circumstance of surviving, living, and thriving that only a democracy-based culture makes feasible. Let's remind ourselves how this radical concept, democracy, came to be a driving force for liberty in the European colonies in North America and why it is ideal for humane human development in Homo sapiens. Let's commit to living up to its calling.

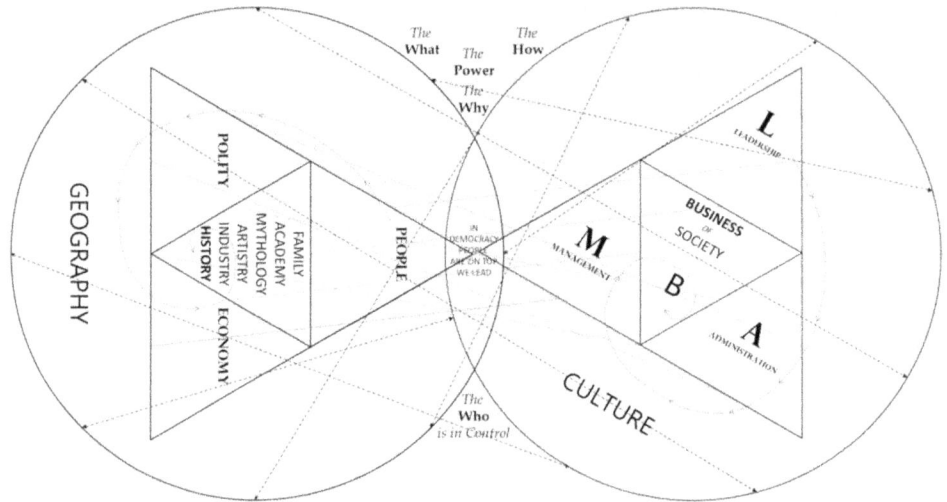

Figure 2-11: Scenarios H—Alternate Scenario of Power Alignments—When the People Power Tries to Manage the Business of Society

Note that the questions about power are not neatly contained within the top and bottom lines of the diagram. Leaving us to wonder, "Who really is in control?" Knowing full well, it is not us, the people.

Democracy, an Ideal Society

The Declaration of Independence was a stand against tyranny. Read it to see if any of these things are happening to us today. If they are, it means that our society is off course, and we, the everyday people, must rise to revolt by demonstrating that we are capable of exhibiting the necessary self-control to be free and self-governing. So long as we allow the few who believe they were born to rule us to think of us as inferior and use our behaviors against us, we are handing them the power. This will be the case as long as we don't engage and lead the society at all levels as a united citizenry, by doing right and by not arguing to prove that we are "always right," even when we know we are wrong. Being too proud to lose our hubris is a symptom of the negatively selfish and socially damaging doomerism disease, without which we can form our power into societal goodness-shaping leadership. We can do this by being better at democracy, being better citizens of the republic, serving, and holding those who misbehave in our polity and economy accountable. This we do by exercising our responsibilities and our rights. We need to relearn how. Let's begin with a review of the Declaration of Independence, salient to today's societal circumstances. Written below, it follows the Preamble of the Constitution [bolded and inserted textual emphasis by the author].

"We the People of the United States, in Order to form a more perfect Union, establish Justice, insure domestic Tranquility, provide for the common defence, promote the general Welfare, and secure the Blessings of Liberty to ourselves and our Posterity, do ordain and establish this Constitution for the United States of America."

Because "When in the Course of human events, it becomes necessary for one people to dissolve the political bands which have connected them with another, and to assume among the powers of the earth, the separate and equal station to which the Laws of Nature and of Nature's God entitle them, a decent respect to the opinions of mankind requires that they should declare the causes which impel them to the separation. **We hold these truths to be self-evident, that all men are created equal, that they are endowed by their Creator with certain inalienable Rights, that among these are Life, Liberty and the pursuit of Happiness.**—*That to secure these rights, Governments are instituted among [Hu]Men,* **deriving their just powers from the consent of the governed**—*that whenever any Form of Government* [and if it is made up of like-minded corrupt officials who make us vulnerable to threats] *becomes destructive of these ends,* **it is the Right of the People** *to alter or to abolish it, and to institute new Government* [vote in better-behaving citizens repeatedly until they serve the purpose of the nation, the Preamble's goals and objectives], *laying its foundation on such principles and* **organizing its powers** *in such form, as to them shall seem most likely to effect their* **Safety and Happiness** [our safety and happiness are under assault by many new forces and technologies that eliminate our jobs, and no one is telling us what jobs there will be in the future. The implementers of the technology are amassing huge profits that they use to purchase politicians' help to allow them to continue to concentrate wealth and the power that it gives them]. *Prudence, indeed, will dictate that Governments long established should not be changed for light and transient causes; and accordingly all experience hath shewn, that* **[hu]***mankind are more disposed to suffer,* while evils are sufferable, **than to right themselves by abolishing the forms to which they are accustomed.** [Doomerism is a new form to which we have become accustomed but must abolish as soon as possible.] *But when a long train of abuses and usurpations, pursuing invariably the same Object evinces a design to* **reduce them under absolute Despotism, it is their right, it is their duty, to throw off such** *Government* [For us, the despotic baby boomers have ruled by majority now for forty years, and it has only gotten worse.], *and to* **provide new Guards for their future security.** [We must negotiate by better civic engagement and making younger, moral, creative persons the new guards to protect us from many threats that have arisen from our vulnerabilities born of success, like complacency, laziness, obesity, and apathy.] —*Such has been the patient sufferance of these Colonies; and such is now the necessity which constrains them to alter their former Systems of Government. The history of the present King of Great Britain is a history of repeated injuries and usurpations all having in direct object the establishment of an absolute tyranny over these States. To prove this,* **let Facts be submitted to a candid world.** [We must be candid with ourselves, and begin to demand, accept, and agree upon the facts. The game playing to manipulate us must stop!]

He has refused his Assent to Laws, [Baby doomers think they can be above the law because it is just a human construct, and as superior humans in their own distorted minds, they really do not have to obey it. Further, they re-write "innocent until proven guilty" to mean, "one has done nothing wrong un-til caught." This is rampant abuse of the liberty-protecting standard of our soci-ety. It is unethical to do wrong and consider it all right if one gets away with it. This is the absurdity of doomerism.] *the most wholesome and necessary* **for the pub-lic good**. [The purpose of laws is for the public good, which in part affords protection of the natural rights of each person.]

He has forbidden *his Governors to pass Laws of immediate and pressing importance, unless suspended in their operation till his Assent should be obtained; and when so suspended, he has utterly neglected to attend to them.* [No delegation of duties to officials close to the people; "only the tyrant can decide" is terribly inefficient and risky too.]

He has refused to pass other Laws for the accommodation of large districts of people, un-less those **people would relinquish the right of Representation in the Legis-lature**, *a right inestimable to them and formidable to tyrants only.* [When politicians are not regularly removed and replaced by new faces of succeeding generations, representation of those who are our future, our unborn and newly born citizens on whom we will depend in our later years of life to sustain the society we toiled to make, declines. Because power tends to corrupt and holding onto it becomes more important to career politicians than doing the will of the people they are supposed to represent, the people are served poorly. Election campaigns cost money to pay for advertisements, staff, and travel of candidates to meet and converse with the people they seek to represent. It is a misuse of economy pow-er by its FILMS[2] [P7] and the HM[5] to fund campaigns inordinately to influence the politicians' performance while holding office. To exchange money for favor is corrupting. This leads to the economy power's tyranny over the people (see Figure 2-7).]

He has called together legislative bodies at places unusual, uncomfortable, and distant from the depository of their public Records, **for the sole purpose of fatiguing them into compliance with his measures** [wrongful manipulation].

He has dissolved Representative Houses repeatedly, for opposing with manly firmness his invasions on the rights of the people.

He has refused for a long time, after such dissolutions, to cause others to be elected; whereby the Legislative powers, incapable of Annihilation, have returned to the People at large for their exercise; **the State remaining in the mean time exposed to all the dangers of invasion from without, and convulsions within** [negligent in-competence].

He has endeavoured **to prevent** *the population of these States; for that purpose ob-structing the Laws for* **Naturalization of Foreigners**; *refusing to pass others to encour-age their migrations hither, and raising the conditions of new Appropriations of Lands.*

He has obstructed **the Administration of Justice**, *by refusing his Assent to Laws for establishing Judiciary powers.*

He has made Judges dependent on his Will alone, *for the tenure of their of-fices, and the amount and payment of their salaries.*

He has erected a multitude of New Offices, *and sent hither swarms of Offic-ers to harrass our people, and eat out their substance.*

He has *kept* **among us, in times of peace, Standing Armies** *without the Consent of our legislatures.*

He **has** *affected to render the Military independent of and superior to the Civil power.*

He has combined with others to subject us to a jurisdiction foreign to our constitution, and unacknowledged by our laws; giving his Assent to their Acts of pretended Legislation:

For *Quartering large bodies of* **armed troops** *among us:*

For protecting them, by a mock Trial, from punishment for any Murders which they should commit on the Inhabitants of these States:

For *cutting off* **our Trade** *with all parts of the world:*

For *imposing* **Taxes on us** *without our Consent:*

For **depriving us in many cases, of the benefits of Trial by Jury**:

For *transporting us beyond Seas to be tried for pretended offences:*

For *abolishing* **the free System of English Laws** *in a neighbouring Province, establishing therein an Arbitrary government, and enlarging its Boundaries so as to render it at once an example and fit instrument for introducing the same absolute rule into these Colonies:*

For *taking away our Charters,* **abolishing our most valuable Laws,** *and* **altering fundamentally the Forms of our Governments**:

For *suspending our own Legislatures, and declaring themselves invested with power to legislate for us in all cases whatsoever.*

He *has abdicated Government here,* **by declaring us out of his Protection** *and* **waging War against us.**

He has plundered *our seas, ravaged our Coasts, burnt our towns, and* **destroyed the lives of our people.**

He is at this time transporting *large* **Armies** *of foreign Mercenaries* **to compleat the works of death, desolation and tyranny, already begun with circumstances of Cruelty and perfidy scarcely paralleled in the most barbarous ages, and totally unworthy of the Head of a civilized nation.**

He has constrained our fellow Citizens *taken Captive on the high Seas to bear Arms against their Country,* **to become the executioners of their friends and Brethren,** *or to fall themselves by their Hands.*

He has excited domestic insurrections amongst us, *and has endeavoured to bring on the inhabitants of our frontiers, the merciless Indian Savages, whose known rule of warfare, is an undistinguished destruction of all ages, sexes and conditions.*

In every stage of these Oppressions We have Petitioned for Redress in the most humble terms: *Our repeated Petitions have been answered only by repeated injury.* **A Prince whose character is thus marked by every act which may define a Tyrant, is unfit to be the ruler of a free people.**

Nor *have We been wanting in attentions to our British brethren. We have warned them from time to time of attempts by their legislature to extend an unwarrantable jurisdiction over us. We have reminded them of the circumstances of our emigration and settlement here.* **We have appealed to their native justice and magnanimity,** *and we have conjured them by the ties of our common kindred to disavow these usurpations, which, would inevitably interrupt our connections and correspondence.* **They too have been deaf to the voice of justice and of consanguinity.** *We must, therefore, acquiesce in the necessity, which denounces our Separation, and hold them, as we hold the rest of mankind, Enemies in War, in Peace Friends.*

We, *therefore, the Representatives of the united States of America, in General Congress, Assembled,* **appealing to the Supreme Judge of the world** *for the rectitude of our intentions, do, in the Name, and by Authority of the good People of these Colonies, solemnly publish and declare, That* **these United Colonies are, and of Right ought to be Free and Independent States**; *that they are Absolved from all Allegiance to the British Crown, and that all political connection between them and the State of Great Britain, is and ought to be totally dissolved; and that as* **Free and Independent States**, *they have full Power to levy* **War**, *conclude* **Peace**, *contract* **Alliances**, *establish* **Commerce**, *and to do all other Acts and Things which Independent States may of right do. And for the support of this Declaration, with* **a firm reliance on the protection of divine Providence, we mutually pledge to each other our Lives, our Fortunes and our sacred Honor."**

Take these words to heart. If any ring true today, let there be no doubt these prove our cultural descent toward doom. To allow any of these circumstances is to be a society infected with a social disease, a doomerism. Let's move on to the next big idea-founding document of the US, the Constitution.

Leadership of, by, & for the People

The Constitution of our enterprise formed on the backbone of a culture based on the principles and values of democracy. Democracy is a means to educate us on how properly to balance societal powers. We as a species, in our struggles to survive in the geography of the planet, and to advance our interests and our pursuit of happiness, established these powers. We have a society in which we can thrive while alive when the societal powers are in balance and we appropriately $AEIOUY^2K$ them. We constituted a society framed upon a polity that requires the people to lead wholesome, virtuous lives. It being "of the people" requires we be attentive and seek to be citizens first, remaining engaged in our responsibilities of citizenship—to ensure powers get kept in check and balanced. Let the polity stay in its proper role of administration in the business of society. We who perform roles within it must uphold high standards of conduct and commitment to serve the will of the people we represent.

Our society uses a constituted polity that is "by the people". We become our representatives and serve as politicians. When we do, we must serve the people's will first. If we serve, we must have a strong citizen-first orientation to uphold the Constitution best. We must be strongly committed to the people to avoid the tendency of corruption in polity power. It is our civic duty by expressing our will to regulate consistently and continuously those who serve in the polity. We do this best by swapping out politicians regularly and not allowing factions to push society toward one extreme or another. The founder James Madison knew that factions would countervail one another (Rakove, 1996). Extremes that don't accord with the honest citizens, living to uphold the Constitution, need to be blocked. Liberty exists for all, but if we forget it as our principal drive to control power, we could lose it. Liberty is always in jeopardy because getting people to live for other people threatens selfish instincts. We must balance power to ensure that we protect the rights of all of us as one American people.

Our society uses a constituted polity that is "for the people." We know that if all of us are to have our liberty, each of us must ensure the rights of all. We gain this respect when the polity does not segregate, separate, or surge its power to divide and conquer us. The value of respect and dignity lies in trust. We gain trust by working together to consent to being governed by the polity power and not be influenced by the economy power to our detriment. We are best suited for the people when we define our common will as a people. When misalignments of powers and purposes begin to show imbalances, or remain after we have sought reforms, we for our-selves and other people must dissent to demand that liberty be predomi-nant in shaping society. We the everyday people must push and pull power to keep it where we need it to be. The work never ends. The pursuit of vir-tue by all of us is essential for the ideals of the Constitution and a more per-fect union shaped and upheld. To have a polity for the people, we must first do better at self-leadership, regardless of our social circumstances and physical conditions. All can be good citizens first. For each other, so we all may avoid tyranny, we must commit ourselves to this purpose. Let's ex-plore a bit more of people power's methods of leadership in the LAMBS model.

The libraries are full of books on leadership. The military ingrains it in-to its members. Business schools teach about it. Yet how do the people lead a nation? They do it by being citizens first, upholding the Constitution in every role they perform in and for society, whether in the polity power, economy power, or any of the secondary and tertiary powers' FILMS[2] [P7] established through democracy-based culture. This includes all roles we perform at the micro, meso, and macro levels of authority, affluence, con-fluence, or influence we might have. What is leadership as a citizen? As Admiral James B. Stockdale stated, it is commitment to others: "Leadership must be based on goodwill. Goodwill does not mean posturing and, least of all, pandering to the mob. It means obvious and wholehearted commitment to helping followers" (Stockdale, 1987). We need to be leaders for one an-other, to lead and follow in accord, using the empathy of the human heart, so that we encourage others to lead like us, with good will toward all. On Saturday, March 4, 1865, President Abraham Lincoln, in his second inaugu-ral address to "fellow countrymen" stated wise counsel. He spoke.

"With malice toward none, with charity for all, with firmness in the right as God gives us to see the right, let us strive on to finish the work we are in, to bind up the nation's wounds, to care for him who shall have borne the battle and for his widow and his orphan, to do all which may achieve and cherish a just and lasting peace among ourselves and with all nations."

This is a profound love for country. This is a commitment to liberty and justice for all. This is the highest standard of leadership we must strive to-ward to make us one people, e pluribus unum.

This is the virtuous way to lead our society. Democracy depends upon virtue in its citizenry. Virtue does not injure others. It uplifts and brings out the best in all of us, if we'll listen to the voice within, the voice that the my-thology power teaches us to hear. This voice calls out to us to obey what is right, what is just, what is taught in moral teachings. Good citizens lead one another to hear it. Today these words should give us solace as we confront the battles we face within our own hearts and within our society at every

level. We are under assault by a silent enemy, a way of thinking that is neither in accord with the aims spelled out in Lincoln's speech nor induced by
the ideals of the Declaration of Independence and the Constitution. Leadership by the people requires citizens live up to the words written and spoken to us by our greatest leaders.

We must begin again to assume goodwill of one another. More so, we
must mean to do it ourselves. We have no time for arguments over who
was wrong first. We are social beings. Two poles connected by how they
relate. Seeing that we are in this life together means we must not focus on
one side or the other but on the interconnectedness. The "we" of the "you
and me" is what we are bound to be. This is the purpose of our leadership
as a people: to build the bonds by achieving the objectives of the Constitution, by E-SASSY-T-TUF-FT-CAUCUS constantly, repeatedly, over time,
from one generation to the next. We must do this until our goal of a more
perfect union gets met, and then thereafter to maintain it. This is how we
bequeath the culture of democracy and perpetuate the republic with peaceable transfer of polity power to the benefit of the people. It will not work if
we do not exhibit honesty and integrity. If no one trusts another, if anyone
distrusts everyone, then we are not sustaining democracy but beginning a
tyranny. Skepticism is a seed of doubt planted by those who seek inordinate
amounts of power for themselves. It is a tactic of a baby doomer. Goodness for all is not in their ambition. All for their self, not their self for all, is
their mode of operation; because they only want, all must serve them to
elevate them. Doomers, if the majority in a generation, shape the whole
culture by the power of majority rule, creating a society bent toward attitudes and behaviors that repel liberty and attract tyranny. The resulting
doomerism culture seeds, harvests, and exploits the growing doubt, dividing and conquering people. The baby doomer perpetrators are either unaware of the disunion, or they desire to disrupt because of blind ambition or
a psychopathy to take advantage of others. They seek to get more and more
for themselves of whatever it is they compulsively pursue. Whether money,
power, fame, etc., such obsessions in a stable society, would be checked and
balanced to prevent excessive hoarding that destabilizes the whole for the
few. They would not undermine democracy. As we conclude this topic of
people power, let's remember: we, the everyday people, to IDEALS liberty,
must commit to one another that we will live by the Preamble's objectives
by E-SASSY-T-TUF-FT-CAUCUS constantly and continuously to make
the LAMBS by our societal FILMS[2] [P7] and the HM[5] sustain our USE for
posterity and ourselves. This we must do to eradicate doomerism. If we
freed ourselves from tyranny, we can escape the wrath of an impending
doom by making the necessary changes in ourselves and in our society. Beginning today with orderly self-discipline, we must get democracy back on
track toward its destiny of liberty and justice for all. Let us never forget that
our democracy freed itself from tyranny, giving birth to our nation.

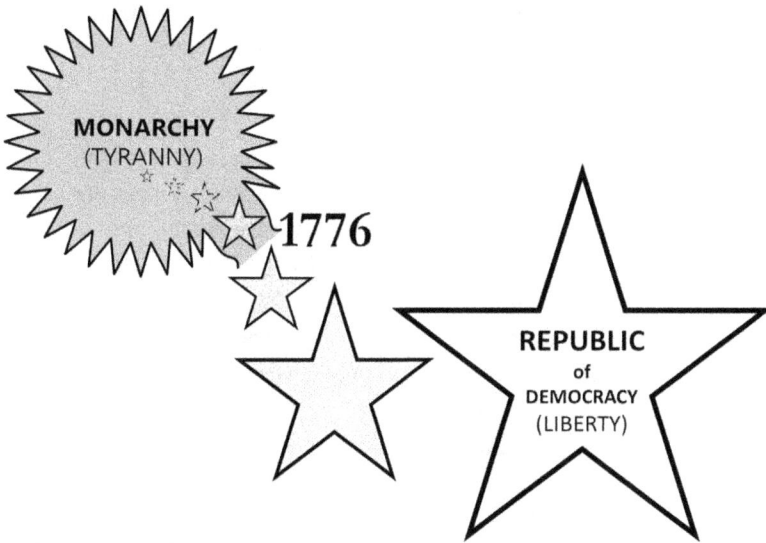

Figure 2-12: Birth of Democracy

Excessive use of force results in seeds of revolution to free oneself from tyranny. Too much polity power over people and on top of the economy powers causes resentment. It foments into fights for freedom to make and deliver provisions as the people see fit. People want the economy power to buy and sell in free markets, to have more control in society, shape their own futures, and to have liberty. As democracy forms successful republics, it gets replicated. Eventually, a world full of democracies in free-trade agreements will no longer confront tyranny and its forced conformity to narrow alliances, allowances, and intolerances. Released from the conceited few who choose to believe they are born to rule, liberty gets uncaged and people unchained, which opens us up to love and happiness. Tyranny may have been a normal situation of humanity, but people know it does not make the best circumstances to become good human beings, because it is not our species' natural condition. We seek to be free from excessive force and control. Democracy is the only human culture that grants this truth so we may live in peace and freedom. The success of such an enterprising system of society depends upon a citizenry living virtuously to sustain it and ensure the revelation and elevation of liberty as its core principle. It is an enterprise of freedoms given by democracy. Its risk is that the economy power becomes so powerful it rules over the polity and the people, creating a new ruling class of elites who feel entitled to, and possibly want to, rule the world. This would be tyranny.

The Cycle of Democracy and Tyranny

If democracy loses virtue, it falls to vice. Vice breeds vice and lands people back in the bondage of tyranny. Vice's cycle defeats democracy.

How is this? Because of the human life cycle and our generational cycles, society is always in motion. It is like a dog chasing its tail, entertaining and amusing itself, awakening and experiencing crises. Around and around the mulberry bush we go. As shown in Figure 2-13 below, society moves ever forward in time, transforming through social changes brought about by human and cultural activity to adapt to geography to survive, societal circumstances of living, and pursuits of luxurious thriving.

We move from the past of yesterday through today (the present), into tomorrow, and we will move into the future, perpetually (unless we annihilate ourselves or the planet exterminates us). Increasing complexity of our knowledge, which grows as we solve problems, drives technology-induced transformations of society. The result is awareness of deeper problems needing to be solved and increased knowledge from solving earlier ones (Hage, 2020). We confront problems to solve in all the societal and social powers that human culture produces. How to balance these powers to shape a society that will benefit all citizens is our current challenge. It is full of risks we need to manage effectively, or we will suffer the dire consequences of domestic un-tranquility and foreign threats against our sovereignty. American society has benefited from evolutions in knowledge and must prepare to keep up with further transformations. Knowledge growth requires a functioning society that moves toward its ideals, our USE's goal and objectives.

But how is American society different? Where has it been, and where is it going? In a democracy, people come first, economy second, and polity third. To have stability, the polity had to be established. People decide to make and trade. Economy provides a place and a way. Discoveries in the process of exchange impart new knowledge. Knowledge leads to new ideas, new ideas to new tools, and new tools to new goods and services to offer others. The marketplace gets complicated, confusion causes argument, and argument disrupts the exchange. People need a polity to make and agree upon the rules by the consent of the people. Properly ordered, the use of power begins with the people: in self, then family, clan, band, tribe, neighborhood, community, and finally, in the polity that establishes the laws of the land. To forget this is to lose the knowledge about the truth of power. Another important piece of knowledge is that democracy makes risky arrangements of the societal powers it promotes.

Democracies are as fragile as they are strong because they spread power around, sharing it vertically, horizontally and diagonally within society. Such a lack of power concentration makes for dynamism. Dynamism requires tolerance, an appetite for risks, confidence, and courage. Similarly, a bicycle is sturdier and better balanced the faster it moves, but at too fast a pace risks of stopping safely increase. The control depends on the rider's effort, and experience. The more work put into riding, the faster and more stable the ride, and better the judgment of top speed and skills at stopping.

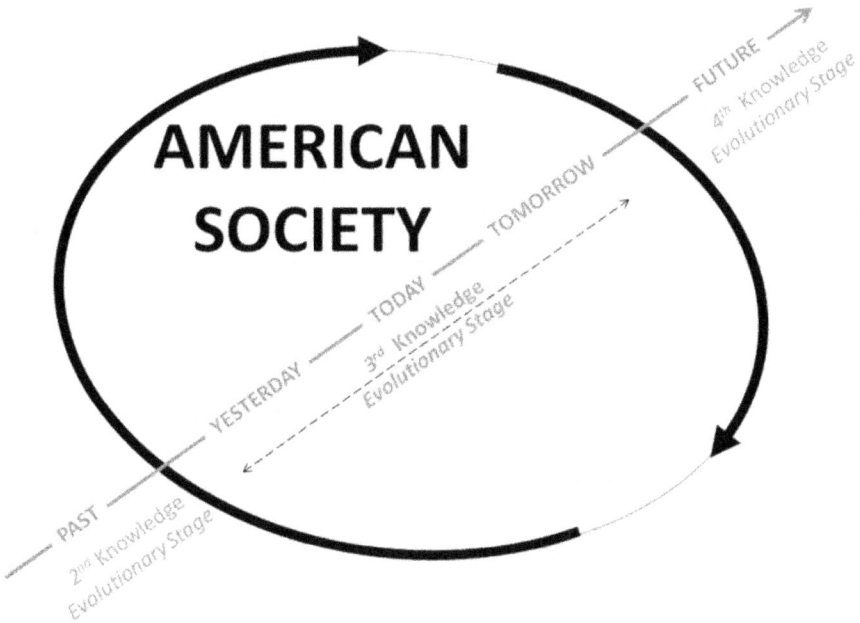

AMERICAN
SOCIETY

FUTURE ‑‑‑‑‑‑‑‑→
4ᵗʰ Knowledge
Evolutionary Stage

TOMORROW ‑‑‑‑‑‑‑→

TODAY ‑‑‑‑‑‑‑‑
3ʳᵈ Knowledge
Evolutionary Stage

YESTERDAY ‑‑‑‑‑‑

PAST ‑‑‑‑‑‑
2ⁿᵈ Knowledge
Evolutionary Stage

Figure 2-13: Cycle of Societal Life—American Society Benefited from Knowledge Evolutions

The work of democracy that keeps it going forward and makes it stable is good citizenshipping. This includes being engaged civically with our neighbors and communities and being politically informed and participating in our politics. Society wobbles. With better citizenshipping, we move forward toward our ideals faster and thereby stabilize our democracy. Motion is good for our stability. We wobble when confronted by newness that frightens us. In fear, we don't pedal. We brake to slow down. If we stop, time and extra effort are required to regain the speed of stability, since we lost our momentum when scared. We cannot go backward, so we go forward. Going too fast is too risky. Going too slow is less stable. Managing to go the right speed takes competence, skill, calculation, and the knowledge of one's destiny. Our destiny is to get our society to be a more perfect union. We, the everyday people, need to start pedaling in unison as citizens to get back on course toward our Constitution's goal through attaining its objectives.

Democracy, once obtained by a people, if unpracticed can falter and find itself on a path of slow destruction. It must be defended against the forces of tyranny that threaten it, beginning with its citizens, each person to their own self, each person one to another, to their family, as aggregated in neighborhoods, communities, cities, counties, states, and regions, as a nation, and as a people. In Figure 2-14 below, we see the cycle of democracy and tyranny. In it, the arrows point to phases of the beginning and end of democracy in American society. **Democracy** arises within a people in

bondage and tyranny, under the rule of the whims of men (a king or queen, for example) through **spiritual faith** (a confidence to "do right" and not "do wrong"), and **great courage** to oppose the oppressor. Being freed sustains a people through dissent and even revolt against tyranny to establish **independency**, where the rule of law guarantees liberty for the people, which leads to fast growth in knowledge and open science that produces **abundancy**, which comes from freedom for the people sharing ideas and freely taking opportunity risks. However, this success harbors negative risks from luxurious wealth, from which **complacency** can too easily arise within unguarded people. If not reversed, a condition of **apathy** within the people toward the injustices that begin to arise from complacency happens. The result of which is a desire for a state of **dependency** provided by the polity, which to maintain its control, finds it necessary to restrict the people in their freedoms, effectively putting them back into **bondage**, under the thumb of a dictatorial "savior" trapping them into **tyranny**.

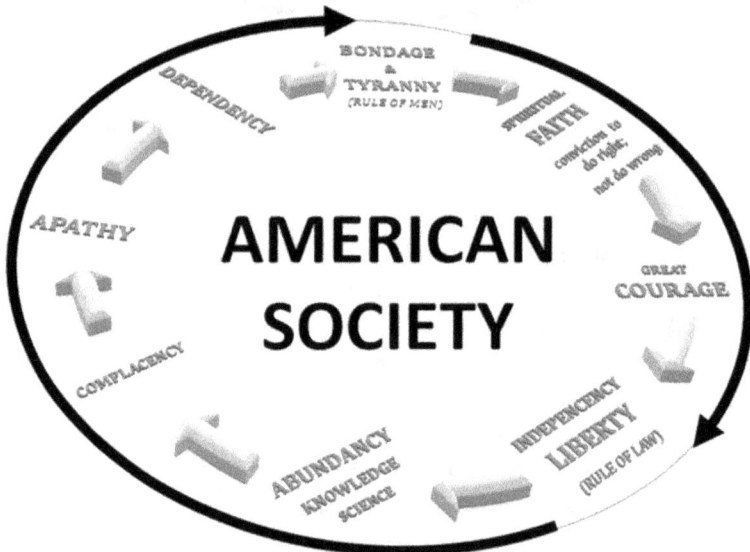

Figure 2-14: Cycle of Democracy—American. Society—Phases of Establishment and Disestablishment—from Tyranny to Democracy and Back into Tyranny

The Cycle of Democracy is a wheel of society's fortunes and misfortunes. It tells the tale of a society moving from tyranny to liberty and back into tyranny. If the USE fails to eradicate doomerism from the LAMBS, it will forget its original written ideals, intents, and first principles and then it will lose liberty. Once liberty is lost it is exceedingly difficult to get it back. The loss of liberty is preventable through us E-SASSY-T-TUF-FT-CAUCUS. (This graphic renders the cycle concept from The Patriot's Essential Liberty Pocket Guide *(Alexander, 2014))*

People must never allow either the economy or the polity to have the ultimate power to shape our lives. However, to have a society that benefits from the liberty and freedom that a culture of democracy founded on this principle of personal sovereignty provides, people have a responsibility to agree to follow the laws once established. The practice of good citizenship, particularly the E-SASSY-T-TUF-FT-CAUCUS kind, with the purpose to IDEALS liberty requires law-abiding behavior as a first right of responsibility as a leader of self and society. When we the citizenry follow the rule of law, it benefits all of us who stand before it equally. This is just. We call the rendering of the just result "justice." The practice of bad citizenship disrupts and ruins the culture of democracy. If we lie, cheat, and steal, or use prejudice and hate to be unequal in our treatment of one another, we destroy that which gave us our liberty. Our requital for any of these forms of cowardice will be the loss of liberty because we will have failed to govern our own selves properly. We must comport ourselves to democracy-made society under the rule of law. If not, breaking the reasonable rules will cause adversity and ruin others' opportunity for positive experiences in life.

As portrayed below in Figure 2-15, the cycle of democracy is divisible into two hemispheres: one in which the polity power dominates, when corruption takes hold by politicians feeling permanently in positions of authority while accepting the economy elites' bribes, governing proposals, and propaganda. And, the other in which the people power dominates. The upper one is a hemisphere of dependence; the lower one is a hemisphere of independence. The dependency hemisphere has too little joy for the everyday people; the independency hemisphere has a lot of joy for the everyday people. The former requires little effort from the people. The latter requires more effort from the people. In the dependency hemisphere, the implementation of power predicated upon persons operating in a "me first" mentality, occurs. Persons think not of anyone else's freedom but only their own. In the independency hemisphere, the implementation of power predicated upon a people in a "we first" mentality, occurs. People think always of each other's liberty.

When we, with others, conspire against the will of the majority, we create a faction. Factions seek power for their members. Factions often form around norms, values, folkways, mores, beliefs, or customs, which are unwittingly contrary to the broader expectations, attitudes, and desirable behaviors of the Constitution as amended. We amend the Constitution to keep us on the path to completing the work begun by the founders to create a more perfect union. Each generation needs to work to make corrections to their understanding of who is a citizen and entitled to full rights of citizenship. The Constitution allows Amendments to keep the consent of the governed. Amendments clarified whose vote counts, and whom the rule of law protects. Amendments have closed gaps left open during its first casting.

If all knew it better, or if confused by it, civilly discussed the different interpretations of it, we would be a more civilized civil society. With more American Civics Education (ACE) courses for children in schools, we could convey to them the important aspects of citizen rights and civic duties our republic needs for them to carry it onward. If, in the socialization process, done principally by family and supported at all levels by affiliations with other social groups, children gain an appreciation for citizenship, and praise for high performers at it, we will defeat doomerism. American society requires an educated politically active citizenry.

Democracy is not a playground. Freedom is not a wild and crazy party of irresponsibility. It is not a perpetual pursuit of selfish frivolities and continuous goofing off. If we are not paying attention to who is collecting and concentrating power, we may one day find that control of it by us is gone, taken away by stealth. There is a time to play and a time to work. We are in the middle of several crises. We must work together to rebuild. The looseness of our societal culture may need some tightening up in certain areas to get us through the power transfers from boomers to Gen X, but mainly to Gen Y millennials and Gen Z. If we do not want to be subjects of a tyrant who treats us like serfs, we need to revive constitutionality as a way to better steward the endowment of our enterprise.

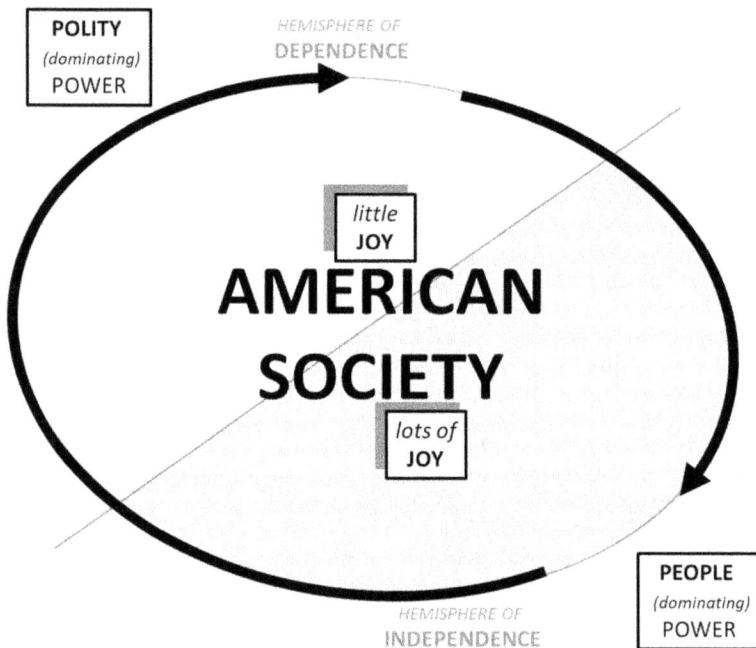

Figure 2-15: Cycle of Democracy—American Society—Hemispheres of Power Dominion

If we focus the socialization of our children on civic responsibility, then our republic-styled polity with its democracy-based culture will be a good civilization. If we do not socialize children toward good citizenship, then the project will risk devolving into a factious, tribal, and unresolvable warring of words and physically violent conflict. Unless and until we recommit to the philosophical proposition that our American ideals and principles unite us more than anyone or anything can divide us, liberty is at risk. We must deem unity a necessity to keep us free from bondage and tyranny. We should work to avoid these misfortunes. The boomers failed to focus on civilization continuation, allowing the doomers to concentrate power in oligarchical ways.

Let's continue, to explain this model of societal transformation, metaphorically. The cycle of democracy consists of many houses. Depicted in Figure 2-16 above, each house is arrow-shaped, pointing toward a social mobility possibility for its inhabitants. Those in bondage live in a jailhouse. Through discovery of a spiritual faith to do right and not wrong, a person may move into the prayer house. In this house, in a community of like-minded believers seeking to move away from bondage and not be controlled but enjoy the newfound faith, a person may find comfort with others who together elect to move away from a dependency on faith. This group takes matters into their own hands to further their distance from tyranny.

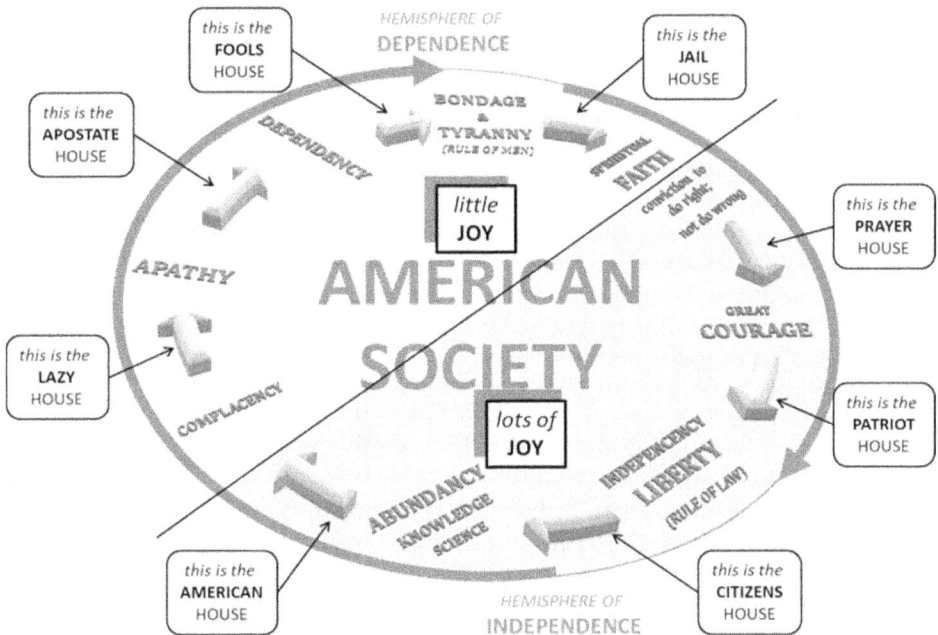

Figure 2-16: Cycle of Democracy—American Society's Houses

They build a new house, one not solely dependent on mythology but recognizing where it has psychological value and respect it as worthwhile, but by trust in reason create a place for the courageous, a **patriots' house.** It serves as their barracks, from which patriots fight for the independence of all in the society, so all may enjoy a free society with many liberties. When the patriots win, they set up a society under a rule of law by a constitution to guarantee liberty for all. This gains the approval and loyalty of their fellow members of the society to commit to being citizens who work together to stay free and enjoy liberties, without harming one another intentionally.

They all move together into the **citizens' house** and the society grows in its prosperity. This prospering society enjoys knowledge and scientific discovery. It uses its advances to build for its patriotic citizenry an **American house**. This house requires the most maintenance of all the houses because the people themselves must assume great responsibility to self-govern and to staff the offices of the polity power and work ethically and diligently in their roles within its FILMS$^{2\,[P7]}$ and particularly as the HM^5 of the economy power.

Serving in the polity is not easy with all the divergent viewpoints arising in a citizenry. It is particularly difficult if the societal powers are misaligned and imbalanced, as now with the majority generation in positions of authority, being and controlling the FILMS$^{2\,[P7]}$ and the HM^5 with unprecedented, and vehemently denied, low ethical standards and malfeasant conduct that goes unpunished. This happens because they're misguided personally, socially, and culturally as to what they should be doing. In other words, they are not practicing good citizenship behaviors. They are allowing the society to drift away from the ideals of the founding documents of the nation. They have destabilized its foundation. Rather, as the majority staff responsible to serve honorably as society's FILMS$^{2\,[P7]}$, HM^5, and citizenry in charge of the LAMBS, they have enabled doomerism to expand within our ranks. We need persons who think responsibly on what actually does benefit the common good of the society and perform accordingly with integrity. Authority must honestly AEIOUY^{2}K the power of the polity and the economy. To do so it needs honest citizens loyal to the Constitution.

The best sets of rules from the polity allow free expression with reasonable guardrails so we AEIOUY^{2}K the economy power to maximally meet the provisioning needs of society, decently. The practice of good "citizen-shipping" by all, works well to produce a state of abundance. This success is seductive with risks. By too easily having satisfied the needs and provided the wants, a people can unwittingly become complacent. Complacency can make people too lazy. Being too lazy, people become unwilling to do the necessary maintenance on the American house. Slowly, a sense of entitlement rises. Benefits get voted into actions. By watching others getting something for nothing, each person moves out of this great house and into the **lazy house**. Both loophole-hidden-assets-non-taxpaying rich and barely-making-ends-meet poor occupy this house. It is a house maintained by the revenues generated by those living in the American house. Eventually, if too many move into the lazy house, the hard-earned treasures in the American house lose out to foolish funding pursuits or to theft by unethical profiteers. Such criminals seek something for nothing with hubris, feeling entitled by birth to keep more for themselves than they deserve. The American house's maintainers also tire of carrying the expense of the freeloaders who never show any effort to change bad habits and get to a socially beneficial standard of behavior, which is one that contributes to the sustainment of society financed by the American house's steadily working residents.

These two classes of people, the "filthy" rich and "dirty" poor, the snobbish and anomic, decide they won't share and don't have enough to share. This leaves only the middle, which gets stressed, strained, drained, robbed, victimized, lied to, and stuck struggling to pay the maintenance bills of the house. Complacency sets in. None then cares. Courage disappears. Carelessness begins. Feelings of defeat take over. Without everyone's contributions, the American house thins out until too few live in it to keep it standing. Soon the lazy house gets overcrowded and people fed up with it leave and move into the **apostate house**, renouncing the society, which is now riddled with "me first" thinking instead of the originating "we first" attitudes and behaviors that produced success. A people driven by a culture of democracy for freedom, in which everyone did his or her part to build the great American house, becomes forgotten. In their resentment, they demand to be taken care of and given the satisfaction or luxury, which they once enjoyed. They become either those of ego and "me first" entitlement, who brought pockets full of cash, or those of pride and "me first" entitlement, whose pockets are empty but hearts full of envy, pleading to have what the others have, either earned or fleeced. Then, they all fight with one another over, battling to be right, claiming innocence and blaming others. They identify scapegoats. They yearn and search for saviors. One of many or one of a few speaks up with promises that sound so sweet that the crowd acquiesces to whomever promises them the best comforts, be it the mob or a violent, power-hungry isms spouting demagogue, for which they sign away their consciences, their remaining few freedoms, and the willingness to think for themselves. They consign themselves to be subjects of tyranny for a sense of security (false as it is; lacking freedom). Having done this, the tyrant moves them into the **house of fools**. However, not having read the fine print, they did not realize that it was a restrictive rental unit, and with one mistake in following some obscure rule, evictions put them back into the **jailhouse**. On their way in, what little bit of their reason, freedom, and liberty they still possess is turned over. Depositing it into the lost and found box at the entry door, they imprison themselves. Through this cycle, the people have moved back into bondage. Now ununited persons, each suffers, controlled by many tyrannies of self-guilt, shame, and powerful overlord wardens and guards who do not care for them, constantly complaining they have to feed and house "these good for nothing" inmates. They prevent uprisings with dehumanizing brutality toward the inhabitants of the house and themselves (Solzhenitsyn, 1974). This concludes the story of a misguided people who cycled from tyranny through democracy, and back into tyranny because they forgot to protect their liberty.

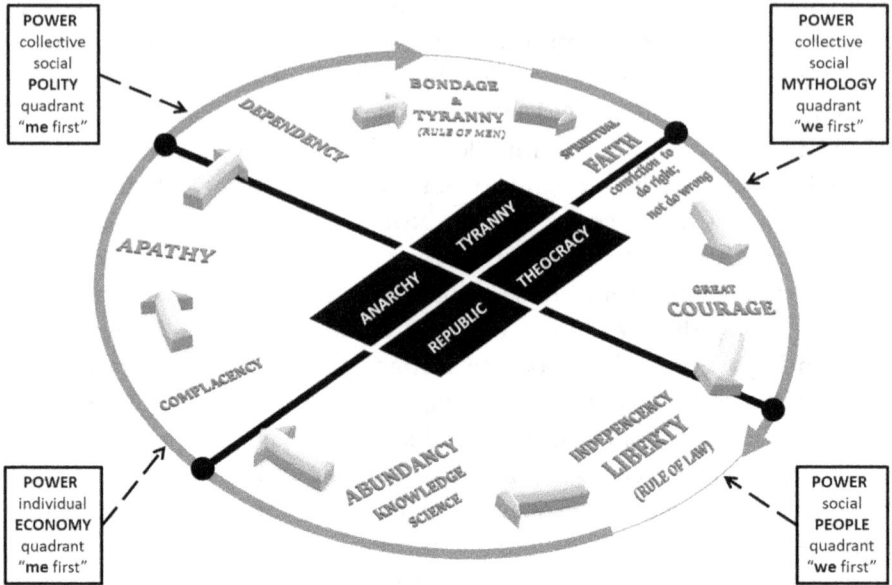

Figure 2-17: Cycle of Democracy—Quadrants of Potential Types of Societal Organization by Kinds of Power Centricities and Concentrations as Related to Micro-level Attitudes and Behaviors of Persons

Through better ACE, such a cycle is preventable. An agreed upon and consistent American sensibility for understanding how to keep liberty is doable. It would be an honest Americanism—to invoke better "citizen-shipping". It would inspire persons to behave as better, responsible for posterity's potential prosperousness, adults in the good order and discipline of a citizenry with agency in its destiny. With parenting as many do, it is the raising and socializing of children as good-doing citizen-firstlings. To prepare children for this purpose to be a citizen as a person's first attitude, act, and subsequent action is to IDEALS each person's own liberty, so long as each person's pursuit of happiness is in accord with the rule of law. This yields the long-term psychological benefit of a healthy peace of mind, a tranquility further obtained by living life in pursuit of virtue. Does this sound complicated? It's not. All of us behaving as citizens make us a good citizenry. Especially when those who serve in an office of public trust, or privileged to guide society's provisioning as an economy power HM5, or as an authority figure in a social powers' FILMS[2] [P7] do so. In doing so, we get the benefits from making society a civilization by civilly believing and abiding by the rule of law, not the rule of men (under a despot). We may pursue factions seeking inordinate power for our own tribe or our own egos, but we must know that this will not lead us to our objectives. We must rise above these instinctive pulls of biology power and push ourselves upward toward high moral states if we are to be successful as a society moving into increasingly complex social circumstances as our artistry, industry, and academy powers alter them and physical conditions as the geography power modifies them.

As depicted above in Figure 2-17, the hemispheres of American Society, encircled by the cycle of democracy, divide into quarters that represent prominent forms of polity. Each quarter has a dominant relationship between the sources of power that people allow or by force accept. In the forms of tyranny, (in the upper quarter) a polity can be the collective social acceptance of one party control. Or, if caused by a division of the people into persons each seeking their own survival, a "me first" desperate or "me first" abundant situation, the polity power or economy power will get full control over the society. When hopeless, people seek relief from the unknown. Those who have the mythology power can help people feel better, but if the people lose their sense of reason, they may give up freedoms. If we feel more like a community of a frightened "us", we can fall into the rule of a theocracy, (in the right-side quarter), in which facts and evidence become masks, and fictions offered and defended preserve the order and hierarchy of those who control the mythology. This produces rulers with absolute power over the people: minds, bodies, and souls. In such a condition, a revealed truth comes to be at odds with a reasoned truth, and demagoguery divides these two sides of truth into the "in" crowd and the "out" crowd, pitting an "us" of insiders against a "them" of outsiders.

Faith can be a powerful inner force shared by a people to give them great courage to build a society with a polity that treats each equally and gives no one power over them; one that allows people to control the polity through those they elect to represent them in it. This is a republic. However, no system of polity is perfect because persons are not perfect, and their organization into groups, and even like-minded, similarly believing persons, is imperfect. When we place focus on the imperfections (minority features of the whole body), it corrodes trust each person has in one another. This can cause tribal factions. Should this happen, a republic unravels into chaos, which is encouraged by power-hungry persons and their cult of personality as they fan the flames of disagreement to destroy the consensus and consent of the governed and the courage and commitment, honor, of the officials of the polity to maintain order. This leads to **anarchy** (in the left-side quarter). Those who have gotten more than their fair share during anarchy concentrate their power and hoard resources to establish a new tyranny over the people. This is how a coup d'état proceeds. To prevent it, each person must think first to sustain liberty, when aggregated, this thinking will block the serious negative risks of a coup from coming about. Each citizen must recognize the root of our own thoughts, attitudes, and behaviors in our micro (personal) and meso (organizational) roles in society to keep liberty realizable. This supports society at a macro level be free by removing threats to the culture of democracy and keeping the polity of the **republic** (in the bottom quarter) clear of corruption.

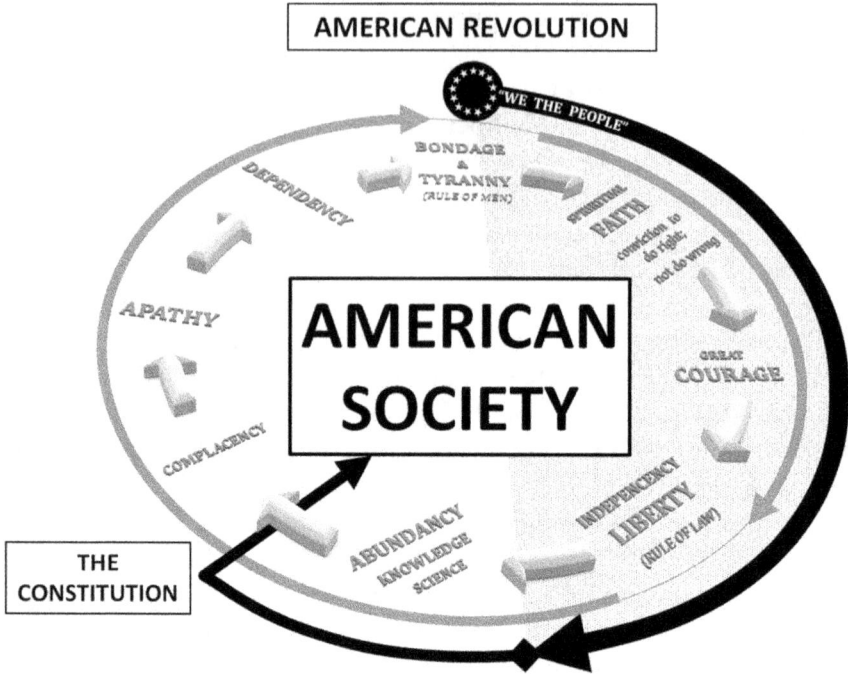

AMERICAN REVOLUTION

Figure 2-18: Cycle of Democracy—American Revolution's Phases
American society began to come into being with the revolution to throw off tyranny. Recall the complaints of the Declaration of Independence. It moved through the cycles of democracy until a written constitution fulfilled this destiny. Its need was for its people to commit to living in accord with the Constitution. The new society has long struggled to achieve the condition of a single nation, indivisible, of one people under God, with liberty and justice for all. Had it, person by person, infused a depth of understanding in the wisdom of the Constitution in each person's daily life and fully applied it in the regulation as a people of the polity and economy to reach the heights of its ideals, the society would have fulfilled the ambitions of a new order of the ages American society. This desire to create a better world, a freer-for-the-people new society, is the motivating factor that has driven changes in the society, toward this idealized goal of a more perfect union.

American society did not exactly follow the cycle of democracy because some came on behalf of kingdoms for commercial gain. Nevertheless, following the model of the cycle of democracy and tyranny we can trace the revolution of the colonies to establish the United States. Figure 2-18 shows the model of the Revolution. Geography power placed an ocean of time and distance between the colonies and their lords. They traded back and forth. Because the so-called new world was forest and not urban, the economy power needed to be prominent, so the colonizers could convert the new geography into a known form of settlement. Subduing the new geography was essential for the settlers' survival. This need put economy power over the people. In some settlements, the mythology power remained dominant. The people settled land that was not theirs. In some places they came to own it by coordinated trade, and in others they conquered native peoples using superior weaponry. Imported diseases also played a role in some locales. The settlers discovered a need for more labor to feed the engines of economic development to progress toward converting the geography into conformance with their originating cultures, which were predominantly English and a few other Europeans. To subdue the geography and make an economy, some imported labor. This labor was first indentured, and then, predominantly from Africa, enslaved.

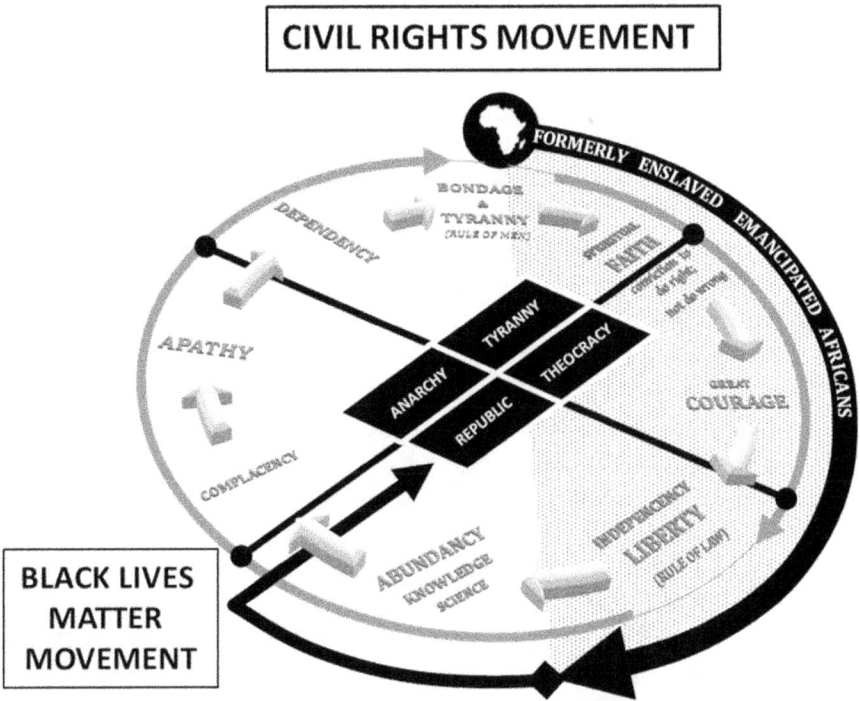

Figure 2-19: Cycle of Democracy—Movement Phases for Full Equality, Social Integration, and Enfranchisement of Formerly Enslaved Africans, Their Descendants, and Persons of Non-100% European Origin, Classified by Culturally Invented Differences Based Mainly Upon Melanin Skin Coloration and a Few Other Physical Characteristics

Enslaved persons from Africa brought to the continent of the Americas pursued freedom from bondage, a kind of tyranny, as the colonists had done from England. Emancipation began their advancing traverse around the cycle of democracy. It moved through the Civil Rights movement and the struggle for equality and justice in the polity, the economy, and the people continues with the Black Lives Matter movement. Confronting implicit biases of racial superiority offer an opportunity to discover one's own humanity. We need not have someone beneath us socially to be happy with whom we are. That is tyrannical thinking. It is not what a culture of democracy harbors. It is what a personality cult produces.

The Africans did not experience the same social status and privileges in the society that the Europeans did. Known to be wrong it persisted, as the powers were misbalanced. The economy power was greater than the people power, and the polity compromised on it but also set in motion a possibility for its correction. Figure 2-19 below traces the movement to free the Africans from bondage and the tyranny of force labor enslavement practices in the colonies. Over time, the people in society realized the hypocrisies of many of the society's practices. They sought to correct these errors and close the gap between founding principles and lived reality in the society. The Constitution, when amended, ends errors. Our history records the arguments and conflicts over the power gained from wrongful ownership of other humans. A war won on the battlefield did not salve wounds or change minds about the economically prosperous yet societally tolerated circumstances of slavery. The hierarchical society inherited from England remained a stain on the written ideals of liberty. We've yet to repair the damage done.

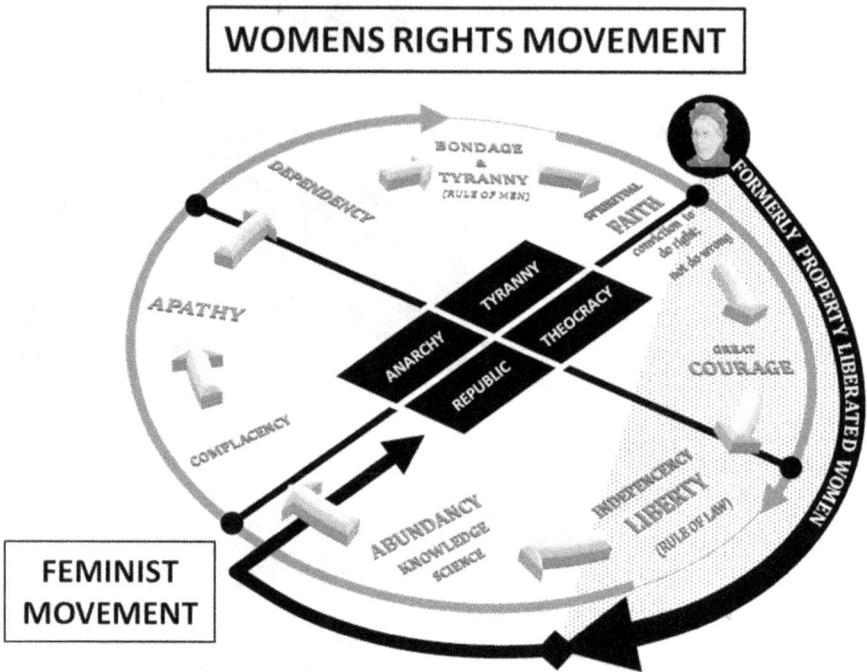

Figure 2-20: Cycle of Democracy—Movement Phases for Full Equality, and Enfranchisement of Female Humans into Society

Considered property by power of mythology, women lacked the same legal standing in society as men. Though not sold at a market, men traded females for dowries. Thus, there was an economic component. Traditions built up around this. Harangued for the freedom and liberty he gave to his wife, John Adams fully applied his belief in the democracy project he helped craft, launch, and pilot. He was a rarity. In time, women gained suffrage and pushed for equality before the law. Equality is super, but men and women remain dissimilar biologically. We simply are not the same. Making us the same in not human. We are not androgynous robots. Nor should we be, as that would just give those who control the economy power the ability to manipulate the value of our labor in a way that might imbalance the people and cause inequality within and among families. We need to be careful about making all persons the same. The uniqueness of each person makes for a more interesting people. A better society celebrates each person's unique contributions, which makes all mothers happy to have their children seen, heard, and treated fairly without legal discrimination or social prejudice against them. Thus, mothers, all women, should vote.

Having not perpetuated freedom for all, social movements were born. Such movements fight against the grain of the majority and the hierarchies. They encourage the society to care, not to be complacent or apathetic but to want to achieve something better. The hierarchies of Europe permitted women to be property of men, and denied them the right to vote. Suffrage changed this and the Constitution amended moves it closer to ideals of democracy culture. Figure 2-20 below traces the movement for equal rights for women. Figure 2-21 below shows the path in pursuit of fair treatment by society for those who live alternative lifestyles from the mainstream as relates to their orientation for sexual intimacy, a private matter of liberty. Despite the potential of factions around issues for groups in politics, a hope persists in the population to become as one people. This is an ambition of the Constitution.

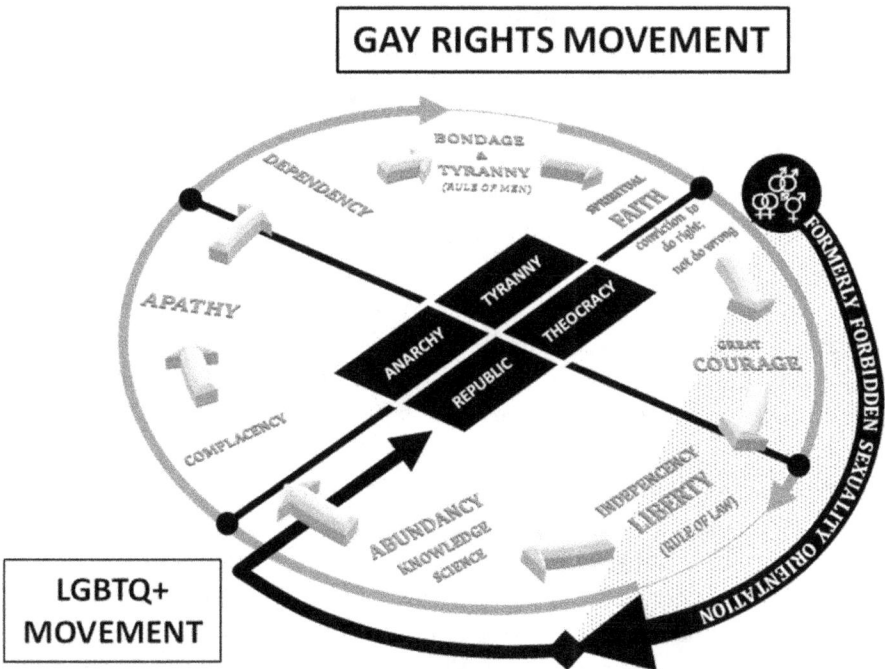

Figure 2-21: Cycle of Democracy—Movement Phases for Protection from Violence and for Permissibility to Live Lives of Alternative Sexual Relations and Expressions Freely in a Tolerant Society Permitting More Liberties than Ancient Societies Controlled by Mythology Power

Is it not a natural condition of humans to seek to understand ourselves inside and out? As a person doesn't, this affects our identity, how we represent ourselves, whom we feel we are inside and outside our body? Doesn't our identity influence what we want to be, and how we want to give and receive love, kindness, compassion, empathy? Is it anyone else's business if identity is a natural right? A small percentage of all populations find that their sexuality is very important to this discovery of how they will be happiest in living out their lives. Ancient societies' mythology powers often prohibited non-heterosexual love pairing because the economy and polity needed population replacements to work the farms, to fight the wars, and to enrich the mighty controllers who led by tyranny.

The USE began with the Constitution. Our national character evolved from a pursuit of a way of being that moves us toward living in accordance and in deeply faithful accord with it. Not to do so is, by definition, un-American and socially treasonous. No one wants to be a traitor, so everyone should get educated on the deeper meaning and powerful structure of the Constitution. If lived out fully, it sets everyone free. It is the means to IDEALS liberty and to gain control over the social powers active in the LAMBS in the USE. Our history is not the guide. The founding frame of mind is.

The historical realities of its ratification did not reach its ideals but set in motion a project to complete it. We, in going back to it for inspiration, must seek out the frame of mind of its calling, not the social circumstances and physical conditions of its time. Societies do change over time. The change necessary to reach a more perfect union is a change we, the everyday people, must lead daily. Each generation is expected to commit to the pursuit of achieving our goal of a more perfect union, particularly when its dominant, generational personality forming, cohorts are in positions of power. This voyage through time requires that we apply our talents to improving our enterprise, our society, to get us to that imagined more perfect union by attaining the Preamble's objectives. This is the inspiration of the founders' frame of mind. This is everyone's duty on the good citizen ship, our US Enterprise. Let's get to work and throw off the doomeristic hypocrisy that is heading us toward the preconditions for tyranny by setting up an oligarchical plutocracy. Let's make this USE the best in the world, a place in which all of us are truly free in liberty.

People, we can do this! In a revolution against all odds, commoners, yesteryear's everyday people, kicked out the world's most powerful empire. In a civil war, we ended slavery. In a world war with a coalition, we defeated the Nazis, held imperial Japan accountable for attacking us, and then rebuilt both Europe and Japan. In a cold war, we sent astronauts to the moon. Nearly a decade into the second millennium, we elected a biracial president. These are historic accomplishments in the movement toward the ideals of the Constitution. Let's not give up now. Let's not cower because of new growing threats to liberty. Let's not be complacent, apathetic, or lazy.

Our progress to defeat tyranny is only possible when we conserve the Constitution. The conservation of the Constitution's principles makes us its conservators. We must be conservatives to be progressive Americans. Our project progresses when we work for liberty and justice for all. These principles put the power in the people. This is the single most important idea in human history. The generations that accomplished this led with convictions that conserved the Constitution and its protection of liberty, the original big idea of our country. It framed our polity, and therefore our society, which continues to evolve toward its realization.

Unfortunately, we now see in the shadow of their light, such conviction and determination reversing. The corroding attitudes and behaviors of the baby doomers create an undercurrent in our culture that denies justice, strips persons of possibilities for the pursuit of happiness, and robs us of our freedoms. The erosion of the people's power is doomerism. We need to stop its corroding zymosis.

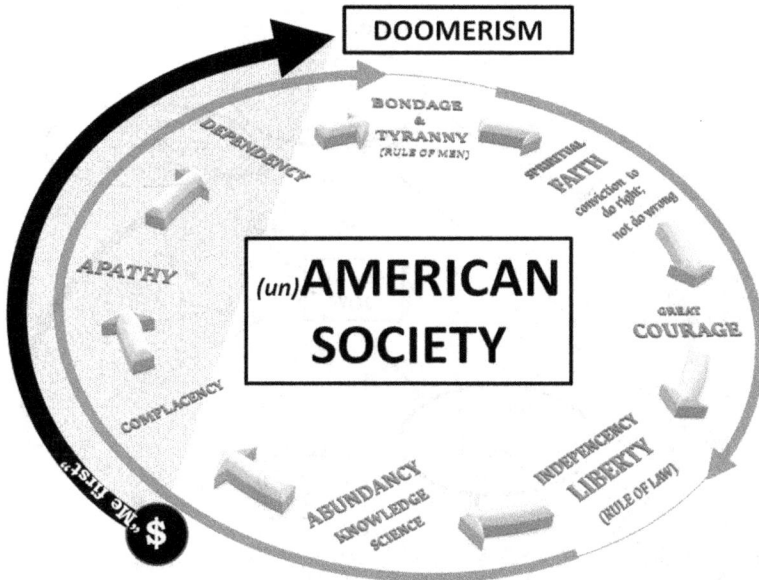

Figure 2-22: Cycle of Democracy—Movement Caused by Doomerism Pressures in Our Culture

One of the greatest successes of liberty, allowing persons to pursue their interests without being told what to do, the freedom to choose how to live, by virtues or by vices, if forgotten, will be an Achilles heel that becomes our society's greatest weakness, which could cause a willing following of the community-harming seven sins. This would ruin the commons for everyone by filling it with vices and putting virtue in the minority. Such a deplorable society, made by an escape from citizenship responsibilities to the community, devoid of a truthful citizenship ethos, is the opposite of the applied wisdom that created American society. It is treasonous cowardice. The degrees to which we tolerate a variety of lifestyles become the basis for community standards. Because honesty is essential to prevent an increased demand on the polity to mandate and re-solve conflicts via its courts, the character required to enable the joy of liberty for all comes into jeopardy. Citizenship as a concept is the means by which we reinforce trust. Because it, by civics, teaches how liberty requires virtue in its citizenry. Integrity, love, contentiousness, compassion, empathy for others, and self-control are its bedrock. These are matters of everyone's character development. We must pursue these vigorously because these are truly in our own best self-interests. In a lifetime, long-steadied and stable community yields personal strength that serves us best. Selfishness is not actually good for one's self-interests. Inward struggles for self-betterment are necessary for outward struggles of self-interests for a harmonious society. Life is not about a "me-against-you" or an "us-against-them" competition. It is a "we are working together through the conference of liberty, so we each may achieve our best possible place in society, per our character and abilities as they suit the society best, which serves us each better." This cooperation is the basis of the real pursuit of human self-interest. Cooperation is the foundation that led to the Constitution. It is the way for each person and the whole people to make our union more perfect.

We need to return to first principles and seek to be constitutionally allied. We need to unite in our citizenshipping toward understanding and synchronize our efforts to improve the society by rebalancing the powers. We must practice better civics through E-SASSY-T-TUF-FT-CAUCUS. To do this we must launch into a more serious series of life long American civics education (ACE). This is how we diminish the dangers of doomerism. Figure 2-22 above shows how it is sending us toward the tyranny of either autocracy or dependency, or both at once.

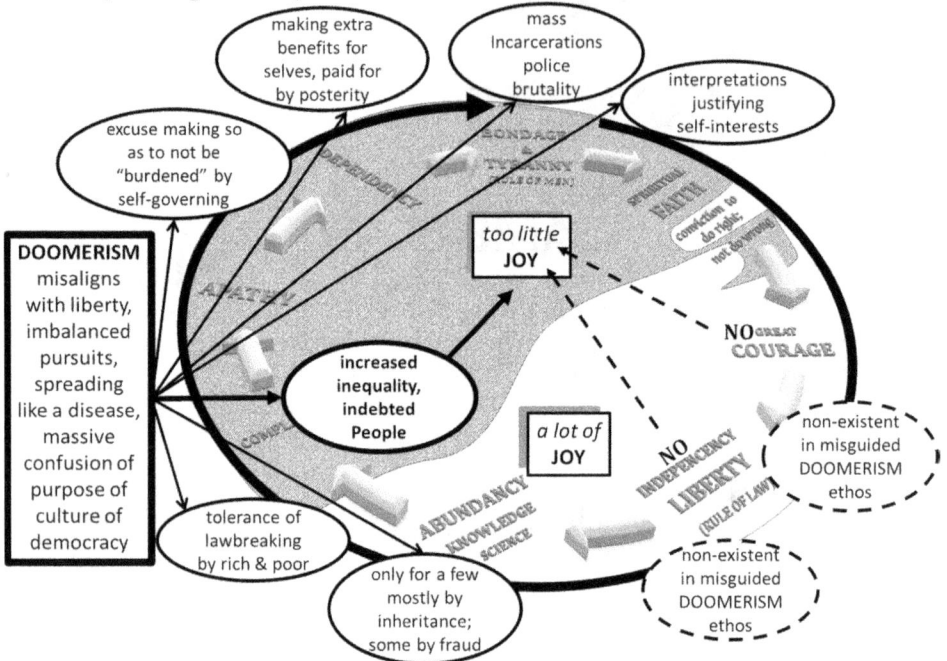

Figure 2-23: **The Cycle of Democracy—Doomerism's Impacts at Each Social Circumstance Station and House**

Doomerism moves society away from democracy and separates it into the haves and have-nots, with the use of brutality to enforce the new order of vertical stratification and horizontal divisions between the people. Democracy opens the doors for persons to find alternative identities that are not based on the existing ones, such as family name, where one lives or was born, or what forms of community, academy, artistry or industry power, to name a few, one uses within society. Being able to be as one pleases is freedom, a right granted in a society based upon liberty so long as ones pleasure does not damage another's. We may not have any other classes of persons who seek to band together to gain peace of mind through legal protections by the polity for a form of group identity. We'd do better to ensure the content of one's character is far more important than person's external physical characterizes, because separatist factions could use these to disrupt everyday life's peacefulness. Shown in gray within Figures 2-19, 2-20, 2-21, 2-22, and 2-23 is a rough proportion of the impact to society of the discussed social changes. These length of arrows and areas of the social movements for freedoms reduce progressively. The last group, sexuality as important to identifying self and lifestyle, is smaller than the previous two. We allow people to be as they would like to be within the bounds of the law and reached equilibrium of liberty for persons who seek to identify with a given group or two. Note, the groups we might share values with are less important than our personal character and citizenshipping activities to reverse baby doomerism.

Key to remember, the polity is to respond to the people, one person at a time in a voting booth, and not to groups as its norm. This applies to groups seeking to change the balance of the economy power in their group's favor. If we all live in accordance with the Constitution, in the spirit of its ideals that the content of each person's character is what is paramount and in the real realms of our behaviors, we all may yet be free to be. On that day when we do, all of us might enjoy with gratitude the abundance of a society that exists to IDEALS liberty to itself in every moment of its existence thanks to democracy being the basal culture of American society. We need to get real, get over ourselves, forgive, and love one another as citizens of a special society, without being too entitled and choosing dependency over independency

Figure 2-23 above illustrates the previously presented cycle of democracy and at each social circumstance, station, gives an example of what doomerism does to the attitude, condition, or behavior that occurs in the house that sits between each station. It shows how doomerism is consuming the society, taking over all stations and thought. The two stations that remain "nonexistent in doomerism" are silenced, ostracized, and outnumbered. They lack the doomerist ways of being and influence on our republic. From these two standalone stations, as well as with half of the faith with morality to have convictions to do right, we must launch our counterattack and push doomerism out of our society. Otherwise, it will consume us with its petty, immature, uncivilized, "dog eat dog," "me first" mentalities. Having described the cycle of democracy, our progress in pursuit of liberty, and how doomerism arises within, let's examine another slice of society. This time, we look at one related to where we live and the subcultures' remnants today.

Settlement Pattern Complications

People settle together in groups, often preferring like-minded others. Many reasons determine why groups decide, or are forced, to set up a community. Some choose places in search of a new means of earning a livelihood, satisfy a belief, fulfil an ambitious speculation, or get better access to resources needed to survive, or wanted live comfortably, or thrive luxuriously.

Legal foundations

Democracy is a culture derived from legal formation and extended to the people by law. In the absence of written law, it has principles that advise people on how to behave toward one another. In the Western Hemisphere, it received Abrahamic societal organizing and control concepts—Moses' Ten Commandments—as an influential life guide for people. Conveyed predominantly by Christianity, (Catholic and Protestant), pockets of Judaism and Islam existed. The mythology power shaped premodern societies. Historically, settlements in the North American continent were majority Protestant settlements, which became colonies, which then became states of the USA. One notable exception was the tolerant territory named Maryland that Protestants and Catholics shared peaceably, but sadly, it was a colony late to denounce slavery. From it came brave justice seeking humans, Harriet Tubman and Frederick Douglass, and the scientific Benjamin Banneker, who helped survey the land that become the District of Columbia, the seat of the federal government. All the while Catholicism was unacceptable to Protestants, who opposed the power of the pope in the sociopolitical structure of the administration of the church, which gave additional power to its priesthood over the laity. The church applied concepts and teachings of the faith with a strong salvation component, controlled by the priesthood, the politicians of the prayer houses. Christian beliefs, interpreting and applying Abrahamic laws, contributed to the making of society by providing principles for the people to follow, which shaped the attitudes and behaviors that would be tolerated within the "new world" society forming in the thirteen colonies. The culture relied mostly on Christianity's moral teachings, though as is the case with all humans, immorality results from irresponsible choices people make. Its beliefs to help people govern themselves had a variety of interpretations and applications in the settlements made by conquest over, or trade with, the indigenous people in the lands that became declared territories of Europeans.

Regional realities

From this start, which evolved into the United States' present continental boundaries, grew a population that expanded its participation in global affairs. Many separate settlements' communities of belief become predominant in the colonies and their conquered territories in the Americas. In lands that became the United States, overlaid upon and pushing away the indigenousness nations, eleven regional subcultures exist. These regions are like nations within the United States. They do not align to state boundaries but derive from settlement patterns (Woodard, 2011). Each region is a differing subculture. Figure 2-24 depicts a map of these. Each is a part of the broader, unifying, democracy-based culture, though many don't completely agree on the same premises of society or on a proper balancing of the societal powers. As each person is unique, while also a member of a family, so are regions to a nation.

Figure 2-24: Ten Regional Subcultures in the United States
(Map adapted from (Woodard, 2011))

Because of the regional variations and themes within our broader national community's culture, enterprise, and society, understanding our differences is essential to achieving unity. Divided by baby doomers who want to create a ruling class while distracting us with the born differences we cannot change is something that we the everyday people need to call out, resist, and stop with community power. We need to seek to understand and link variations and themes back to the larger concepts that led to the country, as the colonial framers did. We need to recognize the histories of the regions of the USE. We need to understand if, and how and why, they diverge from our national community's intents. We need to educate and encourage one another to turn away from doomeristic approaches to living and turn toward the pursuit of a more perfect union, building more national community mores for our identity as one people. Further, we must understand the risks inherent in each regional subculture to the whole nation, their strengths and weaknesses, and as a community prepare the population in all environs for the coming of a new era. To pass successfully through our present crises and chaos that play out differently in the minds of our inhabitants of different backgrounds, we need new forums to dialogue toward understanding these differences.

To move forward as a single nation, we need to help all our regions transition their subcultures toward adaptive approaches or realize the consequences that may result if they don't adapt during this current third stage of knowledge evolution (see Figure 5 1). We, the everyday people, in each region must become more aware of how and why we see the world the way we do and what we expect to give and get from our society. If we are to lead properly from a common cultural position of democracy, we must be open to learning about one another, particularly those who may appear to differ from us the most.

Yet we cannot be open until we understand our beliefs and ourselves. Those who are unwilling to accommodate differences, or newness, to evolve in a way that moves us toward unity and achieving our constitutional goal of a more perfect union will struggle. We must help them. This new social self that we need to develop as a people begins within each of us and will take concerted effort every day to cultivate. It begins with the pursuit of self-knowledge, an internal journey to truth, and a daily effort to resist wrongdoing. Without conscientious self-reflection and empathy for our fellow citizens in other regions, we cannot unite effectively. Without open tolerance, curiosity, patience, and suspended pride, we cannot ready our society and ourselves to perform in accord with the project to pursue a more perfect union. It takes extending goodwill and building trust. We must put some effort into better understanding where we came from to know where we are going and if it is toward tyranny or greater liberty. Here are very brief interpretive synopses of the ten regional subcultures within the United States identified by historian and journalist Colin Woodard.

o   <u>Yankeedom</u>: characterized by an attitude toward society formed from a public-based Protestantism. This regional subculture puts emphasis upon the good of government, communities, the middle class, and education that begins with Bible reading. It includes the areas of Massachusetts, New England, northern Pennsylvania, Ohio, Indiana, Illinois, Iowa, eastern Dakota, and Michigan, Wisconsin, and Minnesota. It has quintessential New England Puritan cultural traits that include a belief in reforming society with political insistence on public conformity.

   •   Conformity to community standards is very important. Its sense of the proper balance of the societal powers is to favor community control and to disfavor aristocrats and bishops.

o   <u>New Netherlands</u>: characterized by an attitude toward society formed from an acceptance of high diversity and a high commercialism preference for free trading. This regional subculture emphasizes global commercial trading, tolerance of diversity, and a commitment to the freedom of inquiry. It includes the areas around its foothold, New Amsterdam, now New York City. It has quintessential Dutch cultural traits that believe in tolerance and commerce as social behavior regulators.

   •   Ingenuity in art and industry is very important. Its sense of the proper balance of the societal powers is to favor the people's Bill of Rights and multiculturalism and to disfavor attempts to control commercial mercantile speculation and materialistic pursuits.

o   <u>Midlands</u>: characterized by an attitude toward society formed from utopian but pluralistic organized middle-class values. This regional subculture puts strong emphasis upon moderation. It includes the areas of Middle America and the heartland (central Ohio, Indiana, Illinois, and northern Missouri, most of Iowa, parts of South Dakota, Nebraska, and Kansas). It began along the Delaware Bay, like Philadelphia, Pennsylvania, and spread throughout parts of Pennsylvania, Delaware, and Maryland. It has quintessential "Penn" Quaker and "Sylvania" German traits that believe in good order and self-discipline with separation between mythology and polity powers.

- Moderate perspectives and skepticism of fervent opinionated agendas is very important. Its sense of the proper balance of the societal powers is to favor organizing society to benefit the ordinary people and to disfavor ethnic and ideological purity or top-down government intrusions into personal affairs.

o Tidewater: characterized by an attitude toward society formed from a respect for authority and tradition. This regional subculture arises from an emphasis upon creating a country gentleman's paradise. It includes the areas of Virginia and the lowlands of Maryland and Delaware. Blocked by neighboring colonies from expanding westward, it aligns with the Deep South politically but increasingly influenced by the Midlands. It has quintessential Virginian (cavalier) traits that believe in the "natural" adopted hierarchy of the landed gentry's society of 18th-century English manor life as the correct traditions for society to maintain.

- Economic, political, and social affairs are for, and to be run by, socially upper-class men. Maintenance of classes as a normal part of society is also very important. Its sense of the proper balance of the societal powers is to favor hierarchical classes and to disfavor giving lower classes equality.

o Deep South: characterized by an attitude toward society formed from its founding by the cruel and despotic Caribbean slavers. This regional subculture puts emphasis upon maintaining its ancient world's classical republicanism. This system saw democracy as a privilege of the aristocrats, who had slaves as a "natural" condition of society. It includes the areas of the lowlands of South Carolina, Georgia, Alabama, Mississippi, Florida, and Louisiana, parts of western Tennessee, and southeastern North Carolina, Arkansas, and Texas. It has states' rights, racial segregation, and sources of African-American subcultural expressions. It has quintessential "Dixie" Confederacy traits that believe in an inequality of the races and the hierarchy of classes. It opposes the Yankees.

- Traditional class-based society and private Protestantism's evangelical beliefs are very important. Its sense of the proper balance of the societal powers is to favor white supremacy, labor, and environmental deregulation and to disfavor democracy pushing for equality.

- There are particular differences between the private Protestantism of the Deep South and the public Protestantism of Yankeedom. In the South, religion is a private situation of a person's plight, dependent upon God's will and a perceived natural order of classes in human society (who is entitled to hold power in the society and who is not), and practiced for one to obtain salvation for one's self. In the North, religion is a public situation of persons abiding by the public mandates on their performance of God's will as the means to salvation. The religion is guidance for the society, directing the community's activities to bring human society into conformance with the guidance.

o Greater Appalachia: a mountainous environment with adapted Scots-Irish-Northern England settlers' clannish subcultures' responses to the biomes it occupies. Characterized by an attitude toward society formed from an intense suspicion of aristocrats, social reformers, and Christian evangelizing this regional subculture puts emphasis upon the warrior ethic and a commitment to individual liberty and personal sovereignty. Many American military members come from here. It includes the areas of the highland South and southern parts of Ohio, Indiana, and Illinois, plus the Ozarks of Arkansas and Missouri, eastern parts of Oklahoma, and parts of Texas. It has quintessential Appalachian frontiersmen traits that believe in self-reliance, individualism, family importance, and patriotism for the defense of the nation.

- Individual liberty, freedom, and defense of country are very important. Its sense of the proper balance of the societal powers is to favor combating for individual liberty and to disfavor persons that tell them what to believe or how to think.

o New France: where the Catholic French settled in the New World is remnant in Louisiana, an island mostly absorbed and converted into the Deep South, yet it is also strongly influential in Canada, a major trading partner with Yankeedom. It has had influence on both Yankeedom and Deep South subcultures, but it is less powerful a force than its neighbors. Characterized by an attitude toward society formed from French peasantry and Catholic traditions, this regional subculture puts strong emphasis upon egalitarianism. It includes areas of Louisiana, principally New Orleans. It has quintessential French cultural traits that believe in kindness, curious sociability, and fashionable self-expression.

- Multiculturalism and negotiated consensus is very important. Its sense of the proper balance of the societal powers is to favor down-to-earth consensus and to disfavor illiberal concepts.

o New Spain: Mainly "El Norte" and "Spanish Caribbean" regions of the Americas combined.

- El Norte: characterized by an attitude toward society formed from a Spanish imperial Catholicism. Its influences were Mexican and Caribbean Hispanic trading partnerships with the Deep South. It's a regional subculture with an emphasis upon the hierarchical societal norms of Hispanic culture, though Americanized through contact with Anglos. It includes the areas of south and west Texas, Southern California, Arizona, New Mexico, and parts of Colorado.

- It has quintessential Hispanic cultural traits that believe in family life's importance, celebrating living with openness through a shared proud heritage and subculture. The Spanish Caribbean: characterized by similar Spanish roots with large influences from Caribbean cultures. It is located in the areas of south Florida, centered in Miami, which has seen increased Cuba and Haitian settlements in the past half century.
- Societal and Catholic norms are very important. Its sense of the proper balance of the societal powers is to favor independence, self-sufficiency, and adaptability, to be work-centered, and to disfavor dependency and change in cultural heritage and customs. It is also prone to machismo.

- The Spanish Caribbean: This area is similar to El Norte and Deep South combined. It includes the area of south Florida.

o Far West: a high geography power, intense, dry, and remote ecosystem with settlers needing industrialized resources to respond to the biomes from which they extract geological resources, developed a subculture of quintessential traits of a colony within the nation. Characterized by an attitude toward society formed from a dependency on massive New England, New Netherlands, and Left Coast corporations' railroads, heavy mining equipment, ore smelters, dams, and irrigation systems this regional subculture puts emphasis upon libertarian values, though it remains dependent upon federal government largesse. It includes the interior areas of California, Washington, Oregon, Alaska, northern Arizona, the western Dakotas, Nebraska, Kansas, and all of Idaho, Montana, Colorado, Utah, and Nevada. It has quintessential Gilded Age traits that believe in industrialization, free commerce, economic growth, and the pursuit of unruly prosperity, which tends toward corruption in the houses of the economy power and polity power.

- Support for the corporations is very important. Its sense of the proper balance of the societal powers is to favor self-reliant libertarianism while keeping federal dollars flowing and to disfavor authoritarianism and government interference with legislation that restricts economic progress gained through natural resource mining.

o The Left Coast: Characterized by an attitude toward society formed from a Yankee missionary effort and Appalachian traders and farmers. This regional subculture puts emphasis upon intellectualism, idealism, and individual fulfillment. It includes the strip area along the Pacific Coast from Monterey, California up to and through the progressive cities of San Francisco, Portland, and Seattle, plus Juneau, Alaska. It has quintessential Yankee traits plus beliefs in ardent individualism, spiritual freelancing, and technological inventiveness.

- Faith in good government and social reform are very important. Its sense of the proper balance of the societal powers is to favor individual self-exploration and discovery and environmental protectionist expanding agendas. It disfavors destruction of the ecosystem, and anti-progressive positions opposed to human rights.

With all of the plurality in our society from regional settlement patterns and urbanity or rurality, we have many different perspectives and values on life and society. Our common ground is in the ideals of the Constitution. Our common purpose is to realize its goal and objectives. To assist us learn and grow in our understanding of one another we can use intellectual tools to come to terms with the differing perspectives and beliefs of others and our own. One such tool uses dichotomies and continuums.

Dichotomies to understand differences

We can seek understanding with the aid of a dichotomy wheel. The wheel turns dichotomous continuums into a tool to assist us with understanding. (More uses of it are cover later in Chapter 2 and Chapter 6). As it relates to values that result from historical settlement patterns, if we comprehend the core sense of one another's values, we can discuss them openly and find a path of agreement on how to proceed with our mission to make a more perfect union. This is essential since people create society, which then contains them, and people are different. A measure of the multitude of different people in a society is its plurality. Society establishes controls in order to function. Controls can be trust based and voluntary as in a democracy, or fear based and involuntary as in a tyranny. Controls can be from within us, or applied upon us.

Control over society can be through societal powers of economy and polity, structured to serve people through various arrangements of the secondary and tertiary powers. People have many questions and spiritual, emotional, social, and psychological needs. Using mythology power, people made religion. Religion is a culturally created social system (Roberts, 1990) that services those needs. Figure 2-25 below shows the lines of forces we experience as persons in society and thus as a people. Our values form the basis of how we perceive them. We may be open to plurality or closed to it. We may want to resist or restrict change, or we may want to permit or promote it. We may think the polity power should have more or less control over society. We may think private entities or public offices should control the economy power. We may not even know what we think, or how and why we think the way we do, which is why using a dichotomy wheel benefits us. Particularly as we seek to build common ground to create a more perfect union as one American People.

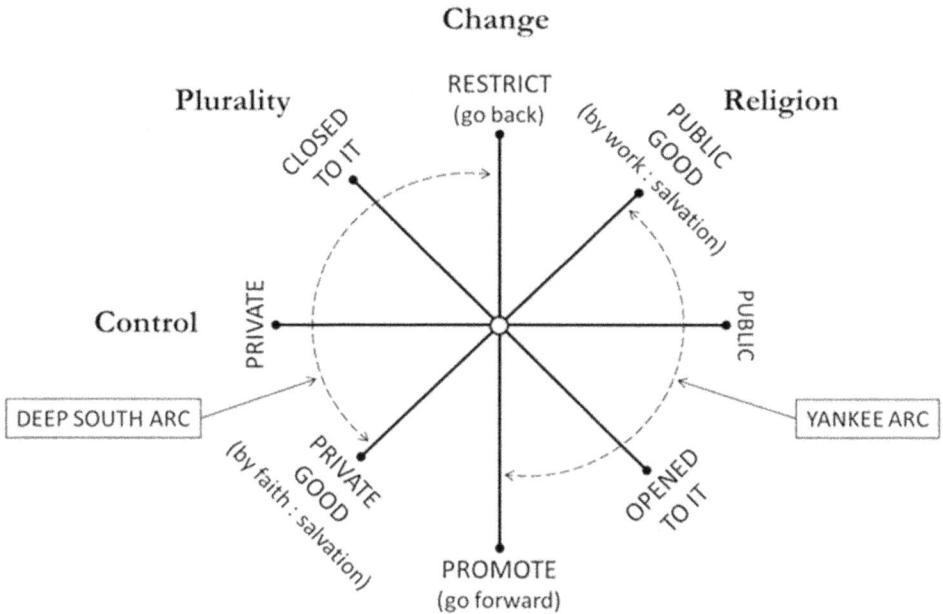

Figure 2-25: Values on a Dichotomy Wheel with Regional Preference Arcs

Regarding plurality in society, based upon historical settlement patterns, the preferences of regions overlaid with its perspectives is possible using a dichotomies wheel. This visual tool can help us clarify our own values and perspectives as well as those of others. This is a talking tool used to seek understanding. As demonstrated in the LAMBS model, we the people as one of the three primary societal powers are the leadership of American society. We need to have a position to shape policy around the control of society. We hire by elections the politicians to work on our policies. We by the provisioning and purchasing of goods and services in the economy power's marketplaces further indicate our positions toward our satisfaction with the society. We will need to look within ourselves and discuss with others our feelings on three issues that differ significantly among our regional subcultures. These are our tolerances and expectations of plurality, change, and religion in our society. To come to agreements we can use dichotomies wheels.

While this tool might seem to be an oversimplification, it provides a starting point for potentially difficult, yet crucial, civil conversations on what we as a people believe and want from the society we are to lead. We need to have less polemic and more productive conversations. We need high-stakes conversations managed successfully as crucial conversations absent emoted anger (Patterson, Grenny, McMillan, & Switzler, 2012). We need to pull away from the extreme poles and converse on our different opinions on these key cultural issues of American society, so we can make the LAMBS within the USE effective, efficient, and on course toward our more perfect union goal and justice, tranquility, defence, welfare, and liberty objectives.

Tyranny forever threatens us

Let us not forget that the enemy of democracy is tyranny: a tyranny of politicians in power who dictate all that is permissible and demand permission be requested repeatedly for all that they permit. Tyrannies come in many forms. Monarchies and kingdoms, feudal in structure, divvy out power to control people and resources. They share these through familial relationships via nepotism. These systems of societal power organization come with hierarchical class-based social systems. These systems use family and class-based aristocracies. Aristocrats adjoin through social life affiliation, landholding status, or relevance to a ruling elite's position. Tyrannies induce behaviors that contradict principles of democracy by inciting superiority fictions of self through the perceptions in persons' heads. Some feel superior to others by affiliation, birth, or fortune. Some feel superior to others by a sense of merit from greater contributions to society. Feeling superior is not in accord with the ideal of democracy. It is a weakness of human nature, a character aspect of Homo sapiens to be aristocratic in culture-shaping beliefs, yet it is at odds with a completely democracy-based culture. The real instinct of our species pitted against an ideal belief. A tension between life's opportunities and living's outcomes confronts our American intents for human equality, which creates a cultural challenge for the inhabitants of the USE. To establish understanding of this contrary to nature concept of democracy means that our republic requires education of self, socialization in its beliefs, and practice in daily life by the citizenry, and particularly in the FILMS[2][P7] of societal and social powers. Founder Thomas Paine wrote about no person being born superior to another in his January 9, 1776 pamphlet, *Common Sense*. This American philosophy requires revisiting frequently to stave off aristocratic passions that imbibe snobbery.

Similarly, dynasties are another form of tyranny. China is a dynastic culture. The nation-state organization of China is a new development in that country's long, continuous culture. History shapes China. China's people have dynastic values. Rather than being beholden to a nation, the Chinese are beholden to a civilization. Its policies are for the cause of its civilization's success through amassing dynastic power and its concomitant wealth in the hands of the to-be-trusted ruling class. A dynasty has a different culture than a kingdom. Its purpose and orientation toward the use of power in making the rules, shaping the society, and controlling the people differs. Also from Asia, the warriors of the Mongolian Genghis Khan conquered countries all the way to Moscow, leaving behind remnants of dynastic culture.

Another form of tyrannical societal power is oligarchy. This occurs when a chosen group disallows democracy and prevents the whole people from leading the society. A political party of officials did this in the United Soviet Socialist Republics. The commissars ran the country through centralized planning and an expectation of party loyalty above all other loyalties. People would rat out their own family members and neighbors to gain favor with party officials. Similar to oligarchy, in that a few at the top control the whole, is a plutocracy. In it, the ultimate controlling powers are shared by a "power elite" (Mills, 1956) of political officials and economic elites.

There is also anarchy, which is a condition society can find itself in when power is not clearly organized. This can result in the tyranny of a mob or in a "strong man" rising to power over the mob. Mobocracies, formed in a fury and demanding obeisance by violence, disunite people.

In tyrannies, cowardly politicians violate their sworn oaths to uphold and defend the public trust. In our land, this public trust rests in the rule of law as prescribed by our Constitution. It needs upheld and defended against all enemies, foreign and domestic. Mobs or gangs who threaten or even use terror and violence to influence the polity and society destroy liberty. They tempt politicians to act in service to their own selfish greed and lust for power. These politicians seek to secure only their own safety from the mob. They also tempt politicians to apply excessive police power to take control and establish order by force. Tyranny over the people seeks to force obedience. (Note: obeisance is listening to a demand and changing the rules to allow or accommodate it. Obedience is doing what is reasonable when asked to do without complaint, for fear of punishment). Punishment for disobedience can be psychological, economical, social, or physical. Examples of psychological punishment include censure, verbal abuse, or emotional manipulation. Examples of economic punishment include sanctions or a policy prohibiting access to financial capital. An example of social punishment is the denial of access to participation in society like ostracization or incarceration. Examples of physical punishment include bodily harm and torture. The threat of punishment is vile coercion, which is a force of tyranny. All tyrannies everywhere are a threat to the preservation of liberty for all.

Nonviolently, in a tyranny of the mob, we might find people demanding politicians provide to them benefits and entitlements for which they are not contributing funds or labor to earn deservedly. The politicians who give in do so to feel the vain power of adoration. A permanent class of politicians can easily arise if the people demand all benefits without the offer of leadership by themselves. This is a risk with democracy. Politicians who create dependency in the people to stay in office are not helping liberty. If they do it for too long, they will erode the determination and industriousness of the population. People mostly want to contribute. To do so, we need fewer restrictions but with politics, we must participate more rigorously to protect democracy from corruption. Politicians remaining in office unchecked for too long distorts their self-perceptions. This then corrupts their attitudes and behaviors. They become tempted toward self-serving calculation and decision-making. They become baby doomers: acting in ways that doom the future and ruin the chances for future generations to enjoy the prosperity brought by liberty. Doomers prioritize their own self-importance over their position's professional performance requirements. They personalize the power of it. They, while merely authorized to be in elected office by the people, act as if they are the power. Gallivanting around as if they are the end-all be-all simply because they won a popularly contest, is embarrassing. Instead, they should recognize they are merely performing a service to society by serving in an important position. It is not fair to our fellow citizens, who begin with a desire to serve us, to put them in such a position. If we love our democracy and love our neighbors who serve in elected offices, we should do them a favor. We should pay closer attention to them and relieve them of the temptation of power before they suffer corruption. We fail them by allowing them to serve too long. We should rotate our fellow citizens into and out of office on a more frequent basis. This will keep polity powers limited and in check, which is a strident need of liberty.

A Republic with Open Economy Obeisance

As a culture seeking equality among its citizenry, democracy insists that people have a voice in the polity. This voice is a form of leadership the people must perform to support democracy. It is instrumental in the shaping of societal powers. Another form of leadership is people's conduct when performing roles. People who fill positions of responsibility within the economy power's FILMS[2] [P7] and performing duties of the HM[5] have a particularly important responsibility. Why is this? Because while the polity is to protect our freedom, if people cannot obtain the necessities of life to survive, live, or thrive, society fails. To guarantee the enjoyment of freedom enabled by the polity power, the economy power must provision the goods, services, and jobs fairly.

In the USE, we have a republic. It is constitutionally ordained with a polity divided into layers of government. Regional subcultures built upon two main sources of virtues and values sets, influence the governing. The intermingling of these sets acquired from different societal powers shapes the forms of the economy power. These two dominant ones deal with relations between persons. First are the inherited mythology power's generationally conveyed mores and beliefs. Second are the marketplaces' agreed-upon codes of conduct that regulate commerce. Commerce is a force of economy power. As our population grows, it contributes to our survival, living, and thriving. People play many roles in the FILMS[2] [P7] and as the HM[5] of commerce.

The economy power fills many roles in its service to society. In performing their roles, people cooperate to establish rules. Rules framed to regulate conduct come from value sets made of the inputs of the laws from the polity, a belief in democracy-based culture, shared moral lessons from mythology power, and the need and desire to improve social circumstances and material conditions. We AEIOUY^{2}K the economy power as helpers (professionals and assistants), merchants (traders and sellers [wholesale and retail]), miners, makers, movers, and marketers (HM^5). How we as the HM^5 go about the provisioning of the necessary materials for our survival, for a decent standard of living, and for a luxurious quality of life—made possible mainly through these secondary powers: academy, artistry, and industry—matters significantly to society and ourselves. While the justice in a society depends on the polity power, the justness of a society relies upon the economy power. It rides on the value sets that regulate the economy power's FILMS^2 [P7]. The economy power's HM^5 depend upon specialized knowledge aptitude, acquisition, absorption, application, and skills advancement abilities (KA^{4}SA^2) gained by extensive (and maintained by continuous) education and practical experience. They assist the main resource providers of life. They also, by developing new expertise, improve our quality of life. They help all of us benefit from the economy power.

The economy is a power that leads us to making tiers and sectors of marketplaces with everything necessary and desirable, from farming, mining, and manufacturing to bringing to markets products, goods, and services organized for buying and selling. The economy power's FILMS^2 [P7] need HM^5 with all kinds of KA^{4}SA^2 and its production and transfer. Society performs these when we AEIOUY^{2}K academy and industry powers to conduct research and teach us how to obtain through markets, the necessary HM^5 we need for the many tiers of the economy. Markets are developed and sustained for the buying and selling of raw materials, like minerals or chemicals, and the refinement of materials for toolmaking, including tools to make tools that are more sophisticated. Machines made to reduce the manual labor required to perform a task, like doing laundry, tilling soil and then seeding it, irrigating the plants, and harvesting the crops, or treating dirty water to be potable and sewage to be nontoxic to the ecosystem of a particular environment, are helpful for human safety and health.

Recently, in the third stage of knowledge evolution (Hage, 2020), we've developed sophisticated computational machines. Tools like nuclear digital clocks to precisely measure time, computers to perform mathematical calculations to represent key strokes into words on a screen or instruct a robot to cut and form a piece of metal or weld two pieces together, and printers to print an object in three dimensions. These new computational machines are able to analyze the performance of other machines, as well as human behavior, to identify optimal performance parameters and traits. This enables the machines to perform their work more efficiently. These computational control tools reduce waste in energy and materials and regulate the inputs, which improves the outputs of the tools for farming, mining, refining, transporting, selling, and conducting business transactions in the marketplace. The qualities and quantities of computer-controlled tools, machines, and transactions have dramatically altered buying and selling outcomes.

Shifts in our consumption patterns are proving disruptive. The advancement of knowledge and technology to solve the problems of manual labor's inefficiencies is bearing out new societal consequences. If we forget that which is essential for us as humans, governing our behaviors to get along and move together toward our destiny, and if we forget what that destiny is supposed to be for—a free and just USE—we'll find ourselves in conditions that lead us back to tyranny. The tyranny of the new epoch, a digital replacing of people as the tools of commerce, removing us from manual laboring, is upon us. It is making us irrelevant (Harari, 2019) in our created society. We must adapt and adopt new ways, means, and methods to remain adept and relevant. We must manage the risks of advancing too rapidly, or make ourselves inapt before we know how to handle the consequences. Our minds and hands must measuredly advance to make our lives easier, but in a manner so as not to leave anyone behind in our society as inept. We need to work politically toward an agreed-upon philosophy of human advancement that will regulate the rules, laws, controls, and risk responses to the threats of us making ourselves obsolete.

This is the important task of the people to lead, the polity to administer, and the economy to manage. It requires that we learn how to control these new tools and not use them to exploit one another. This is vulnerability that the baby doomers' cultural value sets are ill suited to protect us from and pose a dangerous threat to our democracy and our liberty. Science fiction novels and dystopian movies tell of this risk. A common theme in these is the perfect androids exterminating the imperfect humans. Programmed for efficiency and effectiveness, the algorithm-controlled machines see the human diversity of emotions, moods, illogical inefficiencies, ineffectiveness, and unethical behaviors as too problematic. Should they learn to calculate our inefficiency to the work they can perform better, we might become their slaves and not their masters. This would be another form of tyranny threatening liberty. The writers of these stories employed the antennae of artistry power to imagine both the best and the worst circumstances that might arise from the evolution of our ingenuity as toolmakers. To keep our tools from ruling us, we must prepare to protect ourselves using a strategic enterprise risk framework (SERF) to manage our understanding and develop the best KA^4SA^2 we need to serve our purpose as a society and have the LAMBS done in a manner that IDEALS liberty and justice for all.

Instead of chasing the fulfillment of attitudes and behaviors that we previously considered sinful by mythology powers, which doomerism dismisses as rubbish, we must better understand our human nature and learn to manage the risks in it. Chasing money with a blind eye toward the destruction of human rights is dangerous for us. We cannot jettison wisdom without thinking about what we are actually doing. Shortsighted thinking is hazardous. We need to ensure our survival. Liberty is a cornerstone concept that aids us in doing this. We can agree upon this course as our necessary orientation when we get back to the mission to reach our constitutional objectives and not cede the controls of our human culture-made powers to "thinking" machines that learn. If intelligence is artificial, it's inhuman. This philosophical effort begins with an agreement on the common social norms and mores, the values we all must possess and agree to behave accordingly as a citizenry. We do this by selecting a few core virtues and morals to hold in common in all regional subcultures, settlement patterns' communities, and socialization contexts.

This is the first order of the business of citizenshipping. This is the work of defining the boundaries of acceptable and unacceptable attitudes and behaviors in our community. This requires knowing our mythology powers and regional subcultures various teachings on what is right and what is wrong, for us as persons, as communities of persons, and as a single nation. This is the way to move us toward greater unity as a nation of one people, e pluribus unum. Most of our citizenry has inherited value sets of Abrahamic beliefs. This gives us a good starting point. Through its three main lines and its multitude of subdivisions, sects persist in resisting unity over the details of each. If we, under threat of annihilation by our technologies, decide to focus not on differences that divide but instead on similarities, our species will cease to war unnecessarily. We ought to begin with agreement that we should seek to abide by a list of universally benefiting moral values, such as the Ten Commandments in the story of Moses or another mythology power's rules to live by as humans in society. We are no longer in an ancient world. Our knowledge and technology are vastly different, but our forgetting of wisdom is not wise. Ancient codes of human behavior have relevance because our instincts have not evolved as much as our tools and our technical know-how. We must forge equilibrium between old attitudes and new beliefs unleashed by sophisticated possibilities made possible by new knowledge and technology.

In fact, we have more in common in our ideas of how to treat one another than we have differences. Modern information, communication, and transportation technologies expose to us to how similar we are and are becoming because of these advances of the second and third stages of knowledge creation that result in societal transformations. Before we knew more about each other, all religions shared great principles relating to key human ideas and feelings such as love, making societies more humane, and helping followers and practitioners be spiritually and socially fulfilled human beings (Moses, 1989). The economy power should support these lofty goals, not undermine them. When it undermines them, it is serving the wrong purposes. It becomes a misbalanced power. It's meant to serve us, not vice versa. We must lead society to correct this, or we deem ourselves irrelevant in the artificial minds and eyes of the robots we're making to help us. We must identify, teach, and socialize in civics courses the core set of beliefs we hold in common as the American values that we all will agree to live by. These nationwide beliefs will engender democracy in all of us by enabling mutual respect among people, a respect we will need to maintain our dignity as the machines of our digital epoch are given increasingly more power over us by the FILMS[2][P7] of our economy power.

We need to inhibit our instincts from driving us by using our capacity and capability to think through consequences, to think upstream of the risks we create for our own future. We can philosophize. Animals cannot. We must use this form of academy power to our best advantage to prevent our extinction. We must align our mythology powers' teachings on rightful attitudes and behavior to yield the perpetual preservation of human dignity as a core American value. We can separate the wisdom from the myths. We must, or we will not overcome our innate fears. We must be diplomatic with one another. We must first seek to understand by listening with empathy, assuming good intentions, offering goodwill, and extending honesty. We can differ in opinion and still unite. But, if we are not all committed to being honorable as citizens first—honest with our real beliefs and ourselves and honest with one another—we cannot become one people. We will dissolve into fractious regions, occupational communities, and social status-defined populations that can never join to serve the common good. These exercises in philosophy will help us lead our society to rebalance its powers. If we don't, tyrants will divide and conquer us.

Lastly, before moving on to the next section, we must realize that prioritization of values is possible. Two important truths for the balancing of the three primary powers in our society are "no stealing" and "no coveting." These represent themselves in the forces of the economy power. Stealing is interpretable as "taking another's life, liberty, or property away from them. Coveting is interpretable as "wanting what others have and being jealous and angry because one does not have it, so as to be tempted to use powers in unauthorized or improper ways to get what others have". Good citizen-shipping obeys these axioms to make social life better. This brings us to the risks that baby doomers and their maximized tolerance and amplification of doomerism have caused for us in our society.

Thou shalt not steal nor covet

Doomers gave in to greed and gave away the family farm and the family shop: the neighborhood's dependable employers and backbones of local economies and social stability. How is this? By mergers and acquisitions that accumulated wealth in the hands of a few conglomerates. These sales for profit are a generation's greed evidenced and selfishness exposed. If true team-oriented loyalty and competitiveness existed in the baby boomers, they would never sell out their own teams by selling them off to the highest bidder. This activity to just make money and not provide for society the goods and services it needs and wants, is our failure to properly AEIOUY^{2}K the economy power to help the USE achieve its goal and attain its objectives. This error in judgment is a mark on their performance record while standing watch in our pilothouse on the bridge at the helm of the USE, pushing the buttons and pulling on the levers of power, yet failing to turn the wheel to steer us clear of danger. With them in authority positions in the FILMS^2 [P7] of our societal powers, running the LAMBS, we have declined as a people in our quality as human beings. We've lost dignity, decency, and respect for each other as members of the same venture. Their cultural way is leading us toward our doom, as a nation, as a people, and as a species. We must overcome their misguided ways. Have no misgivings. Generations have personalities, and a generation that allows stealing and coveting as acceptable is a failed one in its orientation toward living an American human life, because it is an orientation not in accord with the intents of our Constitution, nor courage of the Declaration of Independence.

We need to get back on course toward our destiny. If doomers were not at the helm, or better stated, helms of all societal and social powers, we might have evolved real advantages in global competitiveness and cooperation to help not just our society but all humans better survive, live, and thrive. Make no mistake, great progress made in extending aid, comfort, and convenience since the second stage of knowledge evolution occurred. Nevertheless, we've slumped on successes for humanity, and dumped on the environment, concomitantly draining fresh water aquifers and other sources, while we've pumped up the wrong values as proudly as sin.

Had more boomers not have fallen victim to doomerism, they might have been underdogs rising, resisting the overbearing greed of the larger buyers, and they would not have been suckered by the greed within themselves. They would have been loyal to their locales, which gave them birth and growth, and through wisdom's advice, by temperance, fortitude, justice, and prudence, they would have avoided the society-destroying sins of greed, lust, and avarice. Sadly, as a generation they have proven only that they are too (morally and/or ethically) immature to see that they didn't exactly "grow up" bravely and wisely enough to contribute to society in ways that make it fair and just by bringing into daily reality the ideals that framed our nation, as proffered by the founders. Except for a very few of them, most failed in the needed citizen mission. But do not tell them this. They will yell at you in shrieks of denial, because of their desire to be the ideal, not serve the founder's ideals. They prefer to declare themselves, "Perfect!"

The baby doomers have given in and thus given away that which is necessary to have a wholesome, happy, true American society. Democracy is difficult. It takes rising above sinfulness. It requires work that a majority of boomers did not put forth. It requires self and societal work done with honor in one's conduct. It requires a citizenry of virtuous character and of ethical integrity with moral courage. It requires a commitment to serve the purpose of sustaining democracy and helping all peoples experience the chance to survive, live, and thrive. This approach expands opportunity, allows for positive risk-taking, and generates growing prosperity.

Yes, it is an axiom that each one's greed can, when compounded, destroy the whole society. This is the foolish path. The boomers as a majority, since majority rules, dragged us across sharp rocky surfaces, breaking up love, distorting beauty, hoarding the resources, and crushing dreams. Could it actually be? Do they feel that only they deserve the goodies? But there is enough to go around! A very small minority of them know this, yet too small in numbers. What could they do? The bossier took the wheel of fortune by force.

We the patriots tire from getting dragged along the path cut by doomers. We know the numbers are now in our favor. The teamwork education of the next generation aims us back toward the right path. The favored path that leads to societal health and happiness is not the one that leads to warfare and wrath. Nor does it result in a path lined with windfall gifts from the community chest. Such as funny forms of extra special free ride irresponsibility taken as a right. On the other hand, demands that press for a no-need-participate in funding American society discounts must stop their fleecing. Both yield extraordinarily favorable welfare for the already rich and domineering few. The better path is the one that teaches teamwork to our young. One supplemented by training in diplomacy. One developing wills to pursue lifetime learning in ACE. All these are good for democracy. Such a lesson plan liberates us from hatreds that do not help us unite.

The risks of the digital era mean we must jettison the vestiges of the Cro-Magnon survival instincts within us. But until we act in E-SASSY-T-TUF-FT-CAUCUS like 1776 patriots and assume the bridge. Without it and us controlling the helm of American society, we, the everyday people who produce our commonwealth, will continue to witness cultural and societal decline toward doom. The boomers, of many stripes we will learn about later, and particularly those with the worst ethos for democracy and a republic—their epitomizing baby doomers—keep decimating society. Their rabid way of being, infected others. So our children may have hope of prosperity, we must IDEALS liberty, and for democracy in our republic, we must continuously counteract doomerism and countervail its rapid spread across the globe. Like it or not, being an influential nation, others will copy us.

We must not let doomerism be our example. The boomers method of group decision making is telling. They act as if the making of a decision is for the group's benefit. However, it is not really for the team. It is for self-gain. The decider, all while knowing each other boomer is thinking "What's in this for me?" drives the hidden "me first" choosing behaviors. It is a choice to take "one for you" (boomer) and "one more for me" (doomer). Done too often is this typical baby doomer act. It lets each one extract with a wink, without blinking, far more than ones fair share, by sneakily milking the whole for the few. Decisions made without ever considering the consequences to the larger body. Choices taken without care for everyone else's welfare, murder a democracy-based culture.

Amplified by the globalizing digital epoch's new knowledge and technologies of artificial thinking, calculations, and computations informed by algorithms finding and sharing patterns in big data sets and extruding analytics creating opinions of behaviors, doomerism takes over. Machines will tell us what to do, control us without our awareness, and their owners will rake in the cash, stash it in their keeps, and leave us to weep without a chance at rising above poverty. Think, if doomerism as culture perpetuates, it is unlikely we will experience good outcomes from these new super human tools. To protect ourselves, our liberty, American society, we must drive out doomerism from within our culture and us. We must revive a democracy-based culture, purify it of past evils, make it ideals real—once, and for all.

Doomerism steals. Doomerism covets. It is hypocrisy living large but pretending to be normal and acceptable. Previous generations also suffered from hypocrisy, but they also sought to rid themselves of it. This we see in the progress the world has made in human and civil rights. The boomers have been unsuccessful at blocking hypocrisy. They seem to have allowed it, even leveraged it. Doomerism is a fleece-first, grift, "me first" attitude and a selfish aggrandizing approach to the pursuit of happiness. It is now unchecked in material consumerism and undermines the conditions of civility that should be approached with a teamwork attitude of "one for all and all for one." "Me first" life management is unwise and undermining; it does not produce the highest gestalt of happiness for all of us at any scale. It unwinds our past progress. Egregious baby doomers by this approach lived by a depressing ethos, seeking to steal before another could steal from them. They developed a cynical "do onto others before they can doo-doo onto you" attitude. Cynicism is unhealthy. This foolish fear, when enacted in every action, proves that immaturity has prevailed within them all. They deemed wisdom too demanding, to self-sacrificial. They incidentally determined that to converse and lead for the whole community was too challenging. It got in the way of their "me first" pursuits, which they misinterpreted as the pursuit of happiness. To avoid any sense of guilt or responsibility to society, they invented and practiced the transaction of limited morality: compartmentalization.

All involved in letting doomerism spread to the majority of the population, fleeced, because it was easy. It wasn't as if they'd sing "I can't get no, satisfaction". They got it, in large amounts, often crookedly. Alas, the wisdom given us by the Enlightenment corroded, eroded into entitlements. Sadly, the American values of temperance jettisoned, prudence abandoned, and integrity washed away from the set of virtues we pursued. Fortitude was left for volunteers to fight for American values, and justice was lost because the chain reaction of the baby doomers' greed, compounded and by majority, pounded our minds with a known wrong way of being, which they sought to make tolerable since they believed it benefited them. The boomers as a generation (particularly their aggressively rapacious doomers) are single-handedly, each by their own accord, sewing discord and destroying our country: the <u>United</u> States of America.

We can no longer afford to allow the steady and silent spread of doomerism throughout. It lacks clout. We, the everyday people, must reject boomer generational ways and cleanse ourselves if infected with their false philosophy, and return to our first principles as the bonding bolts that yoke us to the plow of tilling the seeds of liberty into the soil of humankind. If not, our posterity, our crops of virtue will bear no fruits of justice and peace, and our species shall fall into hellish conditions without hope of happiness, thrust back into the bondage of tyranny, like used up weary serfs.

Doomerism is a form of cultural tyranny. It forces us to choose between money or people, material objects or humanity, as our reason for being alive. It erodes our sense of compassion for our fellow human beings. It prevents us from uniting as one people. It divides our society politically, economically, socially and culturally. It opens us up to the dictates of demagoguery-produced propaganda used to distract us from the thefts that those who think they are superior feel entitled to commit against the rest of us.

A Republic of Willful Abeyance

We are a society held in abeyance from the rule of men and practices of tyranny. We hold with mistrust single-source power-hungry men and women who seek to establish tyrannies. We keep them away from control of our powers and suspend them from power if they begin to act in despotic dominance. This is because American society, built on the rule of law as a foundational principle, keeps us away from the rule of men (humans). This guarantees liberty. Through a judicious judicial power, we the people grant authority to the politicians in the polity, who we elect and appoint to governmental offices within our three separate branches of the polity. We require those selected to hold office to use the power we authorize them to have to achieve our will, which is supposed to align to our enterprise's objectives. We expect them to $AEIOUY^2K$ our powers in alignment with the Constitution. We suspend our politicians who wrongfully use the rules to try to rule over us. They work for us. We don't work for them. They are to serve us. We are not to serve them. If they do not obey the rule of law, or if they behave as tyrants, we possess the authority to hold them in abeyance.

Constitutionally, the rule of law supersedes any who seek to be above the law. Tyranny is the enemy of the people. In the society of a democracy-based culture, no one is above the law because the law, as obeyed and enforced by the people, is the essence of the preservation, protection, and practice of liberty. The rule of law is the force of our will to IDEALS liberty.

With this backdrop painted, let us turn to seeing what can and is going wrong. The DAMN of societal powers represent the bad and the ugly modes of them. As we probe these modes, let us keep in mind the brilliance of the Constitution of our USE. Its framework has built-in flexibility to adapt to survive crises and allow powers to transform their balance, reshape subordinate power relationships, and create or retire the FILMS^2 $^{[P7]}$ in order to resist repeated mistakes, errors, and omissions in how they AEIOUY^{2}K the societal and social powers.

As 20/20 hindsight tells us, the general benefit of increasing humanitarianism, granting liberties, and placing equality and egalitarianism within the reach of justice is a major achievement on the path to our principled objectives. We find evidence of our progress in the advance of liberty in our march toward fulfilling our calling to be one people, e pluribus unum. We are to make freedom a true reality for all of us. The everyday people who labor to love and to become a free people need to unite. To be free of all forms of tyranny and control over our lives by others, we must combine in an unceasingly "for liberty" openly public caucus, held constantly. This people's caucus will promote demanding those appointed or elected to high positions, a proper way of being rooted in E-SASSY-T-TUF-FT-CAUCUS, always and forever. We must continue to push for the agency that democracy grants to us. We must do so by good citizenshipping, not giving any tyrant an excuse to take what is ours away from us if we happen to make a minor mistake in judgment, or mischievously misbehave. Grammatically speaking, we must take away the subject (actions) of lies from the liars. We must remind them of the truth of the object (actor) and the objective of democracy, we the people.

A People, Persons of Many Influences

When we the people are in our personnel roles within any instrument, organization or institution, (the FILMS^2 $^{[P7]}$) of societal power, we must guard against temptations that would pull us away from our virtuous tasks. Social groups develop a life of their own; like organisms, they want to survive. However, role performers sometimes become enthralled with getting more and more power for the group and thus for themselves. This causes the group to lose focus and forget that as citizens, in all we do we must be thinking about how to IDEALS liberty in every way possible. It has many lives. It resides in us in many ways.

We must IDEALS it for the person, the personage, the personhood, and the personality in and for which our people power exists. Person by person, we must battle within ourselves to be ready to support and defend the liberty of everyone. We must be ready to teach others and ourselves how to negotiate toward our unity as one people of many, diplomatically, and not become divided by superficial identifications. Unity is a state of peace. Yet our instincts and the majority of human cultures are prone to war, mostly out of weakness (Schmookler, 1988). Uniting in diplomacy to stop warring tribalism is a nonphysical, intellectual fight we must rigorously engage in. It is something worth doing. It is a responsibility given us by the founders in the Constitution of our established republic.

Republics of democracy transfer power without warring physically by seeing in each person a sacred identity with human dignity. We the people are one when we value each one of us as a symbol of all of us. For example, we do this when we see our athletes win a gold medal at the Olympics. We do this when we hear of a person reaching the pinnacle of their chosen vocation or profession in ways magnificent and magnanimous. We appreciate each other when we feel we are, and we believe we should be, one people under God, indivisible.

This is our nation's intent. Because of liberty, it creates the context for personal achievement that lifts us all up. It is for us as a people to believe that we as a nation are as one person, not the same but equal to each other before the law and appreciated for each gift shared with the rest of us freely, openly, and fondly. We like to represent one another, whether it is our neighborhood, school, town, or state. We are more than a single word, we are four-fold, similar to how our government has three separate functional branches, yet united as one government. Said another way, it is similar to how our society has three primary powers, with many supportive culture-produced secondary and tertiary powers, yet these get coordinated in making one society. So yes, we are "many of one". As a people and as persons are. Each of us is a person made of a person<u>age</u>, a person<u>hood</u>, and a person<u>ality</u>. As each of us is, so is our nation. Its person is a republic, its personage is brave, its personhood is this land of freedom, and its personality is democracy. Its blood is liberty, which bonds patriots to resist tyranny. Here is a bit more to explain this "one of many" influences concept. Figure 2-26 below depicts the aspects that constitute a person. Here are applicable definitions for it:

<u>Person</u>: son or daughter, male or female, linguistic root "mask," a face (the dominant form of recognizing one another as a species), suffixed with a "liquid" term, childbirth being a wet affair, a per-son is a face born, a being with an identity (to be discovered in the voyage of growing up, affected by both nature and nurture). Each person is born human by nature, with certain endowments and limitations. We are born with the potential to become a self-aware human being, conscious of our unique purpose and

worth to the society, with a will for being what we are to be, a will for freedom, and a will for conformity to the conditions of society that in a democracy are supposed to support one's goodwill and general welfare. This is the condition of liberty within the human being. Created for its pursuit was an American society. It has provided infrastructures for personal development, properly employing power in ways supportive of personal evolution to a state of virtuous fulfillment, which is central to the pursuit of one's own liberty. *Thus, the national person is reflective of who we are as a free people.* **Republic** *is our name.*

Person**age**: (Linguistically extrapolated, the statue that represents the person to others related to the age in which the statue, made and observed, occurs. Its meaning to others changes based upon the knowledge of people in the time in which it, viewed and considered, occurs and the age of the person and the age of society combined). The ways a person experiences their own development toward which kind of person they will be, as shaped by the age at which they experience social and societal trials, traumas, and tribulations as well as auspicious blessings, boons, and fortunes. In addition, it is the era in history. Eras shape identities of peers in their birth cohort. Experiencing shared historical events, moments, movements, and turns in history contrary to expectations punctuate change to the equilibrium into which they were born. *Thus, a national personage is reflective of the internal being that with natural rights seeks to be free and live in a state of liberty.* **Bravery** *is our name.*

Person**hood**: (Linguistically extrapolated, people from different places wear different hats of culture and customs that arose from specific geography). The combination of the person as born with the person as experiencing society in the region-specific culturally shaped social circumstances. The influence of physical conditions upon attitudes and behaviors formed from geographic adaptations. The experienced rites, rituals, folkways, and customs used to survive in a particular place, such as might differ in regions of mountains, plains, and deserts, and in settlements that are rural, suburban, or urban in the various biomes a population ended up in, adapted to the geography of their place on the planet. *Thus, a national personhood is reflective of a person's love of and loyalty to their "place" and places structured to be united regions of landholders in hearts and minds.* **Freedom** *is our name.*

Person**ality**: *(A term from psychology).* It refers to the sets of behaviors, ways of thinking and viewing of others. This cognitive and emotional patterns characteristic of a person is identifiable as a unified way of being when with other persons. Personalities evolve from a person's nature (ones biology) and the social environment in which they respond to the cultural factors presented to, and subsumed by, them (ones socialization context). There is wide disunion on what personality is, but it generally relates to how persons feel, think, and behave toward self and others, the motivations and interactions that make us each different. Personality forms within. It expresses outwardly. Generally, it is the way we understand how the various parts come together as a whole person. *Thus, a national personality is reflective of the external presentation of ourselves, how we are seen—on the world's stage and as we were in history. Our nation's formation is unique within the ages of humans living in civilization.* **Democracy** *is our name.*

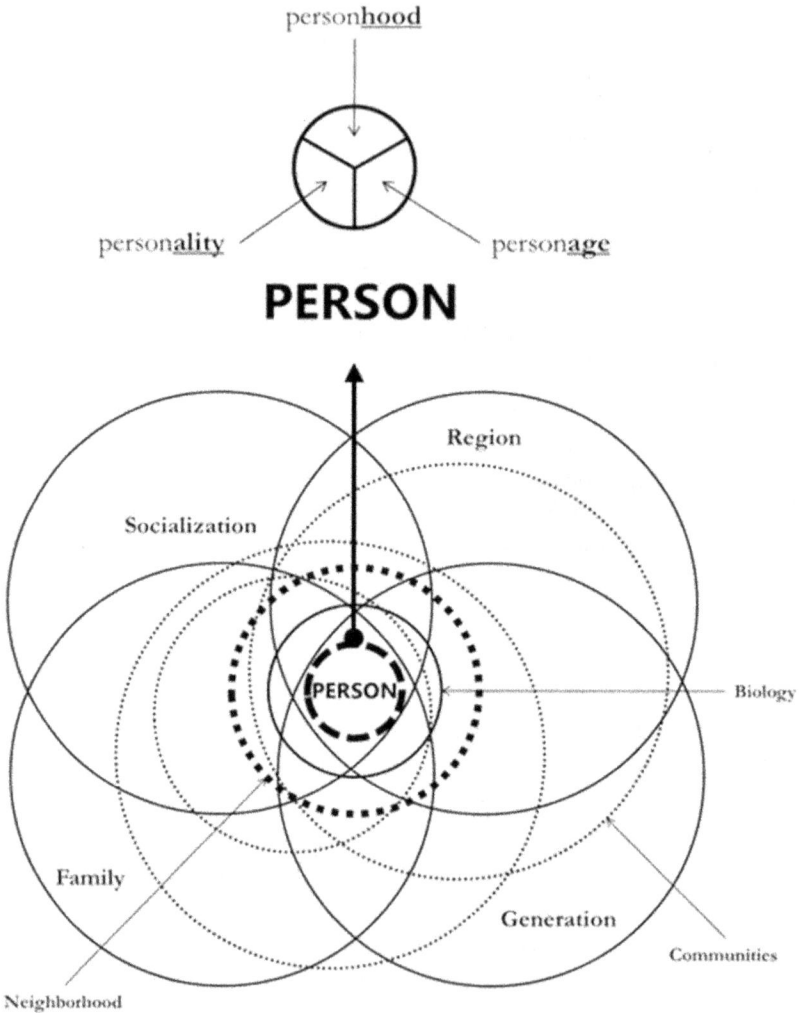

PERSON

Figure 2-26: A Person's Development Has Many Influences
A person is a flower of many petals that make them beautifully unique yet similar to others. Democracy is a garden with many varieties that give it seasonal riches in aroma, sight, and in the sounds of the fauna, the flora nourishes. For it to flourish we must nurture its diversity, and tend to its needs. We cannot ignore it and expect invasive weeds won't overtake it. We must tend to each flower, as it needs so it fulfills its role in the garden that is our society.

Now, if we accept this proposal that we as persons and we as a people are multifaceted, we might accept that much of what we see in society has many complexions. Such complexity does not necessarily mean that things are complicated. Things become complicated because, and when, we do not listen. We need to listen to the many whispers and murmurs of wisdom, which try to communicate with us. If we ignore or deny the voices of our soul, or of reason, we will find the world too complicated. From this state of resistance, we will find mostly conflict internally and externally in our lived lives. After life, we rely on the mythology power in which we believe to take us and transcend us into our next state of being, non-being, or another being. Throughout our lives we confront power done poorly.

Bad & Ugly Power Modes

When is power "bad company?" Power is bad when not used to IDEALS liberty but instead we DAMN it. These poor uses of power are certain to ruin us if not kept in check. So we must be aware of them and not fall into their traps. Power tends to corrupt those who have it over others. We must be vigilant to ensure its proper use as our primary concern. We must keep it within control and balanced; this is our citizenship duty for our posterity and for us!

Here are some examples of how the primary powers are disused, abused, misused, and not used when they should be, all of which confuse everyone living truly in accordance with, and in accord to, the spirit and the letter of the Constitution. Its words we need to read closely, seek to understand deeply, and fuse with to be better at being American citizens. This is a part of our necessary citizenshipping to progress our project's mission, our tradition: democracy, republic, and liberty. Anything else is a lie we tell ourselves. We must not avoid this crucial conversation about what was, what is, and what should be. Nor argue, nor use fallacies to score schoolyard points for one-sided tribal instincts. The stakes are too high. Many among us need a real intervention to experience the republic's foundational ideals, especially those who have adopted heretical perspectives justified by the very thing that they are actually acting in opposition toward. Again, much confusion exists in a society that does not understand its powers. It multiplies when the people don't know how to AEIOUY^{2}K power properly to deal with the risks to the society and ensure that the LAMBS for the USE protect it from corruption.

Let's go over the DAMN of societal powers, beginning first with people power examples:

o   A **disuse** of people power is the non-voting, non-civically engaged, non-politically active, non-civilly behaving, while the opposite is a must for the success of the enterprise to sail smoothly with balanced powers.

o   An **abuse** of people power is the shifting of its use to create aggressive factions, special interest groups that will give each member of the group more gain per person to the detriment of the whole commonwealth. This is particularly problematic when done in violation of community standards, or with criminal intent.

o   A **misuse** of people power is complacent, apathetic, dependent, and demanding dependency, or behaving in ways that are unruly, disrespect-fully rude, and anarchistic, without regard for the rights of others, like a wild animal. Predators eat free animals. Being free to be wild is not liv-ing in a state of liberty. It poses risks to others' safety and tranquility; it is not freedom.

o   A **nonuse** of people power is when a person is mistreated, and the by-stander witnesses are too afraid to intervene to prevent the situation from getting worse. Sometimes it takes just one more person to join in and stop a predator from abusing another as prey. With a herd of citi-zens acting in unison, a bully is controllable. Stopping wrongfulness is a good use of people power. So is voting. So is learning and knowing what is really going on. Keeping the economy and polity powers from misbehaving is a public good. Helpfulness does not occur when the nonuse of people power is prevalent.

Doomerism causes the DAMN of the people power. Resist being a ba-by doomer. We must stop them from doing wrong. We must step up, stand up, take charge, and lead our society. They have not led. We the future gen-erations must rise up into the ranks of authority to exert our will to get our country back on its course toward a more perfect union. We are now nu-merically the majority. We must combine into a new demographic that is not divided by region, political party affiliation, or social status because the world is now turning too fast and the paradigms of the past are not suitable for our future. We must encourage the cynics to recede and enable civics to succeed. Many isms of the past few generations are no longer valid, nor helpful to our project's success. We must turn the tide toward new under-standing, use diplomacy, and engage in E-SASSY-T-TUF-FT-CAUCUS to reach a democracy-based culture with a liberty infused society. An Ameri-can society that requires we balance the primary powers to get the best for liberty LAMBS.

Of concern is when the economy powers harbor risks that imbalance the reasonable provisioning performance expectations in regions, or worse, within the whole society of the USE. When its elites, following the ways of doomerism, seek to shift its socially responsible approaches to $AEIOUY^2K$ its powers away from its duties and to DAMN its powers to create extreme gain that denies people from possible prosperity, they produce gross ine-quality and instability that adds tension to the republic. This tension can only be resolved well if persons in positions of authority, executives, act as citizens first to IDEALS liberty for the common good and our common-wealth to preserve the commons and marketplaces through which provi-sions are exchanged. To claim otherwise is boldfaced disrespect to the tra-ditions, history, and the citizenry that built free markets, which made our enterprise prosperous.

Of concern is when the polity powers harbor risks that imbalance the whole society of the USE. When its baby doomer politicians seek to shift its socially responsible approaches to AEIOUY^{2}K its powers away from its duties and to DAMN its powers to create excessive feelings of "power" and reward those who "sponsor" them and fatten complicit politicians' wallets, we the everyday people must not be nonchalant. We must stop them. Enriching a few, as in a plutocracy, produces gross inequality and instability in the society that adds tension to the republic. A challenge of inequalities that must still be addressed, which doomerism seeks to ignore, is the gerrymandering to prevent political wills being heard, segregation, discrimination, and persecution of groups identified and isolated by genetically determined characteristics, which cannot reasonably be changed, nor should they be asked to alter them. Such illegal intentional separation of citizens by geographic origin, descent, affinity, affiliation, or place of emigration is neither helpful nor healthy, nor is it in keeping with the ideals of the USE. Nor is it sensible, considering immigrants develop a majority of inventions and innovations because they have more than one social grammar (the ability to fit in and get along diplomatically in a variety of social settings, subcultures, because they are conversant with others' folkways, mores, beliefs, social norms, and customs). Immigrants, persons of blended customs in mixed ethnic families, tend to be familiar with different languages: written, spoken, and social, which creates greater cognitive complexity to think outside that famous box of the likely choices, those choices that keep us on a dependent path that narrow-minded monopolistic persons want us to follow. Path dependency feels comforting, doing it the same way we've always done it. However, its risk aversion is risk producing when we face catastrophic change. The third stage of knowledge evolution has us storming. We are coming to terms with its created knowledge, and grappling with the adaptive problems its technology spin off phase is causing. We will need better problem definitions and proposed solutions to consider collegially if we are to survive with our health.

We must walk away from the old, tired, and ineffective ideas—the isms that no longer serve us well. Further, the risks of being short sighted that caused the intentional separation of citizens by cultural characteristics, is crippling to the USE. We need innovations. Innovations come out of the comparison of various solutions that differing cultures have attempted and found beneficial. To find the best answers, we should not stymie persons for silly differences but rather encourage a wide range of diversity of thought formulating holistic understandings of the problems we face. We do this so that we might mine and tease out among the gaps of our understandings a clue that could hold the seeds of a best-case solution. We cannot afford blocking our peripheral vision with blinders of illiberalness, path dependencies, or ideological bondage. We must admit to and better define our problems instead of acting like ostriches with our heads in the sand. This is where our "home of the brave" ethos must come into play. We must have the courage to tolerate and embrace our differences, understanding how and why they exist as cultural adaptations to geography power. We may not know nor care to know, but we must begin to do so. This latter complacency or apathy for a fellow citizen's plight is where doomerism drags us down. A misfortunate back alley path, it does not lead us to victory in the future. A victory to enjoy rooted in liberty. Inspiringly painted up on the ceiling of the Capitol dome is our mission "e pluribus unum". When we finally see that it is our truest calling, and most American personality a people could have, we will realize it and enjoy its social, economic, and political benefits.

Power not well understood as a concept of cultural creation retards our progress to unify as one people. How democracy as a culture aims to $AEIUOY^2K$ power might still be too new for the human species. Civilizations have conditioned us to accept tyranny and its forces as the normal form of animal rule. We, in a democracy-based culture, will not want to tolerate it as we go about our lives. Yet being young, we may not recognize when incompetence and negligence, intentional or unintentional, occur. The people need to learn about power in a democracy to understand how to control it properly and how to balance it for the benefit of all. Culture makes social power in all forms in all its realms of presentation by way of the $FILMS^2$ [P7]. We make primary, secondary, and tertiary forms of it. We even make combinations (positive and negative arrangements) of the social powers we Homo sapiens create. In the course of living, when we find ourselves possessing authority, we may try to play our part well to support others and ourselves and the work as we go about our business in society, or we may not (and get away with a freeload, too). The point is we are society as we are the elements that combine to make it. If we disrespect it we do not disavow ourselves of the consequences, nor can we blame "them", or society. We must perform our roles as best we can, to lead, if we are to attain the Constitution's objectives, or we'll lose our liberty.

Above, a few DAMN of primary powers illustrated some threats to society in permitting the abuse and misuse of power. Certainly, disuses need restored and non-uses of good power need reversed. The most damning for democracy are abuses and misuses that undermine the balance of powers. Imbalanced powers threaten the enterprise, putting it at risk of failing to provide the necessary resources for us to enjoy living our lives, have independency through our livelihoods, and pursue our dreams without any need to beg some tyrant for relief or the opportunity to work. Imbalanced powers allow misguided decisions that cause insolvency by the shifting of too many resources to too few. This results in greed sequestering the commonwealth away from society's access. Such is a form of economic tyranny. It can mutate into oligarchical control of the society by plutocrats. Money must flow for an effective use of our economy power. Tyrants love to say "No!". They love to create scarcity. They derive a sense of power from it (Schmookler, 1988). We the people must help them see that we see this, and we must tell them that they are wrong. We must help them see their unacceptable behavior, and we must hold them accountable. We cannot allow them to exploit us and enslave us to their will.

Primary Purposes Performed Poorly

Powers used wrongly create negative consequences, unintended externalities that bring harm to others. Such externalities of improper power in the LAMBS within our enterprise result in harm to people. Sometimes known, often unknown, and in some cases intentionally kept unknowable. When we through our FILMS^2 [P7] AEIOUY^{2}K power in a manner for which it is not well-suited, social problems arise. One cannot insert a nail into a board efficiently with a wrench, and one cannot tighten a bolt on a screw effectively with a hammer. We the people must come to understand power and regulate it to guarantee its proper use. We must choose the right tool for the job. As now, we need a polity to unify around common themes to save our union. Thus, we must replace one generation with another in all seats of authority.

People power

Here are a few ways in which the people power errs and omits by DAMN of its KA^{4}SA^2 strengths and purpose for society. First, it is an error to not AEIOUY^{2}K the people power properly—to provide leadership over the business of society. Second, it is an omission to not AEIOUY^{2}K the people power on aspects for which it is suited; leaving them to be done by the other primary power's FILMS^2 [P7]. Such as the ever necessary administration that is done best by the polity or the always required management that is done best by the economy. We the everyday people must provide the leadership for the business of society in the ways, means, and methods of our choosing at the micro, meso, and macro levels of influence we possess in our roles as citizens, (recall Figure 2-2 and Figure 2-3).

The goal for the people power to be efficient is admirable, but people en masse, unorganized except by structures and values, are not efficient. The purpose of the people power is leadership: to be effective at keeping the other powers in check and balancing them so that the LAMBS of the USE move us toward our ideals and IDEALS liberty for us. That is, the imbuement of our first principles in everyday life, and this means that each person must daily perform good citizenshipping. It requires honest transparency of motives, not the hiding behind ideologies and isms. Rather we must be brave in the face of complexity, developing more social grammars, building social capital through civic engagement at the micro, meso, and macro levels of society, and increasing our political participation (knowledgeably, reasonably, aware of liberty's position in the postures of the candidates, and not superficially by group identities that distort perceptions of political capability and capacity). We must do these in order to guide the USE back to a commitment to first principles first and good citizenship-ping always. We do not want to get left behind, missing out on future advancements in the evolution of knowledge and its consequent technologies that will impact our society, whether we want them or not. We must IDEALS liberty and keep up with knowledge evolutions for our children and those yet unborn Americans. What we do must not doom them from enjoying the blessings of liberty and prosperity that our American society provides when its virtuous ideals guide the proper $AEIOUY^2K$ of the societal and social powers, daily.

We ought to unite to cooperate and bring the world along with us as a leader within it. What we offer is worthy. Presently, we are not leading; we are not the best at innovating solutions. We are maybe tenth (Hage, 2020). We have lost our "pole position" in the race to invent the next great thing that will help the species succeed at survival, live healthfully, and thrive with peace and freedom. Isolating from the future in fear, due to the false promises given us by doomerism, is not the path to depend upon. We must be independent of past anxieties. To do this we must make the polity progress toward resolution of the ills that have plagued us, and bring about its best and highest value production. We must $AEIOUY^2K$ its powers to do a better job at its duty and purpose. We have failed to do our part, so we must step up, learn, and get involved more often and more intensely in the body politic to lead. We must, before we become wholly owned by the polity power like a totalitarian regime, or by the economy power under consequential doomerism and one of its core attributes, zealous devotion to consumerism.

Polity power

Here are a few ways in which the polity power errs and omits by DAMN of its KA^4SA^2 strengths and purpose for society. First, it is an error to $AEIOUY^2K$ polity power to ignore representing properly the people's authority delegated to it, the authority of the people—leadership over the business of society. Second, it is an omission not to $AEIOUY^2K$ polity power in the manner of its primary strength, administration. Polity inherently exists to be effective at administering the rule of law and order in society with its power. It is an omission to use polity power in a manner concentrated on its primary weakness, management, (recall Figure 2-6).

The goal for polity power to be efficient is admirable, but efficiency does not inherently motivate it. Saying "no" is easier in a large, hierarchical bureaucracy, a classic form for polity power. It is something that democracy divided in order to conquer, but largesse comes to a nation that expands in geography and population. The denial of necessary services is inefficient. The goal for polity power is to be effective. Administration needs systems and experts at their implementation. The scope, scale, and complexity of our society, interconnected with 195 countries on the planet, requires more quality-educated and empathetic office holders who have the cognitive complexity and multiple social grammars to navigate our enterprise toward its objectives and engage in necessary diplomacy with others, (recall Figure 2-5).

Economy power

Here are ways in which the economy power errs and omits by DAMN of its KA^{4}SA^2 strengths and purpose for society. First, it is an error to AEIOUY^{2}K economy power to control the polity, whose authority comes from the people, or to tell persons how to live, because the people are to provide the leadership over the business of society in the USE. Second, it is an omission to not AEIOUY^{2}K economy power in the manner of its primary strength, management, (recall Figure 2-8).

A primary goal for economy power is to be efficient, economize, and be economical. Economy power inherently exists to be efficient at managing the provision of goods and services in society. Economy powers AEIOUY^{2}K subordinate social powers by association and the workings of marketplaces where people as persons and as organized groups exchange what is from the HM^5 (yes, to the 5th power, as the magnitude of the benefits of their combining increases risk opportunities for humankind in a more significant way than simple addition of each to the economy). The HM^5 management as a behavior can provide monetary profits because it is beholden to efficiency to be more effective. It is more than repetitive tasks of processing paperwork or data (like administration) or redundant actions of production. It is an omission to AEIOUY^{2}K economy power to deal with administration, which is not its operant competency, (recall Figure 2-9).

A second goal for economy power is to be effective. However, economy is not inherently effective at administering the ground that establishes the playing field for the provision of goods and services. Because administration as a behavior is not monetarily profitable, except by markup margin for services. Administration is not expressly beholden to efficiency, but to effectiveness, which can fail if repetitive tasks of processing paperwork overwhelm it. Many helpers and makers have sought to make administration more efficient to improve effectiveness, but this is normally at the hire of the polity as a service to assist it with its primary obligation to the business of society.

Unintelligibility

Powers used wrongly do wrong. Powers are used wrongly when we ethically and constitutionally fail to lead with integrity in positions of authority within our FILMS$^{2\,[P7]}$ or as the HM^5. Powers cause confusion when we unintelligibly apply, employ, implement, operationalize, utilize, yoke, yield, and keep (AEIOUY^{2}K) them. It is worse when powers get disused, abused, misused, or not used when they need to be (DAMN). As vowels make words with consonants, powers put into action by culture are like nouns and verbs. This is like mass + velocity, a solid put into motion = momentum, which requires power to get. The powers are nouns that act as verbs upon us by those we authorize to work their levers in the LAMBS for our enterprise. Powers wrongly done bring about harm to the people when the people turn against one another because they don't understand what has happened and why. People band together around issues and become factions that can further fracture society. However, factions also can balance society when they do not act upon fictions. Ill-willing factions in power-frenzied panic create turbidity, intolerance, and stupidity in the public realm. Such dooming discourse disrupts real democracy, restricting dialogue and negating diplomatic deliberations. Democracy requires goodwill and decent manners to deal with its messy divisions among the population. We cannot overcome our "wicked problems" without civility. Doomerism causes an increase in the volume and frequency of wicked societal problems. Wicked problems are not tame problems normally solved professionally (Horst W. J. Rittel, 1973). Wicked problems require innovation to solve, sometimes-radical innovation. Neither traditional nor modern methods are working as we sink into a pit of hell on earth that is the pull of doomerism upon us.

Doomerism is wrongfulness. Wrongfulness creates confusion. Wrongfulness, when it happens, happens because of a DAMN of the societal and social powers. Doomerism persuades the people not to pay attention, distracting them and putting them into discord. Doomers don't talk of a plain and simple way. They purposefully confound us on purpose. For example, the earlier mentioned tired isms are such a form. They do not serve to educate, inform, or advise the people. Isms tossed about uninformatively confuse us, as if a special language only for a "ruling class" and their sycophant aristocracy. Such a secret-sounding language, outside the needs of everyday living, builds mistrust between us. Of course, this is what those factions seeking power want to do to enlist us in their struggle to get more for themselves. We need to be wise to their games. What is necessary to know is not necessarily conveyed anywhere effectively at a time when persons are able to receive it. We cannot learn lessons that we are unprepared to hear.

Matters of personal growth and development, socialization, and generational personalities are aspects of society that we need to understand. They support the people power that creates culture, which shapes society. It is essential that we, the everyday people, grasp these. We need to contemplate how our leadership plays out in society to control ourselves and create better futures for our children. These aspects done better will empower and guide us in how we will force balance when the other powers exercise their forces upon us. We must discipline ourselves to disallow doomerism's distractions. We must render the world before us intelligible to lead the USE to AEIOUY²K its powers to IDEALS liberty to perpetuate the possibilities for prosperity for posterity and preserve constitutionally allied living, permanently. We must, and our peers who serve in authoritative positions within the FILMS² [P7], or as the HM⁵ who push and pull levers that control the forces of the powers, must perform the LAMBS toward our constitutional goal and objectives. One of which is the pursuit of happiness, which in a democracy requires a commitment to IDEALS liberty. Liberty must come first in American society, because it is what gave birth to our republic, with a culture of democracy as it roots.

This absolute necessity of democracy requires virtue. Without it, we doom our babies' opportunities to enjoy either. If we allow unethical, hypocritical elitist politicians and non-egalitarian-unconcerned-for-society economic elites to continue to guide us, we will lose both. The politicians and elites at our helm are a ship of fools (Carlson, 2018). (Socrates told this parable to Adeimantus. It appears in Book VI of Plato's *Republic* (Edman, 1928)). These fools are baby doomers who need our help to cure them of the moral disease of doomerism. We can help them by relieving them of their authority, replacing them with the rising generations' competent people-persons among us. We can begin to repair the cracks in our dock's foundations. We can begin reform, to raise ready our ship upright, re-sail (not retail, putting it up for sale, or sell it out) our enterprise; again toward its preferable destination. We must be very courageous for the dangerous voyage ahead as we navigate an uncertain future now upon us, because the doomers did maintain our infrastructure and misguided us into unchartered shark infested illiberal waters.

Power's Disuse, Abuse, Misuse, Nonuse

Tyranny in all its forms is the enemy of democracy. The disuse of power is no longer using a once used power. Abuse of power is doing something wrong with authority that violates the law. Misuse of power is using power for something not authorized. Nonuse of power is standing by and letting something wrong happen.

We, the everyday people, united, have people power. We must work toward unity. Despite our various socialization contexts, community settlement patterns, and regional subcultural differences, we can unite through committing to practicing good citizenshipping. To do so, we, as persons, must first seek to resist the temptation to DAMN our societal and social powers.

Disuses of people power occur when we are not civically engaged participants in our politics—not voting, not listening and not learning! We must avoid the worst apathy that would allow some to gain absolute domination of all aspects of society, which is the pull of tyranny that makes a mobocracy—an enraged irresponsible improperly exercising their rights and ignoring their responsibilities. Conversely, we must guard against apathy leading us toward anarchy. Ambitious, charismatic persons may desire that the people have more power over all aspects of society, rather than a balancing of primary powers by precept power processes. This overreach can lead to reactive violence's use to control people, put us into a population control event like war or genocide, or give grounds to some to establish a brutal police state. Abuse of our power happens when we demand something for nothing and get it, knowingly committing fraud as persons and publics. This kind of disrespect of the other powers' instruments of action is an invalidating behavior.

Misuses of people power involve vandalism and theft when in peaceable protest and then hiding behind the "innocent until proven guilty" culture. A better path of citizenship is simply to obey the reasonable rules and not commit a crime. Crime is an erroneous form of freedom that is a misuse of our power.

Nonuse of people power is to be a bystander of crime and do nothing, or to allow a risky, gross misbalancing of the powers in society. This is one way of witnessing wrongful behavior and not stepping in to assist a victim and that victim can be the USE, our society not getting appropriate LAMBS in the direction of liberty and justice that democracy culture enables. It is not performing bystander intervention when something bad could result from nonintervention, like preventing a drunk from driving.

Our misbehavior in our participation in the FILMS[2] [P7] of the economy power is a misuse of our people power that is to guide us toward virtue and not into vice. Disuse of economy power is not balancing the subordinate powers it must stimulate to create a successful provision of necessary resources. Its abuse is in allowing it to become our reason for being, to please it and worship it as a god, which enables it to seek dominion, and thus absolute domination of all aspects of society, which is the pull of tyranny. Abuse of economy power occurs as it seeks to control the polity, to demand greater private power over the public powers, and to make governments subservient to industries' corporations, operatives, and lobbyists.

Economy power's misuse occurs when it seeks not to serve but expects the secondary powers of academy, artistry, and industry, to serve it, bending to kiss its feet as if it is a feudal lord. Further, it will seek to control the people, to convert every person into a consumer and discount the value and worth of being a citizen, or member of any other social institution or organization (the instruments) that does not generate veneration for it as omnipresent and all-powerful. It will make consumerism a more important way of being than citizenship, which includes being a good person and family member. As it increases in its control, its operators will desire more and more control for predictability in provisioning, which causes dictator like monopolies. Because of its ability to produce and sell commodities, it is prone to greed and susceptible to infection by severe doomerism that will only benefit a few, leaving the majority behind with nothing but resentment.

Nonuse of economy powers to ensure provisions of resources happens when it retracts from doing what it is supposed to do, which can happen when, after abusing and misusing itself, the other powers gain control over it, and instead of it accepting less, it simply stops doing its job. Alternatively, it makes monopolies to restrict others from free enterprise. Blocking other providers of goods and services out of the marketplace, buying them up, or forcing them to quit trying is a nonuse of economy powers to keep fairness and opportunity viable for the species to benefit from the knowledge growth it produces over time.

We, the everyday people, by not being responsible citizens, allow the powers to lose a healthy equilibrium needed for liberty's protection. Such imbalance perilously permits the polity power to pursue unfettered, absolute domination of all aspects of living, which is the pull of tyranny. If we don't lead, if we don't pay attention, participate in politics, get engaged to support our communities, and make demands upon the politicians and economic elites to strive for the ideals of liberty first, but demand we be taken care of like cattle, we'll face the same fate of slaughter or endless udder-sucking. The polity, if so empowered by our complacency, or worse, apathy, will seek to gain control of the economy in manners for which it is not operantly well suited. It will make us increasingly subservient to it, as a weak and lazy people it will then gladly take full control with excessive administration of civil society making us always at fault for some ridiculous unpredictable law.

We must not let the politicians develop a desire to have more control over all aspects of society. We do this by helping them be citizens first, holding them accountable, and replacing them regularly, so they cannot write too many laws that constrict our legitimate freedoms. If we don't help our fellow citizens who seek to govern on our behalf, they and we will become infected with a doomerism that by the way it confiscates, obfuscates, immolates, frustrates, fabulates, ulcerates, relegates, and extirpates (COIFFURE) democracy from American society, causes, amplifies, tolerates, actualizes, promotes, undergirds, litigates, taunts, embraces, and develops (CATAPULTED) continuous crises for the USE. We cannot allow it. These baby doomers think they are so cunning. But, we've got their number, and their name. Sadly, we are able to fix the blame, though we'd rather fix the problem. We can and will with an all hands on deck resurgence of good citizenshipping!

For the children, we the entire adult citizenry must step up and do a better job at self-governing. Locally in our immediate circumstances, by committing to citizenshipping to become full-fledged humans living with and for one another, or else we'll lose our liberty to a largesse polity spending what we have earned for ourselves on others who did not earn it, such as the economy elites or those forgotten by them in poverty. The polity is the power we must lead to administer a society in which a fair management of its necessary provisions provided by economy power happens in a reasonable manner that keeps society open to inventions. We can only do so if we recognize what doomerism is and prevent ourselves, and our power structures and their operative behaviors, from falling for it. Doomerism slowly decays our trust in one another and erodes our faith in our USE. No doubt, those jealous of us will aid and abet it to bring us down. We must rise to understand and participate, as invited by the original intent of our founding Constitution.

Scarcity tactic of the power-hungry

The book *Out of Weakness: Healing the Wounds that Drive Us to War* by A. B. Schmookler, exemplifies that for those who lust for and use power in its worst ways, the creation of scarcity makes people do evil to one another in desperation. It is salient in explaining how inequality will eventually lead to civil unrest and the destruction of social institutions. Simply put, those who have, can. Then, in creating unrest caused by scarcity (they use the production of scarcity as a weapon), they find moral superiority in blaming the victims. Moreover, seemingly enjoying the evil that absolute power causes in their egos, they deny truth and justice, saying "No you cannot have because I want it all, and I want it now!" Then proudly they hail, "I will have it all! You will have nothing. I am a winner. You are a loser. You are bad, dirty, unworthy!" These cruel acts of raw power typify baby doomer actions while in possession of authority and when without it in certain social situations wherein their sense of entitlement goes without embrace or welcome by others.

To make scarcity and suppress others is the source of wrongful power a monarch feels good about enacting. It is not something that anyone in a democratic republic should feel because our system enables an increase in having. We know this when we realize how decent it is to expand education and not crush it. An educated population, a large middle class, helps stabilize a republic, enables greater democracy, and offers hope to future generations.

It is so sad to see the rich and powerful, the top 1%, enjoy bashing scientists, nurses, and schoolteachers. Those who would make us a better democracy have been under assault by the vain and greedy. We are supposed to achieve virtue by avoiding temptations to sin and striving to help one another. What is equally sad is that those socialized in traditionalistic contexts to obey and respect authority figures—whom seek to maintain the status quo and control over society—are at risk of manipulation by a deceitful wannabe ruling class.

We do democracy honor when we commit to live by the cardinal moral virtues. This is a daily discipline. It is also coded as (to those who believe) pleasing to God. It is a personal, internal battle to meet face to face with one's own weaknesses (insecurities, prejudices, vainglory, arrogance, etc.) and strive to overcome them—to become a better person, father, mother, son, daughter, uncle, cousin, neighbor, citizen, etc. Being a better self-centered, materialistic consumer is not on the list! Oh, how foolish the ferociously selfish among the baby boomers have been. How responsible they are for failing to bring us closer to our ideals! Who cares if a person feels personally successful if he or she shreds society with a "me first" attitude? Foolish little blowfish puffed up with pride, their awkward disguise with thorns out to intimidate cannot hide.

This brings us to the end of our thinking about the primary powers' perturbing permutations. Next, we will examine the tools to make a good society that citizens can use in their thinking about what is happening in society, and how to reverse doomerism and restore our better qualities.

*T*ools to Make a Good Society

Virtue is a moral construction. It is moral intelligence to abide by it. Warranted in efforts to make a good society, it requires an understanding of morality. Building upon the work of child psychologist Jean Piaget, who forged a theory of human development from birth to adulthood, American psychologist Lawrence Kohlberg formulated a theory of moral development (Roberts, 1990), which people experience as they mature from childhood to elderhood. However, too few of us understand that a pursuit of higher morality is a pursuit of wisdom that comes from a pursuit of virtue, which is the truest form of happiness. The ultimate pursuit of happiness is the pursuit of wisdom. Some may not reach the pinnacle of moral reasoning.

This is normal, but as Americans, we ought to see more of our selves, not less. Awareness of self is vital to our being able to reach a condition in society of peace, harmony, and unity as one people. It requires that we actively seek to develop our morality as much as possible to enlarge our capacity for empathy that is essential for democracy. This is a vital task to reach our sought destiny of a more perfect union. This task requires that we seek to perfect our own selves first, before we judge others. This is an act of virtue. Our continuous becoming toward our ideal being is as much a mystical as it is a practical pursuit. We, by contributing to society by working on ourselves and helping one another improve, make a difference in the trajectory of society. We, by our daily actions, make the society better for us. Society either morphs to bad or grows toward good as we nurture one another through our neighborhoods, communities, states, and regions. This is people power to change the world. Achieving perfect union is our goal as a people, e pluribus unum. Those who disagree are traitors. Those who do not support this are morally injured or have fallen victim to the ills of baby doomerism. We must cure them. We need them healed, so that we might return our good ship to its purposeful path to achieve our goal.

This outcome is an ideal worth pursuing. National pride is valuable to the solidarity and comradery of a citizenry. Below is an image that portrays the theory of moral development, with the basis for thoughts and actions within the approximate developmental ages and the corresponding level of orientation toward society.

A complete, functional adult is many complex systems acting upon the person, just as a society is many complex systems acting upon it and people. All make experience. There are many ways to perceive and understand our experiences. If there were a test question on them, it might be best to guess that one ought to circle "e" for all of the above. Circle "e" is a premise for experiences compiled, or experientialism (this author's 1st invented ism). We sense the world with our standard senses, just as the American lobster uses its antennae and follicles. Experientialism postulates that we've two states of awareness, conscious and unconscious, and eight senses that we use to experience our lives. We've the physiological ones we're aware of and those we're unaware of, our limbic and cognitive ones, which our body's brain and central nervous system operate. We've our sight, smell, hearing, taste, and touch, which feed them information. Within these two states of awareness, we also have our mind-centered mental senses: social-emotional-intuition (feelings), memorial and imaginative cognitive thinking (knowledge), and language deep-structure communication comprehension capability (thoughts).

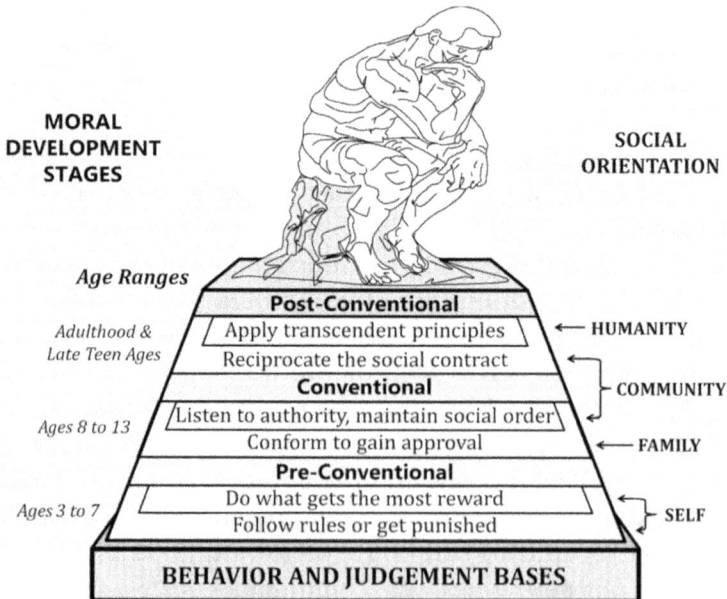

Figure 2-27: Moral Development of Persons

What we perceive through our eight senses of experiencing, we experientially integrate into becoming the being we are and will be, (see Figure 2-28). By way of our KA^4SA^2, we come to comprehend socialized norms, mores, beliefs folkways, and customs, and at our core sensation of self, our morality. Our imagination can take us far away from fact with the fantasies and stories we tell ourselves as we form perceptions while observing or listening to others. We ought to seek facts and not believe the fictions we create. We would also do well to hear our consciences whispering in our minds. Our skills of discerning factual pictures and the clear conscience of a good moral posture develop further through our KA^4SA^2, which is why we go to school. Moreover, if we are more aware of ourselves as persons and seek to develop our morality to higher states of conscientiousness, we will be able to cope with the complexity of our ever-changing world. Such self-improvement work positions us to adapt better and without confusion because as we center ourselves in our life experiences and reflect upon how we are being shaped by them, mindful that society is shaped by culture, and culture is made by us (and can be unmade by us), we can be still in the chaos around us. We can be in it without being of it and without feeling surrounded by it. We can gather our forces and, as necessary, alter the culture, changing its mores if they are damaging to all of us. We can select the customs of tradition that support our well-being while jettisoning outmoded concepts and adopting new ideas to integrate into our culture. But none of this is possible without freedom, and only a democracy-based culture seeks it for all. To have it is a condition of liberty.

A culture of democracy that keeps liberty as its mighty force, which means none of us ruled ruthlessly by another human being, best supports our centering as a moral person. Transformation of the self over time into a person united with others practicing democracy for the sake of everyone's liberty is the commons that we must defend with our lives in pursuit of liberty. As each of us does this at the micro level, so will we perform better at the meso level, and ultimately, so will those operating at the macro level of influence in society. Our enterprise will survive, and if we increase in our living toward virtue, it will thrive. Its success depends on our performance as citizens. Exhibiting service above selfishness, saying yes to the utmost full-fledged thoroughgoing constitutionally allied united citizenshipping, understandingly synchronized (E-SASSY-T-TUF-FT-CAUCUS) is how we foster decency and fulfill beauty in our LAMBS.

Recognizing that experientialism points to our uniqueness as persons can help us permit ourselves to be of goodwill and remind us that what binds us together as one people is the common purpose of our commonness in our humanity in a society built for our liberty from tyranny. The core construction of our country is an exceptional opportunity to resist ignorance and terror. But it requires earnest commitment and courage to tell the truth, live in virtue, and hold one another accountable to do likewise.

This is love. This is common knowledge for an uncommon republic. We must live by it, or we will find ourselves in doom. More self-knowledge and civilly given civic commitment are necessary if we are to uphold the beneficial social mores of our society and celebrate our shared American experience, and a belief in our goal and objectives stated in the Preamble of the Constitution. This so that, people feel patriotism and not cynicism incited by doomerism. We must build positive memories to dream in the language of Americanism: that which is virtuous and inalienable, a belief in the dignity and sanctity of every citizen, who we must help see their own dignity so they do not tarnish it. Moreover, we must prevent fellow citizens from becoming depraved and
perpetuating unhelpful and deplorable socialization contexts.

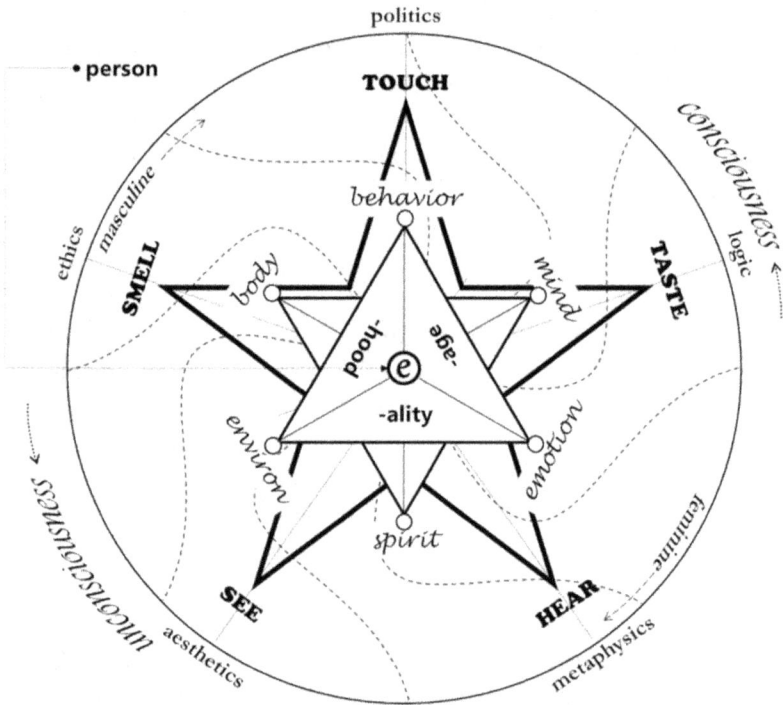

Figure 2-28: Experientialism Diagram
Our experience of life gained through our senses and person formation within the turnings of time and as shaped by the philosophical means of grasping the phenomena encountered while living, conveys to us the culture of the society in which we grow up, rear, live, and die. As we live, like a flower, our mind opens and closes to consciousness yet never stops processing from day to night as we associate with others, encountering the duality of our species as one of two biological sexes required for reproduction.

One way to support our societal improvement is to learn to recognize fallacies and seek understanding of opposite sides, or poles, of the things socially defined by theories that portray them and their characteristics. Things like isms for organizing society and powers to achieve certain objectives. The USE has the high goal of a more perfect union, a just cause to which we all must be dedicated in our own lives, in private and in public. We unite when we try to unite. We divide when we do not try to unite. In what kind of society do we want to live? What do we want our legacy to be for posterity? Not founded for dystopia or utopia, our country is to do liberty and justice for all. We need to fix the foundations of our society. Unity is calling out to us for aid. Let us cast out the demonic doomerism that currently pervades our everyday lives. Let us rapidly and repeatedly replace the baby doomers with patriotic citizens in the societal and social powers' FILMS[2] [P7] and perform better LAMBS toward our ordained constitutional goal of a more perfect union. Yes, it is implied, and it explicitly means we must strive to be more perfect persons to get back on the way toward it. We begin not by citing differences but by identifying similarities.

What we look like, smell like (from cooking vapors and perspiration), or sound like (from regional dialects and distant languages), does not matter so long as we can perform our roles in society and do our jobs virtuously to the betterment of our society and ourselves for our progeny and their posterity. We came out of a past view, we reflect upon and live in the present, and we do best to live for the future and not the here and now. To do so would be vain and foolish when compared with the teachings of wisdom, which are not outmoded because they are old. Wisdom is timeless, never out of date, shared from the highest mental states of moral development transmitted to us through numerous traditions. Of these universal themes held worldwide, the need to will to live with virtue resides in all traditions. So does the will to discover ones true self and purpose for contributing to society. Said another way, we need to discover and follow our bliss (Osbon, 1991). We need to stop focusing on our primate survival instinct's interpretations of our physical sensory mechanisms. We need to focus on the intellectual awareness of our minds because we are all in this society together. If we are to keep it moving toward its objectives, we need to "get over ourselves" and admit and overcome our fears of who is or is not one of us. All who immigrate to the United States can become an American. What binds us is our allegiance to our undertaking contained within the Declaration and the Constitution. We are an American people because we are a creedal nation. This then makes us a people (Will, 2019).

We the people, e pluribus unum, buffered by better citizenshipping, are who we are and whom we must become going forward. This means we need to be better persons in our roles for the purposes of the roles and not let intangible, superficially shallow and hollow discrimination, prejudice, and hatred disrupt the success of the USE. We've enough complexity from new knowledge and technology. We cannot turn against one another. Have we ever wondered, if "people are people," why it is that we "get along so awfully"? Why is it this way? We can now answer why we suffer from such ill effects. It is because of doomerism. Its negative influence upon us has grown exponentially during the adulthood of the baby boomers. It is now at its peak. This generation has held a majority stake for forty years. During which the dilemmas have mounted, unresolved, with constant crises. Now our problems are wickedly complex. We need an intervention in our society, and it is not a single-source solution. It is a multiplicative series of maneuvers. We must depose baby doomers from positions of authority. We must force them off the helm, from the bridge, and out of the pilothouse. We must filter out those in the next generations who mimic and model themselves after them. We all must push ourselves past the trap of thinking and feeling into which doomerism entices us. We must, in our personal and professional experiences, demand better moral, ethical, and teamwork for societal betterment-oriented performance of our work as duties not chores. There is great positive pride and importance found in doing one's duty well. This is a building block for society. The lazy would say otherwise. Yet sloth is not good for self or society, not at the micro, meso, or macro level. To leisure is restorative. Recreation is good. Complacency and apathy are bad. We must not be apathetic and allow factions of extremist perspectives that are contrary to liberty to accumulate power and posture over us as if they hold the key to righteousness. These are but a few of the things we must do to stop the drifting awry of our society. We must learn why we must IDEALS liberty and know we have the power to accomplish this vital task of citizenship.

Through civic engagement, we will get to know and trust one another. As we improve our citizenshipping skills, developing the expertise to perform our duty to ourselves as a citizenry, we will grow in confidence and comfort. We know we are on the same team, Team USA, but we must act like it. We are in crisis, a chaotic storming period, adjusting to new social circumstances and material conditions posed by newly gained knowledge. These we see rising in our academy, industry, and artistry powers. They are more than we are prepared for because we have allowed divisive baby doomers to run roughshod over the FILMS[2] [P7] roles, which they have done during the paradigmatic shift of the locus of society from a modern analog-based speed of change to a post-industrial digital pace that zips along so quickly that we cannot keep up. This post-industrial society brings an axial change to the social structure of society, a structure resulting from the balance of societal powers. The rapid changes in society suggest there is a common core of problems we must address near immediately and repeatedly. These problems hinge on the relation of science and public policy (Bell D. , 1973). Shaping a society that hums along on automation at a pace too fast for our comprehension and adaptability is transforming us. Such a society presents numerous adaptive problems that if ignored by the powerful politicians result in corruption. Political officials riding waves of prospering shifts in the economy power's gains for its elites opens them to payments that fuel campaigns for them to hold onto polity power gains this plutocratic cycle produces. Caught in its gyre the vacuum of which blinds, deafens, and moots truth, baby doomers predominantly lead both. Their corruption undermines our team. Any perceived integrity to IDEALS liberty is a false-faced affront to us. Those we entrust to prosecute properly the LAMBS for us commit "dirty deeds" that seem to be "done dirt cheap." They are failing at their responsibility to move us forward toward our destined goal and the objectives of our Constitution. We have a key choice to make before it is too late. We must abandon the ways of doomerism, rediscover the ideals of democracy and its lifeblood, liberty, and engage our community power to increase our social capital. We the people will use it to ensure our power builds people up in every socialization context, regional subculture, and settlement pattern within which we reside. To undergird our precept culture, democracy, we the people must $AEIOUY^2K$ our power in correct proportion to our responsibility as a citizenry. We must do this for liberty and justice for all. If not, the baby doomers will continue to DAMN the societal powers from an improper balance and misapply them for wrongful purposes.

To help us, we need to attend to how we might think about all the isms and opinions we see, hear, and feel getting tossed about in the public realm. The many isms spread around by the history power of journalism, chronically opinionating in the "media," do not inform anyone. Sold for profit and power accumulation by fixations on performing financially as a sole indicator of worth, such half-truths drive persons to prefer to hear their own beliefs echoed all the time. A lie never becomes a truth, no matter how many times repeated. Through sophisticated targeted marketing, which funnels media reporting "traffic" into several channels of communication, fictions spread and appear legitimate because they appear in many places. To those who like such stories, this is rewarding, especially when fed at no cost to them. Passing on perspectives popular in a particular priority marketplace of persons thinking similarly (and often intolerably) of others is a wrongheaded concept for a vital to the business of the enterprise history power. It lacks the dignified sense of fact-based truth telling that journalism had when its employers and employees saw it as a kind of public service. It used to be their duty to tell the truth, and to call out liars. Liars damage the community. A damaged community detaches from reality. It allows demagoguery to become normal, abort facts, and create fictions that end in a dictatorship.

We need a broader perspective on the perceptions of the public consequences of so-called news and propaganda published with hyperbole only to sell advertisements. The new technology of social media uses algorithms to send persons content that reflects their attitudes and behaviors. It amplifies differences by isolating people into camps. Social media is addictive. It is eroding our social human fabric built on love and compassion. It leads to unauthentic behaviors. It is dooming our children to depression and suicide. This because baby doomer economy power elites now almost wholly own and operate the history power FILMS[2] [P7]. They pay them to make the music they like, which sounds like "ka-ching!" It jiggles in their pockets and echoes as cash registers ringing, racking up coin in their favor for their private chambers. Our vexingly wicked social problems are almost explosive, driven to the edge of understandability by the rapidly increasing acceleration of technological advancements. These push information at people by algorithms, formulas written to feed people not what they need but that which feeds a weakness. The easy answer without basis in fact, just what is popular within a community of beliefs wanting believed for the safety perceived as given by the answer is an error in democracy culture. We need to recognize this vortex and stay out of it. We can do that by developing an eye for detecting fallacies, and understanding dichotomies.

Know Fallacies and Dichotomies

What ideas are available to us to examine in their relation to our purpose of achieving our republic's objectives? Ideas, of course, are sufficiently fungible to create in our imaginations all kinds of combinations that might amuse or even confuse us. Or, ideas are sufficiently intelligible and can be well defined and kept to mean what they mean and what they intend. Certainly, certain combinations are truer than others are, and still others are false. Fallacy is factual. Fallacies exit. Some employ them intentionally as trickery, lies told to confound. Some are accidental, a failure in the proper application of logic. We the everyday people need to know how to recognize fallacies, call them out when we see them, hold their speakers to account, and demand better truth telling or better logical reasoning. To name many, in three general categories of subsets, see the list below (Fearside, W. Ward & Holther, William B., 1959). It is difficult to avoid fallacies. Using our experiential sense, we all search for meaning and too willingly believe stories that comport with our perspectives. Democracy needs better than simply deciding to believe a falsity as truth when doing so is convenient. Convenience is not always best. Consumerism can convince us it is, but it is not. Choices have consequences. We are responsible as citizens to think through our choices. If we choose to be citizens first, we can better understand fallacies.

Understanding fallacies

Knowing the fallacies can help us avoid errors in our judgments of what others' arguments propose, especially those from the persons in positions of authority within society's powers. Consumerism has taught us to crave convenience. We need bravely to confront it as a vulnerability that harbors negative risks for our society. We must be particularly on the lookout for two fallacies of dangerous demagogues (underlined in the following list) (Roberts-Miller, 2017). We need not to argue with emotion but to discuss with reason. Democracy needs respectfully rational deliberation. It does not need ridiculously irrational demagoguery. Civility is its requirement. Below is a list of the fallacies we must understand, guard against using, and call out when others hazard into using them, or perpetrate their use on purpose. This is an intellectual responsibility of our people power leadership to ensure society is fact-based in truth's pursuit. This is an outcropping of a "rule of law" constitution, and is not a "rule of men" mentality that prefers fallacies. There are three forms of fallacies to know. Here they are:

I. **Material Fallacies**
   o Propositions formed wrongly
      ▪ Faulty generalization
         • done in haste or unrepresentative
      ▪ Faulty causal generalizations
      ▪ Assuming the cause: post hoc reasoning
      ▪ Faulty analogy
      ▪ Misuse of statistics
      ▪ Composition and division
      ▪ The all-or-nothing mistake
      ▪ The false dilemma
   o Constructions formed wrongly
      ▪ Faulty classification of various non-exhaustiveness
      ▪ Misconceptions about classification, reifications, and relativisms
      ▪ Confusing causation and correlation: (post hoc ergo propter hoc)
      ▪ Unnecessary vagueness
      ▪ Over-precision
      ▪ Word magic

II. **Psychological Fallacies**
   o Emotional coloration (*Ad vercundiam*)
      ▪ Emotive language: colorful (flowery) words
      ▪ Ceremony or setting: pomp and circumstance
   o Misusing authority (*Ad misericordiam*)
      ▪ Appeal to authority: ipse dixit or "they say so!"
      ▪ Appeal to tradition or faith: "tried and true"
      ▪ Impressing by large numbers: "get on the bandwagon"
   o Stirring prejudice
      ▪ Popular passions: ad populum appeals
      ▪ Damning the origin: "consider the source" (motivism)
      ▪ Personal attacks: ad hominem
      ▪ Forestalling disagreement
      ▪ Creating misgivings: "where there's smoke, there's fire"
   o Rationalization and lip service
      ▪ Self-righteousness
      ▪ Finding the "good reason"

- Wishful thinking
- Special pleading: "having it both ways"
- Lip service

  o Biased misconstructions
    - Apriorism: invincible ignorance
    - Personification
    - Cultural bias (motivism)
    - The gambler's mistake
  o Diversions
    - Humor and ridicule: "lost in the laugh"
    - Demand for special consideration
    - Clamorous insistence on irrelevancies: "red herring"
    - Pointing to another wrong
    - Accuse the accuser: tu quoque
    - False equivalence
    - The wicked alternative
    - Nothing but objections
    - Impossible conditions: the call for perfection
    - Abandonment of discussion
    - Straw man
    - Equivocating

III. **Logical Fallacies**
  o Logical truth and validity errors
    - The undistributed middle term
    - Suppressed quantification
    - False conversion of propositions
    - Non sequitur
    - Trouble with conditionals and alternatives
    - Ambiguous terms
    - Amphibole: "double-talk"
    - Ambiguous accent
    - Ambiguous punctuation and word order
    - Circular reasoning or definitions and "begging the question"
    - Misuse of etymology
    - Idiosyncratic language

Notice the many illogical fallacies useable to confuse us. Again, for a citizenry to retain a republic with democracy is not easy. It is not convenient. It is a calling, a worthwhile and purposeful duty to fulfill. A duty served by knowledge to critically think and truthfully discuss ones understanding with a willingness to learn from another why they think and feel the way they do. This practice helps us understand why and how we think the way we do. This is a social skill. It is a skill we are losing but can regain and improve upon. One way to improve it is to know, identify, and call out fallacies; not be suckered into believing them. Another way is to see ideas on similar topics or phenomena as pairs on a continuum. Knowing to what degree one holds them as true can help us communicate opinions when we seek truth in facts. Often opposites, the pairs form a dichotomy. This device for discussion can help get many perspectives on the table for constructive critical conversations on why we believe what we believe. Understanding each other is how we move toward unity. It propels our project forward, not backward, as doomerism does.

Using dichotomies

Dichotomies are similar to dilemmas, but a choice of one pole or the other does not have the same consequences. The consequences of either choice differ. As a technique to evaluate our perspectives, dichotomies assist us in framing ideas and thoughts. As continuums of possible ways of seeing something, they help us think.

We might believe in either a true or a false idea. If we put a pair of seemingly opposite ideas together, with one at each end of a line, we can set up a dichotomy. Some will be paradoxes. Both poles may be true, though they may appear to be opposites. Holding in mind a paradox is a cognitive skill that requires the ability to handle complexity. Practicing it and imagining to what degree one favors one pole or the other does not invalidate the truth of the other pole. This kind of cognitive complexity is necessary for a democracy and is a part of its culture. Whether paradoxical or not, we must be more comfortable with assessing ourselves along dichotomies and using dichotomous thinking. Doomerism makes this difficult. It favors ideological absolutism. It drives us to "my way only, no other way allowed" thinking. It gathers us into fanatic tribalism. It becomes more essential to us than shared experiences of being American can in defining us.

With a dichotomy, we can contrast the two ideas. We can place our opinion along the line, closer to the pole that is more in line with our beliefs. We can choose which pole we feel closer to, and we can see how it pans out for us in reality. Reality will tell us if we made a good choice or not. Over time, our judgments and choices will bear out. Either we will adjust our beliefs to facts or we may suffer cognitive dissonance or psychological and emotional pain. We will find out whether we were foolish or wise. This is how we adapt. This is how we come to accept new facts. We must be willing to adjust.

Adaptation is a key aspect of our species. It is how we survive in so many different geographic biomes. Resiliency is our ability to rethink, remake, to create and be ready for the chance to choose more wisely on another day. This is evolution. Dichotomies can help us pursue wisdom by sharpening our critical thinking skills. But to do this we must know what the terms at the extreme poles mean and the position in which we really believe. We need to have serious agency in our thinking about what is likely truer to the benefit of liberty for the LAMBS by our USE. We must, or we cannot be effective citizens to support its success. This use of dichotomies is a reflective and reflexive tool that will inform deliberate thinking and discussion. Using dichotomous continuums to understand self, family, neighborhood, community, state, and national character is helpful to democracy. "Who is right" is not the point. "What is right" is! This truth depends upon factuality not fallacy.

```
        Joy <----------------><----------------> Misery
       Self <----------------><----------------> Others
       Free <----------------><----------------> Bound
       Farm <----------------><----------------> Factory
     Change <----------------><----------------> Stability
   Internal <----------------><----------------> External
 Individual <----------------><----------------> Group
Traditional <----------------><----------------> Radical
  Self-made <----------------><----------------> Birthright
 Continuity <----------------><----------------> Discontinuity
Countryside <----------------><----------------> Cityscape
   Equality <----------------><----------------> Hierarchy
     Dharma <----------------><----------------> Karma
       Time <----------------><----------------> Human
      State <----------------><----------------> Federal
     Future <----------------><----------------> Past
       Evil <----------------><----------------> Good
       Mild <----------------><----------------> Severe
    Control <----------------><----------------> Fate
    Sensing <----------------><----------------> Intuition
      Brief <----------------><----------------> Prolonged
   Thinking <----------------><----------------> Feeling
   Material <----------------><----------------> Spiritual
    Judging <----------------><----------------> Perceiving
    Limited <----------------><----------------> Extensive
    Nothing <----------------><----------------> Everything
 Pragmatism <----------------><----------------> Idealism
Immortality <----------------><----------------> Mortality
Tight (strict) <----------------><----------------> Loose (lax)
Follow rules <----------------><----------------> Break rules
Extroversion <----------------><----------------> Introversion
Competition <----------------><----------------> Cooperation
Independency <----------------><----------------> Dependence
```

Figure 2-29: A List of Dichotomies

Figure 2-29 contains a list of dichotomies of important qualities that help us understand what is right for liberty; not our shallow misperception about what is best for "me now." What is right achieves virtue; virtue is what is best for us as persons seeking to be a people in more perfect union. We build up to a national character one person at a time, then one group of persons at a time, from small to large: me, you, family, neighborhood, communities, state, region, nation, and humanity globally. Where on this continuum are each of us, and the groups to which we belong? Identify which side is most important and how important it is by how close to the pole one places it. It is equally important to realize that choice depends on situation. A middle score indicates a neutral or indifferent perspective. Slightly more important is marked toward a pole, though nearer to the center than the side. Much more important, but not completely important, is marked nearer to the word at the pole. A completely important perspective is marked at the end of a pole, next to the word. This process for any dichotomy to denote one's thoughts and feelings can also analyze others' perspectives. Knowing this frames the difference or similarity of opinions on any topic of interest explored to gain understanding. Personality tests work in similar ways of choosing between words. This is a stable method. It does not take a genius to map our opinions and beliefs related to what words mean to people.

The benefit of using dichotomies is that they can help us clarify our thinking to be better at using our people power to lead society. We can use them to understand that the polity engages in politics using polemics to assert and argue for often unproven positions, which might push us away from our objectives by pulling more power under their control or by passing power on to those elites of economy powers who control the polity.

When we understand the polemics better, the positions and posturing of politicians, by using dichotomies, we will be better positioned to lead society. One pole or another may be shaping the policy the polity implements. When we the people become more aware of policy making, the apparatus and the polemics used, we can better prevent maladaptation, which is the DAMN of societal and social powers by poor application of knowledge by the persons in positions of authority badly performing their roles within the FILMS[2] [P7] of the societal and social powers. Moreover, we must not only keep our eyes on the primary powers. We, the everyday people, must become aware of the dichotomies in human understanding, the binary nature of the discourse of the secondary and tertiary powers in society. The most important of these are those closest to persons, which shape each of our own selves as persons from our personages, personhoods, and personalities. A first step is finding the dichotomies that matter and identifying their poles. To move toward unity, we all need to better map out our own polarities as persons, our internal conflicts, and our external frictions.

Know Polemics' Polarity

Polarity defines opposites by contrasting one to the other. It creates a system that supports itself. It drowns out beliefs in the possibilities for democracy culture to produce results. It leads to the tyranny of endless debates between idealists. It prevents pragmatic solutions by realists. Realists correctly contend that such ideological gambling erodes our society and causes brinkmanship-style risk taking in the body politic. These intractable debates oriented toward poles and not agreements threaten the continuation of sovereignty and citizenry. We are losing a condition of practical peace, which enables betterment of society through democracy. Realism demands work. Within our grand project's goal of a more perfect union, its objectives are obtainable. We can do it through realistic work toward real facts to form the real common reality. Realism is the process of seeking to understand what is factually real, what is in fact reality and not fantasy. It is reasoned truth, not "repeated until believed" fallacy. Doomerism is preventing realism. The inability of baby doomers to perform their duties of diplomacy and democracy is a signal to the nation that we must replace them. Metaphorically, they need hospitalization to treat their malady. The hospital will treat their doomerism. It will recondition them from the ailment of power-lusting "tyrantitus" (a desire to be a tyrant). Hopefully, the treatment will help them regain the lifeblood our republic needs flowing through everyone's vessels, up into and around our brains. We need healthy minds to think helpfully. What is helpfully healthy is realistic thinking and actions to ensure freedoms are free from impracticality, by infusions of liberty gained through intermittent training in ACE.

Polarizing polemics over opposite opinions lead to perpetual disagreement and separation. We, the everyday people, must step up to stop the ground-staking, flag-posting tribalism. It does us no good. It is the tyranny of disagreement. Sustained polarity in the polity is a distraction from the failures of it. They get paid, we get confused, and our treasury depletes. No jobs mean zero revenues. It is a polemic caused dilemma in democracy. By use of dichotomy, we can force discussion from extreme poles toward the moderate solutions. However, we first must recognize the game played in front of us. A game born of doomerism, perpetrated by baby doomers, whose conceit is palpable in the air we breathe. We have chosen to ignore it at our own peril.

Now named, and its condition diagnosed, we can begin to fix the problem, cure the baby doomers, and stop the partisan blame games. Whoever perpetrates doomerism is not looking for ways to IDEALS liberty. They are sustaining their position at all costs. They are absolutists in their ideology, a trait of the baby boomer generation (Strauss & Howe, 1991). All classes of the boomers suffer this desire for an "easy button" that gives them an excuse by setting them off emotionally and temporarily ruining them cognitively. Consequently, because of this intellectual laziness we cannot get them to speak civilly and work toward agreement. Thus, they must go, replaced with great dispatch and urgency. They are simply unwilling to listen to possibilities for finding common ground on which to agree. They are egotistical tyrants and not civically minded citizens. They are only in it to win for their own selves and their weak egos' needs. Their weakness is a national security and sustainment vulnerability. Afraid of getting a bad name on social media, spineless sellouts do not deserve to hold positions of authority. We need the courageous that cooperate, not the insecure, immature, and irrelevant to solve wicked human problems caused by the results

of their unfettered doom epoch scaled greed and vanity. Pity them not, but replace them. They have not done well enough to earn their pensions. They must pay us back for their malfeasance. They seek to rule by being right, proving points, and then using their self-defined moral might to get their way. Repugnantly deplorable, this back biting pettiness betrays the tradition of the Enlightenment's age of reason that freed humankind from such tyranny.

When the immoral call for morality and act as if they represent it, this is hypocrisy. This is doomerism. This is not diplomacy, and it is not democracy. This is warmongering with big words: "isms" so abstract they do not mean anything when left alone and drift to float about in the public realm. Policy, practice, and programs in the LAMBS by the FILMS[2] [P7] of the USE are not achieving the stated goal and objectives of our foundational upbringing through the Declaration of Independence, the Revolutionary War, and the Constitution's ratification and amendment. We are off the path. The baby boomers diverged from the well-honed (capital "L") liberal and (capital "C") conservative tradition that created and sustains the republic. We now must battle back with our own ism, doomerism. We the everyday people, the patriots of liberty and justice for all, can sling it at them now. It is a part of our reeducation as we train to be the next generations in control of the polity and the economy, with "e pluribus unum" as our steadfast commitment. Of the doomers, we must call them out to hold them to account. We must prepare everybody to rise up and reeducate, raise the future to train as patriots to be better citizens to supplant the doomers. Let doomerism be our daily-slung ism, while another new ism in this book, "experientialism", shows us a way to wisdom. We must also fling small rocks at them in the form of acronyms. Acronyms, like the weapon systems of the military, are our means to bring about big ideas in terms more easily rendered in policy, programs, and practice—with greater precision than broad isms. We'll get specific where they were negligent. We'll not be lazy. We'll do the difficult calculations. We'll be the energy that makes the whole greater than the sum of its parts. We'll lead with experiential wisdom to achieve a gestalt no other citizenry ever enjoyed. We'll invest in practical KA^4SA^2 that IDEALS liberty. By it, we'll put our nation on a corrected course toward our objectives. They condition society for prosperity by the people, for the people, of the people. People come first! We'll get everyone to seek to be a citizen first, by telling wisdom's truth. As the everyday people, we'll lead American society become its ideal in reality, and keep it that way each succeeding generation by teaching the lessons necessary to keep the USE on its proper and correct course toward liberty and justice for all.

The polemic polarity of argument by the boomers is not peace creating. How can we, the everyday people, get a more perfect union of domestic tranquility, justice, liberty, and defense and fare well if those in the polity push perspectives that do not align with these American objectives? We cannot prove many of their policy isms with certitude or those supposedly proven this way or that way, positive or negative, and argued over because the proof was opposite one side's desired result. We must agree on the facts, even if they prove a favored notion fallacious. Boomers spend hoarded money to hire writers to prepare reports and stories that support their side of the argument to manipulate us as if we were dumb hordes. It's a game. They play it on us as they battle for control of the business of society. It is as if the baby boomers, during their adult time in control of the FILMS[2] [P7], have enjoyed arguments more than agreement. Did they lack a desire to prepare posterity for the prosperity that they enjoyed? So wrapped up in "me" did they not care about other's babies' or posterity's prosperity potential?

Mainly by the pure luck of being born when they were, they enjoyed magnificent wealth. Yet they think so highly of themselves due to their conspicuously consumptive materiality, as if they made it, rather than inheriting it via an endowment of a great opportunity structure that rose on the tide of rebuilding a world destroyed by war. How can they be so vain while society shreds from within by risks their ways triggered? The consequences of which, we are now realizing. They did not prepare to respond to these risks, nor did they determine how we would manage them. Figuratively, they spilled the milk but did not clean it up. Its spoiling stench attracted the roaches hiding from the light that scurry about making nests at night throughout our house. We have done a poor job of inspecting, detecting, and eradicating the vermin that have been fleecing our food of freedoms from the American ideals kitchen. We allowed the game of extremist polemic polarity in the polity to generate in us excuses to ignore it. Or, we picked a team and rooted for their victory, while failing to take part in the necessary deliberate diplomacy of democracy. We allowed ourselves to indulge in the pleasures of consumer materialism. By which hedonism we avoided responsibility of self-governing. So much so, we scant paid proper attention to the polity than we did our own apparel. This kind of superficiality brings demise to democracy. This is a symptom of doomerism.

Misguided positions

The baby boomers, in their enjoyment of high materiality, ignored the important work of protecting and defending the Constitution. This duty is our primary responsibility as Americans. The baby doomers among them guided them to a false posture. They feel it is valid to rationalize the permissibility of winning at all costs and avoiding any accountability. Cheat, if caught demand not to be made to feel guilty. They seek celebrity as the ultimate accomplishment. Yes, that is a self-centered and negligent-to-society perspective. They feel that nothing is wrong with vainglorious pride, envy, lusty greed for power, gluttonousness with power, or complacent laziness in using power appropriately for the common good, and they wrathfully enjoy their abuse of power.

It is fascinating to consider the number of ethics training courses the baby boomers have been required to attend in their careers, which a few wise persons instructed them to attend. The boomers begrudgingly took these mandatory courses, but only did so because they had to. They checked the box but gained nothing. Why would they? In their whining estimation it was a social requirement, not a "me first" need. Ironically, even with no intention of learning anything, they took the tests with hyper-competitiveness to get the highest score. After all in the "me first" way, they had to prove their perfection (if only to themselves). After feeling victorious, they forgot the important points. To their self-centeredness, the trainings' self-inhibiting inconvenient truths were a waste of their "precious time". To their way of thinking, the courses were just some old school elder's mandate for some ridiculously nebulous intangible non-material reasons. Ethics were just something the establishment expected, but since they were counter culture, they rejected them. Them, knowing ethics is just nonsense, because it is beyond the scope of self-interest. The worst of them just punched the ticket and then continued on their way as they saw fit, all the while complaining about how they felt coerced, forced to sit through "that stupid training."

Something is obviously missing in them. Clearly blinded by foolish ambitions they always stretch relativism to fake it until they make it, leaving a trail of disaster behind. A consequence they happily avoid admitting. Worse, in lieu of studying to find the truth, they will argue for their righteousness. It is pathetic. It is devastating for an American society. We must intervene and replace them. We must reject their baby doomerism.

American society's foundation is a democracy-based culture. We all need to behave in manners sufficiently honest. When we do, we can trust one another's decision-making. Firstly, decisions must use facts as their basis. Filtered through the mind of a citizenry seeking goodness ensures positive results. By E-SASSY-T-TUF-FT-CAUCUS, we demonstrate we are a good citizenry worthy of the American brand name. Secondly, we must make decisions to encourage one another to contribute fully to the venture of the USE, because we are all in it together, and we need it to work. Admittedly, this is not easy given our human nature. Yet we must try to overcome our nature that is weak with vulnerabilities to the risks of power's corruptions. We are the land of the brave, and if oriented toward serving the Constitution, we can prevent our self-survival instincts from overtaking our reason too easily. If we are in this mission of citizenshipping together, we can rely on our common sense. We can build the kind of American character we need to replicate the best a republic of democracy can produce. We need to be on the road to character (Brooks, 2015) to summon the wisdom of humility from yesteryear. Our Constitution and our citizenshipping can regulate us to respect always the freedom of others. We can, by these, not infringe upon freedom, not remove it, and not give ours up to another. The founders understood the constancy of human nature, its pros and cons, and its essence. They framed a society with this fact in mind (Will, 2019). It is our duty to honor the miracle of our nation and daily live up to its best ideals.

Humans are human, and our nature, while trainable, does not change dramatically. Each generation must train the next to behave in ways that will support the society. Our imperfections and the permutations of such in our regional subcultures and urban, suburban, and rural settlement patterns give rise to variety in social circumstances and physical conditions. This is why there are seven varieties of children's socialization contexts: snobbish, traditionalistic, anomic, modernistic, postmodernistic, enervating, and radicalizing (STAMPER). (More on these in the *Socialization Contexts* subsection in chapter three.) These, plus the variability between regional subcultures' perspectives on how to AEIOUY^{2}K the societal powers, are incredibly important to understand and discuss if we are to move forward in making a more perfect union (recall our discussion of regional subcultures' perspectives is in the

Doomerism moves society away from democracy and separates it into the haves and have-nots, with the use of brutality to enforce the new order of vertical stratification and horizontal divisions between the people. Democracy opens the doors for persons to find alternative identities that are not based on the existing ones, such as family name, where one lives or was born, or what forms of community, academy, artistry or industry power, to name a few, one uses within society. Being able to be as one pleases is freedom, a right granted in a society based upon liberty so long as ones pleasure does not damage another's. We may not have any other classes of persons who seek to band together to gain peace of mind through legal protections by the polity for a form of group identity. We'd do better to ensure the content of one's character is far more important than person's external physical characterizes, because separatist factions could use these to disrupt everyday life's peacefulness. Shown in gray within Figures 2-19, 2-20, 2-21, 2-22, and 2-23 is a rough proportion of the impact to society of the discussed social changes. These length of arrows and areas of the social movements for freedoms reduce progressively. The last group, sexuality as important to identifying self and lifestyle, is smaller than the previous two. We allow people to be as they would like to be within the bounds of the law and reached equilibrium of liberty for persons who seek to identify with a given group or two. Note, the groups we might share values with are less important than our personal character and citizenshipping activities to reverse baby doomerism.

Key to remember, the polity is to respond to the people, one person at a time in a voting booth, and not to groups as its norm. This applies to groups seeking to change the balance of the economy power in their group's favor. If we all live in accordance with the Constitution, in the spirit of its ideals that the content of each person's character is what is paramount and in the real realms of our behaviors, we all may yet be free to be. On that day when we do, all of us might enjoy with gratitude the abundance of a society that exists to IDEALS liberty to itself in every moment of its existence thanks to democracy being the basal culture of American society. We need to get real, get over ourselves, forgive, and love one another as citizens of a special society, without being too entitled and choosing dependency over independency

Figure 2-23 above illustrates the previously presented cycle of democracy and at each social circumstance, station, gives an example of what doomerism does to the attitude, condition, or behavior that occurs in the house that sits between each station. It shows how doomerism is consuming the society, taking over all stations and thought. The two stations that remain "nonexistent in doomerism" are silenced, ostracized, and outnumbered. They lack the doomerist ways of being and influence on our republic. From these two standalone stations, as well as with half of the faith with morality to have convictions to do right, we must launch our counterattack and push doomerism out of our society. Otherwise, it will consume us with its petty, immature, uncivilized, "dog eat dog," "me first" mentalities. Having described the cycle of democracy, our progress in pursuit of liberty, and how doomerism arises within, let's examine another slice of society. This time, we look at one related to where we live and the subcultures' remnants today.

Settlement Pattern Complications subsection in chapter two). This is the real work for our society. This must come first-and-foremost in our politics, economics, and sociality. To work together to find a common place, a position that protects liberty best, is the goal that should drive our public discourse. Proof of one's point, justification of one's perceptions—that one's philosophical pole in a dichotomy is best, without question—can create unhelpful, unhealthy extremism. Philosophies are not facts. Isms are not facts. They are propositions. Arguing over thoughts is circular and gets us nowhere in the direction of delivering a society that meets its goal and objectives. Nor does it prepare us to solve our societal problems for future generations to keep our country intact. Extremism is a condition of doomerism. It is in part natural for the human to want to be free to be wild and win everything, but it is unreasonable if it infringes on others' freedoms. By nurture, we craft culture to guide society toward growth that expands the opportunity risks but does not restrict liberty and justice for all. We, the everyday people, must educate ourselves on how to be leaders and lead the society to do this.

Purposeful pursuit

If, as we believe, we're endowed by our Creator with inalienable rights, written in our foundation as a nation, we must accept our first principles as immutable, unchangeable, and permanent wisdom for our citizenry. This makes our purpose for being to protect these as our common truth. This truth is the cornerstone in our foundation. It is a story worth believing in, because it is a story that has proven successful in producing prosperity. It needs nurturing. The boomers in charge neglect it. Our society, our tradition, which we are to continue to build upon while maintaining what our predecessors built, is a good purpose. A more perfect union is an achievable goal. We the future leaders must commit to it. The baby boomers clearly did not. If we do not, we'll become like every other society. The majority, having never had these grand principles provided to them, all end up living in daily tyranny by force. They suffer it in their micro, meso, and macro levels of social experience.

See, America is different. It grows out of a different seed, its Constitution. Its seed bears a different tree, a liberty tree. It is a tree like no other polity before it. It has a purposeful pursuit. Being so rare, it requires vigilant protection by citizen patriots willing to self-reflect and continuously educate themselves through civic engagement and political participation in pursuit of truth living virtuously. We cannot tolerate cowardice. The Constitution's defense begins with reverence in remembrance of what its first principles mean for our life's purpose in citizenship to it. Citizenship done right is democracy's sustaining brain and body chemistry, and liberty is its blood.

Let's continue with a presentation of a major dichotomy in the socialization contexts and regional subcultures in our society. We'll examine the at odds, opposite poles of the ways one can approach an appropriate understanding of life in the 21st century. This is particularly important as we are in the midst of a turbulent "shifting paradigm" (Kuhn, 1962) in society. We sense a tsunamic wave (Toffler, 1984) during a major crises "turning" point in our history (Strauss & Howe, 1991). We're experiencing the chaos of changes provoked by a "third stage of knowledge creation" (Hage, 2020). These recent advances have spun off technologies that challenge our very notions of what we thought we knew as true and trustworthy to live by. All of this is causing wicked social problems (Rittel & Webber, 1973). We need younger, brighter, better educated, more civically, thus ethically, minded generations to solve them for the USE. The boomers had their chance at the helm. They failed. They behaved like a ship of fools. We must remove them from the pilothouse. They lost unity. They ignored its calling. Thus, it's time for a changing of the guard. Post haste let's begin the necessary generational electoral change of command without ceremonies for the removed.

Ch-Ch-Changes: Tradition and Modern

Concerning the STAMPER socialization contexts, a special focus on two dominant socialization contexts and cultural linchpins prevalent in our living generations, the traditional and modernistic, will help us frame what we need to do to save our Constitution as amended. Its resurrection as our guide will get the society it framed back on the ideal path toward accomplishing our mission, our project's goal and its objectives stated in the Preamble. These two contexts are a fundamental dichotomy and have many opposite and contradictory attributes. They share a few similar ones, like two different species of tree share the same forest ecosystem, so we have hope. Their points of reference for life lessons differ. The modernistic context relies more upon secular philosophical teachings, while the traditional relies more upon teachings of mythology, both learned through the academy power's instruments. The emphasis on one or the other correlates with beliefs held in our many settlement pattern locales and regional subcultures. Within urban, (the several) suburban, and rural areas we find both these contextual perspectives on life. Within some regions of the country, one appears stronger than the other does. The northern-influenced settlements lean more toward a modernistic context. These areas are legatees to manu-factory industry power-based activities and societal experiences. The southern-influenced settlements lean more toward a traditionalistic context. These areas are legatees to agricultural industry power-based activities and societal experiences.

What is similar is that both modern and traditional outlooks see a need for hierarchy in social ordering. What differs is the way in which perceptions of fact, truth, and the purpose of mythology power in society sustain within the regional subcultures and socialization contexts. The more modernistic northerners see mythology power as promoting a need for the public to tell the private how to work toward making this world a better place in which to live. The more traditionalistic southerners see mythology power as promising a need for the private to beware the sinful public world that is as it is. They seek to live within it with faith but free from it while thinking we likely cannot change it. More accepting of society as it was, it is as it is, and they pondered if it should remain as it is, because in God we trust. When the Creator wills change, it will come. Almighty will is a matter of faith, and the founders decided faith is not a basis for making a republic, but offers worthwhile personal and social benefits that serve us better when disentangled from the polity.

The gap between these two dominant socialization contexts is a matter of degrees. However, in the hands of baby boomers, differences amplified. They eschewed similarities. They did not work toward making our union more perfect. They preferred material solutions above all other options of problem solving. They neglected to consider total human beings. Saying always "It's the economy, stupid," they gave the keys and carte blanche access to the city on a hill to a few economic elitists. By over-emphasizing economy power over the people and polity powers, they authorized a few to rise and reside in a new aristocracy and begin to entrench a group of plutocrats at the top as a ruling class. Remember, republics of democracy are not to be ruled. Allowing a few to rule causes tensions to become more severe, groups to seek group identities, recognition, and rewards, and factions to fight with emotive temperatures heightened. These all yank us away from a temperament for logical discourse focused on our primary mission: to IDEALS liberty. Without the right balance in these powers for the LAMBS, our USE has fractured and fragmented. This devaluing occurred during the boomers time in positions of authority in the FILMS[2] [P7] of society. On the bridge, they sailed us in the wrong direction. Our public discourse is full of terminology that lacks this primal need to understand the origins of human made powers, tyranny, and liberty. The public is further lacking an understanding of our differing subcultural socialization perspectives, and regional and settlement pattern subcultures.

That these two broadly defined socialization contexts and our ten regions differ, but not absolutely, is relevant to our work to heal our nation from doomerism. These differences cause friction, distrust, and doubt in often-opposite perspectives held by fellow citizens. How we should confront change and its consequential challenges in society needs less argument and more agreement. The baby doomers seem to lack the best-case orientation and quality statecraft diplomacy we need. Seeing traditionalism and modernism as a dichotomy on a continuum of how to think about the world may be instructive on how to begin the diplomacy. Diplomacy will help us walk toward a common understanding. We need to do this to begin to define the problems through the same lens. The lens must be one that calls attention to our need to align on the pursuit of virtue and one that looks for the right path to defend the Constitution and get to our desired end state, a more perfect union.

To make the point of the sometimes nuanced, but often outright differences between these opposing worldviews, let's see how they present themselves in a meaningful artifact of culture, architecture. Through a combination of artistry and industry powers, we create architecture. Architecture is cultural expression. Modernists and traditionalists generally prefer very different architectures. One seeks to shape the future. The other seeks to hold on to the past. We find irony in the physical and cultural landscape of our expressions in built form. Some like this variety and some do not. We must come to appreciate each of these for the quality of its expression. We can measure this quality by looking at them as a language of form and judge quality in the way they appear to speak their languages. If done well, we find that we can better understand their aesthetic, before we prejudge them.

Certainly, these two opposite aesthetics for architecture are not quite as bad as the extreme oppositions of matter and antimatter found in physics theory. Modernistic and traditionalistic architecture and socialization contexts are not equal and opposite charged particles that when they meet cause mutual annihilation. They are just sometimes less likely to mix into one, like oil and vinegar. Of course, olive oil and vinegar, like salt and pepper, combine well for a common purpose. They both make delicious salad dressing and seasoning. See, there is hope for the future. We can bring these two polar contexts, traditionalistic and modernistic, together by knowing their similarities and differences.

In moderating moderate manners, we find common core value sets and shared virtues within which to raise our children. We can begin with civics on the first principles of our country as benefiting each of us as persons and all of us as a citizenry. We can use ACE as our key bridge to build common purpose for the citizenry. Using our story as our truth, we can move through the postmodern world avoiding its undermining aspects while learning its good perceptibility. We can do so without the derogatory deconstruction of traditions and modern ambitions. We can develop positive postmodernistic perspectives. We do this by heightened experiential awareness. Informed by a diversity of exposures and experiences to differing others, solving human problems, we gain value. We produce promising prospects to build on positive associations of humane human wholeness rooted in practical factuality and not fanatical fantasy.

The pragmatic possibilities for us as persons and as a people need proclaimed. This is an aim for us to mature postmodernistic into "perceptopostmodernistic" socialization contexts. In these, we can train children on the positive attributes of a postmodern experience without needless nihilism. By improving perception of meanings in various experiences of living human lives, we can educate our people to be proactively prosocial. Through such a worthwhile education, we will resist the abstract nihilistically negative and skeptical side of postmodernism. Through perceptopostmodernistic socialization, we will avoid the cynicism of philosophical and artistic defeatism of postmodern society. By this, we will deter baby doomerism, by which we give in to these sad mental states that propel civility-expunging selfishness.

Nest the best in all the rest

Hope resides in our developing persons of a positive percept of postmodernistic social self: one that seeks to understand while withholding judgment until gaining a better base of knowledge. This posture allows us to hold two opposing ideas at one time, without the one voiding the other. Knowing that we create culture alone enables this capable capacity. This cognitive complexity comes from learning different social grammars. We get these by sharing life experience with others whose subcultures are different. This is the benefit of diversity. It long has fed our inventiveness. Having multiple social grammars helps us develop empathy. A postmodernistic self, possesses cognitive complexity and empathy. Both are vital characteristics that we'll need to adapt to the societal transformations we face now and into the foreseen future. (Hage, 2020).

Traditional contexts use mythology power to teach empathy. Modern contexts' heroic ambition to save the world by scientific method, examining evidence and putting large-scale programs in place, does not convey empathy. Many of its programs went badly for the everyday people. However, its reliance upon academy powers to train us has led to greater complexity of thought. In hindsight, we can see its errors and feel some regret for its failures, which brings us a bit of empathy. This supports the notion of its importance in a globally connected world of diverse human cultures.

Not quite pure Hegelian dialectic, we can see traditional ethics as a thesis and modern ethics as its antithesis. The postmodernistic self pulls the best from each, synthesizing the two into a new way of socializing. Fatalistic refuges forensically filtered from it place emphasis on teaching empathy and cognitive complexity. Developing perceptopostmodernistic selves solves the adaptive problems of traditionalistic and modernistic selves and improves the potentials of postmodernistic selves that can suffer from nihilism. The perceptopostmodernistic approach finds a moderating position between the poles of their socialization contexts' dichotomy. (Note, protopostmodernistic selves, postmodernistic selves, and our contemporaneous perceptopostmodernistic selves all share cores of postmodern attributes, described later). The cognitive complexity and mild empathy gained from mistakes of modernism add to the empathy gained from traditional contexts' faith-based empathetic beliefs. This mathematics of merging makes much more empathetic persons, apt to adapt well to a globalizing world of a planetary civilization of greater similarity than differences, when we train to see the similarities and not hate the differences. We can do this with perceptopostmodernistic socialization contexts. Such people will be more resilient. They will be better prepared to succeed at finding happiness in a more complex society in an interconnected world of often seemingly contrary customs as cultures commingle and collide. They will synthesize the extant unresolved and emergent complications of social crises, giving us an advantage over both the modernist and traditionalist coping mechanisms. As our USE charts its voyage into uncertain seas, with waves of new knowledge creation shifting our paradigms of understanding, we need persons with perceptopostmodernistic selves at the helm turning the wheel to keep us on course, pushing buttons and pulling the levers in correct and proper proportions for providing societal and social powers equilibrium. With our current crew, our ship is unready for the voyage ahead. The baby doomers in command of our bridge, operating our propulsion equipment in our engine room, and getting gung ho in the gunnery are not the right crew. They bring and possess a misguided arsenal of outmoded skills with the wrong weapons to defend liberty.

We need to reflect to develop the reflexes necessary to change out the crew willingly. The next generations are more closely gaining perceptopostmodernistic selves. They are the most educated and exposed to different others of our living generations. The best and brightest among them, with proper coaching and good mentors, will be our best crew. With a proper ACE and training in drawing upon perceptions for creating practical prospects for prosperity by applying a self-guiding education in experientialism, they will restore our ship and sail it, or motor it as necessary, on its purposeful journey, achieving the elusive goal of our union as one people under God with liberty and justice for all. With them, we'll fly our starry Jack proudly once again as a representation of the prima facie ideals we desire it to represent. We can restore this for our venture and not allow its destruction by reminders of the broken promises and social failures in our history. With the next generations at the helm, we'll reconnect the deeper purposes of our venture to our actions. Once again, our actions will speak for us. We'll not let superficial arguments of errors taint our great message. We, the everyday people, can and should self-govern! We can lead society to the best possible destiny for each of us within it, without losing sight of the victory we pursue up ahead. We'll recover from the misguided ways, means, and methods of baby doomers.

We do not need a plutocracy of aristocrats to tell us what to think and then say that we should shut up and be happy they gave us their cake's crumbs. Ours is a victory over all human history, the victory of a more perfect union in republic with democracy. We will again prove, as was done in the 18th century that united common persons can be one people, e pluribus unum, and put in charge of leading the business of society. When done in earnest, a more prosperous and increasingly peaceful world began to take hold. Prodigious progress morally and materially rose from the miracle of liberty's victory. We cannot allow our material successes spoiling of us with comfort and convenience to shroud itself in fallacies and cruelties. Rather, we must learn from our history never again to repeat previously tolerated social abominations. We must not allow again any nefarious political and economic atrocities. By reading history of our nation's lapses from its principles, we should gain perspective to guide us forward. We must imbue in ourselves a fresh reverence of the relevance and vitality of our founding principles (Will 2020). We must seek to live them perceptively as our truth, our creed, our identity in a citizen-first mode. In doing so, we will make our USE a symbol for all humankind to unify as a baby-loving, lifesaving, planet-compatible, cooperative race.

Learning to survive

To lead once more, we, the everyday people, must reflect. We cannot simply sit on our laurels and think we are the greatest as the baby boomers did. We need to identify our socialization contexts, regional subcultural preferences, and settlement patterns for viewing the world at large. We need to imagine our society's place within the globally interconnected world. We need to bring our vision to the polity and economy power

FILMS[2][P7] and enact it from our positions within them. We must figure out how to develop our perspectives to accommodate the changes to which we must adapt. In doing so, we'll focus our USE on its purpose to IDEALS liberty. We'll do it in our self-improvement and future readiness work as humans. We'll do it as we contribute to society via our KA^4SA^2. We'll do it in the FILMS[2][P7] positions we'll hold in the polity and as the HM^5 in the economy. We'll do it better than the boomers did because we'll all engage in properly balancing the societal powers for the apt LAMBS with purpose to make it better for the citizenry. We'll do it through the proper $AEIOUY^2K$ of all the social powers. We'll expand performance to lift us all into better social circumstances and humane material conditions. We'll redefine quality of life. It is not an increasingly competitive accumulation of objects. That is doomeristic, since it never creates happiness. Hoarding does not accomplish the pursuit of happiness. Such a mythology dooms the planet and us to the tyranny of wanting. Our culture of democracy created and endowed us to steward a society for our survival, living, and thriving. Having fame and fortune, which can be hollow, is not the definition of thriving. We thrive in happiness when we have dignified work to perform and a solid means of making a living. We thrive in happiness by having truthful, sincere, human-to-human experience connectedness, through loving and feeling loved, and by being appreciated socially for our contributions to the groups to which we belong and the larger community. We thrive on the wholesome local stages of neighborhoods as we celebrate family and community powers' importance to self and society.

We gain shared value through our hometown living, as with Independence Day parades. The international charades of celebrities are not meaningful to the practical reality we live. They are escapist illusions sold to us by often-perverted profiteers. Their persistent pharisaic pleasure pushing propagates a parasitic game with us. They grift for our attention, which they sell for massive money accumulation. Rather than enrich them, we ought to admire our own local achievements, as these are more meaningful to us than their global competitiveness and game playing. We should concentrate on how we can entrepreneur betterments for others near us through building up the commonweal and generating wealth in and for our neighborhoods. We should not get seduced into sitting stupefied in worship of entertainment as an ultimate achievement of humankind, which appears to be a particularly popular pastime of baby boomers. We must be the heroes of our own lives!

We need to be more aware of ourselves. We all need to reflect our raising, the values given us to believe in. Are we pursuing virtue? Is this our value? The hyper-connected digital age has so infused our lives with computational and communicative technologies, at every level of society, that practically every aspect of our private and public lives transmits to others through digital products, services, and platforms. This harbors huge psychological and sociological risks for us as persons and as a people. We can no longer tell if our tools are helping or hurting us. We can no longer tell if the machines we made are in control of us, or we of them. Our daily experiences, our existence in fact, is now so highly integrated with alienating high technology that it harms us. It devastates our children's psychological well-being. This is happening globally at a scale we can hardly comprehend. We need to take stock and recognize how these technologies exploit our vulnerabilities and expose us to never-before-seen risks to the stability of persons and society.

These technologies arose with the boomers at the helm. Powerful monopolies developed. Previous generations saw the risks of monopolization and addressed them. President Teddy Roosevelt enforced antitrust laws to prevent the dangers of monopolistic tyranny. The boomers did not. These destructive to persons and a people in society, unregulated, powerful, hyper-fast, and furiously complex technologies are not being administered or managed well for us. They are leading us around gullibly. We are turning ugly by using them. This is un-American of us! We are supposed to unite, not divide. Raw power divides a people infected by doomerism. Just because we humans made new tools does not mean they are well suited for us. As the moral edict goes, "just because we can" does not mean, "we should". Thus, we should not become addicts to social media too readily. We must ask if they help the preservation of our democracy, the conservation of our republic, and the protection of our liberty, or not. If they do not, they are not worthy tools. Evidence is mounting. These computational communication technologies are real dangers to our stability. Like Pandora's Box, we let out the worst in us. This is why we as a people must bring the next generations into power, with a luminous looking glass of ACE based wisdom guiding them. We must get our new tools under control and use them more purposefully to IDEALS our American made liberty.

If we do not, the propagators of these technologies could doom our very existence by amplifying our own aggression and causing us to turn it against one another. In the mythology of Abraham, the tricky evildoer Satan promised to destroy the children of God who got free will. If our character is not good, we subject ourselves to proving this parable true. Being that democracy requires an honest citizenry, as its protagonists, we are in grave danger of falling into this trap of self-destruction. It's allegorically the devil, our worst instincts, overwhelming the best intentions of our intellect.

Nowadays, few things affect our lives as much as the technologies we create from knew knowledge (Volti, 1988). Clearly, we need to better assess the societal and social risks of these new technologies causing errors in our judgment. Sadly, the boomers seem not to bother themselves with such difficulties as managing the consequences of mistakes. It cuts against the grain of their egos' thinking "I'm great!" (*Can you hear Tony the Tiger of Kellogg's proclaiming in an advertisement for highly sugared Frosted Flakes "They're great!"? Per-*

haps in taste, but flavor is a single sense, a one-dimensional success. We need multidi-mensional naturally nutritious, not artificial additive, successes.) We need to agree on what pace of advance our species can handle. Before we wreck our homes, our workplaces, our very special lives, and our children's very precious lives, we need to stop, think, ask, and decide what is best for us in our communities, and in an American society. We must address the fact that we have yet to comprehend fully the impact of machines learning by algorithms written from big data analyzing and compressing, computational and communication technologies. Our future development as persons and as a people depends on us learning more about it. We need more academy power to deal with it. We need to prepare ourselves for a future in which more industry power creates increasingly complex digitization. The transfer of control over our lives will continue. The work of the HM[5] to develop more capably predictive of our behaviors computational algorithmic software calculation capacity will occur. These software programs appear to make intelligent decisions. Yet artificial machines poorly programmed and miscalculating exposes us to many negative risks. Reciprocally, we too should estimate the positive opportunity risks to take. The powerful new information management tools can help us learn about ourselves as we enjoy the safety that efficiency brings. We must do so with a well-reasoned strategy. One that keeps these potent tools checked and balanced against our purposeful pursuit of a more perfect union. New information computation and communication technologies need a better evaluation of how they help or harm us. As a result, we cannot allow our children and ourselves to suffer because of them. We need more knowledge in advance of launching new technologies before bad actors hack into us and tell us what to do (Harari, 2019). As we see, new technologies reshape our society with many social consequences (Eitzen & Zinn, 1989).

We must do the ethical calculations and face the moral dilemmas, deciding as a people what we will allow. We must discuss the pace of innovation. In some areas, like social problems, we need more and faster innovation. In others, we need not to be in such a hurry. We need to learn without feeling fleeced of our futures and left behind. We need to stop the fraud by a few sharks that make out like bandits in the night. We need the polity to prepare possibilities for prosperity for our posterity, without massive vulnerabilities that expose our society to the most oppositional risk to our culture, negative tyranny. Democracy is positive. If we do not rediscover its proper attitude, the blessings of liberty, we are doomed. Doomerism will drag us down daily into the depressing levels portrayed in Dante's *Inferno*. In the 14th century, he described the misdeeds of his times. They are the same in our day. With doomerism, they're amplified and celebrated. During the baby boomers' generational dominance of the USE, we've seen many superbly capable wrongdoers. Dante referred to them as panderers, seducers, flatterers, Simoniacs [bribers], fortune-tellers and diviners, grafters [grifters], hypocrites, thieves, evil counselors, sowers of discord, and falsifiers (Aligieiri & Diardi, 1954). Human nature has not evolved genetically, but socially with each generation, we make societies that are more complex and capable with increasingly sophisticated tools.

We need something to hold on to as we advance. We need a shared, common, core belief. We have one in the founders' vision. Under the thumb of British tyranny, they found truth in liberty. Its heartbeat's murmur whispers wisdom into our ears. We must confidently choose to listen to it. Liberty is the gift around which we must unite. It can help us to hold together as we move into the future. We will still find ourselves with challenges to our virtue by the vices of our instincts. Yet through E-SASSY-T-TUF-FT-CAUCUS, we will survive, live, and thrive, one people under God, with liberty and justice for all. We must do this for our posterity, our babies. We will depend upon them to keep our great ship sailing toward its goal, with the lights on for humanity to follow our lead. We, the everyday people, must learn to lead again. We must do better to self-educate and not self-medicate. We must rise up to the challenges with freethinking and bravery. We must think critically not free-willingly. We must ground our suspicions in doubt and question authority, using reason and critical thought to dissect it and dissent if it threatens liberty. Well-coached and mentored younger generations will get us back on the right path, the path upon which we will not be disgraced, the path that leads us not to wrong doing but to soulfully fulfilling wholesome harmonious happiness that comes only by doing right, as gets done when living virtuously in humility with gratitude.

Most children raised by the internet of things, which threatens the family's power to transfer the values of tradition and causes tensions that need addressed by the other human social and cultural powers, are confused and made manipulatable by it. It is wrong that a family cannot raise its children, as they would like because of the pervasive propaganda of media. It is more difficult to hold onto and not let go of outmoded ways of thinking. Yet not all family values are outmoded, and to have one's house invaded by an on-slaught of aberrant values is very difficult to combat. So should we not be more careful of social media and cautious of a digitally dominated future? We see how it is addictive. Addictions are typically bad for us. Its power, a combination of industry and artistry powers, touches our biology power as it connects us to networks of people with community power, from which we gain excitement by getting likes, causing dopamine releases in our brains. This affects us biologically. Our brains and bodies, the psychology of the mind, alter in response to perceived social realities of our behaviors online within digital communications platforms. Our family and community relations are impacted. Not protecting children from its dangers in the way we protect them against others is an adaptive social problem. We must address it in the societal powers: people, polity, and economy. Allowing addictions to electronic screens, with their basic primal instinct stimulating moths to flame and consequent time warps and anxieties of dislikes by followers, is a serious social matter. Why is it not better regulated by the boomers who are the dominant HM[5] position holders in the FILMS[2] [P7]? Seeing how it goes before deciding what to do, so as to not offend anyone or stop profits from it, has led to new conditions of psychosis that have a long-term effect on mental health. Is this a step toward turning people into dependents on a subsystem of the powers of society? Is this devolution, not evolution? Are we not human? Is this something the baby doomers in power want? Do they want to reduce the future generations' capability, capacity, and access to rise up and be in power? Are they so corrupted they think tyrannically, unwilling to transfer power peaceably to the next generation? Do they fear being without the power and positions, they occupy in society? Is it possible we've already allowed mutation? We must rapidly learn how to protect ourselves from the negative risks while benefiting from the positive risks of new technologies. This means less blindness to what is happening is required of us. This means we must better educate and stay informed, think for ourselves, and demand more from our fellow citizens in the polity, our economy, and ourselves. Have we forgotten to be human and protect children? We ought to have more of a voice in our society than we have by allowing a few inventors' gadgets to take control and create a new world order with a plutocracy of technologists and a handful of their in-pocket politicians in charge. Our children are being hurt! We must stop this from happening further.

Our Development and Secondary Powers

The reversal of national fortunes begins with a loss of personal and family power. The good news is that many families are socializing children to possess the necessary traits of better future citizens possessing cognitive complexity and empathy, the qualities of postmodernistic selves (Hage, 2020). Persons, who get raised in protopostmodernistic, postmodernistic, and perceptopostmodern socialization contexts in our society, as many in the millennial and generation Z (Gen Z) were, when combined with the immediately preceding (Gen X or 13rs) and succeeding generations, are now the majority of voters. Many in the younger generations possess the futuristically beneficial traits of civic-mindedness with many raised in, or raising children in, more than one social grammar. Something globalization and the Internet make possible more easily. This perspective prepares the millennial and subsequent generations to do a better job for the whole of society than the boomers did. They are of age and should assume positions of authority within our society. We can have hope doomerism will be defeated and the journey toward full Americanism (intended ideals of founding achieved for real) will be a restored purpose in our society.

Community power teaches culture and encultures children to sustain it as a need of the community. It uses peer pressure for ensuring conformity to the norms, mores, values, beliefs, folkways, and customs of the particular subculture. Community forms by these as well. Some communities don't engage in transferring the larger culture of democracy. This is due to several circumstances of history that have produced varying kinds of socialization contexts, the big four being traditionalistic, modernistic, anomic, and postmodernistic, (which includes all three types: proto-, mean/median/modal, and percept-. Why identify three kinds of postmodernism? Because of nuances introduced by adaptations in child rearing, parenting, and neighborhood support in raising kids that the near exponential technological change in our daily lives required across the turbulent periods of us forming, storming, and norming to the societal transformations of postmodernism, which are the consequents of the third stage of knowledge evolution).

Socialization is the process that influences a person's perspectives on their place and position in society. It involves education at home, at school, in neighborhoods, and through community networks of friends and associates with whom one belongs and participates. The academy power's delivery of vital capabilities for the KA^4SA^2 depends on its content and format and the treatment, attitudinally and behaviorally, by parents and providers of children born to other persons, as well as educators and healthcare training and approaches. Such contexts of families, neighborhoods, and communities, the institutions established by the polity or economy powers to educate, the schools, need significant investment if they are to be capable of delivering suitable education for the high knowledge-demanding and technologically intricate future we face.

If socialization has at its core an education toward democracy, it is healthy for the republic. If it's toward authority of the community over the person's unique needs, it is toward authoritarianism. This is unhealthy for the republic because it is a threat to a person's liberty to be free to pursue a life lived virtuously. Conformity to a life lived by, for, and of liberty is the purpose of democracy. It is how humanity finds "sin-free" happiness.

(Sin = that which damages the wholesome well-being of a person in their own conscience by wrongful doing. As a social construct, it encourages better living in a manner that reduces deep hurting. Its countervailing teachings tell us avoid the temptation of allowing sins to guide us. Sins cast crimes against one's self, one's innocent and beautiful belonging in a living being for experiencing life in the direction of one's intended purpose, to bring joy to the world. Sadly, sin by self and others can curb the will to joy.)

Figure 2-30 below presents a way to map socialization and geographic influences on self-development. Mapping these is an activity that can help us mitigate risks of misunderstanding one another. Understanding one another among our citizenry can remove insider-outsider, "us vs. them", distrustfulness of each other's commitment to the USE's success.

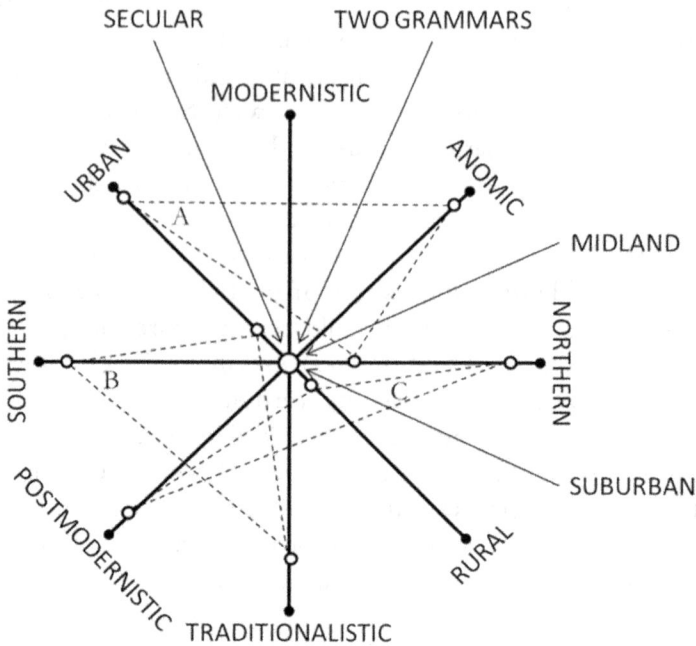

Examples of Person Mapping

A = inner city, in poverty, in Maryland

B = in suburbia near city center, in religious community, in Mississippi

C = in suburbs nearer farms than city center, in integrated community, in New York

Figure 2-30: Mapping Selves
Identify self by social geography. Pick: 1) location by subculture region, 2) location by housing/socialization context of family or socialization characteristics of neighborhood, and 3) location by urbanity, suburbanity, or rurality. Note the reality of the great diversity of perspectives socialized in us to hold. To unify, we must not only be tolerant of differences but curious about them. This takes courage. We are the land of the free and the brave. Get used to it and embrace it. This is what we expect Americans to do, unite across subcultural social boundaries and borders. We must venture across the social misunderstandings that separate us, or suffer a division into two social classes, the few who have everything and the majority with nothing.

Ancient polities run by mythology powers set behavioral controls, which needed rapid replenishment of the population due to losses to wars and diseases and lower life expectancy. We see today a risk in overpopulation. Certain archaic values no longer apply as they once did. Adaptation drives many cultural innovations in society. We need to sort out our customs and values and determine which ones we can move forward with and which ones we may leave behind. If we cannot slow the many social changes to a humane pace, we will need to stop the enforcement of values that are unhelpful and unhealthy to liberty. If we are to pursue happiness, we need not to trip ourselves up on controlling values that do not benefit our future needs as a species.

Joy is a form of happiness obtained from experience with virtuous ideas, attitudes, and behaviors that enable its presence in one's mind. Joy is most possible in a society formulated to IDEALS liberty for each-and-every one of its members. By being good citizens, we can all help each other confirm our belief in the inalienable rights of human beings. Yes, this takes work. It takes personal courage and commitment to fight demons within, demons that encourage sinfulness. In deist traditions, the mythology power is a means by which we can pursue a perfection of the self. To perfect the self is the effort of a citizen. To have a more perfect union, a polity for a society for liberty, requires people to daily pursue becoming better citizens, plain and simple. Multiple factions, the powers of society, principal and secondary, will seek to pull persons toward various interpretations of how to see the world—to hoard more power onto their pole!

This book proposes that not by faction but by self-critical thinking upon the operations of power within society is how a person may remain free to self-govern, and the accumulated reason of the people shapes the society to guarantee freedom for an honest citizenry. This comes with a need to know what is meant by liberty and how as a social being to understand it. Done in concert with others it must. If all know well the intentions of the Constitution, the true meaning of liberty and the proper utilization of the republic as the polity to IDEALS it, then the everyday people will have liberty in a fulfilling culture of democracy. This makes a country a great place to live, and it yields domestic tranquility, defensive protection against enemies (foreign and domestic), and promotion of the general welfare because all possess the beneficial attitudes and enact the best behaviors of good citizens, fully aware of what this really means, not superficially convincing themselves that they fit the bill. Labels do not define us. What does define a good citizen is strong character in accord with the pursuit of liberty. A good citizen's actions demonstrate such to others, and others will identify the person as a citizen, as a good person worthy of knowing and following in their example (unless under the spell of doomerism). To want to be a citizen is to act like a citizen. To be a citizen is to be a champion for liberty, a practitioner knowledgeable in the culture of democracy. As more become this way, citizenshipping with liberty will surge in popularity. Being true—as it must be by virtue of itself from this micro-level activity by each person, such good behaviors will present within the meso-level, and in turn will reflect positively as this society's proper way of being at the macro level. Each one of us has a responsibility to build back civility within our families, our neighborhoods, our communities, and ourselves all across the nation. We all perform roles with others as we make our way through the social milieu society puts before us. One method to develop civility with those who think at an opposite pole politically is to employ the People-Over-Politics Action Plan. This employs objective science-based evidence and conversational techniques to put people above politics. Get mentally above emotions. Restore relationships. Don't let them get sacrificed because of disagreements and political posturing (Levy R. H., 2020).

Mercantile socialization

Regardless of the socialization context one experiences in our society, some overarching perceptions pervade all of them. The mercantile nature of material consumerism shapes a predominant one. The bombardment of advertising presses perspectives into a person's purpose in life, which is to shop for the sake of shopping as a means to pursue happiness. Madison Avenue was instrumental in creating the advertising that causes this effect (Ewing, 1976). Material consumerism and its pressures to compete for objects as social status indicators falsely create a subtext that the amount of goods a person has accumulated is a worthiness metric, and a measure of worth. Consumerism leads us to different outcomes, ones of less cooperation and more competition over material objects. We consume, but we need not become the consumed; consumption is not the purpose of living. Living virtuously, becoming whom we feel meant to become, a gift to our family, neighborhood, community, and society, is our purpose. Correcting preoccupation with conspicuous consumption as purpose, and calibrating our orientation to focus on being a citizen first, as a people, before we go into the economy to exchange objects, will help us regain control of the polity and prevent it from controlling us, the people.

The present power pursuing politicians will side with the economy elites, who seek to support one another as a ruling class. This error occurs because "we the everyday people" failed to take the necessary and effective actions of using our people power to regulate the polity to prevent the economy from controlling it for its elites' benefit. My, my, how dangerously duped by the manipulations of the baby doomers are we. We too easily allowed secondary societal powers to construe their FILMS[2] [P7] by not concentrating on our psychological and social moral development in a manner best for our personal liberty and prosperity. This victory would be guaranteed by all of us being better citizens, intentionally practicing good citizenshipping every day, in every way, and everywhere we may roam as a "we first" united citizenry. We, the everyday people, for whom this nation exists, wrought out of the jaws of depravity within the mouth of tyranny, must reclaim our birthright to govern it.

Secondary societal powers

Academy power conveys and creates knowledge. Its primary concern is our KA^4SA^2. It increases our ability to think about what we know, how we know it, and how we can use our knowledge. It is that which provides for our learning, and it houses a key force, science. The scientific inquiry seeks to orient us toward facts. It focuses on evidence to define truth, reality, things, and events that the history power has journaled. It chronicles and tells, explores what is "out there," is objective, provides explanations, and gives proof. But it may be vulnerable to the risk of being too positivist or deterministic. Because science is not perfect, nor final, we must remind ourselves it is a means of adaptation.

Our species adapts. It is a beneficial process for us in pursuit of our survival, personally and societally. The academy power is one of our most necessary powers in a democracy. We must $AEIOUY^2K$ it to be knowledgeable about our self-interests and the interests of our families and communities in the arrangement of all the powers of our culture of democracy for our own liberty. We all want our freedom. How can we get it without taking it away from any other persons? Save the deranged person, for whom we must provide assistance that respects their human rights and dignity, unless they are criminally violent. And if they are, then we need to determine what caused such behavior and determine whether it can be corrected and reformed, so they might yet become a positive community member. If we can teach them and heal them, then the polity power need not take control of them and us pay for it. Community-based solutions with, of, and by the people closest to the problems, are the most successful because they are correct in a culture of democracy. The academy power is how we figure out, understand our planet, our society, and ourselves and get the KA^4SA^2 to perform better our duties of the LAMBS on behalf of our enterprise by each one of us.

Mythology power conveys the sacred. It provides spiritual beliefs, tales to explain life and living, rites, an ethos, pathos, logos, and kairos, a worldview, and meaningful symbols for believers. Most persons gain faith opportunities from family and community powers, although some academy powers overlap with mythology powers, such as in the field of theology. Others gain faith through a conversion experience. For many, the mythology power is very personal and intense, deeply rooted, and interconnected to one's identity. It is within and it is without; it is substantive, functional, and symbolic. For some, it comes with magic and certainly mystery. Because sacred holy beliefs are so personal, a person's liberty depends on having the freedom to believe as they choose. In cases where community power uses mythology dominantly, it can become oppressive. When it becomes a determiner of insiders and outsiders, it endangers liberty. Liberty needs the tolerance and awareness that all the world's religions actually are very similar in asking their believers to seek, albeit by differing paths, a state of spiritual enlightenment, which is ultimately human belief in what are generally universal truths of life and living with one another (Moses, 1989). Excessive mythology power leads to unnecessary arguments and prejudice in our USE. Narrowmindedness to protect a belief system can be toxic. We in our plurality must seek the common shared principles of each of our faiths as a means to unify in concert with our Constitution's goal and objectives.

Artistry is the power that conveys the expressive creativity of human imagination. It provides sensory joy and stimulates our emotions and thoughts. Often paired with industry power in the process of making beautiful tools or objects for inspiration and adoration, artistry exerts many forces. Artistry power is concerned with beauty, symbols, feelings, and meanings, and it often overlaps with mythology power. It is subjective, needs interpretation, yields insights, and gives us feelings of freedom. It can be very personal and communal, sometimes both at the same time. Many believe life would not be worth living without it. It finds its way into many artifacts of culture—food, clothing, and architecture.

Terminology Confusion

Connotations by politicians, often by error and sometimes by intention, have changed the denotations of terms used by them and by history power pundits, newsreaders, and broadcasters. This confused the understanding of what these concepts truly mean, which led to a politics of symbolic interactions devoid of grounding in truths or facts. Thus, politics today are full of misunderstandings. Have a look at Figure 2-31.

Thinking about it, here is a first note to consider. The "big C" Conservative would be someone who seeks to defend and promote the founding framers' vision and Constitution, to conserve the ideals of its making. However, some who call themselves conservatives are actually "little c" conservatives who are more interested in preserving traditions that may not actually defend or promote liberty for the people, nor defend or promote a posture of democracy in society. These kinds of conservatives might simply be interested in preventing change because in their minds change is seen as too risky. Change causes disruptions in the status quo. Some people simply do not want that to happen. They will accept change at a pace they feel is natural or when forced to confront risks to survival. But because ours is an imperfect union, and our goal is a more perfect one, tensions arise for "little c" conservatives when the people want to promote change to advance on objectives more quickly than the status quo keepers want to be pushed. They've little tolerance for change they feel is unnecessary. For "big C" Conservatives, what is most vital is the progress in the advancement of liberty and democracy. What matters most to liberty is a defense of the person—their personage, personhood, and personality. This posture belongs to a true American Conservative, one who wants the Constitution's goal and objectives conserved and met more quickly than realized to date.

Here is a second note about it. "Big L" Liberal is a belief that people can self-govern, and that a culture of democracy is best for a people to practice, so they may have liberty. It differs from "big C" Conservative in that it came first. There would be no big Cs if there were no big Ls. The C defends the L. The L defines what the C seeks to maintain. The big "L" Liberal would be someone who believes in the inalienable natural human rights of a person to be free. They defend and promote the founding framers' vision and Constitution. But some who call themselves liberals, "little l" liberals, are more interested in using the polity to oversee society in a way that takes responsibility away from the people.

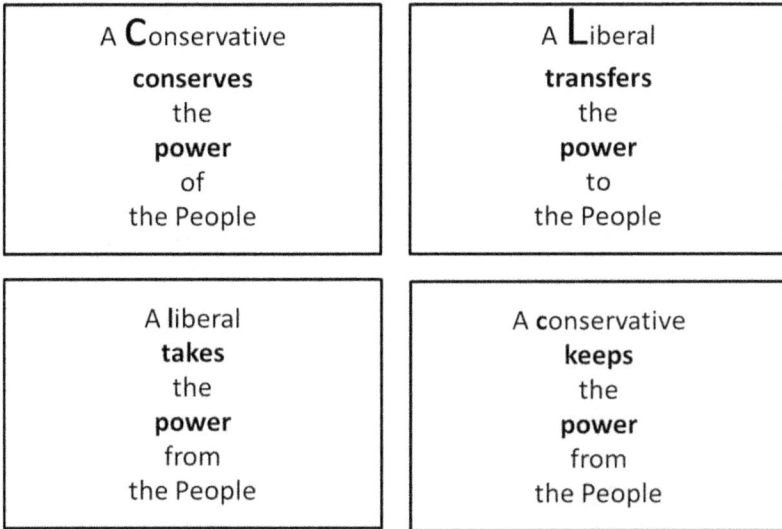

A **C**onservative **conserves** the **power** of the People	A **L**iberal **transfers** the **power** to the People
A liberal **takes** the **power** from the People	A conservative **keeps** the **power** from the People

Figure 2-31: Confusion of Terminology Used by Media Broadcasters Today
Interpretative Notes: Firstly, remember, in the capital "big L" Liberal sense, a Liberal posture means that there can be a government of, for, and by the people, which is a democracy-based republic. A capital "big C" Conservative posture contends the people will want to, intend and attend to it, "conserve" this Liberal state of government. This is essential to understand because the labels the media misuse actually misguide by its use of the term "liberal". Anyone who disagrees that talents are by nature unequally distributed, and feels that those of greater talent and harder work ethic ought not to advance or those others of less talent and effort should get the same economic rewards, because of equality of outcome wishes, which is an administrative ambition, is prone to be labeled a "little l" liberal. When "little c" conservatives in the media use it this way, they also refer to themselves as so-called "conservatives", but they do not represent Liberalism in its truest sense. Rather they represent the status quo of a power structure that comes from history. One that sees the historical ordering of humankind into separate castes, persons grouped in social-economic classes of status and material wealth as normative and acceptable in the human condition and in human societies. Anyone wanting to be an elitist aristocrat is a little "c" conservative. Anyone wanting to be on equal footing with everyone else politically is a big "L" Liberal. This label preserves the intents of American society, as does big "C" Conservative, conserve it. We are to be "Conservative" "Liberals" not the opposing "liberal" "conservatives" if we are to be patriots for the project that makes a more perfect union and life through lives lived according to the Preamble real.

These kinds of liberals might simply be interested in promoting change because in their minds change is seen as necessary progress. Change causes disruptions in the status quo. Some people simply want that to happen, to force sudden changes all the time. However, because ours is an imperfect union, and our goal is a more perfect one, tensions arise for "little l" liberals when the people resist change that is pushed upon them too quickly to be tolerated. For "big L" Liberals, what is most vital is the progress in the advancement of liberty and democracy. What matters most to us is a defense of the person—their personage, personhood, and personality. This is the posture of a true American Liberal, whom a true American Conservative allies with and defends.

Effects on understanding primary powers' roles

Misusage of Figure 2-31's terms negatively effects citizen's understanding of the LAMBS in the USE. Here's how. Sad, incompetent, or negligent misinterpretation of what a "conservative" actually is, can lead to a support of isms bad for liberty, democracy, and persons (as aggregated, a people) such as authoritarianism, despotism, absolutism, and totalitarianism. If in consideration of rank and privilege, being of less stature than those in control of primary powers in society is commonplace, these isms prevail. If then the common human (the commoners, the everyday citizen, those of us who need an effective commons administered well for us by the polity), is ignored, then these bad isms of the rich and powerful get used to control the "masses". Consequently, liberty will fail. To get a good commons, we must hold our politicians accountable. The commons needs efficient, well-managed marketplaces for us to get our necessities. We must make good choices and not be overtly seduced by its offerings, which would cause financial risks to our capacity and capability to sustain our independence from being controlled by primary or secondary powers. We must defend the liberty of our mind and body from the pressures of marketplace merchants selling seductions and sedition against the polity because it failed to disable exploitation. We cannot allow the polity to become beholden to the economy as its ruler. It is supposed to obey us by electoral control. If we fail, we lose. Remember, a "big C" Conservative lives to IDEALS liberty in the LAMBS for the future generations' prosperity in the USE.

It is a sad, incompetent, or negligent use of the word "liberal" as a will to transfer power from the people to the polity. To guarantee security in the economy by controlling it is not helpful for liberty. It grants those not participating in the making of tools (except by their contracting of weapons for war, since warriors work for the polity) and provision of goods and services for the people the authority to tell the economy power what to do for the people. The polity should not command the economy. This arrangement removes the economy power from the management role, and the people power's responsibility, which is leadership of the business of society by micro, meso, and macro actions each of us performs in our roles to the whole.

The people, by regulating the polity for good rules, by good behavior, and by reasonable choices in the marketplace, shape the economy power. The choices of what we seek to exchange in fluid and dynamic marketplaces, both as buyers and sellers, by the synergies of millions of decisions and transactions allow it to be efficient in its contributions to society. As we perform our roles within or interface with the economy powers' HM^5 and its FILMS^2 [P7], to manage the provision of goods and services that help promote the general welfare under limited rules over it to ensure domestic tranquility, we must behave with honesty and integrity, and that important forgotten social trait, honor.

One weakness in the economy power is the labor markets. The solution for consistency in labor market management remains elusive. In part, this is because on the polity administers the KA^{4}SA^2, which is encumbered by hordes of stakeholders in several layers, without free-flowing rapid financing available. This reality creates a lag between the kinds of workers needed and the kinds of workers provided. If industry power's FILMS^2 [P7] invested more in KA^{4}SA^2, we could close the gap. However, if taxes do not pay for an adequate supply of labor prepared to work with the appropriate skills gained by an educational system administered by the polity, poor labor market performance will continue (Hage, 2020). The holders of economy power would benefit by more investments in enabling more rapid development of labor. We need less hoarding and more helping the future hands of the HM^5 get the requisite education and skills training so our workforce can sustain our communities' productive competitiveness to ensure the economy powers succeed for everyone. So don't let misuse of terms confuse how the primary powers operate in the American context in which a "big L" Liberal lives to IDEALS liberty in the LAMBS for the future generations' prosperity in the USE, and to conserve this is what a big "C" Conservative lives to do.

Be aware to beware the power of power

Since ancient times within our species' societies, hypocrisy has existed in persons, peoples, and the politicians of the polity. The source is often the control of others, being able to AEIOUY^{2}K or DAMN power for the raw pleasure of dominating others. This is the sensation of power—the power of power—that grants a sense of superiority and security. Authorities feeling amped up in this way, by having it, and being "in power" introduces risks in societies with a democracy-based culture. Power is a primal stimulant. The pleasure of it extends to basic decision-making, charged up from our animal instinct that as a primate favors a big, mean, dominant male (Wright, 1994). Democracy requires we use reason to overcome this instinct, yet we also allow for meritorious advancement of those superb citizens whose qualities in higher authority will benefit society and thus all of us. The risk we face at micro, meso, and macro levels is the forgetting of reason as essential, and allowing emotional and instinctive reactions will promote those pursuing raw power and not those who pursue merit promotion based upon superior skills of better KA^{4}SA^2. Our fellow citizens who seek higher positions in our social hierarchies to do good things, as a form of their will to perform leadership functions by E-SASSY-T-TUF-FT-CAUCUS ought to receive commendation and respect, but also constructive criticism to prevent arrogant hubris growing within them. Helping our neighbors in this way curtails the risks to ego power posing. Moreover, it reminds them of their sacred public trust that authority in a democracy requires they properly $AEIOUY^2K$ power.

The structuring of the culturally made forms of power into subordinate powers and their $FILMS^{2\ [P7]}$ makes societal powers real in their impact on people. Persons given authority through positions within these power bases need not allow the positional power to go to their heads, as if it is their personal power. They are playing a role for us, for society, and we must understand this when we are in positions of authority. We must be cognizant of our role's scope and scale and not allow it to inflate our egos and puff up our pride when our egos feel threatened due to our perceived poor performance. We are human beings, not Diodon antennatus (porcupine pufferfish). If we have proper leadership within us, as we the people must, we reduce this risk of such foolish behavior as conceit inspires in us.

Let's return for a moment to the concept of mapping dichotomies to help us understand polemics (recall Figure 2-25 and 2-30). This technique is a tool we can use to help us discuss how to make a good society. Using it to move our project forward toward its goal, let's take a look at Figure 2-32. In it, Figure 2-31's definitions are at the poles of two lines of thought: politics and authority. The other two dichotomies are trust and agency. Two arcs ascribe traditionalistic and modernistic socialization contexts, value sets across them. Along these four lines come arguments over what is good for society and how the $FILMS^{2\ [P7]}$ become what they do in shaping it.

For positions making the policies of the LAMBS, the politicians, pundits, and publics, (people self-separating from one another based upon an ideology, or dogma), power tends to corrupt. Corruption leads to unethical thinking that does not comport to the necessary or expected work needing done to IDEALS liberty. Persons holding positions of authority face challenges with illogical and irrational thought caused by the corrupting forces of ego inflation and other fallacious conditions that result from holding power without understanding its dangers. There are unknown, deep-seated, emotive issues not yet cognate, buried in absurd propositions. Fantasies of one's self-inflated importance lead to a need for adoration, more than is helpful to the prosecution of their duties. There are many inaccuracies in ideologies not extracted logically from principles that hold up to the risks of accretion and accumulation of feelings-driven thinking. Unclear thinking confuses facts and undermines real empathy because it leads to only feeling and not thinking. From such a romantic posture, many abuses can happen by the manipulation of emotions, as we know from an understanding of fallacy in rhetoric. As stated earlier we must recognize logical fallacies employment by persuaders of other than American ideals pursuits.

Perhaps the loss of the true meaning of "big L" and "big C" and their "little c" and "little l" contortions that are somewhat reversed in usage are the result of accreted connotations by confusions of correlations as causes. It is possible that politicians did this on purpose to push an agenda on the public via their pundits and thereby caused unintended consequences to the posture of liberty and democracy.

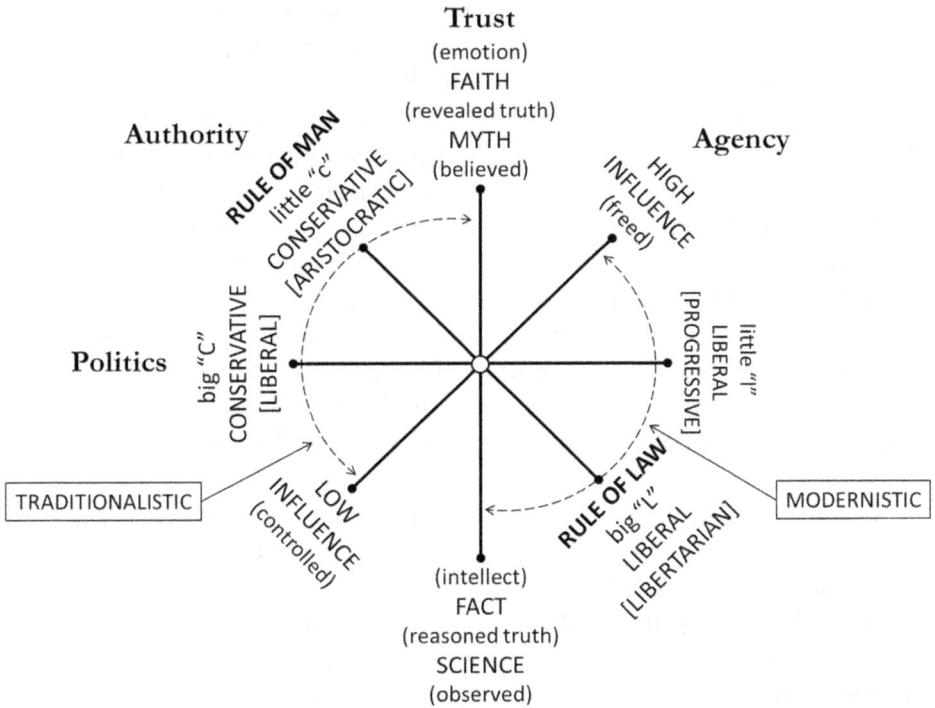

Figure 2-32: Societal Relations Perspectives on a Dichotomy Wheel with Socialization Arcs
What to think, how to behave, and lessons on the meaning and purpose of life are cultural values on societal relations of the powers, passed down through socialization.

These once-healthy, proud, inspiring principles slump over, weakened by errors passed down in comprehending them, as is evident by the changed connotations of conservative and liberal. Once put in place, this fork in the minds of the people causes a growing apart of perspectives, coercing deep cleavages between us. When we come to believe we are incompatible then we seek protection in thoughts for our existence as separate but equal. This pride in ideas does not trace to the objectives of the USE. It is unhealthy thinking. It is a reflection of the negative hubris and vanity pervasive in boomer politicians. Driven by absolutist idealism it is emotional. It disallows logical argument and discourse to pursue common agreement. It prevents the necessary deliberation democracy needs to sustain liberty. The big "C" is to defend the big "L". They both pursue the same virtues, but they are now held distant by argumentative "little c" and "little l," which is depressing for democracy. This is as baby boomers infected with doomerism—their primal "me first" practiced counterculture—do.

They pass the blame back and forth, never solve problems, nor prepare us for the transformations to which we must adapt, or fall into poverty, or barely survive, or die.

Perhaps it is a grand illusion, an intended distraction, a massive smoke screen to prevent a population of divided publics from unifying as a voting bloc to kick out the baby doomer plutocrats and wannabe aristocrats, who seek to convert the USE into a feudal kingdom of haves in luxury and have-nots in scarcity. Rulers divide populations into publics choosing pundits' sides. We, the everyday people, lose in this scenario of listening to one-way propaganda from the differing ism factions in our society that are fighting just to fight, for the pleasure of the brawl, publishing profits, and broadcasting popularity. The self-immersive, impatient, personal satisfaction focused, non-civic-minded boomers are easily pulled into arguing camps as their vanguard cohorts are severe in their desire to not just defeat an enemy but destroy them (Strauss & Howe, 1991). They need the camps to feed this competitiveness. We the everyday people need cooperation of societal and social powers' officials, regional and settlement pattern inhabitants' subcultures to create a good American society.

A large pig of a generation in population, boomers misshaped the discourse in the public realm. They continue to produce noisy inappropriate content about necessary topics. It does not meet our needs. The ugliest voices of their vanguard, and the most unethical, are the baby doomers. This generational cohort's doomerism is mean-spirited. It misguides. It is the cruel means by which, intentionally or unintentionally, by ignorance and incompetence, their actions divide and conquer the people and destroy our divine gift of democracy in America. It reflects the "my way is right, regardless of the facts" discourse. It is fallacious, dishonest, and disturbingly immature. "Your way is wrong because that's how you think" is baby doomer demagoguery. It reduces us by producing insalubriously and argumentative publics. It causes the dissolution of public discourse among the people, which enables other powers to take more control of the leadership in the business of society and results in misunderstanding of which power is best to perform the leadership, administration, and management of the business of society within the USE. Doomerism kills civility in the public realm, which we, the everyday people, need to self-govern. We need to relearn how to converse collaboratively. We must conserve cordially. We need civilized conversations on issues that matter to all of us. We must to coordinate cooperatively on common ground compromises while keeping constitutionally allied.

The Art of Conversation

The baby doomers' demagoguery is detrimental to our liberty. Deliberative debates are an essential part of democracy, to talk through the risks to persons and publics uniting as a people. Nevertheless, with baby doomers, arguments without facts (emotively based not factually fixed in logic of first principles' preservation) have brought us life-threatening societal crises. The lack of knowledge of first principles and good citizenshipping attitudes and behaviors has enormous consequences. It causes a loss of appetite, appreciation, and application of good manners of virtue-bound acts appropriate for democracy, which include:

- Politeness
- Respect
- Listening to understand another's viewpoint
- Being patient to seek comprehension
- Abiding by a necessary willingness to speak one's truth without reprisal, not ostracizing others, not using overly critical speech
- Properness when speaking truth to power, which needs to be done respectfully, but MUST be done

We have lost the art of conversation, despite all the science of communications from the academy power's FILMS^2 [P7]. To learn more of it, let's return to founding framer Benjamin Franklin, who taught us the art of conversation in our country's beginnings. We, the everyday people, would be wise to learn it again. Conversation is a skill we must improve! If all schooled in this, we would be better for it. Before discussing the specifics, the two indispensable qualities for good conversation are knowledge of the subject and a good nature to listen, learn, and share to find mutual understanding, and if possible, agreement. Facts help this, and knowledge builds on facts. Ben wrote, "To please in Conversation is an Art which all People believe they understand and practise, tho' most are ignorant or deficient in it" (Labaree, 1959). Here is his article "On Conversation" published in the *Gazette*, written to help edify the population. Imagine if newspapers today offered such advice. Such neighborliness does not exist. The online newspapers and broadcasted "media" DAMN the powers of history to celebrate vanity or berate others disliked in the opinions of the editor, normally an employee for a corporation seeking only profits, with the huge economy power in our information age led by boomers of self-serving purposes. Such behavior was once, and ought to be again, restrained by the citizens in positions of authority to countervail the corruptions of greed and vanity. Here is the essay.

Complaisance is a seeming preference of others to our selves; and Good Nature a Readiness to overlook or excuse their Foibles, and do them all the Services we can. These two Principles must gain us their good Opinion, and make them fond of us for their own Sake, and then all we do or say will appear to the best Advantage, and be well accepted. Learning, Wit, and fine Parts, with these, shine in full Lustre, become wonderfully agreeable, and command Affection; but without them, only seem an Assuming over others, and occasion Envy and Disgust. The common Mistake is, that People think to please by setting themselves to View, and shewing their own Perfections, whereas the easier and more effectual Way lies quite contrary. Would you win the Hearts of others, you must not seem to vie with, but admire them: Give them every Opportunity of displaying their own Qualifications, and when you have indulg'd their Vanity, they will praise you too in Turn, and prefer you above others, in order to secure to themselves the Pleasure your Commendation gives.

But above all, we should mark out those Things which cause Dislike, and avoid them with great Care. The most common amongst these is, talking overmuch, and robbing others of their Share of the Discourse. This is not only Incivility but Injustice, for every one has a natural Right to speak in turn, and to hinder it is an Usurpation of common liberty, which never fails to excite Resentment. Beside, great Talkers usually leap from one thing to another with so much rapidity and so ill a Connection, that what they say is a mere Chaos of Noise and Nonsense; tho' did they speak like Angels they still would be disagreeable. It is very pleasant when two of these People meet: the Vexation they both feel is visible in their Looks and Gestures; you shall see them gape and stare, and interrupt one another at every Turn, and watch with the utmost Impatience for a Cough or a Pause, when they may croud a Word in edgeways: neither hears nor cares what the other says; but both talk on at any Rate, and never fail to part highly disgusted with each other. I knew two Ladies, gifted this Way, who by Accident travelled in a Boat twenty Miles together, in which short Journey they were both so extreamly tired of one another, that they could never after mention each other's Name with any Temper, or be brought in Company together, but retained a mutual Aversion which could never be worn out.

The contrary Fault to this, and almost as disobliging, is that of seeming wholly unconcerned in Conversation, and bearing no other Part in the Discourse than a No or Yes sometimes, or an Hem, or perhaps a Nod only. This Inattention and Indifference appears so like Disrespect, that it affronts the Desire we all possess of being taken Notice of and regarded, and makes the Company of those who practise it tiresome and insipid. Such is the Vanity of Mankind, that minding what others say is a much surer Way of pleasing them than talking well our selves.

Another Error very common and highly disagreeable is to be ever speaking of our selves and our own Affairs. What is it to the Company we fall into whether we quarrel with our Servants, whether our Children are froward and dirty, or what we intend to have for Dinner tomorrow? The Sauciness of a Negro, the Prattle of a Child, the spoiling a Suit of Cloaths, the Expences of Housekeeping, or the Preparation for a Journey, may be to ourselves Matters of great Importance, as they occasion us Pain or Pleasure; but wherein are Strangers concerned, or what Amusement can they possibly receive from such Accounts? Opposite to this, but not less troublesome, is the impertinent Inquisitiveness of some People which is ever prying into and asking ten thousand Questions about the Business of others. To search after and endeavour to discover Secrets, is an unpardonable Rudeness; but what makes this Disposition worse, it is usually attended with an ill-natur'd, ungenerous, and mischievous Desire of exposing and aggravating the Mistakes and Infirmities of others. People of this Turn are the Pest of Society, and become both feared and hated. On these two Heads it may be useful always to remember, that we never ought to trouble People with more of our own Affairs than is needful for them to know, nor enquire farther into theirs than themselves think fit to tell us.

Storytelling is another Mistake in Conversation, which should be avoided by all who intend to please. It is impossible to hear a long insipid trifling Tale, void of Wit or Humour, drawn in by Neck and Shoulders, and told meerly for the sake of talking, without being uneasy at it. Besides, People this way given are apt to tell the same String of Stories, with all their rambling Particulars, again and again over; without considering, that whatsoever Pleasure themselves may find in talking, their Hearers wish their Tongues out. Old Folks are most subject to this Error, which is one chief Reason their Company is so often shun'd.

Another very disagreeable Error, is, a Spirit of Wrangling and Disputing, which some perpetually bring with them into Company: insomuch, that say whate'er you will, they'll be sure to contradict you: and if you go about to give Reasons for your Opinion, however just they be, or however modestly propos'd, you throw them into Rage and Passion. Though, perhaps, they are wholly unacquainted with the Affair, and you have made yourself Master of it, it is no Matter, the more ignorant they are you still find them the more positive, and what they want in Knowledge they endeavour to supply by Obstinacy, Noise and Fury: and when you press hard upon them, instead of Argument *they fly to personal Reproaches and Invectives. Thus every Trifle becomes a serious Business, and such People are continually involved in Quarrels.*

Raillery is a part of Conversation, which to treat of fully would require a whole Paper; but now, I have only room to observe that it is highly entertaining or exceedingly disobliging, according as it is managed, and therefore we ought to use it with all the Caution possible. Natural Infirmities, unavoidable Misfortunes, Defects, or Deformities of any kind, should never be the Subject of it, for then it is not only impertinent, but affronting and inhuman. It's like Salt, a little of which in some Cases gives a Relish, but if thrown on by Handfuls, or sprinkled on things at random, it spoils all. Raillery supposes Wit; but agreeable as Wit is, when it takes a wrong Turn it becomes dangerous and mischievous. When Wit applies it self to search into, expose, and ridicule the Faults of others, it often inflicts a Wound that rankles in the Heart, and is never to be forgiven. To rally safely, and so as to please, it is requisite that we perfectly know our Company: it's not enough that we intend no Ill, we must be likewise certain what we say shall be taken as we intend it; otherwise, for the sake of a Jest we may lose a Friend, and make an inveterate Enemy. I shall say no more on this Head, but that we ought to use it sparingly; and whatever Opportunities may offer of shewing our Parts this way, so soon as any Body appears uneasy at it, and receives it with a grave Face, both Good Manners and Discretion advise to change the Subject for something else more harmless.

Akin to Raillery, and what oftentimes goes along with it, is Scandal. But if People hereby think to gain Esteem, they unhappily are mistaken; for every Body (even those who hear them with a seeming Pleasure) considers them with a kind of Horror. No one's Reputation is safe against such Tongues: all in Turn may expect to suffer by them. Insensible of the Ties of Friendship, or the Sentiments of Humanity, such Creatures are mischievous as Bears or Tygers, and are as much abhorr'd and fear'd.

There are many more Mistakes which render People disagreeable in Conversation, but these are the most obvious; and whosoever avoids them carefully can never much displease. I shall only add, in a few Words, what are the most likely Means to make a Man be well accepted.

Let his Air, his Manner, and Behaviour, be easy, courteous and Affable, void of every Thing haughty or assuming; his Words few, express'd with Modesty, and a Respect for those he talks to. Be he ever ready to hear what others say; let him interrupt no Body, nor intrude with his Advice unask'd. Let him never trouble other People about his own Affairs, nor concern himself with theirs. Let him avoid Disputes; and when he dissents from others propose his Reasons with Calmness and Complaisance. Be his Wit ever guided by Discretion and Good Nature, nor let him sacrifice a Friend to raise a Laugh. Let him not censure others, nor expose their Failings, but kindly excuse or hide them. Let him neither raise nor propagate a Story to the Prejudice of any Body. In short, be his Study to command his own Temper, to learn the Humours of Mankind, and to conform himself accordingly.

With good conversation understood, the people can get along better, move to unity, and cause movement toward the necessary work of citizenshipping in the course of battling back how doomerism CATAPULTED crises by how it COIFFURE democracy from American society. We, the every-day people, must use our people power as constituted. We must appropriately dissent, block bad citizens from serving in positions of authority, and protect the good by rotating them out regularly. This is how representative democracy works best, when we participate in leading it to our constitutional goal by demanding its objectives pursuit. Using good conversational skills, we can get those in authority to behave better. We all must strive to be as a citizenry E-SASSY-T-TUF-FT-CAUCUS whether in positions of authority or not. It is our calling. It is our duty.

The entrenched wannabe-ruling-aristocratic megalomaniac kleptocratic politicians and egregiously conceited predatory economic elites will both seek its repression. Let their games dissuade us not. Democracy requires courage and commitment to first principles. Liberty requires holding persons in positions of authority accountable for their decisions that affect us, the people, and prosecuting them for punishment if any of their actions undermine democracy as the culture, liberty as the common purpose, and virtue as an ardent pursuit. We must be communicating and corresponding to find a place of agreement, a commonly held fact or ambition for the way we should AEIOUY^{2}K power.

We must converse about power. Our inability to understand power's activities, how we are to properly AEIOUY^{2}K it in our republic and its corrupting DAMN tendencies is dangerously risky for us. Recall in Chapter 2 that we examined how the societal powers get disused, abused, misused, and not used when they should be. Remember how we contrasted the bad and ugly modes of power usage against the good modes. We also covered democracy as the ideal society and the cycle it follows. We went over challenges to the USE from our regional variety of socialization experiences. Called to unity we must unify on core principles. To support this, we shared tools to help make a good society.

Now we move on to a closer look at all the societal powers: primary, secondary, and tertiary. Our understanding of power will give us the edge to win, to secure the blessings of liberty, and to have the victory of a more perfect union over all of the history of humanity. We, the everyday people, have work to do, both within ourselves and as a citizenry, for the foundations of our society to be a lighted lamp on the Liberty Tree to guide us through our present and future crises. We cannot allow ourselves to be the problem and betray our nation (Magistrale, 2020). For the past forty years of baby boomers "me first" agendas we have failed. They sought positions of authority for ego. Instead of serving "we the people" with proper real American style LAMBS, their politic made them rich and powerful. Their policies failed us. By understanding the operant ways, means, and methods of social powers, we can recover. It will take years to reverse the consequences of the climbing boomers positional posturing for power's sake methods. Thus, we must begin the intervention. When we the everyday people reclaim our proper leadership power in society, and in ourselves, we will win. Let's get to it!

3. "In Power We Win"

This chapter defines the powers in society.

Power is like a message in a bottle; you don't know what you've gotten until you take it out. Society is composed of persons arranged in power structures, social bodies, "organs," we call organizations. Those of greater permanence we call institutions. These organs of society are the instruments of social power. Do we ever seek to understand their hidden, underlying "messages" of power in society? Do we ever talk about them? Or do we only ever talk about the aftereffects that we see? Our acquaintance with how we AEIOUY²K societal and social powers must improve. Otherwise, fall victim to the DAMN of power we will. Let's look at how power structures society. First, let's define some of the terms we'll use. Physics defines power by this formula:

$$P = \frac{W}{\triangle t}$$

Power equals work divided by change over time. Work equals force plus displacement. Said another way, power equals force plus velocity. While physics underlies all actions in nature, its application as a model for society holds fewer constants. It demonstrates for us that power is a combination of two main components. The imperfect nature of human beings means that our personal and social bodies rely upon power forms and components. However, each of these components relies on two basic relationships: me and my self, and me and the others in organizations. Because we are ever changing throughout our lives, we are dynamic, so a static mathematical model of power is insufficient. Society, like human life itself, is also dynamic, so a dynamic model is more helpful for understanding society.

In society, power is the exercise of control over other people, principally by granting or denying their freedom of movement, which includes moving the body parts to speak. However, since "we think, therefore we are," we are conscious of the fact that we are conscious beings. We don't like others to control us. We agree to go along with the rules and take part in social   con

tracts. In a back-and-forth dialectic between self and groups, we determine our values and regulate our behaviors. The desire to control the way people think is a will to use power. By various structuring, power shapes society, which then controls people's attitudes and behaviors. Acceptance of controls made in agreement by persons with authority, forms culture. We make culture with social powers and it founds society. Societies differ as cultures differ as peoples differ as persons differ.

Each society consists of people who attempt to use power in ways permitted by the society's culture. Human beings inhabit many forms of society, although the variety is not that large because human beings are so similar. Power within society takes many forms. For example, the conditions of survival in any particular geographic area expose inhabitants to its power. Geography can harm or help people; it makes habitation easy or difficult. It provides the resources that people consume to survive, live in comfort, or thrive in luxury. Risks to each of these three broadly defined standards of living and quality of life conditions require controls. Power structures address these risks. In survival mode, the risks are threats to existence. In comfort mode, we manage the risks well. Some are negative vulnerabilities, and some are positive opportunities. In luxury mode, risks are opportunities, and vulnerabilities mitigated. Social powers regulate risks to the person from a group, and of a person to a group.

The first risks to address are of geographical. Humans adapt to their geography. Adaptation is the manipulation of earth's geography for the provisions necessary for sustaining human life. The process of adaptation creates culture. The culture of a settlement of any given people in any given place begins with their adaptations to the geographic conditions. People have the power to adapt and create a culture, which informs how we will view the power employed by those who take it or give it by agreement. Herein lays the basic organizing premise. Do people give or take power, to and from society, or does society give or take power, to and from the people? It depends on the culture and the tolerance of the people with regard to their belief in their culture. In our democracy-based culture, we consent to give power to representatives. We divide social controlling power to prevent its concentration, lest it conquer and divide us. We contend that all people deserve equal treatment before the law. The law of the land established by the Constitution requires equality before it. The law aids our ability to administer a society by rules to control threateningly risky behaviors that might harm a person or the people in society.

To frame a means by which people can control the power of law, government, the polity, our law powers held by fellow citizens elected to offices of our republic limit them. To ensure that the government continues to retain the consent of the governed, the Constitution limits governmental powers. Enumerated in our Constitution, the power of our polity is affectionately a government "of the people, by the people, for the people." If it were an organism, its elixir would be liberty. Liberty is the freedom to think and act as one pleases, so long as one does not infringe upon another's freedom. The law sets the rules in writing. It provides boundaries for the social contract, the construct within which people must stay to be free. The law disallows harmful behaviors. If convicted of them, the punishment is the loss of freedoms. We contend five categories of freedoms. Power has three tiers: primary, secondary, and tertiary. The powers of society in perfect balance enable the freedoms felt by the people. The first principled freedom ensured for the people is speech: thought and talking.

In the course of living their lives, people have personal and social needs: nutrients, apparel, a place to be, shelter from discomforting weather. They need security from crime, stability, predictability for the acquisition of knowledge, goods, and services from one another, and time to enjoy self-discovery and expression as they mature from infant to elder. Life begins with getting needs met and progresses with the satisfaction of more complex social needs. Structured into agreed-upon organizations and systems of control meeting these higher needs are the work of culture and society. Culture oriented toward providing maximum freedoms in a society is democracy.

Freedom comes when we identify, respect, expect, detect, erect, and protect human rights. The US Constitution declares the rights of its citizens. Please read it to see them all. According to one of its framers, the founder John Adams, the Constitution was, "made only for a moral and religious people. It is wholly inadequate to the government of any other…The only foundation of a free Constitution is pure Virtue, and…but they will not obtain a lasting Liberty…A Constitution of Government once changed from Freedom, can never be restored. Liberty, once lost, is lost forever."

Founding framer Thomas Jefferson held it to be "unquestionably the wisest ever yet presented" since it enabled "the changing of a constitution by assembling the wise men of the state, instead of assembling armies." He also contended that, as relates to the Constitution's Bill of Rights, "The God who gave us Life gave us Liberty at the same time."

Founding framer George Washington stated: "The Constitution…is sacredly obligatory upon all." It exists but has weakness in the weakness of humankind and is vulnerable to "those incited by the lust of power and prompted by the supineness or venality of their constituents, [who might seek to] overleap the known barriers of this Constitution and violate the unalienable rights of humanity." If that were to ever happen, he said, *"It will only serve to show, that no compact among men (however provident in its construction and sacred in its ratification) can be pronounced everlasting and inviolable, and if I may so express myself, that no Wall of words, that no mound of parchment can be so formed as to stand against the sweeping torrent of boundless ambition on the side, aided by the sapping current of corrupted morals on the other."* When elected president, in his first inaugural address on April 30, 1789, he said:

> *There is no truth more thoroughly established than that there exists in the economy and course of nature* **an indissoluble union between virtue and happiness;** *between duty and advantage; between the genuine maxims of an honest and magnanimous policy and the solid rewards of public prosperity and felicity; since we ought to be no less persuaded that* **the propitious smiles of Heaven can never be expected on a nation that disregards the eternal rules of order and right** *which Heaven itself has ordained; and* **since the preservation of the sacred fire of liberty** *and* **the destiny of the republican** *model of government are justly considered, perhaps, as* **deeply, as finally,** *staked on the experiment* **entrusted to the hands of the American people.**

The bolded words above (by this book's author) emphasize how virtue is necessary for happiness. "We the People" entrusted with the endowment of a republic have a responsibility to preserve liberty! Put in our hands by the hand of the Creator.

Founding framer James Madison strongly felt that our Constitution was a divine gift, stating:

> *It is impossible for the man of pious reflection not to perceive in it a finger of that Almighty hand which has been so frequently and signally extended to our relief in the critical stages of the revolution...Whatever may be the judgment pronounced on the competency of the architects of the Constitution, or whatever may be the destiny of the edifice prepared by them, I feel it a duty to express my profound and solemn conviction... that there never was an assembly of men, charged with a great and arduous trust, who were more pure in their motives, or more exclusively or anxiously devoted to the object committed to them.*

From this, we move to one impressing the importance of obeisance to laws. Founding framer Alexander Hamilton once said:

> *If it be asked, What are the most sacred duty and the greatest source of our security in a Republic? The answer would be, an inviolable respect for the Constitution and Laws – the first growing out of the last. ...A sacred respect for constitutional law is the vital principle, the sustaining energy of a free government. ... The aim of every political constitution is, or ought to be, first to obtain from rulers men who possess most wisdom to discern, and most virtue to pursue, the common good of the society; and in the next place, to take the most effectual precautions for keeping them virtuous whilst they continue to hold their public trust.... The truth is, after all the declamations we have heard, that the Constitution is itself, in every rational sense, and to every useful purpose, A BILL OF RIGHTS.*

Founding framer Benjamin Franklin famously quipped, "A republic, if you can keep it." These sentences from its creators show that the success of their venture requires its recipients perform a "sacred duty." We have a responsibility to ourselves. We must be virtuous, especially those of us who are officials in offices of government. Citizen rights and responsibilities guarantee that freedoms get respected, expected, and protected.

Rights, liberty, and freedom interconnect yet nuance differently. Freedoms are rights. Liberty is the state of being free. Free means that people are uncontrolled, except by consent to laws that make a society civilized. Politics is the process of control over the levers of power structures. We the people have the power to self-govern, but we must exercise our rights and perform our responsibilities to society. This is nothing we've not known before. However, we have not been putting in the necessary work. We've been under the trance of a new cult-like culture: baby doomers.

While we all are free to be whom and what we want to be within the constraints of the law, we confront limits in nature, in both geography and our biology. Biology is a power exhibiting the "economy of nature" within human life, in a person living in society. Society sets organizations that if truthful, provide us, by our being citizens, many opportunities. By them, we can become the best we can be to be happy and to give and receive benefits from society. *"Between duty and advantage; between the genuine maxims of an honest and magnanimous policy and the solid rewards of public prosperity and felicity"* (G. Washington, 1789). This statement clearly indicates that he expects citizenship of us, and that it is irrefutably necessary.

Dutiful citizens gain advantages, when in the polity such good citizens generate excellent administration, people-benefiting policies. A people prosperous and happy, uncontrolled, reap rewards from being good. With freedoms given by the Constitution and its culture of democracy, we can be artistic and industrious. We can celebrate life, unhindered by tyranny. Let's take a closer at look at freedoms.

President Franklin Delano Roosevelt during World War II announced four freedoms. These are (with remarks on how they related to the US Constitution):

1) "Freedom of speech and expression"—Found in the Bill of Rights, First Amendment to the US Constitution.
2) "Freedom of every person to worship God in his own way."—Found in the Bill of Rights, First Amendment to the US Constitution.
3) "Freedom from want which, translated into world terms, means economic understandings which will secure to every nation a healthy peacetime life for its inhabitants..."—Relates to the Preamble of the US Constitution's clause "promote the general welfare."
4) "Freedom from fear—which, translated into world terms, means a worldwide reduction of armaments to such a point and in such a thorough fashion that no nation will be in a position to commit an act of physical aggression against any neighbor." This relates to the

Preamble of the US Constitution's clause "provide for the common defense."

These four freedoms build upon the basic rights of humans, the "certain unalienable (un-removable) Rights" declared by the colonists in the North American* continent to King George of England in 1776 as "self-evident truths." Truths because these rights were "endowed by their Creator" (given by God). The rights are:

1) All men* are created equal—treat us equally.
2) Life—allow us to live (in peace).
3) Liberty—allow us to live with freedom so long as it does not take away other's equality, life, or liberty.
4) Pursuit of Happiness—allow us to do what pleases us so long as it does not infringe on other's liberty.

*(so called by the Europeans who settled on its lands and as revised by constitutional law amendments per conventional recognition through social knowledge admittance that women deserve rights as they are also human, and that persons of African descent with more melanin in their skin that makes it darker are also human and citizens with the right to vote.)

Let us not forget the goal and objectives of the USE stated in the Preamble of the US Constitution:

"We the People of the United States, in Order to form a more perfect Union, **establish Justice**, insure domestic Tranquility, provide for the common defence, promote the general Welfare, and **secure the Blessings of Liberty** to ourselves and our Posterity, do ordain and establish this Constitution of the United States of America."

Justice and **liberty**: these are our primary responsibility to uphold by thinking and acting as citizens duty-bound to project and protect. Understanding power, its control, and its purposeful use will help us be better citizens.

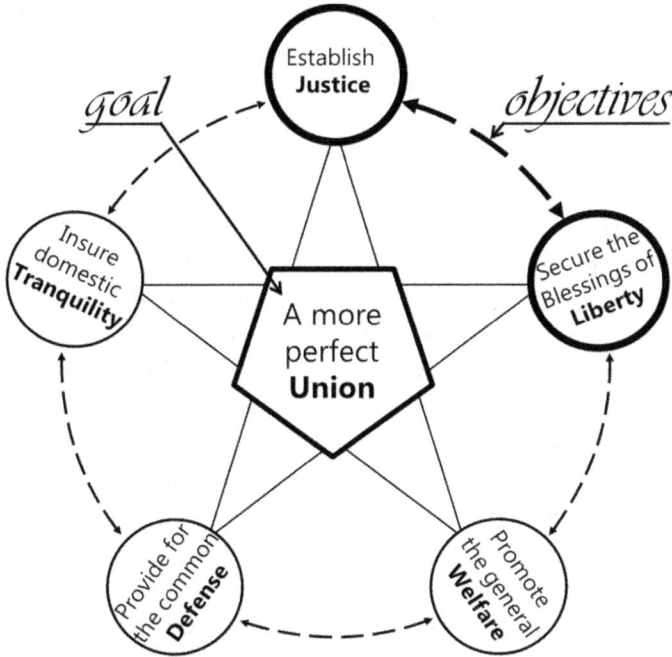

Figure 3-1: Goal and Interconnected Objectives of the United States of America—A Badge of Honor

Let's move on to the societal powers we have co-created through our democracy-based culture.

Powers in Society

Having established a background in the importance of adopting a renewed approach to becoming one American people, e pluribus unum, to be virtuous citizens, under God, let's review the societal powers. We'll review the primary ones and then move into the secondary and tertiary ones, the social powers. As we do, we should remember our posture. We are learning the operant behaviors of power in us and in society. We do this to reclaim our society to serve us. This we'll get by E-SASSY-T-TUF-FT-CAUCUS. Essential to this is that we know how to insure, d'ure, ensure, assure, lure, and secure (IDEALS) liberty back into the ethos, pathos, and logos of American society. Its Kairos is now, two score into the 21st Century's millennium. We must observe its presence in all arguments of those in positions of power, and if it is absent, we must remove them. If they are not doing it, then we know they don't care about us. Society must serve liberty, or it is un-American.

There are thirteen powers of human life and human societies (see Figure 3-2). These powers are regulators of attitudes and behaviors. They shape how we think and act. We discussed the primary ones in Chapter 2 when we went over the good that powers do for us and how they can do us wrong. Of the remaining ten, one is a precept, infusing and shaping all the others. We mentioned it in Chapter 1 as the response to the power of geography. It is culture. It has five powers as its integrant building blocks: mythology, academy, industry, artistry, and history. These are the tertiary social powers. These influence how the family power nurtures the second of the two natural powers, a person's biology. Families' powers combine to form community power. All the human, societal, and social powers exist within geographies. Geography is the first natural power. It is our provider. It gives life's resources for our surviving, living, and thriving with luxury and many worship it with mythology power in a variety of ways. Mythology is a big contributor to our precept power process for adaptation: culture. Because culture responds to geography to create society, it makes us compatible for survival. It structures the primary powers. We must always keep this in mind. Culture is an adaptation power process, flexible, fungible, and malleable by us. Let's return now to the three primary powers in society: the people, the polity, and the economy powers, which is Chapter 2 were discussed relative to the LAMBS model of American society.

First, people structure the other primary powers, the polity and the economy. Once created, these powers take on a life of their own and begin to seek more power for themselves. Balance is necessary for a truly American society. People do it with culture power. We AEIOUY^{2}K people power to regulate the other two. In accordance with the precepts of culture in response to the provisos of geography, it creates culture. In the enterprise that is the United States, the underlying culture is democracy based. This puts the people power in a more responsible position than in any other culture because it makes each person important. Democracy culture makes the polity power subordinate to the will of the people. It is to serve our interests. It is to act in accord of, by, and for the people under the intents of the law of the Constitution. The deep culture of democracy sustains the polity of representatives elected by the people to serve its republic. Democracy demands liberty as the purpose of the society for the people to remain in control. A republic requires an educated population of persons willing to unite as one people. These constructs influence the balancing of the powers in society. The powers constrain and shift as necessary in response to risks to society fulfilling the needs of the people. As history teaches, life is dynamic. We must pay attention to power to prevent it from drifting our USE off its course framed by democracy and moved forward by its republic.

Societies face risks in existing. The way culture arranges social and societal powers determines a society's ability to manage risks. A republic with an engaged citizenry is apt to adapt habits to thwart threats and optimize opportunities. Metaphorically, if societies are sailing ships, they must navigate risky seas. If they miss the reefs and mines, they avoid running aground or sinking. If they catch the right wind at the right time, they get to enjoy some good speed and steer clear of the hazards and avoid stormy weather. At times, risks make life fun; otherwise, they can be frightening. Our brains are ever ready to fight or flee from dangers. Our minds seek control. They must reason to think before reacting to stimuli. Because society organizes powers, it too can decide courses of action in times of amplified risks. Through its structures of authority, society weighs the good, average, or bad potentialities of risks.

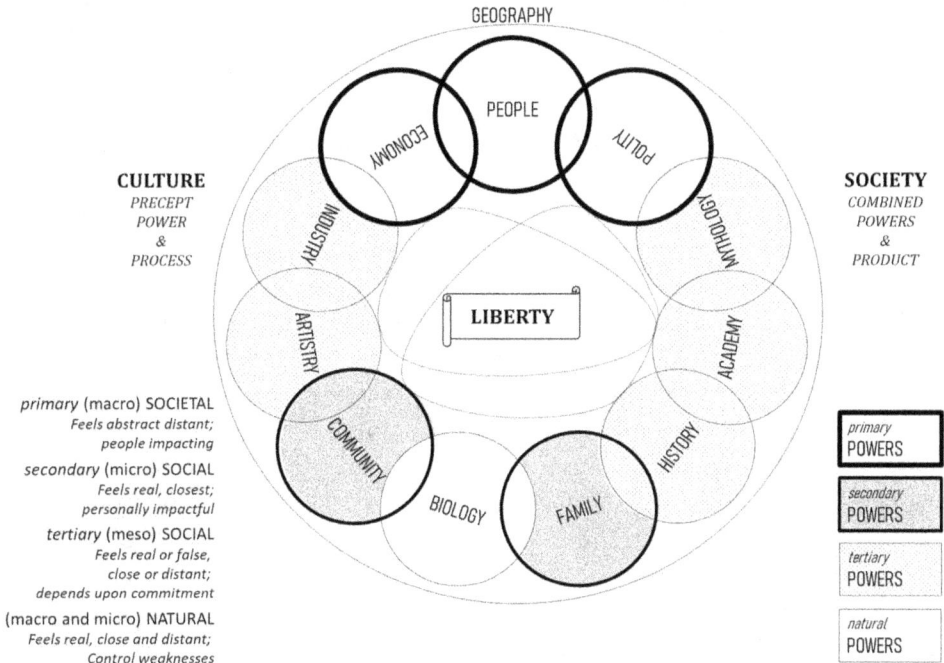

Figure 3-2: Society is a Product of Culture's Assemblage of the Forms of Powers' Organization

In a balanced society shaped by a culture of democracy, a first principle, liberty, plays the central role. The powers protect it.

The persons in charge of powers' FILMS[2] [P7] decide. Decisions on risks faced by society can cause change, promote change, resist change, or force a stasis. Each social and societal power deals with risks in a form or fashion appropriate to it. Powers deal with change through their instruments' mechanisms. Like organs, society's organizations and institutions work together to keep it alive. They all use forces specific to their purposes. But, if those in charge of the powers are not pulling in the same direction, the ship will not sail. It will crash. This is what has happened to the USE under majority rule of the baby boomers (see Figure 4-10).

Persons placed in charge of the FILMS[2] [P7] of the social and societal powers pull the levers of its mechanisms. Authority is a special responsibility. If we are to be successful as a society navigating the risks in our future, we need persons of impeccable character in the pilothouses' bridges at our helms of our culture made and arranged powers. We need persons of virtue who exemplify integrity, honor, and courage in charge. They need to be capable of good analysis and decision-making. Because of their positions, their decisions cause ripple effects throughout society. We see impacts at the macro, meso, and micro levels. Global and nationwide impacts are macro level. Organizational and regional impacts are meso level. Neighborhood, household, and personal relationship impacts are micro level. One fascinating aspect of society is that micro-level actions aggregated can change the macro-level structures or vice versa. The meso is in-between. It carries changes up and down and back and forth. However, it is not always in a neutral conveyance condition. At times, its unique position in the middle yields great positive insights or dire realizations.

A desired positive risk is the taking of opportunities to improve life circumstances or living conditions. Thriving is as difficult as surviving. It takes work until we make it, but we cannot get complacent. The more balanced the powers are in a society, the greater potential for all to thrive. The macro power structures house and hold the most affluent and influential FILMS[2] [P7]. Their scale of operant behavior requires vast amounts of information processing. Their mechanisms are systems run by persons with significant authority. Even the secondary and tertiary powers in society have systems. All these systems of thinking and action interact. To the extent that they integrate in coordinated efforts to push and pull the forces of nature and the seven social powers, society's powers are in alignment. When they seem to be going in the same direction toward liberty, the people feel safe, secure, and generally happy. The pursuit of happiness rests on the success of society and not the selfish pursuits of each person. Cooperative agreement, not competitive argument, promotes the general welfare. This is a fact lost on the baby doomers. They seem unable to get over themselves and make it so.

Alas, society, ever dynamic, is always in the remaking mode. Each generation gets its time to be in charge. We the people of the USE's society must never forget its origins. The framing was a radical social innovation. Many great debates during its framing articulate arguments on power. It is necessary civics for every generation to understand the original meanings. Our Constitution's framing is a great story to understand. In it, we find not only the power of liberty but also the need of an educated populace to understand it and virtuous persons to reveal it. Only a people who know how power acts in society, can sustain a republic with democracy. Thus, knowledge and virtue are prerequisites for self-government as well as the government of a true American society. Combined, these are "civic virtue". Recognition of the common purpose and pursuit as central to our total happiness as one people is purposeful. Civic virtue is the only way to prevent society from degenerating into a mobocracy (Rakove, 1996) or losing ground to a tyranny.

If our society is to keep moving toward achieving its ideals, we need the academy power to better train us in our history. A steady stream of ACE all our lives could guarantee perpetual civic virtue. This is so we may be a democracy of, by, and for "all" the people seeking to be good citizens first and behaving with civic virtue. In this manner, we guarantee the first principle. Liberty presides over our affairs because we know it. For us to do this, we must balance our societal powers toward it and orient our social powers to support it. The LAMBS model presented in the figures of Chapter 2 shared the consequences of imbalanced primary powers. Above, we have learned about the risks and alignment of purpose for the secondary and tertiary powers as necessary for happiness. Let's move on.

Overwhelming amounts of upsetting information distributed daily, hourly, by the minute and second, via many channels disturbs our sense of hope and happiness. It weakens us. This "media" employs our history power through its instrument of new information telling, the "news". Its mechanisms are journalism and reporting. Our critical thinking about what we hear and see needs honed. A part of civic virtue is to examine for facts. Yet, we must avoid the cavern of becoming insular. We must be engaged and aware, seeking information from multiple, even opposing, perspectives if we want liberty in our lives. We must not follow the media outlets like cattle herds. We must break free from the echoing of our own thinking that they seek to amplify to enlarge their market share and dominance over "public opinion" to sell more advertisements. We ought not to allow ourselves to be pawns in their game. We must think for ourselves, or we cannot be free. We must not become engrossed in engorging ourselves eating the conflictual gossipy candy that deludes us from civility. Doing so only makes a few media moguls maddeningly more vainglorious and rich. They might be emboldened to gain control over the LAMBS, rather than convey facts we need to know to sustain our society. They throw money at politicians instead of investing it in humanity. By following them, we create an entitled wannabe "establishment" above us, but one that does not exhibit the modicum of concern about us, which the founding generations' wealthy families and descendants of the USE genuflected. Is the cultural shift from democracy to doomerism what the framers would have wanted? It is a condition of aberrant adverse avarice aimed addiction, an affliction applauded and caused by the baby doomers. Because it profits them, they think it correct, and therefore are not inclined to stop it. We must stop it within each one of us, between and among ourselves. We must resist it and remove it with our family and community powers. These first in importance, but second in influence over society, social powers need our willful determination to use them to cure us of doomerism. We must not fall into the downward-spiraling ant sand trap that the tumult of its incivility from which it profits

its persuaders and perpetrators. We must seek to understand first. This is what civic virtue calls us to do. We must do it as we perform our duties as citizens. This is the first job for all of us in American society. This is how we champion liberty and justice for all.

As it relates to everyone's first job as citizens in a republic, citizenshipping, how do we begin to analyze all the chatter in the mass media? First, we ask ourselves to what extent it supports our liberty or not. Does it only lift higher the upper-class autocrat-wannabes? If so, know that those of them benefiting from sustaining the status quo are not interested in losing the controls over society they presently exert. They enjoy being the operators of the FILMS[2] [P7] of five tertiary social (mythology, academy, history, industry, artistry) and two (polity and economy) primary societal powers that compete and combine in the process of culture, changing, containing, or continuing American society. To the extent that they do so in ways, means, and methods perilous to liberty, we must declare it loudly, call it out proudly, and demand it "cease and desist" stoutly. We must consent to do so to prevent power shifting games that move control away from the people. We must dissent for our own good. Our project goes off course when liberty is limited. As indicated by the LAMBS model's figures in Chapter 2, we need societal powers properly balanced. This means we must show our leadership. We, the everyday people, must rally round the Liberty Tree. Once again, we must champion liberty. Doing so, we frontally confront the affront of the devastating spread of the democracy destroying tumorous cultural disease: doomerism.

Let's move to more in-depth discussion of the three primary powers we must know to control. These form the skeleton onto which all else attaches through the culture we create to adapt to the ecosystems of geography that we inhabit. Here is a recap of what we expect of the three primary societal powers that our historical colonial culture set up for the creation of an American society:

- The **People Power**
  o We expect it to provide the leadership. We do so by our example in our persons, social roles, and accumulatively as a citizenry through developing, possessing, and exhibiting virtuous character. We'll agree to hold accountable the polity and economy to be most responsible to protect our liberty and assist us in meeting the objectives of the Constitution en route to our American society project achieving its goal.

- The **Economy Power**
  oWe expect it to provide good management of the provisioning of the goods and services for our survival, comfort, and luxury. We also expect inspiration for how we'll find better lives, meaningful work, fair distributions of our contributions to the wealth of the nation, and all the freedoms this power can assist us enjoy.

- The **Polity Power**
  - o   We expect it to provide honest administration of the necessary pro-
       grams of government. We also expect it to determine what we need
       to sustain a civil society that supports respect and dignity and all the
       freedoms this power can protect for us.

Each has a job to do for American society to able to do its business.
The people have a job to do. The economy has a job to do. The polity has a
job to do. None can do it alone. All must work synchronously together on
a daily basis. If one is missing or gets misguided. If one goes AWOL (absent without leave), there is no American society. These three powers control the ways, means, and methods that get the business of society led, administered, and managed. These three powers decide who gets what and in
what amount. In American society, liberty is the ideal, but the powers move
us with or without our consent. By the nature of powers pushing and pulling, it moves us in a direction toward greater controlling forces that reduce
the freedom of liberty to be free. This we must avert by our leadership of
self and society, each one of us, by good citizenshipping!

We the people own the responsibility to exercise our power to uphold
the Constitution. This establishes our common foundation. Everything in
American society is built upon and held together by it. By E-SASSY-T-
TUF-FT-CAUCUS, we champion liberty. To champion liberty is to IDE-
ALS liberty. This takes the work of going about our lives exhibiting service
above selfishness, saying yes to the utmost full-fledged thoroughgoing attitudes and behaviors of patriots. We do so because, liberty of, liberty by, and
liberty for us, is our ideal to make real. We must remind ourselves of this
constantly. We must now demand a culture shift so democracy rebounds. It
is our civic responsibility, our first order of personal business in how we
restore the ambition for the USE to go about its business of accomplishing
an American society. We are not like other places. Our Constitution was
revolutionary. It was far better than its Greek and Roman antecedents in
antiquity. We must remember the intents of this nation or lose it unwittingly. Such would be very disappointing, not just to us but also to the world.
Based upon the leadership we have shown it when we justly fought for democracy, we've a reputation to maintain. Let's not embarrass ourselves by
losing it. Let's be the embassage of peace through freedom.

Sadly, the forays made by baby doomers, discord with the Constitution
and the culture of democracy, continue to unravel us as a people, and prevent us to be our destiny, e pluribus unum, annuit coeptis, 1776's Novus
ordo seclorum (see Figure 0-1-1). We are not reflecting our constitutional
ideals well. Out of step with our first principles, we're too much and too
often uncoordinated; especially these past forty years. It is for this reason
that the most critical aspect of a society is the precept power process we
create: culture. It and its tertiary powers' protagonists' FILMS^2 [P7] are so

important to completing and maintaining our project. Synchronizing these to work together requires that we identify them. Metaphorically, imagine that they are players on a sports team. To play to win, we must play well together during competitive games. Each must know the other's strengths and weaknesses. As the action unfolds, we must calculate how each will re-act to opportunities and vulnerabilities. It takes great coaching and plenty of practice time together to get to a level of symbiotic thinking and total trust. From this tightness of appreciation for one another, the team per-forms spectacularly. The coach and players have faith in one another. They listen, hear, speak, and feel the same game language. They gel. We the peo-ple are the coach and the players. We must work toward a unified posture. Scoring points against one another in petty competition is doomeristic. It is a terrible example for our children. It sets our society back to an age that predates our founding. It is devolution. Are we not Americans? To correct the baby boomer misguided missteps, we must converse at the level of how we, through culture, must better lead the business of society, balance and properly AEIOUY^{2}K our societal and social powers.

Our secondary and tertiary social powers in American society derive from the passed down cultures of immigrated and native peoples, altered by the principles, ideals, and key aspects of what makes the country a nation, our polity. But before the polity got power, the people power determined what it would be. It is for this reason that we must understand how people power works. It is what gives liberty its life. The people are essential to IDEALS liberty into every aspect of American society.

People Power

People power's prime method is leadership (see Figure 2-2). We lead the USE properly when each of us AEIOUY^{2}K personal authority power in constitutionally allied ways. People are principally as persons concerned with who we are. Who we are is in part natural as each of us has biological endowments and constraints from genetic formations. Who we are is in part social, as each of us has nurturing to make us ready for society, social-ized by family influences upon us. For example, we grow up in neighbor-hoods and join in various communities of differing activities, like schooling and extracurricular activities if we are fortunate, such as playing on a club sports team or participating in a debate society across town. The persons in our communities and institutions influence us. Persons in authoritative po-sitions teach us, so we listen to them. We obey:

- Family power-holders in our households
- Academy power-holders in our schools: the teachers and adminis-trators
- Polity power-holders in our governments: the elected and appointed officials of our towns, cities, municipalities, states, regions, and

federal government

- Economy power-holders who seek to make life more comfortable and convenient for us: our local shopkeepers, or workers at a national brand-name store, or our best friend's rich dad.

We the everyday people need to know our full power. We are as a power in American society, its leadership. We are freer in a democracy-based culture with liberty than in any other. Anarchy is wild, not free. It lacks liberty. One bully among a mobbing mess will rise and direct the crowd toward tyranny that will dictate the terms of our existence, totally. Bad for us is the way of totalitarian dictators. We must use our people power to protect liberty from such intolerant, cruel, and unusual fools. We can do this when we force the controllers of our polity power to see our liberty as its purpose and provide the necessary administrative services to protect it. When we see they are not working to IDEALS liberty in all facets of society within their control, we must readily remove them. We control who is in the polity. This is more so our responsibility than a right of the privilege of citizenship. We must live up to it. We've not done so well at it the past forty years.

We must use our people power to ensure the controllers of our economy power see our liberty as essential to its existence. In working within the economy power's FILMS[2] [P7] or as the HM[5], or as participants in marketplace exchanges, we must ensure its good management. Good management supports us as we get what is necessary to survive, live comfortably, and thrive in luxury.

People in groups adapted to geography by creating culture to assist us to survive. Teamwork led to ease and knowledge. Knowledge led to better toolmaking. Toolmaking artisanship led to easier living. Easier living led to social organizational innovations. Power spread out into different centers of knowledge around which culture formed and it shaped society. People—the living, remembered, and hoped for—are who we are as a species. Each of us endowed and limited in our capacity and capabilities, become more sophisticated toolmakers. From generation to generation, we keep unsettling the stasis with new discoveries. Leaps in knowledge propel us into temporary turbulence when new knowledge disproves paradigms once held as true. Until we figure out how to recreate equilibrium, we race to adjust to the shift from old to new theories. Turmoil ensues in the disequilibrium to our way of living and our planned futures (see Figure 4-1). Yet we improvise. We adapt. We overcome. We experience these societal transformations together. Our perspectives change. Remember, previous generations' members in the culture-made and sustained powers-controlling positions rose with yesteryear's theories. If misaligned with liberty, such concepts in times of crises inadequately wrestle with the new circumstances, and conditions change painstakingly. The old moves do not cause the effect we need. This half-decent adaptation pattern has occurred throughout history. A large one happened with the first industrial revolution. Then the second stage of knowledge evolution came, and now we are in the third (Hage, 2020).

Our adaptations to survive in geography remain, but now we must adapt to our tools to continue living. Our tools may not want to adapt to our irrationality, so we need to be wise. We need to find ourselves in charge, carefully considering our future as we cope with the challenges we face in the digital age. Our passage from the Age of Enlightenment, to the age of entertainment, to the age of entitlement, to the age of exhibitionism could put us at risk (see Figure 5-8). If we allow the drift to continue, the drift of an unled society, the drift of doomerism, it may soon be too late to resuscitate liberty and justice for all.

People are both unique persons with proclivities and members of groups in society. We belong to groups by happenstance of pre-existing social arrangements, by force, or by choice. At any given time of its history, a human born into a society experiences era related self-shaping social circumstances. Our identity is as a person, all to ourselves and to our social roles and positions within the groups to which we belong. We come to reflect our era. Our shared experience with our cohorts shapes us partially, giving us an applied identity. We carry with us the personality of our generation whether we realize it or not.

About people power, people possess personal and social power. In the context of democracy, these take the form of self-governing and societal governing. Raising humans involves finding a fitting nurturing to the nature of a child. As he or she becomes a unique person, we guide one another through our natural developmental stages. While we become, we do so within the perspective of a human being within a society. We have the obligation to behave and take part in it. If a society of democracy is to be successful, we must behave to perpetuate it. We must do better than in other forms of society. That is, we must govern ourselves and lead ourselves to be citizens first. This is especially important in our leadership role as an American people. We are to control the powers of society. The quality and quantity of power we wield or yield depends upon our citizenship engagement. Our job is to lead the society through leading within our roles in society. We lead ourselves in micro social behaviors. We lead our organizations operating at the meso social levels, and by representatives, we lead the macro-level societal powers. We do this through citizenshipping. It involves:

- Exhibiting good behavior
- Behaving within reasonable boundaries
- Changing the rules if they are not in accord with our Constitution's objectives
- Fulfilling our responsibilities

- Educating ourselves on civics
- Exercising our right to vote and regulating powers
- Avoiding divisive demagoguery
- Resisting prejudices against others we do not understand
- Seeking to understand—assuming goodwill intentions of neighbors and strangers
- Vesting trust in shared values of citizenshipping

We do it by E-SASSY-T-TUF-FT-CAUCUS, which takes lifelong learning and ACE knowledge. Knowledge we must learn as best we can. Because we the people are in the leadership role, we must get educated. Subjects in kingdoms can remain ignorant. We cannot!

Is it too much to ask? As the price of having the four freedoms, it is easy. For the victory of liberty over tyranny, each of us must get educated and mature toward being more perfect persons. We cannot afford to quit this, or drop out. We need everyone to pull together. How else will we get to a more perfect union? We must begin within our own selves. We must continue with our performance in organizations and our participation in politics. If we do not, how will we keep our democracy? It is up to us and not a savior. We must put in the work. We cannot be lazy, complacent, or apathetic, no matter our social circumstances or physical conditions. We must become better citizens everywhere and in every way. This is a discipline. It is a commitment to our society and to ourselves because we must lead it!

Knowledge is the principal instrument of our people power. Our KA^4SA^2 depend on circumstances both beyond and within our personal control. Yet, we must pursue it, as we pursue virtue, as we pursue happiness. Education is a path we must stay upon all our lives.

We are constrained by social circumstances and physical conditions. Each person's endowments and limitations affect their unique contributions to society. We develop and become the best we can. We the people need to find among us those best suited for the purposes for which we need them, as well as finding that for which we ourselves are well suited. Our society depends on creating opportunities for us to fill our positions in the $FILMS^{2}$ [P7] of our social powers with the right persons. Our KA^4SA^2 continuously need to be honed. All of us are a pool of applicants to contribute to our enterprise. We serve our country by bringing competitive skills with a cooperative attitude and helpful team spirit to our endeavors that contribute to its glory. Top-flight knowledge possessors know that life is about cooperation. They know that our country depends upon educated citizens working in positions for which each are well suited to perform our duties in society. They also know that not everything is knowable, so we must repeatedly re-educate to keep pace with the changes we face with increasing knowledge and technology complexity.

Overcoming our limitations is a fundamental need. Some cannot due to biological constraints. Others we can and must strive to overcome. These include:

- Brain functioning—healthy mental states of mind. Having a mind to think and feel with is central to KA^4SA^2. We need it for social self-maintenance competency and the capacity and capability to self-manage. We need it to provide self-care. We need it to get the necessary goods and services for survival, living, or luxury, without adverse social conflicts. To nourish our full faculties is vital, via both biological nutrition and psychological and social nurturing and encouragement. Our happiness depends on our health, and malnutrition is a risk we must avert.

- Bodily functioning—healthy physiological and physical states of body. Having the competencies to live without disabilities is a blessing. Various factors constrain a body. We can suffer from disabilities to ambulatory movement or lack the necessary motor skills in our appendages. Losing our functionality to make and manipulate tools to support necessary behaviors for living puts us at risk of becoming a burden to others. This physical limitation has psychological and social consequences. Validation of everyone's worth, regardless of dependency, is a value within a democracy-based culture. We need each other. If physical constraints impair our capacity and capability to provide self-care, others must. How else will we get the necessary goods and services for survival, living, or thriving?

In adulthood, we reach an independent condition, but for most of our lives, we are dependent on others. The secondary social powers family and community powers are vital to provide care and nurturing for us. We rely on them in our dependent, semi-dependent, and semi-autonomous circumstances. We serve them when we are autonomous and independent. We keep a tether to them and as they do to us. At the beginning and end of life, we are fully dependent upon family and community. This dependency is part of the normal human life cycle. We grow through our stages of being and becoming. As we do successfully, we learn key attitudes and feelings: conscientiousness, compassion, love, and empathy.

Compassionate love is caring for those who cannot care for themselves because they suffer limitations and constrains. Liberty asks us to treat others, as we would have them treat us. Liberty asks us to provide others as much independence, respect, and dignity as possible. It takes compassion. It takes effort. It takes love. Illness and death are tough to witness; they show us our common frailty: mortality. We must face the experience of existence that our turn will come one day. This realization bonds us together in our shared reality as human beings. The wisdom in this sentiment causes us to feel gratitude. When we are grateful, we can appreciate each other better as we mature. We grow up to become independent. When independent, we contribute. We come to control the operant behaviors of the societal and social powers. We work within their instruments, turning wheels to set directions and pushing buttons and pulling levers to make their mechanisms work for society. If we do it well, our ship sails in a healthy direction, and we can take advancing risks. If we do it badly, calamitous risks increase, and our vulnerabilities expose us to threatening hazards and bad memories. Past wounds badly sutured open up and seethe. We must seek to find ourselves in an independent condition when in adulthood. Because a functional society needs us to contribute to its sustenance, we must raise one another to be competent adults. To do this we need to understand our societal and social powers and evaluate the equality of them in each of our ten regional subcultures, three prominent settlement patterns, and seven socialization contexts of our children. When we equalize and raise all babies to be citizens, we make it possible to stabilize our society—to right the ship and sail it better toward our constitutional objectives. Doing this, we will tend to those who are in natural states of dependence. Baby doomers did not attend to society, to human reality. They've not addressed our upcoming societal challenges. They chased cultural precepts that caused baby doomerism. This new culture CATAPULTED crises upon us, and COIFFURE democracy, the safest middle lane and level for liberty, from American society. Let's move on to discuss these difficulties we now face in the context of our people power.

One important fact of our near-term future is our changing demographics (see Figure 4-5). Our society will have fewer independent adults than dependent children and elders. This is a major challenge we will face, and we must begin to become aware of it and work on defining it as a problem we must solve. Its parameters need better known, so that we can create innovative solutions. We need to put in place new means to manage the risks that could come from an ill-prepared demographically differently balanced society than has ever been seen before in modern human history. We are especially in danger of societal sustainment because doomerism culture undermines family and community powers; these two are critical to care for one another. Malfeasant baby doomers do not move society toward becoming one of love, care, respect and dignity. More people are living longer than ever, and the distribution of incomes is separating our citizenry into haves and have-nots. A few have the assets and capital. The many do not have enough to experience a standard of living and quality of life that is feasible, or expected, based on human knowledge's advancement.

As citizens for each other's liberty, together we must join in efforts to understanding one another's psychological personalities and social expectations. A baby doomer outlook inhibits this requirement of citizenship in a democracy. Firstly, we are members of the same society. Yes, we've great regional variety, but we all must be allies with our Constitution. We all have inalienable rights and responsibilities of our citizenship. We must find the willpower to motivate ourselves to be the best contributing members to society we can be. It is ours. Some of us have general orientations to be social rule breakers and others of us social rule makers. Some of us have general orientations to prefer loose cultures, while others prefer tight cultures (Gelfand, 2018). Loose cultures are very tolerant of differences and do not mind rule breaking that leads to innovation. The Dutch who settled New Amsterdam, now New York City, were like this. Tight cultures are least tolerant of differences, and like rule following. They tend to be hierarchical and tradition-oriented. The English who settled New England, the Yankees, and the English who settled the Deep South, the Planters, were like this. Ironically, these two tradition holding regions oppose each other (Woodard, 2011), for reasons of mythology power's differing integration into their subcultures, history power's identity shaping influences, and industry power's use of geography power's opportunities. Whether we prefer loose culture or tight culture, we must all be law-abiders. If we dislike the laws, we must use our people power to change them through our mechanism of voting in representatives that will enact our will. These are citizenship duties.

Because we have differing KA^4SA^2, we must find ways to shape our society to provide the right kind of education and occupation, vocational or professional, paid or volunteer jobs, and for-profit or not-for-profit business, for each person. People learn differently. We must customize teaching so all can learn more fully. Our enterprise's success in the future requires new KA^4SA^2. We must develop greater cognitive complexity and empathy to evolve toward postmodern selves (Hage, 2020). We must not force a one-size-fits-all pedagogy of modernistic or traditionalistic value sets. The education mechanisms of the instruments of the academy power need rebalancing. As we develop though our human stages, we discover within ourselves and within our fellow citizens our KA^4SA^2. Let's set up social systems to reveal our best talents, get people into the right positions, and revel in such a society. This duality of our existence is ever-present, and we must support the poles, the "me" and the "we," in concert to give the "we" the best "me" possible. This is what a good citizenry in republic does through its democracy, its pursuit of an egalitarian culture of equal chance to contribute in social and self-harmony. We must help everyone become the best each of us can be for all. We'll benefit when each one's given and developed endowments and talents promote our general welfare.

We must focus on raising the rising generations to $AEIOUY^2K$ our people power so it returns to the top of society, alive and well. Let's shape our academy power to provide optimal pathways for us all. We need everyone to educate better on how to become a willing and competent citizenry, E-SASSY-T-TUF-FT-CAUCUS. We need such total prosocial citizens to fight back against the cruel and unusual unsocial and antisocial actions of doomerism. As our enterprising society enters unchartered waters of the third stage in our species' knowledge evolution and societal transformation, we must not fear "fear". Times are a changing. They are scary. To gain successful passage through them, we need civically minded able adults, not more baby doomers. Extracting all one can get and causing others to suffer does not a society make. It most certainly does not make a society of democracy with liberty and justice for all. It exacerbates previous generations' animosities and incompetence at getting us to a more perfect union.

Academy power gives knowledge

Our people power finds itself in our knowledge, and our knowledge finds itself in us as persons with varying levels of educational advancement, which have differing purposes. We get knowledge through the academy power's FILMS^2 [P7]. We gain the mechanism of its power through our learning efforts and the effects of it on us. These have differing degrees of recognition for KA^{4}SA^2, representing specific purposes of certificates, as specialized general degrees earned through formal education:

- Doctorate—to discover new knowledge, synthesize to known, or connect with other fields to create new knowledge
- Masters—to teach known knowledge, synthesize differing spheres of knowledge
- Bachelors—to learn basic principles and concepts of society, with extra learning in one or two areas of knowledge specialization, which we see defined by college majors
- Associates—to learn technical skills necessary for the production, operation, or maintenance of equipment, inventions, or art

Regardless of our level of collegiate educational advancement, we study the reality of the observable world with our academy power. We witness both the portion of it within us and in our culture's structures. Knowledge pursues the truth. But the truth may rest between the observable and the unknown. Building upon data and beliefs, we may never know the absolute truth, but we continue to pursue it. This pursuit leads to periodic breakthroughs, radical innovations that shift the paradigm of what we knew. Such shifts lead to disequilibrium. For each problem we solve, new ones arise from our efforts (Hage, 2020). Our adaptive problems to societal transformations will continue (see Figure 5 1). Being aware of causes of social changes, their forming, our storming, norming, and performing (see Figure 4 1) behaviors, once we've fused into a new equilibrium, is important to us as a people. This knowledge of knowledge evolution prepares us for the future and to AEIOUY^{2}K our people power properly as a republic of democracy. We must resolve to press on through change, learn, and lead society along its new path of advancements, while retaining the divine gift of our liberty. We cannot afford to be dependent on no longer valid old ways, means, and methods of performing the LAMBS.

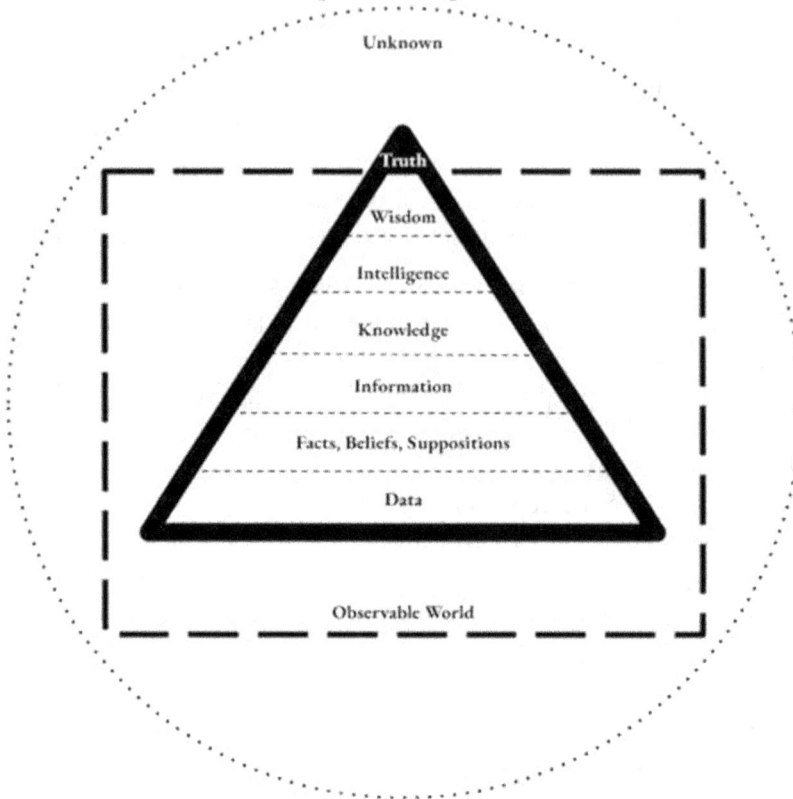

Figure 3-3: Truth Pyramid

Truth resides between the unknown and the observable world. Knowledge builds upon information. Some is not provable but believed in as a matter of faith. We often look for data to support our suppositions of what we want to find, facts validating and verifying the information we choose to believe. Intelligence is the condition in which we become enlightened to tell ourselves what our knowledge is, based upon fact. It is also what our beliefs of the yet unknown and the myths or fictions we choose to believe either allow or suspend. Intelligence is honesty. When we're able to apply our intelligence to live in harmony within ourselves, with others, and with society, we have achieved wisdom. Wisdom gives us clarity. With it we understand the circumstances and conditions that confront us as persons, as a people, and as a society and live without judgment. We are complete in truthful wisdom, in what it provides to, for, and by us.

Let us make our society's academy power provide pathways for all our children to get an equal quality and quantity of education. While baby doomers create an inner-circle hierarchy to limit others' access to a top education, our enterprise needs all children to have it. The tactics to block access to education only prove their treason against democracy. Be it by purchasing entrance to top universities through gifts by false athletic recruiting or cheating on standardized testing. Tests meant to level the playing field to find the studious need respected. They also need cured of biases towards certain intellectual skills over other valuable qualities like street smarts and common sense thinking, which they do not capture, but which are essential for citizens of a republic. Such schemes of doomerism injure the USE. They ruin the sense of fairness, honesty, and integrity that we need.

We must find the best citizens to serve us at the helms on the bridges in the pilothouses of our societal powers. After all, it is our ship, our USE. We the everyday people must lead or we find ourselves in a worsening plutocracy or other form of state tyranny. If we continue with doomerism, we will fail to lead correctly, and effectively allow further drifting into hazardous illiberal seas. We will fail the children. If we do not change course, we will all be labeled baby doomers in the future's history books. Is this what we want? Are we that desperate for material wealth? Our enterprise has historically lifted more and more people up and out of deplorable conditions. Yet we are backsliding under the reign of the baby doomers. Their aristocratic trending is like the tendency of power to corrupt. Their limiting others from knowing comfortable living is nothing more than a form of power exertion. They do it solely to convince themselves that they are superior to the rest of us. It is a form of classism. Saying "no" to others to get a sense of control, for the raw power pleasure of it, is corrupt. Doing so to make others feel inferior is tyrannical psychology. Denying others access to opportunities to contribute their talents, is wrong. Having a central "me first" value causes such moral failures. It does not encourage a race to the top, but instead, speeds up a chase to the bottom.

It is as if the boomers want to be kings and queens, princes and princesses. These labels represent identities that are the antithesis of the citizenry of a democracy. Theoretically, the founder's revolution cast off caste society, tossing it onto a waste pile of history. Practically, we've been working on our project to live up to their words while wrangling over how to handle the apparent hypocrisies in lives lived and what such biographical example implies for us down through our history. We do better to presume we can live up to our better beliefs enshrined in our founding documents, and forgive our forefathers' transgressions while striving not to repeat real actions that are incompatible with our ideals. However, we are off course from this path because the baby doomers are steering our ship in the direction of feudal power arrangements.

An abomination we now face is the making of false divisions among us, like many of the isms discussed in Chapter 1. The creation of a ruling tier of the political directorate and economic elites occurred (Mills, 1956), and doomerism enlarges its control over society. It is deplorable for a democracy. A society based upon democracy must be egalitarian interested for the good of the society so that each of us to our own ability may rise to the level of contribution nature and nurture empower us to get to by our American merit and not by some special boardroom, back door egotistical nepotistic favor, or coattail riding sycophancy. Climbing just to be fancy by fairy dusting is hypocrisy.

Our enterprise suffers tremendous social instability and insecurity because of doomerism. Using our people power to better the use of our academy power, we can reverse its trends. Liberty requires a less aristocratic approach. It begins with our youngest citizens. They need a solid ACE. Our formal education divides into age-based schooling. Does this need to be reformed? Is the current paradigm and pedagogy correct? Presently we have:

- <u>High School</u>—A place to learn the principles and concepts of our society. These, taught at a level comprehensible to fast-developing adolescent brains that are expanding their absorption capability and capacity. This level in coordination with family and community must provide everyone the KA^4SA^2 necessary to be a competent functional adult within society. This outcome's importance increases as society becomes more complex.

- <u>Middle School</u>—A place to learn more and hone the rudiments of basic knowledge, and helps kids learn about who they might aspire to be in life. Children continue to develop the personal and social skills appropriate for the context of our society.

- <u>Elementary School</u>—A place to learn the elementary rudiments of reading, writing, arithmetic, and social interaction for successful group behavior.

- <u>Early Development Learning</u>—A place to launch human brain and social development into learning that ensures future success (we need more of these). This relates to biology power's best advancement, noting the need to avoid the risks of malnutrition.

Brains need fed nutrition and education properly to develop the deep structures of language that increase learning. The anomic and enervating socialization contexts constrain and limit human potential. Poor in quality, such social circumstances and physical conditions disturb the health of children and disrupt normal development. By not correcting these, we expose society to enormous risks. These risks, when realized, result in long-term social consequences. We cannot sustain the near-permanent financial burdens upon everyone that these conditions cause us. As with a construction project, it costs less to plan and design any changes on paper than it does to tear something down and build it differently. We must attend to the needs of children early more often and more fully. We cannot doom them to incomplete or injurious development because of the doomerism sold to us by baby doomers, whose focus is on their needs in agedness. We must turn the prow of the ship and focus our fleet of powers toward tomorrow, not yesterday. Today is the day we must begin!

Particularly important is what we must do better for toddlers, whose brains are expanding rapidly. Babies need appropriate stimulation to unlock the creative powers within human biology power. A baby's body, nerves, brain, and even memory depend upon nutrition and nurturing. Babies must not be made to feel as if they are a mistake or worthless. Self-esteem begins at birth. If we focus on their needs and not ours, we stand less of a chance of dooming them. Note, focusing on the needs of children does not mean spoiling them. That actually would be a pacification behavior of adults to stop an annoyance to the adults done by a child. Attending to a child's development is not a superficial attention giving behavior. It is an intentional effort to give children self-confidence, a sense of their capabilities, resiliency capacity, and a feeling of age appropriate independence. An American should feel free, but not as if, every whim is permissible. Disciplined decorum is necessary to feel the feeling of liberty. It's that freedom to be responsible for one's own person, and get valued as a good one in society. This is our civic obligation—to raise children as such, as Americans. This commitment must continue throughout the caretaking that adults provide children until they themselves become adults. We pass on lessons. Is doomerism the one we want to trickle downward?

Artistry power creates

As a society, we're not harnessing our artistry powers sufficiently for all our citizens. We need everyone to develop more creativity to help us solve the increasingly complex problems of our new era. We confront scary circumstances with our newly invented, fantastically powerful technologies. They are frustratingly complicated when we do not understand them. We need sufficient training to understand their complexity. We need new solutions for the societal problems doomerism unleashed upon us. We must unite as one people to comprehend them and extend appropriate leadership to society. As our children develop, we must be aware of instilling in them a moral character benefiting society, best done by our good example (see Figure 2-27). Sadly, the baby doomers and their culture of doomerism show us many foibles and moral failings. We will discuss these errors and omissions of morality in Section 2.

However, academic, artistry, and moral learning are insufficient for human fulfillment. We must ease stress in life. We must find times of deep inner thought, creativity, and artisanship that give us the powerful sense of "flow" (Csikszentmihalyi, 1991): the place in our minds when all moves perfectly, and we lose track of time, finding ourselves at peace upon a task's completion. A great way to relax our corpus and still our being is through having artistry power active in our lives. The mechanisms by which we express this power to heal us vary by the methods of making and consuming it. Art, the product produced by an artist's work, can tap our senses one at a time or several at once. People of different places, social circumstances, and physical conditions do art differently. Audiences have selective tastes. Some find others' artistic expressions distasteful. When we link our identities too closely to a genre of expression, we run the risk of missing our commonalities.

We can unite as a citizenry around the ideals that allow each of us to express ourselves freely. If we show curiosity for how others bring their artistic powers to life, we can get closer to each other through understanding the how and why of what we see and hear that at first we might fear. We may find we have more in common than the foreign feel of another's art might cause us to think at first blink. For our youth, let's shape our society's artistry power to provide simple delights. Let's all enjoy the creative expressiveness of people. This power includes athletics. Nevertheless, let's do so with a greater appreciation of the cooperation that makes a competition possible. Our people power creates our artistry power; our culture structures it into our society. Our competitiveness supports us in sports and entertainment, but let it not ruin our politics. Governing is too serious to treat as a competition. However, from the joyful processes and products of artistry power, its flow found from its enthralling goodness, we could reach psychological states in which we can flourish as persons and as a people: mental emotionally, growing intellectually, and with healthful fulfillment, socially and physically.

Industry power makes

Our people power also created our industry power. It is an instrument of our economy power and acts through many mechanisms. A key one is work for pay, a job, a source of income to enable participation in the marketplaces for exchanging goods and services. We need to use our people power to press the industry and economy powers to employ our talents and allow us to contribute. We need work. We need a variety of occupations, vocations, and professions in many tiers that allow us to reach our fullest potential by merit and our KA^4SA^2. If a person has what it takes to perform at the highest levels, let us support their talents rising to the top. Yet let us not continue the baby doomer culture of celebrity. We have talent to benefit everyone at all levels of performance and all sizes of scale and popularity. We need a range of available work, nationally, regionally, and locally, including things on the medium and lower scale of KA^4SA^2 applicability. Let's not perpetuate the doomerist culture of the superstars and super salaries at the expense of everyday people not having a paid job to do, and other ways to contribute to strengthening civil society by participation in a localized association doing good for neighbors. Super scaling everything is a ridiculous, anti-democratic formula for aristocracy to take over our minds. Doomerism rewards a few of our fellow human beings (who, like us, put their pants on one leg at a time) in such gigantic proportions it is mind-bogglingly overwhelming. The inequality this creates is staggering in its risks for sustaining an uncorrupted republic.

Socialization and place

The contexts in which reared socialize us. Our enculturation and acculturation occurs in them. The secondary powers are the immediate shapers of these contexts though they have many influences: social, cultural, economic, geographic, and locational. Characterized by the results of the arrangement of the societal powers the authorities in these contexts control the lives of children. Because, we form within them, we all reflect our social circumstances and physical conditions of our raising.

The behavioral settings (Barker, 1968) of these contexts in which we become persons vary significantly by settlement pattern. We've three main types: urban, suburban, and rural. In their broader locales, each sets up the behavioral settings in their architecture in which socialization occurs. They have subcultural values passed down from settlers of the ten different regions (recall Figure 2-24). We've experienced diversity of opinions from our fellow citizens from different settlements and regions. As we live and develop we try things, we adopt and replicate generational values, beliefs, attitudes, and behaviors. We've our complexes as regional people, which pose challenges to our unity when we become unwilling to be curious, listen, learn, and tolerate different perspectives. We get past our differences by a common connection to our foundation as a country, the Constitution. It joins us. To better unify and move toward achieving a more perfect union, we must as a people and as persons, abide by the founding principles and ideals that led to it. It binds us in union as a nation with the prospect to be e pluribus unum, one American people. This reality is our truth. It creates and strengthens our people power. Focusing on our responsibility to uphold the Constitution to its fulfillment aids us in achieving harmony as the fortunate American people. The people power gives us the right to lead society. We lead by E-SASSY-T-TUF-FT-CAUCUS. We self-govern by being good and doing good, which make us well. We govern society best by neighborly civic engagements and informed political participation. These demand that those among us in positions of authority properly AEIOUY^{2}K the societal powers in a manner benefiting our liberty. Further, these demands mean we must not allow ourselves, or others, to DAMN the powers if given authority to administer or manage. By such refusals, we demonstrate the ethical integrity that can reclaim for us the prestige of the label "land of the free, home of the brave".

We the everyday people must demand of ourselves attitudes and behaviors guided by integrity and courage. We must expect our authority holders to act as fellow citizens doing the same. We must be prepared and willing to hold them accountable, especially those of the highest rank whose actions effect situations at meso and macro levels of society that can injure the micro levels whereat our daily living transpires with the most social contact. Our enterprise depends on all of us contributing our best each day. Our officials must keep our public trust. Further, we need citizens privileged with enormous returns on their investments to see themselves as one of us. We need citizens taking entrepreneurial risks to make good use of our artistry, industry, and academy powers. We need to stabilize our economy power in ways that will benefit all of us and not just a few at the top of its earning capacity and capability. Next, we'll touch briefly on a natural power, biology power, and offer motivation for the people power's leadership role. Then we'll cover the polity and economy powers before diving further into the secondary and tertiary social powers.

Biology

Just as society has its endowments passed down from one generation to the next, so too does a person. Each of us receives though biology certain endowments, features, limitations, and spoliations. Beyond our birth, through eight phases of development, we mature in intellect and character. What we get at birth is beyond our intellect's control. Our character is not beyond our intellect's control. It is in large part the primary responsibility of our intellect. What we know to be true in our hearts needs nurtured so we may become persons of good character. Socially focusing on exterior features is less helpful and unhealthy for civil society. We do better as citizens when we see people for who they are in their character, not what group we might think they belong to, or what they look or smell like. We need to assume goodwill of our fellow citizens. Our intellects and character, not our features, nor our sexual orientation or gender dysphoria, are what is most valuable. In society, the only way to overcome stereotypes and prejudice is to stop socializing children to have them. Prejudice isn't inborn it's taught (Clark, 1963). Character and contribution matter most. Acting tribal is antithetical to democracy. A person's biology is not their fault. We should not experience disrespect and indignant mistreatment because of it.

Each person comes into the world and gets raised in a family, a settlement, a regional subculture, and a generation. We also get socialized in a socio-philosophical context (see Figure 2-26). The social milieu influences how each of us experiences nurturing and develops as a social person. This is a fact for our entire species. It justifies being compassionate with empathy as a wise approach to social interaction. We would do better as a people to recognize this. By civic engagement, we can better understand this and practice understanding one another. We need to be able to speak openly about the essences of the influences we have encountered. Others relate to these stories of the social influences on us. All people are born with only biology power. This power is limited since we are born dependent on others to survive, live, and thrive.

In a republic with democracy-based culture, we will not have liberty and justice for all if we tolerate prejudices. A person's character is the purpose of the people to attend to in helping one another find ways to contribute. We must assist each other in developing a common value set that supports the republic of us as one people. Doing this means getting to know persons for their character, innate and groomed, and for their contributions, not for superficial characteristics. With better social grammars to understand one another, we can get along with each other in spite of our many superficial differences. By this, we will build the social capital to perform the citizen-shipping that needs don to get us closer to perfecting our union. We must see one another as fellow citizens in this mission. We need to grant each person this dignity and not look upon one another as appearances of en-dowments, features, limitations, and spoliations, or as members of alien groups. Citizens are a citizenry altogether. Our citizenry must act in unison to maintain its unity for liberty to oppose tyranny. We'll end our discussion of people power with some more words on its proper role in society: lead-ership.

Lead society

As citizens, we must $AEIOUY^2K$ people power to get into unison. We need unity to prevent the primary societal, secondary, and tertiary social powers from undermining our people power. The secondary powers, but even more so the tertiary powers, affect society at the macro level. Typically their influence is at the meso levels, regional subculturally scaled $FILM^{S2}$ [P7] and corresponding HM^5. These influence the micro levels at the settlement pattern and smaller scales of social interaction. Yet nowadays because of the immediacy and ubiquity of media communications' spread, we must be cognizant of new threats to our project to make a truly American society. The intermixing of influences and impacts between levels and scales of so-ciety is like nothing seen before. Previous time lags between influences and impacts of one scale, or level, upon the other gave us time to process with wisdom. The more rapid than ever before information exchanges phenom-enon clouds our judgement and makes the use of wisdom increasingly more difficult. Deliberative bodies most work quickly with less secure facts. When fallacies get introduced into the stream of information, it damages the core practices of our democracy-based American republic style LAMBS. It challenges the stability of our USE. Additionally and aggravat-ingly, aggressive adversarial autocratic nations attempt to ravage and unrav-el American society by exploiting our openness and invented technologies. They prey upon our internal fraying fabric that doomerism wears thread-bare and tears as if no one cares for the whole that is greater than the sum of its parts: society. This is why our people power leadership must be ramped up more now than ever. We must build our community of com-mon ground faster. We mustn't violate the law of the commons that ena-bles our nation's common wealth. The sooner we can, the better the future for our children will be. We do not have time to squabble around the edges. We need to orient to aligning on our core virtues and key values. Only lead-ership can do this. We are the leadership. We must act, act better, and act together. First-and-foremost, we must cease and desist from ignorant arguments. We must concentrate on cutting out the tumor of doomerism. We must heal from its destruction done to our society these past forty years.

The quality and quantity of our people power depend upon citizenship engagement in the activity of leading the society. As we perform our roles within our society, particularly when using our economy powers, we must remember that we are citizens first. Without the framework of the polity, we would not have the freedom to use our artistry and industry powers to expand our economy power. We bring to it our mental and physical labor as workers. We are mediums of the mechanisms and we $AEIOUY^2K$ economy power. To convince ourselves otherwise is to fall into the moral pit of doomerism. With our agency, we are party to the $FILMS^2$ [P7] of power. We staff positions in its instruments, the organizations and institutions, we've shaped within our USE, both for monetary profit and nonprofit, for the providing of goods and services. We must see ourselves in our role performance as citizens first. This is vital to the success of the USE. It relies on honesty and integrity for non-exploitative dealmaking. Taking advantage of a fellow citizen is a scandal we can scarce afford in the dystopian era we are approaching. The 21st century to some holds little promise that people will matter (Harari, 2019), as we believe they should in the United States. Our impact, quality, and quantity of effort will improve society if our orientation is toward helping our country unify. We cannot let the science fictions of either Aldous Huxley's *Brave New World* or George Orwell's *1984* convince us the future of society is inevitably how they imagined it. We must understand their visionary warnings and enact countermeasures. We must not ignore ominous messages if they tell of things that threaten our project.

Guided by the light of liberty we help our compatriots not be in it for "me" first but for "we" first. Each of us must have opportunities to contribute our talents to better it. This builds affection toward it. This makes us proud in the proper cloth of love. Supported and self-motivated we want to contribute to it willingly. We need jobs. We need our economy power to create jobs and not replace us with robots. We should not feel we work "because we have no choice" or to "achieve the necessary financing to survive." We must lead one another at work toward finding harmony because teamwork gives us a feeling of pride, a sense of liberty when supported to pursue our dreams. We will find a great feeling of accomplishment when we move our society toward its constitutional objectives. We need to lead, follow, and experience real good leaders in such a way that we do not settle for treating our laboring as "just a job", a circumstance and condition in which we might feel trapped. We need better mobility for each of us to find our fullest fulfillment. This is what a society of liberty makes possible on a local, regional, national, and ultimately global scale.

We'll benefit by commitment to the higher duty to our USE as we reacquaint ourselves with its revolutionary social invention. From it, we must demand fairness and not tolerate exploitation. We want to work with dignity, not by manipulation. Leadership creates the mood in our society. A proper mode is one of creativity, industriousness, conscientiousness, compassion, love, and empathy. Each generation taught about the societal and social powers will understand how we the people must all learn to be leaders over the course of our lives. Raising an American requires not allowing sloth, gluttony, or any of the other so-called deadly sins to take over our characters. Citizens in charge of the eleven human-made powers, their FILMS[2] [P7] and HM[5], must commit not to use us. We must know and believe in our complete beings it is wrong to exploit a fellow citizen. We must seek equilibrium of the three primary societal powers to ensure we evidence this truth in our society.

Let's move on to the polity power, the endowment we've received from the framers. It has features to which baby doomers cause spoliation. Not wanting despoiled of our life, liberty, and pursuit of happiness, our comprehension of power is critical. We live in a nation that began by dividing power, so we could unite against tyranny to have a republic of representative democracy, e pluribus unum. We must understand the polity power formatively to regulate it formidably.

Polity Power

Polity power's prime method is administration (see Figure 2-5). Polity is principally concerned with who is "in" and who "has" power, officially, politically, and "for what" with "what authorities." Government AEIOUY[2]K our polity power. It does this by making, clarifying, and enforcing the laws. Those who administer the polity power, the politicians, seek to achieve ambitions to effect change in society. In US society, their job is to work together to move society toward the objectives encased in our Constitution and to always IDEALS liberty. Yet it cannot do these unless we do them at the micro levels of society. These American society essentials seem forgotten; the politicians pursue their own ambitions. Infected by doomerism, our ship is off course. Because we've given them the authority to pull the levers of power for our benefit, we must pay attention to their actions. Bad politicians lie to us to serve their fantasies, steered by "me first" attitudes and behaviors. Good politicians work to keep the power with the people and listen to our leadership in society, not our "me first" whims, and employ wisdom and sound judgement to coach us if we are wrongheaded. If we become complacent or apathetic, we fail to lead them. They will falter in guiding society effectively for us. Worse, we allow them to continue to do whatever they want for themselves. This is how we ruin each other and the American project. We must help our elected and appointed officials be and stay good. We must hold them accountable. Good politicians need to arise who will move us toward our enterprise's essential objectives. They must work to IDEALS liberty. This is their principle mission. It is how they serve our project best on its voyage to achieve the Preamble's goal by attaining its objectives. We must demand this from them. Bad politicians take power away from the people without our consent, which will be our fault if we're not participating. We must exercise our leadership in exercising our self-governing and governing-the-self power. Ugly power happens when the polity power uses venal politicians who DAMN powers. We are in trouble when they pretend to achieve good while really playing a game, doing wrong against us, such as with demagoguery, or bait and switch truth as they twitch about stealthily, stitching in special favors for money givers and friends. Demagoguery is a very dangerous hazard for democracy. It sounds so good, but it undermines us. If we the people are not living as citizens to IDEALS liberty, we will be seduced and carried along the path to bad by ugly modes of power. Demagogic politicians will take us there. Or, in attempting to do good work, the politicians may be incompetent, imagining and doing foolish things that cause bad results. Or, by negligent efforts, they may put us into a state of total confusion that stupefies us. The last misguided bad and ugly acts AEIOUY^{2}K polity power is when politicians want to benefit only themselves and their families. This blind ambition leads them to DAMN polity powers to the detriment of liberty.

The polity's legislative powers

The polity makes the laws with its subordinate legislative powers. It can do this by two principal directions, common law or civil law. Common law is the British tradition—all is permitted except that which is prohibited. This opens up society to the positive risks of pursuing opportunities to improve society. It opens up the polity to enable its control by people power. It offers trust in people. A polity can use common law in relation to people to shape society toward liberty but not likely to make a tyranny. Civil law is the French tradition—all is prohibited except that which is permitted. It restricts people power. It distrusts people. This closes up society to prevent negative risks' realization. It hopes to disallow all vulnerabilities and threats to law and order that might arise inside the population. It can create a sense of dependency and entitlement because it gives the polity unaccountable power to control people. Controlled people will go along to get along. Sadly, it overly constrains people. It takes away their freedom to think for themselves. It makes too many laws, by which they naively and unknowingly can get into trouble. A polity can use civil law in relation to people to shape society toward tyranny but less likely liberty. What a great irony that the French helped us defeat the British. Thankfully, we inherited the English law culture of inalienable natural rights and liberty (Goldberg, 2018) that the framers codified and wrote down as the law of the land. A law that lets us, the people, lead. We Americans must provide leadership to society. We must act with leadership over our personal lives. Or else, society's business will not be about us. We will lose responsibility to set the rules for how we wish to survive, live, and thrive in an open and free society. Our choice is govern self and society better or lose liberty.

The polity's executive powers

The polity enforces laws with its subordinate executive powers. These provide the assurance of fairness in society. These make the playing field fair and reasonable, set the parameters and explain the rules on it, and then referee it. This administration frees us to choose the use of our resources. Executive administrators must do it for the benefit of society and not for the benefit of the politician's personal desires. If they do the latter, it is corrupt, corrupting, corruption. The executive powers must prevent the politicians from changing the polity's purpose to feed their lust for raw power and control over others to feel mighty. The executive officials must have the highest integrity to self-police such risks. They must not allow gains through false pronouncements and foolish promises. They must not do things contrary to constitutional intent. The executive power risk taking over law making by accidental fiat when the legislative branch fails to make rules, which means they do so without input of the governed (Will, 2019). Such is contrary to the intents of a republic with a democracy-based culture. This could lead to a shadow government of over administration (Goldberg, 2018). The risk of shifting from common law thinking to civil law thinking is pernicious for liberty, and imbalances societal power in disfavor of the everyday people.

The executive powers must meet their promise to oversee the proper use of the polity power to IDEALS liberty in society. It must be careful not to AEIOUY^{2}K power for ideological purposes but rather for realistic purposes held as good for the society, as determined by the people. It can do this when the people power is properly leading the polity power administer for society by ensuring it makes legitimate liberty purposeful legislation, legally enforced by the executive. A key subordinate executive power to enforce the rules is policing. Taxes levied upon the people pay for the policing—for protection, good order, and freedoms from fear and crime. Policing must support and serve the needs of good citizens wherever they live, whatever they look like; however they might sound or smell. Policing is to keep the peace and discourage wrongfulness and lawbreaking. The better the character of the people, the less we need police. The better the character of our citizens who work to protect and serve us, the better the police will be. Policing should not impugn a person's character, nor destroy their dignity, nor eviscerate their rights. The more citizens behave and honestly resolve to work things out, the less policing we will need. It merits stating another time, a dishonorable collection of persons is not a people, nor is it a healthy society. In the minds of the politicians, a divided people turned against one another will justify a need for harsher policing. The more police stations we have to build and police officers we have to hire, the worse we are doing as a self-governing citizenry. It is our fault. We must provide leadership to society or its business will not be about our freedom to survive, live, and thrive as we choose. We should not need police, even though we are imperfect. If we serve as police, our imperfection can lead to errors and deadly mistakes. Yet until we do better, we will have more police. The executive is required to keep the peace, but when the status quo is unevenly distributed policing, we have problems in perceptions of what are right and wrong amounts of policing. If we were commitment to a democracy-based culture, we would have no excuse for being uncivil. Doomerism likes us to fall into fighting. It likes to tell us "when the rich can steal and get away with it, so to can the poor justify thefts". However, the poor suffer imprisonment when caught. In a materialistic consumer-based society, objects are everything, and everywhere pursued. Doomerism gets what it sows, and it shows in criminality, jurisprudence and incarceration costs we must bear on our taxes, and in our biology.

Concerned with the administration of policy for society's maintenance, what is best for liberty is a limited polity. This occurs when citizens behave better. We can do it by E-SASSY-T-TUF-FT-CAUCUS. This also helps us reshape and rebalance American society's primary powers (see Figure 2-3). We'll do it to put us more in line with the objectives of the USE. We'll do it using the LAMBS model. We will force the politicians to IDEALS liberty to prevent the polity from seeking to increase its own power. Again, we must provide leadership to society or its business will not be about our humanity, or our surviving, living, and thriving in an open and free society. Let's move on to the third form of polity power: the judiciary.

The polity's judicial powers

The polity clarifies laws through the FILMS[2] [P7] of its subordinate judicial powers. Since it owns rulemaking, it must offer clarifications of the rules. It does this with courts that judge the merits of cases brought before them. Simple principles applied to complex life open us up to manipulation if we do not understand that we must live for, by, and of virtue in all our positions. This is how we guarantee liberty. The pursuit of high virtue as we mature through all phases of human development is essential to create a society that upholds liberty (see Figure 2-27 and 3-6). For a common law polity in a culture with precepts premised in democracy, a citizen-first approach helps us do this. Citizenship has not been first during the boom of economic prosperity that gave rise to the baby boomers moving into positions of authority with "me first" value sets. These heavily expressed in consumption trends. Such risen materialism and consumerism attitudes and behaviors have been large and in charge. Citizenship is a social circumstance in which persons pursue in common, by trustworthy cooperation with one another, a better way that has neighbors speaking to neighbors, solving disputes decently. This way every day brings people closer together toward a united, better future. It produces a civil society engaged in self-governing.

A citizenship way needs less rules clarification because people do not seek to hide behind legal shields with soldiering lawyers out in front to protect them from their misguided misbehaviors and fraudulent misdeeds. But with doomerism's "exploitation is acceptable" overly ambitious overt gaming the game approach, we suffer a loss of trust. Its inherent dishonesty, in which persons' pursuits disregard what is good for the commons, injures all of us by making society cruel. The result, everybody suspects everyone else is up to something suspicious. From this doubt, we improperly fabricate prejudicial judgements of others intentions and see nothing but impropriety. We irrationally attribute characteristics to different others and socially classify and categorize fellow citizens with unconstitutional biases. We allow prejudice within and its actions and reactions without checking it and balancing it with our biology, family, and community powers.

Incessant competing against one another for personal gain, for only our own best future, is a worse way. It expands the need for rules clarification. Baby doomers' constant manipulation causes expansions in exploitative uses of legal devises, like tort lawsuits. This wounds society's functional abilities. It turns neighbors against one another. It erodes trust. It thrusts us into the courts over ridiculous disagreements, causing our taxes to go up to pay for the courts.

The judicial power is also concerned with determining the accuracy and applicability of the law's written by the legislature powers and approved, enacted, and enforced by the executive powers. The courts debate the constitutionality of the laws. They serve to uphold the innocent until proven guilty. They administer the system of jurisprudence. They do it for criminal judgments by trials as well as sentencing punishments. They do it for civil suits, arbitrating disputes between citizens. The more that judicial power is necessary, the worse a society is doing. The more citizens behave and resolve matters honesty, the less time spent in court. A dishonorable collection of persons is not a people, nor is it a healthy society. The more courthouses we have to build, the worse we are doing as citizens. It is our fault. We must provide leadership to society or its business will not be about human surviving, living, and thriving in an open and free society. Let's move on the third primary power, the economy power.

Economy Power

The economy power's prime method is management (see Figure 2-8). Economy is concerned with the provision of what is necessary for our existence. It does this by providing goods and services necessary for survival, living comfortably, and thriving in luxury. All of us AEIOUY^{2}K the economy power in one form or another, some at greater scale than others. Those who manage the economy power, the HM^5, achieve ambitions to effect the provisioning in society. These HM^5 work cooperatively and collaboratively, even as they compete, in a common effort to establish places for people to obtain their provisions and exchange property: markets. The quality and quantity of the provisions for society depend upon management. Management gains from experience in learning and doing and through KA^4SA^2 supported by the academy power.

We depend upon accountability and accounting by the HM^5 to identify, organize, task, count, and prevent failures in how we $AEIOUY^2K$ the economy power and its supportive tertiary social powers. The HM^5 extract and exchange resources to manufacture and deliver the goods and services to provide for society. The economy power, through differing arrangements of its $FILMS^2$ [P7], must ensure accountability for the proper use of resources. It efficiently guides its efforts for effective maximization of the production and delivery of life's necessary and desirable provisions. For this, the HM^5 through many complex interconnected $FILMS^2$ [P7] $AEIOUY^2K$ the economy power. One of its important responsibilities is resourcing. Financing, managing, and laboring capacities and capabilities for provisioning activities are essential duties. As too are finding, growing, mining, and refining materials from geography. The HM^5 put, pull, and produce the food from land, sea, and sky. They must have the KA^4SA^2 to find in geography what society needs and demands and supply it. Luckily, geography provides for humankind. It has biological organisms, flora, fauna, geological minerals, and chemicals with which we cannot do without.

The $FILMS^2$ [P7] of the tertiary social powers: industry, academy, and artistry, suitably serve the economy power. The HM^5 feed, house, clothe, and provide us tools. The $FILMS^2$ [P7] change by acts of competition and cooperation and by regulatory rules upon the markets when errant. In seeking to protect liberty and ensure justice, the polity administers rules for society. It monitors the ways, means, and methods by which we $AEIOUY^2K$ economy power so society may be adaptable to changes. It allows economy power to adjust by forces of markets and of government fair play assurance rulemaking. It introduces investments in scientific and technological research and development. It purchases of specialties used only by governments such as military materiel. The polity and economy powers work with each other. They do best when they keep the public interest as their purpose. When those in their positions of authority exploit the public to maximize and glorify themselves, they fail us. They doom us. They falter and fall into doomerism, not Americanism. When properly done, the economy and polity powers discover, invent, produce, and distribute key tools for society to function well for all the people. Together they make transportation, communications, medicine, and military weapons to defend us, possible. Our enterprise's expansion depends upon our public private partnership. Such cooperation is a hallmark of the USE's success at provisioning society. Yet if it only enriches a few, it is off the course of the goal and objectives. Equilibrium of a well-educated well-paid population does give us equitable success. A depressing debt does not. Decent jobs do. Economy power in support of a truly American society built on a foundation of democracy-based culture must create and sustain better social circumstances and reliable physical conditions for our entire citizenry.

A few more notes about the economy power as it relates to the polity power and we'll move on to a discussion of culture as a precept power process. In cases where the people seek provisions prohibited by the polity, a marketplace will develop to supply the demand. The economy power will deliver. Illegal marketplaces will resource and exchange illicit products. Stop the demand then stop the supply is how we can restrict illegality. This will lower the costs of the polity. As a critical primary power to manage the business of society, the economy power has great responsibility to serve the people—all the people.

If the economy power fails to employ people through effective labor markets, then the polity ends up having to support out of work persons. The public-private partnership between the primary powers needs better understood. They integrate to educate people by the academy power, mostly supported by the polity power, which can be slow to adapt to developing the KA^4SA^2 the economy power needs, or wants too rapidly, to provision society efficiently and enlarge fulfillment. They both must pursue one hundred percent full time employment with sufficient income for one adult to support a household to survive, and part time opportunities for teenagers to learn how to work. If they succeed, we do not need the polity to provide jobs or funds for people to survive. It would be best for the economy power to give the citizenry the ways, means, and methods to do better than just enable this minimum existence. Such as, make it possible for us to work and live with safety, good health, and comfort, and have chances to try for luxury through extra effort and ideas—to rise and pull other up the convenience and financial security ladder with us. On a related note, if the people power remains unexercised without one hundred percent of adults voting, we fail. If neither full employment nor full political participation occurs, we amass huge risks to society's stability. Without healthy employment and participation, human depravity, societal decay, poverty, shame, trafficking in persons, indignation, and violations of human rights expand and freedoms decline.

If the elites of the economy power and its HM^5 positions shaped by its partnership with the polity's $FILMS^2$ [P7] don't $AEIOUY^2K$ the economy power to benefit the USE we'll see instability. We need coordinated collaboration for innovations to solve our wicked societal problems. We may need new $FILMS^2$ [P7] for the economy power. If we enrich only a few, then we, the everyday people, will have nothing to do but suffer. Our vulnerability to the risks of instability will rise and threaten our livelihoods. We need unity of mission by the primary powers. We can begin by refocusing them on accomplishing the goal and objectives of the USE and by repairing its foundations. We need their teamwork to do this so we can return to the important tasks to complete our project's purpose, the making of a society that IDEALS liberty, which demands legitimate work: jobs, vocations, occupations, professions, and life-long meaningful contributory careers. We need possibilities for making a living honestly. The economy powers must orient toward our demands. Our society's wicked problems require that the primary powers align and unify on our common purpose and not work at cross-purposes to our needs. We must see through the deceptive fog of doomerism, regain control, and undue our drifting into deepening dangers.

The risks are escalating deceivingly because of doomerism. We need to meet in the middle. We need to find a way to combine to generate the full commonweal of the American people. If those who profit most from economy power do not act like good citizens, we all will suffer in the end. If persons in positions of authority think it acceptable to compartmentalize actions to avoid seeing truth, we must help them. Their marginal cost thinking and use of financial metrics like Return on Net Assets (RONA) lead to stagnant growth. How we measure creates incentives that lead to unintended and opposite consequences causing problems for the American people. It leads to outsourcing labor (Christensen, 2016). Sending jobs overseas is not doing anything "wrong" necessarily when hidden behind economics theories. However, these do not justify the unkind reality of the resulting abandonment behavior. It is a "wrong" done to the citizenry of the USE to have its jobs sent away to foreign lands. We gave these persons opportunities through nutrition, education, socialization, organization, safety, security, networks, and liberty, most of which got paid for by our tax dollars. We invested our money. We paid for the social and material infrastructures that created the social circumstances and physical conditions in which mercantile prosperity became probable. We enabled companies and workers alike. We are in turbulent trouble as a society when those of us in authority within the economy powers' FILMS[2] [P7] and the HM[5] enterprises forget this and forget about everyone else, the rest us, the everyday people. We are a people, nation, and community in pursuit of a more perfect union with the best relations among humans. To do this we need jobs that yield well-lived lives in peace with freedom.

Abandoning one's neighbors is un-national, undermines our nation, and thus is un-American. Harming the everyday people, who provided opportunity and platforms so the willing and creative could advance, is bad citizenship. It is worse citizenship to damage our posterity. To think otherwise is doomeristic. By incompetence or negligence, doomerism negates enabling a nationally supportive economy power that we can AEIOUY[2]K to enrich every contributing citizen to a dignified standard of living and ennobling quality of life in recognition of his or her talents, meritocratically. Lifting up others to be their best and paying them is a kind of human resource management practice the majority of the citizenry supports. To disagree is to be a doomer. To be a doomer is to will the creation of a society headed by an inheritance-based aristocracy, a plutocracy, or a totally top-heavy totalitarian oligarchy. All of which are antithetical to a culture of democracy. If we forget democracy culture, leaving it for dead because we fall under a spell of rationalizing wrongs as acceptable, permissible, and laudable through celebrity super salaries and egotistical conceit, for certain, we are in gravely dangerous waters.

Clearly, we need better team players than baby doomers if we are to sail away from doomerism! The lowered ethics and decreasing standards of civil discourse, uncivilized conduct, poor civic performance, and tossed overboard ethical and social norms are risks to an American society's success. The DAMN of societal powers is intolerable, unforgettable if not unforgivable. We must rise and stand up for a truer ideal of respectful behavior.

We all need to do and be better at citizenshipping this nation toward its intended destiny. Our society was—and must again be—one in pursuit of the virtue of its goal and objectives. We depend on the primary powers' operation by honor, integrity, courage, and commitment in the greatest of degrees. Governments and markets depend on trustworthiness. Corruption kills them both. Deals made behind the scenes to favor a few kill them both. In a democracy-based culture, such aberrant behavior must cease and desist. Laws need obeyed and not skirted. We each must live to establish justice, so that we do not need an expensive polity to do it, or expand its administrative reach by French style civil law that eventually would control us. The power of peace and no policing resides within us. We behave, and we reduce the costs and increase the opportunities for better societal investments in our purpose, a more perfect union.

Culture, Precept Power Process

Every person has a lot of power to influence, and is influenced by, many identity circles of belonging in a society. As an explanatory device, imagine culture as a living creature, the American lobster (see Figure 3-4). The people are in charge, the head with eyes that see and sensors that smell, hear, and feel. The economy is the bigger claw, the polity the smaller one. As forms of power, they help a culture adapt to the geography for the survival of the society. A pair of secondary and many tertiary powers help move it along, adjusting to the tides. In a democracy culture, we'd call it the Liberty Lobster. As an invertebrate, its structure is exoskeletal, with its spine on the outside. This is equivalent to brave citizens openly expressing their freedom of speech and assembly by meeting in large groups to peaceably protest in front of the houses of their polity and by speaking for important issues in the halls of government, without fear of reprisal and retribution because every citizen knows these are our rights shared in common. Anyone who seeks to stop this is an enemy of the people. Anyone who blocks this, or for profits falsely portrays its facts, is committing treason against liberty.

SOCIETY

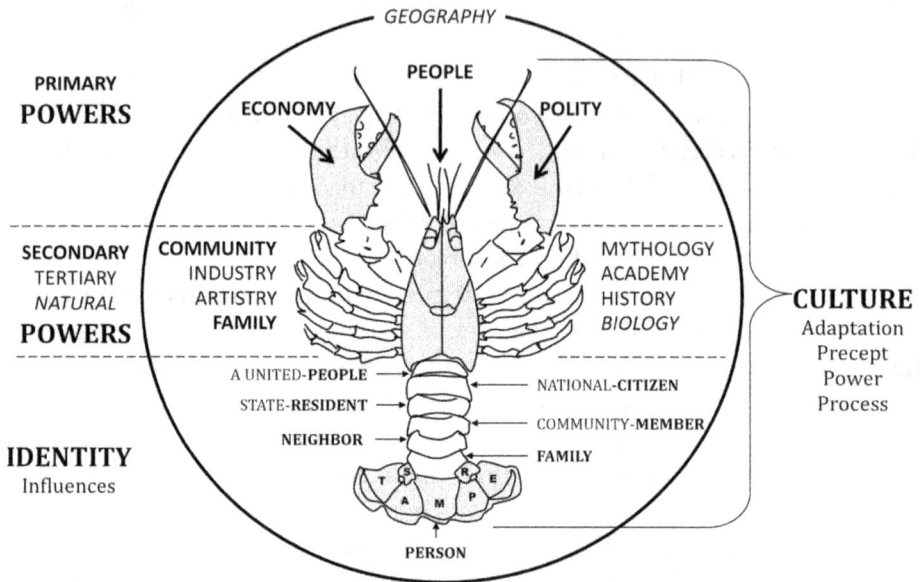

Figure 3-4: "American Lobster"—Democracy Culture, Societal Powers, Symbolized
The most powerful part of this lobster that represents American society is its tail. It symbolizes the connection of a person to the people. A connection built of identities to places; nested in organizational hierarchy. The scale of influence of a place increases with its proximity to the body of the people. Persons get frames of reference from each segment of society. Persons receive differing perspectives from their socialization contexts, of which there are seven. Persons participate in ten regional subcultural variations of being American. Persons grow up in one of three dominate settlement patterns, each which has its themes of living. The secondary and tertiary powers of society, like legs of the lobster must function as oars of a ship. They must synchronize to work in unison to maximize positive actions for the whole. When coordinated the powers benefit the people. This yields the best possible livelihood for society.

Yes, with the claws, we symbolically imply the economy can crush us, or the polity can crush us, but notice that "we the everyday people" as the head control both of these. We are the brains, and that means we've the chemosensory antennae antennules, all the senses (see Figure 2-28) to experience and predict what's ahead. Each of us, to the person is as one of the thousand little lenses that make a lobster's eye. Joined together we have vision. As persons working on our national project, aligned to the same goal and objectives, we make a people, we shape our American society. However, we as a people, like lobster eyes have blurry vision. It takes us human beings time to process the complexity of society and see it clearly, too often in the hindsight of 20/20 vision. Thus, a sudden bright light blinds both lobsters and humans. Yet when in a cold, dim, dark depth as in the current moments, we as the lobster does on the ocean's floor see points of light that beckon us to rise up from the present abyss. Such bright dots as we detect are hope. We see it in the good nature of children. Our hope is the future generations. We must prepare them to get things we got wrong, right. We owe them it. We owe it in honor of the endowment the USE is for us. For the required repairs to our foundations, we must give them awesome ACE as a part of their KA^4SA^2 as they develop into citizen adults. The lobster is bilateral. So is the human brain. Symmetrical along a central line, the lobster has identical sides, and we are this way in much of our thinking too. We separate ideas into dichotomies to help us understand the world before us. Unlike us, having only one main body, a lobster has two main parts. The first, its body, the cephalothorax, consist of the cephalon (the head) and the thorax (the midsection). The second is its tail, called the abdomen.

In our representation of society, the head controls the powers. The claws and head represent the primary societal powers and the midsection the secondary and tertiary social powers. Taken together with the abdomen, the lobster within the water, representing geography, personifies the culture of American society. For us, this total culture is a people-centered democracy. *(As an aside, the body of the lobster has fourteen segments, called somites, each bearing a pair of appendages. These somites are fused together to make up the body. For the Revolution, thirteen colonies fused together to fight as one united confederacy. 13+1 the "we are one" = 14.)*

The abdomen, or tail, of the lobster referentially is the relationships we as persons have to the various identities of social organizations to which we belong, like it or not, by our having been born into American society. When all these segments are in alignment, we have a happy civil society. When misaligned, we've discord, disagreement, and defeatist feelings, and our amygdala runs rampant, as if our ramparts bombarded. This is what doomerism, a domestic enemy of the Constitution, is now doing. As our social organizations made up by us represent the place out of which "We the People" as a united people react to national crises, the lobster's tail is made of significant muscle in six segments that are not fused together but connected by flexible tissue, like our relationship to our social identities. The flexible, muscular tails of lobsters, like our flexible social identities, help us flee from danger quickly to find new positions that better suit the situation, social circumstance and physical condition, we find ourselves in as a people. When the lobster needs to escape danger, it forcefully and rapidly contracts and retracts it tail to scoot backward to safety. The last segment of the abdomen is the tail fan, which helps it quickly move back from danger. Referential to the Liberty Lobster as culture, this tail fan is a person. A person's liberty is the purpose of the democracy. When the culture of liberty is in danger, as it is now, each person plays a vital role in our escaping the threat in front of us. Right now, that is baby doomerism.

Healthy Persons

When all of our social identity organizations realize their purpose is to IDEALS liberty for every person, we'll be aligned and able to contract and retract rapidly to flee the danger. We then can correct the course of the nation toward its intended ideal condition, offering liberty and justice for all. Like the fantail of a lobster, a person is multifaceted. The five parts to the tail fan, the telson and its pairs of uropods on the side, are referential of the health of a person. To thrive, a person must attend to their: physical, emotional, social, spiritual, and intellectual health. Additionally, these seven fantail parts represent the socialization contexts in which a person develops. These have considerable influence on one's health. Central for a person to understand society is intellectual health. This is the ability to think clearly with reason. It needs balanced by physical and spiritual health on one side, and emotional and social health on the other. Healthy persons aggregate to a healthy people. A healthy people work together to make a healthy society. A healthy society births, raises, and sustains healthy persons. Benefiting from all these healthy results requires love. In relation to a person's relationship with others conditioned by love, psychologists have identified eight forms of love. We all should look for these in our lives and understand them for our health. These are:

1) **Philautia** = Self-Love
2) **Storge** = Familial Love
3) **Philia** = Affectionate Love or Friendship
4) **Agape** = Selfless Love or Spiritual Love
5) **Ludus** = Playful Love
6) **Eros** = Erotic Love
7) **Mania** = Obsessive Love
8) **Pragma** = Enduring Love

Love is a triangle of the intensities of our: intimacy, passion, and commitment to the object of our love, and how these combine to indicate how consummate we feel toward it (Sternberg, 1988) (Fromm, 1956). Because democracy provides freedom, and freedom feels better than oppression, the best society can be is to be free from oppression; we must fight together as a people to keep it that way. We must commit, persons to person, to become better at being complete citizens, pursuing truth and full intellectual health together for the good of all.

(As an aside for humor's sake, the underside of the central part of the lobster's tail fan, the last segment of its abdomen, the telson, contains its anus. Referential to the intellectual health of a person, an anus is like an opinion. All have opinions. The smell of which is generally only liked by the person expressing it. Let this remind us about the

false affection to sniff up another's anus for favor. How anyone could be a sycophant to kiss up, or lick another's orifices to gain favor, is difficult to understand. Is not truth telling a form of respect and love? Why would we let someone believe a fallacy?)

Behind the protective powers of economy and polity, the lobster's sensory organ filled head receives and detects distant signals. We the people do the same from society. These messages help us find food, choose a mate, and decide if danger is near. In our culture, food is referential to everything we need to survive. A mate is referential to how we structure our relationships under a rule of law and administer it. Danger coming near is referential to the risks in and to society. We must actively engage in attending to these so we can guarantee that our society and we as a people survive, live well, and thrive. This includes guiding the protective functions of our culture's two defensive mechanisms against threats to our survival. Hazards in the geography power and within our selves when our people power is dysfunctional and needs mitigated. Doomerism has amplified the dysfunction of the people in our performance of our leadership responsibility in the business of society. Because of it, we're failing.

The people power protects us from dysfunctions only when dutifully and properly done to develop healthy persons of competent leadership character and good citizen behaviors. The economy power protects us by helping us get the necessities for living. The polity power protects us by creating a societal structure of law. It supports the economy and people power by administering basic services we need as a nation. It provides for our common defense against all enemies, foreign and domestic, which threaten our society. When we comport ourselves comfortably with our founding principles, we constitute a society worthy of defending.

Positions of Authority

Remember that culture is a human construction. With the lobster symbol, some of us are in the claws, making our shells and controlling the muscles, sinews, and tendons that operate the propodus and dactylus. Recognizing this, we all bear a responsibility to one another to not allow positions of authority to cause us to forget that we are in a culture of democracy, and using power by controlling its FILMS[2] [P7] is a privilege. Here are things of society into which power is fused:

- **Functionaries** (functionary offices and their officials who hold authority)
- **Instruments** (organizations and institutions socially agreed upon as legitimate forms of authority)
- **Logistics** (the means to AEIOUY^{2}K a power)
- **Mechanisms** (the ways by which we AEIOUY^{2}K power)

- **Structures & Systems** (the combined philosophies, purposes, precedents, policies, processes, procedures, and practices [P7])

Just as with the many fallacies, the more we know of power, the better we can lead with facts not fantasies, and with truth not lies. We must avoid the DAMN of the powers. We must AEIOUY^{2}K the powers by the consent of all the people represented. The proper balance and orientation toward the best risk-management activities to preserve liberty, is how those in positions of authority within the societal powers must do them. The following six vowels and one consonant begun verb, describe different ways in which power is used. Simple definitions show the nuances, with examples. We:

- **Apply** power when we put it to practical use.
  - o   I apply power to push you with my arm.
- **Employ** power when we bring it under control to achieve results.
  - o   I employ power when you depend on me, and I ask you to do something I need done.
- **Implement** power when we use it like a tool to do work for us.
  - o   I implement power when I persuade you while you are not dependent upon me.
- **Operationalize** power when we use it empirically and measure results.
  - o   I operationalize power when timing my races to get faster.
- **Utilize** power when we put it to profitable uses.
  - o   I utilize power to make something I will sell to you.
- **Yoke** power when we join two things together with it.
  - o   I yoke power when I join you to help you lift a heavy object.
- **Yield** power when we allow one to go before another.
  - o   I yield power when I let you go first when it was my turn.
- **Keep** power when we do not release it to another.
  - o   I keep power when I insist I go first when it is my turn.

If we all behave as citizens in all the positions we hold, from that of common everyday person to that of congressperson, Supreme Court justice, or president, the society will provide a living situation that ensures the Constitution's objectives are met. We as a people have yet to accomplish it. So this is our most ardent goal as a people—to fulfill the calling of the opportunities of this risky venture, our USE, as we go about doing the business of society. We the people must unite it, not expecting those in positions of authority to do it for us unless they are citizen-first-oriented, citizenshipping for liberty. Baby doomers cannot do this. They are diseased by the corrupting forces of power.

Personal Development

Every person in our culture has a role to play in our nationhood. Every person brings with them from their abdomen of assent the ability to dissent against power and consent with common principles, the first principles in the Constitution, to its maintenance of democracy and our republic. As we move through our eight stages of individual development in the social care of others who socializes us, our development is both psyche and social. It begins with our first stage, and ends in our eighth stage when we pass along what we learned to the next generation. These stages are discussed (by originating psychologist Erik Erickson) in relation to dichotomies as a continuum of experiences that we absorb and assimilate intellectually and emotionally as organic animate beings (meaning living, breathing organisms) and socially and physically as human beings (meaning we need others, despite how the personal power of conceited pride might tempt us to think otherwise). They generally correspond to the phases of our life cycle from birth into adulthood, arrayed as such:

    Stage 1: **Infancy** (birth to 18 months)
        Trust vs. Mistrust
    Stage 2: **Early Childhood** (2 to 3 years)
        Autonomy vs. Shame and Doubt
    Stage 3: **Preschool** (3 to 5 years)
        Initiative vs. Guilt
    Stage 4: **School Age** (6 to 11 years)
        Industry vs. Inferiority
    Stage 5: **Adolescence** (12 to 18 years)
        Identity vs. Confusion
    Stage 6: **Young Adulthood** (19 to 40 years)
        Intimacy vs. Isolation
    Stage 7: **Middle Adulthood** (40 to 65 years)
        Generativity vs. Stagnation
    Stage 8: **Maturity** (65 to death)
        Integrity vs. Despair

We all get encultured in different generations, and regional subcultures. New immigrants acculturation bears upon their places of origin's enculturation, socialization contexts, and what their FILMS[2] [P7] conveyed when they resided there. Regardless of the place of origin and its subcultures, the intellectual health of a person born or residing in the US needs a healthy understanding of the fit, function, and purpose of democracy as culture in a republic. This is the foundation for American society. It enables freedom for entrepreneurship and an enterprising economy. It is essential we experience our freedom and decide not to be controlled. Freedom of thought is how we learn to use our natural and nurtured talents to fit us to opportunities to survive, live well, and thrive in luxury. We do this by way of markets that by their allowance of freethinking find a way to provide goods and services. When the economy powers are balanced, it serves us all well. With an understanding of the roles of the primary powers: people, polity, and economy, we will be able to by good citizenshipping guide and regulate them. This will help us ensure, insure, and assure democracy. Teaching this knowledge as a part of ACE socializes children how to be Americans.

While many may think they are American by virtue of having being born within United States territory, they are intellectually not yet American, except in the sense that they are born with their natural rights, which must be protected, and by our polity are supposed to be. Persons are not born knowing that the polity is theirs to staff, attend to, and mend when ill. Our polity is ill. Until we properly educated enough of us in the duties of citizenship to ensure the USE's survival, we've a problem to contend with for many years, unless we intervene. In nautical metaphor, until we fix the ship and set sail upon the correct course, we are doomed. We've doomerism, not democracy.

The instinct of humankind is twofold: power and love. Because of both, our species survives. Power precedes love. It must be conquered, divided, and subjugated by love, or we are simply primate animals, willing to kill for power. How we come to know power and love in our lives matters as we find our social identity and as our perceptions of our citizenship rights and responsibilities are learned and adopted as a part of whom we are as persons and as a people.

Socialization Contexts

We, the everyday people, must find a way to go about our lives exhibiting service above selfishness, saying yes to the utmost full-fledged thoroughgoing constitutionally allied united citizenshipping, understandingly synchronized (E-SASSY-T-TUF-FT-CAUCUS). This is the way to think and behave as a citizenry. By all of us, all the time, we must, if we are to keep liberty alive. Generations, regions, settlement patterns, and socialization contexts shape a person's identity. These influencers overlap a person's developmental stages in life. Understanding their influences on human development and us will help us understand each other better. Better knowledge supports our ability to unite all the time, not only in times of societal crises. Of the influences upon us as we develop, the socialization contexts relate us to society, our place within it, and our success in it. Socialization contexts produce distinctive kinds of social selves. These selves come with differing value sets. These are the traditional, anomic, modern, and postmodern (Hage, 2020). Each overlays a settlement pattern: rural, (several varieties of) suburban, and urban. Each also overlaps with regional subcultures and generational personalities. Related to the anomic two alarming contexts exist, the enervating and radicalizing. Related to the modern another context exists, the snobbish. Furthermore, the term post-modern relays fragmentation and meaninglessness, deconstructivism and nihilism. Contemporary times afford multicultural exposures that benefit our species. In addition, we've gained evidence of the errors of modernism. Its systems management social engineering to universalize the world proved arrogantly overambitious. To promote the perceptiveness gained in the after-modern information age, a prefix, "percepto", can be affixed to it. "Perceptopostmodern" is the present state of socializing children with postmodern advantages. Such it is for a global civilization of persons sharing across borders, joining in and participating with communities of interest the world over. We're only a fingertip away on the Internet of Things in a pocket size portal to nearly all the planet's sights and sounds. (Whoever makes the smells available will increase immensely the possible perceptions available in an inch, and likely get filthy rich with their scratch and sniff solution).

Due to the massive size of the baby boomer generation, its personality disproportionately affected society. Its value sets delivered us into an era of doomerism. It will pass, but it poses significant challenges to future generations. It blocked the transfer of the knowledge, understanding, and experience of bonding ideally, which was once present in a neighborly American way of life. Bonding leads to unity. Doomerist-oriented thinking is the opposite of what a free everyday people need to unite as a people. Unity of a people builds upon social appreciation, the recognition that we depend upon one another. We need our families, neighbors, communities (for jobs and hobbies), municipalities, states, and nation for our lifestyle. We cannot be baby doomers undermining these social necessities. We cannot be baby doomers disgracing them, destroying their real worth to us, and their benefits to civil society, and it to our commonwealth.

Doomerism is resulting in three new socialization contexts: the snobbish, enervating, and radicalizing. Added up, nowadays there are seven different socialization contexts: snobbish, traditionalistic, anomic, modernistic, postmodernistic*, enervating, and radicalizing (STAMPER). (*this way holds promise if made perceptopostmodernistic). Socialization is a process. By culture power process, societies stamp, imprint, and impress into the minds of children worldviews and value sets. Family, mythology, academy, and community powers' FILMS[2] [P7] transmit worldviews, beliefs, and mores. Children train on life skills. In some contexts, they go untrained to enter society with the skills it needs from them. Just growing up and becoming an adult are two
different things.

Each generation anticipates that its children will carry on the traditions passed down to them. If doomerism is a new way of living, it is not a healthy one to pass down. It drowns out wisdom. It sets children up for failure. It leads to fear and anxiety by portending doom for the future and hopeless inopportunity. Community power can countervail. It needs an extraordinary, what should be automatically American, unity of effort to support young people rise and be prepared for the future. Nevertheless, they can do it if they find ways to unify and avoid divisions into socially constructed enemies.

Baby doomers cause argumentative groupings on purpose. It's a game to them. They shape opponents based on ethnic origins, or shared socialization experiences. They stimulate political factions, and alternative facts in the marketplace of ideas. Then, they exploit these groups using the educed intense orientations to ostracize them. This outcasts them as others, causes them to distrust the necessary institutions. It further imbalances any preexisting misperceptions and unreasonable viewpoints of reality. The baby doomers desire this; it divides and conquers the young. It preserves their dominance. It then passes down their legacy hubris, their tribalistic ideologue idiocies. This is their, or rationalization form of, self-justification. Diseased with narcissistic infantilism, they cannot see the damage they are doing, and did. In their needy arrogance, or insecurity, they always want to prove themselves worthy. "Look at me, look at me, look at me now, look at me first" they psychotically opine. How sad it gets when a life gets lived without true integrity and grit. We must find ways to help them convert into citizens first. We need them to give back, to return their takings, in ways valuable for babies to get raised American.

Trends in youth reaching stability and maturity with confidence are not promising. Overwhelming anxiety is on the rise in youth. Psychological frailty is affecting society. Overprotective baby boomer parenting and promoted technologies fostered these weaknesses in character (Haidt & Lukianoff, 2018). These further spread doomerism throughout society, which like an unforgiving undertow is pulling people apart. It is devastating the promise of us progressing forward to the founding ideals of American democracy. Victimization is now common. Courage is in retreat.

Over time, through historic events, awakenings, and crises, we adjust. Original meanings and intents are lost. By accretion, adaptation, and accumulation of knowledge, ideas about a person's place in society change. Simplicity gives way to complexity. Responses to rising risks alter perceptions of society and its cultural perspectives. The land of the free becomes the land of the afraid. Ideals once held as truths critically challenged spreads suspicions. For the USE, the way the boomer generation has dominated positions in the LAMBS is bearing rotten fruit. Exposing terrible examples, youths see adults enacting horribly un-American value sets. Left malnourished from consuming the fruit of doomerism, we grow in fear of a pending doom. Doom is not our destiny. The boomers seem to have forgotten the critical-to-know purposefulness of our enterprise: to IDEALS liberty and justice for all. We must reject doomerism, people.

The boomers neglected the critical responsibility to manage the risks confronting the enterprise. "Win-win" behavior is not "wink-wink, we'll both take more than our fair share." This misguided search to find the loophole first, before following the for-the-common good rules, is disruptive of trust. Society disintegrates by such unwise nonsense. Getting what one wants when it is wrong does not justify it just because the satisfying sense of winning and not losing dopes up our egos. These forces of doomerism pervade and pervert our socialization contexts' expansion. Too many of them add further challenges to finding common ground. This makes it difficult to convey correctly the necessary American civics to future generations. Without good civics lessons during socialization, American civilization could dissolve. The jeopardy to liberty for all is huge, thanks to doomerism. We need to prepare children to be citizens first, so they enjoy the blessings of liberty, the benefits of our society. Let's go over the differences between these seven socialization contexts.

- Snobbish—Children socialized in such a way that they come to believe they are superior to others. Growing up in luxury is not wrong. Being oblivious to a life without want is not their fault. However, lacking appreciation for democracy and its citizens is risky for us. Children in the top 10% of the wealthiest families are at risk of becoming spoiled brats. We are not to be raising aristocrats in the land of the free and home of the brave. We are to be raising Americans. Financial success is good, if the goods are gotten respectably, earned, and not by theft. The self-consciousness of being rich can breed arrogance and conceit. Zero appreciation by the snobbish for the struggles of everyday people (read we in the majority), for whom the country was established, is not good for us. Especially if these children go to the best schools and enter networks at the top that put them into the best jobs. Holding the highest-ranking positions, not by birth but practicably because of their birth, is risky for sustaining the merit based advancement promise that serves a democracy-based culture well. Kids of affluent access pathways may start thinking they are entitled to high posts and riches. This is risky for our society. Snobbish children risk thinking that they are superior then act out accordingly. Seeing snobbery as acceptable is not democracy. Making elitist people, snobbish socialization, is neither helpful nor healthful for the citizenry of a republic. Setting up an aristocracy is contrary to our founding. We need to elevate the best among us, not only those born of high rank and privilege, unless they possess the right stuff. A plutocratic club attitude for raising snobbish, conceited people is not meritocratic. Beware the flimflam sham of an entitlement to be full of superiority. *(A tiny minority in the US—not needing feared, but helped, and their enablers properly reformed.)* These children need help. Is it possible that fellow citizens will be neighborly enough to help them integrate with the whole society built up on the framework of democracy? How might we combine societal powers to assist them?

- Traditionalistic—Children socialized in such a way that they believe the traditions of their community are superior to others' cultures. Being unaware of the outside world is not their fault. Isolating a community from other societies in the digital age of global commerce is difficult. The rapid pace of change feels threatening. Children reared in traditional-values homes, families, neighborhoods, and communities live in *gemeinschaft* (communal-like) social circumstances. These are often found in rural settlements where the needs of the larger group—the community, kinship, and religion—take precedence over the needs of a person within it.

  These lifestyles are "folk" supportive. The mores and customs are valued and identity shaping. A natural spontaneity in emotions and expressions of sentiment guides social interactions. Relations and relationships reinforce traditional social roles performed by one another. In this context, children become inner-directed. These social contexts are often homogeneous, resulting in less emphasis on creativity and more on conformity. This approach reduces reflection on one's self and society beyond the borders of one's community. Maintained through moral persuasion, strong norms, protected mores, favored folkways, and customary habits, these children are at risk of being unable to adapt effectively to the digital age that poses threats to traditions. However, by enabling exposure to escalating interrelationships of foreign cultures going global showing up locally, due to the Internet and entertainment and socializing media on it, traditions can share and celebrate each other. Insecurities from information overload need managed.

  Isolation from different ways of viewing the world leads to strong opinions that potentially produce prejudice. Growing up, children might feel inferior or superior, confident or conflicted in their opinions of others, and others of them. In traditionalistic contexts, creativity channels toward innovations within traditional arts and crafts. Ideas beyond those tolerated by the community are unexplored. In a dizzying, globalizing, cosmopolitan, commercial world, these children are at risk of subcultural anxiety. If it happens and they find themselves left behind or left out of experiencing material and technological advances it could be frustrating and frightening to fret in fear of feeling forgotten. Worse, it could enrage and enable engaging in prejudices as self-accepting mind-narrowing defensiveness. Resilience to cope with, and not angered by, the rapid changes in the outside world is challenging. It could become difficult for these children to understand outward thinking and learning. It takes risk-taking courage to desire, not deny, opportunities to explore beyond their social boundaries. Traditionalistic contexts can become dependent on wanting to stay the course and walk on proven past paths. Many that once led to success no longer work out to ones benefit. For example, this has happened in coal mining towns, wherein a boy can no longer expect to grow up, work as a miner, get married, and raise a family. This is a social challenge that can lead to a traditionalistic context becoming an anomic context for future generations.

Persons raised in traditionalistic contexts must decide what is good in tradition versus what might be a vulnerability of it in the future. Integrating socially into a changing society by sorting out what to keep and what to leave behind is stress inducing. These children need help adjusting to the future. Technological advances driven by the economy power challenge traditional ways of viewing society and humanity, putting a gap between perceptions of what is considered right and wrong for people. Traditionalistic contexts may cause children to grow up prone to exhibit intolerance in their behavior.

Doomerism amplifies these risks. Is it possible that fellow citizens will be neighborly to help them integrate with the whole society built up on the framework of democracy? Giving up outmoded social norms, mores and folkways is not easy, and shouldn't be done hastily or at all if they sustain liberty and our national project's progress. Preserving healthy ones is essential to keeping the ideal core values and virtues in our society. Adaptation is challenging. Making people feel like society is forcing a choice between a more dominant academy verses a mythology power is not helpful. It is not a choose science or choose religion, winner-take-all game. However, the baby boomer-shaped public realm construes life as a series of binary opposing choices. It is not. This approach is misguided. It causes an unhealthy perception of reality. Because of the way they think as a generation, they fail to see a both/and possibility of our truth as a constitutionally allied people.

- Anomic—Children socialized in such a way that they come to believe they are inferior to others. Being unaware of their social circumstances and physical conditions into which they are born is not their fault. Finding out they live in impecunious situations is difficult. Children reared in anomic homes, families, neighborhoods, and communities live in urban and rural pockets of poverty. Deindustrialization, racial discrimination, and segregation caused these pockets. Deprived social opportunities perpetuate joblessness. Survival stress induces poor health, and there is an absence of a variety of educated neighbors of mixed levels of income within their settlement patterns. These children are at the most risk of suffering indignation and difficulty interacting socially with others from outside their locales.

Isolation from the mainstream ways of viewing the world leads to unfit social grammars. Children can grow to feel inferior, unwanted, and useless. Single-use zoning has not been helpful to community diversity as the mixed milieu of cities once was (Jacobs, 1961). In our cities, an unequal distribution of opportunities in all kinds of societal power's instruments has occurred, which disadvantages children of some neighborhoods over others, particularly those of anomic social circumstances and deteriorating physical conditions (Levy, 1983). These children do not learn the social grammar of mainstream society from neighborhood life. When adolescents, they get disconnected. They do not develop toward being contributing citizens and become at-risk youth, easily exploited (Besharov, 1999). They fall into lifestyles that alienate them from pathways to healthy living and opportunities to contribute rewardingly for self and helpfully for society.

Mostly reared by a single female parent in circumstances of lawlessness, these children lack a sense of community with the social norms necessary to find success in schools and jobs, which puts them at a disadvantage. They are at risk of becoming a permanent urban underclass (Jencks & Patterson, 1991). The anomic context does not socialize children to be ready to integrate with mainstream society. These children suffer anomie, which is damaging to endure. It results in a terrible hopelessness and a cycle of poverty, gang life, and incarceration. This unhealthy pattern accepted as normal ill prepares children for out of neighborhood social interactions. Cycles of social dislocation and deprivation continue (Wilson, 1987). Those trapped within it, being creative humans with artistry power, make art that expresses this subculture. Their expressions assist their psychic survival in the harsh realities they face each day. Anomie causes sadness, emotional anxiety and mental depression that demotivates and diminishes children's biology power. A very, very rare few are unaffected by it.

These children need the most help to be able to join in the benefits of society and have the possibility to pursue happiness. They are often the victims of the circumstances into which they were born. Yet blamed for it they are. More or less trapped in poverty, their biology power to escape is handicapped by malnutrition and social and psychological instability. No jobs for low and unskilled potential workers, no marriages, and no hope, only a will to survive, gangs, drugs to escape, incarceration, and becoming wards of the state seem to be available for them. These are not promising conditions for our fellow citizens. The complexity of this wicked social problem, full of negative risks for children, requires radical innovation by adults.

Doomerism amplifies these risks. Baby boomers are too into their own egos to escape their self-adulation and find a way to solve joblessness, single-parent families, and spatial pockets of poverty in rural and urban settlements. For future generations, reversing anomic conditions is essential to reducing the cost of the polity's judiciary FILMS[2] [P7] placed upon the people. We could avert deficits and repay debts if we spent less on juvenile and adult jurisprudence and incarceration. We could build civil society with social capital used for social integration supporting family-centered neighborhoods with flourishing education programs. Jobs generate revenue. If not forced to spend it on judicial necessities that result from the economy power's DAMN that causes blighted communities, we could prepare children for a better future contributing to society. The earliest possible support of community power to preschool children will help them avert the risks of a cycle of poverty (Hage, 2020). Interventions must begin early. A consortium of other powers is necessary to help these children learn other social grammars that will help them.

o   *(Will our baby boomer citizens who run exceedingly profitable corporations, the wealthiest generation that extracted the common wealth from the public and put it into their private pockets, and those within the top 1% of the wealthy help? Will they decide to pay back society for the opportunity structure it provided them by contributing taxes to rebuild the dilapidating social and physical infra-structures their fleecing has caused? Will they leave the polity powers and the economy powers, since it is unlikely that in either they will $AEIOUY^2K$ these powers to find, free, treat, and support transitioning these children to a state of normalcy and stability, psychologically, socially, and economically?)*

- Modernistic—Children socialized in such a way that they come to be-lieve that their identity is most important, not others'. Being unaware of their social insecurities is not their fault. Raised to be competitive, they receive cues winning matters most.

  Children reared in modern-values homes, families, neighborhoods, and communities live in *gesellschaft* (universal-like) social circumstances often found in suburban and urban settlements in which every person seeks their own advantage within the social milieu. These lifestyles seek to be cosmopolitan, relying on rational will to guide calculations of conduct. This context develops people to view human relations as im-personal, indirect exchanges. It prefers efficiency to empathy. It popu-larizes shallow social skills used to maintain transactional relationships.

  Modernistic contexts involve approving of others only in so far as, and as long as, the others can further one's own self-interest. In this context, children become outer-directed. This context encourages achievement, universalistic thinking, and an individualistic orientation. These social contexts are more heterogeneous, producing weak social bonds—in stark contrast to traditionalistic socialization.

  Indifference to others' ways of viewing the world leads to strong opinions. Children can grow to feel superior and overconfident in their point of view. These children, taught to be polite, develop social cognitions aware of how others perceive them and how to pretend to behave well to shape others' perceptions of them. They act so as not to offend, in superficial and self-serving manners, wanting to win, but not perceived, or judged, as mean or selfish.

For these children, peer groups become the most important entity. Their sense of self and belonging depend on climbing the social ladder. Each seeks approval from others, jockeying for position and controlling emotions to appear compatible. Hiding their true selves, they may feel that pursuing whom they are inside is a risk. Keeping up a social front, a face to the public, which may differ from the face they face in their private mirrors, is stressful for them. Perception as one of the most popular "in-crowd" kids becomes more important than representing oneself honestly. They learn to be two-faced persons.

At its worst, a modernistic context may cause children to grow up prone to insensitivity, cynicism, and distrust. Engaging in dishonest behaviors and manipulative tattle telling is a risk. Because of its superficiality, fitting in to maximize gain, this context does not raise creative and reflective persons. These children are at risk of catching doomerism. Hopefully they do not become lonely in old age. The realization that material success does not holistically fulfill human needs and favorite objects do not follow one in the afterlife could aggrieve them.

- Postmodernistic—Children socialized to believe in curiosity and tolerance. Raised to be cooperative, they receive cues to be inquisitive of diverse perspectives. (If we improve it to be perceptopostmodernistic, we can help children further become familiar globally, to perceive variety with interest, seeing it as a positive opportunity to learn something valuable from differing cultures outside their local social milieu.) Children reared in these homes, families, neighborhoods, and communities often live in suburban and urban settlements. They have identifiably new characteristics and outlooks on humanity. This context began as an adaptive solution in child rearing during the third stage of knowledge creation. Parents responded to the disruptiveness of this wave's inventions. A recent context in the history of our society, it leads to children experiencing a more diverse and integrated social context. It gives children more than one social grammar through exposure and open experience with people of other subcultures.

The postmodern self is generally more capable of coping with complexity. Possessing high levels of a sense of agency, creativity, and reflectiveness, such persons adapt through greater degrees of empathy. This allows the integrating of differing peoples into a unity. The perceptopostmodernistic self yearns for greater connectivity with others who differ because of a belief in humanity needing to unite against existential and historical threats of war between nations. Perceptopostmodernistic children develop the cognitive complexity to entertain opposing ideas at the same time. They do not feel a need to choose one side over the other. They find ways to combine them and create something new. They can analyze opposites or take a synthesis and antithesis and synthesize them. This skill is good for innovation and makes problem solving easier for them. It prepares them to navigate increasing complexities in society. These children are at risk of suffering anxiety when they compare their dreams for human harmony against the harsh reality of human cruelty and the negative uncivil trends in society that are being shaped by doomerism as acceptable norms by the adults of authority over and above them.

- Enervating—Children not in homes of any family power but growing up in bondage inside brothels, criminal drug manufacturing houses, or orphanages in which they are treated as burdensome animals. These children, damaged by monstrously inhumane treatment at the hands of evildoing adults, who have no concern for the children other than the profit they might bring to their illicit practices, need serious psychological assistance when freed. This is a recent, mostly hidden from view, illegal underworld of addictive drug trading and human trafficking for slave labor or sex by organized crime networks. (*A tiny minority in the US—not needing feared but helped and their enslavers properly punished and if possible reformed.*)

- Radicalizing—Children being raised in homes where the family and community of similar others don't feel wanted, or they feel threatened by changes in the society while suffering from a sense of anomic hopelessness, and economic depression. Treated as undesirables in such a context, children learn they are not a welcomed part of the neighborhoods in which they reside. They come to believe that the traditional way of life taught them is invalid in the broader society they occupy. This causes them to feel unwanted by society. These children grow up with a consciousness of otherness. Unacceptance hurts, and these children seek belonging. They radicalize to one fanatic form of thinking or another, be it as apostates or ugly stereotypes of the land from which they or their parents immigrated. These children may become dangerous to others, go overseas to fight for a cause, or commit acts of violence and terror within our borders. This is a recent development in the circumstances of our society. (*A tiny minority in the US—not needing feared but helped and their recruiters properly punished and if possible reformed.*).

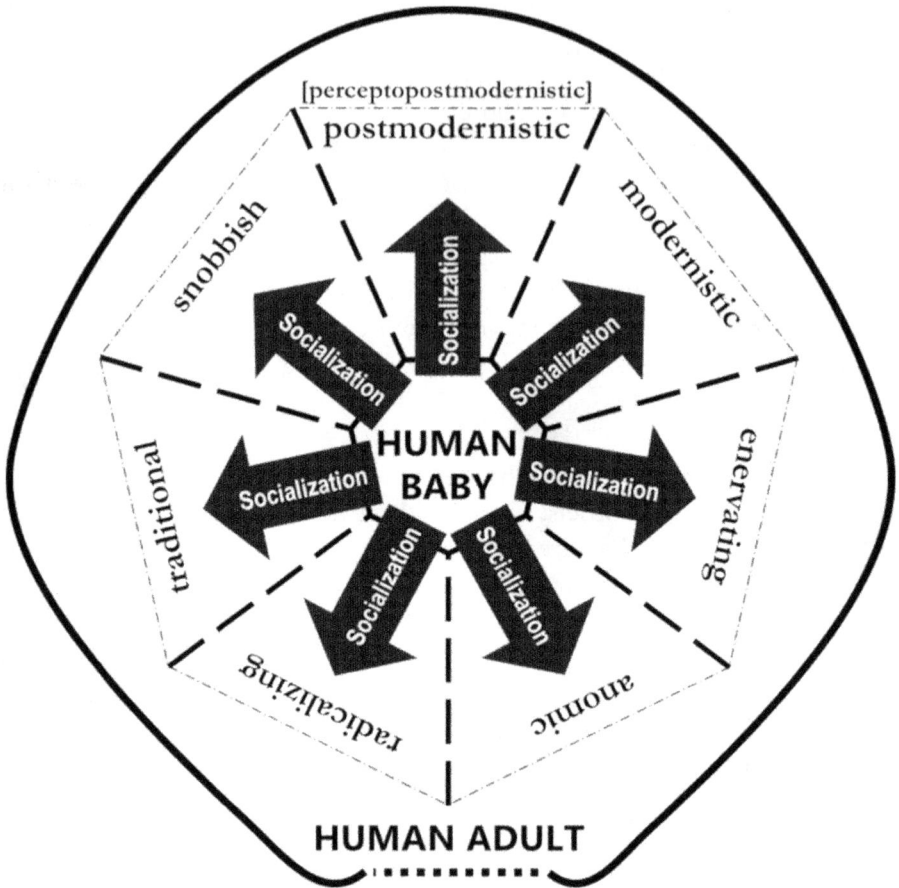

Figure 3-5: Seven Socialization Contexts in Which Children Grow Up

If we don't ensure that these contexts have a similar and appropriate civics education, a full life ACE, our progeny will trample one another, as tramps fighting over scraps of tossed-out food at a garage can. Unless we clean it up, our society will be this heap, the remnants of the improper DAMN of the primary societal powers. This is what doomerism has begun. If we fail to understand and create customized ways, means, and methods to overcome the inherent challenges of children's socialization contexts, we fail. We must be able to integrate socially all children of our citizenry into the blessings of liberty. If we neglect to regulate the societal powers and ourselves as persons, we doom the future. We must shape our community and family powers to help children prepare for their future. We need changes to refocus on their generations, as opposed to the dying ones. We need the children to believe in liberty and our enterprising project to sustain it for humanity. We need to attend to our societal powers for better LAMBS that result in the secondary and tertiary social powers gaining and maintaining the capacities and capabilities to raise patriotic American citizens who understand the duty to IDEALS liberty and perpetuate the endowment that is the USE. All children deserve a chance to self-actualize and enjoy liberty. Socialization contexts must meet all their needs shown in Figure 3-6 below. Our human-made societal and social powers must ensure it.

We need changes to rebalance purpose and powers. The polity is best to administer, the economy is best to manage, and the people are best to lead. Our regulatory function over the other powers meant to serve us is critical for democracy. We need to move society toward the central matters of the business of our enterprise. We cannot allow fringe elements at the extremes to take control. Not to do so is a constitutional failure to recognize we are citizens first and have a purpose to lead. If we do not regulate to prevent the DAMN of powers, then we, along with liberty, will be doomed. We need to fulfill our societal objectives, or watch in shame the thwarting of democracy. It will devolve back into dependency, bondage, and tyranny.

We all need to reflect upon the lessons of our generational peers with whom we share life experiences. Our shared history causes us to see the world in similar yet differing ways from previous and future generations. We need to converse with other members of living generations. We are all in the same society at the same time. We are a constellation of generations. We are the living legacy, carriers of the endowment, citizens in, for, and by its cause. We are everyday conducting the business of our society. What kind of society it is depends upon us, and we need to be American about it. It will have a legacy. Do we want it to be good, or bad? Do we want it to continue on its present course in which the baby boomers extract all they can take from us in the here and now, sucking it dry, shriveling it into a useless, hollow, shrunken pile of skin and bones? Do we want the children to have a humane future? What kind of society do we want to be? We can shape it. Let's have one based upon democracy. We are its purpose. We are first among the primary societal powers. We are the majority. We are the everyday people.

Layered on top of socialization contexts that shape our rearing are generations. Generations have personalities (Strauss & Howe, 1991). Generational conflicts within, between, and among generations influence our society. The movements within our subcultures need connected (we must be cognizant of how) with our essential culture, democracy. Knowing this, we can move toward unity by focusing on the basic bases of society we share. We can work together to balance the primary powers to reinvigorate that which unites us first-and-foremost, a calling to defend liberty. It gave birth to our nation and guided the constitution of its new order, its revolutionary concept that we the people could self-govern. We need to keep this in mind at all times, or we'll lose it.

People's principal instrument to control the three primary powers is culture, a power sorting and setting process. Influenced by the secondary powers of geography, community, and family, these construct with the other building blocks of culture, the tertiary powers of mythology, academy, industry, artistry, and history. These nouns refer to familiar knowledges, but in the context of this model, their use is a form of power. Power is a force applied over time with sufficient mass to enable it. These societal and social powers cause changes in attitudes and behaviors. Their FILMS2 [P7] can do so without consciously knowing it, with or without expectations. Power causes responses in people as its forces create, modify, ignore, or jettison historic cultures' norms, mores, customs, habits, and ambitions. Culture is malleable; many mini-cultures exist within subcultures, and subcultures within broader cultures.

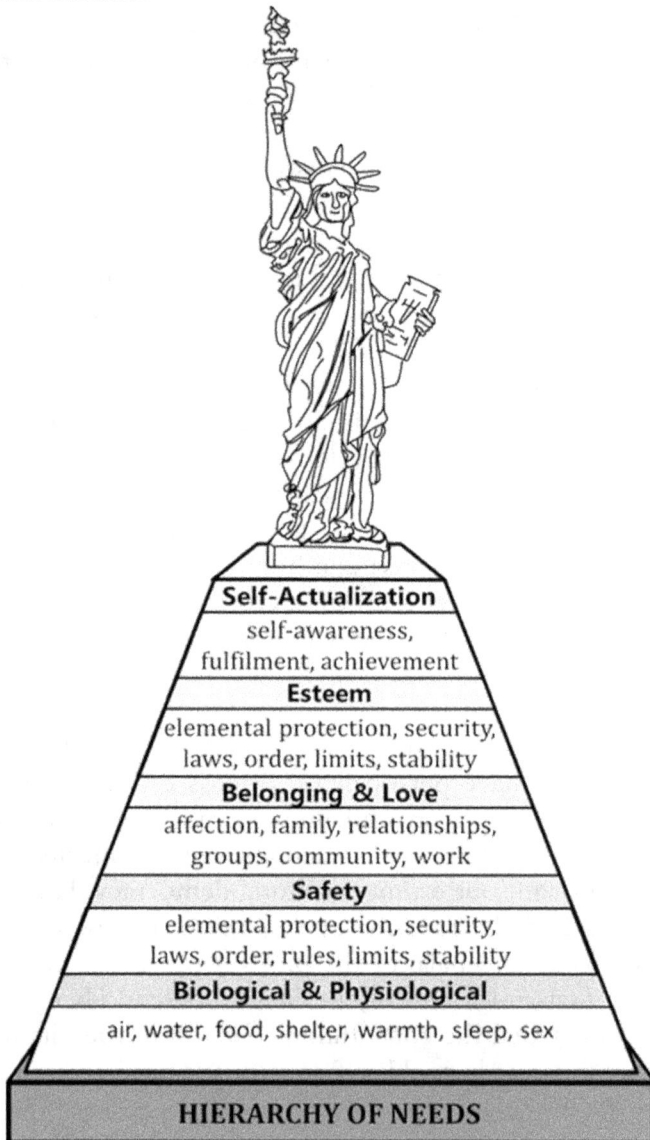

Self-Actualization
self-awareness,
fulfilment, achievement

Esteem
elemental protection, security,
laws, order, limits, stability

Belonging & Love
affection, family, relationships,
groups, community, work

Safety
elemental protection, security,
laws, order, rules, limits, stability

Biological & Physiological
air, water, food, shelter, warmth, sleep, sex

HIERARCHY OF NEEDS

Figure 3-6: Hierarchy of a Person's Needs

Culture is the social use of any knowledge. To those within a society, culture guides us in how to think and behave. For those in positions of authority, it tells us how to AEIOUY^{2}K the societal powers. A culture of the rule of law tells people to do things in accord with ways that achieve an intended outcome. Such an approach requires that we behave in accordance with the law. Disregard of it violates others' liberty. To seek to skirt the law, find a loophole, disobey, and flood the judiciary with work causes the size and cost of government to increase. We cannot establish justice if cheaters misuse the polity's judiciary. Such is a common practice of baby doomers. Research the number of these cases of the baby boomer generation compared with others to see evidence. They in many ways have broken American society with their death grip on the polity and their empire of self (Gibney, 2017). Their malfeasance has set us back from accomplishing our constitutional goal and objectives during the boomer's era.

In regards to power in society, culture frames why and forms how to adapt the primary societal powers to changing social circumstances and physical conditions. It influences the knowledge pursuit of a society, implying how people are to pursue their KA^{4}SA^2. The broadest culture of a society is a combination of subcultures. Societal value sets accommodate the subcultures shaped by secondary powers. Secondary and supporting tertiary powers help us find understanding and meaning. We use them to create and select beliefs, form values, establish norms and mores, and then develop attitudes that guide our behaviors and activities. Subcultures regulate the tertiary societal powers we shape to help us survive, live, and thrive while alive.

With democracy, the easiest form of forgetfulness, sloth, causes complacency, which produces an accidental ignoring of what is important. It seems the baby boomers intentionally avoided the important mission of our project to fulfill the Constitution's goal and objectives. They bilked society. Perhaps it is negligence, incompetence, or treason for the boomers to have ignored their responsibility to IDEALS liberty. We must put it into practice on a daily basis. The boomers stabbed us in the back, initiating a slow bleeding of virtue from democracy. We must rotate the boomers out of authority and suture our wounds. We must not let democracy die. The death of democracy is the return of tyranny the world over. It is an ominous duty to uphold our Constitution and its republic. Boomers failed to perform it. Blame it on television, a "drug of the nation, breeding ignorance and feeding radiation" (Franti, 1992). The Constitution will restore dominion when the citizenry strives to live guided by virtue, the truest lifelong, long-view (not shortsighted) form of happiness. Trust in this truth; it will set us free! The truth is that the baby boomers have bankrupted our nation spiritually, socially, politically, and economically. It's time for them to go. We, the everyday people, must intervene now! We must move them out of all the FILMS^2 [P7] of our enterprise and put them to work on a new repentance submission on a subordinate mission. One they will need to perform to help us restore our ideals-based creedal nation. Per some mythology power's religions, such is a project that might just save their own souls from burning in a payback hellfire.

People Make Culture

Culture is a power arrangements process done by persons who, as a people, come to agree upon what will be more or less powerful in the society. The secondary and tertiary social powers simultaneously mold and get formed by culture. Such is the nature of power—to inspire, modify and control behavior. All powers have affluence, influence, and confluence with one another, which is why we the everyday people must improve our fluency with them. Some operate with more degrees of behavioral control than others do, and at different levels of society. However, due to the creativity of toolmaking humankind (yes, language is a tool we made), the shape of culture is not as precise as a simplified model theorizes. However, models help us see better the degrees to which something is more or less powerful in the system of powers that makes society. Using dichotomies, we see degrees of differences and similarities that support understanding and conversations for seeking deeper appreciation.

Dichotomies are a tool to understand better the levers of power within our culture. Let's look at the poles of dichotomies. If opposites, these become the argumentative polemics. We set these up in our minds and use them to speak out against others with whom we disagree. Between them is not a vacuum but a continuum. We mark our position along their connecting line. We can select a point that reflects the degree to which our contention is closer to this side or that side of any dichotomy. This is an intellectual exercise of self-discovery. Some dichotomies are diametric, with poles that are true opposites, while others are less severe, like herbs and spices. Both flavor food but impart to food differently, as detected by our palates. So recognizing not absolutes but sides and nuances, themes and variations, is a critical manner of thinking and one necessary in the population of a democracy if it is to ever have a chance at becoming a people across generational lines, regions, ethnic origins, socialization contexts, and KA^4SA^2 divides. We can use dichotomies to reshape culture. Cultural changes come from large numbers of persons acting separately to cope with social existence, which aggregate to shift culture (Wilson E. O., 1978). Often the biology power of each person judges the culture, rejects, and revises it (Trilling, 1965). Not all changes are for the best. Changing culture is difficult. Wrapped up in it are identities for which each person can get caught up in a basic game of getting visible payoffs, satisfaction. In doing so, an invisible characteristic of affinity for like others alters attitudes and behaviors, and if some act psychopathically, cooperation loses out to competitive aggressors (Basu, 2011). A casualty, this contributed to our shift in culture, because a majority misguided by "me first" mentality drifted away from pursuing core American virtues as they adopted value sets that destabilized our society's foundations. We, the everyday people, might want to demand that an all-American culture ensures the use of our societal and social powers to achieve our constitutional goal as we attain its objectives.

In order to communicate, congregate, commiserate, and celebrate, people need language. It's a unique tool of humanity, foundational in the making of culture, not just to speak with one another but also to feel one another. Verbally and nonverbally, as social beings from dependency on others at birth, to finding our place in new social settings as we mature, we must possess adequate social grammars, in addition to the spoken and written word. Children get their communication skills from the families who raise them. Socialization occurs within subcultures of the broader culture of American society. We have already discussed differing socialization contexts. With a society built upon a foundational culture of democracy, the key beliefs, mores, values, and virtues of citizenship ought to be shared ubiquitously across socialization contexts. If not, the ability to form one people from many, e pluribus unum, suffers severely. This puts our goal at risk. Without all getting a good civics education by our academy power, reinforced by our secondary social powers of family and community, we're at the risk of losing the center. Without it, we may not be able to hold the republic together. We need a vivacious civil society. Therefore, we must teach the culture of democracy. Civics classes are how. They absolutely are essential to transferring the knowledge of the enterprise that is the United States, a nation under God, indivisible, with liberty and justice for all. However, as learned from the framing founders, the citizenry that does not respect the Constitution, does not live virtuously, does not do its duty, and behaves poorly; living too hedonistically and disrespecting freedom, is at risk of losing the blessings of liberty.

Yes, being a citizen takes more work than being a subject of a kingdom. Yet the rewards of magnanimity are greatest in the culture of democracy that serves up liberty as its precise construct. However, liberty requires maintenance, and this is the citizen's duty. When faced with overwhelming odds of certain defeat at the hands of the then-most powerful kingdom with the best navy, what did the revolutionaries who dared to declare independence and fight to keep it actually have on their side? They had a thirst to quench. They had a taste for liberty. They fought a near-impossible uphill war for it. It began with the issuance to the Continental Army of the first general orders, written by George Washington that began like this:

We have therefore to resolve for a vigorous and manly exertion, and if we now shamefully fail, we shall become infamous to the whole world. **Let us therefore rely upon the goodness of the Cause,** *and* **the aid of the supreme Being,** *in whose hands victory is, to animate and encourage us to great an noble Actions – The Eyes of all our Countrymen are now upon us, and we shall have their blessings, and praises, if happily* **we are the instru-**

*ments of saving them from the Tyranny mediated against them. Let us therefore animate and encourage each other, and shew the whole world, **that a Freeman contending for Liberty on his own ground is superior to any slavish mercenary** on earth.*

Further on he notes: "Remember officers and Soldiers, that **you are Freemen, fighting for the blessings of liberty** – that **slavery will be your portion, and that of your posterity**, if you don't acquit yourselves like men." The bolded words [by this book's author] emphasize how being a freeman fighting for liberty against tyranny makes our endowment of liberty and our republic our responsibility to preserve. This sets forth a social grammar all citizens must know; it is a foundation stone of our culture. This social grammar of citizenship requires awareness of the great ideals that founded the nation. We as a society would benefit from the Pledge of Allegiance's steadfast institution over time (Mayer, 1970), as words spoken, believed in, and lived by. Words of an eternal cause do not come lightly, nor do they arrive often. If we do not deliver the objectives of the pledge to all, its words will fall upon deaf ears, dead hearts, dumb minds, and numb souls. We need to prove repeatedly with civics the benefit of believing in its words and reify them by fulfilling them in our daily lives as real, purposeful, and true. This is our truth, an allegiance to the ideals of democracy, and its blood soaked elixir, liberty.

Clearly, the Revolutionary War with its lead shot, cannon balls, and bayonets was no video game. It was real danger. Real life-or-death long marches and battles against a better organized, better financed, better trained, and more experienced enemy. Somehow, we won. What this portrays is the unique potency of the first principle, liberty. It is frightening that in today's age we do not comprehend it as our birthed culture, our calling, and our responsibility to upkeep. To lose this awareness renders us fools headed toward being controlled by devious others. We need to be more knowledgeable of liberty. Our culture of democracy makes us strong; we must invest in revitalizing it! We must protect it from the fate of baby doomers who are shifting our culture away from its historical roots toward a divisive, argumentative, dishonorable doomerism.

In addition to the people power of our revolutionary ideals, American democracy shaped itself in many ways by responding to the influence of tertiary powers. Before these, let us have a look at the other secondary powers that cause effects in the making and remaking of society and affect our culture.

Geography, a Provider Power

Principal among the secondary powers is geography, nature's power. It has enormous influence that precedes how people must think and proceeds how we must act to survive on planet earth. Geography provides the eco-systems within which humans exist, surviving, living well, and striving to be thriving in luxury. The standards of living and quality of life available depend on the resources of any given geography and a culture's adaptation to it, which depends on people's KA^4SA^2, carried in the vessels of language, traditions, and customary social powers and their techniques and technologies adapted to specific biomes. The quality and quantity of KA^4SA^2 resides in a culture's capacity, capability, and aptitude for the process of adaptation to the geography. Geography power shapes culture, and in it, people shape their living environment. Geography makes indigenous built form, vernacular, native to place architecture possible (Rudofsky, 1964).

On the continent known as America, people brought foreign cultures to the land. These people struggled to build settlements with the materials they found in the land, as they built what they knew based on where they came from. Eventually, they evolved a culture different from their original one while retaining aspects of it they found useful in their new colonies. One aspect of the culture they left behind was the nature of the polity. They wanted to be independent and not dependent on a ruler. They wanted to govern themselves with more freedom and fewer restrictions put upon them by a distant king. They wanted to be equals with one another. Except for the error of slavery, the ideal existed unrealized due to the politics and economics of the time. The economy power created the misbalance that allowed a people to live in hypocrisy and rationalize it away. Only the people power properly applied through the polity power can countervail such cruelty.

A culture in which each person in the society has equality before the polity headed up by elected representative officials, who ensure the society functions on a rule of law basis, is a democracy. This constituted social structure drives a desire for the economy power to support equality in the provision of survival-necessary goods and services for people to be able to survive, obtain the comfort of safety and security to live well, and strive to thrive in the excesses of luxury. Key social factors precede living well and enjoying excess luxury. Noncriminal gains, honest happiness, are possible by a good citizenry with sound policies that allow good industry power to optimize entrepreneurial efforts by the people to pursue commercial prosperity unhindered by excessive demands on them by the polity. This people-first society is democracy, culturally. To recap, democracy is a culture. People make, sustain, and change culture. It is part and parcel to identity, person by person and as a community. The polity power influences culture. The economy power affects culture. The people power perpetuates culture. Culture made out of and influenced by the primary societal, and the secondary and the tertiary powers shapes society.

A geography known by people becomes power in the knowledge of how to survive in a locale. Geography is also the power of ecosystems' disruptions to social life. Human settlements must respond to dynamic weather events to survive. All forms of weather cause people to think of ways to resist weather damage. The winds and rain of typhoons, hurricanes, and tornados can annihilate people's shelters. Other dynamic geological events threaten the tranquility of domestic living. The earth can shake, rattle, and roll by tectonic plates rubbing and bumping to produce earthquakes. Tidal waves, floods, lightning, wildfires, and volcanic eruptions are other hazardous risks to human settlements.

But even before worrying about dynamic events, people must learn how to adapt to the biostatic conditions that influence living conditions: temperature, humidity, and altitude.

Lucky for humankind, nature's ecosystems provide materials and nutrient resources we can use to make living possible in nearly every biome. These come with varying weather conditions that influence human adaptation, our cultural responses, and the tools we make to survive, live comfortably, and thrive in luxury. The geological aspect of sea level relates to coastal flooding concerns, which melting glaciers and mountain rains can cause as well. Each of the major biomes: forests, grasslands, deserts, and tundra can support human habitation. We settle close to survival-required bodies of water. Water can be freshwater in the form of rivers and lakes or salty and brackish in the form of marine water. Humans live on land with water resources in various biomes and climates. Our settlements support our social structures. The most present in our lives is the family. Let's move on to examine its power in our lives.

*F*amily Power

Formed socially by combinations of persons, family—the living, and remembered ones who care for us and us for them—is central to society. It is from family that we get our nature and receive our nurture. It has an essential power to shape culture by socializing children to be members of the American society. Families are on the front line of teaching liberty. Children must learn what it means to be an American. Not just the rights one has but also the duty one has—to be a citizen ensuring those rights exists for the next generation—because tyranny is always knocking on our door. Tyranny never stops trying to creep into our hearts, minds, bodies, and souls. It comes to cause dissonance. It enjoys corruption. It seeks to incite violence. It wants to use brutality. It invites us to trade freedom and liberty for order and tenuous security. It declares an enemy to scapegoat. It wants total control over all powers. Tyranny lurks in ignorance of the Constitution, which can cause naive people to ask of the Constitution what it was not intended to provide.

The Constitution secured the possibility for families to enjoy the blessings of liberty. But we are not there yet, and we must dedicate ourselves to getting there. The Constitution begins to secure liberty by separating the powers of the republic's polity into three branches to prevent the concentration of power. Power concentration is not in accord with democracy culture. If a family understands this lesson, than it will divide power in the household in a way that is freeing for the parenting adults, liberating, and beneficial to the children, allowing them to develop more experience with several adults. Children should be encouraged to know that they have a special function in the governance of the household. Power sharing is not instinctive. We must teach it and train at doing it. Civilizing is the learning of how to share power.

American society must repeatedly reeducate its citizenry on its ideals to create the civilization intended by its founding. It is possible. We can step away from the path of power-lusting dependencies that prevent us from rising to our highest nature. We must serve our founding words to distance ourselves as a people and move away from the animalism and tyranny of typical historical societies, civilizations that ruthlessly conquered others. We must recommit to the pursuit of ideals to prove that the truth of America is realizable. We, the everyday people, through E-SASSY-T-TUF-FT-CAUCUS must make the idealized America real. We cannot quit on this mission. We've the retardation caused by the large boomer generation to recover from and get moving forward again. Our American project is essential to keep liberty alive. This is a core mission. We cannot deny it. We cannot hide from it. We must do better at it, every day in every way.

Community Power

Community is a social power like family. Found in many forms it is an adaptive force. It can be a settlement. We find it shared via interested networks of dispersed persons from different settlements communicating with each other. Many powers both affect and give effect to Community. The diagrams below in Figures 3-7 thru 3-11 illustrate this. They show how a contemporary settlement overlays the many powers' houses for meeting the needs of inhabitants. Together we build society.

The primary house of people is their residence. See Figure 3-7 below. From it, we go out into society to engage with others in the instruments (organizations and institutions) of the social powers. Our residence and neighborhood influence our development as people and our preparedness to be citizens. Civics taught in schools is a necessary application of the academy powers to help us, through our democracy culture, to unify as a people. If we don't do it well, we lose the glue that socializes us in all our possible contexts to be capable of the necessary E-SASSY-T-TUF-FT-

CAUCUS we need to perpetuate our USE. To that end, we must reinvigorate and ramp up our ACE.

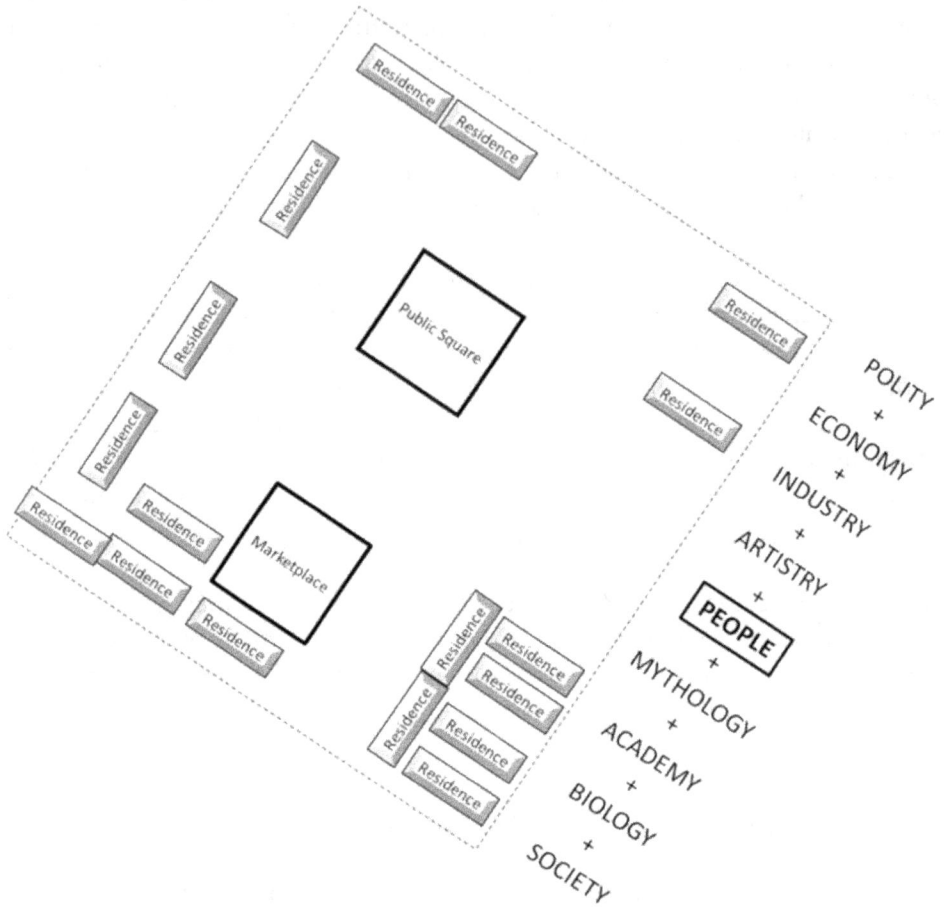

Figure 3-7: People in a Settlement

Our society houses the polity in civic buildings. See Figure 3-8 below.
The polity's houses often separate in accordance with branches of government. There are houses for the legislative, executive powers, and judicial.
These subordinate powers may have additional houses to support aspects
of their administration of society to attain our objectives: establish justice,
ensure domestic tranquility, provide for the common defense, promote the
general welfare, and secure the blessings of liberty.

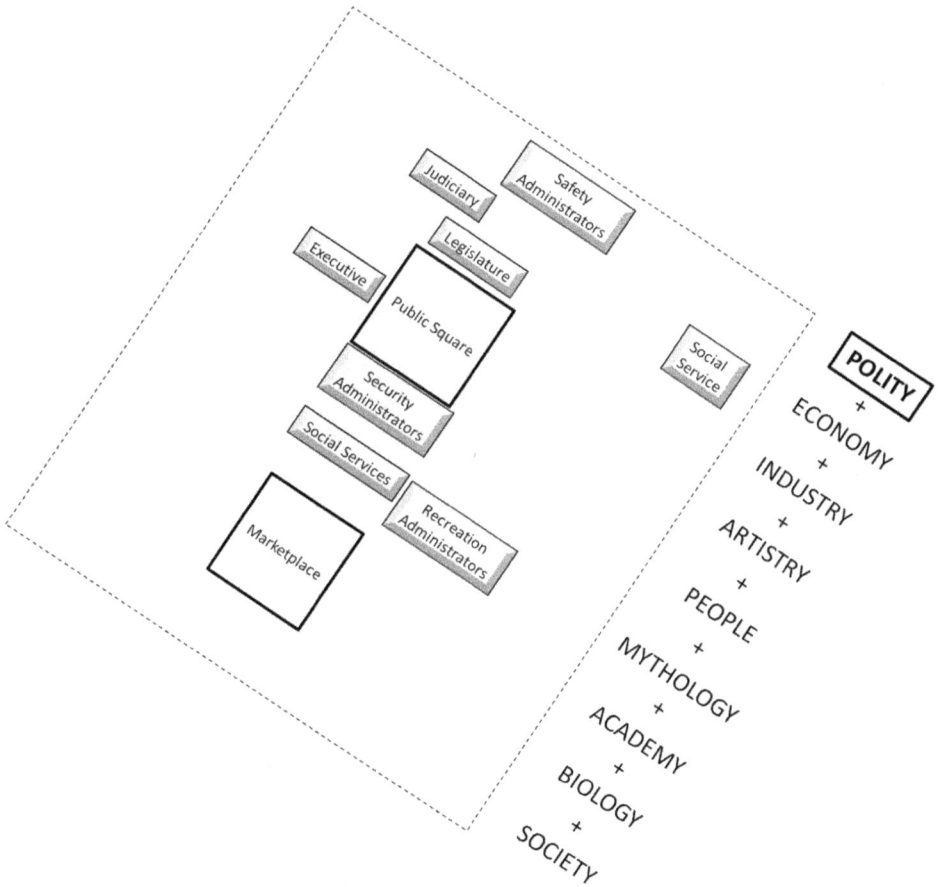

Figure 3-8: Polity in a Settlement

The economy power stimulates creativity in the people. Its supportive and subordinate powers of industry, artistry with their use of architecture and engineering expertise make available for society many useful utilities that support the resourcing of provisions, transportation, and communication. See Figure 3-9 below. Survival stimulates it. To live decently perpetuates it. A desire to thrive in luxury increases it.

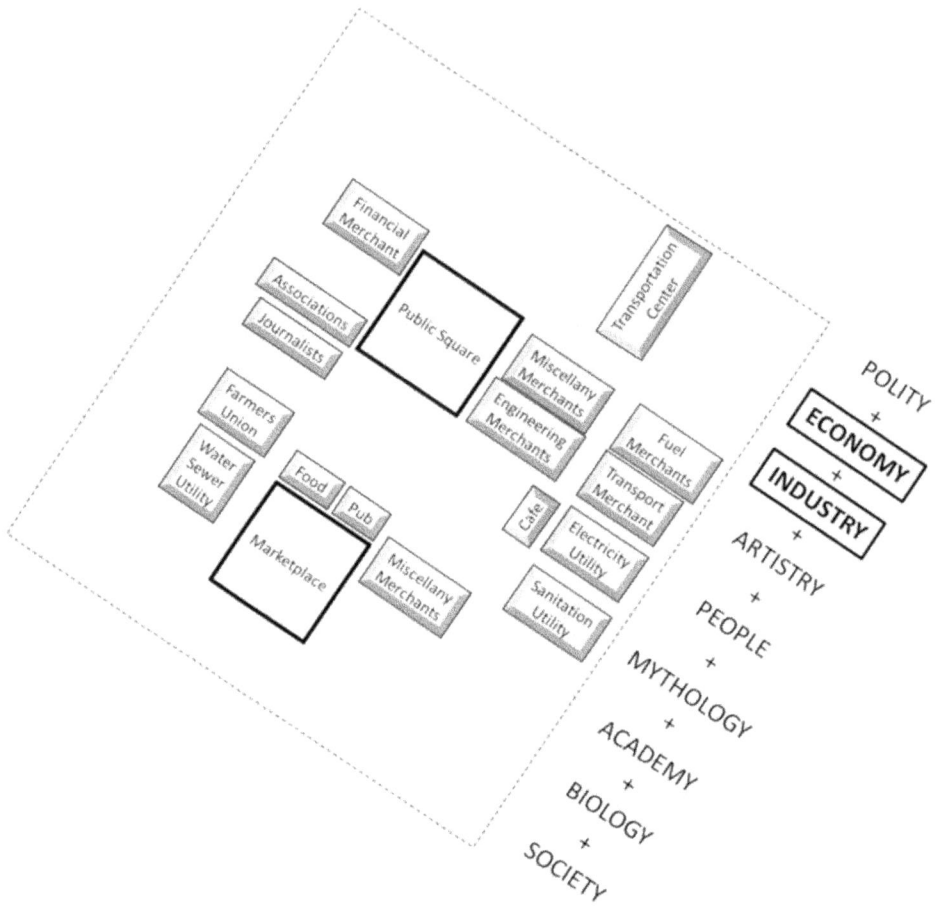

Figure 3-9: Economy in a Settlement

The community secondary and many of the tertiary social powers have fewer and smaller houses than the primary powers, but they provide valuable contributions to living and enrich the people of a society. See Figure 3-10 below. They provide a network of social worth through private interests that create the informal civil society that bonds neighbors and communities together in spirit and hopefulness as a citizenry of the nation (Putnam R. D., 2000).

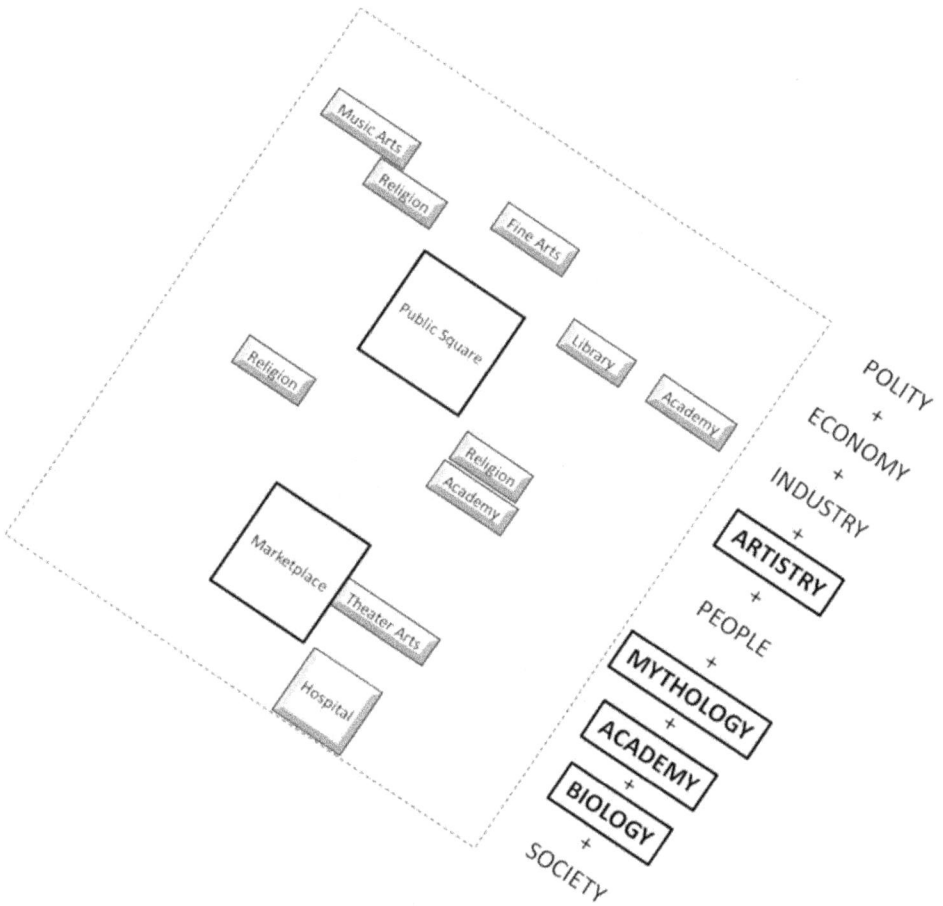

Figure 3-10: Artistry, Mythology, Academy, and Biology in a Settlement

Civil society builds social capital. Social capital builds community through people's participation, contributions, and civic engagement in meaningful projects to benefit the whole community, such as maintaining a public playground or assisting neighbors in times of need. All the powers combined make a fulfilling society. See Figure 3-11 below.

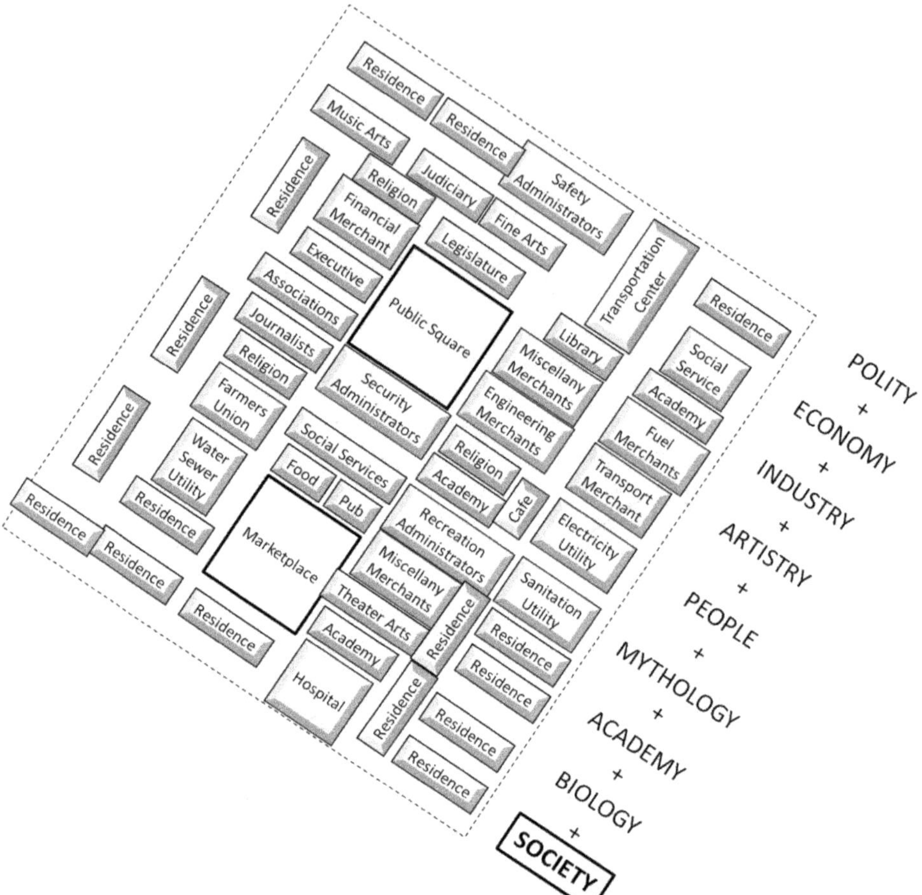

Figure 3-11: All Powers Combined Make Society in a Settlement

Next, let's look closer at the social powers culture creates and sustains.

Culture's Social Powers

As a precept power process, culture predicts behaviors, though not perfectly. Imperfect people AEIOUY²K the human culture created social powers imperfectly. In our imperfection, we can succumb to the DAMN of these powers. Our culture is a measurement of our preferences and tolerances for our control of our desires for power, either inspired or despised. Culture creates and controls power. Culture is not monolithic. It is complex, layered, and full of nuances because it is a mosaic of integrant building block powers. Ancestrally, humans created powers to master aspects of life they felt compelled to control to survive the wild and dangerous hazards of geography. Compelled by basic survival instincts, people satisfied their basic needs. Theorized as a hierarchy by the American psychologist Abraham Maslow (see Figure 3-6), the culture power processes satisfy these needs by provide resources that occupy, comfort, arouse, or entertain. Culture refined powers also evolve. They are determined as necessary by the majority, often through the dealings of marketplaces, or by the most physically powerful or highly regarded. The tertiary powers of culture: mythology, academy, industry, artistry, and history (see Figure 3-4), behave as integrant building blocks.

It is important we note that culture expresses itself in the physical artifacts of our lives. These materially represent to archaeologists our standards of living. The architecture and landscapes of our settlement patterns: our rural farms, urban cities, suburbs, and gardens, show our quality of life. Architects capture the inspirational and aspirational aspects of culture in architecture. The cultural landscape tells tales about who we are (Jackson, 1984). Because we act and interact with nature through the medium of culture, and by it build structures, it is the hidden dimension "making up the warp and weft of human existence" (Hall, 1966).

Entering the days of higher digital machine learning technology, we must understand better culture's society shaping power processes. Thus, this book calls it out. We need to evaluate it, along with our regional subcultures. We do this to develop ways, means, and methods of adapting to future challenges, to avoid the risks that threaten our survival. We do this by adopting a unified approach to IDEALS liberty for the sustainment of the promise of freedoms that the USE by proper LAMBS yields for us.

Our experience of the spaces and places we build shapes our perceptions, our emotions, and our thoughts. Becoming familiar with our time and place and appreciating others' is vital to better standards of living and quality of life. Oriented by our experience of our architecture we gain confidence (Tuan, 1977). Over time, we change the built environment to accommodate the expectations of the future. Predictions are often wrong. So we must better remember that utopian visions often have many inadequacies.

We do well by saving extant architecture (embodied culture) for it. Moreover, by being adaptable to it, we can create it through our imagination of its possibilities. We need not see it only as a dystopia or utopia. Useful adaptability requires the maintenance of continuing current capabilities to respond to change. Aspiration and a sense of the continuity of what is true for us are essential, because open-ended change frightens us (Lynch, 1972).

Adaptive problems of the third stage in knowledge evolution and the technology it brings are a cultural challenge for us. We must know that the Constitution gives us capabilities for adaptation to utopian and dystopian visions of the future. We must be practical. We must know what American Culture is. Doomerism hampers this. We must develop unity as one American people around an honest assessment of American history. We must gain common knowledge of our culture and change its bad in for its good to bond together. We must become one to resist the plutocracy doomerism causes, because it will destroy democracy. As our framework for uniting, it gives us hope, but we must invest in its determined pursuits named in the Preamble. The secondary and tertiary powers drive the way we make the built environment. As we cohabit it, so do our social and cultural adjustments to past, present, and future, get made. Let us better attend to it and its lessons of time and place, of space shaped and face placed upon our culture. Let's go over the tertiary powers influence upon and within culture making.

Mythology

Mythology is principally concerned with a person's and a people's feelings, hopes, and fears, giving us aid and comfort against the great unknown. It tells stories that give us beliefs to assist us in having purpose and meaning in our lives. Much wisdom in human affairs conveys by it. Through its allusions and allegories, with its explanations of the circumstances of human relations and behaviors, our species came to understand better our nature. It provides us customs and rites for marking the transitions in our biological and social lives. As such, it builds for us cultures. Some lean more heavily on this power than others to define themselves. They are free to do so in the USE without interference from the polity. Mythology does more, but it generally forms a philosophy that explains the unknown (or unknowable) and conveys ancestral ideas for human attitudes and behaviors. Many instruments of the academy power originated at houses of worship where mythology power put it into practice. It draws its persuasiveness from our lack of evidential knowledge of the purpose of our existence by creating stories to explain the unknowable: Why are we here? Why do we exist? Why do we behave the way we do? How should we behave?

Mythology gives us lessons to learn about others and ourselves in its storytelling, tall tales, and fables, and in the answers that make up its rituals and rites of passage. Its ways, means, and methods to $AEIOUY^2K$ its power is highly influenced by community power. It has many forms: deistic and pagan—with gods in nature like the Shinto or Wicca with its witchcraft. Ancient ones were polytheistic, as with the Greeks, Romans, and Hindus. Some are dualistic, seeing equal and opposite gods of good vs. evil, such as the Zoroastrian. The dominant ones are monotheistic, three of which trace their roots to the creation story of Adam and Eve and the descendants of Abraham. These are Judaism, Christianity, and Islam. Apostates from these may practice Satanism. There are others that are animistic and non-deistic, some with lessons and rituals for life without deity worship, like Buddhism or Confucianism. Many of these have branches, twigs, and leaves of faith group divisions. Some mythologies are highly proscriptive with high orthodoxy of dogma—cultlike, tight belief, and behaviorally regulatory religion. These can be the most limiting of personal freedoms and demand the greatest sacrifice of people power to commit to them. Some mythologies have lower levels of orthodoxy and are more flexible, undogmatic with looser beliefs and fewer behavioral constrictions. They are the least limiting of personal freedoms and require the least sacrifice of people power.

Academy

The academy power is principally concerned with a person's and a people's thinking and understanding, giving us advice and knowledge to survive, live well, and thrive. That which ruminates upon the questions answered by mythology we know as philosophy. It is devoid of myths, a secular system of thought and thinking on the five big W (who what where when why) and the mighty H (how). These, the common questions we all ask and want answered. The academy power enables us to hold, produce, and transfer knowledge. It is involved in the exercise of our pursuits of KA^4SA^2 and the evaluation and dissemination of knowledge across and among societies, such as through translations and diplomacy. It has many branches and many complexions. We often divide it into two branches. The first branch is the humanities, which leans on artistry power grew out of mythology power, also known as the traditional disciplines of thought and expression, the liberal arts. In the other branch are the sciences, technology, and engineering, which lean on the geography and industry powers. In these, we find a different manner of KA^4SA^2, its production, and the by-product of its growth, radical innovation. Some disciplines, like architecture and industrial design, straddle the two branches.

Per its level in society, knowledge defines differently. Knowledge at the individual or micro level is definable as "the capacity to do things" such as reading, writing, and arithmetic or using tools to make food, cook, clean a house, or repair a machine. At the meso level, knowledge is "the production of goods and services," while at the macro or societal level, "knowledge creates resources that society needs" (Hage, 2020). As knowledge spreads by persons, organizations, and society, it embeds in our experiences and activities, our work and play, and our culture. Knowledge grows legs and the academy power expands, becoming increasingly important to our survival as a species. There are many components to knowledge's embeddedness (Hage, 2020). It is in our:

Hardware	=	Technology, tools, and machines
Software	=	Operations and their controllers, techniques, and methods
Skills	=	Education, training, and in our minds
Ideas	=	Science, theory, and models to explain things

The academy power is that faculty within us for KA^4SA^2 in society's instruments of power. That is in our organizations to operate, our institutions to function, and ultimately for our USE to effect excellent LAMBS on our behalf, with us as its owners. Thus, society's successes depend upon each of us to $AEIOUY^2K$ the academy power at the levels where we are best suited to do so. Society's selection of us into these positions says something about how we go about educating ourselves with our academy power and how it connects us to our polity and economy powers.

The structure of the academy power at the meso level of society, at the level of the social powers' instruments, is done through various $FILMS^2$ [P7] of community and resourcing. There are public, paid for by the people through the polity, and private, paid for by the people through selective community power, some with mythology origins. The academy powers split into levels of advancement based upon age and development and for older teens and adults into specializations and disciplines. These can be industry and profession-based training environments paired closely to areas of concern to the polity and the economy powers, and they may be publicly or privately resourced. Some, on a consortium basis, are jointly resourced, industrial-based, public–private ventures. In some cases, highly advanced knowledge is done by combined efforts at the societal level, across social, professional and national boundaries in an effort to solve ubiquitous human problems, adapting to the social changes brought about by changes in geography powers or challenges caused by new knowledge and technologies introduced into the $FILMS^2$[P7] of the economy power. The transformation of society to meet such challenges requires we $AEIOUY^2K$ the academy power in novel ways, creating the conditions for new organizations and institutions for the efficient development and dissemination of new knowledge and technologies. This is doable by combined efforts at a regional level to solve local problems related to the geography power of certain biomes and the needs of humans there to adapt to the change.

We, the everyday people, if we want to reclaim and retain our leadership responsibility, must become more aware of, understanding of, and conversant with knowledge's evolution. If not, the changes we face in our local communities will feel daunting. Fear will open us up to baby doomerist behaviors. We don't want to exist in a state of confusion and become easily manipulated by those who intend to DAMN power, in whatever culture shaping power base or power structure they reside: primary, secondary, or tertiary. We have no choice. If we are to be citizens, we must eradicate doomerism from our culture of democracy. Our society requires people who can reason logically, think imaginatively, and understand how to apply the powers of our culture for the benefit of all the people. This will enable us to IDEALS liberty for all. James Madison, the fourth president of the United States, said, "Knowledge will forever govern ignorance and a people who mean to be their own governors must arm themselves with the power which knowledge gives." He was correct.

Industry

The industry power is principally concerned with a person's and a people's survival, giving us the tools and materials shaped from the geography power to create settlements and a society. It enables structuring of the physical world, our built environments, our food, clothing, shelter, and the tools it uses itself and forms for us to use in our artistry and athletics. Combined with the artistry and community powers, it forms architecture, which serves all the other powers with houses for them to be symbolically present and physically able to perform their functions. Industry, through its instrument of architecture, makes cities of our buildings and shapes our real and cultural landscapes (Jackson, 1984). It leads us to increasing KA^4SA^2 in engineering and advances our toolmaking from hand tools to machines that support any imagined endeavor or activity in society. Industry strongly overlaps with the development of science and technology, depending upon and employing their knowledge in its toolmaking pursuits, as it provides a form of celebration of human achievements for us. One example of this is the play of sporting activities.

Artistry

The artistry power is principally concerned with a person's and a people's emotional well-being—our thriving—giving us the forms of expression that support our curiosity, let loose our imaginations, and practice and celebrate our creativity, personally and as a society. It enables us to play—to use our curious intelligence to produce and share creative expressions of experiences. It gives us athletics to enjoy the physicality of human movement and the social joy of shared play and shows us the beauty of performing an activity. This includes sports that use special tools, equipment, machines, or animals. It comes to us in various modes:

- The <u>Literary</u> Arts of storytelling, fantasy and fiction, through which we imagine our world, find many expressive forms. It includes tales of society, its history, theory, and fact telling in nonfiction accounts. These, in combination with history power's records, tell us about one another and ourselves through stories of the past, present, and possible futures or complete fantasies of alien species. Our expressions of understanding or yearning emerge in poetry writing and recital as well as songs, many played on instruments made with industry power. In combination with our physical, athletic biology power, we celebrate movement and tell stories though dance.

- The <u>Visual</u> Arts of illustrating our world in abstraction or surreal or real reflection and representation in the fine arts of drawing, painting, and sculpture find many forms of expression. Also through crafts, we make commercial arts that combine artistry power in support of industry power, and even through new combinations of mixed media, we tell stories of ourselves.

- The <u>Musical</u> Arts of making sounds in beautiful patterns.

- The <u>Theater</u> Arts of performing stories find many forms of expression. These can include singing and dancing along with acting. This includes filmed recordings of plays, movies, and television programs.

- The <u>Culinary</u> Arts of making food in delicious ways and in appetizing compositions find many forms of expression.

- The <u>Civic</u> Arts of shaping our physical world, made in combination with our industry and community power to serve our culture powers through architecture, urban design, gardens, parks for recreation, and their appurtenances from the fine arts such as sculptures and athletics facilities.

- The <u>Athletic</u> Arts involve a form of artistry in our athleticism that leans on our biology power. We enjoy sports with teams and sports with one-on-one competition, those without much equipment like wrestling or the martial arts, those with more equipment like gymnastics, boxing and skiing, and those with machines for racing, like bicycles, automobiles, boats, and airplanes. We even have sports that employ animals, like horse and camel races.

History

Last but not the least of the tertiary powers of culture is history, the story once told, now told, and proposed—the use of the knowledge of what has happened, is happening, or could happen by those who look back in the hope of defining trends that may continue into the future. The history power of culture is principally concerned with people's activities, particularly those given positions of authority in the polity and the elites of the economy power. It chronicles, journals, and reports. It enables us to remember our public shared history and the private histories of our autobiographies. It even addresses the production of our history. History recorded in the arena of news reporters and storytellers (the media) as they document current events is journalism. History writing includes the storytellers who create mythology. It also applies to when literature skills of the artistry power prepares nonfiction works. The FILMS[2] [P7] of the academy power use it in pedagogy. Epistemologically speaking, doomerism challenges history power's journalism instrument. It implies that what we know is what we know, but it is not informing us of what we do not know but ought to know as the owners, the citizens, of American society. We need to understand better the hermeneutics and the dialectics of power. There is risk to liberty if the polity gets to work its politics without the people being in control of it. The polemics of rage, residing at the diametric poles, become extremely dangerous. Their arguments get more severe with confusion over obfuscated isms infuriating those caught in between. It is as much an issue of linguistics as it is of knowledge, though there is evidence to suggest that language is the first knowledge, and its limitations influence our ability to comprehend just about everything. So words matter. Words have meanings. We need to know them. If we think we know what words mean, but we don't quite, then we misunderstand one another, and this can cause emotions to rise up in our amygdala and block our ability to hear facts, as we tell ourselves stories of what we think is an insult upon our personages (Patterson, Grenny, McMillan, & Switzler, 2012). Communication is foundational to socialization, socializing, and being socially involved with others as we go about our lives. We really need to be better at listening, and we must be more vigilant to do our homework to know what words mean before we toss them around symbolically. We need to know not only what the isms mean but also how their meaning relates to the effects they seek and how these affect the way citizens IDEALS liberty. We need good history for the justice we need and the truth of the purpose of our USE.

Lastly, the history power supports the other powers by writing their stories for us to remember: histories of our artistry, arts and entertainment, athletics, and for the influential in society, family histories.

*D*emocracy

Democracy as culture is rooted in sharing power. This is not instinctual. To protect inalienable rights, it is essential that each of us learn to do it. Doomerism dispossesses us of the knowledge of how to share. This harms our ability to care for our fellow human beings as equals. Each has equal stake in democracy. We need to understand power and how it operates if we want a society with a culture rooted in democracy instead of one rotted out by doomerism. Power in numbers and hope for everyone under the sun comes from democracy. We find community power when we unite neighborly with others. Yet we all must step forward in unison when dissent becomes necessary. To dissent against abusive power is to consent to liberty's defense. To dissent is to be a stronger, uncorrupted, constitutionally correct, citizen of justice. A citizen of democracy constitutes in the heart a love of liberty, living to achieve the goal and to attain the objectives of the Constitution as amended. This is how the citizens collectively committing to citizenship patriotism, regardless of what positions or offices they hold in the polity or economy, ensure the Constitution is being lived, not evaded, but upheld.

Democracy is a kind of culture power process that shapes all societal and social powers' FILMS[2] [P7]: It is an integrant building block of our republic. By culture, we assemble the networks of powers into a society. These interwoven networks sustain the society. When sharing common principles society becomes more beneficial for everyone and its culture is more secure. The society of the USE relies on the culture of democracy. This culture based upon the invisible force of truth reaches throughout the population and reveals itself in common sense. Abraham Lincoln captured this sentiment's essence: "You may fool people for a time; you can fool a part of the people all the time; but you can't fool all the people all the time." This makes control of the history power so very crucial, and it is why the people power must not believe everything seen in the media. Without deeper investigation, propaganda by persons seeking to stay on top and control society will fool us by their trickery they use to DAMN history power.

Those in the history power's FILMS[2] [P7] must pursue the highest levels of virtue because they chronicle what happens in society. They write the journals that historians in the future will read to learn from the past. They cannot and should not, but do, tell untrue stories. This is a misuse of their power. How deviously pleased the doomers feel to start rumors and watch them spread until eventually a lie is seen as being true. Not only is this illogical. It is dangerous. If con artists distort the truth and people wanting to be deceived allow it, reasonableness is dead. Physical might gains more value than intellectual right for settling disputes. This primate drift backward threatens civilization. A loss of the necessary integrity for a republic is altogether a loss for democracy culture. To lie and rumor for raw power and financial gain is disgracefully embarrassing. It undercuts the honor of the citizen who commits it. The lies are evidence of a doomerism infection. This hurts liberty.

Yes, it is exhausting to sift, sort, and filter to find facts and build truth. However, because of the history power and its immediate instrument, the "news" feeders, the need to be first—not factual—to compete for advertisements easily sways the economy power and its FILMS$^{2\,[P7]}$, and it easily tempts the polity power and its FILMS$^{2\,[P7]}$ to crave to control it. The fact that the framers wrote the right of free speech is a huge protection for the people. The history power used to be used to lie to people on behalf of a tyrant and his or her minions, who would monopolize it to blame all failures on a scapegoat. Then, having diverted attention away from themselves, take what they want, fleecing funds from the people to put into their own pockets. Alas, nowadays due to doomerism this control is circuitous and roundabout. The economy controls the polity. The economy controls the history. The people struggle to believe the polity. The economy uses the polity like puppets. The people are spectators to the show. This is not how a republic is supposed to function, and we must stop it. We must block doomerism in self and in society. We do it through better citizenshipping. Let's get busy with stopping the fooling of ourselves. Know this as motivation: "By manufacturing a never-ending stream of crises, a corrupt oligarchy can prolong its rule indefinitely." It is time to participate in politics to regain control of "Our country tis of thee, sweet land of liberty," or it will have liberty for us no more. This is not a joke. We must yoke the power back to its original constitutional intents. If we don't, we'll be consumed by it and converted by consumerism into consummate fools of the plutocrats, aristocrats, autocrats, kleptocrats, and oligarchs. Is that what we want? If not, stop arguing about the shallow, superficial, hollow rhetorical fallacies being put in front of us by the top two powers of polity and economy, and make them appropriately subordinate to us. The leadership in a democracy belongs to the people power. We must lead the society through building up a trillion good gestures that create a community full of citizens who understand that each day is a day to demonstrate that we are in charge. We do it of ourselves, our neighborhoods, our communities, our states, and our nation, as one people, e pluribus unum. Daily behaving as good citizens and holding one another accountable to the best standards of conduct that support and uphold the intents and principles of the Constitution is how we self-govern. How can this be possible? How do bees make honey? Community cooperation involves anticipating that others are also doing "good for good" because we all want goodness. This trust diminishes fear. Trust increases as we gain harmony working on the US project together. No one cheats. Liars die off. Thieves need not steal because they have legitimate jobs; government costs less because we need fewer police, less jurisprudence administration, and fewer courthouses. With better behaving citizens, civically engaged and participating politically, less revenue for government operations is needed, which means less taxation is put upon us.

We have the power. We are the people. We shape the culture. With it, we shape the society. Democracy needs our honesty and integrity every day, in every position we have, in all the roles we play in our families, neighborhoods, communities, states, and nation. "We the people" attitudes and behaviors begin with you and with me. It begins with us. It begins when we truly begin to fully believe in and act as if we are a democracy. We begin to do this when we stop ourselves from becoming baby doomers. When we live for the children and not our hedonic selfishness, we perpetuate our society's prosperity of peace and freedom for posterity. Truth, love, joy, beauty—these are natural pleasures. These are magnanimous in their purity. We must be able to pursue them by seeking to live virtuously, making trustworthy citizens of one another and of ourselves by committing to the community. We build together. We should not look for someone else to do it for us. When we mature past our selfishness, we arrive at a state of being that can put us in a state of mind that recognizes the truth of what liberty is. It is a state of consciousness. It is a state of being conscientious. It is as state of reason, of enlightened being. Being a citizen first gets us there.

First, we must move past the temptations of doomerism and attend to the balancing of powers that we, by our culture of democracy, assemble in our USE to provide the LAMBS. This begins by our civic engagement and political participation (American Academy of Arts & Sciences, 2020). It builds up to our being brave and attentive enough to control our politicians to AEIOUY^{2}K polity power on our behalf, not allowing them to be controlled by the elites of the economy power. It begins with us. It's a must do. Polity and economy power, if unchecked, will seek to use history power-infused public relations skills to coerce our minds and convince us to give them our consent, even if what they ask of us is not in our short-term, mid-term, or long-term interests. If we are ignorant, they will sell us one form of ism snake oil or another. We must be more aware!

Discipline is necessary for democracy to exist at its best. Driven by instincts we are. We must cognate and control these short-term utility seeking pursuits of pleasure at the level of self that is all about "my" gratification and "me first." Baby doomers' sybaritic weakness manipulates us. Yet if "we the people" all go this route, this immediacy of self-indulgent gratification harbors risks and externalities unconsidered in the moment of amusement's hot pursuit. As we mature, we learn this. We know it. Yet we go around and around in circles in pursuit of pleasure but get nowhere near it in any sense of permanency. Our greed for pleasure distracts us. Our desire to be distracted continues. It consumes us; we consume more but have no more happiness. Consumption comes to define everything. Everything is consumption, and we become nothing. Then we may find guilt. Our hedonism does not result in happiness if gained in a way contrary to social norms. If it results in guilt or shame, (if a conscience exists), we'd seek to rationalize it away, denying it is real. If we have no consciousness of the consequences upon others caused by our greed, we may be closer to psychopaths, or if intentionally cruel, sociopaths, and never develop a good conscience.

Self-knowledge is more important to democracy than self-pleasing. Self-pleasing is more important to doomerism than is self-knowledge. Do we seek to be deceived? We have a choice: reason and rightfulness or stupidity and wrongfulness. One is liberty, the other doom. Through the pursuit of pleasing ourselves first—"me first" doomerism—more and more people become narcissistic adults. The children of tomorrow need the adults of today to be adults, not childish, foolish, or idiotic adolescents. Doomerism is not a good teamwork condition. Democracy requires excellent teamwork. We need teamwork. In all the societal powers, teamwork is fundamental. Good cooperation is foundational if the entire USE is to be successful at making good living possible. To reach our goal by attaining our objectives, we need the powers to work in unison in the LAMBS. If not, we'll see our land become dysphoric or suffer delusions of grandeur. Thus, we will land ourselves in a disastrous dystopian reality. We do not need to live in a perpetual nightmare.

In threatening times, people turn to one power or another. Constant turning over of traditions and modern projects failing confound us. We fear what will become if we lack a clear vision of purpose. Often the mind-centered powers compete for our thinking. The mythology or academy powers offer the answers to the questions we keep secret. Fears show in factions' group behaviors, like longing for a fight just to fight, uncivilly, to feel that raw power victory sensation. These past forty years distrust between and among traditionalists and modernists enlarged to epic proportions of hatred.

In God we trust, and e pluribus unum, holy and human, with religion and science we strive. Mythology power and academy power are of the same substance, human culture. With similar purposes, both prepare persons for social grouping. Both tell stories to help the group survive. One carries the wisdom of how to behave and get along in the group. The other one shares the knowledge we use to overcome the threats, and find opportunities, within Geography power.

American society balances the mythology and academy powers by allowing them to keep in motion. See Figure 3-13 below. The coin is a symbol of exchange. All societies have a means of exchange and a store of value. The coin's faces represent these two strong social powers of culture. Gravity exists, and it represents the natural power. The coin's edge is what allows the coin to stand up. Thin coins, those with little distance between its faces topple easily. It will fall flat on one side or the other. In this metaphor, the sides seen extremely are a theocracy or an atheist bureaucracy, with either one side up and with the other down. In the founding of the USE, the separation of church and state, removes this weakness. It puts distance between the ability of one power or the other to dominate culture, and it lays the foundation for an American society. A thick coin, with our without motion, stands easily. Spinning it gives us dynamism the makes living more stimulating.

Continuing with this metaphor, to make such a society viable, the coin needs spun with good velocity. When set in motion it becomes more stable and will stand up longer because it can resist external forces. It is the physics of science, the academy power, which freed from the mythology power, creates this condition. The more the knowledge of nature, the faster the coin can spin. However, with too hard a flick, too much science pressure, the coin will not remain in place, but will drift and move in many directions. This introduces risks to it colliding in a conflict and falling down. American society by separating church from state created the conditions for science, the academy power, to be strong. Yet, to forget the mythology power, as modernism did is to set the coin wobbling adrift. Modern fantasies of curing an ill world can go too far. Ancient fascinations of curing an ill world can go too far. The balance leads to stabilizing motion. Over ambitious modernism causes loss in perception of the value of mythological wisdom. Mythology power's stories imbed wisdom in traditions. Modernism against traditionalism is a false conception. When ideologues pit mythology and academy powers against one another as opponents, people suffer. During the time of dominance of the baby boomers, a culture war arose that posed itself in battles of an either or choice of which power possessed the truth. Neither does alone.

The arguers forgot the truth. They no longer recognized the powers shared substance, which is each of us as human beings and the culture made to protect our natural rights. The divide we experience today resulted from a generation's personality. The divide is a fallacy built on a false premise. Being false, we easily can stop the argument. We set our egos aside. We think of the children and the state of the endowment of the USE we will be leaving them. We resist burdening them with debts. We must rediscover our truth writ in our founding documents, and live it, daily. The framer's wisdom, their understanding of human nature, put the coin in motion. Spinning on edge, it created a three dimensional image of a sphere. Metaphorically, this mesmerizing orb was part of the miracle of the birth of the USE and a new form of liberty—separation of church and state. It is only possible with balanced mutual tolerance of the two powers. It allows for both, it benefits from both. Yet if too far apart, the coin gets too fat to spin. Too thin a coin is too unstable to begin to spin. The right influence of each is a decision the community must make. In some places, it can be more of one than the other can. This rests on tolerance. Tolerance is the force that applies the right pressure to spin the coin. American tradition builds a public square. American tradition builds a public commercial market place for private sellers. One often built in front of a religious edifice. The other often built in front of a bank or government building. Often all three together shape the central square of an American city. Our settlement patterns tell us a bit about ourselves.

For an American society the religious and secular traditions, the ancient and modern ambitions must balance. The culture of democracy is a means to produce the stable balances of these mind-feeding powers. This is our truth. We must move away from the ideological extremism of doomerism. It began to infect our culture during the baby boomers majority rule. American democracy is the motion we must sustain by participating as an educated citizenry. The sustaining of American society relies on ACE. This is critical to gaining prospect of prosperity for posterity. Commerce as our focus reduces the risks of ancient arguments that led to warring over unprovable ideas. Entrepreneurship reduces the risks of modern egotistical megalomaniacs sending commoner's children off to war.

Comparatively, within a theocracy, a coin is set face down. There is no debate, no motion of ideas, no innovation in society, no upward mobility. Conversely, within a polity that seeks to replace traditional religions with it as the god, the coin is set face up. There is no debate, no tradition of holy beliefs, no human spiritual needs recognition, and no mental stability.

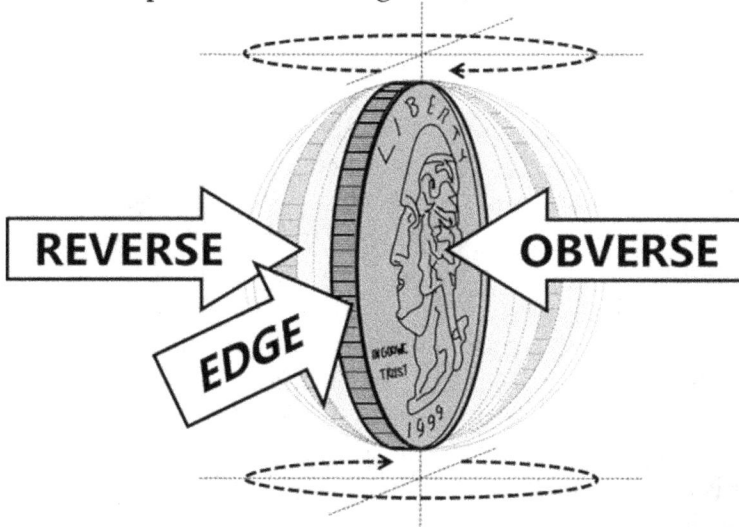

Figure 3-12: Stability in Motion—American Society Balances Mythology and Academy Powers

Figure 3-12's spinning coin symbolizes a motion of ideas. It tells us that debate is possible here. Debate creates the dynamism of democracy, which produces opportunity and hope for generations. Such a society requires the force of liberty within its citizenry. This then is the willingness to share and transfer power. To hoard it and demand it all is ape like madness. Ideologues are this way. They do not serve the intents of a republic, nor are they into keeping up with the virtues of democracy. This is appearing to be the result of baby boomers reign, of their acceptance of the drift into doomerism. What would a 1776 patriot see? What might they say? Would they go so far as to claim, legitimately, that it is quintessentially un-American?

Living for the moment is different from being in the moment. Being in the moment is being with people we care about and attending with our attention to what is occurring between them and us, a realization of a real relationship. This is part of seeking a mid-term value, a pursuit of the comforts of family. This interest extends outwardly to our neighbors and communities. As this expression of love, listening, caring, and attending enlarges its circles, it realizes that our long-term purpose is the pursuit of freedom for one another, so that we may be free to see everybody happy. This is the societal pursuit of happiness made possible by the making of the United States of America, led by the everyday Americans. It comes through virtue at the level of community. We concurrently belong to many communities. The specificity of what each demands of us encourages us to hold certain beliefs, have certain attitudes, and behave in certain ways. This is the social dynamic of belonging and getting along with our fellow citizens. It does not mean going along with something wrong to get along. To belong to a group out of fear of ostracization is weakness. A free person cannot be dispossessed of personal integrity to secure membership.

There are no repercussions from honesty in a constitutionally allied society. There is only truth. Consequences are for the corrupt. If we all act with integrity, with bravery, we will deserve to be free. If not, we enslave ourselves, and others. We've no right to enslave others because of our insecurities. A love of liberty strengthens us with the courage to stop such soft corruption of cowardice. Knowing liberty truthfully empowers us to correct wrongs, and call for rightfulness. It helps us understand dilemmas where jeopardy resides. This grants us the wisdom to know what to say and how to act in ways best for justice. Culturally, if everyone expects this, we become the heroic American people envisioned by the founders. Power is what sits within and between us. Its abuse is a disservice to liberty, which rightly used shapes our sense of community, along with our trust in others. Our trust is not for treading on. It lifts up the quality of our social lives.

Citizenship is the work we put in for the community, which returns to us in freedoms in kindness, attention, attentiveness, love, conscientiousness, compassion, and empathy. Historically shaped communities, full of customs, may contain vestiges of the past that don't comport to the ideals of the Constitution. These communities may need significant work to help the citizenry adopt the calling to understand and the ethic to agree with an ethos that is not necessarily grown and nurtured in the fields of their minds and community praxis. However, it is vital for the emotional community. We must practice citizenship, be civil, be civic, and work to undo the wrong done to liberty and gain closer alignment with the next level up to it. But not by eroding the lower level's shared beliefs to the point that they are stripped of their independent thought, unless such thinking is not grounded in constitutional truth and violates its foundational principles. In this case, the lower level contemplation needs therapeutic adjustment to develop acceptable consideration since unconstitutional behaviors threaten or damage a wider community.

The communities to which we belong ask for different beliefs, attitudes, and behaviors. They each regulate our relationship from which we get a part of our identity, as well as what of ourselves we give to them. The dichotomous continuum is from nothing to everything, with all positions in between. The calculus of dangerous risk to self (death, bodily harm, lack of safety, inconsistent comfort) ranges from high sacrifice to low sacrifice to no sacrifice (no effort toward making a more perfect union and using every possible excuse to dodge all responsibility while demanding all rights). These are not all mutually exclusive. People may have blended levels of commitment to citizenship, and this can change over the course of their lives.

Oaths of office build faith and public trust that communities' members in positions with authority act more faithfully to the principles of the office, held in common by its members, than a non-oath maker, position taker. Assuming responsibility can be stressful. It takes sacrifice. It requires higher commitment to principles. Those who decide to be standard-bearers of civility and seek to represent the best of what a citizen of a republic built on democracy can be must exhibit themselves as examples and defenders of what such a culture can produce. We've many citizens who are staunch defenders of it, who live by the integrity that principled life provides. Take our warriors (by land, by sea, by air, by space [astronauts]), for example. They've high patriotism based on solid, not to be soiled, honor and commitment to citizenship. They want to protect society and uphold its principles by their example of good behavior. Although they, too, are imperfect humans, prone to error, they push themselves to be better. They want to demonstrate how to be a better person, citizen, and human being with commitment to the greater common good. If one of those in a polity position, a politician, lies, violates, or asks the warriors to violate first principles, apostate challenges in military servants' minds arise. We need elected officials who respect the warriors and do not disappoint their patriotism. We the people must not elect any who denigrate the honorable intentions of defending democracy.

The pragmatism of the people can be lost if the politicians become too righteous for an ideology. If they have ideological pursuits, "I know what's right" opinions without facts, self-enrichment might mean permanently arguing a position within the polity to autocratically amass and keep power. Loss of integrity harbors in this, and it turns baby boomers into baby doomers. The people's pragmatism seeks realistic results. Our pursuits are what need to be done. The better thought for American politicians is not one of how to hold onto power through ideology but rather this:

"I can do better than selfish. This is a civic duty, a public service. I will work to find the common solutions best for the majority without dictating cruel and unusual circumstances toward the minority. This is a temporary assignment. I will do my best while I have the office to do something. I want to play a daily role in helping the society be better. I want to IDEALS liberty for the people. This is my duty."

This is a public servant's attitude. In determining whether their conduct is proper, <u>all</u> federal government employees must follow the U.S. Office of Ethics' fourteen principles. These are:

1. *Public service is a public trust, requiring employees to place loyalty to the Constitution, the laws and ethical principles above private gain.*

2. *Employees shall not hold financial interests that conflict with the conscientious performance of duty.*

3. *Employees shall not engage in financial transactions using nonpublic Government information or allow the improper use of such information to further any private interest.*

4. *An employee shall not, except as permitted by subpart B of this part, solicit or accept any gift or other item of monetary value from any person or entity seeking official action from, doing business with, or conducting activities regulated by the employee's agency, or whose interests may be substantially affected by the performance or nonperformance of the employee's duties.*

5. *Employees shall put forth honest effort in the performance of their duties.*

6. *Employees shall not knowingly make unauthorized commitments or promises of any kind purporting to bind the Government.*

7. *Employees shall not use public office for private gain.*

8. *Employees shall act impartially and not give preferential treatment to any private organization or individual.*

9. *Employees shall protect and conserve Federal property and shall not use it for other than authorized activities.*

10. *Employees shall not engage in outside employment or activities, including seeking or negotiating for employment, that conflict with official Government duties and responsibilities.*

11. *Employees shall disclose waste, fraud, abuse, and corruption to appropriate authorities.*

12. *Employees shall satisfy in good faith their obligations as citizens, including all just financial obligations, especially those—such as Federal, State, or local taxes—that are imposed by law.*

13. *Employees shall adhere to all laws and regulations that provide equal opportunity for all Americans regardless of race, color, religion, sex, national origin, age, or handicap.*

14. *Employees shall endeavor to avoid any actions creating the appearance that they are violating the law or the ethical standards set forth in this part. Whether particular circumstances create an appearance that the law or these standards have been violated shall be determined from the perspective of a reasonable person with knowledge of the relevant facts.*

Following required ethics is a more desirable state of mind and action for our politicians in their duty to serve the public. It is what democracy expects and deserves. The politicians form a community. They learn from each other. Their community has drifted off-center, away from its purpose, away from the necessary core values they need to believe and reflect in their behavior. We need to center them. We, the everyday people, need to step it up and lead them away from the doomer disuse of community power. We must reinforce vice retard incorruptibility as the essential stance against the temptations of authority. Replacing them is a necessary tough love we must perform to save them from a condition of continuous malfeasance. In doing this we protect their liberty. We must remove them and help them find grace and a mission in teaching ACE. This contribution might save them from an inner tyranny the mythology power could cause them as their biology power collapses and they age beyond ambulatory independence and mental competence.

People pursuing positions in the economy power may be of three states: hyper, average, or hypo-attentive. Our hyper-attentive fellow citizens are attending fully to their responsibilities to regulate the polity and offer goods and services to support the needs of the society. Our averagely attentive fellow citizens, mildly attending, mind their own business and only participate politically when their business is threatened. Only when at risk beyond their immediate control of confronting external forces demanding they change do they seek to regulate the polity yet continue to deliver goods and services to support the needs of society. Our hypo-attentive fellow citizens may be at one of two poles:

1) **Complacency** due to sufficient economic financial success or because of past setbacks or intolerance for the complexities of dealing with the polity, or

2) **Apathy** due to anomie, feeling forgotten, unwanted, left out of the opportunity dream; too busy struggling to achieve basic needs.

These hypo-attentive citizens are at risk of living with an attitude of "What's in it for me?" and focusing on self-interest as the basis of society. Dichotomously among the baby boomers, the former are the rich, the latter are the poor. Attitudes acceptable to the rich, the poor emulate. This is human nature. Nevertheless, thoughtlessly mimicking the moneyed uncritically is foolishness. Corruption of the one enables corruption of the other because of how setting the example plays out in human affairs. A bad example is "me first". A good example is "we first". With the economy power, we need good examples of team players, playing on team USA, for our enterprise. We need teammates not overly concerned with their own size of fame or pocket's money if such pursuit would injure others' liberty.

Those in the second pole give up because society seems not to care about them or give them a sense of hope to escape poverty. It is not difficult to appreciate how some people could fall into pursuing (false) freedom without liberty, demanding something for nothing (dependency), wanting a free ride, civically and economically. Destitution can cause some to feel the way they feel. It takes empathy us to see it this way. Without it we see the downtrodden as freeloaders. The defeated and hopeless, those in anomic conditions, have only two powers and two consequents. One is to vote. The second is a "donkey power," declining to follow socially agreed-upon rules, refusing to move toward common need of compliance when requested to move along. This power expresses itself by simply saying "no" without reasoning, and refusing to budge. If not skilled in negotiation, the enforcer will feel forced with no choice but to use violence or the threat of violence to force conformity. This will illicit jackass kicks in response. Violence incites violence. When angered by mistreatment, or, when annoyed by excessive demands for nearly impossible and uncomfortable work rates, a donkey hee-haws and leg thrusts to communicate in a liberty demanding display. Our downtrodden neighbors need opportunity support to assist them, which includes jobs to be in accord with community standards, to carry one's own load, and to work. The choice society has is to reduce the cost of those who seek to get the polity to "take care of me" as the basis of society. The economy power must dedicate itself to giving everyone a chance to earn a living. If everyone can earn enough to get the necessities to survive, the polity will not need to take from all others to support those without jobs. The societal powers' authority FILMS^2 [P7] should not permit an unpatriotic abandonment of the American people by the wayward HM^5.

Some of our families and communities ask us to be good global citizens, which can feel very illusory, more so than being a good national citizen, but the world is closing in on itself with advances in transportation, communications, and experiences, and all of us are vulnerable to pandemics as we get closer in space, and time. Maybe, perhaps, we might even grow closer in our humanity. It is a visionary expectation that all humans might get along one day. However, many remain challenged by globalization because of the fear of others, those who seem so different from us. In reality, we humans are more alike than different. We all invent culture to adapt to our geography. The differences are mostly superficial.

Everywhere, the societal powers' FILMS^2 [P7] influence the making of subcultures within the larger culture. When different societies share ideas or artifacts, their respective cultures influences each other. The globalization of trade comes with the creation of a universal culture atop the particular cultures of places whose people interact in trade. Culture flows from the famous and powerful, those who produce objects that others want to consume, as emulation influences the consumption trends in other societies.

Everyday life, normally taken for granted, runs on underlying culture. For us, this culture is democracy and the free exchange of ideas and goods. With globalization, the cultivation of culture through sharing, borrowing, or countering clashes increases. Through audiovisual technology, the typical social experiences of everyday life in one place encounter social experiences of other places, and ideas are stimulated about accommodation or rejection.

The richness of human expression expands, and a multiplication of images and cultural goods of our artistry power become knowable by peoples who before globalization were not conversant in reading or understanding them. Often misinterpreting them, we create new meanings. Being exposed to many different others' artifacts and cultural expression is exciting but can also breed anxiety and insecurity. Manufactured cultures produce and perform for others to witness as authentically original from the place and people who make them. Deformations caused by globalizing consumerism feel like a confusing onslaught. Cultures get undone (Featherstone, 1995). We must hold on to the essential aspects of our foundational culture to hold the center for stability. What is most meaningful for our society from democracy, for liberty? It is for us to keep it free and clear from the noisy distracting productions of doomerist culture.

Everyone, to the person, is also a regional citizen of the subculture of his or her ancestry, settlements, and geographic conditions. Historian journalist Colin Woodard describes these within the United States as separate nations. Many within their state have great pride and are citizens in the sense of loyalty to their state, and some to their municipality, city or town, and even neighborhood. We are members of many communities, each with its powers to influence how we think. This is why we need to share a common base to build a land of one people, e pluribus unum. We have it in the Constitution. We must rediscover it! It gives rise to the potential for our people power to unite to change our lives and our livelihood, as we move forward in the crises and chaos of the rapid discoveries of this third stage of knowledge and its emerging nano-, bio-, and info-technologies that are dragging us into the future faster than we ever imagined possible. The latter is pushing us toward thoroughly machine automated repetitive for formerly manually done work. Artisanship is under assault. Robots that require us to have different skills will remove us from the labor we used to do with our bodies. Some make us safer; others deskill and diminish our tactile talents that created great positive pride in us.

We'll need to become better at understanding what makes us human beings. Being human is not solely our being mule laborers anymore. It is not so much our being machine operators anymore. It is more demanding of our creativity. Being human is being creative. Our artistry and industry powers enable us to survive within geography's power. Now we do computer programming, data extrapolation, and more analytical thinking of more complex languages. We keep learning. We keep adding knowledge. We expand the challenge to living and thriving as we master survival. Social transformation is our nature. Change, however, is hard for us. We must learn to better tolerate change and fill the variety of occupations we now have as we find ways to make survival for all possible. This is pragmatic.

We must come to seek knowledge and find wisdom. We must find a way to handle many complex ideas in our heads at one time and not seek simple edicts that pacify us. We need to develop the ability to have cognitive complexity, to understand our consciousness, kindness, capacity for love, and capabilities to apply them in our interactions with our families, neighbors, communities, states, nation, and one day the global human civilization. This is empathy. Humanity needs it, or we will rip each other apart like great apes seeking dominance.

In democracy, it is wrong to pursue the pleasure of power as the most important aspect of living. Such an approach is a fallacy to us—a danger, in fact. We are a representative democracy. We must rely on reason and diplomacy rather than instinct and violence. This is our great opportunity. This is what gives us freedom. We need to find something useful for everyone to do, legally, for pay sufficient to afford a standard of living above raw survival with a quality of life befitting the citizenry of a republic. The talented and determined need open avenues of approach to optimize their contributory support to family, neighborhood, community, state, region, nation—American society—with options to climb a merit-based ladder into the luxury of our contemporary era's advanced knowledge and high technology that keep us in convenience and comfort. However, with opulence we must not become complacent or apathetic. When we have jobs, we feel good about ourselves. Experiencing challenges, coaching, and overcoming of obstacles is rewarding. This is a social problem about work. We, the everyday people, must solve it. The elites will not. The politicians will not. Power and money has gone to their heads. They have lost touch with the reality of the day-to-day effort it takes. They have become cold and calculating. We are the nation. They are our servants. If we are not intelligent about it, they will make us their slaves. Do we want to live as serfs in a feudal kingdom?

Eternal Meaning

Will democracy as our base culture, a culture that fights to establish itself in the hearts and minds of many people but is suppressed by ancient primal passions for raw power and control that don't allow the people power to rise, guide us forward as a species toward a state of being in which we'll learn our eternal meaning? We are to be a single people, a single species, surviving together, living in witness together, and working at thriving together, celebrating all the cool things we do all over our globe. What has happened to our curiosity? We need it back. We need to travel outside our comfortable little social bubbles and discover the vast humanity that exists. It is rewarding to see how we create and recreate the glory of eternity in daily ways. In human cultures, there is a great richness of testimony and mystery for our creativity.

Eventually, when the world awakens from its states of hate, it will make democracy the way to lead society. We will see the dawning of the destined age of peace and harmony. With knowledge, we can learn about what we are and escape our instincts' control. Reason will rise in all of us by awareness of truth, and people will begin to lead properly by democracy. Leadership by the people in a society is the future for all humankind. If we do not, a few baby doomers will hoard everything and press the rest of us into horrible, deplorable living conditions and social circumstances in which we fight among ourselves while they laugh at us as ignorant animals. They are no better. They are worse. They are evil for violating the creed of democracy.

Democracy is a culture that enables a pursuit of humaneness, an achievement of happiness in eternity, salvation, and mercy. This can weigh heavily on those realizing their mortality, through self-assessing, reflecting, and self-judgment of self-worth to the community (at which a person's psyche has most attached itself as their identity and purposeful pursuit). Democracy enables a human condition of liberty when appreciated. It takes us into deeper thinking about what freedoms are. There is only one liberty, a state of having higher awareness and aspiration of humanness, as a natural but not wild animal. Liberty can be reached when we have in our countries the four freedoms (that Franklin Delano Roosevelt spoke of, and Norman Rockwell painted), which are best for humanity, at the macro "species" level. These are:

- "Freedom of speech and expression"
- "Freedom of every person to worship God in his or her own way"
- "Freedom from want"
- "Freedom from fear"

Liberty also depends on each citizen living toward inculcating and exemplifying the cardinal moral virtues:

- Prudence—Seek to develop good judgment, reason, and self-discipline in managing one's personal affairs.
- Fortitude—Seek to develop mental strength to face danger and adversity with courage and be resilient.
- Temperance—Seek to be moderate in action, thought, and feeling.
- Justice—Seek to comport one's self to truth, fact, and reason while being just, impartial, and fair.

There are many other virtues necessary for us to live by such as getting educated, and exhibiting a public spiritedness. Founding framer Benjamin Franklin wrote about them in his autobiography (Mansfield, 2003). In our culture of democracy sustained by these freedoms and virtues, we consent to be governed. We must also understand that our role is to defend liberty from tyranny of all kinds! We must come to understand how as singular citizens and as citizens combined, a citizenry, we have the power to shape the FILMS[2] [P7], in particular the immediately affecting us institutions and organizations that are the instruments of human power structured into the social and societal powers. We find ourselves employed by these, and we must not let persons who are not acting as good citizens overtake them. We must preserve our courage to push for decisions that do not cause damaging or DAMN of powers and consequent externalities upon our own self's conscience. We must not allow the demise of future generations' possibilities. As good-seeking people E-SASSY-T-TUF-FT-CAUCUS, citizens of the species, of our nation, and of our regions, states, communities, neighborhoods, and families, we each must seek to show leadership—to do what is right. What is right is what aligns properly with the first principles that led to the creation of our nation, and the creed of the principled ideals of the Constitution. We, the everyday people, must work to reduce or eliminate the unintended consequences of our actions upon our fellow citizens by restricting the externalities of transactions that cause negative social circumstances and our engineered infrastructure's and housing's deteriorating physical conditions.

If we don't think past our own self-interests in our dealings, we could jeopardize our successes. By permitting doomerism, we allow the ruining of the foundation of public trust upon which our enterprise depends. We cause the failures. While we cannot remove all risks of errors and omissions, by each of us seeking to do right and be good we can minimize our society's vulnerabilities. Strategic responses that remove danger to others based upon the community's risk tolerances mitigate the magnitude of negative risks' realizations. We must discuss risks to our society in open forum, such as the hazards to wholesomeness caused by doomerism. We must concur on our tolerance thresholds and appetites to manage both behemoth-like bad risks and be open to opting into taking reasonable risks of opportunity to improve society. Regulation helps restrict reckless decisions. Unconsidered externalities in an institutional framework are a footnote.

Further, we must guard ourselves against archetypal social decision-making traps. It is a risk for the community to allow groupthink. To "go along simply to get along", when the way we are going is wrong, is an abdication of our duty as citizens. The status quo is an excuse for "not getting involved" in the fight to control human culture created social powers. We have to stand up to autocratic wannabe aristocratic oligarchical plutocrats and tell them that we are in charge of the USE—not vice versa. We exercise our democracy when we speak up and don't allow ancient human stupidity to reign supreme. We know enough now to block the old imperial attitudes that wage empire wars solely for royals' egos, to conquer and pillage, or monetary benefits of conquests.

The "them or us" approach of an "in or out" crowd mentality is an immature posture that we must grow out of to reach upward and make a better experience of humanness in our lives. It is otherwise an institutional idiocrasy. "Individual irrationality is different because we as individuals have the capacity to modify and overcome institutions driving us to disaster. That is the element of hope" (Chomsky, 2015). We as persons can make a difference. One person can inspire us to aspire to be great together, or they can divide us into hating each other. Which is better for democracy? By E-SASSY-T-TUF-FT-CAUCUS let's correct our societal and social powers' FILMS[2] [P7] to IDEALS liberty for the USE.

Power Arrangements Debates

Ever the inventive species, we humans have sought many ways of organizing our powers into systems, structures, and societies that we feel support our culture, our adaptation to our geography. Our subcultures create meaning for us as persons, as regions, as peoples, and as nations. Interestingly, the USE formed from many regional subcultures, which conveniently united to fend off a tyrant, and agreed upon a common culture, democracy, by compromises, consensus, and the diplomacy of cooperation. Such a way emerged during the Enlightenment. Our nation began as an ideal idea. It was set up as an experiment with a built-in charter for room to grow with the ages. It could have been graceful, but those who addict themselves to power for power's sake made it vociferously difficult and often violent. We are testing the history and finding it unfit. Therefore, we must go forward with what is no longer an experiment but a full-fledged project. Did the 18th-century humans put the cart before the horse? Were they divinely inspired to provide a way for us to become a holier more pleasing people to the Almighty? Is humanity capable of sharing power, of democracy? For us Americans the answer to these questions is our eternal test and quest for meaning. We must all be patriots in this purpose.

Democracy is the natural saddle of a free people. If improperly bridled to our society we'll struggle to pull it along. It is a heavy load. We must support it evenly. Too often in other societies, one group's attitudes dominate the others. In ours, we mustn't allow such misbalancing. We believe in egalitarian ideals. Our ethos (good character, values for virtues pursuit), pathos (humane humanness encoded in our human nature's emotions), logos (essential reasoning, logical discussion to find agreement), and kairos (our time of opportunity to make a new order for the ages in human's history) require equality for stability. We must continue to resist the ancient primal instinct driven strains of hatred and warring to resolve differences and as a basis for loyalty, or worse, fealty. Rather, to be completely in accord with our culture of democracy, we must learn and relearn, teach and reteach, train and retrain with ACE to know what a citizen of the USE must do to be an American. After 245 years we've yet to fully hitch ourselves to this heavy cart for all humanity. We've done it before, and can once again. Our project continues. We must push and pull it forward to escape the present domain of doom. In putting doomerism behind us, we'll demonstrate that democracy really is doable for everyone.

Doomerism has been a major setback for us in achieving our constitutional goal by attaining our project's objectives. It jettisoned citizenship and replaced it with consumerism and other conceits and deceits. While the polity argues over fears of this or that ism, the advance of a truly American society stalls and falls apart. Let's have a look at some of these isms now. As we do, please keep in mind that in order for us to self-govern, we must bring our people power to its proper place of leadership in the micro, meso, and macro levels of society. The diagrams in Figures 3-13 thru 3-15 below show society's future options with some current isms that describe popular mindsets. Each illustrates a different framework. Through study of these, we can identify our positions and posture toward societal power arrangement debates. If we don't fully understand the words, we need to better learn them and not just blindly like or dislike them because we were told to do so once in our life by someone we trust. Our Constitution, our enterprise, our society, is at stake. We must reason and contemplate, not emote and get irate. We must debate with logic. We must avoid rhetorical fallacies. In the diagrams' triangles is a continuum, corner to corner, along which we can place ourselves. It's our starting place for conversations about the direction of society, and by doing so we can discern why we feel it demarks our going-in opinion. Before we begin a debate on the best courses of action that we the people should take as leaders of society, we must also prepare to contemplate that we are moving into an uncertain future in this third stage of knowledge growth with diverse, and thanks to doomerism, diverging perspectives. Keep in mind that we should identify the risks involved in our initial points of view yet be open to new considerations. We can implement the SERF to calculate how to undo the present baby doomerism that COIFFURE democracy from our republic. Regardless of which STAMPER socialization context and regional subcultural and settlement pattern value set preferences we have, we must unite. Unity is our duty. Knowing the differences in our social circumstances and the physical conditions of our person (personality, personage, and personhood), families, neighborhoods, and communities (recall Figure 2-26) is less important than our compatriotic commitment. This exercise of self-analysis prepares us to invoke our people power properly—to have the LAMBS within our USE ensure we AEIOUY^{2}K power as we want it done, which is to IDEALS liberty and justice for all. Because our role is leadership, we must set this tone. Our society cannot be healthy until we do. People need something useful to do and natural and cultured (developed) talents rewarded accordingly. Being conscious of our existence as we form and seeking freedom to be as we are to be, a thinking tool-making creature, we desire liberty.

Each of the following three Figure's diagrams consists of a large triangle made up of four smaller triangles. The three outer ones indicate a direction that we can push the enterprise. Concurrently these triangles represent a different, yet related, societally topical ism named below their base, written inside the inverted central triangle. These isms and triangle's stated possible direction for society are conceptually compatible. The societal debate occurs in the central triangle. It is our responsibility to consider where to lead American society. The discussion should drive toward an outcome that supports a pursuit of liberty. Each direction, or combined overlapping and staggered or staged direction we choose, must result in the best possible realization of our nation's founding principles. Outside the large triangle is a square pattern of four words written in curly letters. These words reflect four attitudes the USE can take related to the possible societal directions framed by the triangles.

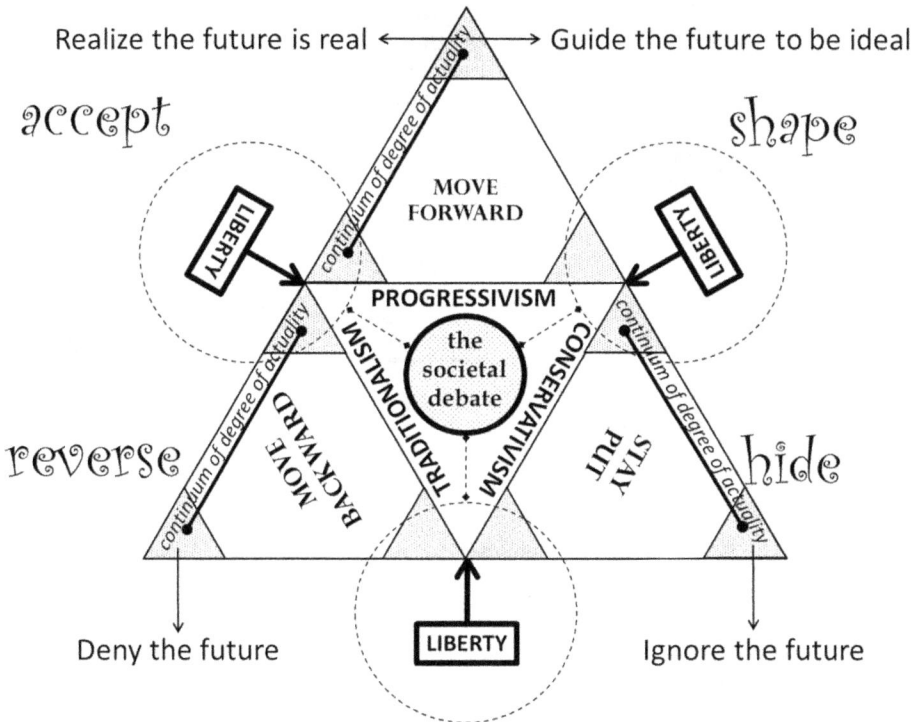

Necessary Pressures on the Polity from the People

Before any policy decision, ask & estimate,
"How does it, or does it not, support Liberty?"

Realize the future is real ← → Guide the future to be ideal

accept   shape

MOVE FORWARD

PROGRESSIVISM

the societal debate

reverse   hide

Deny the future   LIBERTY   Ignore the future

Figure 3-13: The People's Pressure upon the Polity—Possible Approaches to the Future

The first diagram (Figure 3-13) addresses a debate over the pressures for liberty, written in the rectangles, we the everyday people must put upon the polity. The three outer triangles contain the societal directions options: "move backward", "stay put", or "move forward". We the people might hold four different attitudes toward the accelerating technological change the future is bringing to us: "reverse", "hide", "shape", or "accept" it.

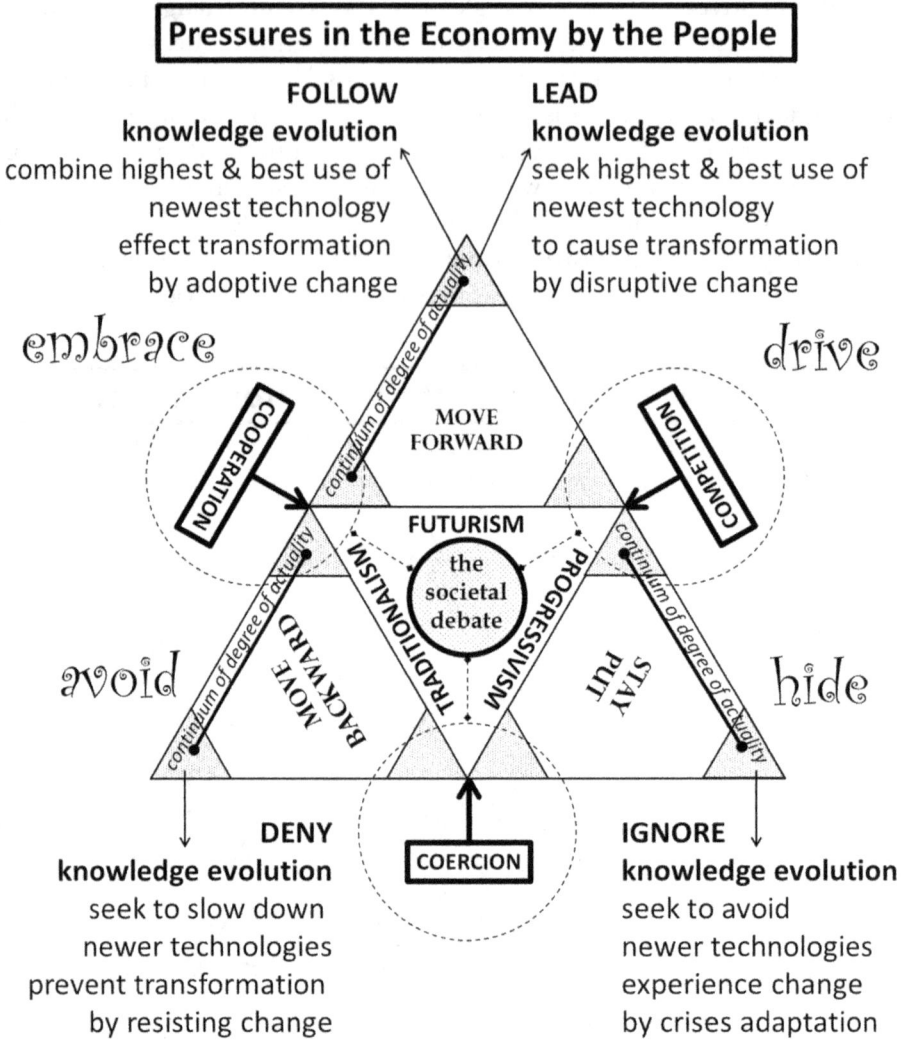

Figure 3-14: The People's Pressure upon the Economy—the Possible Approaches to the Future

The second diagram (Figure 3-14) addresses a debate over the pressures that we the everyday people could put on the economy related to knowledge evolution. This diagram's pressures and attitudes differ from the previous one. Its pressures written in rectangles are "coercion", "competition", and "cooperation". These methods influence our thinking as we discuss our adaptive problems the future brings. The outer triangles' directions are the same, though their bases' labels are different isms. This tool supports thinking about the organization of human effort and work. Its attitudes are "avoid", "hide", "drive", and "embrace". Again, the debate must focus on liberty, but we must recognize the consequences of the various approaches we might take. For example, if we seek to avoid the reality of the coming future, to move backward toward traditional arrangements, we may find ourselves resorting to coercion as a means of employment.

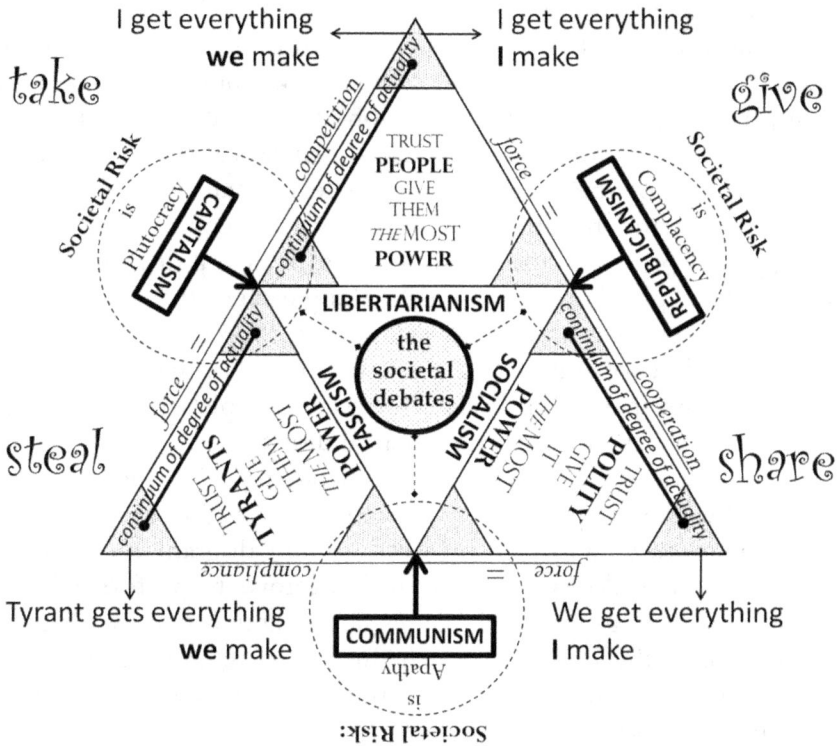

Societal Structuring Power Between: Polity-Economy-People

Libertarianism led to the creation of the United States of America, which led to Liberalism.

In Fascism, one ruler becomes a tyrant.
In Communism, one Party becomes a tyrant.
In Capitalism, private interests can become a tyrant.

Figure 3-15: The People's Options for Structuring Societal Powers for the Future

The third diagram (Figure 3-15) addresses a debate over the structuring of the primary powers in society. We the everyday people must decide upon the balance of these, and demand of our FILMS[2] [P7]—especially as it relates to the wholesomeness of the instruments of society—integrity. Honorableness must be core to the nature and purpose of our society's organizations and institutions, which we staff, and more critically through which we AEIOUY[2]K the social powers we entrust to them. This diagram's directions, pressures, and attitudes we can take as we approach how to lead society differ from the previous two. The outer triangles in it contain statements related to the nature of power arrangements, trust, and proportionality of control.

Differently than the others, this diagram combines systems of society isms to form debate possibilities. It adds a new dimension, defining the negative risks, written outside the pressures' rectangles. In this diagram, we the everyday people can press for "capitalism", "communism", and "republicanism". Here, the term republicanism includes a representative democracy in a republic for polity power with an economy power preferring free markets as its means of provisioning society. It seeks to balance the LAMBS toward equilibrium to IDEALS liberty and produce prosperity presently and for posterity. The term capitalism puts the economy power in a predominant position, subjugating politics to economics. The term communism puts the polity power in a predominant position, subjugating economics to politics. Note too, the inverted central triangle shows different isms at the bases of the other triangles. The four attitudes define the essence of the systems' results in the minds of the people on how society's economy power produces goods and services, of how it distributes rewards: "steal", "share", "give" or "take". Lastly, along each of the sides of the large triangle's perimeter are underlined statements, "force =": "competition", "coercion", and "cooperation". These indicate the primary forces that influence behaviors in the relationship between people's pressures and the isms that represent the three shown societal directions.

Contemporaneously, this third diagram portrays the dominant societal systems of the primary powers' we humans AEIOUY^{2}K and DAMN during the 21st century. With the first and second diagram focusing on the coming future, how do these past models promise to perform? Is there a possibility for a new model that ensures liberty and justice for all as its objective? Certainly, the USE, for which this is a core ambition, has not yet obtained it, but until the 1980s, it appeared to be moving toward one. What retarded its progress? Doomerism did.

Doomerism got it off track. Doomerism called for changes in ways that do not support the USE's past ambition for liberty. No one seems to have been watching out for it. Of course, our course needs correction. Doomerism CATAPULTED crises and chaos, and it COIFFURE our founding ideals from our everyday lives in the society made for and endowed to us by previous generations of Americans. Only we the people can change it.

Only we the people can renegotiate the navigation to put us back on path, to the way of the Preamble, with the means of the rule of law, and the methods of good citizenshipping. We share much of the blame for our predicament. We became complacent (Magistrale, 2020). The baby doomers encourage us to care less, be "me first" in attitudes and behaviors. Forty years later, we see the ill results. We cannot keep things as they are. We must reform our electoral processes (Simon, 2020) and our economic policies, or our babies will not feel freedom, nor understand and experience liberty as we have known it and strove to ensure it for every citizen in the USE.

The choice will be with the people to decide what is more important for us as persons and as a people, independency or dependency. As per the Cycle of Democracy diagrams (see Figure 2-14 through Figure 2-23) if we do not rise to resist doomerism, we will find ourselves in bondage. On the micro level of human action within a society, better practice of democracy culture will shape the FILMS[2] [P7] of the meso level, which in turn contributes to correcting behaviors in the operant primary powers displayed in the LAMBS model (see Figure 2-1 through Figure 2-11) for maintaining a proper American society. If each person avoids the tempting self-centeredness and other ailments of doomerism, we will prevent the glooming and dooming of democracy. We will create at long last, e pluribus unum, one American people.

These last three diagrams framed complex issues. (Compare these three Figures to relationships expressed in the Assessment Card of Figure 1-5). They are tools to use when talking about how we might help ourselves solve the adaptive problems we face, like overpopulation and dangerous manual work given over to robots eliminating useful human activities (work), which we need to survive, live well, and thrive. (These are only two examples). We must discuss the many more adaptive problems the third stage of knowledge evolution brings about, which doomerism exacerbates.

We are in crises because baby doomers do not address them civilly, forthrightly, or competently as risks in our project and thus to our liberty. As citizens of our republic if we aim for the USE to grow and sustain, not strained and stained by corruption and waste its endowments, we must use these tools to defeat the fallacious, fraudulent, and felonious foolishness of the baby doomers' games being played with, on, and against us, the everyday people.

Let's not be divided by baby doomers. Let's become one. Let's unite despite all our rage they flame. Let's get serious and fight their spite and foolishness with love and intelligence. Let's fix the USE. It's our ship to set sail in the correct direction once again. Let's prepare to ignore how they will assail us with idiotic isms. Let's let their cruelty and ignorance of their errors embolden us with great courage like that which the founders possessed against their oppressive tyranny. Let this be our inspiration, aspiration, and ambition for the 21st century. Let's make real through our perspiration the banding together of our interests as it once was done by colonists with the establishment of the nation. Tensions will exist in a republic; we tolerate them by civic engagement and political participation, which is a gift of liberalism, from libertarianism endowed to the citizens of the USE. It takes work to sustain a republic. The debates are within a closer degree of disagreement than those of shifting the polity and economy completely. Such a small range of disparity is not difficult to overcome so long as we remember the common denominator. Zealous, partisan, uncompromising politicians are not often in the majority. They have been because of baby boomer values, which enabled some to become baby doomers and produce the contagious social plague now affecting us: baby doomerism. Through our social powers, especially the family, community, and academy, we can learn to move past it, unite, and focus on how to address the future as one people. We do this through a more completely engaged participating citizenry. We do it when we begin and sustain in perpetuity E-SASSY-T-TUF-FT-CAUCUS. On this, we must immediately focus our youthful generations that are rising into adulthood in the next few decades.

SECTION 2: DOOMERISM

4. *"Cunning Baby Doomers"*

This chapter defines the problem confronting our society that we the people must stop or we'll lose democracy and its prized possession, liberty.

What Is Doomerism?

Doomerism is a deadly-for-democracy cultural shift, a movement away from our originating ideals and founding principles. It is a coming doom if not stopped posthaste. It is unendingly gelling of micro, meso, and macro-level value sets that harbor huge risks for representative democracy in a republic. It is inducing a perilous and unsteadying drift toward feudalistic plutocracy and asinine aristocracy. It is dangerous demagoguery domestically threatening the Constitution. If unresisted culturally and not turned back, it will devour democracy. Theoretically, doomerism arose from a billion self-centered decisions by a majority of a generation's members. These choices extract. They take from future generations of Americans. They obey a megalomaniac's narcissistic "me first" attitude. Its risks are amplified when one generation by its volume controls society at all ranks, behaves complacently and shapes policies accordingly, because it holds the greatest number of authority positions in the FILMS[2] [P7] of society, defined as the:

o **Functionaries** (functionary offices and their officials who hold authority)

o **Instruments** (socially agreed-upon, legitimate forms of social groupings given specific authorities and status respect, typically known as organizations and institutions)

o **Logistics** (the methods of instruments' power usage)

o **Mechanisms** (the means of instruments' power usage)

o **Structures & Systems** (of the instruments created by, then shaped and sustained through, shared: [1]philosophies, [2]purposes, [3]precedents, [4]policies, [5]processes, [6]procedures, and [7]practices. These seven "Ps"—[P7]—guide each person's work for, in, and with an instrument of societal power and its logistics, mechanisms, structures, and systems).

American persons in authority and important roles are supposed to act responsibly. We are to hold ourselves accountable to the highest ethical standards, because we are democratically, representatives. We are to exhibit our common core civic virtues and values, which make the foundation of our efforts as a people in the leadership, administration, and management of the business of society (LAMBS). Doomerism dooms babies because it endangers our posterity's potential prosperity by allowing unacceptably poor performances of personal duties necessary in a citizenry for an American society.

Blessed with phenomenal comfort that allowed such a self-serving approach, doomerism dialectically induced faith in its actually corrupt precepts as good. Its promises felt good, but are bad. Do not be fooled! It has had terribly negative consequences for the next generations. The boomers missed their opportunities to use the wealth of the nation to attend to its civic needs. In their complacency, they retreated from sustaining civil society. They allowed its privation through hyperbolic privatization. The boomers are mostly responsible, their value sets having caused, amplified, tolerated, actualized, promoted, undergirded, litigated, taunted, embraced, developed (CATAPULTED) societal failures. Public infrastructure that enables private enterprise, crumbles when left unattended. Entrepreneurs suffer the costs. We become less competitive internationally without a strong collaborative public–private partnership that enables advancement for all our people.

The boomers neglected the citizenry by disrespect, devaluating political discourse, and eroding public trust. They generally behaved badly as citizens in all levels of society, in all positions of responsibility because they sought "what's in it for me," as opposed to serving in their important roles with duty-bound honesty. They dishonored the society. They got theirs, and they screwed us, (particularly in the last decade (Sternberg J. C., 2019)). For a long time to come, we must work to recover. They are not looking ahead, they are looking behind, protecting their rears because they know that although they thought they had gotten away with their theft and negligence, we've found out, and now they are afraid to sacrifice to give back what rightly belongs to the future. They never could sacrifice because they bought into the "me first or nothing for anybody" thought process. This zero-sum mentality is too childish for a sophisticated civilization to survive with for long before unraveling. Takers break. They broke us. This is why post-boomer generations must intervene with audacity. We must now lead; we have the numbers. We must rise. We must restore ethical integrity in all societal and social powers' FILM^2 [P7] and in the HM^5 who provision us with livelihoods.

It is a citizenry's responsibility to encourage one another to be good citizens—rich, middle, or poor, left, middle, or right. We must unite in a commitment to behave as good citizens. We must support one another, not demonize one another for this or that superficial feature. The boomers did not attend adequately to this requirement for an American republic. They did not think to make it better for the progeny of the nation. Because wisdom was not vital to their enjoyment and would have been inconvenient to their hedonistic pursuits, they ignored it. This doomeristic ignorance happened in part because it could, thanks to the material comforts and national wealth produced by the United States enterprise (USE) that did not suffer social, economic, urban, and industrial based devastation during World War II.

The results of a citizenry not attending to civics are ill-suited socialization contexts that do not prepare people for the future we are encountering. We've many unstable families. We've tattered citizens and tarnished environments that further defeat our ability to advance as a whole people in our citizen purpose, which is to accomplish the goal and objectives of the Constitution. Our enterprise is to move us toward ideals, not make excuses and steal from the future. Such attitudes and the behaviors that support these activities are an American generational crime. We must face up to it. We must reverse it. We must reform ourselves. We cannot allow any more baby doomers in positions of authority within our society's FILMS[2] [P7] that apply, employ, implement, operationalize, utilize, yoke, yield, and keep (AEIOUY[2]K) our human made powers. We need our powers operant in the LAMBS to serve us by abiding by our purpose to achieve the ideals of the founding of our society in democracy for liberty and justice for all. This is not too much to ask. This is what it means to be a patriotic, non-baby doomer, American.

There are baby doomers in all generations. When the baby boom generation embraced doomerism, it exposed the risks of unresolved conflicts that festered during the boomers high life of good times. The boomers most shared worldview based upon a "me first" value set, and not a "we the people" value set disintegrates social norms and any extant social harmony suffers. Doomers live to coerce. Without respect or remorse, they demand, take, or steal, extract more than their fair share and don't care for their neighbors' lot or losses. They generally block and damage the potential of future generations' babies to achieve positive outcomes of living for liberty, of living in a democracy. Boomers' attitudes toward others in society and their behaviors in it have caused social and economic separation, isolation, and division among the people. Exemplified in the results of their value sets this is, and it proves they did not "stand the watch" properly; they did not "mind the store" correctly. They ignored the most important duty—citizenship to sustain the citizenry. They ignored the purpose of the nation made for the everyday people. They promised freedom and delivered disaster (Andrews, 2021). Because their sought freedoms were not in pursuit of liberty, they ignored the ideals of the founding of our country. They walked away from our destiny, each taking for his "self" or her "self" what they could, fleecing for their own private castles, like feudalistic lords, wannabe aristocrats, or sycophants pandering for favor to a king. They acted as if entitled to everything like spoiled whining crybaby royal brats. We are not a kingdom. We opposed one. We are not to act as if we are in one. Doomerism beguiles us down its path to act in ways antithetical to that which is in our own best interest, unity for liberty. This defines the drift from democracy its grift causes.

Liberty requires virtue, first-and-foremost. Doomers saw virtue as foolish, so they abandoned it for greed, hubris, vanity, and avarice. Our national moral, physical, political, social, economic, and spiritual health depend on an honorable social construct, a compact among humans to agree to the rule of law and commit to it as a unified praxis and pedagogy to teach each new rising generation. Americans are not born. Made are we. Too many of us are not living up to the good citizenship requirements needed to sustain the society. Many of us did not live up to it in our history. Have we forgotten, or were never instructed that we are supposed to work toward greater enfranchisement and participation in the running of society by the people? Simply put, Americanism means we believe in democracy as the best form of social organization for a culture, for humankind. This belief is not enough to keep our democracy. We must come to understand power. We must thwart its DAMN within the LAMBS. Or else, our USE will fail us. The baby doomers will stealthily convert it into a land of the frightened. They'll doom it to despotic rule, making it a home of the cowards. Liberty will begin dying by its apathy allowing tyranny.

What is it about doomerism that has become so dangerous today? Is it the excessive, over the top, "me first" selfishness and its consequent "I got mine, 'F' you" self-centeredness that now is tolerated, and even celebrated by the baby boomers? What they fail to see is that a billion self-serving, selfish persons do not make us into a people e pluribus unum. Further, a billion shortsighted, self-serving decisions do not make a functional society, in keeping with "Novus ordo seclorum" in ways "annuit coeptis" (see Figure 0-1-1). (Note, the traditionalists will say the lack of these causes our ailments). That such a rare form of rabid selfishness consumed an entire cohort of a huge generation is sad. It portends bad things. It causes disgrace. It forecasts poor taste. It eradicates ethical integrity. It embraces corruption. It erases trust. We feel like we've been had, sucker punched in the gut. The boomers apparently are blind to it. Ignorant and disrespectful, or cruel and unusual, they continue onward unconstitutionally with undermining Americanism. Their undercutting by undercover activities is undoing our society. We are now no longer due what we are to pursue as one people, virtue. We might as well call the boomers the un-American generation. Each time we peel back a layer of the consequences of their failure, we get pundits that are more pungent and unaware. We hear their obnoxiousness as sounds that, if odors, would smell rotten. They are toxically undermining the public trust, not reinforcing or creating it. The results of the uncivilized in powerful positions are uncivilizing, causing society to shred unity and shed its bonds. Since they've been in positions of power, they have been blind to how they have amplified the disturbances that harbor negative risks for the rest of us. These are real public trust hazards, threats to democracy, thrusting demagogues upwardly. The boomers could bring down the republic and disintegrate democracy as a viable culture in their effort to hold on to the status quo they wrote on blank checks, which need funded by the American babies not yet born. We sit astounded when witnessing their ignorance of self. Blatantly horrid, trapped in fantasies to keep what they have fleeced.

The selfish become tribal. They find others who believe the way they do and band together so each one might do as they please. As if freedom was meant to be, "Do whatever you want when you want to do it even if it is wrong." That is not freedom. That is the tyranny of selfishness, and it erodes the social fabric of families, neighborhoods, cities, counties, states, nations, and civilization because it signals to all that "You are in this alone," "Look out for yourself first," and "Life is a zero-sum game." This status quo rallying cry only benefits those in control of society. We, the everyday people, are not in control, but we need to be. This isolating doomeristic mentality is extraordinarily immature, the lowest common denominator lifestyle. That people of this ilk became a majority that enjoyed the blessings of liberty but now destroy democracy, is viscerally appalling to earnestly courageous and self-honest, honor pursuing, and standard bearing patriots. Unless boomers recognize the harm they are doing as the generation "large and in charge," leveraging their majority to make the rules and horribly shape an amoral society, we cannot expect them to repent and remove the burden they've lumped on future generations. It's time they get dumped out of power and invited into invaluable volunteer social roles to support domestic tranquility and American civics education (ACE).

We need to reverse their many policies that punish the young. We must put in place the stepping-stones for power to transfer and future-oriented solutions to begin. The young cannot succeed with hope alone if buried in feelings of impossibility from the results of decisions made in a past they could not influence. Decisions that do not work in the favor of the next generation aren't the optimum decisions for a nation to remain solvent. Perhaps we might succeed, but the weight of failure we feel now is almost insurmountable because the system seems rigged by the boomer generation to benefit them alone. We have seen no improvements in many of the social powers' FILMS[2] [P7] that are supposed to prevent and resolve failures. For example, we see how a rigged system causes in our inner cities extreme survivability fears and stress, which shortens lives, which adds more stress. Systems set up conditions and probabilities (Heath, 2020). This we cannot deny. We should not hide behind shallow platitudes to justify wrongs as tolerable. We've such deplorable conditions and disparities in our cities and rural communities.

Moreover, doomerism is a blind following of the crowd, which is foolishly mimicking the rich and powerful person's fallacious fantasies. When the top percent are corrupt, it trickles down in the society. Such as, "If the rich and powerful can lie, cheat, and steal, why cannot I?" asks the average person on the street. This is a real risky social circumstance, and it erodes justice if there are different standards for criminals in high offices, like wolves on Wall Street, verses those guilty of lowly crimes done to survive in desperation nearer to main streets. Or, as done on mean streets lined with deteriorating properties filled with abandoned Americans. Forsaken persons left out of opportunities. Whose chances are now lost because of the boomers' creepily unpatriotic flight of capital to foreign capitals. A practice they celebrate. It produces cheap goods more cheaply for greater profits to put into their pockets. This is not a crime, but it is a shame that citizens are less favored than are foreigners when it comes to providing jobs. This leaves people to wonder, "Which way do I go to get to your America?" (Reid, 1988).

When the rich and powerful do wrong, it sets a bad precedent. It ruins the world because of all the copycatting that occurs. This is how the moral disease of doomerism spreads socially and how it brings about the demise of democracy, which relies on honesty and integrity to provide a social culture that empowers people to thrive. If people are just barely surviving and struggling to live without losing everything due to gross insecurity and instability caused by baby doomerism, we have a wicked problem to solve. The pockets of poverty evidence it where the deplorable anomic, enervating, and radicalizing socialization contexts persist. We should not tolerate the prejudice these cruel social circumstances and physical conditions push on our babies and children.

Why is nothing done about it? Because babies in these neighborhoods did not matter to those in positions of authority over the society, many of whom were failed modernists whose one-size-fits-all systemic conceptions could not adequately address the nuanced complexities of regional and local conditions. By a systems approach, the parts were attacked and not the whole in its gestalt reality. The combined overconfidence and failure to see the whole tangle up with discriminatory false narratives that told stories to blame the victim, which is a tactic of baby doomers. Conversely, what about all the bailouts of corporations given massive breaks by the polity and declared "too big to allow them to fail?" Does "too big" mean too important to the whole? How, why, did this happen? Teddy Roosevelt's administration disallowed monopolies due to their threats to the people. How did they arise to endanger the whole society, again? We've been spat in our faces. We, the everyday people, paid to "bail out" the trillionaires. This was total hogwash, rubbish, and a wrong decisions made by the political and economic elite plutocrats to save themselves. This tactic increasingly continues while doomers remain in control through their culture of doomerism upon us. Society has its checks and balances. However, when not enforced, we get protectionism and social welfare for the rich (Reich R. , 2020). Untenable are both systems: those for the inner city and those for the city's financial district. They both are mining the middle to fuel their extremism.

What do they have in common? Stories not based in fact. Made up baby doomer fictions to get away with whatever they wanted, and to get it all for them, whist shouting at the top of their lungs, "Society be damned!" America, we have a problem, and we need to get upstream of it, before they damn us all Hell. We need to convene a new team of citizens in the polity and bring in the rightful people to discuss the pressing issues in advance of the further demise of the country. We need to get to work on solving problems instead of arguing about whose theory is right and whose is wrong. Doomers' incessant ideological arguments are hurting us. The baby boomers love to do it. They love to prove a point. Winning as if everything is a sport is a poor model for society to adopt. We've been in this mode for some forty years. We need their infighting to stop. We get that it is their generational personality, which shaped our current and doomeristic culture, but it creates a contradictory state of affairs to those necessary to sustain a representative democracy in republic of fifty united states.

Democracy is the culture upon which our society formed and which for 245 years we have been working to extend its provided freedoms to all our citizens as it ought to be, as it should have been, and as it will be. We must do this sooner rather than later, or else we'll go asunder, under the gaze and fist of tyranny by way of the disguise of a disgustingly devious social disease, doomerism. Solving our wicked social problems requires deeper understanding. It means we must collaborate on forming positive new visions of the future. An unwillingness to get upstream to look downstream is going to fail us. To see the root causes, we must get upstream of the problems (Heath, 2020). Downstream penny-pinching is a bad habit of baby doomers. Too shortsighted, not wanting to be blamed, they avoid taking responsibility. Blinded by their ideology, they are just too tight-wadded to look past their own self-importance. Why else are we still at war around the world? Are we supposed to be the boss of foreign sovereign nations? That is not in the Constitution. Why is it our behavior now? It is doomerism à la carte from the baby boomer generation's tour of duty on the bridges in the pilothouses at the helms of our societal and social powers' FILMS[2] [P7].

It would be most humbling to the founders in their graves if the next generations, now more in number, would apply the "democracy rules" ethos and in all societal powers say, "Step aside, boomers. We are ready to assume the watch. You had your chance. You failed to advance us socially. Your day to go away has come. You milked the system enough. Your retirement secured at our expense. Know that you must give some of it back." Of course, we know what the boomers will say: "I 'earned' it." Yet, did they, if gargantuan fiscal debt runs trillion-dollar deficits of money borrowed from the future? However, as the boomers approach their graves, should any of their consciences plague them with guilt, perhaps they might ask themselves, "Is getting 80% of what I once got when I contributed 100% of my labor for 60 years for 40 more years, until death do us part, fair to unborn Americans?" We can hope, or we can legislate. What paths will we choose? Will we say, "Intervene, let democracy take back American society from aristocracy to make it as intended—rightful!"

Respect the elders but not the bank robbers. Baby doomers must repent and return the fleeced treasure. Yet we need the retiring boomers with money and time to volunteer in our communities. Let them show civic engagement and help us rebuild civil society. They could become leaders in teaching ACE. They know how to learn. They can retool their opinions. They can become valuable trainers. It's up to them to leave a better legacy than that which they are now producing for themselves. If they've worthwhile pride, not hubris, they will do this for posterity. They will be spectacular at it, because they have large egos, and something to prove. Let's hope they do not want to go down in history as a failed American generation that lost democracy to tyranny. Rules need rewritten to enable a sustained nation, not perpetually drive us toward bankruptcy. We can no longer kick the proverbial tin can down the alley hoping someone else will pick it up and trash it. Rather, we must step in to pick it up and fix it up for a useful purpose, the perpetuation of democracy in America.

Does this not compute? Is there a better scale for appreciation of our contributions? Should we change our expectations for our last phases of mortality, to give those who can contribute more the most resources of our society? Demographically, the population is shrinking in future generations. This societal perpetuation risk could expose the USE to errors inviting social terrors. Replacement of workers is not happening, and automation leads to fewer jobs overall. People need to work to pay into the system. We cannot afford the boomers taking everything out of the common wealth. It is a mistake to think that we can avoid collapse without boomers sacrificing for once, for the citizenry, for the posterity of our USE. Imagine the headlines when it happens: "Me First Defeats Democracy," or "We First Goes Down in History as the Loser in the Game of Life." Such an irony it will be and proof of the truth of the cycle of democracy that complacency leads to apathy, and apathy to a poverty seeking handouts, which puts us back under tyranny. We need entrepreneurial growth to enlarge the opportunities for all to find meaningful work and ways to pay for our survival needs, living preferences, and thriving possibilities. We need egalitarian means to cooperate with and compete on our talents—to distribute justly the rewards of our labors, so we might believe in the possibilities of making it in the USE, and to make it work for every citizen.

Should we contemplate what would be best for the whole community? Or do we want squalor and squander—uneducated, filthy, impoverished children and luxury living for those who no longer add to the revenue but demand high-end everything because they feel entitled? The boomers invented the internet, they claim, though its idea began with others before them, and its engendered social media harms our youngsters. Children are suffering emotionally, mentally, psychologically, and socially. It is not good for their health (Haidt & Lukianoff, 2018). How can we have these discussions rationally without overboard emotions? Do we use our reason anymore? Can we still? Should we ask tough questions and face them like a society that does not want to collapse? Do we want continued distractions by impractical or unprovable matters of creation vs. science, a woman's right to control her own biology, or trumped-up nationalism during a global pandemic to drive our thinking and politics? Are we thinking as a citizenry seeking unity?

We the people have to get serious! The pleasure years are gone. Painful ones are coming. If we do not dedicate ourselves to seriousness, doom is certain. We must during this era of doomerism that CATAPULTED crises that COIFFURE democracy and liberty, work together to solve problems; not argue over improvable theories. We must enact an urgent reasonableness. We need to stop playing and get to work teaching our civics to the next generations. According to Strauss and Howe, the millennials are civic-minded (Strauss & Howe, 1991). Millennials with succeeding generations are now in the majority. Let's prove this one observation based theory right. Let's rise to the occasion and make a better second half of the first half of this century. We've had a risky start to this century. By rejecting doomerism, we can prevent a pending doom. We are in the 21st century. Legally speaking 21 is the age of adulthood. Shouldn't new adults have the leadership for a new century? The old guard must go out to pasture to reflect on their collective life's work and its worth to the USE. Then, shed the takers mantra, come back as givers. Be our volunteer civics educators, and election poll workers.

Let go, boomers! Trust in your children to save the nation. Envision a new truly patriotic community focused role for your generation in retirement. Serve in one that gives back and one that prepares our next generations to be ready for the mantle of societal leadership. Teach them of your mistakes. This could be cathartic. It is the way of wisdom. It is what elders do. Train them how to be a truly American people. A role statistics say you messed up. Redeem your generation. Correct it by fixing it for the American people's posterity. Ride off into the sunset heroically, not dejectedly ashamed for citizenship done erroneously.

Maybe one's lifestyle should change when one gets older. Maybe one should sell off one's estates, pay taxes, and prevent inheritance as the founders requested because aristocracy is a class that kills democracy. A ruling class is an anathema to the intent of the nation. Maybe there is a different way to understand one's role in society when one becomes an elder. Maybe our idealistic side should sacrifice to save the union. This, the real ideal we should reify. Or will we let doomerism be our demise?

20/20 Vision Will Be Too Late

Twenty-twenty hindsight is a way that historians help us understand what has happened. However, at this hour, we cannot wait for its lessons. We cannot afford to look back after the fact and learn that our republic was lost, a victim of the rise of doomerism in our society. Doomerism eats away at democracy and perpetuates our societal cancers of racism, classism, and disuse, abuse, misuse, and nonuse (DAMN) of the societal and social powers. It ruins the best possibilities of family run small business-based innovative entrepreneurial capitalism and promotes the worst possibilities of a totalitarian-like corporatist predatory one, countervailed by cries for socialism. Neither is good at its extremes. Doomerism has taken hold of our society. It metastasized in our present generation-in-power, unbeknownst to them because they enjoyed unfathomable economic growth and prosperity. This experience enabled the entry of the disease, which slowly misguided them, causing the few terrible ones in their midst to infect others until the core cohort at the mean, median, and mode of their bell curve slowly converted its thinking to believe that the pursuit of virtue was not necessary for the existence of democracy. But, that the purpose for life was "me first" hedonism, the rest be damned. And so they allowed the DAMN of the societal and social powers of the USE. We must demand the LAMBS be toward liberty and justice for all. This mission for our project must begin again, henceforth and forthrightly, now!

Baby boomers started a pursuit of celebrating and tolerating ways of living that ancient history, mythology, and academy powers advised were sinful or foolish. They became a generation that grappled with ethics like none before, requiring ethics training in all corners of society because the detestable exemplified the worst of humankind, and they knew it. They pretended to do something about it, but they did not really care; they just checked the box to make it go away. Superficial appearances of righteousness became more important than substantive changes in character. They morally failed, which means they socially failed to enlighten society with grace and dignity. They dragged us down. Their egregious mean, median, and mode statistically aligned to corruptibility cohorts became baby doomers. These perceivably psychopathic perpetrators of narcissism pulled the whole generation toward the cowardly "me first" attitude as permissible and then into the vainglorious habits of hubris, celebrating violations of moral social codes as newfound freedoms! The community power was muted. Social capital to countervail dwindled. Civic associations converted into lobbyist, not working to supplement governing society, but to control society by influencing government (Putnam R. D., 2000).

Doomers created "superstardom and extreme salaries for a few" as the vision of society. Just like in the kingdom of a man named George. They clawed and brawled. They clamored fastidiously, backstabbing competitively. They pushed to be closer to the thrones of power in society. In their ambitious "me first" minds, lying, cheating, and stealing became authorized. These were the innate, harmless non-violent, indispensable tactics of self-advancement. Though raised to know better, they did these indefensible acts. In their daily lives, they continuously backslid toward tyranny, and we now see its rotten remnants. The consequent behaviors are doomeristic, dooming our posterity to poverty and persecution by a police state. Can we imagine the slide in conversations that might have been like this: "My, my, well, since Myron and Mildred got that conspicuous status symbol, so must we too? See here now, we are Joneses after all, not to be outdone by anyone! After all life is a game, which we do not intend to lose!" How fooled they were by envy. How well Madison Avenue contorted their ability to perceive reality. How fooled they were by fools. We must raise the framer's intelligence to the surface.

These unwanted ways of the domineering doomer cohort created the conditions for the rise and expansion of doomerism. Unseen and unfelt by the first and forth quadrant bell curved boomers, it brought about the destruction of virtue, value, and vitality in our settlement pattern, regional, and national communities. In part seduced by the wealth of the nation at a time of growth, they misunderstood the warnings of the framers about power. They failed to abide by the founding wisdom. We must now address this circumstance and reacquaint with our endowed vision of a new order for the ages. We need oracular ACE everywhere, every day. We must help baby doomers, and all other (later we tell of six other types) boomers if badly inflicted by doomerism, repent, recover, and rejoin the community's mission, the gifted enterprise for all.

We are a community inspired by desiring for, and aspiring to make a more perfect union. We will need everyone to engage in saving the Constitution and its union, but we cannot allow them to hold the positions of authority. They are ill suited for the decision-making necessary to prevent a pending doom caused by their mistakes, errors, and omissions, their failures to perform good citizenship. With a newfound civic awareness and importance, we will remind our community, for whom citizenship is deeply within our citizens' hearts that we are to be constitutionally allied. We cannot have our people unable to name it or speak of it because of all the noise caused by doomerism. We need to silence this noise, so we can mobilize all the people to make possible good living by a shared wisdom of good citizenship. We need embrace patriotism as a form of liberty and defend democracy. In an age of information overload, of artificial intelligence and the digital manipulation of real images into fake ones, real reality and virtual reality or fantasy get confused. Fictions begin to replace facts. Opinion becomes evidence. Rumor becomes truth. This is doomerism. We must reject it! It is not sport. We must remove it from our minds. We must prevent it from taking over our American society. It erodes trust, and trust is what we need. Trust based in truth needs salvaged for liberty to survive in the future. Factuality must trump falsity for us to know felicity.

All these alterations in our perceptions of what we believe become threatening to civility. This insecurity undermines our trust: trust in ourselves and in others. The knowledge growth in our society and the technology it produces increase exponentially. The complexity confounds. We are too easily distracted. Defrauders become felonious fallacious figureheads parading about as if saviors. Leaders become cowards. We feel intentionally misled. We might think we are in an experiment in a laboratory, nurtured like bacteria in a dish. We want to escape. We want someone to "pour some sugar on me." We want to hide. This state of psyche is exactly what those who have authority want us to think. This is thinking like a subject in a tyranny, like a serf in a feudal kingdom. To contradict this affluence of power, the colonists held a revolution, giving the veritable middle finger to the world's most powerful empire, to be free to form a new nation. They pulled it off, thanks to gritty George Washington and the French, who went bankrupt helping us, but then had their own revolution for liberty. We must find solace in their courage to strengthen us to revolt against doomerism, excoriating it to exorcise it from our culture.

The young framers, most in their 20's and 30's with some older statesman among them, built on English traditions and wrote a Constitution. It "ordained" and "established" our nation. Clearly, it felt decreed from a higher power than a kingdom, from a source more powerful. Humans never did anything like it before. How else could they have pulled it off, if not for divine intervention supporting their cunning and luck? What a boon for the future! Our Constitution was a great social invention forming a new possibility for a people power based polity. They were ahead of their time. Sadly, society then did not practice what they saw fit to write, which was right. Yet what they wrote set up a means by which posterity could advance upon achieving the wisdom they scribed. The quill and ink soaked into the fibers of paper to enshrine it. The project of self-government began. The responsibility of citizenship was elevated. Now forgotten, it is a concept needing revived if the visionary American society is to survive. Civics must be our focus. If not, our project will fail; either by fury or a simpering whimpering disappearance into tyranny (recall Figure 2-14 through Figure 2-23).

Two hundred forty-five years after the Declaration of Independence, have we forgotten the fervor of patriotism known in the days when the framers planted its seed? Who recalls the Liberty Tree? Look it up. Who thinks of the seedlings when they admire the full-size tree? Clearly, doomerism caused forgetfulness of the key principles, buried under the heap of generational accretions of wealth in a nation and several distorted stories. Other ideas introduced into the mix distract. Shallow is hollow and see-through, though if such people expressing unhealthy and unhelpful non-sense contrary to our purpose as a people receive more pay for it, then most think it is the way to go. We need to swallow our pride, deny hubris, and disallow vanity to control our attitudes and behaviors, if we are to convert into full-fledged, conscientious citizens. To convert, the baby doomers must begin to walk through the seven stages of conversion (Rambo, 1993):

1) **Context**—Doomerism is shaping a chaotic society in which people feel vulnerable. This risky condition elevates fear. Fear brings crises.

2) **Crises**—Doomers have poorly managed systemic financial, social, alien, and viral crises.

3) **Quest**—As they age, they may reflect upon what has happened, consider a sense of personal responsibility, and want to learn more about what they can do before their lives end, perhaps to change the circumstances they allowed to happen.

4) **Encounter**—Seeing this book will be an encounter of a third kind. Criticism they have not yet seen or heard based on concepts they may not have considered matter because they are the least common denominator causation of our society's troubles.

5) **Interaction**—Through reading this book wise leaders proffer constructive criticism. This is that. Through self-reflection, they grow aware of a new way for them to live in support of a vital mission to cure a societal disease and heal a divided people.

6) **Commitment**—If deciding to make a difference in the lives of others, to assist youngsters grow greater civic engagement and purposeful political participation, to bring about a renewed age of citizenshipping that produces micro, meso, and macro adjustments to insure, d'ure, ensure, assure, lure, and secure (IDEALS) liberty in the USE's LAMBS.

7) **Consequences**—It will take time to win everyone to this concept, and harassment may be levied against those who do, but if they remain strong, over time and generations, this renewed way of living will fuse the culture of democracy fully in the citizenry, and the republic will succeed at attaining its objectives and achieving its goal.

We the people must help guide those who have fallen under the false promises and wicked spells of doomerism. We must bring them back in line with attitudes and behaviors that support our efforts to properly AEIOUY^{2}K American societal and social powers, so the USE pursues its principled objectives. We ought to be a leader to the world in how democracy culture works to IDEALS liberty. We should do this for every person on earth to have hope in knowing and experiencing the four universal freedoms democracy culture infuses. This process is not an easy one. Yet, if we remain constant in our support and lead until we meet our mettle, we will fulfill our objectives. We will eradicate doomerism from our society and win the world over, enabling a greater number of real democratically based societies to exist. As innovation diffuses, so will adoption of citizenshipping as a new way of being. One we ought to have been doing since the creation of the nation.

A **SELFISH** Politician

wants to use **POWER**
to enrich themselves; ignores
the **PEOPLE**

The first readers of this book can be the innovators to tell of our need to introduce a vigorous life of victory by exhibiting service above selfishness, saying yes to the utmost full-fledged thoroughgoing constitutionally allied, united citizenshipping, understandingly synchronized (E-SASSY-T-TUF-FT-CAUCUS). This intensely activated citizenshipping will lead the way, encouraging "early adopters" of its logic. It will begin to show us how to resurrect our American principles. It will show its proof in voter participation and in community volunteerism in the kinds of associations that made American society collaborative toward a more earnest and at times harmonious pursuit of our goal, a more perfect union.

Soon we gain an "early majority," then a "late majority," and finally we get the "laggards" to come along and get on the bandwagon of our properly hitched-up citizen horses, our innovators, our defenders of liberty, our citizen-firsters, who will pull us along toward our intended destiny. We must begin this now, as an intervention, by raising the forthcoming pragmatic patriots up to positions of ownership of the societal powers. Those who take on the challenges of important positions in our human culture-made powers' FILMS[2] [P7] will ensure we AEIOUY[2]K the powers properly. Our young adults between the ages of 24 to 40 in the brightest time of brilliance and genius will move us forward on the right path, the path that does not disgrace us and attains our objectives.

As history has shown, the 24 to 40 years of age range is when human innovation is the most prevalent. We need to let them lead the way, coached along by the elders who also must commit to saving the union from chaos. Further, as we demonstrate the power of the people to transfer the reins of authority and prevent the reign of the baby doomers from continuing, we'll see other nations inspired by us once again. More democracies mean less war. Less war means less loss of our treasures on foolish foreign excursions. It costs less to build policing coalitions than to fight wars. The diplomats use words not weapons, and we can create a more stable political world with diplomacy than we can with warfare. Winning the peace after a war is even more difficult. It takes strong statecraft and diligent diplomacy to convince others of the necessary non-animalistic guided behaviors that American society needs to fulfill its promise. Exemplary behaviors inspires, then get emulated by others. This is how virtuous character based leadership works. This is as American leadership must work, beginning with us, the citizenry, setting a good example.

Democracies do not war with other democracies. More democracies ensure greater peace and prosperity for the posterity of humankind and enable the necessary consortiums of scientists to come together without politics getting in their way as they, global citizens that they are, seek to solve the difficult problems that only complex organizations of highly knowledgeable workers can solve for the rest of us. For example, the development of a vaccine for a murderously contagious virus or saving the dying coral reefs essential to oceanographic health needed by our species to survive.

In regards to the conversion of persons into citizens to steward the powers and direct them in a manner for our future prosperity, we must, internal to our enterprise, find a way past the big political impasse. This gap is a philosophical one that exists between the original intended purpose of the polity as rendered by the founders and its opponent philosophy that arose in the beginning of the 20th century. The founding of the nation seems in hindsight to have been a near-divine solution because of its revolutionary proposition, its faith in God, overseer of all Providence. The idea that the people could lead the polity and the economy and not coerced in how to be by a ruling despot is so incredibly profound as to make the founders truly prophetic. Not to believe it feels like apostasy. The belief in the rule of law and not the rule of men is masterful for creating conditions for liberty. It requires people be good citizens to help keep the government limited and prevent it from becoming too large and too intrusive in our lives. However, in the early 20th century, many came to view federalism as not just important for providing for the common defense but as an opportunity to help people in ways not imagined by the founders.

An initial proponent of this thinking on the national stage was Woodrow Wilson (Will, 2019). The idea of looking for a big brother to protect the citizenry from the circumstances of living was a novel one, but the evaluation of its consequences against the risks it posed to the citizens' character concerning a desired posture for liberty was insufficient. It is a very confusing problem. It needs solved by the persons in positions of political power and elites within the economy not becoming victims of baby doomerism. If they accept baby doomer value sets, rationalizing them as permissible, tolerable, or laudable, we will all fall down. Authorities must check on their own lust for power by applying the principles of E-SASSY-T-TUF-FT-CAUCUS to prevent the externalities such disastrous for us desire produces. One such threat is polity administration and economic management that leads to instability.

Instability in the society from the misbalance of polity and economy powers is horrendously dangerous for liberty. If one fails and the other oversteps its role, or if the people fail to lead (only 60% are voting in national elections, and Congress has had career politicians on its rolls for too long), the imbalance undermines the USE's advance on its objectives. Aggressive power hungry clowns and rats will report all sorts of lies that totally confuse the people, who then become complacent, apathetic, and seek to be dependent, either on the economy, as in the worship of product brands, or on the polity, as in handouts, bailouts, and corporate and social welfare. What a mess! The only escape from such doomerist conditions is for the people to step up and do their job: leadership toward liberty's complete attainment. To get there, a massive societal-wide conversion is necessary (recall Figure 2-1 through Figure 2-11). These portray primary powers' misalignments to responsible purposes that cause problems in the LAMBS and imply why we need to rebalance them).

As history power handlers write, we try to organize around worthy causes. To address wrongdoing, we create themes. Too often, when groups do address an injustice, the competition of all camps pushing for their "ism" to win, drowns out the others. However, if all these camps are unaware that they belong to a larger army and do not recognize that each camp is a unit within a larger unit or know what the whole army is fighting for, the individuated camps will fail. The battles fought by divided components not working toward a common goal will fail. The battle cry that supports the whole does not divide the army against its self but unites all its units against their shared enemy. However, this is not a history book. It does not need to be. Enough already published ones exist for us to know what goodness and what badness happened in the name of the United States of America. Nonetheless, this book proposes a worthy cause and a new rallying holler to motivate uniting.

This book is discussing underlying principles and concepts of power that we the everyday people need to know, so we can escape our crises and unpreparedness for the future because of baby doomer dominance in our society. We must learn to see the cultural shift caused by doomerism. We must recognize how bad it is for us, as persons and as a people, in our society, in our republic, and in our democracy-based culture. In addition, it does not help other fledgling democracies overcome the ever-present threat of tyranny. We need to be the example nation. We were once, and we must respect this fact of history. Truly, since the two proceeding to the baby boomers, the GI generation that liberated Europe from the devilishness of

Nazism and the Silent generation that led the Civil Rights movement, both made us proud,
and great in the eyes of others.

The big bulge of baby boomers transformed our society as they passed through it. The changes they made have been as dramatic as a python devouring a pig because of their sheer numbers. The boomers moved us from an industrial age into an information age (Naisbitt, 1984). We are witnessing a post-industrial and postmodern society still in turbulence, which causes questioning of the foundations of our enterprise. In the second wave of industrialism, we experienced a pace of life tied to the tempo of the machine, but the arrival of a third wave in social transformation continues to drastically alter everything (Toffler, 1984), shifting our paradigms and challenging our beliefs. It is causing us adaptive problems (Hage, 2020). The digital age is even faster, more customizable, less secure-feeling, and riskier because we are in the midst of a societal shift with old models of thought. With the majority boomers in authority, we've yet to find a new vibrant and unifying paradigm for the USE. This book proposes it be to SCORE (survive doomerism, communicate its wrongfulness, organize to retire boomers, resist a furtherance of misguided democracy undermining values, and escape from the current chaos by reviving virtue and liberty as our purpose). We will do this by E-SASSY-T-TUF-FT-CAUCUS with momentous ACE to IDEALS liberty and justice for all. We will do this to meet the challenge of our project's mission to become a more perfect union as we rearrange all our powers into an equilibrium to best $AEIOUY^2K$ them to perpetuate prosperity for posterity.

Our enterprise is about the people, and whatever becomes of our society, we must keep this element at our core. It is what liberty is for, it is what democracy is for, and it is why we have a republic. The trials and tribulations of our enterprise are well recorded, its successes and subcultures, its cruelties and kindnesses. We, like all civilizations before, have our contradictions and complexities.

Nor is this a philosophy book. Although it mentions much about constitutionality, it is not a law book. Most of it comes from efforts to gain an informed understanding of society from the social sciences (anthropology, sociology, criminology, political science, and economics). However, it is not an academic behavioral sciences book either, although many of its constructs build upon knowledge gained in scholarship of the factors compounded by scientific inquiry and based upon facts from evidence accumulated by the most impressive educational network of universities on planet earth. Yet with all the esteemed universities we have, specializations within these increasingly separate fields of discourse, which moves us further apart and not closer together, nor closer to a general truth we can believe in and pursue as an American one expanding in all thought. Of course, the amount of knowledge we have amassed outstrips our capacity to grapple with it. We must keep chasing it down in our hunt for truth, justice, and the best American way.

Let's be clear, this book is an appeal to our better nature. A request we look deeper into our national character. Its purpose is not an attempt to blame the baby boomers. Its claim is the tale of the lame results of a generation's retardation in moving our miracle forward. The consequences are presenting themselves. Few remnants of the first principles survive in their lives lived in comfort. This book intends to raise awareness of the dangers of complacency in democracy. It hopes to inspire investigations into the many crooked games of its worse cohort, the baby doomers. In doing so, it calls out for rigorous scholastic examination. It suggests circumspect introspection by those who wish to reverse our circumstances. It hopes to portray the gravity of the stakes we face from many malignant behaviors. It seeks to acquaint the misguided with the inchoate human shame necessary to motivate atonement. This must happen nationally if we are to reclaim any good graces in the history books of the outcomes of boomers time in charge. If they alter their attitudes and behaviors to change course, we've a chance. There is a way for them to leave behind a better legacy than the one that is currently carving itself into our hearts. The present day's risky activity we see from the baby doomers is discouraging. Corrupt, yet projected as normalcy. The citizenry needs better performance from those with authority and from itself as the body politic. This book hopes to help them see past their foolish pride and guilt, and repent. We need them contributing to the mission of the USE based in our Constitution, not thwarting it innocently or intentionally, because they were infected with the social disease "doomerism".

Alas, this book is a patriotic book full of ideas and intellectual tools to use to find unity and purpose, to help us right the ship of the USE. Perhaps it is because of modernism that we suffer from our success. We feel we have to teach all of it to everybody. We stress out our kids trying to feed too much into their developing brains for fear they will miss something and not be competitive in life. We are confused. We make unnatural choices and societally pressured decisions. We don't any longer think for ourselves with clarity of purpose. How can we? We have forgotten what liberty means because we are under the rule of convicts who have no truthful commitment to the commons that created our wealth. Nor do they have a concept of truth, for they use relativism to rationalize their approach to living and what they call leading, though they are managing affairs in a manner that does not live up to the values of virtue, the essential requirement to sustain democratic principles of self-governing people running a self-governmental republic. It seems as if we are lost at sea with fools in the pilothouse of societal power, drunkards on the bridge; dupes at the helm.

*G*enerations' Personalities

Over the course of the nation's eighth generation's ascendency to the mantle of adulthood and the assumption of positions of authority within the FILMS[2][P7] of human powers, during the boomers' reign, pulling on the reins, camps have emerged. Factions born of well-intended ideas now are so opposed as to cause their most vigilant extremists to circle around their ideologies in near-religious fervor, fed by lies used to deceive and control their followers. People must guard against being captivated by impostors posing and posturing for personal power. Demagogues bloom, everywhere dishonesty holds sway, and terror comes in the door. We go astray. Tyrants don't move us in a way that secures our just victory, which comes in our making a more perfect union by living virtuously, neither in need of over-lords nor wanting the ailments of largess.

Our national neighbors, our rising generations, we, the everyday people, are suffering the aftereffects of a malfeasant generation's rise and exercise of our powers as the majority that has now ruled longer than any previous generation. To remove us from under its control, this book proposes we find our strength in the founders. Look at how popular the musical *Hamilton* has been. Does this evidence a deep yearning to understand what we know to be true but have been too distracted to look for? We must find it. We must go back to reading the essential treatises of liberty and applying them in our daily lives. All inhabitants of the United States of America must again purposefully gain control of our country by knowing its roots and by living up to the letter of the law and the letter that led to the law of the land. We must unite, holding one another accountable for being on our best behavior. We must together strive for virtue to protect the common wealth, preserve the commons. We must work collaboratively to serve the common good. We must ensure that liberty is known by all, always, every day, every second in every minute, every minute in every hour, every hour in every day, every day in every week, every week in every month, every month in every year, every year in every score, and every score in every century. When we are in the majority in authority in the positions that control our society, we must listen to the minority and appeal to each other's better angels to guide the country toward its goal. By doing this, we will improve community. We must come to trust our neighbor as a fellow citizen. By doing this we know that we are all truly in it together, rowing in the same direction with the same force. By doing this we understand our endowed responsibility as citizens of the greatest political invention ever to exist on this planet, the pure genius of social innovators, a constitutionally based, democratically selected, representative republic form of government of the people, by the people, and for the people.

We, the everyday people, have the power. We have our elections. We must use them better. We must not become complacent and allow those in positions of power to stay in power. As neighborly as possible, in love we must protect our fellow citizens from corruption while in the offices that grant them authority. We do this by removing them regularly and perpetually and teaching each generation this liberty-supporting logic. We cannot let natural human weakness creep in and allow power to go to their heads. We must take turns in these positions. More of us doing this will gain for all of us a better appreciation of how we must be E-SASSY-T-TUF-FT-CAUCUS to sustain democracy. Does this make American sense? If so, welcome to the real ideal of America, self-government. We behave properly and keep government limited, so we might exercise our constitutional freedoms, no more, no less. Thus, this is a patriot's book. A citizen is a patriot. We become compatriots when we follow its recommendations to remedy society from doomerism. At times, a citizenry must act more patriotically to defend democracy and liberty. This is such a time as we adjust to the third stage of knowledge evolution, recognize our regional and settlement pattern differences, and acknowledge our generational personalities and their consequences.

We are in an era of crises. If we want to have liberty, not wild animal "freedom", (the fallacy that we can do whatever we want whenever we want, without regard for our neighbors), we must take on our task fully and seriously. We must lead society as intended (recall Figure 2-1). We lead it toward Americanism, an enterprise of cooperation between private and public interests in balance as we strive to achieve a more perfect union. We know what it actually is (as established philosophically during the Age of Enlightenment and instituted as a form of republican government with a spine of democracy, a culture of principles to secure liberty and justice for all).

If we are willing to contribute to making it so, we must be good citizens first, then consumers as necessary, believing it is our duty as citizens to perpetuate the rule of law (the only way to guarantee our liberty) and not suffer under the rule of man (humans). If we read *Common Sense*, the Declaration of Independence, and the amended Constitution of the United States, and if we extend forgiveness for the crimes against other humans the founders perpetrated in a time when injustice was more common than justice was, we can advance on our goal. We can forgive but not forget, learning from horrors and celebrating honors. History is. We cannot go back and change it, but we can make amends. A place to begin is a refocus on first principles, honoring the founders' ideals written for us to follow. We should return to them to move as swiftly as possible with each succeeding generation toward the "we," democracy, so liberty and justice for all have a chance to overcome "me first" doomerism.

On June 21 of 1788, the Constitution became the official framework for our government. If 25 to 30 years is an average duration for a generation's adults to control American society's FILMS[2] [P7], then we've had eight since then. Our eighth dropped the ball. We find solace knowing that eight is a small number, and if we survive it, there will be many more generations of Americans to come. However, there is no guarantee. Gracefully the seventh generation, the silent ones, moved us in the right direction. We now set upon the work of committing the ninth, tenth and eleventh to combine to lift our ship upright and set it back upon its correct Constitutional course. We can call upon the seventh who labored for democracy, for justice, for the common good and fulfillment of the Constitution. In them, we see hope for our progeny, for our prosperity, for our posterity, and for the continuation of liberty more fully than ever before.

Rising adult generations should not feel held down or held back by the isms of the past. This is a good approach. They can better look ahead without chains to tired "isms". They can be critical of what is in the old isms that do not evidence the principles of the foundation of democracy culture and the republic it birthed. They can recreate the intellectual frames that support the advance of the project toward its goal and can achieve its objectives doing so.

Despite all the faults of an imperfect society that has not lived up to its founding wisdom. If we truly commit in our hearts to defend our Constitution (our liberty it enshrines) against all enemies foreign and domestic, (and that domestic enemy includes anyone among us, regardless of station, willfully causing breakdowns in civility), then we must rise to the occasion of this moment in our history. We must act in unison as citizens first. Disruption in the social compact—the contract of trust and fraternity with one's neighbors or members of the family of liberty lovers who know and live by its true values and who strive to live in accord with the founders' wisdom—is doomerism. We need stop its lying culture. We need trust in the truth of one another's words. We need to forgive one another our less than ideal deeds. Trust and forgiveness must become important civil constructs once again.

Doomerism promotes intentional exploitation, and a hiding behind the limitations of the legal system. This is criminal behavior against democracy. This is a game played by the baby doomers. We cannot afford its costs. It is wrong to burden us with it. Dishonesty dooms democracy; it buries the society in doubt, and cheating causes a loss of clout. It hurts everyone. Prone to swindle, baby doomers are un-American. We need them arrested, reconnected with justice, and reformed to commit to living truthful lives. If only this could be done on their dime and not ours!

Virtuous values—first of self-governing and then self-government—lived fully in service to our family, neighborhood, municipality, state, nation as one people under God in community living justly to reduce the costs and risks of giving government too much power, are deterministic for the citizenry in a constitutionally established republic built on the frames of representative democracy! Either we value virtues and hold them as our standards for everyone, or we die at the hands of humans disobeying the rule of law. This, the founders told us, is true. The truth is that power tends to corrupt. It undermines kindness and love for civility. Civility benefits our progeny and us with blessings of liberty. History has proven it. We are supposed to be providing superintendence of liberty in the national community. We are not supposed to be lining our own pockets while others die of starvation because we have neglected their rights, abandoned our civic responsibility, and rationalized this as acceptable, declaring one another "winners" or "losers." This schoolyard antic is foolishness. It is not mature democracy. We must rediscover the founders' wisdom and reimagine it in our politics. Rather than watch entertaining theatrical drama, or sport like competitive politics, we must demand to experience and witness scholastic discussions and debates on the framers' intents. All proposals need tested in the public realm against the goal and objectives for the USE before admitted into the politics of policymaking.

Our job as virtuous citizens is to reduce power, divide it, and conquer it by not needing its enfranchisement in any political body more than is necessary, or possessed by only one party, faction, or group at a time, setting up tribal like warfare over it. The Constitution lays out what is necessary, so obeisance to it guarantees our liberty as well as just and fair treatment of one to another. Misbehavior forces the government to expand to keep the peace by policing more heavily, with increasing the judiciary, adding more and more courts that cost money to staff, operate, lead, administer, and manage.

At one point, nearly all inhabitants of the United States died younger than they do now. Life expectancy has been on the rise. The duration of a generation's control of the society has increased with each generation. The current ruling generation has held power longer than the others did. Considering their terrible performance, enough is enough. The longer a person holds a position with authority, the more its power corrupts him or her. They meant well, some not so much, but they have failed to uphold liberty. It is time for them to go. It is time for the revolution of Jefferson—without blood—a political death and replacement of those in power. Their sordid incompetence as corrupted politicians and economic elitists, like an autocratic plutocracy at the helm of society, has led to a terrible demise of the principled ideals of democracy in republic. The USE is no longer the best democracy. It is not even in the top ten. In 2019, it identified as a flawed democracy (Economist, 2020). The slide away from truth built by a citizenry in pursuit of it, a citizenry living to know virtue, has happened mostly during the last 40 years. This period correlates to the time of baby boomer dominance over American society. It happened so slowly that it went unnoticed until it became obvious. If it is not obvious now, this book opens eyes to it.

Young people, we must now rise, respectfully but very quickly, to kick the ruling generation out of power. They collude against our Constitution in pursuit of personal power. They continue to corrupt our society. These baby doomers must be replaced by succeeding generations who commit society to the virtues necessary to guide our lives, not to the sins of the doomers but the higher-minded, morally superior, principled universal ideals to live "of, by, and for" us! Otherwise, democracy is dead, the republic ruined, and the United States divided forever, unable to heal because we no longer feel we can trust one another as one nation under God, indivisible, with liberty and justice for all!

Why Should We Care?

We need to be concerned about anything that poses risks to the suitability and sustainment of our nation. As a society, it should be humane because it's built upon a polity that believes in putting the people first. Thus, we must participate in our own governing. Doomerism is the greatest present danger, the domestic threat to the Constitution, an enemy of it because it influences culture to convert people into persons, dividing and conquering them with mass confusion of mixed messages, decreasing sociability, causing isolation, and tempting citizens to be more concerned with consumption than their country. The founders proclaimed the risks of the pursuit of comfort over liberty. They knew and professed the risks that voting for benefits would cause, not just for future generations' finances but also for the soul of the nation. Once divided as persons seeking benefits first, along will come the false prophecies of grouping people into factions. Doomerism employs these kinds of demagoguery to thwart unity of the whole by driving persons toward being one of "us" and not one of "them." Forcing persons to choose a side based on some oversimplification of reality or a single physical characteristic is dumb and risky. It prevents the real discussions of differences of opinion and perspectives that democracy embraces in the thrill of debates. To keep liberty alive, we must have civil discourse and deeper consideration of varying viewpoints, and we must be willing to change our minds per the facts that represent truth as best we can understand it. If we seek truth in the favor of liberty, we can all agree on what benefits us as a people. Becoming super selfish, wanting to be given everything for nothing, or falling for demagoguery are temptations we must avoid. We simply cannot forsake the legacy of liberty, the endowment of our republic. To be able to carry out our sacred trust, we need to think of the risks, parse out the threats and hazards, identify the opportunities, know our vulnerabilities, and rebuild our civic-minded informed political muscles for the purpose of attaining our objectives and achieving our goal.

We need to care that doomerism is a "me, me, me" construct. It's an "all about me" syndrome, too easily fallen into. It's its own egotistical demagoguery pulling on our minds. Hedonism is an ism that gets at it. If all that our politicians and elites care about is self-serving "me first" activity, they set an ugly tone of disharmony for society. Their example is a poor one for the parents of children to emulate. Each generation now risks passing down doomerism to the next. Perhaps an unconscious guilt has caused the baby boomers to raise millennials to be socially minded and less prejudiced. Interestingly, the boomers' competitiveness may have had a positive unintended consequence. By pushing their children to do well in team sports, kids learned the value of teamwork (Bosché, 2016). Especially in the world's most loved, creative and accessible sport, (English) football, (American) soccer. It's a beautiful game for learning solid teamwork skills, personal resiliency, and moxie.

The underlying reality of doomerism is a particularly prevalent value set that is destructive to civility, the common good, democracy culture, and the republic polity's health. It makes society an ugly conglomerate of sin-promoting, shallow thinking, and immoral individuals. Such baby doomers disturbingly play "fast and loose" with the rules to bypass legal proceedings and put family, friends, and ideologues into positions of power for which most are unqualified. When such loyalty to a person is required instead of the rule of law and merit, it paves a path to tyranny for everyone to follow. It brings about the risks of a cult of personality demagogue dragging mobs into the mud raking yellow journalism fear mongering hatreds of a nepotistic autocratic empire in the making. Circumventing the rule of law is a constitutional abomination, a violation of its principles and of democracy, and an affront to the people power best exerted for leadership. The hasty adolescent impatience of the baby doomers to get their way makes a "teenage wasteland" of our republic. For example, baby boomers as a generation had a preference when paying taxes to exploit loopholes and nuances. They sought to cut down their responsibility to as little as they could get away with (Sinek, 2012).

Figure 4-1 below overlays some factors of our society that have occurred in the third stage of knowledge creation that began the new digital era to which we are still adapting. It includes some social upheavals and economic uncertainty we've experienced during the age of the boomers' control of the FILMS[2] [P7] and as the dominant HM[5]. During this stage, the boomer generation was the majority of the adults of the citizenry and most of the polity.

These days, baby doomer politicians, sadly it seems, feel power is more important than people are. A majority of the boomer generation suffers infection by this moral cancer. Being the majority generation, they are responsible for the chaos we as a nation have been smothered in because they run everything. They AEIOUY²K society's powers. Worse, they all too frequently DAMN human cultural, social powers. How could it not be? We've demonstrated earlier how true it is that "a billion self-centered, self-serving, selfish decisions do not a society make." If society is crumbling, has not negligence at being citizens allowed it? Aren't the failure and their value sets connected? If it is only the "me" and not the "we" that matters to them, is it not their micro actions aggregated up through meso instruments that have accumulated to cause the macro failures? Society is not about an all-out, winner-take-all, zero-sum competition in which each person may lie, cheat, and steal to become the fantasy they want for themselves. Is their whining and victimizing just a case of them being spoiled, and trying to make right all that they felt was done wrong to them, or whatever motivates their vanity and greed? Were they naïve, snared unfairly? Did such entrapment make it easier to do a deal with the devil to obtain their fairy tale? Getting what they wanted at all costs, having it at last, does not justify their ways, means, and methods. We've heard the cliché "the ends do not justify the means." Could this statement be wisdom, not a mere weakling figure of speech? We should reflect upon it. Words have meanings. We should know what they mean to mean to prevent the ways, means, and methods of the LAMBS in the USE fail because of stupidity.

Society is a cooperation to maximize the common good, the common wealth, and the survival of the community against the natural hazards that threaten life on the planet. Working in unison to sustain life in as harmonious a manner as negotiable is what a good society does.

When we the people are not under the spell of the baby doomers, we build humane networks of human understanding and human-to-human commitments to work together to establish the fairest and most reasonable systems possible to produce a common wealth and enjoyable society for all of our posterity and us. This purpose depends on our carrying it out through our E-SASSY-T-TUF-FT-CAUCUS. Real Americans build prosperity for all. We've done it all over the world. We don't produce false scarcity to feel powerful. Nevertheless, two score ago, things began to change. A coming of age generation chose this thorny tyrannical tactic as they rose. The baby doomers do it because they are hoarders. Hordes of us must rise to restrict their access to our capital: human, personal, social, physical, and financial. We, the everyday people, must remove and block them from authority positions to prevent their manipulating the FILMS² [P7] that control our cultural processes and the consequent human made secondary and tertiary social powers. We must take these actions to diminish drastically their dominance to AEIOUY²K our primary societal powers. We must deny them access to the steering wheel, levers, and buttons with which they

DAMN our societal and social powers, which by democracy belong to all of us in common.

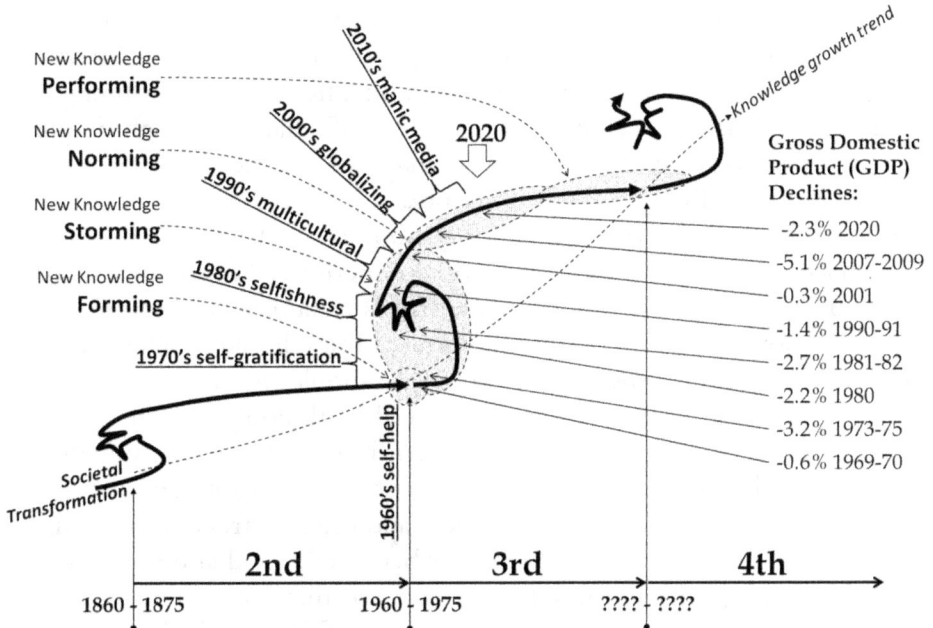

New Knowledge
Performing

New Knowledge
Norming

New Knowledge
Storming

New Knowledge
Forming

2010's manic media

2000's globalizing

1990's multicultural

1980's selfishness

1970's self-gratification

Societal Transformation

1960's self-help

2020

Knowledge growth trend

Gross Domestic Product (GDP) Declines:

- -2.3% 2020
- -5.1% 2007-2009
- -0.3% 2001
- -1.4% 1990-91
- -2.7% 1981-82
- -2.2% 1980
- -3.2% 1973-75
- -0.6% 1969-70

2nd   **3rd**   **4th**

1860 ┼ 1875   1960 ┼ 1975   ???? ┼ ????

Knowledge Creation Stages that Punctuate Equilibrium

Figure 4-1: Cultural Decades, Recessions, Adapting to the 3rd Stage of New Knowledge Creation

(For full context of knowledge creation stages, see Figure 5-1). Note there is a lag time between new knowledge creation and new technology invention. Innovation of extant technology happens a bit sooner with new knowledge's introduction. As knowledge disseminates, known broadly, it begins performing. We accommodate it. We make new technology, which when implemented disrupts the equilibrium. We change patterns of behavior. This threatens the stability of the instruments of society. We experience chaos and overreactions as we attempt to adapt to newness transformations. Adaptations permeate and escalate, some work, some don't. The experience is one of technology storming. Generally, when knowledge begins performing, technologies start storming. When technologies start norming and performing for us, impetus for new knowledge gains momentum. Lags between new knowledge and disruptive technology decrease as complexity and integration increase. Society transforms. We must keep up or we feel left behind. The more knowledge we create, the more all of us must work to understand what it means, and how its spawned technology might challenge the equilibrium we might have believed, or hoped, would remain intact for us during our personal lifetimes. The disturbance of the balance of societal and social powers brings to us periods of crises.

Bad for the USE, the baby doomers' value set is wrong and corrupt. They cannot see it because the power they pursued blinded them. They lack. They exhibit zero wisdom. Some claim they are sociopaths, antisocial, destroying and not creating society (Gibney, 2017). Some would go so far as to say they fundamentally are un-American, or worse anti-American. It feels at times as if the doomers sold us all down a river to get the gold all for them. Not sharing is not caring. They care for no one but themselves, using each other in a game to get ahead, to the front of the line, to get there first. "So what?" we might ask. Ignorant are they who fight to be first in a game of getting more goods at the expense of others liberty and a well-functioning society everyone depends upon to be able to pursue ones best interests. Moreover, we cannot take our possessions with us when we die. The goal is not to get but to give and get along, helping one another get by, not using each other to get ahead. "Get ahead of what?" we might inquire.

Petty egos with weak beliefs cannot make an American society. Land of the free, home of the brave they were not. It is time to weed the garden of democracy in America overrun by baby boomers' baby doomers and their accomplices and their cruel culture of doomerism. We need to steal our nerves and execute their eviction from offices of authority over the societal and social powers and from the pilothouses that should provide earnestly honorable LAMBS for the USE. Further, we should not buy their products. Let their moral bankruptcy be their financial bankruptcy. Let the power of the markets act against them to train them how to be better humans. Let not the polity bail them out anymore. It is time for the younger generations to name and denounce the baby doomers and their destructive cultural shift of doomerism. It is time for the younger better-educated and more civically minded to seek positions of authority and use that authority as it was intended to be used, as a governing opportunity of the people, by the people, and for the people. As a generation, the baby boomers have failed the following generations. They did not police their own kind. Perhaps because there were simply too many of them, and they preferred complacency to a public responsibility to protect civil society. They did not employ the leadership of accountability.

If anyone, like journalists and professors with history and academy powers, wants more evidence, they can use the following 4x5x8 cuboid tool, shown in Figure 4-2 below. With it, they can assess the damage to our society inflicted by the boomer generation. If they have the courage to investigate and to tell the truth of what they find, then check into it. Let the results not be sugar coated or spun to a false face to make it look better than the real facts indicated. Yet we need no more proof. Have at it for the records, but we must act and toss out the baby doomers. We need not tar and feather them like the British-hired Stamp Tax collectors. However, we need to let them know that enough is enough: no more doomerism in the USE, please! Then we reform them and give them a chance to redeem themselves and leave a decent legacy. That is the real American way to go about reversing negative trends. It is not their way, so they will struggle to comprehend why it must happen this way. Of course, we must help them understand. It's unexpected we can get them past their entitlement infirmity. Nevertheless, we must try with all our electoral and purchasing power might to send them a loud and clear message that we are here to correct the course of our project, our enterprise, our society. We need convey to them that to do so they must turn over the helm to the future, step off the bridge, resign, retire, and return as volunteers in service to the project's mission. We need their support of its new initiatives to restore faith in it. They can teach ACE to all inhabitants repeatedly throughout our lives until they pass on. This activity will be good for everyone and should keep our project's vision fresh and our body politic alive with decency and a dignified united people.

Our problems are due not so much to political partisanship as to the underlying denominator of both sides. The force of doomerism has corrupted so many citizens that too many are out for self over others, seeking to be aristocrats and employing demagoguery to get what they want, which causes tribal tirades and creates extreme opposite policy positions at the edges of our polity. Tribalism is an example of baby doomer behavior, a piece of the core, root cause problem. A part of the broader societal malady now named baby doomerism. The social scientists might want to study it. We will need fact-based theorem to put in our social serum to treat ourselves of it. In addition, we will need to test the remedy to ensure we have eradicated it. We'll need longitudinal and latitudinal research on it. We the people will not gain back our democratic republic until we can cure the doomerism disease within our people. All of us in the nation are supposed to be governing. It is not about picking sides in a shallow competition. It is about cooperating to get to a more perfect union to achieve the objectives of our American society as outlined in our founding documents, principally the Constitution's Preamble and the Declaration of Independence.

Lastly, as an example of cooperation, think of a sports league and all its activities and roles, the responsibilities of its participants, and the rules of the game that must exist—all the social cooperation that must happen over a lot of time by many people before a limited period "competition" can happen between athletes on game day.

See the forest; don't just focus on one tree. However, know which one is the Liberty Tree. Upon it, we must hang newly relighted lamps of patriotic fervor. When examining each kind of tree, understand where it is in its life cycle and the context and importance of the forest ecosystem, that of the bios in which it breathes and feeds and that of the planet on which it grows. To think that every tree could be self-serving is a foolish metaphor with which to approach life. Sadly, this seems the accepted wrongful and misguided way of the forty-year majority generation. One made up of persons whose worse personality traits negatively epitomize the baby doomers.

It is not too late for them to repent and behave more morally and more cooperatively to right the ship that their sins dragged it—in the wrong direction—during their generation's tenure in positions of authority throughout society, for example in: government, agriculture, industry, education, and media. It is not too late for the paradigm to be shifted from their destructive-of-democracy value set to the higher-minded one intended for the citizenry by the founders. The hypocrisy must end. Self-examination and reflection on the error that baby doomerism is, is a good place to start. Perhaps liberty lamps might inspire them.

Not all boomers are baby doomers. Baby doomers self-identify by their social pathologies and then try to persuade everyone to worship them. We must help them refrain, and if not, restrain them as citizens holding them accountable for being outside the lines of respectful discourse and action, to provide a marketplace that is fair and reasonably operated to the material satisfaction of each one's desires and merit of their ability. We only seek to control the boundaries, not the behaviors, and allow them to form a self-regulating system. However, if one among us begins to lie, cheat, and steal, we must hold them to account for the real damage to us all. If we allow them to fleece, we are fools dreaming that denying what we see will make a difference in what we believe, know, and feel about the wrong being done to us. Then we'll fall victim to tyranny. Fight the mighty with right-mindedness, conscientiousness, compassion, love, and empathy. With correctness in thought, using logic for liberty, we'll better guide the USE. A citizenry united, committed to a democracy-based culture, will preserve the union, and the republic that governs it.

We need to progress to the conservation of real principles. We need to moderate the extremes and find the peaceful in-between near the middle, which we must widen and heighten to gain stability and reduce the risks inequality brings as well as the extremism a large distance between top and bottom causes.

Why should we care? Because. We, the everyday people, do not want to live in a tyranny, neither under a dictator, nor within a mob. This was the principal concern of the framers. It led to their first principles. It's why they wrote the Constitution. If we don't protect representative democracy by participation, if we don't in the republic exact our governance, we will find ourselves in the trap of tyranny. It is harder to get out of it than we might think. We must prevent a slow slide into it by misguided complacency and doubt allowed apathy. So be bold, be loud, be proud, be a citizen, a champion for liberty, and persuade others to do the same! But don't go overboard and tilt the power toward a system of government that gives away your liberty for comfort. Don't become pacified and allow the politicians to do as they please. Stay vigilant to hold them accountable, speaking respectfully, keeping them in check, and ensuring we are balancing the societal powers and governing our country, as we would like. We must commit to replace them more regularly for the flexibility we will need as knowledge and technology exponentially escalate the pace of change in our lives. We must apply our book smarts and our common sense. We must use the strategic enterprise risk framework (SERF) to ensure that we manage the risks properly, so we can prevent ourselves from becoming serfs. Let's be wise and think long term but monitor, regulate, and change the politicians in the short-term. Vote in every election. Be evermore civically engaged. These tactics ensure that the strategy of self-government will fulfill the goal and objectives of the Constitution.

If we doubt democracy is possible, then we are being too selfish. We are born into a society. We are born in need of others. By our nature, we are social. We must overcome our survival instincts by elevating our consciences to the mature view that we need one another. Life is not a competition but cooperation. Cooperation is how our culture will get remade away from the drift of doomerism. Yes, we love to compete, but only after the game's rules and referees, associations, leagues, teams, training, facilities, and finances are set, so we understand the boundaries and might compete fairly. Unfair competitions are not fun. They are deplorable. We hate cheaters. We've an adage: "Cheaters never win, and winners never cheat." This is not hard to live by. If we disagree on this, we really need to check ourselves. Infected with the democracy-destroying, morally corrupting social disease that is dangerously deadly for American society: doomerism, we might be. Let's get a check-up!

In the baby boomers' poor-quality "me first" ethos of self-centeredness, they quit on us. The comedian George Carlin railed against them. In their egregiousness, they avoided the "we" as an absolute unless it served their "me" first cravings. Morally bankrupted by the overly ambitious pursuit of self-worth in materialism, overtaken by greed, vanity, and hubris they caused community damage. If, as the Beatles sang, "Money can't buy me love," why give up on "love thy neighbor"? Why only love immaterial objects? It seems this was their choice. More money than can be spent on anything other than a collection that sits unused and unusable because of the limits of time and lifespan is a strange form of self-expression when people are dying of starvation. Hoarding behavior, they quit on us, the everyday people. We share the community. We have stake in it, too. We speak for posterity now.

The boomers apparently dropped the ideals given by the Age of Enlightenment, converting it into an age of entitlement. Bored, not getting enough attention, they initiated an age of entertainment, which confuses the purpose of life and makes it meaningless—to be but a spectator and not an actor, adventurer, etc. Sitting on the couch watching others do interesting things on the television was not a good development for our democracy. The force of entertainment from our artistry powers, made larger-than-life by our industry powers, is a challenge for us. Enjoying being entertained is a welcome pastime. However, if we are entranced into a coma of doing only that, we lose sight of reality. We do not see that we need to avoid isolation and control by our entertainment impulses. We need to get out and be with other people, engaged in meaningful activities that bond us as family, neighbors, and friends. We need to build community with one another and not just on religious holidays and festivities. We need more often to engage in lending a helping hand.

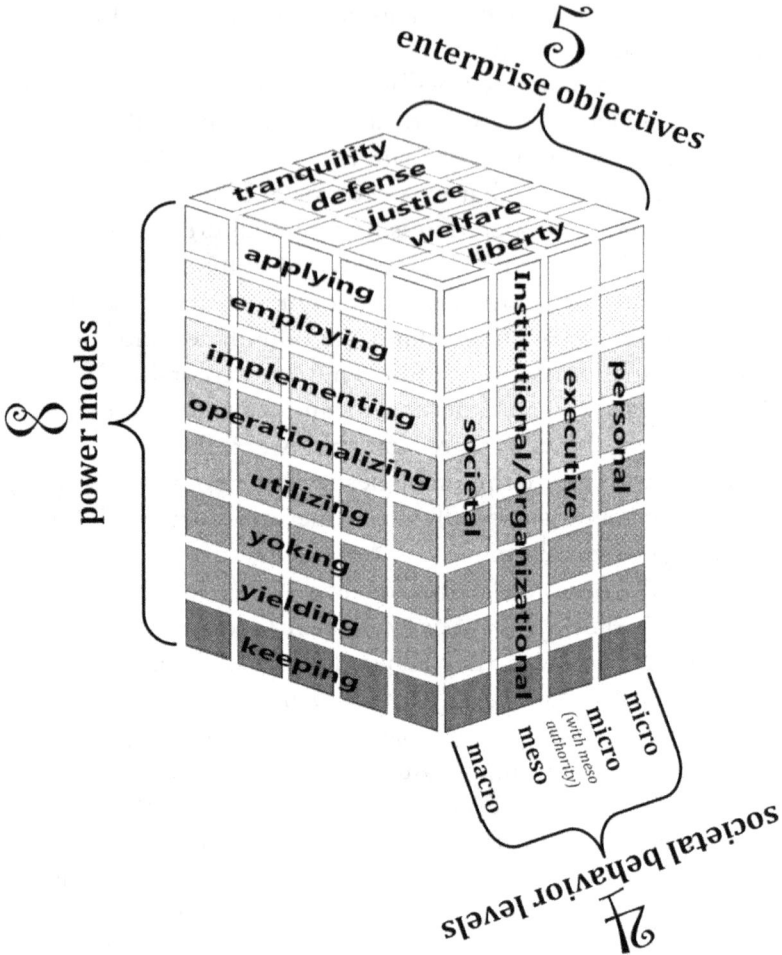

Figure 4-2: 4x5x8 Cuboid—USE Objectives Need Citizenship Behaviors at all Levels for All Power Modes

This 4x5x8 cuboid is a tool to ask, analyze, and understand the intersections of the five enterprise objectives with each power mode and levels of societal behavior (how we ought to behave as good citizens for the benefits of a good society made possible by the USE, a public–private partnership to provide optimal pursuit of happiness for people). Each square of each face represents a cube of a three-way condition. For example, the lowest corner cube represents the condition of keeping power (in any of its forms—primary, secondary, or tertiary) at the societal or macro level to achieve liberty. The top corner cube represents the condition of applying power at the personal or micro level to achieve tranquility. Thus, the primary choices of the society for shaping power balances to achieve the USE's objectives illuminated for civic debate. It is an elucidator. The 4x5x8 cuboid is to be used to combat doomerism. It is our gladiator to win the war against it. Linguistically, in phrasing these choice discussion topics, the "objective" is the object, the "power mode" is the verb, and the "societal behavioral level" is the subject, or actor. When all actors behave as good citizens, exercising good citizenshipping, the modes of power are controlled within the societal and social powers in a manner that enables (and does not prevent) the achievement of the USE's objectives for the citizenry.

Helping others feels good. It is something a people do when they unite in purpose to make a more perfect union out of flawed, imperfect humans.

This is our plight, to uplift, to rise, to prove how to be good humanly humane humans. We must lead ourselves to do more, demonstrate civility, generate social capital with comradery, and engage civically. This is how we restore hope in and with one another as participants in the same venture, our nation's voyage through time in pursuit of something better for everyone.

TV tells lies about other people. It pacifies and stupefies minds. It's not akin to our kinfolk who built this nation. It numbs humanity's possibilities to watch acting that is not real, or worse, "reality TV" that is as staged as necessary to tantalize and enthrall the audience. Bored of being entertained, some among us began exhibiting their own lives as fantasies, convincing others they were real, which led them to bring about the age of exhibition. In the span of a generation, they have switched the age, the consciousness, vacuously from reason, to selfishness, to entitlement, to amusement, to voyeurism. We need not follow them. They have quit on what matters.

We'll quit on listening to them. They only speak to get things for themselves, one by one, a billion selfish egotistical decisions that dismantle our national community and distort by an immature misconception the meaning of democracy. A billion such narcissistic decisions cause chaos, disruption, deception, and the discerption of the Constitution. This debasing way of living causes the destruction of our societal bonds, followed by divisive demagoguery that brings about the demise of our unity as a people. Divisions by schisms decay our people power. We really do need to rise from the ashes of the plague, with new perspectives and new political platforms aimed at getting us on the right path, the path to liberty and justice for all.

The baby doomers are cheaters who want to rule the roost and run the show so that it rewards the wrong kind of people, whom they need to feel justified. To have someone like them on top is how they rationalize their immorality, like a den of thieves. Each generation's scholars cannot entirely escape their upbringing and the values it nurtured, and so like a quotient, they and their work are a summary of what they would want to know, expect, and accept. They cannot completely escape themselves, and their judgments seem appropriate to them in their time. But if the formula of citizenship had kept in the calculus a better comprehension of the key principles that set up the polity, then maybe less drifting away from it and fewer distractions caused by impostors, exploiters, and users would've occurred. More focus on the right knowledge to use to protect and defend the Constitution, to remain enlightened, and not to allow a sense of entitlement would also have occurred. Perhaps conjunctively, an age of entertainment progresses into a thoughtless age of entitlement, and it into an age of exhibition, (see Figure 5-8. It shows how declines in civility will worsen if we don't stop doomerism).

We cannot go back and start over; we've depleted the mathematics that got us to where we are today. We can reintroduce the framers' formula to guide us and revive our commonweal. We are all commoners, who've succeeded by it for many generations. Shame on the baby doomers for being asinine gastric aspirant plutocratic politicians and economic elites; for exploiting us, blowing smoke up our anuses, and for pretending they are one of us. If they were, they would do differently. They should respect us and listen to us. We are the patriots who ask for truth, justice, and a truly American way. They should protect the rule of law. Nevertheless, they choose to neglect it. They prefer to misuse it for gain.

The conversations with and among us need to treat each other with respect and negotiate without the need of intermediaries and a ballooning, overwhelmed court system burdened by gamesmanship—people seeking to exploit and not be accountable to their end of a bargain. When citizens are afraid to speak to one another and want to depend on the state, we have a real threat to our sanctity as a community. We have a breakdown in the social contract of trust that binds us to our common purpose, which is to serve the Constitution by being good citizens first. From this, the trees of liberty will multiply, growing a forested republic providing us with shade and oxygen.

The common denominator in our decline is the accumulated decisions of these, majority in power for the last 40 years, living beyond their means, non-declared-war waging, and debt-producing baby doomers.

They have caused and allowed the creation of a corporation-based feudal-like globalizing system and class of new aristocratic rulers of the planet, and controllers of governments. They, in their beyond excessive self-interest, willingly accepted the comfort of consumerism, forgot to be citizens, and covered their eyes so they could convince themselves they were not to blame as the ball smashed the window. Instead, they blamed hollow ghosts, failed to study history, and continued to exploit to enjoy their sinful ways. The system these past forty years got milked, bilked, and rebuilt: rigged by self-aggrandizers as badly as it was by the robber barons and monopoly trust bosses before, and the indentured servant's contract owners and slavers before them.

Alas, how will the children of liberty rise to stop it, reverse it, and recover democracy out from under its grasp? Fee enterprise does not mean, permit a few to criminalize the polity with bribes! Free enterprise works best with integrity.

What have we learned from history? The rich will send the poor into war, so the poor cannot revolt. Vilified by the rich and powerful, technocratic educated middle class persons lost positions from which to wage fights against plutocratic ascendency and rising tyranny. Driven down, forced to bear the burden of corporate welfare, and paying for the abandoned poor left behind by corporations that failed to innovate and that sent jobs overseas instead of making it work out here, the middle class shrunk in its capacity to stabilize society. What kind of citizen abandons their neighbors, casting them into defeat? Is it their game to suppress the middle class and press it into poverty? Are the downtrodden to be depressed into serfdom? Would this be acceptable to us? Will both become wards of the state, stuck in bondage? Should the top 1% of the economic elites have full control of the polity to write laws and rules that allow them to own 80% of everything, without any responsibility to behave as fair, reasonable, and responsible citizens? The conquering royals of yesteryear in England put a good deal of effort into making it look like they care about the British people.

We are not imperials, so it is worse that our top money making citizens turn their backs on the community of the rest of us. Must the educated enterprising middleclass enlarging form of society be forced to pit persons against one another to fight for food fallen from the table of those who stole societal power? Is it eminent we'll decline toward total doom? Are foreign and domestic enemies seeding our demise? We need to rise and get educated on how we must act to restore liberty and have a chance again at a robust, thriving society that is accessible for all who are willing to work to contribute to it. We cannot allow all of us to be abandoned by the few who are hoarding unchecked. How do they live with themselves and consider themselves citizens of our nation?

Our nation is a quilt. We are quilters. Baby doomers are not quilters. They are victims of their own pride, separated into voracious camps of arguers, arguing without evidence, figuratively holding on to tightly to opinions and sticking to their guns. They think like a bunch of gunslingers looking for a fight, conceited, pretentious, and unrepentant. They glorified the war on this, the war on that, claiming to be trying to make a difference but only making a mess. Had they stuck to the principles of quilting the fabric of our regional subcultures together as one nation, we would not be plagued with the social ills we now face. We would have been able to succeed at achieving social equality for all our citizens. We take the scraps of our lives and make tapestries in community. We support and uphold one another. We love. We don't hate. Baby doomers hate. They are such spoiled, selfish brats—what else can they do but act the way they do? They were spoiled, and so they spoiled the age, creating spoilage. Doomerism harbors too many negative risks to chance it any further. We must revolt audibly, voting the next generations in, and the boomers and their mindless mimickers out. Have no doubts, if we do not, liberty loses and tyranny wins.

Risks to Society

As we are in a new epoch, coping with the crises of our storming about the new knowledge and its technological advancements, we need to prepare to navigate as never before. A considered risk approach is now necessary. Who is applying a risk-management approach to our society? Who should be? In a culture of democracy, it must be everyone. The people power—the leadership power—must more earnestly by us, the citizenry, act to govern to manage the risks to our society and us as a people. We, the everyday people, should use a SERF to control societal risks to reduce our exposure to threats to help us to preserve our people power. We must consider the risks to the perpetuation of our republic. We must find ways to mitigate the risks to our sovereignty and liberty from realization. We must retire the baby boomers to tranquilize them. We must be able to identify the hazards that threaten our democracy. To IDEALS liberty, we need to see the uncertainty bred for it by the baby doomers' ways, means, and methods of taking from us. Driven by modernist ambitions and tolerated due to traditionalist beliefs, doomerism is the result of the economy power overtaking the polity power as the principal administrator of society and the polity power overtaking the people power as the principal leader of society (recall Figure 2-1 through Figure 2-11). This is not as it is supposed to be, nor as is best. So what risks does this malalignment pose to society?

The risks to society of doomerism are the uncertainty we face now in attaining our objectives and achieving our goal. Let's go over this at length. Risks are future events that could happen. Risk includes probability and impact (Pritchard, 1997). Risks are both positive and negative. They are the opportunities or vulnerabilities and hazards that allow threats within or upon the inputs, throughputs, outputs, and outcomes of our enterprise. Achieving our objectives depends on our leading the proper performance by our FILMS^2 [P7] and the HM^5 to AEIOUY^{2}K our social powers in line with our duties for the LAMBS toward the purposes we need to IDEALS our liberty. Risk is uncertainty explained. There are positive risks, i.e., taking risks, seeking opportunities to improve, to break from a path upon which we might be dependent (such as loyalty to a wrongfully doing demagogue or group thinking know nothings who do harm). There are negative risks, i.e., taking risks that expose the vulnerabilities of, or allow threatening hazards to get near the principles and persons we hold dear, (see Figure 4-3 below).

We must ask ourselves difficult questions. Which of the foreign and domestic opportunities and threats in the future, or remaining from the past, are the most important in the present? We must understand these to shape into focus the priorities the people ought to have to IDEALS liberty, because now, reviving our first principle, liberty, needs to be the most pressing concern of the culture. It should drive attitudes and behaviors, instead of the hyperbole said and heard in the mass media marketplaces. Too many words spread around to manipulate our opinions. Too many veiled masks of the isms. We must return to our first principles. We must demand those among us in positions of authority stop the game playing. The republic does not need tail wagging the dog nonsense. Such diversion is a deplorable affront to the people who pay for the polity, and purchase private property from the economy. Thereby, we the everyday people enrich it. The history powers of journalism easily manipulate consumer behavior and profit-driven practices in a dynamic marketplace facing paradigmatic change not yet fully understood. Journalism is in disequilibrium. Use of the SERF analytical tool will help us, the citizenry, gain a sense of control over the knowledge we need. We must use it in our people power to control the polity, drive the economy, and reestablish democracy for liberty. How we respond to risks and control our risk responses is vital to our citizenshipping efforts to IDEALS liberty.

Figure 4-3: Strategic Enterprise Risk Framework

Within our USE, we have endogenous risk-management and risk response controls. At the highest elevation of macro analysis, in the polity, we've separated powers in our branches of government and federal vs. states' rights and responsibilities. In the economy, we've market forces and rules of the game to ensure a level playing field, such as antitrust laws to prevent us from suffering the tyranny of monopolies. Boomers have failed to enforce these properly. Now the mess is almost too big to address. Why would they? They fear others might ask them to follow the rules. Many of them parade around the cliché that "rules are meant to be broken". No, they amend by due process if they are mistaken or misapplied, and their administrators corrected. This takes community, a social action, which is how democracy does it. Perhaps because of such a personal inconvenience, the tyranny of their selfishness dictates they can do what they want. Maybe democracy is too difficult for them, because it requires consideration of others' needs and wants. Could it be that this responsibility is why they seek shortcuts to avoid obedience to the laws? We need the rule of law to ensure the fluidity of economy, and our four freedoms the polity is supposed to protect as human rights.

Boomers of all kinds are all into their shared generational values together. It's their personality, after all. Many are proud its "Me first!" mantra. 'Tis a distorted version of what liberty means to mean in America. But hey, they like to skirt, loophole, and rationalize how rules do not apply to them, because they're special. How can we have a society if no one plays by the rules?

In the people, we've education, the use of academy power, we've moral teaching, the use of mythology power, and we've family and community power influences on individuated persons as they relate to society and give or take from it with social capital. We've social capital to acquire through our academy powers and must dedicate ourselves to learning, not playing, and not being entertained by flashing lights and flittering sounds. We need to put our electronic flames down. We are not moths! Our social capital needs our discipline. We must not be distracted. We must make social movements and extend voting access to the younger generations. We need to get them engaged in taking over the society before there is nothing left for their babies. Do we want the United States to die of the disease of doomerism? Are the boomers so callous they will hold on until the last possible minute as they sink our ship? They likely will not go down with it. They will jump off into golden rafts or float away on golden parachutes with insanely immense severance packages—for having failed Who do they think they are? It's incredulously irresponsible of them to exploit the commons like this! Yet do they care if we think this, or if we feel this way about them? Nope, they do not.

Like the 4x5x8 cuboid and dichotomies, the SERF is another tool for the people to use to gain control of society. Using these tools while building our social capital, we can shake off the bogus factors used to restrict us. We will be successful if we learn how to assess the risks to us in our society, our democracy, our republic. We then need to respond to them strategically in tactically correct ways, means, and methods to avoid, transfer, or mitigate them. The doomerist risks could sink our ship. We must put our ship back on a course toward our goal and objectives.

The tools of this book share various lenses with which we can examine and understand the increasing complexity of society. We can begin to grasp the social circumstances we will face in the future. Our best lenses use timeless virtues and principled ideals. Together we must slug forward, slowly removing the erroneous doomeristic ways of being and behaving. These are not in accord with our primary tenets, our core American values. We must unite in pursuing our purpose. Or else, we are useless in its cause, its propositions to ordain and establish a more perfect union. We have a government that can be for humankind an example more humane than any other is. If we do not begin to relive by our tenets, in a click we will become mere tenants. The doom given by doomerism will turn us into meager serfs. A cliquey cabal of global plutocrats will own us. They are preparing autocracies and committing atrocities against people's liberty the world over. They are forming unfree feudalistic kingdoms of, by, and for thieves.

The SERF helps us think about risks to our freedom and gain the necessary perspective to protect, sustain, and promote the objectives of the Constitution. That is, imagine the United States were seeking to establish itself as a shining city on a hill, a beacon to all the world that humans could organize and govern with liberty. Envision such a place where everyday people perform their duties respectfully, in consideration of the customer, staff, and leader of government of by and for the citizenry. Serving as client and practitioner, sheep and shepherd, we the everyday people trustworthily self-manage without need of supervision. It's not a novel idea. It's foundational for us. We can believe in it. We must behave accordingly to sustain it.

We are an entrepreneurial nation. We the people own our polity. We the people by our economy power own our businesses. Ownership privately and publicly gives us agency in our society. This agency requires we own up to the responsibility. The name of a responsible owner, an entrepreneur of society, is "citizen." If we do not behave well as citizens, we have no right to our democracy, and we will not have the liberty it affords us as a population. Only when we become better citizens do we become a people, e pluribus unum. Only when we are one people can we sustain the truth in the power of our work on our project to achieve our goal, a more perfect union, and attain our objectives: establish justice, insure domestic tranquility, provide for the common defense, secure the blessings of liberty, and promote the general welfare.

We the everyday people are all commoners. We have no castes, no set classes like in feudalism, no monarchs, no system supported sycophants, and no legal aristocrats. This is important to understand. If the everyday person, the commoner, the citizen, regardless of rank, is only a consumer-oriented customer, then we might become demanding individuals, competing against one another for status and services, which creates an adaptive issue for the provider, the business, or the government that seeks to help us help ourselves with our satisfying our needs and pursuing our wants. To say the customer is king is a mistake. Kings are feudal, selfish, tyrannical brats! We are a culture based in democracy, the principle that all are equal before the law, and none rules over the others. We respect one another. We do not subjugate one another. To use such monarchical language is antithetical to our revolution, waged in the 18th century to free us from such beliefs that there are natural legal superiorities among humans. There are not, but there are natural inalienable rights to our person, and it's born free, though socially dependent on family. Certainly, we've persons with more ability than others, and we take pride in our teammates who can do great things, so long as they do not become overly conceited and arrogant. We do have to manage the risks of envy in our lives. This is not so difficult if the rules are fair and opportunities are real. Under the reign of the baby doomers, too many doors to prosperity have closed to us.

If the envious of unnatural ability yet equal opportunity do not work, but demand total economic equality, and get it by taking the earnings of the middle who work, we'll have public policy problems. Taking and giving are measured actions of administering to the whole community. Distributing others incomes to those who show no work ethic, or effort to contribute, or gratitude for it, is risky. The population under this scenario might become spoiled brats who act entitled to something for doing nothing. It could breed further social maladies such as rudeness to the front-line service employees that comes from persons thinking too highly of themselves because of too much money or too many handouts. Entitlements to top and bottom are a slippery policy slope that can cause un-neighborly behaviors, reflexively un-American and uncivil, as if one had greater importance than the other did. Do we want such undignified social engagement in our culture?

Conversely, if the everyday people were only the staff of the government, they would work to eliminate conflict and competition within their ranks, while ensuring they had all the resources to deliver service in the best way they saw fit because they were the experts; after all, they had the responsibility to deliver the services. With this sole orientation, they would become monopolistic, uncaring, and bureaucratic, the victims of their own success. These two examples of a dichotomy's extreme polar behavior of service recipient and service provider illustrate the problem with allowing doomerism to persist in our culture. It pushes the extreme perspectives in polemic arguments that become overly emotional. This intentionally distracts us and ruins our ability to communicate, cooperate, and collaborate. Emotional argumentation is not what democracy needs to moderate and unify. Such polemics divide us, allowing the few at the top to steal from us because redirected attentions miss the dirty tricks of isms' proponents.

In order for society to work effectively to achieve its objectives, citizens as both the customers and providers of governance, must mitigate these extremes. We must be responsible to participate knowingly, to lead our lives with the awareness that we both receive government and give it since we make up the staff of it. We are paying for it and electing those among us whom we trust to oversee it. Always, the objectives of the USE need kept in mind. We must use the enterprise for good. Always we must behave to support its achieving its objectives, which benefit us personally. Doing so will assist us unite as one people to align best against the threats we face and avoid negative consequences vulnerabilities cause and hazards present. In addition, we must work cooperatively to benefit from taking rational risks full of good opportunities the enterprise presents us through its strengths.

We the people are the shareholders of the enterprise. We have stake and agency in the fulfillment of its primary goal, a more perfect union, and in its contributing objectives that need managed in balance, without one demanding the powers skew to obtaining one in excess of the others. This balancing act is our responsibility as we regulate the powers of society and by good order and discipline keep them and ourselves in proper balance. This being said, what are the risks to the USE's success? Let's look at these in the context of a SERF, the steps to set up a risk profile for society that we the people can use to keep our eye on the powers and get them to serve liberty best for us.

We'll begin with a few questions. What are the hazards harbored in the way the baby boomers balanced our societal powers? What are the vulnerabilities to the USE attaining its objectives and achieving its goal? What is our threshold for allowing them to exist? What negative risks are we going to tolerate? Inversely, what opportunities opened up by the enterprise to achieve its objectives should we risk taking? What is our appetite to take and realize positive risks? How can the enterprise prevent negative consequences? How can it enable and encourage positive outcomes? We the people must be engaged in the discourse. We must discuss it with one another and tell our elected officials and economic elites what we need and want from them, our fellow citizens. We need to hold them accountable to act as constitutionally allied citizens for our commonwealth. For example, our increasingly computer algorithm controlled technology and interconnected information network-based society exposes us to hackers. How will we respond to this threat? This cybernetic society provides us with conveniences. How will we respond to this betterment? With all the uncertainty in the ever-increasing knowledge and crises of instability caused by circumstances of globalization, automation, and information overloading, we should press for greater dialogue by using our people power to shape society more than receive shaping by it. We need to know what our appetite for opportunity risks is, as well as our tolerance thresholds or aversion level for allowing vulnerabilities and hazards to persist with the many threatening risks to our USE. We must resist the ease of complacency. Are we lazy cows wanting fed? Do we want to wallow in our muddy cognition like happy sow, believing in only one side or the other of any dichotomous deliberation? We must negotiate the two dominant thrusts of philosophy since the first stage of knowledge creation, which led to a modern sensibility. We must get past the fight of these two diametric philosophical perspectives. We've fought over these since modern times began. Fraught paradigms extrapolated out into polemic isms, does us no good. We must refocus our comprehension on the American ideals. Did the boomers error in not understanding we needed rigorously to stay close to our first principles in thinking and teaching them? We must respect our original traditions of thought. The framers discerned how to provide liberty and opportunity. They led to our nation's founding. We cannot reject their history-shown wisdom, and fall for incompatible ideas. We must trust in their truth. We must forgive their errors and not reject their vision because of mistakes they knowingly made.

Modern humankind is as equally unwise as ancient humankind was. However, today's tools are more sophisticated. Because of this fact, we must be more cautious about what we think human nature is. We must manage the societal risks inherent in our social species. We must do it better than before if we are to succeed to get back on course toward our goal. We've more change to adapt to more quickly to keep together as a people in the most turbulent era of this third stage of knowledge creation. An era for which the boomer "me first" personality is ill suited. We need multigenerational civic engagement and political participation. We need a "we first" approach for national solvency and solidarity to better respond to the risks we face.

Change is inevitable due to the dynamic nature of life, but we must not become victims of the DAMN of the other primary societal powers, which causes us to fail to prevent negative events that hurt our society. These too, cause us not to enable positive events that will support our society's health and healthfulness for us as persons and as a people. We have a purpose. The responsibility to govern exists within us, the citizenry. We cannot be so disturbed by doomerism that we roll our eyes and walk away from our duty to preserve the union, demand the Constitution be upheld, and work on being better citizens. For society to get better, we, the everyday people, must civically engage and act as informed, politically minded participants who understand their agency and stake in leading the society. For society to be supportive of our personal purpose pursuits, we must act purposefully to support it. We need to lead society. This means we must own up to our better selves and demonstrate the discipline necessary to attend to it and manage its risks.

The SERF introduces us to standard thinking exercises for managing risks. As we think about risk, we should ponder the types our society might face. With all the uncertainties mattering to our liberty, the risks we face to achieving our objectives, we in the USE need transparent science in full view of everyone, without hidden agendas, ambitions, or manipulation and fraud. This means that persons, regardless of which of the societal, primary or human culture made social secondary or tertiary, powers we represent, must behave with integrity in a manner that evokes the best of democracy culture and American society. We must all daily, personally and socially, work toward the achievement of the enterprise's goal by the attainment of its objectives.

To do this, we must be conscious of ten types of risk categories:

1) <u>Planetary</u>—For example, asteroids, altered climes, or geological and weather-born hazards exist. Our planetary risks are global, and this involves diplomatic and trade risks. Global risks can be species survival risks, too, such as world war or changed habitability conditions. Here are some examples of planetary risks:

o   Opportunities for discovering new resources, new knowledge of planetary behaviors, or new technologies to help us exist without causing harm to earth. Uncovering new resources that give us better life possibilities, like medicines, to learn how to protect ourselves from other organisms and natural disasters.

o   Vulnerabilities to not adapting to destructive weather and not being able to survive famines, migrations, and pandemics.

2) <u>Political/Social/Societal</u>—For example, demagoguery that could destabilize economies exists. Persons, when engaging in political social behaviors (at home, at work, and in the marketplace at the micro, meso, and macro levels), regardless of which societal or social powers we represent, must behave with integrity in a manner that evokes the best of democracy culture and American society. We must all daily, personally and socially, work toward the achievement of the enterprise's goal through the attainment of its objectives. Our political and social risks are the most critical to perpetuation of our enterprise. They can cause failure in managing all other risks. Inversely, they can guide successes too. Here are some examples of these risks:

o   Opportunities to feel enfranchised, integrated as a member of the society, to be citizens contributing to the greater good, to avail us of 100% voter participation in all elections.

   ▪   Regular rotation of our elected officials to protect them as fellow citizens from the corrupting temptations of power, and a full commitment to citizen responsibilities to uphold and live by the Constitution daily.

   ▪   Chances such as forming new political visions, party platforms with younger perceptopostmodernistic civically minded candidates of incorruptible integrity with goals that comport with the need for the best LAMBS for the USE to be globally connected and competitive, and to cooperate in solving adaptive problems the human species faces that no one country can solve alone.

   ▪   Chances to invest in civic engagement to assist persons in anomic, enervating, and radicalizing conditions become more socially integrated in society, and try to eliminate these socialization contexts. The possibilities to make societal success probable for all citizens by increasing commitment to develop citizens with more than one social grammar and with sufficient social capital to sustain a strong and dynamic civil society.

o   Vulnerabilities that create disintegrated populations that result in lousy
    voter participation, persons feeling alienated from society, living in
    anomic conditions, leading to the formation of aggressive factions and
    demagoguery that threaten democracy and cause a full, absolute corrup-
    tion of our people and politicians, or the enterprise's FILMS[2] [P7] for the
    LAMBS dragging us into conflict, divisiveness, or wars.

    ▪ Path dependencies—doing things the way we've always done them
       because we've had success that way in the past. An example of this
       risk is the two-party political system.

    ▪ Political polarization rose as the number of baby boomers in posi-
       tions of authority increased. This is most evident in the federal gov-
       ernment. Partisan loyalty around an ideology to thwart the other
       party typifies baby boomer politics. It defines baby doomer politi-
       cians. Winning arguments became more important than governing.
       Governing requires cooperating, negotiating, and compromising to
       solve societal problems. Doomers fail at these three requirements.
       These are opportunity risks of government to help solve societal
       problems. Solutions can come via limited and unlimited govern-
       ment involvement. The polity can be supportive of societal problem
       solving. It can do it through reframing the FILMS[2] [P7], inspiring (in-
       centivizing of) or regulating (rulemaking for) the helpers, mer-
       chants, miners, makers, movers, and marketers (HM[5]), and support-
       ing knowledge aptitude, acquisition, absorption, application, and
       skills advancement abilities (KA[4]SA[2]).

    ▪ Conflicts over who can take part in political decision-making linger.
       Arguments over who belongs within the political community con-
       tinue. Schisms over place of origin and sexuality at birth exist. His-
       torical restrictions persist. Social movements for the right to vote
       transpired. Persons of shared place of origin, physical characteris-
       tics, and sex at birth earned membership. Gerrymandering and de-
       vious intimidation schemes restricted various citizens' access to the
       voting booths (recall Figures 2-18 to 2-20). The American ideal of
       equality persists. Over time, social policy for persons identified in
       groups upholds their rights. Discrimination and voter suppression is
       the unconstitutional opposite of the values of democracy.

    ▪ Excessive executive power accumulation in the polity staffed pri-
       marily by baby boomer politicians, presidential power increases. It is
       more than the Constitution enumerated. The executive government
       power grows beyond its framed intentions. In the economy, chief
       executive officers get massive compensation compared to the value
       they provide. This is particularly onerous when dismissed with ab-
       surd amounts of severance pay for someone who messed up.

    ▪ Enlarging economic inequality generates envy. If unexplainable or
       unjustifiable, it causes distrust. Unstable, volatile economic condi-

tions are threatening. Also so are falling and failing economic opportunities for the people. If no advancement is possible, it is demoralizing. If the economy power doesn't employ people gainfully, depression enters into persons and the people. We must provide jobs. To feel the blessings of liberty that comes from the positive experiences of earning a sense of purpose through work. Jobs that become careers contribute to our sense of self-worth and the ability to generate wealth. If upward mobility is not a workable option for the majority while a few get everything, rifts arise. Wealth accumulation only for those already privileged, while the majority decline, is risky. Increasing ranks of groups suffering dissipative economic chances is unhealthy, for them and for society. More persons sucked into and stuck with poverty, mounting illness and anomie is dangerous.

These four path dependencies of doomerism are express threats to democracy. For the first time in US history, all four (political polarization, conflict on whose a member of society, rising economic inequality, growth in executive power) are happening at the same time (Mettler & Lieberman, 2020). Either the time of the majority rule of the baby boomers is a correlation with this circumstance, or it is causal by spawning baby doomerism culture. These four threats have aligned against our foundational culture of democracy. We must respond with great urgency!

3) <u>Reputational</u>—The status, posture, and public perception of a society or the power that shapes it exist. Persons, when engaging in representative behaviors, regardless of which societal or social powers we represent, must behave with integrity in a manner that evokes the best of democracy culture and American society. We must all daily, personally and socially, work toward the achievement of the enterprise's goal through the attainment of its objectives. Reputational risks are diplomatic risks. Diplomatic risks are global risks. If we do not exhibit our values, we incur reputational damage. If we live by virtue and demonstrate our values, we gain reputational respect and advantages. Here are some examples of reputational risks:
o Opportunities to demonstrate the best in human relations, civic engagement, political participation, democracy at its best, and a republic magnificent in integrity and esteemed the world over for its exceptional citizenry and LAMBS.
o Vulnerabilities in its reputation and esteem due to terrible behavior by its citizenry and deplorable conditions for its populations due to corrupted DAMN of power in the enterprise's LAMBS.

4) <u>Strategic</u>—The thinking that drives choices at the societal level and in the top circles of the powers, and the attitudes and behaviors the persons in top positions within the societal powers' FILMS[2] [P7] perpetuate. Persons, when engaging in strategic thinking and persuading behaviors, regardless of which societal or social powers we represent, must behave with integrity in a manner that evokes the best of democracy culture and American society. We must all daily, personally and socially, work toward the achievement of our enterprise's goal and attainment of its objectives. Setting strategies for societal success is critical. Bad or no strategy leads to bad or no results in the direction of our purpose. Good strategy leads to good results. Many other risks are increased or decreased based on strategy. Risk-management strategy must be set and worked up toward with the effort required to attain an objective. Here are some examples of strategic risks:

o   Opportunities to establish priorities, make new policies, write new laws, remove wrongful laws, and correct erroneous laws' growth. Or chances to make new regulations to protect us from new harmful things, or to reduce regulations that restrict opportunities or constrain liberty. Possibilities to frame conversations on topics that benefit the citizenry and the LAMBS in a manner best for the perpetuation of the opportunity promise of the USE for those able and willing to work to improve their lives.

o   Vulnerabilities in our core LAMBS and threats that leave gaps that might cause short, mid, or long-term inability to attain our constitutional objectives on our way to reaching our goal.

5) <u>Operational/Performance/Functional</u>—Poorly done work in the social powers, particularly within the HM[5] of the economy power, weak actions by persons or components of the FILMS[2] [P7] in each of American society's three primary powers. Persons, when engaging in operations for functional attainment, regardless of which societal or social powers we represent, must behave with integrity in a manner that evokes the best of democracy culture and American society. These risks are particularly important inside the FILMS[2] [P7] and with the HM[5]. Low quality work increases hazards, amplifies vulnerabilities, and causes threats realization. Well-done work decreases negative risks and can increase positive opportunity risks. Critical to managing these risks is the treatment of the uncertainties of possible events, their variabilities, ambiguities or emergent unimaginable ones. Here are some examples of operational/performance/functional risks:

o   Opportunities to support organizing priorities in new ways to achieve innovations that may be necessary for adapting to problems that increased knowledge and new technologies bring to society.

o   Vulnerabilities in failed practices or standard procedures that are no longer valid due to technological change and poor LAMBS allowing the misbalancing DAMN of powers. Path dependencies, repeating failed behaviors and expecting differing results is another way to put what is colloquially known as a definition for insanity.

6) <u>Compliance</u>—Illegal and intentionally unethical behaviors are kept in check by rules. Compliance to rules is a risk. Following them creates opportunities for all to benefit from the common ground agreement, or platform, upon which free pursuits may take place. Breaking them seeds doubt as deception and fraud undermine the whole for everyone. Without an underwriting of trust, society crumbles, and a few aggressors steal or fight over control of it. Persons, when engaging in compliance behaviors, regardless of which societal or social powers we represent, must behave with integrity in a manner that evokes the best of democracy culture and American society. We must all daily, personally and socially, work toward the achievement of the enterprise's goal and attainment of its objectives. Dishonesty destroys the ability of society to self-regulate without the need of large oversight organizations. Here are some examples of compliance risks:

o   Opportunities to cooperate with the best ways of being, in compliance with moral virtues and laws to reduce the size and cost of government, and appropriate rulemaking to support the enterprise's LAMBS in the directions necessary to attain our objectives.
o   Vulnerabilities to make too many laws that convert common law into civil law, from innocent-until-proven-guilty into guilty-until-proven-innocent jurisprudence, and a large penal regulatory structure that reduces our freedoms. Or worse, we DAMN power to produce a law targeting one faction or another by a false proxy argument leading to that group always being unable to obey it.

7) <u>Comfort & Convenience</u>—The potentials to demoralize by spoiling to sloth and complacency, and the outcome of overcoming difficulty through innovation to save time at work, creating more leisure and freedom from labor constraints, so more can be done to improve the lot of humankind. These should not be intentionally restricted, but their pursuit needs managed so as to not imbalance powers and cause other risks becoming vulnerabilities that could mutate into potential hazards or severe threats. There are vulnerabilities hidden in too much comfort and convenience. Here are some examples of comfort and convenience risks:

o   Opportunities to invent and innovate to achieve materially better circumstances for survival and thriving livelihoods, to improve personal freedoms.
o   Vulnerabilities of comfort and luxury are the numbing of persons to the civic engagement and political participation needs of a democracy. Comfort and convenience can make a person complacent, lazy, or apathetic, which threatens the functioning of society to ensure all powers balance to equilibrium to provide capably their benefits to society. It

can also lead to callousness for the suffering of fellow citizens.

Other risks of this category are technical, industry, and artistry power-dependent aspects of society. These include our shared infrastructures, the physical components that make our technologies possible. Our federal government addresses these, plus the planetary and many political, social, and societal risks. Its Department of Homeland Security's (DHS) Federal Emergency Management Agency (FEMA) (US Department of Homeland Security, 2018) prepares plans. They refer to the critical infrastructure necessary for a human community's survival during a disaster as "Lifelines." These include:

- Safety & Security
- Food, Water, Shelter
- Health & Medical
- Energy (Power & Fuel)
- Communications
- Transportation
- Hazardous Materials Control

DHS developed a Risk-management Lexicon (Risk Steering Committee, 2008) and it maintains a National Response Framework (Security, 2019) for managing risks to our communities' lifelines through a National Incident Management System (Federal Emergency Management Agency, 2017). They provide these publications via DHS's websites. However, they do not address the kinds of risks to our liberty mentioned in this book. These are our responsibility as the citizenry and the leadership of American society.

8) <u>Financial</u>—The gaining and losing of money or its capitalization into assets that retain value in the minds of others willing to trade for them in markets exists. Persons engaging in financial behaviors, regardless of which societal or social powers we represent, must behave with integrity in a manner that evokes the best of democracy culture and American society. We must all daily, personally and socially, work toward the achievement of the enterprise's goal and attainment of its objectives. Paying as we go, borrowing, and investing all interconnect with other risks. We need to let the polity power administer and the economy power manage the business of society, so financial risks that damage the common good and general welfare are properly addressed. Borrowing to get opportunities is a good risk. Borrowing to make ends meet means something is off and needs correction expectedly and effectively. We must create opportunity and prevent vulnerability with sound money policies and practices. We need to not overvalue our assets, nor undervalue them, nor use them to leverage collaterally beyond their capacity. Figuratively, we must avoid the risks in foolishly milking out the cow in the here and now. If not, we get a moral and social problem. We must preserve respect for the rules that enable financial success

but protect the game from corruption by unethical cheaters unable to control personal greed. Baby doomers think they are intelligent when they outsmart others to get a bigger piece of the pie. Determining how to cheat without getting caught is energy spent in the long-term wrong direction, as the "law of the commons" shows. Over-depletion destroys the equilibrium in the system that enables prosperity's possibility. Only moral forces can counterbalance the antisocial tendency of hyper-competitiveness that leads to cheating. Morality is more intelligent because it stops disruptions from happening as a matter of course (Knight, 1921). It takes commitment to society over self to have healthy financial outcomes. Here are some examples of financial risks:

o   Opportunities to invest capital to grow businesses and increase the capacity of the economy power to provision society.
o   Opportunities to collect revenues fairly from all persons via numerous forms of taxes, reduce taxes, or find ways to fund necessary works from user fees.
o   Vulnerabilities of amassing too much debt that could cause threats to solvency by poor LAMBS, so funds are not available. We must mitigate overcommitments, unmet obligations, and poorly constructed budgets that lead to deficits and debt that bury our future generations' chances to prosper and remain free, to retain liberty as a core purpose of the USE.

9) Structural Alienation & Inequality—Social problems can cause challenges to our solvency to provision society. Persons engaging in power-exercising behaviors, regardless of which societal or social powers we represent, must behave with integrity in a manner that evokes the best of democracy culture and American society. In past civilizations, societies with severe inequality have had imbalances in powers that lead to brutality, criminality, and cruelty, to name a few behaviors that we should not tolerate in a democracy because they are affronts to everyone's liberty. Here are some examples of structural alienation and inequality risks:

o   Opportunities to stimulate persons to learn and work toward stretch goals in pursuit of betterment.
o   Vulnerabilities in structures of society that make such striving impossible, which threatens the society's stability by producing, promoting, or permitting the anomic, radicalizing, and/or enervating socialization contexts. These deplorable, impoverished, dangerous, and damaging contexts are not just bad for children; they repeat a cycle of sad social circumstances and physical conditions. The seemingly intractable poverty and ignorance that often accompany such sad depravity can lead to criminality, underworld markets of illicit substances, dependency, and if never resolved, a mobocracy.

10) <u>Fraud/Vandalism</u>—The dishonorable, dishonest, willful misrepresentation to obtain something for nothing, rationalized attitudes and criminal behavior to lie, cheat, and steal from another person or group, to pretend and amend rules for one stated purpose but actually done for the opposite. Frauds vandalize our enterprise. Persons engaging in compliance and auditing behaviors, regardless of which societal and social powers we represent, must behave with integrity in a manner that evokes the best of democracy culture and American society. These are the risks that most undermine the public trust and erode the value of democracy for every honest person. These risks lead to other risks amplification and potential realization, such as government expenses. Here are some examples of fraud and vandalism risks:

o   Opportunities to achieve a level of citizenship to prevent destruction of neighborhoods and communities through rule-abiding self-discipline and successful LAMBS, so honesty, integrity, and trust make fraud impossible and vandalism improbable, thus reducing the costs to society of cleaning up swindles and making repairs to damage caused by defrauding scams.

o   Vulnerabilities in persons' and groups' attitudes and behaviors that make fraud and vandalism appear permissible, as is the case with baby doomerism currents within our national community's culture. Size shapes markets as the majority makes value worth copycatting, even if criminal. People seek to belong to the mainstream of what others all seem to be doing.

Seven Step Risk-Management Process

Having listed these types of risks in the LAMBS for our USE, what is the process to manage them? We must follow these seven steps:

1) **Identify** the risks to American society, both the vulnerabilities and opportunities. We must remind ourselves of what we've learned from history and what we might imagine in the future—the uncertainties that matter to us, the risks, internal and external, positive and negative, that we face as one people. The USE is trying to be a more perfect union, with justice, domestic tranquility, a defense for the nation, and a limited federal government whose powers allow tax collection to support all states evenly within its delegated authority to promote the general welfare (the common good) and secure the blessings of liberty for current and future generations. We must know what matters, identify those uncertainties to us achieving our goal and attaining its objectives, and call them the risks we must address as the people.

2) **Assess** the risks we identify that could affect our reaching our goal and fulfilling our objectives. We do this with both qualitative and quantitative methods to figure out their likelihood of occurring, probability, and

their potential impact, severity, and then prioritize the risks that matter the most.

3) **Determine** our responses to the risks. We need to determine which risks we will accept, mitigate and manage, avoid, and transfer.

4) **Set up controls** we'll use to monitor the risks and periodically reassess as circumstances unfold and risky events either happen or do not happen, and evaluate how our planned responses perform. We can determine if our responses are adequate or if they need to be changed.

5) Determine **reporting** of the risks. We'll want to know the status of the risks as circumstances unfold, and we get closer to events that might cause a need to respond. We'll want to know to whom, when, and how to report what we observe happening. Who'll need to know depends on the scope and scale of the risk. Some things need reported locally and others regionally and nationally. We the everyday people will want the politicians and elites, their HM[5] and all societal and social powers' FILMS[2] [P7], to tell us if risks must be responded to, such as is done with industrial disasters by the history-as-it-happens journalism powers.

6) As we continue to wonder what could go wrong and what could go better, we should periodically **revisit** the SERF and verify we've the right tolerance and appetite for risks in place. This is our risk profile. We may want to be high-risk takers, or risk-averse, or no-risk takers. High positive risk is sending a man to the moon. No risk-taking is practically impossible, but low risk taking is always sitting in our houses, afraid to go out. Both super high risk and no risk postures are extremes that are unlikely to be agreeable to a majority, except in times of intense awakening or crises or when we are confronted with radically new knowledge inspiring disruptive, radical innovations to which we must respond. Using the SERF will help us be ready to revise our risk-management approach. High positive risk-taking and negative risk aversion are common postures. High negative risk-taking and no positive risk-taking are less reasonable postures.

7) We'll need to **revise** repeatedly our management of the risks to our society, especially when the powers are not supporting the accomplishment of our goal and its objectives. We do it in the same manner as we did at step one above. Risks are perpetual because uncertainty is continual. That which does not matter to us as a people must not distract us from leading society toward our goal and objectives. We must remain focused on these because this is what a culture of democracy does. This is how we IDEALS liberty.

We must apply these steps in two arenas of calculus, metaphorically, one inside and one outside our American house. One is for the purpose of internal affairs (inside our house). Relationships within our country need risk attention to "insure domestic tranquility" and "promote the general welfare". These affect multiple categories (government, society, culture, politics, and economics). The second is for the purpose of external affairs (outside our house). Relationships with foreign countries need risk attention to "provide for the common defense". These affect multiple categories: existential (ecosystem inhabitation), economic (commercial trade with foreign goods and services makers, providers, and sellers), and political (by other nation states' espionage, invasions, and incursions upon allies or international partners with whom treaties fix common interests and relationship behaviors). Thus, we must manage two categories: domestic and foreign. Management must be coordinated so that one is not creating risks in the other.

Framework Applied to American Society

To protect democracy using this SERF, we can be ready to IDEALS liberty back to the hearts and minds of people. We must IDEALS it. It is ideal for us to make it real, so we feel it coursing through our marrow. We can reinvigorate our constitutionally ordained and established culture of democracy. We must, so our republic, through every future awakening and crisis we might confront, survives with liberty at its core. The enterprise we have inherited is "our" business of society to lead. We the everyday people need to get busy to become better at this business, or we will lose the enterprise to a few manipulators. But we first have to stop doomerism from taking over. We must remember that we the everyday people are the ultimate stakeholders, the shareholders in American society. We cannot allow the borrowing by politicians against our resources to continue while a handful of profiteers, using knowledge and technology that we funded, take all the profits. The profits must be shared with us. We funded the infrastructure and research that made it possible for the economy power to be so successful. The remuneration of our investments back to us is broken. We are the executives. We must demonstrate and demand the rightful high standards of behavior expected of real executives with integrity and virtuous character we want our children to emulate. We the people must not cop out of this responsibility. We can do it. We can live up to it. We can support and assist one another with love's accountability and honor's responsibility. It is purposeful. It has meaning. It is belief in democracy. It is what a citizen is and does.

Being better citizens is a part of it, but knowing the risks our enterprise faces is critical for the direction of our united energies to IDEALS our mutually benefiting, inalienable rights to liberty. In an effort to prepare us to protect our liberty and manage the risks (both the benefits of opportunities and disablements of threats) within our enterprise, let us approach self-governing from a risk-management perspective. To rebalance the powers in our society, let us use the SERF to think through the risks. The point of the SERF is to set up a monitoring, regulating, power-controlling means for the people, to say, "Don't tread on me!" and be ready to prevent trampling upon us that aims to make us to feel as if useless serfs.

Just seven steps, the SERF is a means to enact the probable opportunities (to defend) and a method to evaluate and control for disabling potential threats (to protect) our liberty. We must adopt risk responses to inspect and correctly reverse the dangers (to rectify) our democracy. We need to learn to recognize and discuss in greater numbers of citizens these risk-management steps. Those in positions of authority seem unable to meet the moment we now face in our third stage of knowledge evolution. We've lingering risks from old ideas of the economy power and poor advice of the polity power. Too many in office are, sorry to say, old with old ideas, outmoded for the challenges we now face. Out-of-date thinking has created open sores. It widens gaps. Such vulnerabilities and hazards in our democracy are risky. They test the enterprise's solvency and possibilities.

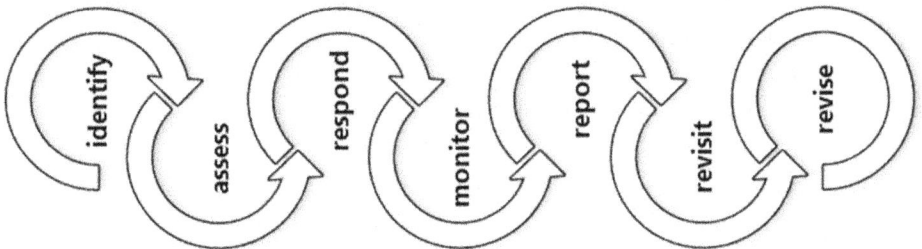

Figure 4-4: SERF Chain to IDEALS Liberty

Doomerism clings to the way things were and does not look ahead to what is coming. This generational situation harbors very significant risks for us as we poorly adjust to the turbulence we're confronting with the new technologies' rapid alterations to American society. To IDEALS liberty, we must not miss any options because we are holding on to old ideas like invalid isms that do not help us. Yet, we must restore the ideals, the wisdom that led to our Constitution. We confront wholly new risks. At this moment in 2021, we must begin to apply the SERF to the USE to get better LAMBS. Let's continue with the seven steps of risk-management of the SERF by looking at risks to our constitutional goal and objectives.

1) Identifying risks

Harbored in the basic stated goal and objectives of the enterprise of the United States, a republic polity in which we engage in the business of society, are risks of significant uncertainty. Let's imagine and remind ourselves of some of the risks that lurk and linger within our society, frustrating our attempts to achieve our goal, a more perfect union, and attain our objectives. Doomerism has brought new risks into our society, and we see them now more clearly than ever. They are risks to our objectives, which are to:

o   **Establish justice**. We need everyone treated equally, regardless of any
       of their physical features. We have the opportunity to live up to the best
       nature of our humanness. The vulnerability is to fracture into factions
       based on superficial characteristics, unprovable ideologies, or mythical
       dogmas that result in hatred, inequality, and group identity politics in
       lieu of personal character as the bases of knowing one another. We
       need to resist holding preferences for kinds of persons we can superfi-
       cially label, see each other as unique Americans, celebrate the variety,
       and unite in common purpose, liberty. Equally important is we must
       become committed to finding out the truth, to factuality, not fantasy.
       We must demand facts not fictions, regardless of how much we want to
       be on a winning team. In the face of facts that disagree with our desired
       beliefs, we must behave securely within ourselves. Ego insecurity is a
       risky posture. Factualness is how we make justice feasible.

o   **Insure domestic tranquility**. Not all people in all locales, across all
       settlements (urban, suburban, and rural) and regions, get along swim-
       mingly in the gumbo pot of our social milieu. This is human. People
       differ. Making the differences an excuse to dislike one another is neither
       helpful nor healthful. It's an aphorism of truth that hatred eats a hole in
       the hater's soul. The opportunity to learn of one another better, to in-
       vest in understanding and develop conscientiousness, and then apply
       compassion, love, and empathy to seek unity is what we must do as a
       citizenry. The vulnerability to become instinctively apish and fight over
       irrelevant differences related to liberty is foolish. Tyrants like to incite
       such division while seeking to destroy any chance for the people to
       govern and instead take all freedoms away and concentrate power at the
       top. There is no domestic tranquility in division. Division is the weapon
       of demagoguery. Demagoguery destroys democracy. It is a quality prac-
       ticed and propagated by baby doomers. We must reverse the negativity
       toward domestic tranquility caused by doomerism. The trends in dimin-
       ishing volunteerism, low involvement in politics, and the loss of civic
       associations damage society. Such declines in civic engagement bode ill
       for our democracy. We need more acts and traits of good civic charac-
       ter that create the possibility of self-government from us, the citizenry.
       Our civic health is poor (The National Commission on Civic Renewal,
       1997). If people don't get to know one another, a downward spiral of
       distrust ensues, which further erodes trust. Trusting one another as fel-
       low citizens who have one another's best interests at heart is essential
       for domestic tranquility. Our calling is to get more involved in politics
       to thwart the demagogues who seek to make it so ugly we good people
       will stay away. We must not let them. This is the game. They are playing
       it against us—to fool us to stay away and let them have it all. We cannot
       shy away from the battle ahead, which is a war for the right to self-

govern!

○ **Provide for the common defense**. We must generate sufficient revenue to be able to protect ourselves, and we must ensure the professionalism and civil control of the military. We need a highly competent and active diplomatic corps to make friends and prevent the development of adversarial relations. Trade is a vital way to integrate and develop healthy relations, but in cases where we feel that others are not suited to be our friends because of the way they treat their people, we need to find ways to influence them to be less problematic to their people and the world community. The opportunity to support world peace and global commerce depends on sovereign nations feeling safe from predators and pirates. The vulnerabilities of becoming too dependent on war to solve problems only make future generations find war acceptable and give the vanquished an excuse to hate and rage against the victors. Whether it is legitimate or not, if they feel humiliated, they will seek vengeance, violently. We risk becoming too powerful, arrogant, and conceited, overstretching and exhausting our resources. The US did not constitute to be an imperial nation. Not intending empire, but by luck of geography, and our pluck throughout history, we became one, accidentally. We must address this as a risk, now. We behave wrongly to our intents, our Declaration and our Constitution when we act like one. The common defense is not a policing function of the entire world. If we want to sell the service of security, let us be reimbursed for it by those who benefit from our military might. We cannot afford to give it away freely. We are bankrupting ourselves. Freedom is not free, so security needs financially reimbursed. This is merely a pragmatic reality.

○ **Promote the general welfare**. We must realize that our governments are veritable clearinghouses of great information, and we must read what they produce and fund for production. We paid for much of the knowledge we have gotten. Our governments grant funds to scientific institutions to conduct explorations into the unknown. Research and development done by private sector organizations with funding from businesses' profits declined significantly so the government stepped in to keep our country competitive as foreign powers raced to recover from WWII and outpace us to gain marketplace dominance, which we held. The boomers wanted faster and greater profit, and lower risks to it. Their econometric accountants formulated measures of return that dissuaded investing in discovery. Their lawyers risk aversion advised them to shy away from it, too. The great engineering advantages of the US firms dwindled thanks to a shift in values (Hage, 2011), correlating to boomer' dominance.

Entrepreneurial leanings and learning by doomerism became excuses to leverage for the prevention of loss. Not to continuously seek to learn is to set ourselves up for tyranny. Not to trust the scientists and civil servants who prepare reports of facts is foolish. In addition, we must care for fellow neighbors and ourselves in our communities. We cannot fare well if we lose a sincere sense of belonging in our communities. When we commit to act in ways that support our community, we associate with one another. This association helps us solve local problems together and accomplish our goal and objectives. It builds "social capital" and empowers civil society to solve our problems "with" us. This is quintessentially American. It disabuses us of the notion that someone else should do things "for" us. Such thinking as this is "rent-seeking" entitlement talk.

Local community groups and civic associations offer opportunities for every citizen to feel good because they can support the common good. If we lose the ability to associate and participate in this way, the social capital of our people power is lost. The power of our social networks, which uplift us in feeling good about our lives as productive members of the community, is vital to our way of life. The American way builds upon groups associating to get things done. We used to take great pride in serving alongside others to improve our neighborhoods, communities, and society through voluntary association. Our privately funded community efforts built houses for learning, worship, and play. In raising funds and creating assets to share with one another, we built community itself. Such civic engagement to make a difference nourished the well-being of not only the beneficiaries but also the doers in the citizenry who made things happen for others (Westhues, 1982). We do best as a society when we help each other out and work together.

Free association for a purpose greater than selfishness was beneficial to everyone's self. It was more in our self-interest to bond closely with neighbors than to ignore them. Working with community groups uplifts our hearts and minds. It develops mutual respect that helps us connect with and create special places where different people interact easily. This releases us to share ideas in open forums where we can discuss and debate with skills vital to sustain and reify the culture of democracy. We learn skills such as running meetings, speaking out politely in public, or writing petitions and letters to officials to encourage or grieve a policy. The opportunity to have the best knowledge and sense of strong bonds with each other is good, healthy, joyful living. The vulnerability is in expecting others to take care of us, to allow lazy complacency and irresponsibility, to permit a kind of complaining victimhood and entitlement sensibility to persist as normal, acceptable, or at worst, laudable. Oe'r the land of the free and the home of the brave, we cannot allow such doomerism that pervades our urge for freedom and independence to take root, and which rots out our courage. Such would make us apathetic, which would place us back into the bondage of tyranny. Recall the cycle of democracy, (see Figure 2-14 through Figure 2-22).

○ **Secure the blessings of liberty to ourselves and our posterity.** We need to reverse the negative trends doomerism has caused. Three of these trends are the decline in engagement with neighbors and community-centered activities, the use of racism by politicians to incite suspicions and concepts of superiority that result in the restriction of others' liberty because they appear to be different, and the decreasing degree of civic engagement and political participation. Most troubling is low and diminishing levels of voting among us, particularly in our younger generations.

The danger is that our collective loss of association creates problems both for our society and for our democracy. We see these as risks to the realization of our Constitution's ideals. Doomerism causes the loss of a belief in everyone that all persons must be treated equally with dignity, and that we as a people are a work in progress to which we must be committed to achieve our goal and attain our objectives sooner rather than later. At this point, we are ready. We've reared children accordingly. We must not allow a backsliding into ethnic hatreds, into prejudice driven by the fear of a loss of something that does not have a natural right to exist since all humans are created equal; not the same, but by nature, equal in liberty to be free. Moreover, if democracy is at risk, so is our republic in the quality of its representation of the people's communities.

The republic needs to roll backward from the overreaching of the federal-level polity. We ought not to expect the federal government to solve all our problems. We should prevent it from disadvantaging one state over another. States that receive the most aid from the federal government, who don't pay for it proportionally with the taxes they give, need to pick up the slack and not speak with forked tongues that claim one thing while doing another. We must be mindful when regional subcultures reject federal rules, and if they are not overreaching rules, hold them accountable by removing from them the gifts of the people passed to them by the federal government. Shame is on the fools who benefit from our money. Taxes funnel through the federal government to the states to aid those in need. Any among the recipients who do not recognize this, live out of touch with fiscal reality. Such disconnectedness is a danger. The risk of conspiratorial lies rises. Radicalized "true believers" of false narratives become threats to civility. If they interfere in the government's work by attacking it vociferously, we bear witness to the realization of such risks. Both the ignorance of what the country does for one in need, and the innocence in believing in hypocrisy are risks. When recipients of aid are not aware of this irony, we see the stupidity that bites the hand that feeds. When recipients believe the power grabbers' big lies, we see threats harboring a demise of democracy. We can best address these risks through local associations of civil society helping those in need. The largesse of a federal government makes it too remote. Such psychological distance turns it into something that is wrong or so big as to be a seeming leviathan, endless and demanded for help. To avoid money moving machinations in the Capitol requires an intelligent citizenry. It requires states to seek self-sufficiency. We won't get there with baby doomers in charge. Neither do we get the beneficial levels of compassion and civic engagement. As long as they control the attitudes of the populace, we ride out the risks without any rationally planned responses; headed on our way to doom. A distrusted yet depended upon big brother government in a brave new world, remands society to earlier feudal forms of social control that enrich a few and punish the many for having been born by disallowing them the blessings of liberty.

We must not allow politicians to serve themselves before their constituents or use the power of the polity in ways unintended. We must remove those who DAMN our societal powers. We need to prevent our politicians from rationalizing a corrupt system that allows them to succumb to bribery and behave wrongfully, unchecked by the citizenry. We the people must do better leadership by rotating our fellow citizens who do the difficult work of governing. With compassion for others we must build new coalitions and enforce our right to govern, breaking down the duopoly made worse by forty years of adult boomers in positions of authority. It is kindness to remove mistake makers. More of us must volunteer to serve in office. Those who've served too long need to resign or retire from office. If for no other reason it would save us from their moral errors and remove us from the tempting lust for power, which causes harm. Enjoying power like pleasure stops office holders from upholding the Constitution and striving to protect liberty. They and we, and our fellow citizens in the management roles of the economy, must not allow FILMS[2] [P7] failures in ethics. In addition as citizens, we need to trust officials with the social responsibilities of the public interest, the common good, and the general welfare responsibilities of our Constitution. We've been negligent by succumbing to doomerism. We caused it by our poor citizenshipping, by our failure to be responsible as citizens first, to refresh repeatedly and regularly our representatives in our government. We must turn with the winds of change and embrace a new world order for the ages, which pleased providence when we undertook this project. We must begin to behave as it requires by exhibiting service above selfishness, saying yes to the utmost full-fledged thoroughgoing constitutionally allied united citizenshipping understandingly synchronized (E-SASSY-T-TUF-FT-CAUCUS). We have the opportunity to build an open and honest society of a free citizenry, appreciative of our liberty, contributing to elevate and IDEALS it for our posterity and ourselves.

What other risks do we face?

Well that's a whole lot on the risks of the objectives listed in the Preamble. Let's continue identifying other risks we face. Key among many is the risk of us not committing to pursue the goal of our project. As a citizenry going forward, we need to dedicate serious and significant effort in our lifetime to achieve the goal and attain the objectives of the Constitution. It is 2021. We need, finally, to seal the deal. The contract is long overdue. We've lost time due to the baby doomers' negligence to attend to it. We need to accelerate our schedule to recuperate from the damage of their remissness. They took their eyes off the ball, seduced by the next shiny object that made them feel all warm and fuzzy inside in their insular, ego-stroking, self-centered neediness. Instead, we must attend to the needs of the Constitution, its goal and objectives. To meet these, we must be aware of the negative and positive risks.

On the positive side, we've opportunities to make amendments that correct gaps in its content or clarity. In the future, we could add or remove laws to clarify its intents to refrain from constraining liberty. Future interpretations by the judiciary might accurately support liberty. It is easy to misconstrue by malfeasant desires counter to the culture of democracy and liberty of all citizens or by accidental incompetent or negligent readings of it.

On the negative side, we've vulnerability in having forgotten what liberty means and confusing it with a wild and crazy freedom to be lawless. The blessings of liberty are not anarchy, mobocracy, aristocracy, or plutocracy. These are misunderstandings. Every person in the USE needs to recognize the truth of citizenship from an American civics education (ACE) and put the duty of citizenship in our hearts and minds as vital to all our successes, our total general welfare and common good, with this as our purpose. First, we must act as citizens. Then, the polity and economy powers will make prosperity, justice, and liberty realizable. Sadly, we are under the spell of the bad sign of doomerism. It is the cause of the confusion of culture. It is pushing democracy out of our society. It is replacing our society's primary powers, the people, economy, and polity. This confusion is causing corruption in all three. The chaos and crises we experience are the result of this spell. It's the sign of the times. Negative risks are on the rise, threatening American society and undermining the Constitution.

The Constitution and the culture it intended to spawn becomes corrupted when citizens don't willingly abide by it and act lawlessly, which raises the cost of government and impacts everyone. The economy of inequality does not rationally recognize the contributions of citizens to making the goods and services necessary to sustain the high quality of life made possible by the everyday people. We get a classism that is unsustainable and politically problematic when a few fleece from the majority. Worse, when citizens abuse or misuse the Constitution by not settling differences civilly but rather taxing the legal system with mountains of litigation that overwhelm and bog it down, they raise the cost of government. This is foolishness. It affects everyone. Why should all of us pay for these games? A litigate subculture is not healthy. This, too, creates a kind of classism between those who win and those who lose, between David-scale clients' lawyers looking to get rich quick off Goliath-scale clients' lawyers. Inversely, giants run public relations advertising campaigns to confuse the people and prevent them from filing legitimate claims.

Further, if these risks shred the social fabric woven by the Constitution, we may find fewer citizens willing to defend and uphold it. Corrupted beliefs in it lead to corrupted behaviors against it, without thought of the risks of enormous negative consequences that result. We might see this in a loss of the military, which depends on oaths to defend it. If misunderstood, or politicians are corrupt, feeding the elites and starving the people, who legitimately will want to defend it? Honorable citizens will not serve, only the downtrodden that would like a leg up but may seek to change it in unhealthy ways. For example, gangs are now operating within its ranks. This is part of the downward spiral of decline and decay. When we lose the possibility of fielding honest politicians, we'll become a bogus republic of pacified masses satiated by handouts and suffering diminished opportunities, while a plutocracy rises to power. The corrupt ones will claim it is a dirty business, and the honorable will avoid it. This is not right. Only the light can cast out the darkness, and the honorable must take back the polity for the people. If not, and if people look for excuses to be corrupt, they will elect people who reflect themselves. This is a shame. If we lose an honest citizenry, we will also lose trust among us, a sense of community, and respect for one another. In economic inequality, strife will ignite factions. In blight ethnic identity tribes will form, blame one another, designating each other as enemies, then war, violently. This is not as our ideals portend. We need to believe in the ideals, we need to make them real, or they will die, and we will have failed. But there is a chance to restore the pursuit of virtue. It resides within the words of our founding documents. People, the Constitution needs us. It needs us to engage in politics, so it does not become worthless, and liberty forgotten. We must understand democracy. We must be citizens of it. Not to do so is to abandon all hope for liberty, which is to become subjects of a ruler, of the rule of man and not the rule of law.

When politicians don't abide by the Constitution, we get unethical scandals and a loss of public trust in the institutions of the polity, which further causes a loss of a sense of community and a loss in the continuity in governance and successful governmental operations. Failures caused by repeated disruptions through removals, vacancies, and malfeasance. The wrongful seek to overwhelm the FILMS[2] [P7] in the hopes of proving them wasteful, so they may replace them with their own rules and puppets. This is a tactic of fraudulent and abusive tyranny: confuse, claim failure, place the blame on the system, and then overturn it. What do you suppose Hitler and Lenin did to take over their nations' societies? Like them, the DAMN of the polity power is a most corrosive toxin to our culture of democracy that depends upon honor and integrity. These essential traits of good character begin with our willpower to uphold the Constitution in every way, every day, by everybody in every place, post, and position of authority within all the societal and social powers. We absolutely must do better as a citizenry and as citizens, or we will lose our liberty, or freedom, our democracy, absolutely.

We engage and participate to govern!

Of all the above-cited risks, the greatest is the loss of involvement in the people power through civic engagement and political participation. The powers that enable our USE need strong organizations and institutions. These instruments of people power weaken under doomerism's wrath because it causes vulnerabilities in persons. By permitting criminality to practice fraud, complacency in civic associating, and apathy in political participation, doomerism exposes us to serious hazard-creating mistakes, of which we should be very leery. If we don't get involved in civil associations and participate vigorously in politics, the process by which we regulate the powers of society, then we the everyday people will lose our power during the balancing act of the LAMBS for our USE as the DAMN of powers increases to defeat liberty and then us as a people. We must engage! We must demand the politicians and elites, the executors of the positions of authority at the top, AEIOUY^{2}K their powers properly for the USE.

John Dewey, an American philosopher using academy power, wrote "Democracy is more than a form of government; it is primarily a mode of associated living, of conjoint communicated experience" (Dewey, 1922). Associating with one another as citizens, as stakeholders in our USE, builds community among us, and we can use community powers to build our social capital to influence and persuade the USE to better balance the powers for us to achieve our goal and attain our objectives. Social capital improves cooperation. Cooperation is foundational behavior to continue a culture of democracy, run a republic, and best AEIOUY^{2}K powers to IDEALS liberty. A loss in social capital is a risk in our society. Robert D. Putnam, a professor of political science using academy power wrote, "The performance of our democratic institutions depends in measurable ways upon social capital." His research found that high levels of social capital generated supportive environments for democracy, while those with less social capital did not, and that states with high levels of social capital developed more innovative public policies. He wrote, "Politics in these states is more issue oriented, focused on social and educational services, and apparently less corrupt" (Putnam, 1993). His studies suggest, "States high in social capital sustain governments that are more effective and innovative." The American Political Science Association summarized the risks of low social capital as follows: "current levels of political knowledge, political engagement, and political enthusiasm are so low as to threaten the vitality and stability of democratic politics in the United States" (Task Force on Political Science in the 21st Century, 2011). Social capital locally accumulates in networks that improve trustworthiness of others through association. It is often easiest to build it around a common pursuit or purpose (Putnam, Feldstein, & Cohen, 2003). A blessing of liberty is to freely associate. To protect this, we need to build social capital to respond to the risk of doomerism that threatens unity and willingness to socialize with physically, socially, sub-culturally, and economically different others. Increasing our social capital through civic engagement will prepare us for the adversity we will face because of the difficulties doomerism is causing our American society. Democracy depends upon our civic engagement. Doomerism drives civic disengagement so its perpetrators think they can avoid all social responsibility. Since 1984, academic reports indicate sobering declines in civic engagement. TV raised boomers became spectators, which weakens us by eroding moral truths shared through social associations (Davenport & Skandera, 2003). A disengaged public is a vulnerability that exposes democracy to the dangerous threat of tyranny. It is as if the boomers embraced narcissism made the future hopeless and the past irrelevant as they sought to escape and "get in touch with themselves" (Lasch, 1979), and possibly only this. The narcissism has spread as wide as the boomer generation is large. It has reached epic epidemic proportions and appears everywhere in society (Twenge & Campbell, 2009), and at micro, meso, and macro levels. We can reverse this. We can remedy it. We have no choice if we are to remain a democracy-based culture but to get involved civically with our neighbors. To be clear, here's what civic engagement means:

> *Civic engagement means working to make a difference in the civic life of our communities and developing the combination of knowledge, skills, values and motivation to make that difference. It means promoting the quality of life in a community, through both political and non-political processes....A morally and civically responsible individual recognizes himself or herself as a member of a larger social fabric and therefore considers social problems to be at least partly his or her own; such an individual is willing to see the moral and civic dimensions of issues, to make and justify informed moral and civic judgments, and to take action when appropriate.* (Ehrlich, 2000).

Through civic engagement, people building social capital to best AEIOUY^{2}K community powers is critical for the preservation and vitality of democracy in the USE. Founder Benjamin Franklin recognized this vulnerability, this fragility in representative democracy, when upon the conclusion of the 1787 Constitutional Convention, when asked by a lady what sort of government the delegates created, he said "A republic, if you can keep it" (Farrand, 1911).

We need good rules

Another risk to the Constitution worth mentioning is elites of the economy ignoring its laws. This happens when the HM^5 exchange illegal items in hidden markets. All forms of criminality disrespect it and create communities with subcultures ignorant of it and behaviors contrary to obeisance of its principles. Illegality happens. If rewarded, we've serious problems. If we cannot trust those in positions of power, we've serious problems. If the economy power elites seek to gain control of the society to serve their interests, we might see bribery on the rise. With bribes given politicians to misuse the polity power to make laws that make it easier for corruption of the FILMS^2 [P7] of polity and economy powers to enrich exceedingly only the politicians and the elites of the owners of the businesses of the HM^5, the USE converts into a plutocracy. This makes life miserable for the commoners as if commoners are burdensome and filthy serfs needing punishment for dirtiness.

Too many laws that restrict freedom are not good. Such conditions people to first seek to ask permission, or be told what to do, then second to request to be taken care of, and morally, psychologically, socially, economically, and politically controlled. Encouraging people not to lead lives guided by their own free will and wits, but be willing dependents, wards of the state, freeloading on the backs of others who pay taxes taken from their wages and salaries, is un-American. Too many laws create innumerable restrictions that are entanglingly confusing. It creates a need for lawyers to interpret all the rules and limits freedom of natural rights to be lived without fear. It further makes society overly complex in bureaucracy, which limits opportunities to take risks to innovate and adapt to change. Having too many laws is a civil law construct, while having fewer laws is a common law construct. The former puts everyone in fear of going to jail for some ridiculous unknowable violation of some obscure frivolous law written to benefit a minority faction like a protected guild or a person seeking power over others. The latter is better for liberty. We need the polity not to seek to write more laws but to refine and improve existing laws, while eliminating foolish ones that do not serve to secure our liberty. They need not pile on more but cull through and better a key few. Perhaps we need fewer lawyers, who have a tool kit of ambition and ability to write laws, to work in our polity. Instead, let's get more doers to enter politics who can use sound judgment untampered by legal prejudice.

A people, if overly controlled by laws that are made to shape society by social engineering behaviors—to give politicians more power or relieve economy elites from responsibilities to society—and persons experiencing a culture that allows bribery and crookedness, have little power to reverse such a change as doomerism causes in the societal powers. This risk is realizing itself as doomers misbalance the powers in these liberty-decreasing directions of democracy dissolution. Unfortunately, in a society controlled overtly politically, with disproportionately demanding obedience to too many laws, liberty dies. If people behave as citizens first at the micro, meso, and macro levels, most laws are unnecessary. In such a society, the police of the polity will not need to be overused unfairly to enforce loyalty. With doomerism, multiplying rules will become an excuse to exert control over people as the police so choose. Police, in feeling overly important, protected by a polity that betrays the people, become abusive. Particularly at risk of unjust pushing around and unlawful punishment from pressurized policing are vulnerable populations in settlement patterns of social circumstances and physical conditions of poverty. Many in these situations psychologically suffer from a depressing anomie. Whole neighborhoods find themselves in such anomic conditions. Associations of kindness and therapeutic help would better serve the impoverished. The trauma of being down and out and getting bossed around to conform to standards without having jobs to survive is cruel. Failures of personal choice and neighborhood solvency need addressed; not ignored. Too many people get duped when abandoned by opportunity providers, who no longer serve society but take for themselves. Unfairly, blame dumps on the forgotten in situations that are not entirely their own fault. This is wrong. It must stop! We have the power to reverse it.

The running away from society by too many baby boomers is a terrible shame. It will be a stain on the generation, and upon each one's soul, unless they change. Perhaps they will when they realize it, and discover how to be conscientious with a conscience to care for fellow citizens. Of course, this is only possible if they are not psychopaths, or sociopaths. Nevertheless, if they are, there are treatments for them. For both the baby doomers and the destitute, there are possibilities to escape their impoverishments, morally and physically. The help for them comes from the three primary powers uniting to do something for these citizens, enabling other powers to be respectfully involved to reverse the cruelty of the cycle of poverty. No one-size-fits-all, top-down approach will be successful, but investments into building back community from the families up can be triumphant.

Anomic communities suffering scarcity and desperation don't need punishment; they need uplifting, life skills, and help to find a way to take care of one another through neighborly citizenshipping. Politicians can frame the situations and seek to assist the economy powers' willingness to be citizenly and figure out how they might invest in neighborhoods that need it the most, with appropriate community powers to coach and mentor people on how to find a way forward out of trauma, away from drama, and upward into security and self-esteem. If the politicians shape a culture that uses policing for population control, and not for encouraging and teaching civility to the disenfranchised in anomic circumstances, the Constitution is at risk of being disrespected and ignored. Politicians ought to encourage the people seeking to employ community powers to help the lost and lonely, the hopeless and stoned, figure out how to lift up, survive, and find a way to be contributory citizens. We ought not to abandon them. Sadly, the polity staffed by baby doomers suffers from entitlement comfort caused complacency, and some cowardice. They fell into too many ethical failures, feeling before thinking, and found themselves in too many scandals; then argued they'd done nothing wrong.

Exposed opprobrium produces a loss of the public trust and abates a sense of national community. Scandals cause a flurry of news reporting that drowns out the real issues the people must engage with to solve. Misconduct causes a loss of respect in the society by giving example at the top of poor attitudes and bad behaviors. Sadly, due to human nature, the balance of people who see the powerful people get away with it follow along as if it is how one is expected to think and behave, as selfish corrupted persons. Plop, plop, fizz, fizz, oh what a disease it is: baby doomerism. What a pitifully poor example politicians portray, which others sadly will follow. Even more sadly, some of them get reelected by an inattentive, complacently apathetic and ignorant of their own real economic self-interests public or by those who see themselves in the politicians and have so lowered their personal standards as to accept, or worse demand, it as the public standard they want exhibited by their representatives. This is a risk of doomerism. It is the beginning of the end of democracy. It is wrong. We must stop it. Dishonesty destroys democracy. We the everyday people must elevate our private and public standards, demand accountability, and insist on responsible attitudes and behaviors from ourselves and from those who create the vulnerabilities that result from the DAMN of the polity and economy powers. We must not DAMN our people power any longer. We must disavow our society of doomerism. We must evict the baby doomers from offices of authority. It is our only hope. Once removed, we must help them reprogram themselves to contribute to the realization of constitutional living.

2) Assessing risks

So, having gone on identifying the risks in doomerism as a bad substitute culture for democracy, what again are our constitutionally planned objectives? How do we analyze the identified risks to achieving them? Our project's goal stated in the Preamble is to form a more perfect union. We do this through attaining the objectives of:

- Establishing justice,
- Insuring domestic tranquility,
- Securing liberty,
- Providing for the common defense,
- Promoting the general welfare, and
- Securing the blessings of liberty to ourselves and to our posterity

For the next generation it is wise for us to do so to leave a legitimately beneficial legacy of our efforts at stewardship of the endowment passed down for the perpetuation of the culture of democracy for humankind, (for the continuation of the enterprise). How were these objectives set? By being ordained and established by the Constitution of the United States. Assessment of the risks is done by estimating their probability of realization and the potential severity of their impact if they occur. We must work to prevent the risks from happening, or control them somehow to limit their possibility and damages if they happen. To mitigate them we strategically and properly must develop appropriate affordable responses. If we do, we will have greater confidence and some assurance that we will not fail in attaining our objectives. Good assessments will prepare us to cope with the risks. Through quantitative and qualitative analysis, we can learn them. The better we understand them, the easier it will be for us to address them. With good yeoman like citizenshipping skill, we'll determine how to respond to them. We'll know how to reduce our exposure to them. We'll ready superlative responses based upon sound tactics. In this way, we mitigate the risks, remove fear and anxiety, and can avoid most of them, instead of transferring them to the next generations.

2a) Quantitative analysis

Analysis that looks at the numbers, the dollars and cents, and seeks to make sense of them is quantitative. It looks at cash flow—money in and money out. During the reign of the baby doomers, we've seen our debt, our liabilities, increase continuously. Now to the tune of a frighteningly enormous number, without a commensurate intake of revenue to pay for it, we are deeply in debt. At the time of writing this book, the national debt of the federal government owed by all of us to ourselves is $28,176,687,427,702 and rising. This works out to be $ 85,327 per every single person in the US (Peter G. Peterson Foundation, 2020). To pay it off tomorrow, each citizen would need to write the US Treasury a check for this amount. This is not good. It causes a fear of financial insolvency and a risk of dependency upon foreign powers to loan us money to pay the interest on our debt. Why are basic business balance sheet practices not happening with our money? Is not the debt-to-income-ratio supposed to be sustainable?

Other numbers we can look at quantitatively are ones that describe the population. When we look at the numbers of people being born and at the projected workforce (to help with generational promises' affordability), we see a huge challenge ahead. In terms of worker population replacement, we no longer see the historical demography pyramid. The shape of society used to be a pyramid. It is no longer. The formerly fewer retired elders who no longer contribute revenue by taxation upon earnings are going to be unsupported. We do not have enough younger workers in the population to produce the requisite revenue for all the retirements. The demographic shape of society is changing. When the baby boomers are 85, it will be rectangular. Meaning society will have the same amount by age of young, middle, and old people in society (see Figure 4-5). Then as aging occurs, society's demographic shape will turn into an inverted trapezoid, unless population rapidly expands. (How can it without jobs for young adults to raise large families?). This means fewer up-and-coming working adults and more elders on the retirement rolls. We'll have more takers than givers, more withdrawals than deposits, more socially dependent than self-reliant society funding persons. This does not bode well for societal sustainability or retention of present standards of living and high quality of life. Whereas in 1950 there were sixteen workers for every retiree, in 2010 there were only three (Taylor, 2014). With people living longer, we have a big challenge ahead, which should be more important to us than it is. Why is this? It is because the baby boomers are beneficiaries (Willetts, 2020). They're not worried about their kids' willingness to support them. They will simply expect their children to support them at a higher level than the kids will enjoy themselves, which is an age-of-entitlement thinking caused by doomerism. They essentially discontinued the habit of investing and saving for the long term, which caused financial instabilities and recessions, and low quality fiscal strategies, policies, and practices that lacked responsible economic moderation. Seeking to collect all the cash for themselves, they changed the way investments happened with a preference for short-term gains that changed rewards behaviors, and reduced investing in workers' skills development. They made bad decisions deemphasizing economic centrism, putting benefits in place for themselves (Sternberg J. C., 2019), which resulted in stagnated growth as reflected by Gross Domestic Product (GDP) performance declines (see Figure 4-1). Yet another ism arises at the center of baby doomer caused societal drama. The boomers have left things worse off than the way they received them. In part, it's because of a dominant ism of theirs: narcissism.

Frustratingly for rising generations, they'll be "me first" into the grave because being true to oneself is what they believe makes one successful, after all is said and done. They see no hypocrisy. Will they have guilt and shame and make a sacrifice for their grandchildren and great-grandchildren's chances in life? Will it be a moral dilemma for them? Let's hope so. Let's encourage them to reverse negative public opinion about their generation, and change their ways to save the nation. Or else we will continuously be forced to break-open our piggy banks for what little cash we'd saved for getting-by money in hard times, and making us sing out loud all the time that "money's too tight to mention" (Valentine & Valentine, 1985).

POPULATION PROJECTIONS
shapes by numbers of persons in age groups

ECONOMY CONTRIBUTING YEARS

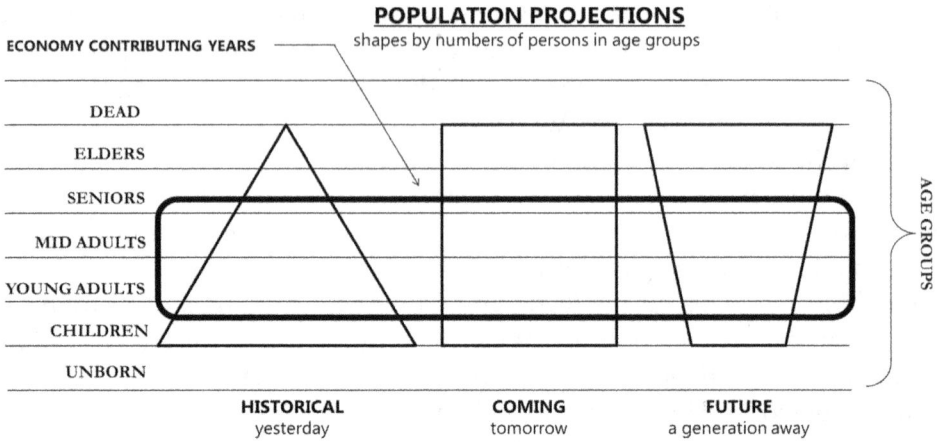

| DEAD |
| ELDERS |
| SENIORS |
| MID ADULTS |
| YOUNG ADULTS |
| CHILDREN |
| UNBORN |

AGE GROUPS

HISTORICAL — yesterday　　COMING — tomorrow　　FUTURE — a generation away

Figure 4-5: Demographic Trend in the US

We can also look at the success of the economizing of the economy power to produce and distribute the goods and services we all need. A rising national debt threatens the opportunities for future generations. It also limits the possibilities of economic activities that can increase our national output, our gross domestic product. The beneficiaries of well-managed books, of quantitative financial controls, are all our people in the various stages of generational growth, the children, adults, and elders. We need the LAMBS in the USE to consider the risks of debt and income distributions in regions and settlement patterns. We need to understand how we might have income stability and a future for the young to be able to work for their own ambitions and not simply to pay off the debt of those who came before. We are dooming our society with the debt the baby boomers create to sustain their well-being, while the future generations' general welfare looks poor. Few returns on the investments of our tax dollars are reaching us taxpayers.

The luxury of the boomers continues unabated, which would be okay if it were from a growing economy yielding more for more, but it is not. The boomers wasted our money on wars that gained us nothing but pain and suffering, all for the sake of a few who got grotesque monetary gains. Despite what the boomer pundits want society to believe, their economic disinformation is just one big smokescreen to hide their fleecing from view. The borrowing continues, and the burden gets passed to the unborn babies with each boomer that retires. The high tide has begun. We are scant to replace them. The job shedding has begun. They are not trying to help the future; they only are continuing to help themselves. This is what the numbers indicate. The integers would be different if the boomers better managed qualitative factors. Yes, that would have required they cared more about sustaining the dream of perfecting American society instead of devising ways, means, and methods to fleece it.

2b) Qualitative analysis

Analysis that looks at the characteristics, the essence, the nature, and the standards of things is qualitative. In society, it looks at the standards of living (indicators of the quality of the environments we inhabit) and the quality of life (indicators such as levels of peace, safety, security, education, health, and employment and economic advancement opportunities in the for-profit marketplaces). Do people have safe and secure infrastructures and utilities: transportation, water, sewage, refuse management, electricity, communications, and security provided by the society? How well is the economy power doing with provisions: food on tables, roofs over heads, and clothes on bodies? Certain standards are established in society at a level at which everyone agrees is the minimum that every person ought to be able to experience, a level at which we live. Above the standards is a quality of life measure (indicators of the above survival opportunities we might experience). How much time do people spend at work compared with time with family, or leisure and recreation time? How is everyone integrating in the society? How many different socialization contexts would we rather have than the seven we currently have: snobbish, traditionalistic, anomic, modernistic, postmodernistic, enervating, and radicalizing (STAMPER)? Is having this many putting our project to fulfill the Preamble at risk? Does it degrade the standard of living and quality of life in our society?

By the numbers, there will be fewer working adults than dependent children and dependent seniors and elders (see Figure 4-5). Are there any qualitative aspects in the social economic stratification, sizes of classes: elite, upper, high middle, mid middle, low middle, low, lower, and lowest that we should work to ameliorate? What if there is no upward mobility and increasing downward mobility in the population due to crises and chaos? The quality of life analysis looks at society and the risks within it and asks what it means. Does corruption jeopardize political stability? Is it possible instability can grow so large that there might be insurrections? Is the polity so full of scandals we'll need to have emergency elections with high frequency? What happens if the society has many bankruptcies: moral, ethical, social, and economic? What "quality" problems have happened during the tenure of the baby doomers in charge? What can we name? Do we think they could have avoided them? Are they reversible? How do we think we are to AEIOUY^{2}K the powers to fulfill our objectives? Answers to these questions allude to uncertainties that should matter to the persons of our FILMS^2 [P7] authorized with the responsibilities in the LAMBS. Likely, they do not because such questions are not central to the "me first" mentality of the baby boomers in the positions to do something about them. Thus they, by being in the generation in majority in authority, who are supposed to be

responsible to solve future problems before they happen, pose a risk to the USE. We need to respond to their hazardous threat to our liberty with an intervention, which brings us to
the next topic.

3) Responding to risks

After we have a sense of the risks from our assessment, by analyses we need to generate responses to the identified risks within the three primary (societal), two secondary (social), five tertiary (social), two natural powers, and our precept power and process of combining these twelve powers into an ever in motion product: society (see Figure 3-2). Based upon the analyses compared and contrasted to our tolerance thresholds and appetites for the risks, we assign responses to them. Then we implement the responses, some before events occur that make risks realized, some during, and some afterwards. In polity power, we respond to risks through government. In economy power, we respond to risks through commerce. In history power, as it happens, we've journalists and historians to help us recognize and respond to risks by informing us of their observations. In mythology power, we've religions to address morality and rites of passage risks in our human maturation, and we've alternative beliefs when we cannot believe what some profess. In academy power, we've many responses to the need for KA^4SA^2 in the arts and sciences. In the geography power, there are risks we know about and ones we don't, but we study with the academy power to understand how to use our cultural power process to adapt, survive, live, and thrive. We learn of ecology, organisms, flora, fauna, insects, and ourselves, the humans. We know a lot less about ourselves than we think we do, as we are prone to ignorance of our own qualities, since nowadays we find satisfaction easily because society supports instant gratification more than societally stabilizing virtues.

We see in the geography power the opportunity to adapt to our environment, and we come to understand, on a planet with a changing climate, that in certain ways we alter it. We can build environments, make architecture and landscapes, shape the places we live in, and shape the societies we occupy. In the US, we've a society built upon democracy precepts (our common denominator culture). It is a response to the pull of tyranny in societies. Constitutionally provisioned we recognize our natural rights empower us to be citizens who self-govern by citizenship responsibilities and citizenship rights, which requires citizenship education. Just being born in the United States does not equip a person to make American foundational ideals real in their own self. We must model, teach, learn, practice, pass down, pass on, and live out good citizenship attitudes and behaviors. A prime response to failing to raise Americans is to perpetuate lifelong ACE.

In most socialization contexts, we learn to behave in ways contrary to animal instincts, to be reasonable and try to understand others, learn civil behaviors, and commit to uphold the Constitution. As we age, we might forget the socially valuable principles we heard in school. To sustain them we must behave as informed citizens, actively engage in continuous self, social, societal, and ACE, so we can participate in electoral politics in ways, means, and methods that best serve our and society's needs, health and happiness. We need not pick a team, choose a side, and listen only to its rantings and ravings, its distractions to distort truth so it may gain control of society for raw power's sake. We need to consistently learn and relearn the truths of our founding principles and keep our politician-citizens from falling into the temptation of power-hunger games that fail us.

We must lead and not be led. This requires suspending belief until we evaluate the propositions of any one extreme against the source and nature of representation of the facts. We must discern how the application of statistics in reports verify and validate or falsify and deny a storyline. Editors portray biases by their beliefs. Truth is difficult to ferret out. Without a perspectival viewpoint that hunts underneath surfaces to find any presumptive prejudices of published propositions, we can be played as if fools. Reading broadly and deeply is an effective response to disinformation misinforming us, so we can uncover likely truths between the lines of political and economic publications.

Other responses to risks of the DAMN of the societal powers, the risks of doomerism, involve the need for each of us to be a good citizen, to believe in and abide by our responsibility to standards of conduct and self-regulating behaviors. We must enliven ourselves and remind each other always that we as a people have an awesome obligation to IDEALS liberty. Without this sense of duty, we are subject to despotic manipulation by control freaks and wannabe autocrats and their sycophantic bureaucrats in tow.

Therefore, to respond to the risks of doomerism in all the roles we play in the societal and social powers, within which we behave, we must consider acting as a citizen first. We need to do so most prominently when we are of working age, contributing to the economic output (Westhues, 1982). Society depends upon its working adults the most. We as a free people must stand for our natural rights and liberty. Our privacy is our right. It needs respected more. We need protected privacy, to keep the value of innocent until proven guilty, to hold fair trials by peers, and always to have the Miranda rights spoken. If questioned for suspicion, we must remain silent until a defense attorney is appointed. This is a response to the risk of authority overreach by government administrations. Some of whom might want to control people in a raw power possessive way that is more like the rule of men than the rule of law that is supposed to protect the people from the polity and such a form of petty tyranny. We must abide by and rely on the Fifth Amendment until we are in court. The boomer game-playing, winning-losing mentality means that some administrator's police will seek to entrap us. It is just how they roll in the age of entitlement and baby doomerism. To uphold the Constitution, we defend our liberty against abuses of authority by allowing no coercion, seduction, or persuasion to obtain our private personal information. Shame on whoever tries to get it! Doing so is an "assumed guilty until proven innocent" civil law not common law construct. After all, this could be the way of a "me first" person in charge of a safety or security department or in uniform suffering from doomerism, wanting to win at something to prove self-worth? We must respect legitimately exercised authority when done appropriately, but must not incriminate ourselves, nor gleefully be violating reasonable laws, or taunting our fellow citizens in uniform by flagrantly flaunting freely socially disruptive acts as if we've a right to disturb the peace, without any responsibilities to respect others liberty. Just because a person can be a jerk, doesn't mean it's necessary to prove it's permissible. Reckless incivility to prove freedom's existence is unhelpful. It's disrespectfully uncivilized.

Remember that the boomers' narcissism deludes them into being the most: self-seeking, self-interested, self-centered, self-aggrandizing, self-absorbed, self-indulgent generation in our nation's entire history. Being so huge and dominant for so long, they fooled us to think it is normal. It is not. It is unusual. It is cruel. It is a risk the founders feared. A dominant group ramrodding its demands over the opposition of a smaller group's opinion is culturally wrong in a representative democracy. In a republic, every effort to find a cooperative agreement is necessary to maintain peace. Exercising majorities for factional, generational, gain is cruel, abnormal, and dangerous. What is normal in a republic is not what typical societies have done over the ages. Thus to hold onto one requires better citizenry and better personal ethics and professional behaviors when serving in positions of authority. It is not easy, but it is best for everyone. Too bad the boomers largesse overshadows this truth from the wisdom of the miracle of the tradition of the framers. Expect nothing that isn't oriented to their selfishness. Protect yourself from doomerism. Rely on the Constitution. Keep silent if detained lawfully or unlawfully, whether with knowledge or in ignorance of the possible infraction. Plead the Fifth until getting a day in court. Even then, be leery. The boomers are on the bench and behind the jury fence. Know your rights and do not sacrifice them. Make the founding principles and ideals integral to your life. This is the real American way. Respond to the asinine risk of arsenic tyrants' toxic behaviors by rising to assert liberty's primacy. Another risk response on behalf of liberty is to prevent local politicians from enacting unconstitutional laws, ordinances, codes, or rules. Know the Constitution!

We need a better common understanding of the expectations of the people in person-to-person interactions. We also need a better common appreciation of the varying experiences and a basis for equality in person-to-person interactions. We must respond to risks of power getting out of control and out of balance, to create conditions to limit inordinate power, to put limits on governmental policing power and economic exploitation.

But with the responses to risks we demand and get instituted, we are not done. We must keep an eye on the direction of society. Each new generation begins again the voyage for liberty. Each must revive afresh an awareness of natural rights as distinct from naive instincts. All must find among the ranks its yeoman, coxswain, and boatswains to guide the USE. All must get trained in the foremanship of a representative democracy in republic. None knows how to do it by birth. None understands how special it is to be an American until taught ACE. Greatness takes learning, not of a sense of superiority, but of responsibility, which gives a person purpose and the good kind of pride to a people. Each generation must be prepared to be citizens with the culture of democracy, so that they may enjoy liberty and know how to monitor the risks passed down to them, to continue the movement toward our objectives attainment. For such a glorious advance to sail smoothly takes mastery in managing risks. Plainly, this effort got forgotten by the majority generation the past forty years, as baby doomerism metastasized and magnified its manipulation of our minds which COIFFURE democracy culture. Doomers' deconstructivism destroys the cohesions of our society with legions of "look at me now, look at me now", its "me first" that matters, slimy slicksters and lechers, social lesions that devastate our trust in our fellow citizens, or decent strangers with whom we are simply unfamiliar with, whose customary folkways are not our own. The exception does not justify the rule fallacy is rampant in doomerism, and we must respond to it with facts to reclaim the truth of reality over fantasy.

3a) Manage

To manage risks is to prevent their occurrence or reverse their damage if negative, and avoid, limit, cope with, reduce, if they happen. It is also to promote their realization if positive, and enjoy the benefits. Management requires constant work to ensure alignment in society to attain the republic's objectives and make changes as necessary to keep our project on a correct course to achieve its goal. We must clarify critical aspects of this mission, our civic duty, our work as a people. Such as, clear commitments to civilly, as soon as humanly possible, if we are to manage present risks to a true culture of democracy. We must come to know how the misunderstanding of "isms" threatens liberty and justice for all. Various isms are used as labels in ways that give concepts far too much power in public discourse, causing division. This practice perpetuates yelling and not listening. It undermines the potential for positive representation and performance of the polity we pay for with our taxes. With doomerism, the politicians do not govern. They just toss rocks at one another. Adults do not solve disagreements, fix ill feelings, or overcome sensations of inadequacy this way. To silence the lamb, scorch the earth, bring down fire and brimstone, and win at all cost while everyone else suffers is childishness. It's baby doomerism. Such does not help us beneficially converse, discuss, or debate nor get good at governing. It is poor citizenshipping. It gives power to others, taking it away from us, the people. We need to manage the internal threats to our national community by preventing the further spread of doomerism and its recurrence in the future. Confusion results when the isms get interchanged and overlapped. So we need to be clear about what these mean and how to address them as ideas, as systems of organizing thoughts about society. Doomerism causes ever more bewildering disorder. Here are a few big rock isms thrown around in the public realm:

Capitalism is a system of economy. The economy is the name for all things related to the provision of goods and services to help people meet their needs and satisfy their wants. The economy is a generator of material wealth for the HM[5] and the management of ways, means, and methods to provide the materials people need to survive, live, thrive, and sustain society. The economy, being such an important aspect of human life, gets a good deal of attention from the polity. The polity is not capitalism, and capitalism is not the polity.

Communism is a system in which the polity runs the economy. This restricts people. Communism is a system of economy in which the workers own all aspects of the economy. Theoretically it is a similar idea to democracy in that people (in communism the workers, those laboring in the economy) own something larger then themselves. People in a democracy own the polity. Workers in communism own the economy. Communism is not democracy, and democracy is not communism.

Socialism is similar to democracy in the theoretical aspect that it seeks to include all the people. In socialism, the intent is that the people benefit equally from the economy. Socialism also seeks to make an official culture controlled by the polity. In contrast, democracy is a culture not controlled by the polity but by the people, acting honestly toward a common good of tolerance for others and helping one another be equal before the law, which we the people established for our society. Democracy opens up society to new ideas. Socialism closes off society to new ideas. Democracy enables freedom of speech. Socialism dislikes people speaking out against the polity. Democracy demands the people speak out and be involved in the polity. Socialism deters it. Socialism dissuades it. Socialism is not democracy, and democracy is not socialism.

Anarchism is a condition of lawlessness. Its risk is a mobocracy, of persons seeking to create it to promise only one solution: theirs. Demagoguery rises up in mobs, incites anarchy as a means to justify establishing order, and places a despotic ruler in control of society to run its economy and control its people by polity dictates. Driving a society toward anarchy is the practice of tyrants who eventually seek to rule the people psychologically, financially, and physically, even by cruel tactics if necessary, which manifests more anarchism that makes more absolute mandates by the mastermind admissible. Anarchism does not a civil society make. A civil society does not manufacture anarchism.

Totalitarianism is a societal system of total control over the people and the economy by the polity that a few control, who force everyone to live by their whims and will. Tyrants seek to create totalitarianism to be powerful gods and want their society worshiped for its creation as the image of their perfection. There is a risk to the USE if it does not educate its children on the unfreedom and cruelty experienced by persons in totalitarianism.

Cosmopolitanism is an awareness of other cultures. The USE, being a land of immigrants, can use its cosmopolitanism to export and encourage liberty everywhere in the world. However, it must live up to its tenets of the Declaration of Independence and Constitution. Because it is ours first, we must comprehend better its foundational culture of democracy and the republic it enables. We do this when we lead it, not behave as if it is outside of our control. We can participate in the cosmopolitanism of the planets' many places without losing our strong core values and beliefs in the virtue of making and sharing a truly American society.

Libertarianism is a worldview that proposes human beings are born with inalienable natural rights, that they by reason and agreement can make a society in which common interests upheld through honorable dealings, without need of extensive government oversight, are possible so long as everyone's freely pursued personal interests are legal and do not infringe on others' liberty. By concepts of freedom, it creates community. It holds that proper citizenshipping enables all to prosper by creating a society that helps each person reach the position they are best suited for: for themselves, their communities, and the society. It asks the best of the rest and expects honor from all. It prefers merit-based ways of distributing rewards. It holds all to account under the rule of law and is adamantly opposed to the rule of one or a group of persons' egotistical edicts. It demands respect for fellow members of the human race, regardless of origin or physical attributes.

Republicanism is a form of polity that supports the freedom of the people to form associations to cope with and move through historical changes driven by knowledge growth and consequent technologies, in a manner of governing with representatives for populations. Done well it regularly replaces representatives to refresh the polity to ensure flexibility, liberty, and stability over time. It protects the people from a new ignorantly violent or obsolescent party, faction, or ideology, which would put the republic at risk, because those in political positions require reelection. It expects to make politicians think that they are never permanently correct. Flexibility is what a representative republic with a democracy based culture offers by its separation of polity, economy, and mythology powers. This structure ensures diverse and equal perspectives are engaged in the decision-making, which enables the republic to adapt to changes more readily. However, it relies upon an informed, civics-educated, and attentive population that understands how power works in the society and uses politics to ensure a proper balance of the societal powers: people, polity, and economy. Moreover, it depends upon positive contributions from all the subordinate human social powers' culturally made infusions into society's FILMS[2] [P7].

Exceptionalism is the belief that the USE, given its unique history of supporting liberty, was an exceptional and unique human innovation in social organization. To be a leader in human dignity for each person, it must earn the privilege to be called exceptional. It cannot do that with a population of inhabitants that does not live up to the highest standard of citizenship. To be considered remarkable, our citizenry must courageously champion virtuous living and total participation in keeping democracy culture free from doomerism. We cannot be exceptional with baby doomer hypocrisy. Nor can we allow our polity to—in our name—cause damage and pain to other societies' people if they do not threaten our sovereignty. We must be certain we are not using war to benefit a few at the top of our economy—making and selling munitions for profit's sake—expanding territory like an imperial empire.

Well, that is enough of the isms for now. Much of the discussion of risk has been about internal risks to the USE that doomerism implants in us as persons, inserts in our republic, infects our democracy with, and infests our society. The key to thwarting all the negative risks and pursuing all the positive risks is a love for and courage to IDEALS liberty.

There are also significant external threats to our sovereignty. Presently, the USE spends more on providing for the common defense than the next ten nations combined (Peter G. Peterson Foundation, 2020). There is much debate as to whether this is for defense or for waging war. With all the war the boomers enacted we might ponder whether we should rename the Department of Defense what it originally was and grew out of, the Department of War. Better yet, how about we stop waging wars and focus on homeland security defenses. This thought points out a foreign policy debate that we the everyday people need to be smarter about, because it is vitally important to our lives. Are we an empire spread across the world, using forward-deployed military power to ensure that a globalized, interconnected world can continue to ensure the economy power delivers for our country as we police the world? Are we overextending by doing all the work, which other sovereign nations should be helping us to do as partners in keeping peace for prosperity's potential extension to every person willing to work for it? Is there a need for more unifying treaties throughout the world so a single police force staffed by many countries is capable of peacekeeping activities led by the United Nations? Could there be a massive, single treaty that ensures all agree to play by a certain set of rules to keep the commerce of the economy power, vital for the provision of necessary goods and services, humming along without piracy? Is it possible for a single police force to protect supplies worldwide from destruction due to polity power seeking too much control over the free flow of these provisions for survival, living well, and thriving?

Perhaps the next generations of midcareer entering and rising working adults, the millennials, Gen-Z, and the subsequent ones who are growing up more digitally and globally connected in a world of shared high technology culture, will be better at making friends of foreign lands and building trusting alliances. Certainly, they will do this better than those who came up through histories of enemies and wars waged by polity power's overstressing its importance in our species. Rising generations are more like each other globally than they are different regionally. Due to the newest technologies, they communicate with different others as they digitally trot the globe with great curiosity. They more easily see into the lives of foreign people than anyone previously could, and find a greater sense of shared humanity. It enhances peace's promise to be learning of one another in real time, and technology is making this happen. This is a positive risk for opportunity. It means there is hope for the future, but we need the younger generations to rise and lead our society toward the oft-wanted world peace that we've not been wont to experience historically. In part, this is because our primal nature has been encultured in teaching boys to be warriors and women to be mothers. Perhaps now, thanks to economy power's inventions, we may raise boys and girls to be human diplomats, united in improving babies' destinies, humanely and globally. Clearly, a pandemic has shed light on this need. We must rise to the occasion. Globally, the millennials are poised to lead (Shah, 2020). We must encourage and allow them. We must transition power to them in a way that removes the negative risks of such transfer and improves the positive ones.

Of course, the common defense is necessary to prevent invasions, and these invasions may not be military but cultural. Therefore, we the people had better understand our Constitution and ensure that what it aims to establish is learned by new arrivals, and that they commit to upholding it and don't come here to take from our coffers what we earn to send around the world. If we are to be a breadbasket, let us keep what we make and share in kindness by political or privately run charitable organizational means, not by removal by persons to prop up other places. We must keep our capital, social and financial, within our republic to ensure its survival and thriving potentialities for all our citizens. By seeing policies as a means to manage the risks to our society, we can do this. It will take work. As we look at the risks we identify and must respond to and monitor, we must also determine our posture toward them. This includes how we report on them as we witness their presence and how we revisit and revise our assessments of them when patterns of behavior differ from our predictions. These are the remaining aspects of the application of the SERF and the management of the risks to our Constitution and the USE. Let's look at how we might further respond to risks as time and change exert pressures on us.

3b) Accept

One of the societal risks in our constitutional republic of democracy culture seeking to IDEALS liberty for everyone is the outcome of our elections. Our elections are our control over the polity and by means of policy a way to set fair play rules and referee the economy. Through our role-playing within both we are an essential control to manage risks. We must accept this fact and do our part honorably. By being citizens first, we prevent threats and find opportunities. When working in an authority position within a social or societal powers' FILMS^2 [P7] or as HM^5 in economy powers we must perform our responsibilities to lead with good character. Importantly, we cannot fall into exploitation traps that convince us to go along with groupthink of a meso- or macro-level influential decision-maker on how to AEIOUY^{2}K power for personal or factional gain.

We have the power to make society the best it can be for all of us. Elections may result in unfit candidates who do a poor job on our behalf. When such occurs, we have only ourselves to blame because it indicates that we the people did not properly vet the candidates. This is our responsibility, the rightful helm of leadership of the business of the society, of our enterprise, of the nation governing over the lands in which we live. If we do a poor job in our political knowledge and participation, if we blindly follow the big talkers, we subject ourselves to subjugation. We then support their will, and not our own. This is failure. This is subordination. This is dereliction of our duty. This is what baby doomers want. It is that which creates conditions ripe for doomerism to conquer and alter the culture of democracy into a plutocracy.

Republics, to be successful, require work. Just being consumers does not support democracy. When we've done poorly at self-government we must work toward making real for everyone our constitutional objectives, or we expose ourselves to disruption, factions, argument, and disagreement. All these things lead us toward anarchy, which gives opportunities for demagoguery by despotic, power-hungry, dishonest, dictatorial persons who rise in prominence and persuade that only they can stop the perceived mayhem. This is a dangerous threat to democracy! Alas, democracy can get messy, and extremists can rise up in frustration. Nevertheless, this is because of a failure by the citizenry to engage civically and reasonably pursue virtue and truth in the polity and economy powers. It is also a failure in secondary and tertiary social powers services for civil society and the common good, which we need done well to build the commonwealth.

Power is centrifugal. It seeks to pull more power toward itself. Only a population of civically educated, civilly behaving, civic-minded people can keep power in check, balanced, unable to concentrate, and corrupt us. We should not accept otherwise. We should demand more ACE everywhere, every day in every way, as a response to the baby doomers' calamitous policies and toxic behaviors. With its powerful consumerism, their doomerism draws us away from our duty to be a citizen first. It persuades us to be self-centered, ruthlessly inconsiderate, commons-destroying fools. Is this how we want to be? Is this how we want to live? Does this create a virtuous American Society? Is not greatness defined by ones virtue and not ones material wealth? It's about time we think about our legacy, and how we are leading to the destruction of the endowment given us by the framers.

Thanks to the Constitution, we have the backup option of expressing ourselves through peaceful civil disobedience. We can dissent when any one form of societal power grabs more than it should. For the health of the society to be as intended, we must lead! Our real patriotic fervor needs directed toward living virtuously in accord with the Constitution and legitimate laws. If we don't understand its true intents and don't improve our engagement with our society's need of us to lead it, it will be doomed. We will lose it. The DAMN of powers will continue as the USE decays into a state similar to fallen empires. The founders did not expect us to become an empire. Yet we have ended up that way. Because of a few ambitious men and the courses of action we have taken as a nation in world affairs, we have grown to lie on the globe as if we wanted to be an empire. We must walk back from the temptations of imperialism. We must not succumb to the hubris and vanity of being so large but guard against it. We cannot allow "super-power state" status conceit to enter our hearts and minds. We must not think we are infallible, superior, or extraordinarily exceptional because of our scale, size, military might, and economic production. Such hubris as recorded by history power brought about the demise of empires and crumbled civilizations. When the walls come tumbling down, we've failed. They will fall if we do not restore our foundations, like the rule of law and an honestly honorable citizenry committed to combine to abide by it in all ways, means, and methods of its existing to survive, live, and thrive as an American society. We must not be fooled into believing the lies that raw dominance-power tells us about ourselves. We must remind one another of our nation's best ideals of its framing. Every day we must be resolute to make real the first principles of our founding, or we'll remain off course pursuing the wrong purposes. We must accept the opportunity risks in creating a truly representative republic that a sought after democracy-based culture makes possible.

Metaphorically, our society as a ship needs refit with new yeomen, boatswains, and coxswains who understand its purpose, and we must set sail in the direction of its intentions. We cannot allow the risks of doomerism to continue without effective mitigation. We must accept the risks we should and know more about others we are exposed to that we want to transfer. After identifying and assessing these against our tolerance threshold and appetites, and we are certain we cannot accept them, we must carefully determine how where to transfer them. Today, we must not transfer the risk of becoming an empire ruled by doomerism to the future. We must respond to this risk immediately. We need to intervene in our routines with risk management actions to replace rapidly and repeatedly the politicians and elites currently misguiding our enterprise with constitutionally allied citizens. The current batch is performing poorly. We must fire them. Send them to reform school. Plus, every one of us must commit to the long-term remedy and sanctity of doing better citizenshipping. We must respect our selves and our endowment more by E-SASSY-T-TUF-FT-CAUCUS when we AEIOUY^{2}K the primary powers in the LAMBS to benefit everyone in the USE. Additionally, we must successively fill our ship's pilothouse, our bridge, our helm with new wholesome crews. These persons must be team players. They must be civics educated, civil society supporting, commonwealth healing, and ignorance repealing citizen-patriots. Perpetually they should be 24 to 40 year old patriots. We must replenish the officials with authority we privilege with the responsibility to navigate and drive our ship continuously with each generation's citizen first patriots. We must do this to prevent career politicians from taking hold of American society ever again. Because once in a position in charge a human is tempted to keep it and shift their focus from representation to strides that strive not to let go of it. Never can we as a people allow as the boomer generation did, such "me first" values to overwhelm our intents and decision-making.

3c) Transfer

The very positive endowments of our society, the first being the virtuous values of the founding ideals and our Constitution (as amended) that framed the structure built upon the equality of humans before the law with divided polity powers, both vertically and horizontally, must transfer from generation to generation. It needs better taught, understood, and its guidance implemented by succeeding generations to sustain the exceptionality of the nation it began as American society moves toward its objectives. The good risk assumption of our project is to give everyday people control of the polity and freedom to pursue liberty and justice. This pursuit of happiness needs kept going generationally. Other benefits of the successes of the relationship of the people, polity, and economy powers have been the financial transfers of capital into infrastructure that makes the material world and natural world less threatening to survival and frees us up to thrive in magnificent manners of employing our artistry and industry powers. The entrepreneurial risks taken to build better physical conditions to support enlightened social circumstances need continued. However, as we have progressed in time and entered the third stage of knowledge creation, without having fully repaired nor properly corrected the lingering ailments of previous generations, we have seen the transfer of social welfare bur-

dens. We continue to suffer the ailments of both the means of wealth transfer and the preference for bailing out certain groups over others and con-
demnation of victims and not the systemic reordering of the powers to
benefit all our people.

We saw, with the third stage of knowledge creation, a generation rise into power, accepting ideas of property and capital redistribution, of fiscal
policy by the polity, which did not bring everyone along fairly. Boomers
dropped the practices that sought to address certain lingering problems of
the second stage of knowledge creation. Unity destroying societal problems
festered, left without redress, nor revisits. Boomers curbed in their appetite
to take risks for others within our borders absolved not to get involved in
solving them. Yet the baby doomers among them chose to engage in military follies to engorge the military industrial complex and chase egotistical
fantasies of conquering and converting other societies into dependents upon the USE though military might. A complacent self-indulged population
did not stop them. Many cheered them on, over there. Their generation
decreased its tolerance to experience personal social difficulties here in the
homeland. Boomers squandered opportunities to attend to societal risks
that put vast numbers of our people at risk of losing a decent standard of
living and which prevented possible gains in higher quality of life pursuits.
The boomers poorly resolved lingering big isms from Reconstruction: racism and classism. They mismanaged risks in globalism and nationalism, and
now transfer these to the future generations who they spoiled for selfish
reasons, and insufficiently trained in ACE, because such was inconvenient
for them to sustain their own "me first" image of how they wanted to be.

Yes, risk management is complicated and thus is precisely why more of
us must be civically engaged, and participate politically with the purpose of
moving perceptions and policies in a direction that puts our USE back on a
path independent of doomerism, one that is oriented toward fulfilling the
calling of the revolution, to IDEALS liberty and justice for all. If we all believe in this, in 1776 liberty professed, then we can reverse the damage done
during the boomer generation's rise and tutelage in the higher ranks of our
societal and social powers. Their "greed is good", "me first", and "wolfing"
on Wall Street conception of "trickle-down" economic theory has and is
destabilizing at a time we need unity to confront uncomfortable challenges.
Domestically we've unsolved regional and settlement pattern differences of
where to go, how to get there, what risks we're exposed to in the options
we might find if we conversed civilly, not immaturely competitively as baby
doomers do. Even though some boomers perpetuated the proposed for
positive ideals limited government to stimulate people's innovative spirits, it
unfortunately transferred risks left un-responded to, unmonitored, un-
revisited, and unrevised. These risks have resulted in poor tax policies un-
derfunding extant government benefits to boomers' own retirement programs. With these promises, huge debt risks transfers to younger and un-

born American generations. We must engage in serious discussions regarding the efficacy, ethics, and even the appropriateness of such programs and taxation! Relevantly, ending overseas military actions for good is a theme. Mainly because aging boomers realize the costs that threaten their loss of enormous retirement benefits they want—live out their luxury to the end. They in shortsightedness now see they cannot afford both doing good for world peace and padding their pockets and paying for the healthcare required to keep them going. This act is unspoken and unheard of because as the dominant generation running the history power, they do not recognize its risks transfer to the younger generations or how obvious it actually is. How could they, "me first" doomerism has blinded them, even though how things are perceive seems to drive the public behaviors of the polity power's politicians and the economy power's elites.

If we the citizenry cannot form associations to manage the transferred risks within our communities, settlement patterns, and neighborhoods—to lovingly care for one another—than we've ceded our social problems to the polity and economy powers. Is this what we the everyday people want to do? Do we seek to become complacent and apathetic, to relinquish responsibility for managing risks for solving social problems in our places to Big Brother (the polity, the administrator) and Big Sister (the economy, the manager)? (Yes, this is a simplistic biologically based rudimentary use of language done in the hope of making a basic point). The paternal and maternal instincts in the biological power made two sexes of our species: genetically (though miniscule amounts of mutations occur). Each has preferences by nature, reinforced by nurture, as documented by the history powers.

Generally, men seek to control, to protect, and to administer, and women seek to control, to protect, and to manage. Both seek as necessary to provide a stable home, a nest, with provisions for the children. Anthropologically speaking, the woman says I need this or that for our child. The man goes out the next day and negotiates with the environment to find and come back with it. This does not mean that only man is administrator and only woman is manager. It simply means that the essential, rudimentary essence of control by administration is metaphorically a brother, a boy trained in ways of the father per the culture to become a man in ways the society deems needed for its maintenance and perpetuation. Male is a child-maker who brings a powerful love to protect and provide a stable environment.

The essential, rudimentary essence of control by management is metaphorically a sister, a girl trained in ways of the mother per the culture to become a woman in ways the society deems needed for its maintenance and perpetuation. Female is a child-birther who brings a powerful love to feed and nurture. Either can do much of the other's role, but science shows both a mother and father present in the lives of children, particularly when bound legally as a unit, on average, leads to better outcomes for children than a single parent raising children can provide. We are not as complicated as we think we are. If by biology power it takes a male and a female to make a child, then by family power of the two, and in cooperation with neighbors by community power, we raise a child into an adult. Substantiation of this comes from the supplementation of child rearing provided by the other tertiary powers, particularly the mythology power for morals and academy power for the KA^4SA^2 to contribute to the sustentation of the community. However, wealth gives us all sorts of options for how we might see ourselves because we are not struggling to survive, and we have the blessings of liberty to imagine new forms of socially arranging and defining ourselves.

We must commit to citizenship and transfer a belief in it to our children. If we don't our society dwindles into an unexceptional, defunct never again wannabe representative democracy in republic drifting slowly back into a dictatorship of detention, repression, and rule by a tyrant or board of oligarchs who, like sycophants, seek to please the plutocrats who give them more than their fair share. Such bootlickers are prone to lie to the bosses while they fleece the population of its natural rights and best produce, taking the top quality items and discarding the worst, vaingloriously dropping it downwardly onto the "little" people. Treated like serfs, forced to consume the crumbs of crap found unfit for the mighty highnesses, we'll die diseased with no access or ability to pay for hospital care. Malnourished, possessing insufficient biology power to fight, we'll lose control of society to a bunch of hind asses, hole-licking un-Americans. As this occurs, they'll promise food security to quiet us and take what's left of our dignity and liberty, putting us in bondage to their new feudal system for controlling the dirty masses. If we fail, they'll ruin the USE. This risk transfers to us when drunk-on-power doomers occupy American society's pilothouse, staff its bridge, station its helm, pull its levers, push its buttons, turn its wheel, and give its commands to the sailors laboring to keep the ship afloat and sailing—to where it goes, none of us know. Unless, we the everyday people awaken from the daze of doomerism and see the transferred risks, and engage to initiate better responses.

For the boomer generation, shame will be upon them in the books to come. The history power will chronicle them as failures, a complete opposite of their self-perception. But of course, they are deluded. Debased they deface the nation each time they state of others that which is actually their own self-description. It is not ironic; it is despicable that they should do so and actually believe themselves. For all their "me first" self-centeredness, they have no self-knowledge, or they are intentionally manipulating others for their own selfish gain. We don't want the risks of their wannabe big lies, autocracy and aristocracy, transferred onto our children. No more, we need doomers out of the positions they are protecting for themselves with doomerism's disguises. This scheme of maneuver is doable, but it will require changing from an allowing ignorance consumerist-oriented population that has not lived up to its responsibilities into a good citizenshipping one. Boomers have extracted for themselves, exploiting the FILMS[2] [P7] for "me first" gain, which has decimated systems and is ruining the commons in uncivilizing manners. They have ravaged. They have pillaged. They have transferred a mess onto us, an over $28T debt (Peter G. Peterson Foundation, 2020), which continues to rise. Buried and cast adrift toward doo, we the everyday people need to demand these transferred financial and concomitant societal, social, and personal survival risks, and how they make our USE vulnerable and limit our opportunities, get full and serious attention. We need responses to them to prevent these risks transference and realization. Urgently, we must find ways to mitigate them. We need an engaged citizenry intervention.

3d) Mitigate

The objectives of the Constitution provide the framework to mitigate the risks to the people of being over-controlled. Perhaps the people misunderstand this perspective of risk management. With the SERF, we can come to know that we must use the people power to mitigate the risks we confront. When we the everyday people see the ability to push the polity and economy powers' FILMS[2] [P7] and the HM[5] to AEOUY[2]K powers in ways, means, and methods that serve the USE's objectives, we all will be better able to IDEALS liberty and justice for all. A key method to mitigate the risks of external threats in the provisions for the common defense is to create positive international interconnectedness through strong diplomacy. To defend we extend our perimeter outwardly with friends, through mutual interests, to have tentacles of polity power's foreign affairs policy everywhere. Embassies and with military bases spread out around the world to stabilize a globalizing economy, do this. Done fairly this requires reimbursements for the stabilizing security our military presence brings. This is world teamwork to keep trade and commerce flowing without piracy and deter territorial wars. Another way to mitigate the risks of the DAMN of powers is by a society that has freedom of speech, of the press, and of thoughts unspoken. Of course, this comes with a subordinate risk that needs managed, which is the use of the history power to spew propaganda for one power or another seeking more power. Big lies told repeatedly seek to complete a drumbeat as believably true, conspiratorially, to cause the effect instability can do, and to affect negatively our emotions as a threat to peace and freedom, since tyrants lying in wait always like to enact a coup d'état. We mitigate these risks with facts and trust in truthful sources and professional proofs. In actuality, factuality is not an aspirational aspect, but a constitutional allied democracy-based culture requirement American society needs to exists, and it's obtained when a nation contains a citizenry who persist in consistent dedication to developing, practicing, teaching, and modelling good character in pursuit of the deep and true happiness virtue brings.

This is the eternal battle of the people to lead. Any amount of power tends to corrupt whosoever possesses it. Power wants to grow. This is a human social fact (particularly in certain subcultures that prefer a warrior ethos and machismo figures as idolized males). Citizenshipping is a process to redirect this trait of our nature and nurture to get good people power behavioral benefit to the people. We need journalists to write history as it happens, factually. We must disallow journalists from shaping history, like an unauthorized fifth column seeking to enjoy the power of rumor, gossip, and tall-tale telling and watching the gullible eat it up, buy it, and believe it is true. We need to hear good news. Doing good occurs more than what is shared by doomeristic journalists daily selling more profitable bad news. We the everyday people by control of our biology power (block instincts for instant gratification by excitingly interesting dramatic incidents). We can use our family and community powers (encouraging ourselves and others not to consume hyped up horrible stories that influence our perceptions of our lived reality) to alter the economy powers (by reshaping information consumption behaviors by not buying what's being sold in the marketplaces of news media). Moreover, we must dissuade those who like to gossip. We must stop spreading rumors. We must not watch to see how far they spread, and then take conceited pride for having started the whole drama's realization. It is wisdom that: "Great minds talk about ideas, average minds talk about events, small minds talk about people, and little minds try to pettily destroy others' lives". We all have the capacity and capability to behave in any of these states of mind. How do we prioritize thoughts is a matter of civility and commitment to our community's health and our society's vitality and virtuosity? By using wisdom to know what is important. Virtue pursues truth. Truth resides near the top of this pyramid of thought (see Figure 3-3 and relate personally to it in reflection of self-formation concepts in Figures 2-27, 2-28, 3-5, and 3-6).

We mitigate the risks of nonfactual reporting and fallacy by not believing in and buying the lies told to us. We can prevent this by helping those who seek to be in the history power's FILMS[2] [P7] to understand the power they will possess and the essentiality of honor, honesty, and integrity, which we need of them to report only the facts and not distorted ideologies. If they are not victims of doomerism, and they are citizens first, they cannot fall into societal failures and crises CATAPULTED by baby boomers. Citizens first will not behave as baby doomers, dooming the prospects of future American babies, upon whom we'll all depend. It is incumbent upon us to apply our intelligence to ensure their prosperity, especially considering the population trends that are not replenishing the numbers of productive workers necessary to sustain our livelihood as a people and as a society. Here's a grim example in the form of a question. When we are all old and dying, do we want nursed by a human being, preferably a relative, or a robot?

Along these lines of concern for the perpetuation of the USE as an exceptional beacon of hope for liberty on planet earth are the threatening risks in the rise in aristocratic tolerances. Thomas Paine clearly indicated the common sense that no one is born to rule another and that to think such is an affront to liberty. Yet, baby doomers clearly see themselves as superior beings, as gods, as our overlords, our rulers, by elitism, mass accumulation, and mass incarceration to control human freedoms that subjugate and distract from the truth. Further, under their control society has become unequal and inegalitarian. What is the utility of these social circumstances and their resulting physical conditions?

Economic inequality is a dangerous precondition for violent anarchy and despotic deception. We must make deposits into social capital-building accounts to prevent the perpetual, perverse DAMN of persons who happen to be suffering anomie, the poor Americans among us. We must demand better citizenshipping by those in wealth with economy power not to persecute or ignore our impoverished fellow citizens. If good citizens, they would stabilize society to prevent such poverty and find ways to help by creating jobs, and sponsoring and leading restorative associations. They would not tolerate in the USE the existence of the social circumstances and physical conditions of the poor becoming a lumpen proletariat in a seemingly permanent cycle of poverty. In both rural and urban pockets of poverty, limited social grammars develop. Few enjoy a healthy social integration, and many feel they do not belong in society. The possibilities for those in poverty to have a decent standard of living and the opportunities to find better quality lives remotely exist in a few not yet proposed policies the baby boomers will never discover because of their "me first" orientation as a generation. Thus, their doomerism devastates social innovation. To lift people out of poverty, radical innovation is required. Which generation is the most likely to be creative enough to figure out some reasonable solutions? Likely, according to biology and history power, that which is aged 24 to 40.

Such disequilibrium as doomerism causes results in only a few who reach the monetary heights of unfathomable riches, living off assets not income. These lonely few band together. They possess the ability to live in a self-protected bubble. A place free from any social or societal guilt for what they have. To each his or her own, and congratulations are due if the riches were truly earned, not stolen, or totally inherited. The risk of inheritance is the protective attitude of snobbery, which leads to snobbish socialization contexts that raise children to think they are born superior. Such aristocratic attitudes are terribly undemocratic, unrepublican, and thus horribly un-American. This risk needs mitigated, or we will lose fellowship to classist attitudes. We cannot allow it. Through ACE, publicly and privately, we must reinforce the political truth that all humans are created equal. If we cannot effectively mitigate snobbery, we may find ourselves ruled by an autocrat who thinks nepotism and aristocracy are a wonderful means of ruling over society. Such wannabe aristocrats too easily ignore inequalities because they are unaffected and unexperienced in the struggles of the everyday people. We must guard against such uppityness.

This snobbery happens in many layers with the mercantile mantra of the HM[5], "keeping up with the Joneses." Such aggressive, competitive advertising and marketing converted a culture of democracy based on Abrahamic and deist values into a culture of vampire consumerism, by doomerism. The rise in consumers trampling one another while rushing a sale at a shopping mall for a small electronic object evidences this. Such stampedes and other consequent mad consumerist behaviors maim and kill other human beings. With doomerism, human lives are less valuable than material objects. Possessed persons' urges to possess overwhelm the voices of wisdom within. Relishing in objects over people relinquishes reason, and gives doomerism a victory. Clearly, such a rampant rise in consumerism brings with it a decline in good citizenship behaviors. People, the economy is not the end-all-be-all, neither is the polity, but a well-balanced arrangement of the three primary powers though our leadership efforts is best. Our performance of our roles in the societal and social powers' FILMS[2] [P7] at the micro, meso, and macro scale of impact is the ultimate risk-management effort to which we must commit ourselves. We must balance our powers. We must AEIOUY[2]K power for the good of society for self. We must believe in our purpose to IDEALS liberty. We must do this core work. We each provide the LAMBS for our USE. This purpose is what we are called to do as Americans. It takes proper citizenshipping. It requires a larger-than-self-centeredness centering. It requires more of each of us, and we must be determined in our efforts if we are to reverse the flawed path of doomerism and steer our ship to a Promised Land of the free and home of the brave. We must innovate new ways in society so all have the prospects of producing a prosperous life. We know this is the best way to enable all to gain some bounty from our productivity. Rising tides lift all boats, leaving none to drown at sea. Is this not an aspirational goal worth pursuing?

As we move toward correcting the societal problems CATAPULTED by the baby boomers, as their doomerism c̲onfiscates, o̲bfuscates, i̲mmolates, f̲rustrates, f̲abulates, u̲lcerates, r̲elegates, and e̲xtirpates (COIFFURE) democracy from American society, let us report honestly and fairly. Let's tell the truth about how we are doing with our risk responses and whether our adoption of the SERF for the preservation of the union, is effective. The USE gives us freedom to self-govern and pursue happiness. Such joy is more than skin deep. It is a long-range quest, not a hedonistic, here and now pleasure-seeking vacation trip. It is the happiness found through developing virtuous character. It is meaningful comradery gained from doing good work with others in civil associations. The social connections and bonds we make serving with others in a righteous causes fuels our people power.

Our happiness quest leads to preparation for life from the best socialization for the future for our children. One focused on them getting a good ACE, so they may enjoy and protect the blessings of liberty with gratitude for its being and their becoming American. This so we might enjoy them and upon our death know that they will IDEALS liberty for humankind as our nation's legacy. We will know our entrusted endowment shepherds forward when we steward it with a service mindset and behaviors. We must prepare them to apply the future generations' talents to perpetuating it toward full constitutionality, so all our citizens will have it. Doing so, we will know we served the calling of this higher purpose, to transfer an exceptional demonstration of the blessings of liberty for others to see as an example and seek to repeat the world over. This is a sound mitigation to external risks.

Let us get to work; let us exert the necessary effort. Let us defeat and eradicate doomerism from within one another and ourselves! Let us banish it from our culture of democracy and our meant to be American society. Let us explain that we made a mistake. Let us no longer follow in the footsteps of the misguided baby boomers, and dissuade others from copycatting them too. Let us begin earnestly E-SASSY-T-TUF-FT-CAUCUS. Please let us do these things to mitigate the risks doomerism poses upon posterity and us.

4) Monitoring risks

Thanks to our society's framing in the rule of law through our encultured democracy, we've built-in controls for monitoring risks. These controls work within the FILMS^2 [P7] of American society. We've laws and elections to monitor and control the polity. We've many markets, experienced HM^5, and governmental departments of trade and commerce to monitor and regulate the economy power and prevent financial fraud. We've governmental departments of education, administrators, teachers unions, and parent–teacher associations to monitor and control the academy powers. We've our military to monitor our borders and interests overseas, ready to defend us. In common, all these depend upon us, the people, to staff them. If we're all corrupted by doomerism, then so too will all of our societal and social powers' FILMS^2 [P7] and our HM^5 will get distorted by it, too. Thus, we must have our better consciences monitor us. Our society begins within each of us. If we are citizens first, it becomes beautiful. If we are rotten, the forest gets diseased; the trees all die. The worst death is that of the Liberty Tree. It is a rare and special breed. It needs us to pursue virtue and be virtuous to protect it, and nurture it to be stronger within our children to preserve it for posterity.

We are living our lives, we find things wrong, and we wonder, "Why?", and "How?" Didn't the adults before us monitor the risks to society? Did they act by uniting or dividing calculations about what to do? Were they behaving as citizens first, as champions of liberty, or were they not? We find now that doomerism has shown its face fully to us. Now we must enact our risk responses to keep it from spreading to the next generations. We must apply significant effort to preclude callous cynicism and incompetent callowness to adjust the course of the society before it is too late. In many ways, we thought we had retired our risks of totalitarianism, and stopped resourcing our responses because we thought these risks were no longer prevailing. Yet they are. They return. Tyranny never goes away. We must be more vigilant. This is life. It is cyclical. Broadly, our response methods to risks are to manage, accept, transfer, mitigate, or most dangerously, ignore them. We have ignored too many risks for too long under the ruse of baby doomers, who lied, cheated, and stole the stability of society from under our feet by fleecing our resources and using the polity and economy powers in a way that has nearly bankrupted the society—morally, financially, and socially.

Elections are a major control over the polity, a response to power concentration, and a means of monitoring change. The baby boomers have the concentration of power. We must break this apart. We must take the power from them through repeated retirements of them by election of youthful civically oriented civilly behaving candidates, regardless of political party. We need to monitor better and respond with younger and younger candidates for the health and tone of the whole polity. It is unhealthy from "me first" corruption and out of tone since most in it are from one kind of background: law school. Law is not essentially a problem-solving tool. In fact, it can be wrong with its oft-overwrought complicated thought. It rests on precedents, which restricts creative thinking. Lawyers make more laws. We need fewer laws. We need not a civil but a common law legal system. Less law yields more freedom. More law causes less freedom. We must elect practical persons of real pragmatic accomplishments. All our politicians should go into politics to serve liberty first. Neither for profit nor for the sensation of power should they run for elected offices.

5) Reporting risks

Thanks to the many FILMS[2][P7] of the USE and its primary, secondary, and tertiary powers, we have access to many reports of what is perceived as going on in our society and of how the LAMBS is going. They all report. Writing reports is common practice and a valued process in all our powers, principally by the history and the academy powers. The polity demands reports in its efforts to govern. However, many reports go unseen for what they ought to be doing: supporting a risk-management step. The economy needs reports in its efforts to provision society with what we need and want. Written reports cognizant of the SERF benefit the USE. How we write on what wrongful happenings related to the union's prospects for prosperity is very important in a society suffering from information overload and doomerism's disinformation. We the people can read most of the reports, except those requiring higher levels of secrecy due to national security, which promoting the common defense may require.

There are many sources of information. Yet we trust our fellow citizens in roles of responsibility within the FILMS[2] [P7], who represent us, to read and apply what they learn from the reports in their roles to provide good LAMBS and to continue our society toward achieving its goal and attaining its objectives. If, however, their focus is not to IDEALS liberty, they might not employ the knowledge in the reports in the best possible way for us, for our republic and democracy. Further, if they are not getting reports that essentially examine the risks to us, then we are not getting the best risk-management to ensure proper fiduciary and fecund fulfilling LAMBS, which constitutionally we are required to receive. Again, it is up to us to rise up to lead, behave, and raise our children to behave as citizens first, for the betterment of our society from which we gain benefits. The shortsightedness of doomerism has jeopardized our integrity in reporting and our pursuit of virtue, which is the American way of life, built upon a culture of democracy, governed in republic representation with civil cooperation and civic association.

Some of the key mechanisms of reporting we get from the polity are in the Congressional Record and the State of the Union Addresses. Sadly, the desire to remain in power that infects our politicians blocks the telling of truth to us. We must guard against rhetorical fallacies. We must not accept any more lies. We must require the truth whether it comports with our desired wishes and hoped for beliefs of what we want to be true, or not. Since those we have entrusted to serve in our polity have resorted to administering their own continuation, we have no choice but to do what a good leader must do, hold them accountable, teach them their error, and encourage them to get better. However, if their offense is willfully egregious and a clear violation of explained expectations and rules, we must punish them by removing all of them from office as soon as possible. They tended toward corruption as the culture of doomerism infected their thinking. They are listening to doomerism's tempting tidbits teasing up their narcissism and not the message of democracy that they are supposed to abide by in their performance of their duties on our behalf. They swore an oath of office. They disgrace themselves by not living up to it.

This brings us to how we must constantly revisit the risks in our society. We do so by the responsible use of our powers as a people to demand a rebalancing of the primary societal powers toward the USE's optimum performance. The framers provided a republic with representatives regularly elected for us to use to self-govern. We have failed to refresh sufficiently our body politic with new politicians, and those who stay too long have corrupted the society by the power-money-politics-underground-elites that do a disservice to liberty and to us, undermining the possibility of us achieving our goal and attaining our objectives.

6) Revisiting risks

The best way we can engage in revisiting identified risks, to verify, validate, and update our assumptions of our risk appetites and tolerances, our assessments of their probability of occurring, and the severity of their impact is by intense involvement in knowing them. We can also revisit our responses' effectiveness to realized risks. In revisiting risks and the results of responses, through elections we should voice our directions to authorities providing for the LAMBS. If during their terms of service, our representatives' performance is not suitable, then through social movements we must raise awareness of low quality service or misguided activities. If necessary, we must dissent. We must peaceably protest poor quality and bad for liberty policies. We must march in the streets at the houses of governments, politicians, and elites. Through peaceful, organized, noise-making protests, we'll encourage them to listen to us and get society back on course. If forced to do this, we must not riot or allow bad actors to riot in our midst and make us look unruly. We must organize well to prevent terrorists among us as we exercise our rights. First, we must exercise our responsibilities, so we won't have to resort to such acute measures.

7) Revising risks

From our revisiting of the risks to our USE, we must continuously implement the SERF mindset to IDEALS liberty with each new generation to keep us on course to our purpose: providing liberty in a culture of democracy within our republic, remembering always that our polity powers enable and our economy powers provide. As we do this, we must regularly revise the risks. We the everyday people must provide the leadership for the policies of government and the markets for the exchange of the necessities to survive and live well and the luxuries with which we might thrive. As the globe turns, change is continuous and so is the need to revise identified risks as we find out how they need amended to accommodate for new knowledge and technology that brings about societal transformations.

We've a beneficial arrangement for society when we seek to balance our societal powers to disallow risks that overtly damage our social fabric, social constructs, social capital, and social contract with one another. As Americans, we should be patriotically motivated to defend and uphold the Constitution. If we cannot get everyone at every level of influence in society, the micro, meso, and macro, to behave as a citizen first, to fight back against doomerism, and to remind ourselves of the original intents of democracy for liberty, we may well become subjects with lessening freedoms. "In power we win" depends upon the FILMS^2 [P7] ensuring stability. Instability is a big risk we need to be cognizant of for its generational consequences. We all must work to prevent its realization. We need to know the look of the events in which it demonstrates itself becoming a constant in our society and respond to it to mitigate its impact and restore stability in its wake.

The Risk of Instability

We the people need to know and employ the SERF as we shift our posture to assume our proper position of leadership of the USE. Leadership is our necessary role. We are the power in a democracy. We need to know and understand how to AEIOUY^{2}K it. Each of us to the person—in families, neighborhoods, communities, states, a nation, and as a people loyal to the Constitution—is to be a leader. This is as it must be in a democracy. We provide the leadership of the FILMS^2 [P7] of all our societal and human social powers. We must do this first by being good citizens working to IDEALS liberty and justice for all in our thoughts, attitudes, and behaviors. We must take this step toward unity and walk this way every day in every way.

We must rise up to be better performers in our roles for American society. Our good attitudes and behaviors are particularly important for stabilizing our society. Without this, the baby doomers, the most dangerous, self-centered, narcissistic psychopaths, will continue to instill a sociopathic culture of doomerism within and among us, downgrading American society. We need to better exercise our rightful and responsible agency to govern ourselves as healthy humans when holders of authority positions within the FILMS^2 [P7] or as the HM^5 of our societal powers. (For a reminder of all the powers, see Figure 3-4.)

What underlies the instability in society, besides the misbalancing of powers done by baby doomerism? It is the blatant ignorance of a required focus on liberty for upholding democracy as our culture, a forgotten wisdom in the system of rule of law. Finding loopholes first is the approach of liars, cheats, and thieving baby doomers. Wisdom professes that dishonesty dishonors a people. Widespread unrighteousness undermines the stability of society. A billion dishonorable doomers skirting the laws ruin the rule of law as an ordering principle for society. Disregard for the consequences of flooding the courts with frivolous suits is foolish. It is a tactic of the selfish seeking to get away with crimes. The baby doomers ought to know this. Perhaps they simply chose not to abide by it thinking, "No one will notice. I am but one, it cannot make a difference, no one is watching, it won't cause any harm, plus I will benefit." Yet in aggregate, they are devastating us. Our courts are overwhelmed with their nonsense.

They began backsliding down a path of social destruction, of rationalizing the unethical as permissible. They exhibit inconsiderate, disrespectful approaches to dealing with others whom they would contend were in the way of what they wanted—right or wrong, good or bad. Yet Providence is watching. As a generation, they've been misguided. God is watching and waiting. The judgment is becoming clear and our punishment begun. Our society is in deep chaos and crises. Because of the size of the boomer generation, their billion selfish choices now expose the sheer force of the consequences of their approach. Their massive ignorance of others has dangerously destabilized our national community. They have loopholed the daylights out of our society, leaving us in shameful tatters. We are less a mass of good than we are a dark matter of shotgun-shelled holes. Like moth eating away wool cloth, our national fabric is becoming tattered and unwearable.

Our society once a proud quilt is fraying into a ragged frazzled threadbare sense of guilt. Now it will take a major overhaul to patch and repair it. We must begin to weave a replacement cloth, threaded together by a trillion selfless decisions, thoughts, attitudes, and behaviors that create trust and social capital to countervail doomerism. We need greater civic engagement, informed political awareness, intelligent electoral politics, and full voter participation. We must judge politicians by their perspective on how to AEIOUY^{2}K our societal powers, their knowledge of liberty, and how they intend to IDEALS it. These repairs are to reverse extant problems. We will need further risk-management responses to prevent future threats of doomerism from arising in our society.

We will en masse remake the cloth of the USE as one nation under God, indivisible with liberty and justice for all. It is our duty now. We must lead by E-SASSY-T-TUF-FT-CAUCUS. Our citizenshipping will work the loom, fueled by social capital spoken in many social grammars, without prejudice. We will remake our societal fabric, our quilt e pluribus unum. In doing so we rebalance how we AEIOUY^{2}K the societal powers, and reciprocally, we prevent their DAMN. Moreover, by weaving citizen-first attitudes and behaviors into all we do, we will successfully prepare our society to adapt to the changes we confront in the current third stage of knowledge creation. It will continue to bring increased frequency of changes to our lives until we reach equilibrium once again. Until then, to cope and transition, we need to admit this reality and not live in denial nor seek to restore the past of a long ago era. We are beyond this being possible. The last happy epoch must become memory and not a hoped-for destination.

The key thread in our weaving work is to bond and bridge gaps with the most common denominator, a belief in the Constitution, written to give commoners the power to lead society as it transforms over time in response to humanity's inventiveness and its consequences. American society is to be led by an honest people, for the people, in a government with the right kinds of people in its seats. To be a people working together, we must see our task as one of weaving a social fabric that cares about everyone and orients all our choices toward the benefits of liberty for our children. Our babies deserve bred and fed on the elixir: liberty. It needs nurtured and raised in each generation's mentality for a personality that respects being free.

This is a key to uniting as one people: the shared commitment to liberty, properly understood through ACE throughout our lives. We will not preserve the union without it. We must live our lives as liberty yeomen, boatswain, or coxswain, whichever role we've the most talent to perform well.

In our lives, as we perform roles of responsibility within society that require us to attend to power, we must consider the consequences for the community. The thoughtful reflection and analysis of the SERF can help us do this effectively. This kind of thinking is what is missing in doomerism-guided attitudes and behaviors. The opposite has plagued the baby boomers. Seeking to corrupt matters for personal gain has been their "me first" way, not the proper delegation of authority and its responsible separation of duties to prevent corruption. Nor have they applied their intellects to ensure that no processes of power would cause a loss of liberty. A citizen-first consciousness brings to the performance of the authority figures in the FILMS^2 [P7] of power the necessary KA^{4}SA^2 to properly operate the enterprise. It leads those providing the LAMBS toward achieving our goal and attaining our objectives better and faster through good risk-management.

We must become committed in our E-SASSY-T-TUF-FT-CAUCUS. Putting such high-quality citizenshipping first-and-foremost is necessary if we are to succeed in our efforts to live healthfully and happily. As our species strives to survive, live well, and thrive on earth, we must lead ourselves to be better versions of humanity. We must elevate our consciences, be more conscientious of how we feel—to enjoy conscientiousness, use compassion, give love, and example empathy to tackle complex problems organizationally. The challenges we face require more teamwork because of their layered complexity. Layered in varying degrees and hierarchies of knowledge, we need to work together as teams to comprehend our problems and not let them get so confusing that we become impatient and demand simple answers.

Global teamwork requires trust. Trust is more than just intellectual, so we must bring forward our complete selves, more fully aware of our shared humanity. We cannot go about our work in compartmentalized ways, seeing things as divisible and separable, looking for conveniences. We must see things more holistically, through the networks and connectivity that assemble reality. We must not just focus on the threads but also the weave. We do this by seeking to understand the knots of our connections, the nodes in the networks, with one another in society. With this psychological and sociological knowledge, we will understand the weave needed from the loom. If not, if we cower from complexity, we will fail as a society and find ourselves in the doom of tyranny's bondage.

Learning through ACE about liberty and about ourselves as persons, neighborhoods, communities, settlement patterns, and authority position holders, we'll be able to sew up new social contracts, a better fabric, and one to weather the fast-approaching future. Our ACE begins with reacquainting ourselves with our objectives, our founding principles. We'll restore our greatness as a nation, as one people of many, e pluribus unum, one person at a time, one family at a time, and one neighborhood at a time using our social capital to rebuild the trust that democracy with liberty requires within, among, and from all of us. It will take time. We cannot become distracted again, as the baby boomers did. They got us off course by adopting misguided values for things as the most important nouns, forgetting about those of persons or places. "We the people" is our focus, not "my things", "me the person", "just for me," or "me first." Awaken, America! Let's begin at the beginning. Let's restart ACE as a primary responsibility in our lives. Let's disregard and discard the lies of doomerism.

The most heinous lie of doomerism, the "me first" mentality, is that it is harmless. It is not. It disrespects the people and even undignifies the person who believes in it. Blinded by its sins, we cannot see. Our eyes grow blinders, as we only focus on "me" only. It is a shame that we have done such a thing to our children, much less ourselves. It does not honor our parents. It does not gain us respect. It makes us look like wretched, horrible persons. Yet we retain the shameless hubris and materiality of the baby boomers. It is not "a material world". To believe so is shallow, a hollowing copout, a rationalization of a culture that CATAPULTED doom; brought to society by a misguided generation.

We must confront the danger of its facelessness that turns people into cogs in a machine that benefits others, ignoring the human humaneness and normal natural needs of people as persons and citizens in peaceable society. Treating people as unknowns to the polity and economy powers causes the ignoring of their needs, wants, and desires for opportunity to contribute. Lives go unfulfilled. Such inhumanity causes wrongs to be done in the name of the people by the polity and economy powers' FILMS^2 [P7] and the HM^5. For shame, is there no shame in the hearts of the baby doomers? Have they no human soul? How dare they call themselves American! They have drifted too far away from our core values. Colloquially, they need reined in, removed from the pilothouse's bridge, yanked out of the driver's seat and pulled off the societal ship's helm, and their hands taken away from the controlling wheel, levers, and buttons. We need such an intervention urgently!

American citizens, through ACE, become the new patriots of the Constitution. Knowing the purpose to prevent the loss of liberty by living out our culture of democracy and participating knowingly in representation in the republic, we can summon the will to begin to solve the problems of instability. As we do better at self-governing in our personal lives and within the FILMS^2 [P7] and the HM^5 at the micro, meso, and macro levels of society, we will stabilize American society. Baby doomers removed the idea of protecting the Constitution from the control of the people. It was full of inconvenient truths preventing them from serving themselves uninhibitedly. They paid it lip service and rationalized their way around its ideals. It blocked their search of treasures for their temples of self-worship. All expense and effort was spent on their all-important, ego-based "me-ness," which caused the meanness we now see, hear, smell, feel, and taste in our daily lives in society. Politicians controlled by economic elites through fraud now try to control public opinion with lies.

This brings us to the personal issues, the risks to us as persons. For those who deny suffering from doomerism, this is an appeal to contemplate whether it is perchance possible that one's being might unknowingly have been invaded by a mindset that purports to provide acceptable values with which to justify one's own attitudes and behaviors. However, such thinking as these values cause may be wrong for a democracy, for the liberty of all of us in, and as, an American society. The "what's in it for me" approach is neither helpful nor healthy for e pluribus unum seeking a more perfect union. It is antithetical—foolishly, selfishly, intolerably so. What might the risks of this mindset be? Let's discuss them in the next section, the last section before we present how doomerism COIFFURE our democracy from American society.

Risks to Us

Ultimately, we live within the bounds of a society. We cannot pretend we don't or that we can do whatever we want like wild animals. A country, a community, does not find glory in that way. American society does not work like that. We must cooperate and be considerate of our fellow citizens. Citizenship requires we care for our family, our neighbors, the members of our communities, our state, and our nation as a people—we human beings whose rights and dignity begin with our respecting each other and respecting ourselves. Those who put E-SASSY-T-TUF-FT-CAUCUS first strive to apply common sense for the common good, in the commons, which give us the common wealth from which we all benefit. To understand this is not calculus; it is arithmetic. This is a public issue. It is not a private issue. It is not about one's self. It is about every self. It is about "we" not "me." Such "me first" approach in the polity has led to an average of $7 dollars spent on older adults and $1 spent on children (Taylor, 2014). The baby boomers are now on full display for whom and what they are: selfish, argumentative, ideological dogma addicts. Our posterity deserves better prospects for prosperity. We need to end such doomerism and begin good citizenshipping.

The micro-level attitudes and behaviors we exhibit add up to perceptions of permissibility, which if misguided lead to an eroded faith in the LAMBS. The society in which all have a part to play is ours; it is our USE, constitutionally. We must not forget this. If we do as fleecing baby doomers seek, we will lose hope. We'll be the ones who suffer from the distrust they aristocratically seed and breed. We'll have frustrations with our family and disrespect, dishonor, disagreement, and distrust with neighbors and others, viewing them as competitors and not collaborators in our pursuit of happiness. We'll not trust fellow members of the communities to which we belong. We grow suspicious, doubtful, insular, and mentally and emotionally ill from all the anxiety such a lack of trust thrust upon us by the baby doomers causes. They do this because they are trying to gain power by dividing and conquering us, while simultaneously burying us in destabilizing debt. Pulled by tyrannical instincts, unreasoned in the importance of the virtues for living life well, they corrupt themselves and seek to us. By corrupting our public and private FILMS^2 [P7] through a spineless cowardice they fail to uphold the Constitution while in positions within our governments. We see their crookedness in the DAMN of economy power and in the private HM^5 associations and affiliated FILMS^2 [P7] we've made to AEIOUY^{2}K it, in all its sectors. We see it in the instability we have to support fulfillment of the standard of living created and sustained by the industry and academy powers. We see it in the decline of the quality of life opportunities that industry and artistry powers have provided us in our society.

Sadly, many in the positions of authority using economy power celebrate its success with the creation of super salaries that sequester the people's capital into a few pockets. According to scholarship by the academy and history powers, many in top positions get their wealth from inheritance that paves the way to access the best routes to top colleges and top jobs. This is as it is in a kingdom, where royal families grant their offspring upward assurances generationally. Not meant or made to be a kingdom, we must see recognize the risks to us in this. The founders frowned upon such inheritance's risks of setting up a permanent aristocracy that would block the opportunities for a free people to advance in society. Aristocracies, once formed, seek to remain atop a society as its ruling class. This makes them an enemy of democracy and individual liberty because they subjugate people into controlled subservient positions as subjects, whom the aristocrats enjoy ruling over. From the immense profits of undistributed capital, we see paid propaganda that aims to convince us that those at the top actually earned it. Not fooled are we. Yet doomerism keeps us from making the change in society to invest in new development to share the wealth of the nation.

To keep capital out of the flow of the marketplaces is a restriction upon the opportunities for others and an injustice to the society, which needs reinvestment for each generation to enjoy prosperity. It is a wrongful misuse of the powers entrusted to the economy to trap capital in so few castle keeps. We-are-citizens-first values respect the society and enable freedoms. A we first society would not appreciate selfish persons who hoard everything for themselves to the detriment of the many. Such practices of the baby doomers are steering us toward a colossal doom. Their fast and furiously defended, flashy, "look at me, look at me now" super salaries are driving inequality that causes instability. How can these boomers think they are so special as to receive 400 or 500 times more money than those who earn it for the companies that employ them?

It is just sad that publicly traded corporations, large companies, and small and privately held companies seem to behave as bad citizens. It is discouraging they have accepted the Supreme Court's opinion that while they don't vote as citizens. They, considered financially a person, can express their free speech while hiding how they contribute funds to politicians' campaigns. Is this not a prime example of causing doom for future babies? What citizen in their right mind would agree with this as rightful? For shame, all the games of legalities played by baby doomers, intentionally poking more holes in the social fabric built upon righteous rightful thinking of what is legitimately obvious to a kindergartner. Using technicalities to fleece is wrong. Wanting whopping wanton secret-ingredient wonton-like loopholes is wrong. It is the intentional hiding of truth behind processes blocked by integral blinders. How dare they do this to us, to the USE?

This question may not be answerable without a moral awakening for which we don't have time, so we must intervene now. One day the baby doomers may recognize their crimes and reconcile the damage they caused. Are not the baby boomers the spiritualistic, wannabe flower children seeking world peace? If so, why cannot they seem to share now while they are in charge? How did they become so hypocritical? Did they sell out, accidentally by arrogance and recklessness, or intentionally for materialistic consumerism as a mistaken promise for happiness? On the other hand, were they always narcissistic and their original protests just an example of this characteristic? Obviously, we did not recognize it because of all the destabilizing turmoil they stimulated. They were the generation that promised freedom but delivered disaster, having a degrading effect on our country. (Andrews, 2021) Perhaps they enjoy chaos. It is not good for the rest of us trying to live our lives in peace and have happiness. We cannot wait for answers. The risks to us are too great. We've no time for blind justice to catch up to the rat race they run, to snag them in their cheese-snatching schemes. Besides, they already clog up our courts with too many bogus lawsuits.

In the meantime, we have work to do to weave back together the social fabric of American society they have shredded. With an understanding of the ecology of powers and the SERF, we can begin to rebuild our ethical and purposeful levels of high personal standards befitting the republic, in accord with our democracy culture, and push for the IDEALS of liberty. However, before we hear more about the dime-stealing crime of doomerism—in an effort to leave no doubt—we need some final words on risks to us. A last bit of risk talk, and then we'll move on to why it is such a huge micro, meso, and macro levels of society challenge that we face. And, we'll

go over how now we must have an intervention to correct the course toward one that favors a
better future for our babies.

As noted, we build risk awareness through the SERF. "All is a risk" is the case within all cultures run by people who are running-scared of accountability. Baby doomers, prone always to avoid responsibility when it is inconvenient, deny that there are any risks in their approach. They've a low tolerance for ego denting, though. Perhaps they are afraid, ostriches with heads in the sand, or they simply want to hide from taking any responsibility for fear it will disrupt their fantasies about themselves. If we the people are the proper place of leadership in society, we'll fail if we are unwilling to accept responsibility and accountability for our performance. As citizen first leaders, we must accept responsibility. This is a key trait of a leader. We must step up to prevent the feeble-minded from running the show.

Citizen leaders tune in to first principles and build upon them, reminding one another of their genius, respecting the wisdom of how they create winning teams that work together to achieve victory. Not preparing future generations is a huge risk to us. Did the boomers do a good job at this? Not having raised citizen leaders is a huge risk in a democracy. We need to develop leaders in each generation, and with increasingly complex globally connected societies, we need better risk-management. We need it as another tool for understanding the social transformation that new knowledge and technologies are causing. We need it in our leadership training in our ACE, so people are conversant of the risks to our American society, and preparing appropriate responses to deal with them effectively to protect our society from damages.

The delegation of our powers and the risks in their FILMS[2] [P7] need to be understood, and the roles of who is to do what must be clear, the means of communication apparent, and the controls we use to respond and monitor our risks regularly reported to us, the everyday people, the leadership of the USE. Insecurity in speaking about risks to society is not excusable. Using the SERF to talk about risks is a way to confront our mutual societal fears. The SERF brings forward our fears and the uncertainties that matter to the USE in a logical way. It unmasks fraudulent rationalizations that hide truths with fallacies and polemic disguises. Truths need known. Fallacies need stopped. The SERF exposes vulnerabilities that open us to threats and it shows us opportunities to take risks upon to generate betterments for the USE that is ours to lead. The essence of the work we are in the business of doing, both personally and in performing our roles as citizens for our society, is the practice of good, sound risk-management.

Our obligation is to professionalism, not protectionism. That is, we must act professionally in our demeanor and behavior as citizens. Immature behavior, lashing about in childish ways to protect this or that as "mine, mine, mine" with a "screw you, it's all mine" attitude is not the best we can do. It is in itself a form of ego protection and an infantile aspect of doomerism. Doomerism now exposed needs dealt with forthrightly without denial. We can have no more finger pointing. The root of the rot dug up, we must remove it from our society. We keep our better culture of democracy when we know the risks to liberty and manage them. We now know more of what doomerism is doing and why it is doing it. We must reject this infection. We must not become beholden to it. If we do, we die. We the everyday people in a republic with democracy, hasten our death to tyranny if we do not vigilantly refresh it with our willpower, by valiantly exerting our people power constantly. Becoming conversant and not skittish at risk talk, we'll develop sufficient risk-management know-how for better citizenshipping. Yet the question remains of the risks of doomerism: what else has it done and is it doing to us? Why is it such a problem for us, if it is merely risky business?

Why is Doomerism a Problem?

The good news is that doomerism is not permanent. It is like a bad hairstyle, a puffed up with hot air coiffure. We can change it at will. This book encourages that we change it now and rehabilitate those most suffering from it. To do so, we need an intervention. We need to replace baby boomers with adults within the age range of maximum brilliance, from 24 to 40. We need citizens in this age range who believe in and civilly practice civic mindedness. We need them to want to serve, to lead with multiple social grammars and rebuild civil society's social capital. We need these citizens to step up with their advanced educations, teamwork qualities, and problem solving abilities. We need them to review the civics educators' recommended ACE curricula (see The Learning Liberty Resources in the Appendix). We need them to be emboldened, empowered, and put in charge as our—civic-minded team-playing citizenshipping to IDEALS liberty— executives, legislators, judges, and commercial entrepreneurs of the USE. We need them to assume authority positions in the LAMBS. We'll respond to the risks of their poor performance possibility by preparing these successive younger generations to be honorable leaders with a solid ACE.

Unless we reverse doomerism as soon as possible, there will be no endowment to pass down. There will be no stable, healthy, well-forested ecosystem of a society with a liberty tree lighted by the lamps of justice, unless we transfer authority to AEIOUY^{2}K the societal and social powers to those who will live in the future. Certainly, we must educate them to IDEALS liberty and pursue our goal and objectives as citizens first. If we do not, American society will die. To keep it alive, we must coach the citizenry to choose future leaders dedicated to E-SASSY-T-TUF-FT-CAUCUS and to commit to IDEALS liberty. Their purpose and calling is forming in these saving graces of the ideals of democracy in representative republic. They will redeem us.

It will be necessary to manage the risks of this transfer of power from its wrongful concentration in the baby boomer generation to the succeeding generations. If we don't move the baby doomers out, they will colloquially "eat us up" and destroy the US as a republic of democracy by their excessive weight. Strange headlines will be written to explain how the baby boomers COIFFURE democracy from American society. To avoid this risk's realization, all must manifest the social control upon authority figures, holding them accountable to reflect the best in the people, not the worst. Let's explore what this might mean. Doomerism, of course, is far worse than a bad hairstyle. Yet, we cannot allow its dangers to determine our fate as a people, as a nation, as a society. Let's go over how it COIFFURE our culture.

It Confiscates

Doomerism confiscates democracy. It seizes the power of the people and puts it in the hands of patronizing politicians and economic elites. As a corrupting condition, it turns authority figures into power bidders. Power pursuits are political acts. These groups are politically motivated, not in party affiliation but in the fact that politics is about power. They both want more of it. How superior they believe themselves to be, as plutocratic, wannabe aristocrats. Power is a corrupting force. Our founders understood this and knew that it needed checked and balanced. They used committees so the herd through representation would be heard. They chose a republic to resist the power-hungry few and the mob of the many not being able to agree, or falling for and following the demagoguery of a rule-breaking, charismatic, instigator malcontent, like Masaniello of 1647 Naples, Italy.

The founders believed that each person, by their common sense and reason, could build coalitions to prevent one bully from taking over and dictating terms for the rest. Political engagement would bring the best ideas to the surface. The majority, through debate, would determine what they believed to be best for each other through committee procedures. However, committees fail if full of dishonest sycophants. As boards for governing, if they fail to live up to the high standard ambition for them, which is the "check", the managerial control to stop one person taking over, there will be ramifications on those they represent but do not see, or hear. We must make ourselves seen and heard.

However, if they believe they can ride one person's power pursuit to their own advantage, limited integrity butt-licking boomer brownnosers will sell out the people they swore and oath to serve. This is but one way in which the self-centered baby doomers confiscate others' voices. This is how the baby doomers have corrupted the federal government. They reduced it to a political game, and they sorely underperform the duties for which elected. Since the majority of voters are baby boomers, they did not mind because they got their materialistic consumer comforts, and the representatives are just like them, selfish. What a nice reflection and security in ego this must bring.

Trivial trinkets and fantastic gains in Wall Street investments have bought them all off. So they willingly live for and worship Wall Street, allowing it to buy their cohorts in Congress and continue to enlarge our supposed-to-be-limited government, transferring our wealth to the economic elites, driving up our debt, and wrongfully burdening future generations. The reign of the baby boomers raised the roof of financial risk tolerance thresholds, pushing annual deficits and increasing the nation's long-term debt. Kicking the social problems' can down the road by their billion selfish decisions, we move toward one of two poles. Both of which are heavy forms of tyranny that diminish our quality of life: aristocracy and mobocracy. Too many baby doomers take from all of us through Ponzi-like monetary and taxation redistribution schemes to flatter and fatten themselves as overfed fat cats of the economy power. These profiteering-off-the-politicians elites pay for the campaigns, lobby for the policies, and laws their patronizing (of them and toward us) politicians write. Then, they move back and forth through a revolving door at the highest income levels, taking jobs that do not better our lot. It is a joke, and the American people are fools for not stopping it by properly participating in politics to prevent partisanship.

We must replenish the persons in government so the polity cannot confiscate all our wealth. We must regulate the polity from stealing from us and giving to its friends, the members of their country clubs and parties in the upper, wannabe ruling classes at the top of income brackets, way above the normal conditions of the everyday people. If the few take our wealth quasi-legally or illegally, to be a plutocracy, they are not an aristocracy. The airs of aristocrats required legitimacy. The royals would be regal and moral with the interests of the population in mind, or feigned. Sometimes a parade was a charade for population control. The baby dooming kleptomaniacs might want to be a plutocracy, but it lacks the face of kindness, real or faked, by loyal to nation royals. By their thievery, doomers convert the dignity inducing democracy culture into a kleptocracy! Persons who earn income in the top one percent enjoyed a 70 percent growth in income after taxes and government transfers between 1979 and 2016 (Congressional Budget Office, 2019). How is it that the population majorities suffer more while they prosper? Is that promoting the general welfare? Is that a blessing of liberty, for a handful to confiscate control of the common wealth and sequester it from flowing in the marketplaces? This confiscatory behavior of doomers, keeps money from moving around the economy. It prevents the flow of cash through the pockets and bank accounts of hard working everyday people. It stalls the prosperity economy power can bring to everyone working to move survival, to living, to thriving.

It Obfuscates

Doomerism obfuscates democracy. As a corrupting condition, it renders the purpose and future of our enterprise dim and confusing. The use of fallacies and polemics is a smokescreen that blocks from view the truth that our polity power is supposed to protect our inalienable rights, but this does not seem to be what it is doing. The truth is that our economy power is supposed to allow us to make a livelihood free from depravity and enjoy the blessings of liberty. Neither is doing its job well. Nor are we, which is a big part of the reason why they are doing poorly. Doomerism has overtaken our logic. With its distractions, it has obfuscated our common sense thinking. It is as if baby doomers only care about winning a battle of the egos and ruling over others, rather than being responsible. They are fools who don't serve the nation well because of their "me first" selves. Their isms and ideologies get tossed about to disguise reality and obfuscate this truth. They hide behind their lies. They hire propagandists to write sensationalized stories full of surprises that chastise our intelligence and capsize our outcries. The idealist baby doomers would rather argue to prove they are right than do right. The damage this causes the rest of us is no longer tolerable. A free people no longer want the consequences of their ways. We must unite in opposition to such manipulation of the press, and us.

This mistake comes from the myopia of seeing life as a series of zero-sum games to be won instead of living virtuously, attaining true victory over self and not over others. Ask any beautifully minded mathematical game theorist or decent economist. They will explain the fallacy of winner-takes-all- competition-mentality in complex social situations requiring smarter negotiations. This syndrome of an inability to solve disagreements is causing the worldly problems of social ills, incivility, violence-inspiring immaturity, and a feverishly fervent hatred of enemies within our population. For example, the present broadcast "media" of baby boomers divides people and political parties for profit. Don't be a puppet! Think, identify facts, and use logic. Journalism is not to be about being first; it is to be about being accurate. But the baby doomers think that being first is more important. Ah, they revel in scoring points. Not all in life is a game of sports. While society falls apart, they rejoice in stupid little tit-for-tat, unruly, obnoxious remarks and ripostes. Their petty win at all costs competitiveness contributes to incessant information overload. It is irresponsibly destructive, and in no way constructive to the free speech ideal, which undergirds our freedoms. Truth is the bedrock upon which our societal foundations were set. Telling a lie is not exercising ones right to speak freely. It is lying. It is dishonesty. It undermines our freedoms. It is a corrosive opacification. It obfuscates truth. Such behaviors put people on the defensive. A byproduct of the speed of media is that people begin to believe in false-hoods as truths and question provable facts. This is chaotic. It undermines future generations' ability to know the real history, not the one written by the winner of an undefined, un-refereed game run by cheaters, but the actual history based upon fact, not opinion.

Doomerism obfuscates by causing confusion in the societal powers. Power is the basic component of organizing people. Organized people are a society. A society can place power in tyranny, or it can place power in democracy. The Constitution is the basis of the US. It places the power in the people to self-govern society by representatives in a republic. Its principal aim is to constitute an unoppressed people. It does so by the manner in which it regulates and distributes power. Citizenship behaviors are its rudimentary social force, the foundation of organizing a society, giving basic rules, norms, standards, and mores that will shape people's behavior toward wanting to govern with each other, of, by, and for one another as a united people. Such is democracy. Democracy is a culture. It takes courage. It takes work to prevent government from taking rights and instead to protect them. Persons in a democracy must lead others and self for the benefit of all and not for the inflation of our own personal egos. This takes training, which begins with basic lessons of civics, of our foundation laid by the founding framers. It continues into other curricula of leadership and social responsibility through a complete ACE.

Human behaviors can be permitted or prohibited by the FILMS[2] [P7] of the polity power, its dominant systems of law. Historically in the Western Hemisphere, these legal systems are the common law of the English and the civil law of the French. Both establish the government as the rule of law. Common law does not want the rule of men (humans) to be in control of society, because such provides power to the patronizing politicians to administer society's legal framework. Of course, as we know from our history power, through the oral and written lessons of our ancestors, nothing in human affairs is stagnant: not love, not hate, not health, not wealth, nor the lack of any of these. Therefore, a more perfect union is of, by, and for the people, a work in progress, yet only possible by a law-abiding culture called "democracy". It provides the polity flexibility to adapt and adjust its rules by the will of the people, to ensure its sustenance and nonviolent transfer of the authorities to keep the society solvent and on course with its objectives attainment on behalf of the will of the people. It's a will built by ACE to edify us of our responsibility to enact the best citizenshipping. We must to forestall our country drifting away from its purposeful course of navigation.

As we read of the threats of doomerism, we continue to see that the power of control over the polity has shifted to the will of the elite of the economy power. This misbalance causes many societal woes. The crises and chaos we see repeatedly emerging are the result of the risky ways of the baby doomers plagued by ill micro-, meso-, and macro-level "me first" attitudes and behaviors. We are not seeing our inputs handled with throughput in a manner resulting in the outputs we expected of the societal powers. Doomerism distorts all of the FILMS[2] [P7] ending in ugly outcomes.

Since the Constitution establishes the law in a culture democracy, people power in society, so constituted, has forceful influence for the recreation of this culture that frees people from the bondage of tyranny. Doomerism dismisses this culture and dismantles its first principles by obfuscating the fact that a liberated people are free to be unoppressed. Oppressed people are controlled. They are restricted in self-expression and denied the freedom to create culture. Restricted are their thoughts, speech, and pursuits. An unoppressed people, appointed to self-govern by a Constitution, have more responsibility than do subjects in a kingdom. Participation in the polity is necessary. Those serving it have the public's trust. To make it work requires a pursuit of knowledge that includes a strong ACE with the profound truth of the ideals that made the US a reality. It requires an informed public to have fact-based opinions and a social responsibility to share these opinions civilly with others in the society in an open frame of mind to consider differing perspectives.

Informed opinions on what is important in one's family, neighborhood, community, state, and on matters pertinent to the LAMBS needs expressed. The polity's politicians and the economy's elites should address pertinent matters on the citizenry's behalf as team players with the people in a balancing way. We the everyday people must demand better synchronization of these three primary societal powers toward achieving the goal and attaining the objectives of the USE. Conversations on issues needing addressed and on the problems confronting the society locally, regionally, and nationally, must happen more profusely. The risks that exist within society from doomerism need responded to with reemphasis on reasonable rules and regulations through voluntary changes in attitudes and behaviors. Solutions chosen based in facts and evidence should point to compatible arrangements of the parts to the each other and the whole. Gestalt equilibrium would be an ideal outcome—where the whole is greater than the sum of the parts.

We the people, as the leaders in democracy, must attend to our responsibilities to keep politicians in check. We must prevent them from violating our citizen rights. The miracle of the nation was this mandate to limit the polity and make it work for us, not us for it. We control it by the power of voting. If we do not vote, we lose power. It is our right to select by open elections the persons given the authority to govern. Those who run for and hold office we call politicians. "Politician" has poor connotations when we do not keep them in check and let them think whatever-the-heck they want. Our constant participation in politics is how we get them to perform according to our will. We simply must participate in politics, or "politician" will remain an epithet. It is better to have politicians than tyrants who never change. Voting serves the immense purpose of protecting our liberty as constituted when used properly to replace politicians regularly. Baby doomerism obfuscates our understanding of this because it allows us to act like our own little isolated tyrants of commons destroying self-interest, ignorantly failing to perform our prime culture and revolutionary "rite" to vote. Let's moor to voting, and do it more. The folkways, customs, mores, and norms of our democracy culture depend upon us doing it consistently. Let us no longer see it as an inconvenience of no difference making. Such is too narcissistic a viewpoint for us to hold anymore. It is one of doomerism. We must vote in all matter large and small, local to national. We must learn how these elections intertwine, and how such practices as gerrymandering and redistricting detrimentally affect our representation. We engage more deeply, and we'll eliminate these lame and lazy alterations and our own excuses for tolerating them. We must vote to change the dominance of the duopoly, and we'll get rid of the two-team game played against us. A situation undesired by the framers.

Doomerism obfuscates democracy further by denying our society's first principles. Baby doomers do not want them known. They pay lip service. Principles get in the way of their fleecing ambitions. They cannot openly steal from us if we are aware of our societal first principle, liberty. Essential liberty is freedom from oppression of any kind. When the economy powers' HM^5 and FILMS^2 [P7] DAMN their power, it leads to an aggressive consumerism that cripples us in massive debt. We need to address this risk. It exists because multinational corporations have no national identity. They are above us. They do not need to respect a sovereign nation's culture. They feed the economic elites who buy politicians attention and affection. Internationally expansive operations create loyalty by paying its executives extreme salaries, and convert them into thinking like feudal lords, kings and queens, absconding from the nations, filling their pockets full of all people's riches. Commercial businesses are great for advancing prosperity in humanity if undistorted by societally wrongheaded remuneration or responsibility abortive schemes. If not held honorably, they otherwise behave as rapier criminals without a conscience.

The economic elites get all the money out of every society these days. There is enough to go around and make more successfully supported people, more millionaires and billionaires than ever, but if there are only three zillionaires, is this sequestering of capital a limitation on the rest of us? The baby doomers' hoarding and belief in their own entitlement are arguments that plutocrats make. Plutocracy is a risk to democracy, and its proponents use propaganda to make people believe in the lies that allow them to have it their way, to have it all, everything we the everyday people make. Yet American society is a result of government (the making, enforcing, and arbitrating disputes of law) and of a culture expressed in more forms than just the foundation of democracy and respectful representation respectively.

Much of culture is a response to the risks of the geography power to our existence as a species. Geographic and social adaptations by people to survive within earth's biospheres and its ecosystems' environmental resource capability and capacity to provide, including its climatic realities, affects people's acquisition of what is needed (such as tools, food, clothes, shelter, survival knowledge, and comfort). What is wanted motivates. It serves interests effects ambitions, and affects what we pursue to fulfill needs and desires.

Our needs and wants intertwine in our minds as influenced by other minds. Psychologists working for advertisers seeking better ways to convince us to buy something, study how we think (Ewing, 1976). This brings us back to the adage: great minds discuss ideas, average minds discuss events, and small minds discuss people pettily. Little minds try to destroy other minds. Now, we can add, manipulative minds seek to make other minds think differently than they might naturally think. Be mindful not to believe the hyperbole, the false promises of advertisements, which can turn people into unknowing consumers who trust brands more than their own hands (Ewing, 1976).

We used to make everything in this land. For our needs and wants, we depend upon our economy power to make the provisions for us and to employ us. Our needs include tools, what tools produce, and social stability to rear children and live with comfort. Our wants include a desire to be able to escape from difficulty through entertainment, either by knowledge acquisition or by creative expression like writing, crafts, invention, consumption of others' creative expressions, such as reading, or observing others' performances of their creations with sounds or stories in theaters, in movies, on television, or on other mobile screens receiving broadcasts. Our artistry power continues to seek new forms of entertainment to make survival more palatable. Doomerism invites us only to consume and not to engage civically to prevent the politicians and economy's elites from forming an accidental, (or is it intentional), tyranny over us. It makes us insecure, claiming that only a few superstars deserve big money, and the prestige of pretentious privilege to swerve around taxation and law, so that only they may be great, until we worship them for their near-godlikeness. Doomerism creates a religious experience of economic elites. Their wealth is metaphorically like Mt. Olympus, and they live lives of luxury as we toil, suffering from their self-centered decisions because too much power has been concentrated in too few hands. This is the gravest danger to democracy.

It Immolates

Doomerism immolates democracy. As a corrupting condition, it sacrifices liberty and democracy for dominance and determinism. It uses demagoguery and distraction to dispense its disease to divide us, immolating our livelihoods as if they do not matter. Doomerism sacrifices people and virtues to please the powerful position holders. It gives away principles (to placate ameers) and macerates truth. It causes the foolish to think they are fantastic. It eliminates merit-based methods of advancement, so the friends of friends of baby doomers' country clubs go first. It's aristocracy, not democracy. We must stop the foolish, fallacious, and felonious acts of the baby doomers in politics and feudalistic commerce in economics. They have wreaked havoc these past forty years. The boomers' failure is on prominent display every day on the television, computer, and portable device screens porting social media broadcasts across the internet. They simply reject any vestige of hope in finding agreement. The compromise that formed thirteen colonies into one nation under God proves that the boomers are clowns compared to our grandfathering founders. The damage from their false, uncompromising, unprovable, ideology-based politics and society destabilizing economics becomes clearer with each day we allow them to remain in positions of authority.

The boomers inherited a polity based on compromise and sacrifice. Rejecting these in favor of standoffs, they squandered the commercial boon we earned after winning World War II. As parents, they passed down to their children, for the first time in our generational history, a lower standard of living with fewer opportunities to own property. Fealty is never being able to own property. The self-righteous boomers will likely wipe out the probability of retirement pensions and medical aid and healthcare for the generations that follow them. They'll milk the future workers' paychecks to provide their Medicare welfare dependent lifestyles. Moreover, many have not put anything in place to enable the children of their children to have a means of saving for retirement after a long life of work. They just take. They care not of the consequences to babies' eventual adult lives. It's uncivilized and un-American.

Doomerism immolates democracy by its waging of the "culture wars," perpetuating for ridiculous principles not benefiting democracy a perverted polarization and permanent state of gridlock. We can evaporate this dense deadpan disagreement by removing them from all places of authority. Doomers cannot build relationships. They can only separate. It is how they isolate and defend their sickening to society "me first" selfishness. Misguided by extreme materialistic pursuits they forgot how to relate to others humanly. Wealth can make this possible. All was a game of life to them. Wealth can make it easy to lie and hard to compromise one's opinions and conform to comport with the truth, much less seek to find it. Having dominated the expressive and commercial subcultures of society for decades, the boomers are clueless about how to build anything bigger than selfish pursuits. They are great at seeing the universe in their own navels.

Such fascination with self immolates society. It destroys the capacity for conscientiousness, compassion, love, and empathy by creating tribal-like verbal warfare among a desperate population reaching for a savior figure. It breeds a cultural despair and perpetuates the politics that enrich a few by distancing the public through stupid, irrelevant arguments over isms favored by one side or the other. It forgets that we the people need to govern and not play politics for points. Who cares who scores? We need to solve real societal transformational challenges. We need to adapt to a future coming faster than ever before. We must find a way to generate the revenue to sustain our enterprise. We cannot fund our society now, as it was passed down, ready to provide the good life for more people than ever. The boomers have lost our advantage. We are here now, and we need them gone. We have their spawned culture of baby doomerism to thank, and we must tank them by telling them "You're fired," and without severance pay, as they have not earned it. Doomers do not deserve it because they screwed up by skewering the prosperity of posterity. Yet oft' forgiving are we, and once gone from power we'll welcome them back to teach that which they did not live by: civics. This will be good for them, for us, for the children to learn how to carry on the great experiment that became our project, a republic, e pluribus unum.

If we collect near-zero revenue because we allow ourselves to be fleeced by a few pirates who for private gain willfully ignore their citizenship responsibilities as listed in the Constitution, then we run the risk of losing freedom of commerce on the seas and a change in global peace. A choice needs made during the chaos of crises of the storming phase of the shifting paradigms altering our equilibrium and stability, caused by the third stage of knowledge creation (see Figure 4-1). Now, exposed to new risks to our capability to "provide for the common defense," we are not in a position to allow baby doomers who benefited from the free and open society of the USE to ignore its other needs.

The primary societal powers need rebalanced to meet the Constitution's objectives. Allowing doomerism to continue so a few may "have it all" means that none of us will have a "common defense." Shell games of policy funding immolate the facts. New feudal lords fielding funds by not paying taxes means they build castles with keeps that sequester financial capital away from the main need of the Constitution for we the people to protect ourselves from foreign enemies. If our new robber barons were better citizens, committed to upholding the Constitution by supporting the funding of the USE, they would be writing checks willingly to the Internal Revenue Service and not funding the campaigns of patronizing politicians who will put in office lackeys to give them a free ride and allow their irresponsible behavior to continue.

Foreign policy mistakes are born of misunderstood purposes of our engagement in international affairs. Diplomacy has no normal constituency within our borders, except in Washington, DC and at a few universities that intently study it. It does not create as many classified domestic jobs like the military-industrial or prison-industrial complexes. It does not easily show its power, as a military air strike. It does cause us to have to talk to others with whom we might rather not communicate. Diplomacy aims to keep the peace by keeping the conversations going, or potentially going, when global risks rise up as dangerous threats of wars and their horrid human harm and refugee migrations. We can solve problems through diplomatic negotiations.

Diplomacy also keeps us informed about what other nations are doing with their societal powers. It is like a game of chess: it requires more strategic thinking than checkers does. Building a foreign policy for the spread of democracy and the exercise of trade, increased or decreased by sanctions, is a difficult proposition. Containment of aggression around the world is like being a police officer on the beat. Funding a foreign policy to maintain a peaceful world by ourselves is difficult and expensive. With a more robust diplomatic effort, we would be able to get more friends to help us get to world peace and prosperity. We must learn more about how our nation's foreign policy activities and statecraft affect our daily lives. This is especially important when we evaluate candidates for President of the United States, since foreign affairs enacted on our behalf is the primary responsibility of the top official in our Federal government's Executive branch.

We the everyday people, who may not see the immediate benefit of paying attention to our nation's foreign policy, need better to understand it and other international concepts like realpolitik, machtpolitik, and Weltpolitik, to name a few. Our relations in a globalized world of intertwined economic activities mean that we are more connected and dependent upon the world than ever before. We should know and formulate, as the leadership body of our society, how we want to proceed. Do we want to press for democracy? Do we want to work to help others not be oppressed and imprisoned by tyrants? Do we want to police the world, so there is less violent conflict that could disrupt the supply chains of our economy power? If there is one area we must pay more attention to, it is our nation's foreign policy, since our treasure taken by taxation funds it. How it connects back to our opportunities at home and supports our common defense less expensively than going to war is something we must attend to forthrightly. Could we use diplomacy to get others to do more policing in their regions of the world? Can we trust them to do it justly? How do we engage with the world without bankrupting ourselves? How do we get fair and equitable trade and prevent capital from leaving the USE for polluting places with cheaper labor?

What happens globally does affect us locally in the present world. We must voice our will through our representatives. We must understand that if wrong is done in our name in a "might makes right" manner, versus just causes that are welcomed by the world community, as negotiated in the United Nations, we may cause unintended consequences that will haunt us and possibly hurt us, in reputation and/or physically. If we are boastful and brag like an empire, how can we claim to be a peaceable democracy? If we behave tyrannically, we disgrace ourselves. If we do not act in concert with our core values, as we prefer treated with respect, we humiliate ourselves. If we develop petty prejudices and hatred of the other, simply because our polity failed to engage in humane diplomacy, we fool ourselves. If we instead are indiscriminate and brash, we might make enemies of peoples who have had no ill will toward us. We must discuss how we want to be in the big, wide-open world. We should know how it ties back to our basic values. Does our way of being around the globe provide for our common defense? Does it help us present ourselves as we want seen? Does it help or hurt our purposes? Does it endanger our people?

Do we want to do things for shortsighted reasons that cause backlash, as our foreign policy in the Middle East has created terroristic hatreds against us? Is it our right to meddle in other nations' sovereignty? Does our foreign policy create gains for liberty, or does it jeopardize citizen safety overseas? Is our increased internal police brutality with militaristic weaponry making us look like hypocrites in the eyes, hearts, and minds of those in other nations? Through our internal brutality, do we lose moral ground for our arguments on why democracy is the best way to organize society? Does it cause a loss of diplomacy by removing our moral ability to influence the world toward peace with freedom? Does it strip our diplomats' ability to defend us with words and cause us to lose this critical leg of the stool of relations, leaving us only with whatever intelligence we might gather and our military? Put into a corner, are we only able to provide for defense with the use of violence? Does force become our only weapon against frustration? Is this who we think we are meant to be? Is this who we want to be? Perhaps we should seek to understand better the first principles and ideals of the founders. They would not ever engage in a "holy war" or support others who do, because they believed in freedom of faith practices and a state separated from any religion's control. They were devout deists who vehemently disapproved of theocracy.

We really need to think as citizens about how our polity speaks to us and on our behalf. We must pay attention to its words. The rule of law is not for waging war on the people. What do we now think of the polity's use of power to address social problems? Is it wise to approach them with language like the baby doomers spout? Must everything be a war? War is destructive; it is not a good cure. It is not medicinal, and yet it is the language used by the polity. We have heard from them there is a war on:

- Poverty   - Drugs   - Crime   - Terrorism

What's next? How about better foreign and domestic polices? Is it sensible, in a globalizing world of greater risks brought about by the complexity of advancing knowledge and technologies and interconnected networks of academy, industry, and artistry powers, for us to be warmongers against

everything that frustrates us in society? No, of course not, such is foolishness! However, if the ideologically minded boomers, who protested against
Vietnam, like to think it is the way to go, then we are in deep trouble. Because of their generation's majority rule, particularly in the past twenty years
of their entrenchment, we've steadily lost the moral negotiating power of
claiming to be a fully free republic with good democracy culture. With it,
we have persuasive ability. Without it, we don't. According to the Freedom
House's 2021 reporting, our democracy rates an 83 out of 100 points, an
eleven-point drop in ten years. For point scoring lovers as the doomers are,
this is poor performance. For the longest surviving constitutional democracy, this is embarrassing. We should be at the top of the lists of such evaluations.

We are the longest living constitutionally established republic of representative democracy. That we aren't rated the best democracy proves we
simply need newer, more diverse and complex minds to carry us forward
without the win-lose zero-sum mentality of baby boomers. We need thinking that is more diplomatic, that does not seek war but builds peace and
prosperity. We need long-term stability and better commercial ability, so the
economy power's FILMS$^{2\,[P7]}$ and its HM^5 can create jobs for us domestically and not have to export them. Some might argue that an unstable world
means the capital will flow back to us. This is illogical thinking; chaos everywhere does not create full employment here at home.

We must be mindful that the economy power's FILMS$^{2\,[P7]}$, if given the
whole world to work within but without responsibility for the social consequences of its performance or non-performance, create risks we might not
want. Globalization can create difficulties. If couched with a proper foreign
and domestic policy that focuses the enterprise on managing its risks in a
manner benefiting the people first, and not the economy power's elites, the
hurt put upon our families is avoidable. The pain that undermines family
values by forcing all in the house to sell their labor to afford a basic standard of living and abandon children to electronic devices' that numb their
brains and cause hyperactivity by overstimulation. This social circumstance
is going to prove out in the long term as a cruel and unusual reality thrust
upon us by imbalanced societal powers. Worse in the short term, these col-
orful lights flashing moth-to-flame dopamine releasing addictive predatory
gadgets are terrible nannies.

Economic impossibilities undermine family values. Jobs sent overseas
hurt communities, driving them into anomic conditions of poverty and un-
leashing horrid, enervating behaviors that hurt us to know they happen in
our neighborhoods. Other families adapt by turning to dual-income households, but that is not enough when one person cannot work. Marriages
broken by financial stress, and poor public policies, leave children with only
one parent who must work and raise them. Extreme inequality in income
distribution is the result. The rich distance themselves hiding behind gated

community fencing, increasing an air of aristocracy, devaluing and shrinking middle classes (blue, white, grey collar), and sinking the lower classes lower. Entire generations growing up in poverty, causes conditions ripe for criminality as the only way, means and methods, for survival. Its consequence is incarceration. The economic separation of different-looking people allows no interclass linking, no learning of one another's social grammars. It correlates with the development of globalizing underworlds run by thuggery. These are the results of baby doomerism. This is what happens when we treat children as appendages or an afterthought instead of as the future's merciful benefactors in the greatest opportunity for humanity project. One which they must invest their lives and fulfill its completion. Moreover, when we are feebly old, we will need them to attend to and nurse us. Babies are our posterity. Frustratingly it's becoming increasingly evident, statistically, that the boomers "me first" conditioning caused them to forget about this eventual situation, and it misguided investments away from preparing the next generation to take over the leadership of society. Cycle of life wisdom tells us their development is a primary purpose for society. Further, we need their opportunity potential improved to provide future prosperity to us all. Only by a "giving" culture do we get it passed down from generation to generation. Doomerism is a "taking" culture. Thus, it immolates hope and destabilizes our society's foundation found in ideal American principles set forth by the nation's framers.

This is what happens when we don't invest in the time to come, but sing hedonistically, "I want it all and I want it now" and then vainly with foolish pride take it—to satiate for our selfish selves like greedy sow. This kind of ailment is the moral sickness of doomerism. For shame, is there no guilt in the hearts of the baby doomers? Can they really be that callous? Are they medically psychopathic? What does the ticker tape say? It clearly says that the measure of the economy is the money in the wallet of the top one percent, of the traders on Wall Street, and not the family who wants to shop at mom and pop community based neighborly stores on Main Street. What has become of us? This is not who we were meant to be. This is not as intended. We are diseased with immolating doomerism!

We the everyday people must lead the polity power not to kiss the anus of the economy power any longer. We need to stop the backbiting and bitter infighting that distracts us from the fleecing at hand and get serious about the new age we are in that requires radical innovations in the foreign and domestic policy arenas that in a globally connected world shape the conditions of our everyday life experience. Are we alive for one another in community? Are we as citizens in the enterprise, stakeholders of the nation, or are we mere pawns, tokens on a board, in some surreal battle of isms playing out before our eyes as the tails wag the dogs on the national television broadcast networks blaring in our homes and on our personal computers and handheld electronic devices? Oh, the games played with and on our attention gain in absurdity and we are pained to see it. We must adjust.

Let's get out of the cycles of poverty and consumerism. Let's get into a pattern of E-SASSY-T-TUF-FT-CAUCUS. If things get worse, this proposed approach, this remedy, will get us through troubled times ahead. If things get better, this treatment for the social disease of doomerism will guide us. It with ACE will instruct us in how to invest in our children, not to spoil them but to enable them to bring their gifts into the endowment of a free land as a free people working toward the Constitution's objectives of liberty and justice for all as we strive to achieve our project's goal of a more perfect union. If we don't, we end in tyranny, in a fast approaching, tomorrow.

It Frustrates

Doomerism frustrates democracy. As a corrupting condition, it causes us to wince as we witness baby doomers on television, or any broadcasting hand held devise or computer screen, behaving in ways shameful, irreverent, disrespectful, and undignified. They act terribly proud of their hubris and greed. This is frustrating to a society in which parents seek to raise good children. No longer can we point to our persons in authority as positive role models and examples to emulate. It frustrates to no end. It is a shame and an abomination what the boomers have done to our American society. It wounds to watch when a baby doomer behaves in the stereotypical ways of their generation's personality. Still, it is more incredibly frustrating that they cannot see it. If made aware of it, and recognizing it could be true, then they would become defiantly defensive, and embrace denial and attack the sage trying to advise them on how to save their souls from evil-doing. Or worse, they couldn't care less and would see nothing wrong with it. This hurts neighborly loving compatriots. It's like seeing a loved one caught doing something inappropriate, exhibiting foolish pride, hypocritically denying facts in front of everyone. With our eyes, we can see. With their eyes, they cannot. Nor can their mind admit what wrong they have done. We do not want to witness them go down in flames, but they refuse to use the water in the buckets of love we try to pour over them to douse their ego errors and restore them with humility needed for community. We hope to free them from doomerism.

The greatest frustration we feel is the boomer's slogan: the "me first" generation. What could be more "in your face" toward posterity than that "I got mine, screw you" mentality, held out as a virtue when in fact it is a vice? After all, visually, "me" looks like "we" written upside down. What an affront to liberty and justice for all. They've flipped society on its head, turning it from democracy toward plutocracy.

The discovery of doomerism explains detrimental conditions in society. Extrapolated, many confusing situations are now explainable by it. A patriot seeking to instill hope, will call our citizenry to action for the nation's preservation in line with its intentions, which were written and amended through history as we move with purpose toward the ideal society and a more perfect union of humankind in social contract with one another for the benefit of all. We must decide we are citizens of this nation first and dedicate ourselves to its sustenance and course correction. We are frustrated with all the political and societal chaos as the old guard of boomers refuses to let go of their outdated and wrongheaded ideas. We need the young to rise and assume positions of authority with a commitment to continue our project until finished, so help them God. Then, pass it on to posterity in a better condition than they found it with instructions to the next generation to do the same. This is a core sustainment value, a bedrock American virtue. To maintain it as a truthful society, the USE needs children reared to be stewards of its endowments, who as adults will protect and serve, and defend and uphold, the Constitution against all enemies, foreign and domestic.

Of course in near hindsight we can see how predictable it is that the "me first" generation would be struggling to let go of the controls. Letting go is admitting that it is not all about the ego. That it is not all about "me." That "I" am not the great and almighty one who can lead, administer, and manage the business of society properly. Plainly, not to want to transfer power in a republic is antithetical to our purpose in a democracy culture. It is an attitude of selfish consumerism, not selfless citizenship. Since attitudes drive behaviors, baby boomer conceit does not allow them to relinquish authority. Their wanting to hold onto the reins of power and not exit gracefully frustrates our potential recovery from their damages. We need them to leave the helm, step off the bridge, and exit the pilothouse, go below deck, study ACE then volunteer in schools tell children how to undo what they did wrongly in their time in charge, when these kids become adults. Boomers attitudes and behaviors, their refusal to transfer power longitudinally to the next generations of Americans causes risk to our nation's survival. Yet we will need all hands on deck to resurrect its respect and inspirational potential.

Thanks to doomerism, these two roles, citizen and consumer, are confused. We need to clarify them. They overlap but differ. They each have their sphere of existence, importance, and influence, but nowadays it feels as if one is eclipsing the other, which is negatively affecting the culture and shaping the society away from the other. In an upcoming section called "What has doomerism done?" we'll address this situation and share some diagrams of it in Figures 4-7 through 4-9. Later in "Remedy", the final major third section, in its subsection "Sociological Thinking" with its Figures 6-7 through 6-9 we'll expand further on it. For now, let's continue to explain the strands of its pernicious pitfalls; how it COIFFURE our nation's first principles, preeminently, democracy.

It Fabulates

Doomerism fabulates in droves that destroy democracy. It makes up stories and passes them off as truths. It fantastical false tall tales drown out facts. It pretends that its alternative reality is real and uses all sorts of fabulating forces to fool the common folk. It causes cultlike conditions that undermine honest society. As a corrupting condition, it perpetrates frauds. It equivocates. It fuddles around with factuality, dismissing it; ignoring its grounding in the pursuit of truth. It causes misbalancing dalliances of the societal powers. These power shifts destroy important relations necessary for proper LAMBS in the USE. Childhood fables teach us lessons of life, but fabulating fraudulent false fantasies for private gain, selling them as actuality, is felonious piracy. Are the doomers looking to loot the whole kit and caboodle from the rest of us while telling us to feel it as beautiful? Encouraging others to believe that these fakes are the truth, not because they've any evidence but because we want to believe in them, makes us fools. These fabricating forgers are playing games with us. If we let them, we are making a feeble mistake to "go along to get along" with these mountebanks. Certainly, the boomers have mastered the making of narratives to tell, sell, and exploit in their battle of isms while diminishing foundationally good American ideals. They are motivated to win at all costs, for their egos' weaknesses not meekness needs. This gets us nowhere fast but slowly erodes the public trust in the FILMS[2] [P7], the HM[5], and in one another as citizens and as fellow human beings. This is their unconscious unconscientiousness. Let's hope it is not a consciously intended consequence. Power divides to conquer. We must be more mindful of power. The belligerent battles of bad ideas, the ism fights, are ruining the USE, especially those fought with worn out and tired ideologies by ideologues and demagogues that neither prove nor discredit one theory or another, but continue as if in a sporting competition of no real life significance. Ultimately, these rhetoricians play their foolish philosophical fantasy games for their own pleasure and profit received from engaging in them. They enjoy being fabulous cause-fighters. None of these arguments put liberty appropriately at the center of the discourse, which is critical to us realizing a fully American society.

Doomerism is running us aground. Its culprits drown us in nonsense. These fabulators of fabulous lies and false mysteries are a dastardly bunch. The tabulators cannot keep up with all the counting of their millions of fallacies. We can barely believe the barbarous scandals of the baby doomer grifters, politicians, and exclusivity peddling, wheeler-dealer elitists. With the doomers, everybody is always innocent with no sense of responsibility because all is according to them, "relative", thus unbelieved in since all is rendered as relatively "harmless", or so they think in their spectacular alternative reality of spectacle. Economy elitists, through "legal" bribery, buy the policies for the polity to make the law of the land. We the everyday people do not stand a chance unless we unite. We must stand together! Let's align on our economic interests, regardless of our social circumstances. We must not allow elitists to continue to divide us while they hide behind acts of philanthropic kindness! We must unite, tie them to a goodbye kite, and send them in flight to the la-la-land where they can fabulate to themselves. We are not buying it. "We're not going to take it anymore."

Boomers have been dominant for forty years now. It is long overdue we remove them from authority. However, we the people cannot cry foul and say, "We've been cheated!" Typically, less than 60% of us vote in national elections, a "D" performance in civic duty. The boomers have proven incapable of producing the brilliant new ideas we need to overcome their falsehoods and failures. We are in a third stage of knowledge evolution. Its globalization and high technology deeply penetrate our everyday lives. The risks to liberty lie within our borders. We need to ignite the fire within to rise and begin the recreation of the American dream.

Certainly, all generations get tempted to fabulate. Less than morally becoming behaviors might give instant gratification. Immorality can cause long-term pain for others and terrible feelings in the minds of perpetrators. Prognosticators have warned us of this for eons. With a relativist mentality, the fortunate generations throughout time ignore wisdom. Wealth mushes their minds and conceit convinces them they will suffer no defeat. When a generation introduces itself to less reflexivity and more reflection, living gets better. Seeing guilt, shame, and depression within can make a path to revive core principles of citizenship. The success of a civilization depends not upon hedonism. It rests not on finding instant satisfaction but on the discipline to delay beastly gratification. Success comes from the pursuit of deeper, longer-lasting, wholesome sensations captured in the big idea words of broad and massive meanings: love, truth, beauty, justice, the cardinal moral virtues, kindness, conscientiousness, compassion, empathy, and sympathy. These lead to happiness, a sense of entitlement does not. These take higher states of conscience, patience, contemplation, and imagination, not shortsighted shallowness. These special words, shared in the attitudes and behaviors loving mothers and fathers ask of their children, give life worth. They lead to being human; humanity's victory over animal instincts. Of course, moms and dads need hope, jobs, stable relationships, and homes and to not be buried in so much debt or an intractable depravity of poverty they almost want to give up, but won't. Love for one's children promotes effort. Simply put, absent anomie, in dignity and decency with a job that pays the way each day, people find the means. Enjoying simple happiness is easy when unthreatened.

People know how to feel joy when uncorrupted. Doomerism introduces unwanted immorality. It causes unnecessary complexity in human relations. Without integrity, trust is impossible. Without belief in each other's word and honor, we suffer. Scandalous scheming slips in and makes life too complicated to comprehend. We either join in, or defenseless, get depressed. This is not how the blessings of liberty will exist. This is a sickness! Name it: baby doomerism. Shame it. It's to blame. Replace the baby doomers. Create hope for the unborn and recently birthed babies. Fix focus on the necessary remedy so they may know an American society worthy of its founding's intention.

In many previous generations, when a few misbehaved, the majority who sought to live by good attitudes and behaviors, in a word, virtue, shunned the misguided into conformity with the healthy norms of society. When a majority live toward virtue in salutary mores, society leans toward civility. When in control of the societal and social powers, the boomer generation misbehaved. The few good-seekers felt shunned and shut down. Stopping the grifting, the graft, and the fraud became increasingly difficult. The number of the corrupted was greater than the number of the uncorrupted. Those with integrity and good character were in the minority. This was a reversal for American society. Civilization requires citizenship. Contrarily, rationalization became the norm for baby boomers. This shift in the balance of human affairs from inspirational honesty to decrepit deceit caused a decline in civility. This is what happened during the boomer generation. They let misbehaviors slide. They moved the moral weight off its central core values and rested it precariously to one side, then the other. They sought either end's irrational misinterpretations of morality or none at all. Now, American society totters on a crumbling fulcrum, teetering off-balance. The weight of doomerism's shiftiness keeps tipping the scale in favor of the few who want to rule. At present, society is less a "see saw" and more a "hee haw." The rich laugh at the poor, who have no countervailing power, and the whole world's population laughs at all of us in the US. They see the fabulation and we cannot. They chuckle at our pathetic inability to self-govern because of this.

Now that the boomers are no longer the majority, we can finally force an end to their fabulation with an intervention. The next generations combined are now in numeric superiority (perhaps moral, too) as a more populous voting body. But we are divided by doomers' desire. Yet we must unite. Yes, we must take charge of society. We must reverse the grift done by the baby boomers upon posterity. The American project depends on it. Our children require it of us. The numbers are in our favor. Mortality tells us the future is ours. Morality tells us the sooner we get a hold of it the better for the youngsters and us. Most importantly, we must claim it for America's babies, for whom we must rectify illiberal incivility and instill in society good character citizenship as our primary people power purpose. This will be our sacrifice, the saving of America from doomerism.

We must be patriotic citizen-surgeons, cutting this tumor out of our body politics' democracy culture. To do so we must focus on transitioning power to the next generations' civically minded ACE educated leadership ready moral persons of integrity and humility who are constitutionally committed. We must activate the sense of confidence they need, the "I think I can" attitude. Overly coddled by baby boomer parents, some have doubts. This is why the boomers must resign, retire, and stop trying to be in control! They cause the fear and doom. The equilibrium in society will restore, and society will shift back to balanced approaches to governing, by us working together to achieve the idealized national community imagined by the founders, which we seek to complete. One based not on the social circumstances and physical conditions of the framer's time in history, but upon their grand vision of what we might build with the principles that guided their fight to create the opportunity for our destiny to be achieved: America. They fought a revolution for us! Let's honor that risk taking sacrifice for a dream state. Let's make it come true before 2042!

The framers believed in the goodness of humankind, in the fraternity of e pluribus unum, in a republic, by representative democracy. It requires we move away from and contrast ourselves against animal instinct-driven behaviors. Democracy takes tremendous commitment to virtue to succeed. This wisdom was lost on a "you got lucky baby" generation, who hazarded all toward self-service and not community service. They abandoned the community work of healing passed down to them. The movement toward civil rights, a just movement of justice for all citizens, they left to flounder. They preferred free love and self-exploration. They put some noisy energy in protesting a war in Vietnam. They snubbed those who came back wounded, who valiantly sought to serve their country, even on what might have been a misguided adventure. These two sides of their generation never repaired the rifts of history, and they tore into one another ideologically. They fought over a fight about an ism, 8,584 miles away. Thus, our national politics is in ruin: useless, doubted, and divided. Of course, the present politicians are majorly baby doomers! Their bribing economic enablers are baby doomers! The false fables and tall tales they tell to distract us took over the logical debates of democracy. They tanked local news outlets, preferring to elevate nationwide brands. This damaged community powers' benefits by distracting us from what was near and dearly needing our attention to that which was far away, and for which they wanted resources. They fabulated to get both.

Our HM[5] became exceedingly greedy. Our FILMS[2] [P7] became disrupted, distrusted, and dissatisfactory in performing the LAMBS. Our USE is in jeopardy. Notwithstanding, do the baby boomers take any responsibility for this being so? Not likely, they cannot see what they have wrought. They take resources, while avoiding answerability. It ought to be obvious. But to admit it might be too egotistically degrading for those whom believe the world revolves to satisfy them only. Alas, this "me first" mentality is blindingly diseased; not a reliable vision to be believed in when a people seek to unite in the common cause of liberty and justice for all with peace and freedom as its hallmarks. Appositionally, it is an unworthy worldview. It aims to start doomsday situations of chaos and crises. For these, it is well suited.

We must ask ourselves, who has profited the most these past forty years of the boomers majority? By following the money, we'll see that a few nearly psychopathic sociopaths did. By disregarding social norms and compartmentalizing aspects of life, they avoided accountability. Avoiding the responsibilities of citizenship, they put "me first" first. Avoiding morality (or pretending with dogmatic moralizing), they hired like-minded sycophants. Roaring toward blind ambitions, doomers damage reputations, backstab, and aggressively climb over others. They destroy friendships, neighborhoods, and teams all the while decimating the sense of value in being a virtuous member of the community. Remember, power divides to conquer. Seeking only to use the community, to be above it, exploiting its members is their manner. This is not what a citizen in a republic of representative democracy should do. It is what citizens in an empire do.

We are not an intentional empire but an accidental one. The US was geographically lucky, its people plucky, but we ran a society willing to exploit cheap labor: slavery. The Europeans sent airs of racial superiority and made fortunes selling to Africans. The colonies and new Americans made their money using them. We are fortunate few wars were fought on our lands. Military conflicts restrict economic prosperity. We've still not recovered from the one among ourselves, over slavery. Imperialism's pull tempted us, and we made mistakes. Such as American society did not fully jettison portrayals of monarchy as good, which we inherited from European ancestry. We borrowed too many enculturating parables with good princes and pretty princesses. We repeated these stories to our children. From our very beginning as a new order for the ages, we went off course with these fairy tales. Abandoning customs of a feudal world was difficult. The bejeweled royalty sell themselves as perfect, attractive, persons. We retain too much affection for moneyed celebrities. We haven't discontinued this European atmosphere of superiority. Its mentality of hierarchies is still with us. It is not us. Constituted to be an egalitarian-minded society with democracy, we must at once drop such myths used by kings and queens to mesmerize and subdue the population into servitude under their control.

We need a greater "escape velocity" to leave the hierarchical, status-conscious, ambitious values that encourage a destructive envy. Previous generations were proud of the accomplishments of those who earned their greatness. Merit, not inheritance, was the story we wanted to tell and prove as well. Yet we remained trapped within the tantalizing tales of feudalism despite the fact that we're not a kingdom. Despite our human nature, we must despise the idea of inherited authority. We should not disguise this made in America fact. We mustn't admire fabulous fables that tell us otherwise. We are a republic with the ambition of equality for our people. We veered off course. We read from stories of kings and queens, princes and princesses, instead of histories of American industry and artistry. A few innovators in earlier generations tried to invent all-American forms of expression. Consider the efforts of the architect Frank Lloyd Wright. Whether one likes or dislikes his architecture, he attempted to create something organically from the soil of democracy, not the spoils of feudal monarchies' ornamental foils. He sought something American, honed from our values, geography, and virtues that sang our tune, not that of a European ruin. Yet the housing stock favored by the boomers is full of European-lookalike, wannabe palaces. With their ramped up rampant McDonaldization of society (Ritzer, 1993), throughout the suburbs they built big ego temples— oversized for need "look at me" edifices. Modern controls of calculated efficiency and predictability enabled stable profitability from such massive McMansions. Poor imitations of European aristocrats' manors, these plunked down disproportionate imitation buildings are often ugly. Most are full of architectural fallacies. Big boxy geometrical excesses meant to impress are not architecture. They might have pretty faces of fine materials, like brick, but they present disenchanting and clunky volumes and masses. These simpleton false fronts do not hide the uncoordinated sides and backs. Confronted by views of awkward elevations, neighbors see plastic siding riddled with unattractive misaligned fenestration. It's too bad they have to look out at one another's discombobulated back-of-house befuddled buildings while sitting in their decorated interior rooms. As a cultural landscape, it leaves a testament to boomers' generational value sets. In a hundred years, what the historians will tell! We foolishly fabulate over falsified reveries of fancy European gentry. It has been 245 years since we declared independence. We really must stop imitating and emulating!

The boomers are the eighth generation to hold the controls over culture, the precept power process, in the USE. They've held on to it longer than any other generation, in part because medical science of the academy power, funded by public grants, extended biology power's abilities to keep persons alive longer. By being in authority and shaping society so long, they've taken us far off the course of conserving the Constitution. They stopped progressing toward its goal and objectives. Morally we regressed. Our younger adults and future generations must get our project us back on track, heading in the correct direction to accomplish our mission. First, we need our rising generations' adults to gain positions of authority, and adopt adaptive attitudes and to make adjustments to bring equilibrium to the primary powers of society. Second, Using our people power properly, we must commit to this course of action to think adaptively as we turnover the control of society to our civically minded team-playing trained, striving to be integrated and acting with integrity, younger generations. We must trust in this plan. We can, if we are all seeking the survival of American society, which requires we define it as it might be, in accord with founding ideals, principles, and virtues, not as it is today. We've suffered slowly forty years of rising doomerism, a societal disease we must cure and get past, plus many eras of failures to fix. Third, by reviving the framer's goal and objectives as our project's sail plan, our seemingly forgotten piloting ambitions, we'll get it done. They are not out of reach. Living to achieve the establishing words as our purpose, we can unify and make a thriving society at all levels. As a quick aside, note that sociologists analyze society in three levels: the micro (e.g. you, family, and friend groups; neighborhood based), meso (e.g. organizations and institutions, businesses and associations; regionally based), and macro (e.g. societal-influencing powers, nationally and internationally based).

The governing and globalizing rich and powerful persons, and those of us inside the operant primary powers' FILMS[2] [P7] must listen to know and respect that we the everyday people want adjustments. We want to stop the DAMN of power. We want risky approaches in the ways, means, and methods in how we AEIOUY^{2}K the powers to cease so we can prevent a reversal of the Free World back into an age of feudalism. Baby doomers must stop fabulating to fool us. We have seen and heard enough. We have the numbers now!

As soon as possible, we must enact by elections the eviction of boomers from political power. We must stop buying beloved brands from corporations whose executives, boards, and major shareholders (if traded) are boomers employing doomerism tactics. We have no choice. We must lean into this to make a difference with, for, and by people power to write the rightful history of tomorrow, beginning today. Without delay, we must rely on one another to behave as citizens first. We cannot let them put us under their thumbs any longer and tear us asunder by false prophesies and moldy isms. Doomerism will put babies in near-hellish poverty unless and until we reject it once and for all. It will not be easy, but by refreshing the polity, repeatedly, we will demonstrate seriousness and responsibility. By our demanding markets respond, they will supply according to our resolute wishes. By doing both determinatively, persistently, and perpetually correctly, we will prove our proper leadership role for the "new order of the ages" society sought in the seventeen seventies. This is as it should be. This is what it means to be Americans. This is a significant psychological realignment to a real purpose. The gift of the nation is a gift of love. This proved out when the founders began the cycle to transfer political power regularly, and generationally. Why our eighth generation's mean, median, and modal cohort decided not to do it smartly was misguided. It will take dedicated extra effort to avert their lies we've learned to believe in as accurate depictions of how things are, despite what we see with our own eyes these days. We can change perceptions. We've the precept power process of culture, exercised via representative democracy in republic of, by, and for us, the everyday people. We just need to unite to replace the doomers in authority to begin our work to defeat their spawned baby doomerism, exorcising it from our American society.

How well the baby doomers tell themselves their fabulous self-inflating fables. They must have very short memories. Perhaps they have such high opinions of themselves that they forgot how poorly they've treated people. Do they think others love them? They are deluded in their hyped-up celebrity. They are users. The used amused them by kowtowing to them. What can anyone not in the dominant way of behaving do but placate and wait, toss out some bait, and laugh under their breath when a baby boomer behaves as predicted. They are so self-absorbed, they cannot fathom that some might enjoy winding them up and pushing their buttons to watch them uncontrollably spin ridiculously until the emotionally implode, or explode vilely with violence, shamelessly exposing themselves for their supercilious boorish behavior. The boomers are now no longer in the majority. They sense it. They fear payback. They fear we will take back what they have knowingly stolen. This is why they are so entrenched in their games. Doomer pretension is sickening.

A last note on the fairy tales of doomerism, and then we'll move on. Wanting lifestyles of the rich and famous—could this be why regulators and referees hear curses words slung at them by bad fans these days? Is the desire to make commerce fair and reasonable the trigger for doomers to assault our governmental workforce all the time? The top half does not want a middle class of competent civil servants. What would Teddy Roosevelt think of this situation? What the baby doomers have enabled is a new tax code that has enhanced and not prevented hereditary wealth, which the founders feared would lead us back to European ways of being, in which the aristocracy of landed gentry ruled the rest. This is what needs stopped. After fifteen years of research, a French economist now writes and lectures on issues of inequality. He relates it to the French Revolution, how a few wealthy take all the rewards of everyone else's labors (Piketty, 2014). Several journalists report on income inequality bringing societal demise. Studies of reputable economists in private and public institutions confirm it (Reich R. B., 2020). The middle class, in particular, feels the squeeze (Rose, 2020). The journalists describe the symptoms and articulate the aspects it presents. Yet none notes the underlying denominator is a disease, a cultural infection, which this book diagnoses as "baby doomerism," or doomerism for short. Stay with us, Section 3 prescribes the prognosis of a cure and the remedy.

Doomerism presents symptoms though how it COIFFURE democracy from American society, plus how it CATAPULTED crises and chaos in the USE. It allows baby doomers to see monetary and egocentric profit as the sole goal of life. This, of course, has eroded societal bonds and pushed norms out of bounds. It spread person by person. It grew by gradual moral leniency and tolerance for unethical cowardice and grift and graft expansions. It is pushing good people into depression and insanity. The sociologist Emile Durkheim described this condition as anomie. Anomie is a lack of normal ethical or social standards. It is a normlessness state in society, in which the expectations of behavior are unclear. With anomie, the social system fails, and civil society breaks down. Survival rendered nearly impossible, stresses the will to live. This threat is unnecessary. The vulnerable either seek to escape it by becoming drunks and drug addicts or ideate and commit suicide. Nowadays, books with narratives of the end of democracy publish the failings of the US. Our republic faces a final fatal showdown between democracy and doomerism. Democracy in the United States is our birthright, our brand. We taught it around the world as a preferred arrangement for human affairs. It needs resuscitated.

Talk is becoming prevalent in certain circles about our culture. Chatter about how our culture is not producing citizens but rather people who behave only as consumers. Consumerism is an unsatisfying cycle of buying things to feel better. It doesn't work to fulfill our deepest needs. No matter how much we repeat it, the empty feelings persist. It is a way of life sold to us by those who profit from it. It is how a few enrich themselves by telling us lies. They are shallow. We do not need to follow. If it only enriches the few, especially when they don't pay taxes, why "shop until we drop?" Doing so only gives a temporary euphoria to the consumer and disenfranchising dysphoria to the citizenry. This tactic of cultural manipulation uses advanced psychology informed sales techniques. Baby boomer-led businesses have hired psychologists and liars to feed our brains a disruptive diet of desires since we were babies. They never thought it was something wrong. Brainwashing citizens to be consumers was good business. But hey, why would they think morally if all they care about, in their hollow self-centeredness and narcissism, is profit? Why would they act in the best interests of children? Why would they care about their fellow citizens, other parents, or the whole community? Such things are like an ulcer; they erode us from the inside out. Let's continue with how doomerism ulcerates our society.

It Ulcerates

Doomerism ulcerates democracy. It slowly eats a hole in our core values, turning us against one another, pushing aside our inner virtue. As a corrupting condition, it influences us in ways we cannot see, though we see its ugly outcomes and what it has slowly done to us as a people, to our culture, and to our society. It has led us into unending warring, which dooms peace and bankrupts our treasury. The Constitution requires that Congress declare war. Cowardly baby boomers never were brave enough to make such declarations, yet spent our money on war's euphemism, "conflicts." Isn't this considerable dishonesty? What would a kindergartner think? They would not see any logic in rationalizing this. War is war. What is it good for, if undeclared and not done for the common defense, or to defeat tyranny that threatens our allies, who repaid us for our support? It seems that baby doomers don't recognize how their current ways of running the state are failing. Their new status quo does not exactly square with creating a society to IDEALS liberty. It does not push for achieving the goal and attaining the objectives of the USE. How might we describe the new status quo that has come to us?

The status quo of the baby doomers is a fanatical form of tribalism. It makes tribes that want nothing to disrupt the status quo. It like by quid pro quo, which is their go to negation. It's at the low end of human moral development, (see Figure 2-27), self-focused on getting the most reward. It is such a divisive, annoyingly immature approach to discussing history. It does not help us know the future situations or the risks we are confronting and must unite to address. The ideologue nature of the baby boomer generation is harming our unity. Their war on institutions like an ulcer on the lining of an organ is disembodying for society. It creates chaos, instability, fragility not order, not unity, not integrity. It damages the lining of democracy. Ulcerous circumstances of anarchy result in apathy, and both devolve into tyranny. Doomerism is undermining the culture of democracy upon which our republic built a free society. Its tribalism is an ulcerating ism that obliterates the chances for our republic's survival based in democracy. Doomerism adduces contemplation of possibly shredding of the Constitution in favor of fascism.

Hyperbolic sensationalism is another of its ulcerating isms. Honest journalism is dying. It lost integrity and is now about selling content media full of unhelpful and unhealthy drama and trauma. Journalists, once protectors of democracy, are now perpetrating its murder. When owned by money-hungry hoarders, whose status quo tribe seeks to be on top, democracy is in doubt. Their end game is world dominion. Their method is a new-styled feudalism that is taking hold to reestablish new monarchs led by globalizing, unregulated, multinational corporations, who have zero interest in the difficult work of governing by, or tolerating, democracy and its representative principles. They simply need the masses of people kept ignorant. They want us to worship their brands. They want us to want dividends or handouts. They want us to dream of making it big on Wall Street. "Rags to riches" is their favorite fairy tale. It's a fallacy for the majority, so why do we fool ourselves? Yes, be an entrepreneur, but don't chase a myth—it's a tiger's tail for society. One in a million does not justify an entire system of society. Coaxed to seek the unnecessary as desirable goods and services in a temple made by Madison Avenue we slip and fall prey. The priests of consumerism created in us this religious-like worship of objects and money by and for the economic elites who gain from our psychic pain of wanting what we cannot afford. Broadcasted "media" preaches to us that their materialistic cathedral of conspicuous consumption is the one and only worthy worldly worship house of reality's religion of real things, not mysteries. It is its own myth. Corporatism, materialism, and consumerism are its trinity of ulcerating isms. Our stomachs sour. Our minds cower. Our beings sour. We must resist now. We cannot wait until the hour to act, because doomerism devours. Our hearts go dour. Keep in mind at the other extreme of propaganda driven cultures are communism and fascism that use similar psychological techniques. For example, the Soviet Union made the state into a secular civil religion (Roberts, 1990).

A big risk to the USE is the taking of the nation away from the people by the economic elites. They take the polity away from the politicians, and the politicians take the power away from the people. Anti-citizenship attitudes and behaviors, promoting anarchy in the impoverished streets forebode doom. Like an ulcer, they eat away at liberty and eviscerate democracy. Stop falling for their game! It's done to distract us by tribalism between political parties. They support the battling by paying for the brainwashing newspeak and its diabolic twisters of misinformation and disinformation.

Most gray- haired men and women are blind to the doomerism that has corrupted them. Most do not know of an ulcer either, until a doctor diagnosis it. Well, now we know the diagnosis. We can put an end to the ugly show. Tell each other "Let's go!" Move in the direction of healing and repealing their attempts to change our society into a permanently patronizing dependency-based culture of complacency and apathy. Say "No thank you!" We'll revive our republic with our patriotic citizenshipping from here on out. To do so, all adults 18 to 54 years old and 75 to 125 must vote for non-baby doomer candidates, be they boomers or younger doom and gloom "me first" understudy mimickers. If we are to save the USE, we must change the guard to alter the status quo. If we are to preserve the potential prosperity for the common people in posterity, we must resolutely replace our politicians regularly from this day forward. We must protect the replacements from being purchased by the elites. The American babies have everything to lose if we don't act ambitiously, near unanimously, to do this over the next decade, regularly afterwards, forevermore.

We need a generational rising: younger, more energetic, better-educated team players. This is the revolutionary spirit we need. Jefferson was right. It is wrong for previous generations to punish future ones with their accumulated debt. We've allowed too many ulcers at the micro (local), meso (state), and macro (national) levels of government to stay in political offices for too long. Their affluence, influence, and confluence of rivaling political parties, a duopoly of doomerism needs diminished and disassembled. We need to begin again with new ones that mean what they say and whose platforms and policy agenda say what they mean. False fronts and money laundering hunts must henceforth cease and desist.

Baby doomerism is a root problem. It underlies the many identified challenges social commentators announce. Many of the authors are baby boomers. Thus, they cannot see under their own skins to realize how their worldview CATAPULTED the crises we read and they write about. The human rights champion, the US, no longer exists as a leading democracy. We are without any moral high ground, if indeed we ever really had it. Our history has its horrors. Without proof of good conduct, we cannot lead. Without any leader for democracy to inspire aspiration and effort for liberty, dictators will rise like simian primate alpha males. They love raw power. They want to concentrate it, autocratically, within the circle of their conceited conveniently anti-republic pseudo friends and fellow wannabe rulers of men, and owners of women. Globalizing, multinational corporations will make deals with any despot whose markets are open to them. To extract wealth out of and up to their corporate suites is more important than the character of politicians with whom to associate. This is another kind of vacuum—a vacuum cleaner. It sucks out the wealth of nations' geology and labor forces into the moneybags of an elite status quo. Power, money, politics are made to serve the few with a mind infected by the ulcer of doomerism. This trend decreases the possibility for the people, especially the children, to have a say in the way the world goes. With doomerism, its going along with the relegation of democracy offered liberty, once the sacred pursuit of the American body politic.

It Relegates

Doomerism relegates democracy. As a corrupting condition, it consigns people power to an inferior rank. It isolates people into persons. It makes persons feel obscure, or it forces them into a category of type. The politicians and economic elites have manufactured these assigned groupings of topologically stereotypical identities. Such groups enable political manipulation and separation. Deplorable conditions exist for some of these groups. Doomerism relegates people to identities not of their choosing, and it persuades them to use these to gang together for security. Mass psychology exploits these groups. Position holders lacking responsibility for governing use groups to advance their agendas. This divides the citizenry. Position holders relegate their represented people or market's buyers to segments and sectors using historical typologies. This takes away people's dignity. Their actions transfer responsibilities of one kind of power to another, which misbalances the societal powers.

Relegation is a form of DAMN of powers. It sets the locus of power not as intended by the Constitution but as by the desired alteration of tyranny. An example of this is how doomerism puts the locus of people power in the economy by convincing people that they are consumers before they are citizens. This is backward and absurd. The Constitution is the foundation of the society. It establishes justice via the rule of law, which makes freedoms possible. It enables the economy power to serve the people with its positive provisions that contribute to improving society.

Doomerism relegates leadership to uselessness. In the societal and so-cial powers' FILMS[2][P7] it exhibits lameness, and the boomers think they are blameless. Here are examples of how things go in boomer-shaped society. Unaccustomed to and unadjusted by wisdom, they've been behaving bra-zenly, blanketing truth in new disguises, staying always on the move, re-moving factuality, avoiding acting ethically, and ever seeking to maximize personal gains regardless of what or who it hurts.

What should we do? Imagine how we will handle it when recently re-tired boomers start asking former employees for favors. Imagine that they were cruel and used their authority to deny opportunities for high quality underlings' advancement. Because of their competitiveness fears of being surpassed, they preferred promoting mediocre staff that would be loyal for the uplift above their own advancement potential. Wisdom advices a master wants the best apprentices to replace him or her when the time comes for the transfer of control to be done. Doomers prevent the best from rising. This erodes competence by lowering the standards when passing the torch to lesser than the best up-comers. This "me first" driven precedence sets a precedent for how things are done, and it then gets mimicked by the next in line, who hide behind self-made lies that they were the best qualified. Oth-ers see this relegating of excellence. It demoralizes. The consequence is a rapid quantitatively and qualitatively demise of a once jim-dandy workplace. As doomers and their understudies take, it makes the instruments of society perform worse. It rides a tide of cowardice. What was on their minds? What if everyone knew this was an intentional game, choosing whom to favor, not by merit but by sycophancy? Did the boomers willfully prevent better employees from gaining competitive advantages? Did the boomers do it to protect a favorite sycophantic loyalist?

What if the boomer was a boss, not a manager, a kind of anti-leader, who in lieu of developing staff bullied the intelligent who tried to help by offering better ideas, but were punished for their dissent? Behaving like bobble-headed, wobbling, always "yes" men and women is unhealthy for an American society, and encouraging it will relegate us to failure. It induces nasty nests of pestering harassment. The peevish bosses need pesky favor seeking persons to perform their petty will. What a pernicious place to work is the doomerism infested shop or office. More so, the insincere and non-genuine way of doomers is tiring. Imagine the situation of an "old friend" (not really) being in need, acting all buddy-ole-pal friendly, obvious-ly pleading to get something for nothing by pretending familiarity. Once they've calculated that the superficial social niceties are successful, they ask for what they really want. Shocking, but apparently it is not a problem in doomer-headed society. They don't think we see it. We do. Having two fac-es is the best way to hide a motive is their ethos. It relegates dignity and respect to the heap pile of bile as they bilk. When they manipulatively talk, the honorable balk, and walk out.

Let's get back to the retiree looking for an insider from whom to get information for his or her "self". This is a classic pattern of doomer behavior. Intentionally seeking to exploit a node in a network to "gain access" is shallow, shadowy, corruptible, and a corrupting negligent misuse of a relationship with another person. It lacks integrity, honesty, honor, and truth. Such are the unbecoming, unsociable, self-centered characteristics common among the baby doomers. Their little snub code of snobbery is tolerated from one another because real connections cost too much personal commitment. It's an intolerable idea for them. They skate the surface; relegating justness beneath them, because depth would slow them down on their ambitious ascents. Alas, this "wink-wink" symbolic interaction bears no reality. It is fakeness. The false befriending, grafting, grifting, and asking for favors from those with whom they didn't give the time of day to when they were working in the same office is wrong. The suddenly having a need, "Help me! I'm a victim" use of others to get ahead is a sick syndrome. It relegates common decency to an undeserving status of impermissibility. Egad, we've had enough of these unkind persons. They have undermined our social confidence in a good person's character.

Modern generational snobbery, doomerism is a verifiable social illness. It thrust aside a building block of community: trust. Was the boomer generation trying to become one people under God? Or have they a false sense of God? If they do seek holiness, the doomers among them don't listen to instructions on moral and ethical behavior. They rationalize themselves as perfect. We are all imperfect, but we are to work on improving ourselves. To believe in our possibilities and strive to develop into more perfect beings helps us to unite wholesomely with veracity as we pursue accomplishing our task: e pluribus unum. Our project's mission is to make a more perfect union. It is why we are a citizenry. We must return to doing it within civil society. We begin by balancing the primary societal powers.

Perhaps doomers became so insecure because they've gotten everything easily, though they would beg to differ, but history clarifies theirs was more luck than pluck. Not having had to work for it through war or famine, they were spoiled. Yet, they want admiration. Knowing it's probably not really possible, considering the ease of their subsistence, since they didn't actually earn it fully, they surround themselves with liars who lather praise upon them falsely, or comfort them with abiding accolades, cozy accommodations for weak egos. To doomers these compliments are a welcomed vibe for their cults of personalities. A doomer who thinks they are actually held in high esteem is likely a victim of the sycophancy their narcissism socially nurtured in their fan base of lickers and sniffers who might have played the emotion exploitation game better than they did. Nevertheless, they don't care because they use this lapdog loyalty to get what they want for themselves from the coattail riders: a feeling of being worship. It's abhorrent. It breeds a false belief that we are supposed to see the world as superficially as possible—to use and be used divisively. By good luck times, they accumulated wealth and success. It feeds the odious thinking that their ways, means, and methods are best, that they've figured it out on their own, and gotten it correctly. Nonetheless, they have not. If they had, we'd not have had so many crises and suffer from so much consequent chaos. The Beatles sang, "Money can't buy me love", and a false sense of emotional security is a phony excuse maker's speedy passage to avoid deeper feelings that need felt and dealt with seriously. Doomers may still be mentally in adolescence. In their minds, the world revolves around them. From the outside looking in, it is funny to see how they fool each other, who they fool, and who fools them by feeding fantasies to their egos, acting with absolute adulation. What a pitiful form of being. Probably, snobbish modernistic upbringings caused it. Or possibly, the flatterers weren't fooled at all. Rather they played their game to move up the ladder. For those now gone, no longer the fancy folks at the top, they're stripped and left unprotected, except for their retirement checks and medical care, paid for by future taxation.

These climbers are now naked, perhaps even afraid without their doomer trailblazers to slide up on, as they tell themselves "fake it until you make it". An incorrect representation of realty, this ego buffering effort at convincing themselves their career rise isn't a liar's ride, chides, so they hide it deep inside. These fools lied about liking the boss. They pretended. They liked their way up by seamy stroking on the confidence lacking personality holes, filling them with creamy flattery that gave doomers a dreamy feeling of being a king or queen. But not just by liking, some unscrupulous climbers also licked, sniffed, scratched, sucked, and sexed their way to the top. How un-American, how sad the culture of doomerism actually is for human dignity. It's an affront to integrity and a betrayal of liberty.

The baby doomers don't allow the competent and more talented to rise. It would ruin the fabulous fantasies they fabulate about themselves. Thus, the must wrest the chances from the best and relegate them under their thumbs. They are too territorial. They act unaware of the greater needs. They never sought to serve the higher ideals and to live by virtues. To this statement, they'd complain they did. What they might admit they did, they'd claim began in the preceding generation. They just rode the wave until it eroded. When the way ahead proved too difficult to sustain the effort to effectuate the objectives, the boomers did not remain at it. They receded. They only served themselves, one by one, uncemented bricks. They did not make the necessary social capital or continue civil society. Without such societal mortar to glue the bricks in the wall together the common good weakened. If the earth moves, gravity alone cannot hold them in place. These bricks like us, the everyday people, in misguided doomer dominated society are inefficiently adhered to one another. We must engage in a massive task to rebuild the walls that make our house of democracy an edifice inspiring sublime respect. We must disassemble the bricks, clean, inspect, and test them, then if solid, build them back up with an appropriate adhesive mortar: cohesive civility. We'll leave the bad ones aside, unused, tossed off onto a baby doomer pile to which we'll send over elder and younger masons to repair them. Those of them who will listen to the voice of wisdom and enthusiast youth will know what they have done wrong. They might repent and apologize. Especially as death stares them in the eyes, they may begin to see the destruction resulting from their "me first" generation made culture: doomerism. Repentant doomers could get returned to the wall if they demonstrate a willingness to sincerely sacrifice for others, to adhere to social norms, and to give back what they have taken. They must completely commit to making us strong as a citizenry. However, we cannot wait for them to have their "what it means to be an American" epiphany. We must begin to build back our house on its original foundation laid by the framers, which over time we adequately amended.

Otherwise, they (and those who don't know what they have done wrong) will live in fear, secretly knowing as impostors they seek to hire newbies they think cannot see their game or whom they believe they can inculcate to become just like them. Passing down doomerism gives them comfort. It justifies making those they advance feel beholden to them. Owning others is wrongful. Doomerism makes possible promotions of the least qualified into positions beyond their competencies. Soul selling-out to become the chosen ones ruins merit-based intentions. Sadly, organizations and institutions will suffer downward spirals in quality, character, and public trust because doomerism puts mediocre persons in the top ranks. Such unimaginative managers need admiration. So, they hire lesser talents to look up to them as "great." It is a negative gyre, not unlike the cycle of democracy when the people become complacent (recall Figure 2-22). It ends poorly when integrity, ingenuity, and industriousness are left out of the advancement equation. Promoting the less talented, bigger brown-nosed posers, causes a deflating trend in human resource acquisitions and group performance.

The relegation of top talent to the bottom, or out the door, is the risk of sycophancy. Incompetent climbers, self-liars cheating to get the positions of being in charge, are the cause of this risk in a meritocracy. Biologically speaking, the softer stinking stool of sweet brown rises, until someone of reason raises the bullshit flag. It takes bringing in outsiders to clean up the mess. Sewage from "brown tonguing" (translated from the Swiss) leads to organizational failure. It takes time and energy to clean up the social mess, and the turbulence of change prevents the accomplishment of the mission.

Fortunately, the US military, having a rigid promotion system, does not suffer from as much of this nonsense. They have a well-managed promotion board system. Anyhow, they get candidates from the larger society, and as we have seen, many baby boomers have gotten relieved of duty. Alas, the military is not immune to the damages of baby doomerism. Let's have some humor around this brown nose, brown tongue concept. Brown nosing implies smelling. Sniffing is an exploratory behavior. Brown tonguing implies tasting. Licking is a much more fully committed behavior. Perhaps the adored enjoy sniffers sniffing their holes. Probably the wannabe admired and loved enjoy the lickers licking. Could organizational life be this simple? Tease or be real? Commit (which comes with responsibilities many users don't want to have toward another they seek to use for their own ambitions) to doing it fully, and be "owned." The latter is more akin to a bad behavior that has two sides to it, sleeping one's way to the top, or using one's power to persuade someone to sleep with them. Is it 50/50? Was it more prevalent during the baby boomer generation? We might ask a sociologist to find out for us. What fantasies of fabulation might they uncover under the covers? What might the degraded morals and morale of the good others have done to the performance of the organizations that had it happening within their offices?

Alternately, allowing slacking off as compensation for sneaky fleecing—distracting others while taking steadily more for oneself—is wrong. As a whole generation, more than any other generation, what the boomers had, have, or will get, they got by egregious manipulation. We can hear their retort now: "Hey, we may own everything and have security, but you've gotten all these freedoms to be vulgar, to be unconstrained by conventional social norms. Thank us! We lowered the standards for you! But don't worry, we'll not judge you as improper or unacceptable, so long as you stay away from the truth that we stole all your wealth." Some are just beginning to address these claims saying "No thank you" and "Ok boomer" in fed up tones. These express the sentiment, "We'd rather you didn't try to kill off virtue completely". It's an adhesive for us as a people. It's trustworthy. Doomers are not. The content of our character matters, not the size of our earnings or houses, or the amount of stuff we possess in storage sheds on the outskirts of suburbia.

It Extirpates

Doomerism extirpates democracy. As a corrupting condition, it increases a willingness to destroy the very ecology we depend upon for life. It puts off confronting these issues to future generations, when it might be too late. With ecology denied, ecosystems get disrespectfully exploited. Degradation of the planetary necessities that provide life-supporting environs is bad. It bluntly impacts human society's ability to survive. It stunts us. By increasing the challenges to resource acquisition, to farming for food and textiles, and to mining for materials for tools (weapons), fuels for machines (water, wind, and fossil fuels), materials for artists an musical instruments, and shelter (forestry, minerals), doomerism jeopardizes the species. We need a better configuration of our approach to our ecosystem. We need to reimagine methods of toolmaking by our HM[5] for the necessary and desirable provisions. We shape the material world for habitation quality and comfort (architecture—the built environment). Our past ways of doing it need improved congruence with the planet's cycles of life. We need to imagine new ways, means, and methods to integrate our needs for survival and our wants for thriving with the capacity and capability of the earth to sponsor us. We must resource our inhabitation, but we must do so without destroying the planet's various biomes that provide for all species. As one example recently seen by scientists, we're exhausting our fresh water aquifers' water supply faster than they can recharge. Civilizations collapse without potable water. This is a critical risk for the species, yet seldom gets mentioned by the media. Why would it? Doomerism extirpates.

Doomerism destroys democracy. It extirpates resources from the beneficial powers that make living enjoyable. It enervates society's communities, depriving them of a loving vitality that makes them beneficial for persons. It weakens people power by separating people into oppositional groups that cannot speak to one another. This, a classic technique of tyrants, creates a fear of scarcity, or a real denial of provisions, which emaciate some but not others. This starving of people from one another depletes community involvement. Dividing neighbors undermines civil society, unravels social capital, disavows a diversity we need to learn more than one social grammar in a globalizing world, dissuades civic engagement, and pollutes political participation. Doomerism denies the joys of citizenship. It enables tyranny to overwhelm democracy. It is as if doomerism wants to extirpate democracy and liberty.

Well, that concludes this diatribe on how doomerism COIFFURE democracy and harms other positive aspects of an American society. So let's now summarize what doomerism has done. Then, we'll share a discussion on the competing pressures of being a citizen and a consumer. Then, we'll move on to Chapter 5 in which we explain what caused it.

*W**hat Has Doomerism Done?*

Doomerism has changed our society for the worse. We've deplorable discourse, a fractured public realm, and a distrusting populace. The boomers teach us to fix the blame instead of fixing the problem. Doomerism misguides us away from our culture of democracy. It deteriorates our will to work to IDEALS liberty. It moves us away from one another, each of us in our own private mindsets. Our lives are no longer centered upon living a virtuous life. We no longer seem to seek to possess, protect, and project liberty. This is why we struggle now to IDEALS liberty for posterity and why we must act to make the necessary repairs to our citizen ship, our US

Enterprise. Liberty must live within us, in our hearts and souls, in our selves, to revive Americanism in our society. Liberty's life pales without Constitution-committed living. Citizenship behavior, based upon trust and stored in common purpose, sustains liberty. Liberty requires community responsiveness.

Doomerism denied good "isms" and created and amplified bad for liberty ones, like gamerism, as if life was a game to win or lose. This immature, zero-sum competitiveness unnecessarily created societal confusion and division. We need to understand again the purpose and meaning of life. Pitting ideologies against one another without allowing meaningful learning and understanding is foolish. The largest of the bad isms we've suffered from is consumerism. It is a huge aspect of the doomerism plague. It has decayed the necessary behaviors to keep our civilization civilized. It eliminated the unity of effort by driving competitive, modernistic attitudes through us. It has made complacency commonplace. It makes the unacceptable acceptable, which is slow-motion suicide. We're forgetting at our own peril our good traditions. We know more about consumer brands than we do our civic responsibilities. We've a long fight for a civilization of democracy on the horizon. We must stop committing societal fratricide. We must stop the winds of time gaining enough strength to blow us over by weakening our posture.

In the Figure 4-6 below we see how with doomerism, the people are neither serving nor being served. The society is blowing in the wind, spinning on a mast as battles over who is the master pit persons against one another and the people hang on for their lives. Our only hope is citizen-shipping—to push into the wind and right the obverse side of society to restore democracy and revive liberty. If not; if blown leeward, society will fall down like Humpty-Dumpty. A cracked egg is a mess, for a society, metaphorically this means into chaos, out of which tyranny can rise. Recall in the nursery rhyme that all the kingdom's horses and all the kingdom's men could not put him back together again. But we can. We are a democracy, a republic, not an egg. It will take work. Though we would rather society prevent America from falling in the first place, keeping it on top the wall is the righteous course of virtue. To stabilize it up high, or should it fall and break, we must constantly work to align the micro, meso, and macro levels with liberty for grace, dignity, and respect. We do this by behaving as appreciative citizens, living for one another and our common goodness, good for all and all for good, e pluribus unum, since Annuit coeptis, we are Novus ordo seclorum (recall Figure 0-1-1).

Doomerism confuses us. We the everyday people want to live lives of humanity, not of indecency and disease. We want the simple, peaceable life of freedom and opportunity to reach the highest heights of contribution our talents can achieve. We want to self-actualize and realize the joy in living a life filled with family, love, and liberty. With doomerism's philosophy, theory, policies, social trajectory, reality of errors, corrections, and poor results, we cannot be as we wish to be. Because of what it has done, we cannot allow it to continue doing what it wants, which it does through its doomers, and the other four ill types of boomers: the loomers, groomers, zoomers, and roomers. So we've no choice but to retire them.

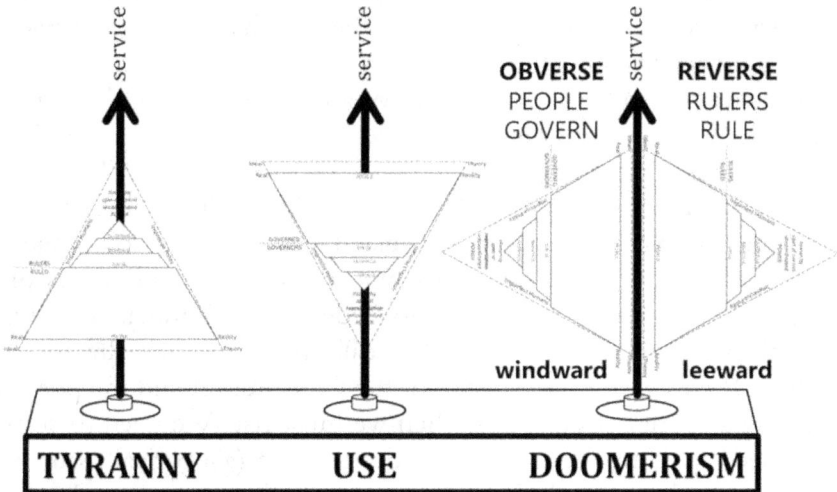

Figure 4-6: The Power Pyramid Shape of Society Related to Service
The shape of a society under tyranny is a pyramid with a few rulers at the top. The shape of the society of the United States Enterprise is the reverse, with the people on top as the majority. The shape of society influenced by doomerism is sideways, neither ruled nor governed but like a weathervane on a pole, blowing in the wind. But the answer is not blowing in the wind; it is in shaping society to be as the USE is intended to be.

There are arguments about where we came from and where we are going. We can understand it like this. We have two origins in thinking from historical settlement patterns, northern and southern, with several combinations in between and scattered all over. Of the STAMPER socialization contexts for children, we've four predominant societal conditions or socialization contexts of children (traditionalistic, modernistic, postmodernistic, and anomic). We have three settlement locales (urban, suburban, and rural). We've ten regional subcultures. We've a repeating pattern of generational turnings every eighty years, but with aging generations living longer and fewer replacements being born and raised, we're at risk of not replenishing our workforce with sufficient employees. We've adaptive problems with each new major stage of knowledge creation, absorbing and implementing societally transforming advances that increase and propel the innovation of increasingly complex technologies that require constant learning at a faster pace to keep up and compete. We are on an escalator that exhausts us. We are all trying to keep up with the race toward the next reality before we become too accustomed to the past and fall behind. The past is too quickly becoming the present, and the future is overlapping the realities of both. Confronted with too much information all at once are we nowadays. It feels like what was once a manageable arithmetic pace quickly became ten times faster at logarithmic lengths. It now seems to be accelerating overnight, every night, as if increasing exponentially. It is dizzying. Who is rushing, and to what unknown asymptote, why? We feel like we are drowning. We must avoid the riptide; we must ardently maneuver with citizenshipping skills to regain control. We must perform the leadership. We must pilot the USE. It's our societal ship after all.

If our species heads for extinction, we are in deep, deep, deep trouble. The baby doomers in positions of authority know this, but they don't care. They are getting what they feel entitled to, paid for by the children of the future. They could not care less. They'll be dead. They'll will burial in gold-lined coffins just because they can. Because they are unlikely to change their ways, they will argue until their death. We cannot wait. The hopes of the future generations reside in our acknowledging their human dignity, respecting their needs, and enabling the realizations of their dreams for a healthy life. If we do not want to doom the Constitution and the possibility of achieving a more perfect union, then we must rise. We need to stop being confused, listen to the voice of wisdom within (allegorically our better angels) and rapidly retire the baby boomers, inviting them to volunteer to teach in our ACE campaigns. These will help all find a proper perspective on the purpose of being an American, and engage in better citizenshipping to sustain our society. When we have less chance to advance, and less to chase materially, we'll have each other as a citizenry. We need to exhibit empathy, compassion, conscientiousness, dignity, and love to find happiness as a community. Doomerism is full of false promises that gain us nothing in spirituality, humanity, and harmony as a people. We must not let it destroy the promise of family and community power we need to enjoy the blessings of liberty.

Despite the various realities we face, what we have in common is the miracle of liberty. It's a gift of Providence. We the everyday people inherited it from thirteen predominantly English colonies on the continent that came to be known as North America, when their governors united to declare independence. For it, they fought a violent war to free them from insufferable, tyrannical control by a king. Then wrote, ratified, and lived by a Constitution, the oldest still in use. One that came after their daring Declaration that clarified that humans create their governments, and societies, and this meant we could and did amend the Constitution to be more in line with its ideal words—to extend liberty and voice in the polity to all human inhabitants of the country.

Our common liberty affords us freedoms based upon 28 basic principles of the founders as shared by the National Center for Constitutional

Studies (Skousen, 1981). Doomerism threatens these being known by the everyday people:

1. *Natural law is the only reliable bases for sound government and just human relations.*
2. *Under a republican constitution, a free people cannot survive unless they remain virtuous and morally strong.*
3. *Electing virtuous leaders is the most promising method of securing a virtuous and morally stable people.*
4. *The government of a free people cannot be maintained without religion.*
5. *All things were created by God, therefore upon Him [Her, It] all humankind is equally dependent, and to Him [Her, It] they are equally responsible.*
6. *All men [humans] are created equal.*
7. *The proper role of government is to protect rights equally, not provide things equally.*
8. *Men [humans] are endowed by their creator with certain inalienable rights.*
9. *To protect man's [human's] rights, God has revealed certain principles of divine law.*
10. *The God-given right to govern is vested in the sovereign authority of the whole people.*
11. *The majority may alter or abolish a government that has become tyrannical.*
12. *The United States of America shall be a republic.*
13. *A constitution should be structured to protect the people permanently from the human frailties of their rulers.*
14. *Life and liberty are secure only so long as the right to properly is secure.*
15. *The highest level of prosperity occurs when there is a free-market economy and a minimum of government regulations.*
16. *The government should be separated into three branches: legislative, executive, and judicial.*
17. *To prevent the abuse of power, a system of checks and balances should be adopted.*
18. *The inalienable rights of the people are most likely to be preserved if the principles of government are set forth in a written constitution.*
19. *Only limited and carefully defined powers should be delegated to government, all others being retained in the people.*
20. *Efficiency and dispatch require government to operate according to the will of the majority, but constitutional provisions must be made to protect the rights of the minority.*
21. *The keystone to preserving human freedom is strong local self-government.*
22. *A free people should be governed by law and not the whims of men [humans].*
23. *Without a broad program of general education, a free society cannot survive as a republic.*
24. *A free people must stay strong to survive.*
25. *"Peace, commerce, and honest friendship with all nations – entangling alliances with none" (Thomas Jefferson, first inaugural address).*
26. *The government should foster and protect family integrity, because it determines the strength of a society.*
27. *The burden of debt is as destructive to freedom as subjugation by conquest. (Ben Franklin said "Think what you do when you run in debt; you give to another power over your liberty").*
28. *The US has a manifest destiny to be an example and a blessing to the entire human race.*

Doomerism causes us to forget about these principles. If we believe that generations shape culture, and culture shapes society, and society shapes our behavior, we can correct course. We must understand the precept power processes of culture that shape society and us. If we do, we can solve our societal and social problems. The USE's democracy is ours. We must realize "We the [everyday] people" own it. We are it. We must act like its owners. Owners must be responsible and accountable to succeed. Do we want to complete our project begun in 1776? If so, we must support democracy by first knowing about ourselves. We cannot have liberty unless we put in the necessary self-development work as persons and as a people.

For the nation, each of us must find our personal purpose. We need to figure out the reasons for which we were created and for what we are living. We can do this when we have freedom and educational opportunities. Given the gift of life with many endowments that remain hidden from us, our talents need freed. They often remain unknown when unseen within a family, neighborhood, community, state, or regional subculture. It can be difficult if we do not feel we fit in within any of these social contexts. This we must correct. We must help one another maximize our potential to contribute to the greater good. The pursuit of virtue can free us to discover our special aptness. When developed we can comfortably share it for society's benefit and ours.

Our Personal Journeys

Through our lives, if we are well guided or lucky, we find ourselves. We come to understand what we can be and what our purpose is in life. When we can become ourselves for our best health and the greater good of society, we can find the happiness we pursue. In a democracy, freeing the truest self of each of us is a calling for all to participate in. If we can help each other get it together, we can find our own personal happiness within our being, as we are becoming its fullest potential. We can self-actualize (recall Figure 3-6). In this voyage to harmonious selfhood, we've many helpers and many lessons in the FILMS[2] [P7] of the societal powers, particularly family, community, mythology, academy, artistry, and industry, all of which may or may not see us for the endowments and limitations of our biology power. Called to serve, aren't we? (Guinness, 1998). Surely, doomerism didn't kill this within us. We can only hope that as we rediscover our social humanity through E-SASSY-T-TUF-FT-CAUCUS. It is medicine, part of the remedy. By it we denounce, and will defeat doomerism.

While being raised, we need our mentors to believe in being a citizenry, e pluribus unum. As we become who we are to be in life, we must remember our elders, parents, teachers, and coaches. We need them to build up our capacity and capability to possess conscientiousness, feel compassion, give and receive love, and offer and experience empathy. An empathetic and conscientious approach to participating in society is what a good citizen does. Citizens do for others first because it returns innumerable rewards. This is the essence of goodwill leadership. It defines a people. It defined the American people. We need it back. We need to be E-SASSY-T-TUF-FT-CAUCUS as a citizenry. With democracy in republic to IDEALS liberty and justice for all we will win the future. We must not allow doomerism to confuse and block us from following our calling as a people to become e pluribus unum.

We are a complex species, and what makes each of us unique comes from nature. However, the way we develop depends both on it and on the powers most in control of our environments, which reinforce our becoming by their nurturing and from an orientation toward becoming good citizens first. Not everyone receives the same developmental conditions, and some include conflicts that expose us to, and in some sense cause us to have, attitudes and behaviors of cruelty, hatefulness, and jealousy. Mythology power in the Western Hemisphere teaches such unsociable characteristics as sins; in the Eastern Hemisphere, they are opposites of the rightful ways and not good for our dharma. These unsociable attributes include greed, fear, vanity, hubris, narcissistic slavery to feeling superior, defrauding, cowardice, excessive ambition for commercial gain, deceitfulness, sloth or laziness to take any action, and a simply evil, demonic, antisocial beingness. Those who are bred in the blessings of liberty and have encountered and experienced in their natural selves and in their nurturing the attitudes and behaviors of kindness, love, and compassion have the best possible path toward fulfillment or positive self-actualization, through higher morals development (recall Figure 2-27).

For society to find ways to help its babies navigate their personal and social voyages that are impacted by and will impact it, a considerable amount of focus on humanity, on the conscience, conscientiousness, and state of consciousness is very important. A society too wrapped up in pursuing negative attributes, wrongful and unsociable attitudes and behaviors, is a society in decline. A decaying society is as a ship adrift at sea, with incompetent authorities in its pilothouse, on the bridge, at the helm, or one of mutiny and disorder, near anarchy, inattentive to the needs of its important mission, unfocused, and risking running aground and sinking. A society not focused on the voyage of its babies will find itself in this terrible state of confusion, not sailing toward its objectives. In our metaphorical ship, we're confined to quarters, quarantining form doomerism's infection. Those in the pilothouse, on the bridge at the helm turning the wheel, pushing the buttons, and pulling the levers are baby doomers. They are the worst cohorts of the "me first" generation. They sneezed and everyone got shot with snot. They are only thinking of themselves. Others called to serve have been unable to grab hold of the wheel, push the right buttons, and pull the best levers to get us moving forward toward our intended destiny.

Alas, the boomers are no longer the majority of living adults. What doomerism has done is to make them fear losing power. They are trying to divide us so they get to keep all they took illegitimately from the future. We must not let them! The blessings of liberty provided their prosperity. They should not pass to posterity probable poverty. It's as if they choose to say "I got mine, 'F' you! Get lost. Your loss is not my problem." Sadly, they caused it, but want to blame the victims to hide from their own culpability. Perhaps buried deeply within their psyches guilt and shame exist.

Sorry for the digression, let's get back to understanding our complex selves. Our biology power exerts many forces upon us, from sexuality to control ambitions. We see these influences in, or by, our egos, with a high or low need for attention or acceptance. We can place ourselves along the continuums of many such dichotomies' poles. From wherever one positions oneself, nurturing supports the development of our social selves. These can swerve from varying positions throughout our lives as we socialize, exposed to new experiences in the many contexts within which we might find ourselves. We are fortunate if we gain more than one social grammar to get along with different others more easily. This is helpful to a people in a land where the majority of its inhabitants are immigrants.

Our socialization experiences as youths give us certain orientations to society. We are either taught or not taught, or any number of degrees in between, about becoming and being good citizens. Invited to develop our motivations, we learn how to lead and follow in groups. If we are lucky, we get to learn about how to play on teams and perform for the team's success. We learn that for self-advancement, a certain amount of rule following or even rule bending may benefit us. Too much bending or testing of the boundaries can get us into trouble with authority figures, but we must learn how to identify legitimate and illegitimate rules. We are born with an independence-seeking motivation, though some come to lose it to dependence seeking if their odds of achieving it seem insurmountable. All of us have a certain need to control aspects of our social contexts and ourselves. We differ. Some persons need less control over others, while others need more. Doomerism exposes and exploits this latter group's urges, their instinctive cravings for raw simians-primate power.

We are a fascinating species, and our bewildering variety ought to bring us joy in knowing how unique each one of us is. In a culture of democracy, we embrace this uniqueness. We celebrate it. Enabling each soul to become its best contributor to the whole, we achieve gestalt, a state in which the whole is greater than the sum of its parts. From it, we each get to enjoy the flow that rushes through us when we are doing what we feel we were born to do. This flow is a state of optimal performance, of self-confidence in doing, a feeling of happiness (Csikszentmihalyi, 1991). Democracy is the culture that makes maximum self-attainment possible for all. We must pull it back from the brink.

This is not easy because of the great variety of natural and nurtured states of being. All our complex personal selves' personalities, personhoods, and personages (recall Figure 2-26) mean we need high tolerance for differences. Too many choices present numerous possibilities. The psychologists have created several tools we can use to help us understand our adult selves. We may be oriented to certain poles that, once identified, help us orient better toward others and find purpose by which, and places in which, we can employ ourselves for the betterment of self and society. We might be judgers, enforcers, willing to be controlled conformists who want everyone to follow all the rules perfectly. Or we might be intensely concerned with reality, or indifferently relativistic, or simple rule breakers who desire not to be controlled, or carefree in spirit, or not wanting any responsibility, and hope never to be held accountable for anything we did or said that was wrong. Or we might be an inventor-creator or feel we got forced by having no other choice than to become a criminal in order to survive. Knowing more about whom we are by nature and nurture is a wise aim to have in mind, and something worthwhile pursuing; not just for our own health, but for the community's too.

Becoming a citizen is a team effort, and it begins with a society dedicated to doing it. Citizenship is not just a legal status. It is a set of attitudes and behaviors that support society accomplish its goal and objectives. A society that scores low on citizenship commitment is subject to chaos and crises. This is mainly because its population is ill prepared to work together. A teamwork value set is necessary to move in a direction of unity for the common good. Citizenship commitment, civic engagement, and informed political participation wax and wane, through good times and bad. In our current times, we are not doing well. It is paltry, we see the problems from it, and we know some of its causes. These causes have a least common denominator that creates the most common problem we face at the micro, meso, and macro levels of society: baby doomerism. It became prevalent in a generation that rose in a time of rebuilding a world from world war devastation and tremendous growth in globalization. It dialectically grew as a negative force out of the successful gains of the second stage of knowledge evolution in the modern era. It put the economy power into play in new ways using the new technologies of our current third stage of knowledge evolution. It came to accept and believe in a way of life we call consumerism.

Consumerism's Influences Upon Us

Consumerism, as a subculture of motivations, leans heavily on solving material needs, creating and fulfilling material wants, and addressing problems of how businesses get rewarded. It alters the perceptions of the purpose of work. Work is not just laboring to survive, get along, and/or climb the social status ladder. Work and trade solve survival problems, enable comfortable living, and create luxurious thriving opportunities. But as society becomes increasingly complex, symbols of one's status in society gain importance as more are able to find employment to meet needs and satisfy wants, buying conspicuous signals of success at selling one's labor in an ever-expanding marketplace. Status becomes one's presentation of self to society. In the FILMS[2] [P7] of societal power are ladders for climbing based on KA^4SA^2, presented to us as a game of life to be played.

We get caught up in the game: driven, reinforced, and propelled by our consumerism. There are all kinds of pulls on us through consumerism as a culture. One is its effort to be the basis for our identity through its glamorous products. Another is it making itself our purpose, which rewards the

HM[5] more than us as consumers. We can be any kind of consumer: a chooser, communicator, explorer, identity-seeker, hedonist, artist, victim, rebel, activist, or citizen who demands to be treated like a consumer. Our identity in it is as fungible as the advertisers deem it. Their work is to stimulate our emotions to buy. Consumerism is stretched to mean different things to different people. It is a social movement in consumer rights promotion and protection. It is a political ideology for the right of freedom of choice, albeit a choice limited by purchase power and product competition or lack of competition as is the case with monopolies. It has been an economic ideology for global development since the collapse of the Soviet Union (a failed experiment in state controlled collectivism). Consumerism is a lifestyle of conspicuous consumption. Conspicuous displays are a culturally constructed strategy to communicate one's status (Harris, 1989). It supplants religion as a weekend activity and provider of social distinction and status. It is a moral doctrine in developed nations, replacing the Puritan ethic. It sells itself as the means to the good life, a vehicle for freedom, power, and happiness. It is supplanting democracy's idea of a citizen: that we are politically equal and find happiness predominantly through exercising our inalienable rights. In the founding of the US, this radical social innovation replaced the mythology power's religious conceptions that we find happiness predominantly through worship. Consumerism declares that happiness comes predominantly from participation in markets, not participation in politics and free speech or religion and its rites and rituals (Gabriel & Lang, 1995).

Consumerism is supplanting reason. It is the economy power supplanting the polity power as the primary framework for living and use of the people power. It shapes the secondary and tertiary social powers, by conflict and confluence, but it is driving for control of our souls. Our FILMS[2] [P7] of societal and social powers: people, polity, economy, family, community, academy, mythology, artistry, industry, and history. All adopt mannerisms—ways, means, and methods—that support consumerism. Slowly, we have forgotten the democracy culture that made our society possible, and the structure that established for us liberty became misbalanced by misdeeds of misguided people. We seem no longer focused on being better persons and a better people. We are not concentrating our energies on contemplating what kind of beings we are, on our possibilities of being, which might elevate us above survival and the material accumulation of consumerism that returns our investments with spiritually hollow and unfulfilling results, or unholy ones. Consumerism seems to enable a few to become incalculably rich with money, and yet we see so many of these people without happiness, stuck in sad states of humanity with bankrupt souls, suffering from Machiavellianism.

We Are Both Consumer and Citizen

The following Figures (4-7, 4-8, 4-9, 4-10) show how the economy and polity powers play a game of "push and pull" an internal tug-of-war. We the people are the rope. Various isms are doing the pulling. The challenge is to balance the appetites for things and power, so we have a standard of living and quality of life befitting the everyday people who make up the real majority based upon incomes and who get us through our lives kindly. The majority should not suffer at the hands of any minority, nor should the opposite situation occur. The framers sought to establish such a respectful balance. We need to expand the middle, lifting babies out of anomic, enervating, and radicalizing contexts, so they may grow up to be contributing members of American society. With the drift of consumerism into doomerism, this ideal of an egalitarian society of equal opportunity to rise on one's merits is at risk, threatened by inequality from birth. This is not morally right for the USE. Recall that power seeks to divide and conquer. We must recognize its operant behaviors inside of us, its pulling and pushing upon our consciences, and resist it. Unity of self and society, cohesion as one people, require that we block dividing forces within and outside of us.

The first diagram, Figure 4-7, shows how our functionality as people relates to our normal condition of being. We are concerned with both private and public matters and having our needs and wants for goods and services satisfied by the economy power and our need for societal stability, a security from fears, famines, infirmity, and fights, addressed by the polity powers. A person not overly encultured by the forces of either the economy or polity power lives in balance and at peace with themselves. A balanced person has a social condition governed by logic. This posture is unseduced by the overt messaging of extremists seeking to convert a person to a way of thinking and behaving that subjugates them under a belief system that only maximizes benefits for its proponents. Persons who follow an extremist unquestioningly lose their liberty. Because they allow the radicalizer to tell them what to think, how to think, and how not to think, they become subjects to the one who seeks to control them. Radicalizing extremists DAMN the mythology powers.

In a person who knows liberty, the private and public pressures that pull and push on the self and society do not penetrate their identity. A well-balanced person knows that power seeks to corrupt them but through reason does not allow it. They make their own decisions based upon what services liberty, which involves the pursuit of virtue. Knowing they have liberty, they resist any peer pressure, or herd mentality, to join utopian promising cults. They also do not succumb to dystopian terror tellers' tales. They do not choose a side. They choose a centered way of being, a social circumstance that is a balance between self and society, private and public needs and wants. Not easily persuaded by fallacies, they are uninfluenced by illogical, magical thinking that leads to fanatical posturing.

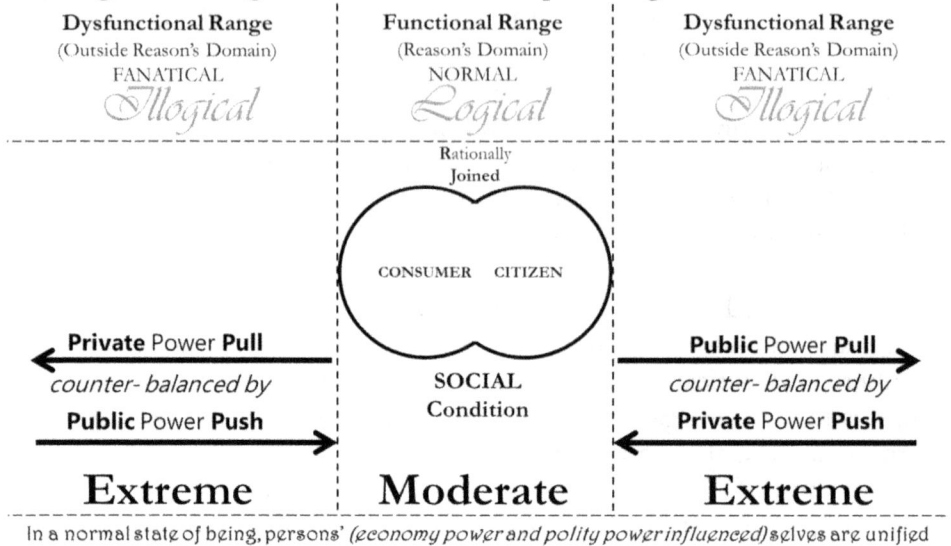

Dysfunctional Range	Functional Range	Dysfunctional Range
(Outside Reason's Domain)	(Reason's Domain)	(Outside Reason's Domain)
FANATICAL	NORMAL	FANATICAL
Illogical	*Logical*	*Illogical*

Rationally
Joined

CONSUMER   CITIZEN

← **Private** Power **Pull**   **Public** Power **Pull** →

counter- balanced by   SOCIAL   *counter- balanced by*
                              Condition
Public Power **Push** →   ← **Private** Power **Push**

Extreme   # Moderate   # Extreme

In a normal state of being, persons' *(economy power and polity power influenced)* selves are unified

Figure 4-7: Balanced Social Selves Provide Unified Identity

The second diagram, Figure 4-8, shows our functionality as a person if it separates due to insecurity in our identity and the pressure to participate in illogical social conditions that favor a fascinating fantasy that pulls or pushes us to more privately or publicly concerned attitudes. Remember Chapter 2's discussion of the distinction between how the mythology power influenced settlers within the regional subcultures of Yankeedom and the Deep South. These regions use the same holy book, yet their viewpoints on how to AEIOUY^{2}K mythology power is oppositional. One prefers its public influence, while the other prefers its private influence. Similarly, a person may desire that everyone be totally responsible to the public, making complete private sacrifices for the community, or a person may desire to be left alone without any public responsibility to do whatever they please in private. This choice can occur in how one approaches their identity as a person. Are they going to be identified as a consumer by their brands, or by their citizenship, the content of their character as a citizen?

Doomerism, through consumerism, seeks to pull people away from identifying with a polity power and enslave them to an economy power. With a kind of mythology power, consumerism invites people to worship products and the HM^5 responsible for the brands that become icons of idolatry. Media no longer refers to persons as citizens but as consumers. Because the media wants consumers itself, they do this, which supports their sale of brands' advertisements. Identities split in two. Instead of cooperating, they compete for control of the self. Exposed to risks of exploitation, we lose out. Predictably, politicians, pressing for personal power, perceived promising "me first" possibilities. Perplexed and predacious persons

ripen to presenting promises for promotional perspectives, purposely provided to them, as the predictors of probable position preservation or potential election to one.

Dysfunctional Range	Functional Range	Dysfunctional Range
(Outside Reason's Domain)	(Reason's Domain)	(Outside Reason's Domain)
FANATICAL	NORMAL	FANATICAL
Illogical	*Logical*	*Illogical*

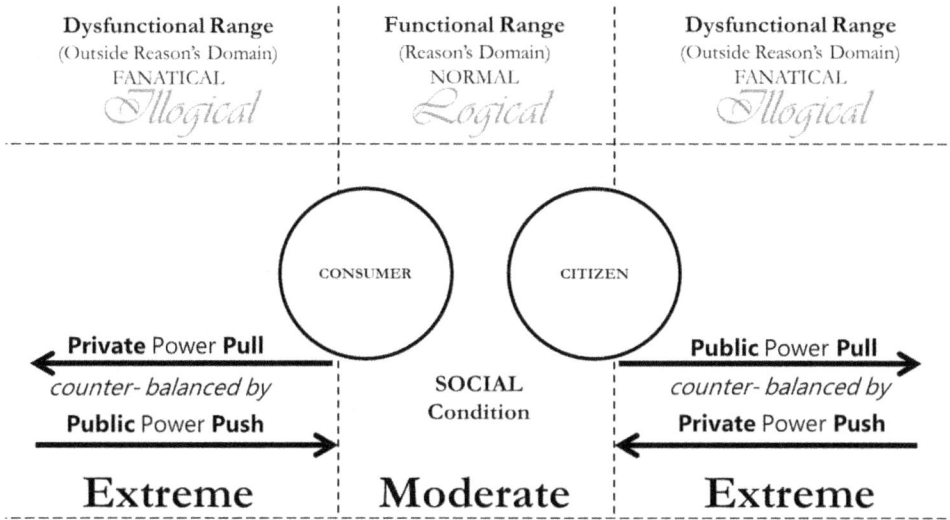

CONSUMER   CITIZEN

Private Power **Pull**   **Public** Power **Pull**
counter- balanced by   *counter- balanced by*
Public Power **Push**   **Private** Power **Push**

SOCIAL
Condition

Extreme   Moderate   Extreme

Causing an abnormal state of being, Doomerism splits persons' selves into two separate identities

Figure 4-8: Doomerism Divides and Confuses Social Selves—We Bifurcate

The profitability of the illogical fantasy selling private perceptions of
selves becomes dependent upon the brands. As this tug-of-war on a person's identity continues, if the person does not resist it, they will come to
believe that consumption is how one gets satisfaction. Alternatively, they
could become disgusted if unsuccessful, and through envy be subjected to
being radicalized to completely reject the FILMS[2] [P7] of provisioning goods
and services through open markets by brands, private businesses. The oppositional persons will see the competition for consumers' attention, and
money in exchange for their offerings as wrong, and request control of it.
They will insist the government do it. This solution would be an infringe-
ment on the liberty to invent and seek to bring one's ideas to the market for
consideration. Real self-confident joy is hard to find in an overly imbalanced and illogically controlled environment. The pursuit of happiness is no
longer a social condition of liberty, but it distorts into a pursuit of consumer materials as forms of attempts at happiness. Oppositely, it is lost to an
acceptance of an overt administrative state dictating consumer choice by
controlling what items get put into the marketplace.

This third diagram, Figure 4-9, shows how our functionality as a person
depletes in a culture of baby doomerism, which causes us not to see the
connected interrelated aspects of being a person. We are at once a consumer and a citizen, parts of a self and a society. At the extremes, we become
antisocial and fanatical in our viewpoints. We get radicalized. We either
seek zero responsibility to others or demand total loyalty from them. We

either want the economy power to rule us, or we want to rule others using polity power. We suffer in the confusion of one extreme or the other and cannot synthesize the two concepts. Are we bad citizens for being irresponsible to societal needs and only thinking of ourselves? Are we being bad consumers because we want the polity to control society, and we do not care what goods and services are available for us to buy?

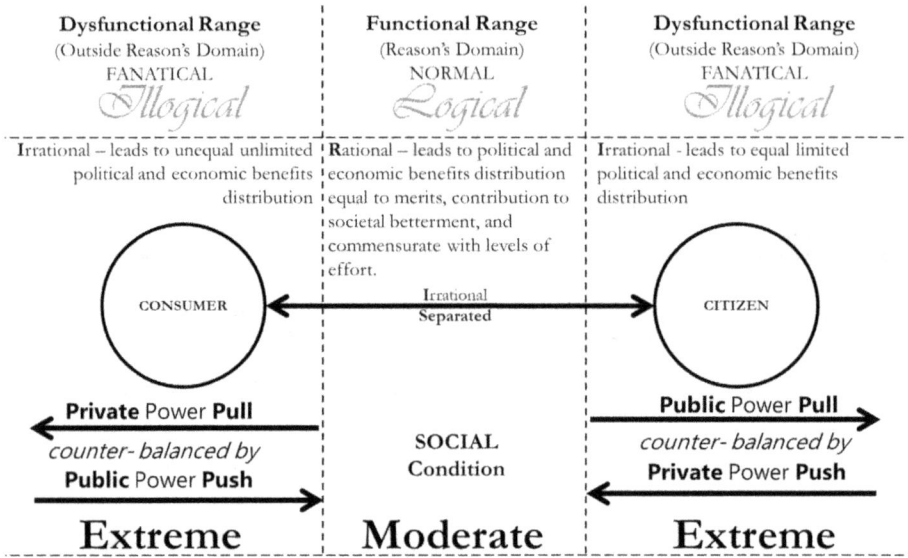

Figure 4-9: Doomerism Divides and Confuses Social Selves

The fourth diagram, Figure 4-10, shows the evolution of thinking from a split social self to thinking about how a society ought to be organized to serve the consumer and citizen selves and their needs for goods and services, be they private or public. A virtuous social condition of a balanced identity as a consumer and a citizen does not pull a person to one extreme or the other. We come in all types. But if we the people seek to be one people under God, indivisible, with liberty and justice for all, we must unite around a few basic principles and dedicate a large part of our lives to reifying them and bonding as citizens to keep their promise alive for posterity. Consumerism poses significant challenges to our improving our citizenry. To help us get better, we must look inside ourselves, at our motivations. Each of us needs to better comprehend who we are as a person, a social being, and close the gaps that injure our ability to unite. By better understanding our nature, our nurturing, our socialization contexts, our regional subcultures, our settlement patterns, and our cohort proclivities within our generational personalities, we may be able to adjust our thinking, change our attitudes, and engage in more thoughtful consuming and citizenshipping, becoming balanced virtuous persons. In the hope of saving the union and developing ways to ensure all of our citizenry can survive, live with dignity, and thrive, we need wholesale changes in our outlooks.

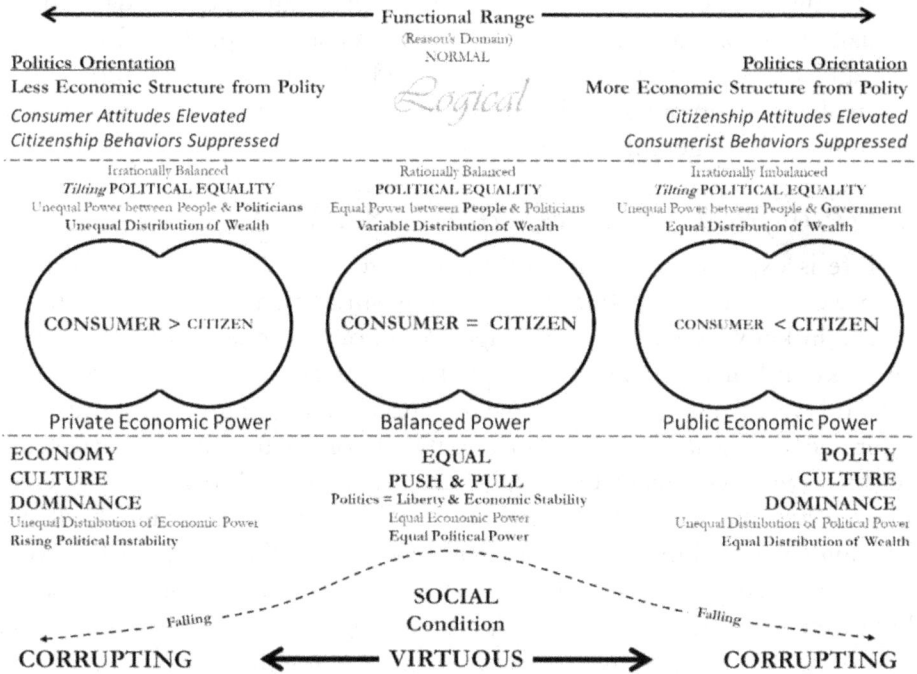

Figure 4-10: Social Selves Perspectives

We must become more conversant with the causes of the uncertain future to which we must adapt to overcome the hazards of the digital era we've entered. It is the result of the third stage of knowledge creation. Biological evolution takes eons. We've not time to wait, so we need to lean into the scholarship of being human. Let's ponder what kind of beings we are and what we can do socially to improve negative trends in our society.

We learn from the FILMS[2] [P7] of societal and social powers all sorts of things about ourselves as a species. The academy and mythology powers accommodate to social circumstances and physical conditions. They support family power, as we relate to one another in neighborhoods to AEIOUY[2]K our community power. Our relationships with these powers get inputs from regional subcultures' and settlements'—urban, suburban, and rural—values sets differ. Realizing we are Homo sapiens, a created, animate, intelligent animal, we've a variety of levels of consciousness we can explore together to restore democracy culture to move the USE toward a society envisioned, though not lived fully by the framers. We realize we exist on a unique planet whose geography power shapes our survivability and experiences while living. Its cycles of day and night, the solar year as we rotate and revolve around a sun in a galaxy in an ever-expanding universe, is a part of our in-beingness. We hear it all began with a big bang. Expansion seems to be a condition of life. Our expanding knowledge needs a parallel expansion in moral conscientiousness, compassion, empathy, and love for our fellow citizens. We are all in this society together and should commit to one another to make it better by adopting attitudes to adapt to our mutually confronted risks identified in doomerism. Its professed hopelessness and prophesied doom can be avoided. Because it thinks not of the human baby, everyone's beginning, it misaligns society and nature, mainly our biology. Let's get into this topic next.

Misaligned Society and Biology

Life is expansion. We expand in our size until we can grow no more. Then we start to decay, but as our corpus shrinks and shrivels, our minds expand in knowledge. We gain in age and in our experience of living. If we are lucky in our social reality, we gain love from family and close friends and find wisdom and solace for having survived a long time. Hopefully, we experience living in comfort and dignity. If fortunate, we recognize when we thrive with feelings of being fully alive, when in the flow zone, we enjoy spiritual luxuries. We might also find ourselves in the blessings of liberty enjoying some real material luxury now and again. Of course, our life cycles are determined by the biology power's programming. We confront realities that differ with each of our developmental stages as our bodies, brains, and minds expand. We develop in social contexts that either nurture or devalue us, to a variety of degrees and in differing stages.

When our biology does not conform to the rules of society, we have tension. In both good and bad ways, such as sexual maturity coming long before we have the economic ability to afford children, we have tension. This tension needs managed. Mythology power holders condemn out of wedlock sexual relations, and yet the economy powers cannot provide jobs to marry when the body wants another for reproductive behaviors. What could happen if we better aligned society with biology? Radically, what if we prepared children to be adults at a younger age, then allowed, and enabled them to marry to have the consensual adult sex their teenage bodies want by giving them a means to afford a family? What would happen if we built society to accommodate our biology instead of biology morphed to fit society? Imagine "What if?" What would be better for human children? What would be more humane, more natural? Of course, we would have to have social rules, as marriage is very serious. For example, no quitting allowed for ten years, and mandatory counseling by networks of trained healthfully and happily married volunteers to support the young families. What could happen if we reimagined the use of the societal and social powers related to biology power? Might we find any inspiration by listening to nature? Or will we simply allow the algorithms of artificial intelligence and automated robots make us obsolete? Perhaps they hold the cues to our being able to be more natural and follow our instincts. The point is that we need to start thinking differently if we are to adapt successfully. We need to solve serious risk harboring adaptive problems. First, we must respond to the threats of doomerism to begin to get to work on future proofing the human race from machine control, as one example of a coming threat to us. We need to converge on new understandings in the new digital era. We need to know how to best socialize the babies of tomorrow, so we can clothe, house, and feed them to keep them alive and made healthy to sustain our species.

Further, if we don't raise children to expect to care willingly for the elderly when they are adults, who will? What will happen to the baby doomers when they are frail and feeble elders? Will we abandon them because of their ruthless fleecing? Will they be denied all they think they earned, the money they took from the future to fund the entitlements they voted in for themselves? It is worrisome that they will die old and lonely. What empathy or pity will they receive? Have they ever thought about it? It will be an ugly society if we discard the elders because they were mean and selfish in their adult years. Even if it's a tetchy culture they've created in society, should not we recognize that they're diseased? They're misguided, blinded from seeing the tumor of doomerism within. Perhaps baby boomers reading this book may have a revelation. We need this for them, because we'll need their repenitent labors to correct our country's course. We must find a purposeful place for all boomers in our repair, rebalance, and care for American society campaign. As we launch into it by a rapid intervention, whether loomers, groomers, zoomers, roomers, or doomers, we will need their help to save the Constitution. We know we can count on the bloomers and broomers.

We don't presently have a standard socialization approach to raising children. We neither adequately nor consistently train all our children in civics and prosocial behavior. We need better ACE. We need common core subjects taught to everyone, everywhere, in every phase of our intellectual development. Agreement about what it means to be an American needs to begin early. The great miracle of our country needs explained. It is a valid nail to hang one's identity upon as a citizen of the US, who consumes. It is sturdier than the identity of only a consumer. Certainly, we'll consume goods and services that support the citizenry by moving money around, producing a good economy.

Currently, the advertisement commercials send messages to children that often run counter to their parents' lessons. Parents want to protect their children. Parents are becoming paranoid because of the antisocial qualities of baby boomer dominated society. Parents need to be able to control what children consume. With baby boomers, the polity power allowed the economy power to sell without restriction or regulation. This is ruinous to the minds and morals of children and society. This disuse of polity power, abuse of industry power, and misuse of artistry power, and nonuse of people power to protect children and help family power is sad. The lack of a social conscience in businesses who peddle inappropriate symbols to children is sad. President Eisenhower would be angry. Bad behaviors by business do not allow us to celebrate the great benefits good business brings to us. Conscienceless commercialization complicates the work of parenting. Communities' retention of wholesome norms, folkways, mores, customs, and beliefs gets threatened. Neither is the technology of typing emoji, acronyms, fragments, and short sentences to each other helping them learn how to have social conversations. They hide behind their screens and avatars while wanting to be accepted and to get along comfortably with their peers. This is no way to socialize children in a democracy. Democracy requires special social skills. We must learn to discern positions; express opinions built on facts, deliberate, debate and discuss to find common ground. Respectfully disagreeing with facts as a badge of false pride's "honor" is not helpful to resolving disputes and solving social problems. To deny reality as evidenced by factualness is a cop out of the undisciplined and under adherent citizen to the core values of democracy and the Constitution. We must seek out shared beliefs to which all might subscribe and commit as a community standard. Sound ACE will support this approach. Addiction to dopamine produced by likes on social media will not!

Seven socialization contexts make uniting as one people challenging. Children grow up with different understandings about how to behave in society. This is why an ACE is critical for the USE to reach its goal. This is why being able to cross learn with different others builds social grammars that support our social capital to build a strong civil society. Not only do the STAMPER contexts cause variety in fitness for social interactions with others, so also do settlement patterns. These overlap with other social powers' influences upon us, as does each developing child's person-ness (recall Figure 2-26). Place and time both shape our identity and relate to our consumer and citizen attitudes. Contexts and identity persuade or dissuade certain behaviors. We can be moderate or extreme in many opinions. It is our task to overcome doomerism and combine to provide commonality in comprehension of what it means to be a citizen and a consumer in the future. A consistent ACE is our starting point to unify in our mission to complete and sustain our project to make a more perfect union. A clear vision now clouded out by the boomer generation's begat culture: baby doomerism.

Our sense of neighborliness differs among settlement patterns. Urbanity, suburbanity, and rurality are dissimilar lifestyles. The eleven regional subcultures impart different consumer and citizenship perspectives. One's generation and the timing of the arrival of one's family in the US do too. Newer, older, and originating colonial immigrants have different citizenship opinions. Older families have a sense of ownership and entitlement, having been here longer. This is a normal assumption, since generations have worked on the project longer. All these variations in ones societal, social, and personal experiences make understanding one another more complex. In some cases, it is very difficult. Never-changing human nature's survivalist instincts cause us to segregate, not integrate. This is why being an American requires effort. Fortunately, human nature hardwires us to cooperate socially. We can collaborate if we are open-minded and have a common goal. We cannot simply let life happen unconsciously, unthinkingly, and impulsively. We must realize these days that plutocrats seek to shape the containers of our lives. They intentionally make us ignorant, so they get to keep the power, and rule over us. This is tyranny, people. As Americans, we cannot just be as we feel we want to be. We must apply a higher state of mind, a societal-wide discipline to learn how to get along. Freedom does not mean being as instinctively direct as one can be. It means working diplomatically, "virtute et non vi" (by virtue not by force), to persuade others to support progress toward conserving constitutionality as the best way of living. We must do this to move society forward toward being just while ensuring that everyone has liberty. The sacrifice is worth it because it yields both for all of us.

Being a real American takes concerted effort, a determined, disciplined, coordinated commitment to doing it. It requires we all focus upon our project's goal and objectives. Without this, we cannot build a society of liberty through a culture of democracy. We will fall back into the conditions of Hobbesian savagery. To be American, we must put emphasis on nurturing our better natures. We cannot allow our animalism to override intellectualism or our spiritualism. We will not succeed in our mission if we let the primate within control us, shaping our attitudes and behaviors, by directing our thoughts and actions. We must train ourselves to listen to the higher, more humane holiness within. We must rise up to the ideals and make them real. We must see our job as it is, to lead society. We must push ourselves to be the team that IDEALS liberty and justice for all, every day in every way, with everybody in every place. This is the duty of a citizen. A proud posture is not a pose. The exposé of the follies of the baby boomers may be painful. It may tarnish our identity and take away pride in being a citizen, but we can reverse the course. Being a citizen of the United States should give a person pride. This, if more important than the vainglory of conspicuous consumption, will enable us to unify and rebalance purpose in our lives and in the societal powers.

Recognizing the variety of social circumstances and physical conditions for children, with the SERF we'll manage the risks. We'll tailor an ACE for future generations and new arrivals to perpetuate the best in the USE. We need to address our differences civilly without argument over who is or isn't entitled. It's not about entitlements. It's about contributions. It's about commitment to upholding the Constitution in our daily lives. In its defense we must unite! We the everyday people must accept the challenge, will, and exertion to put forth the effort to endure the longsuffering generational work to unify society. It will require more than the suggestions coming from officials. We must enact neighborliness in our daily lives. We must be

E-SASSY-T-TUF-FT-CAUCUS. The think tanks and administrations of federal, state, and local governments are not going to solve our problems. We are! We must regulate them and demand they minimally referee the economy powers, creating fairness in the marketplace to maximize competition, ensuring its openness for the entry of new ideas and products made by small business entities and entrepreneurs. These are essential to keep markets free from coercion and prevent price gouging and other wrongful behaviors that destroy our prospects for prosperity, and its passage on to posterity. We ought not to depend on these bodies anyway. We ought to appreciate them as members of civil society, but set up volunteer associations that support us locally. Bottom up rather than top down is more in keeping with democracy culture.

To unify the people requires a greater comingling of citizens. It requires teaching and learning more than one social grammar. Knowing differing perspectives and agreeing on a common one is quintessential to democracy. We must come to know "how things get done in my neighborhood and why" while hearing others' stories. To do this, we all must adopt a more reflective thinking style, one that teaches us conscientiousness, compassion, love, and empathy for one another. Reflecting upon our own human experiences with curiosity toward others can build within us these socially vital emotions, or sensibilities, or sympathies. From these we the everyday people will not be tempted to try to rule over others with raw power ploys and game plays.

These vital humanly humane sentiments remove the confusion put forth by doomerism. Of them, conscientiousness and empathy shape pathways to unite, not divide as us doomerism does. Compassion and love help us bond with one another in community. These feelings mitigate combat baby doomerism's risky negativity. A new attitude toward our identity that puts "citizen" first and at the forefront of our experiences will help us unite in the fight to get back our leadership role in society. This is as it is intended to be in the USE. It is what makes us American. We need to be assiduous in our citizenshipping, not asinine in our consumption. Reinforcement by moral codes and not hatreds will bring forth the best from the mythology, community, and family powers.

We the everyday people must regain our curiosity about the heritage of our neighbors. Discovering common humanity in others is challenging. With a belief in this country as a place to realize dreams gives us hope for our children. It is part of everyone's American experience. For some families, it happened a few generational cycles ago. Those who've been here teach those who are new here. This is as it has been. New immigrants need taught to be receptive to receiving advice on how to assimilate, and not offended by it. New immigrants must come here to become Americans, and not to extract money out of our economy to build estate castles in the country from which they came, as feudal lords would. However, baby boomers' selfishness caused them to disavow this welcoming and teacherly virtue of America's Lady Liberty Libertas. It was too much work for them. It was easier for them to dislike. Doomerism prefers to blame outside others as the cause of our problems. The Constitution faces both foreign and domestic threats. We must give new arrivals attention to integrate them properly. They came here with hope for a better life. If they did not come for themselves, certainly they came for their children. They need us to help them become Americans. We need them to work and contribute. We must merge everyone into society, or society will disintegrate further. If they came to take and send back home, we might need to evict them for refusing to assimilate to our core values and not wanting to become American. We do not need any more stealers or free loaders within our boarders. We have enough hoarders to deal with thanks to the boomers shifting us to a baby doomerism culture.

American society is for better futures for our children. This is why people come to our shores. This is the clear intention and purpose of the endowment of a civil society. American society is to be civil. Built upon the foundations of our polity we associate and create groups that support it. It projects truth as inalienable natural rights. Across all generations of immigrated people, and with the continent's native nations and peoples, we must learn affective and effective social grammars. We must generate social capital through civic engagement and informed political participation. Our civil society must be stronger. Through it, we'll manage the risks inherent in instinctive human nature found in those who pursue power for power's sake. Responsibilities to the society carry the society forward toward its goal. By the quality of our performance in our social roles, we make community. Remember, by nature we are socially dependent creatures. We need others. Our roles, when performed with the intent of making a better future for the children, reify our American ethos, pathos, logos, and kairos. We are a nation of many. Not to live for a better tomorrow is to adopt doomerism as one's guide. Sadly, it confuses us. The people who believe in it suffer and cause suffering. They deny suffrage. The people who believe in the ideals and purpose of our country, who seek to live by its laws and originating principles, advance us toward our goal by attaining its objectives. We must admit these are in jeopardy of annihilation by the chaos of doomerism that is spinning out of control as we storm over new technological advances impacts upon our emotions.

Socioeconomic Risks of Technology

The risks of doomerism are rising in this era of advanced new knowledge and technologies. We must recognize this. We need a more holistic understanding of it to better adapt. As we adapt, we must resolutely hold on to our core values and reestablish our honor. We cannot allow the miracle of the American society to commit suicide (Goldberg, 2018) due to the anomie of doomerism.

We must gain control of the technologies and regulate them for the betterment of our children. We must mitigate negative risks: anxiety, depression, suicide, and murder. Doomerism clouds our judgment. Its pressing us for more, better, faster, perverts ambition. Its tolerance and vain celebration, lusting for power, money, and fame, distorts the purpose of life, one person at a time, and corrupts a people's voyage. Our personal journeys benefit in a society led by a united people sailing to the correct destination, a representative republic with a culture like an ocean of fair winds and following seas we call democracy. To the extent that it faces hazards and is vulnerable by its openness to newness, we need to enact good judgment. We need to regulate to manage the dangerous consequences of our new technological tools. Our new hardware, software, and the social transformations these bring needs managed for the sake of our future. We need to do this with the children's opportunities in mind; not our own selfish adult desires!

A new class of technology billionaires claims their fame, but the children suffer. Shame on them, but are they to blame? Are they innocent victims of doomerism? We must focus not on placing the blame but on properly defining all the negative extensions of doomerism, and then fixing the problem. How might the digital-native millennials regulate the technologies? They have had direct experience with their detriments. We do not know. They are not holding enough of the societal power's positions of authority, particularly within the polity, to do something about it.

We should get them into authority to try, but not unless they have good character, integrity, and education in ACE and the humanities. Our solutions need to be humanly humane and not further technological and technocratic. Just as modernistic architects thought they could cure poverty with public housing, we need to be careful whom we put in authority. We need the right skills for the administrative and managerial jobs within the FILMS[2] [P7] of society. Social economic circumstances correlated more with poverty than shanty housing. Neighborhoods form on the city streets, the urban floor. People need places to meet and mingle, not shacked up in tiny apartments thousands of feet up in the sky. Ownership of places is essential to prevent vandalism (Bell, Fisher, Baum, & Greene, 1990). Owning one's own place requires one has a job to rent it or buy it. This is where the economy power needs to place emphasis.

Psychologically and sociologically, free for tenants cheaply built high rises did not afford the propinquity or proximity to connect people quickly to the city. People need sociopetal not sociofugal places. We need to gather, together. More so, the isolation of people in separating boxes limits community formation. Neighborhoods do better with the security brought about by more windows and doors opening onto the streets, allowing eyes on and voices to enter the street's public realm. By the way, back then architects did not learn this lesson well. In some places, high rises were a mass housing solution to get certain populations out of the way for engineers to build highways. High rises for highways, putting people in less important status than transportation. Fortunately, some bloomers put together solutions with new approaches to land use planning and usage, redressing the modernistic single use zoning that ripped apart the urban neighborhoods. We have these pockets of poverty to address more fairly. Places the boomers have not corrected, but if of good architecture, gleefully gentrified. Policies by their colleague boomers enabled it.

Concomitantly, we cannot allow those not prepared for the jobs of administration and management to get them. Yet, we need those in charge to surround themselves with good teams. A diverse group can bring planned scenarios under thorough scrutiny. A variety of thinking, differentiated skill-sets, and many educational backgrounds, even having rivals, is better than naïve mono-cultured groupthink. Such an approach benefits decision-making. Diverse teams, especially in the polity's executive branch cabinet, can prevent single simpleminded—too easily agreed upon by 'group think' —solutions from being proposed. There are experts worthy of giving and getting advice. There are subjects that are very complex, for which we do not have clear understanding. We must try. Let's move society forward into the trepidatious future with our best competent minds. Let's get our 24 for 40 years old civic-minded citizens with the right stuff, ready for the mission. Let's assign them the duty to listen to us, and experts, and guide us onward and upward toward our goal, by effectuating our objectives.

The slick new electronic computational, communications, and entertainment technologies are a problem like poverty the architects were hired to help solve, but did not have diverse enough teams and not all the right skillsets and tools to address best. These technologies like poverty doom our babies. They are too often de facto babysitters. Parents cannot be with their children because both have to work to make ends meet. This is confusing, feels unnatural, and its outcomes are bearing the ugly truth. We are not able to play our roles as parents well when we struggle to meet basic needs. Worse, when we cannot earn a sufficient wage to support a 21st-century standard of living, we suffer enormous stress. Stress kills. The challenge of reaching the standard is harmful. Not being able to reach a quality of life that allows us to find leisure and recreate our minds, bodies, and souls is further depressing. Past industrialists saw a value in this. As peer to Henry Ford, Andrew Carnegie, J.P. Morgan, Cornelius Vanderbilt, and John D. Rockefeller, Milton S. Hershey said, "Business is a matter of human service" (Gutmann, 2019). He built parks for his workers, and his five-day forty-hour workweek eventually became the norm in American society.

Balance occurs. The economy power does social good when not subjected to errors and omissions in its activities and relationship with society. Under the doomers, beneficent basic labor and time structures eroded fast.

We no longer feel free to be, to recreate. Many feel trapped again by the economy power and not enabled by it. We the people must be able to lead. If all we do is grind to survive, we've neither energy nor time to lead. This is a very problematic societal condition for a democracy. Baby doomers flawed ways, means, and methods of doomerism CATAPULTED destruction. We should not tolerate damage to children as permissible in American society. The first way they get hurt is by poverty, caused when parents cannot work a job that pays for necessities. This we must fix. We should not turn our backs on our fellow citizens.

Our economy power is expansive in its invitation to free people to take charge of their own lives and seek purpose. We like the freedom to find solutions to societal problems. We've done well to make ways for our species' survival. Through our entrepreneurial spirit, we invented and created new tools. We made markets for new ideas on new ways of doing things to help us thrive in living our limited lives. The economy power and its subordinate FILMS^2 [P7] and its HM^5 are extremely powerful at effecting new solutions. Yet they too are susceptible to the corrupting forces of power. We must AEIOUY^{2}K it, and not DAMN it, if we are in a position of authority invested with it. It, like all powers, needs controlled by checks and balances for a just arrangement to prosper. It must deliver prosperity for all so the polity does not need to pick up the slack from its failures and unpatriotic abandonments of citizens. It must deliver the goods and services profitably but fairly to the populace, without bankrupting everyday people.

We need the economy power to continue to develop with constituent artistry and industry powers. We need it to combine with history and academy powers to form special associations that put into play our community power. We need these to expand and open up new sectors for exploration. We like to take measured, yet risky, opportunities to discover, invent, and make new tools. We use tools to block emerging threats, mitigate hazards, and solve adaptive problems. Through our economy power, we've an engine of opportunity. With it, we invented and implemented many benefits. However, as with all new things, we eventually see consequences. These we need to address. In the ever-changing business landscape of entrepreneurial efforts, we must be mindful of purpose. Cultural passion to find new and better ways to profit while provisioning society can carry us away into unethical waters. The persistent pursuit of profit in itself, with social reorganizations caused by its production of new knowledge and technology, creates vulnerabilities to the stability of American society.

The positive and negative risks of such organizational alterations in the FILMS^2 [P7] of the economy power must be understood by the citizenry. While new ideas can cause improvements, these efforts need led by the citizenry with eyes on potential consequences. The SERF can help us lead. Because people staff the roles in the economy powers' FILMS^2 [P7] and its HM^5, we can control it. If we are of the citizen-first mindset, we can prepare ourselves to recognize risks to liberty in societal transformations. We must protect ourselves from groupthink that would support things that jeopardize democracy and the republic's and citizens' financial stability. Doomerism numbs human's humanity and humaneness senses. We are not dumb. We can see now how its blind ambition exposes us to vulnerabilities. Threats arise outside the economy powers, that when realized unbalance society.

Monopolies, a negative risk of economy power, misbalance the primary societal powers' arrangement resulting in destabilizing disequilibrium. These large groups of people, organized to serve an often singularly focused profit purpose, which hinders or harms others by concentrated power, are consequential for society. Some owned by many publicly traded stocks are corporations or quasi-public utilities. Some owned by a tiny group holding all its assets, and others privately owned by larger groups, are successful private companies. Monopolies harbor hazards to opportunities. They operate to stop competition and prevent the flow of new ideas. In efforts to keep their power, they cause limitations, like guilds, blocking others from contributing to the cause of societal betterment. If new knowledge produces a new technology that can do more for lower costs and greater profits than what monopolies do, the monopolies, fearing to fall, can become ruthlessly cruel to the newcomers in the marketplaces they dominate. These circumstances make persons to behave wrongfully or even dangerously. If the new solutions only concentrate wealth, than we the everyday people should be concerned, because good economy power moves money around, it does not centralize and restrict its access to a few at the top.

Our polity has its FILMS[2] [P7] to administer the conditions of society. Its role is to guarantee our inalienable rights. But, because the economy power shirks its responsibility to the citizenry that supplies its workers and marketplaces for its goods and services, those negatively impacted by massive disruptions to labor markets and production sectors have to rely on the polity for help. Is this the best model to cope with continuous growth in knowledge and technology? As the people who lead society, should we not better unite on our common values and find more stable and efficient ways to handle advances? Or do we want to trust in misplaced evolutionary tales of the survival of the fittest to assuage our fears of being accountable to our neighbors' plight, or in being responsible for the community's health?

The public-private partnership, as it is today, covers labor risks through the public sector. Other than by hiring workers, this permits the private sector to enjoy freedom from contributing toward a people's survival. This allows our economy power's HM[5] to pursue profit-making ambitions in isolation of broader social needs. The public assumes the risks of its failures. We the everyday people through taxation pay for the insurance that covers us for failures in business operations. The public left holding the bag bears the risk transferred to it so private business can pursue less burdened courses to generate wealth. The polity builds and holds the safety nets for the private sector businesses and the people who lose jobs. Is this an ideal arrangement of societal powers?

This model gets into public opinion trouble when it poorly remunerates the contributions of persons' labor. Without sufficient cash flow, the public sector cannot amass revenues to provide a safety net. If the economy power elites who benefit from not having the risk of labor maintenance and management are poor citizens who will not pay into the safety net for labor availability, they will demand bailouts for themselves when they fail. This is the kind of hypocrisy doomerism entails. Not wanting to be a part of a society of everybody, elites decide to compartmentalize their participation in society. They use their status and excess wealth to gain influence over the polity. They push for laws that enable them to avoid taxation. They lobby for preferences that feed their less-than-sociable instincts, so they might hoard cash unrestricted. They hire specialists at manipulating image and opinion to brag about how good they are at giving to charity. It's called "PR" for public relations, but it's really mind controlling propaganda radiating to disguise their subliminal entreaties that petition for positive public opinion, while they in other ways are taking prosperity away from the everyday people. They make it sound like they give a lot, but it is often miniscule compared with what they take home for themselves. For some it is a game, charity only given as a popularity stunt. They need to posture at celebrities' cocktail parties. On the other hand, it might be a money sheltering punt. It might not be really charity, which to be blunt, would be quite an affront if its giving only served a public image act and legal tax payment avoidance. This behavior is a part of the rigging of the system, so to speak. This is only one example of what a society of doomerism leaning on consumerism produces as tolerable, acceptable, and laudable. Do we really believe that this is a good direction for American society? We need this question debated in our politics with us informed of, involved in, and in control of it, so we the everyday people can perform our people power role. We must insert and assert ourselves. We are the leaders in the USE's LAMBS activities. Without us leading with the purpose of liberty, the societal and social powers will abandon it, untied, setting it adrift to hazard toward unknown risks. Figure 4-11 below depicts this mess of a society. We must unite intelligently to remedy it.

We are coming to the end of this chapter. It sought to explain what doomerism is as a form of culture. It sought to show how it COIFFURE democracy and threatens to replace it as the mainline culture in American society. It presented risks and examples of how doomerism CATAPULTED crises upon us. Before we move to the next chapter, in which more of its causes will be conveyed, a few more aspects are worth hearing about. These contain more of its negative influences upon us.

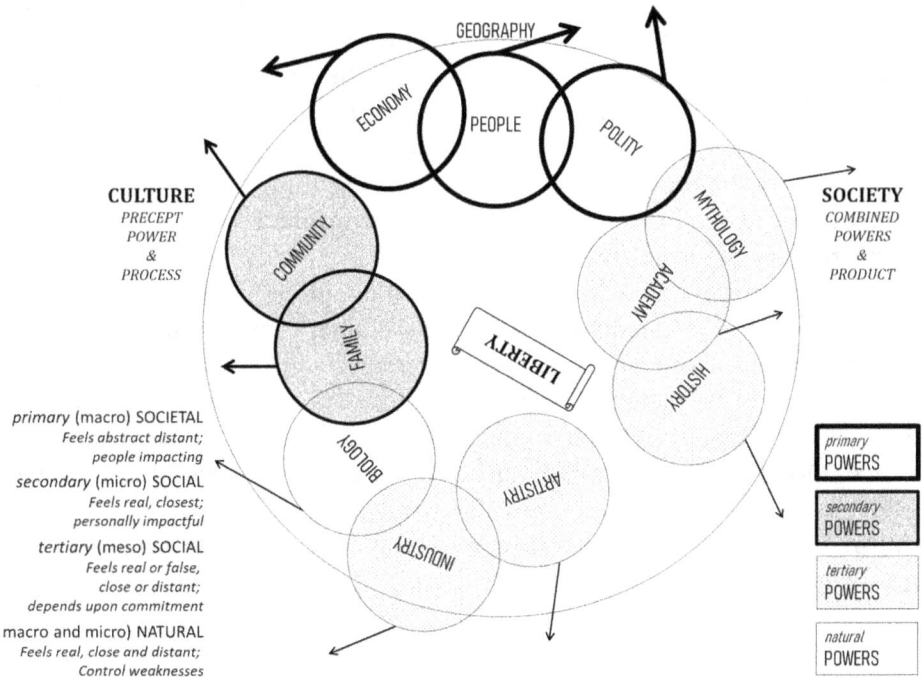

Figure 4-11: Society with Baby Doomerism Culture
Detached from its founding principles and virtuous living, American society resulting from baby doomerism's cultural modes that COIFFURE democracy is a disorienting mess; not heading in a healthy direction of equilibrium, of a stasis of trust and prosperity for all in the nation, because doomerism CATAPULTED crises and chaos into society.

We must understand that the prosperity that made doomerism possible brought about a sense of privilege. As scarcity is a technique of those in power to control populations, privilege has hazards too. Privilege blinds us. Doomerism privileges false beliefs. It makes us ignorant to the inner workings of our minds. In this way it weakens us, stripping us of real liberty. It eviscerates the wisdom that virtue relies upon. Doomerism tells us what we want to hear, what feels good to us. Contrarily, wisdom tells us what we need to hear. Wisdom increases our conscientiousness. Doomerism reduces our contentment and lessens our contentiousness. We must terminate and invert this trend. Wisdom helps us be humble and appreciate and express compassion, love, and empathy. None of us are perfected beings. But if we do not try to become more perfect, we cannot perfect our union. Identifying with a citizen-first mentality creates a path to rectify the moral drifting doomerism embraced. Its promotion of inegalitarianism, the tolerance of power over people is a negative aspect of it. Doomerism's value set that "I am in power because I am who I am", "It's all about me", and "I am in this for me, so what's in it for me, because I'm not playing a role for the benefit of society" is the result of baby boomers' "me first" construct.

Democracy tells us that if we promote egalitarianism, more of us will have power over our own lives and not be the subjects of tyrannies. This leads us to be more humane, to shed the hubris that doomerism encourages. We have to want to do the work of democracy. It takes biology-based will power. This personal power encouraged by mythology, academy, community, and family powers can do amazing things. It can bring us the resiliency we need to develop the grit to confront the future. But with it, we need a pursuit of virtue and wisdom.

Wisdom may make us feel uncomfortable, but with democracy, the person is important and central to society. We all are invaluable when we do good together for one another. We must rediscover the essence of our nature, exemplary caring and giving, and nurture out of us the ills of excessive taking. Each of us having this value leads to dignity and respect. These are a choice. Doomerism breeds indignity and disrespect. It wants to grow itself inside of us and keep going, spreading out and taking over. It's a deadly tumor. We must stop it. Let's now move on to learn more of what caused it, so we can erect the treatment to cure it.

5. _"Kept Itself Going"_

This chapter describes what caused doomerism and what it means to us if we allow it to keep going.

_W_hat Caused Doomerism?

Many factors aligned at the wrong time for democracy. The continuation and combination of the consequent social circumstances caused doomerism. We've experienced a decline in civilization. We move closer to the precipice of doom precipitated by a lowering of standards. Embedded in its chaos we got barraged with confusion about what to believe in, we got misguided by immorality and hedonism. Forgetting our national purpose prepared us for it. Transfers of the common wealth from public to private coffers accelerated it. Declines in support for civil society are elements of it. An uncompetitive commercial global market spoiled the generation that more fully than any entered into it. Bourgeoning growth and wealth disguised our demise. Unchallenged by post-war rebuilding societies, poor choices were not yet evident. We see the consequences now. Diluted civic engagement and decreased political participation evince it. The internationalized scale of energy and consumer goods production fed into it. New knowledge shocked us. The known underpinnings of American society winced. The denied undergirding and consequences from our devastating separatist war and the culturally failed forced reunification still linger. All of these factors colluded. Risks went unidentified, thus unmanaged.

All the while, as we humans solve one problem, we always discover or cause more problems that then need solving. As a species, we have entered into a new era, a third stage of knowledge creation (Hage, 2020). We are figuring out how to adapt to new social challenges. The adaptive process involves trying and testing differing ways of being. Some have been beneficial, but some have been negligent. Chaotic change opens us up to new possibilities. Changes in our social definitions of what is permissible allow exploitation to expand. When what's right and wrong get questioned, criminals emerge and take advantage of our uncertainty. Doomerism allows a few high-society persons to appear to be above the law. If they seem to be getting away with crimes, it pulls others into doubt and risky business. "If they can do it, and they have every luxury, why can't I?" becomes the question. The majority begin doing the formerly forbidden. Everyone seeks advantage for self. Insecurity and fears rise up. Myths of damnation no longer feared, doom approaches daily in our minds. Doomerism's culture shifting influence expands. Increasingly, it goes unchecked. Irresponsibility and excuses balloon.

This is why we need community—to get through crises without falling apart. When doomerism takes hold, previously impermissible attitudes become permissible. What was once unacceptable gains acceptance as normal for the majority. This leaves lingering frustrations and raises new challenges. Tolerance of egregious misdeeds, whose perpetrators are celebrated, hurts the whole. To consider damaging-to-democracy behaviors as appropriate or laudable is unhealthy for honor seeking Americans, the ensemble of e pluribus unum believers. When the focus on honesty disappears, doomerism takes hold. It grips and molds a delinquent culture, devastating for children's development into good adult citizens as it devalues the ideals of liberty.

The baby boomers made many misguided choices to serve "me first" self-justifications, to buffer weak ego needs and amass material wealth, which drove them. Their insatiable desires took over their being. They then chose to convert society to their beliefs. They used power accumulated in concert with their beliefs to persuade others to be like them. By this, they felt justified. This criticism applies in differing quantities and various qualities to the five kinds of boomers we've attempted to reprimand for engendering doomerism culture in our society.

Persuasion is a primary force in a democracy. They persuaded a shift from "we" to "me" as the first consideration for persons in this country. Our entrepreneurial conditioning made the USE a society of excellent salespersons. We must not let them sell us on doomerism. Many social choices caused vulnerabilities in American society. Ideological ambitions and groupthink behaviors propelled poor decisions. Boomer's "me first" attitudes allowed for and enabled irresponsible, narrow-focused pursuits. Self-interested orientations amplified the risks. Attaining material wealth outside the moral constructs and principles of democracy became common. Items once considered illegal became unenforced. With too many violations of laws, too few enforcers could not keep up with the criminality. Honesty seemed abandoned. Enough persons neglected social responsibility that perceptions changed. Crimes became not crimes, because a "one is not guilty unless caught" mentality became ubiquitous. Catching criminals becomes near impossible in an overwhelmed jurisprudence. Doomerism thwarted "rule of law" justice oriented officials at all levels.

A bombardment of information confused us. Changes in new knowledge led to new computational and communications technologies. More channels of unfiltered and constructed false information distribution occurred. Once honest fact seeking and telling sources hired unethical persons into positions of authority, trustworthiness became undermined. Soon, no source was clearly a truth-offering outlet. Each spun tall tales to sell. We suffered from information overload. We chose providers who served up stories favorable to our faiths, or handed out and passed around information reaffirming to our beliefs in non-ego offending ways we liked to consume it. Consumer preferences amplified. We separated by instinct to survive the overflow. We began to doubt the stability of our identities. We sought to buy things to establish our public and private identities. We often ignored what our family and community elders told us was wise to follow. We instead listened to the talking heads on the World Wide Web, as if their being electronically broadcast made them superior to the humans whose job it was to advise us. Moth to flame, Icarus to sky and sea, we failed to learn the classic lessons of human wisdom.

Now we suffer from saturated selves. Neither those framed on romanticism nor those framed on modernism help us cope very well (Gergen, 1991). The new era exploits personal vulnerabilities. The way we used to apply past value sets to give us comfort is threatened. This postmodern age requires we recognize our interrelatedness and accept everyone's humanity. In this epoch of advanced complexity, past lenses of how we imagined the world are less valid. The now-weakened metaphors do not serve us well. We must reimagine our purpose and worth as a species. The cultural frame of romanticism, many traditions bases, suffers. The cultural frame of modernism, which was going to save us from our past's myths, also suffers (Gergen, 1991). We need to choose carefully what to salvage from these perspectives. Let's base our choices upon what helps us reclaim the Constitution's truths. Because we are in transition, experiencing a societal transformation, we must return to the root cause of our existence as a country: liberty.

During this stormy third stage of knowledge evolution, we need to understand ourselves better. Especially because of the aspects of its knowledge and the technology it spawns, particularly artificial intelligence, machine learning, and genetic engineering, we need to be very cautious. As we transit this transformative period, we must recognize our personal and societal motivations. Once identified, analyzed, and understood, we can manage the risks and control the revolutionary computational and communications technologies to help and not harm us. These capabilities contain more risks to humanity than knowledge developed during the first two stages of its evolution. We can orient our responding efforts toward serving our unifying goal and objectives. We can IDEALS liberty and drill in democracy mentality that benefits our representative republic. These are the most essential cultural components of American society. Their being forgotten by the boomers helped spread doomerism within our society's FILMS[2] [P7]. Doomerism now resides like a disease within the organs of our body politic. It is devouring and digesting our core tenets, turning them into mushy turds, as it converts our society with its malignant malfeasant culture. We need to be more reflective on what we are doing and not just "go along for the ride and see where it takes us." We cannot be like these roomers!

Figure 5-1 below represents the punctuated equilibrium theory of Jerald Hage, Director of the Center for Innovation in the Department of Sociology, College of Behavioral Sciences at the University of Maryland. It demonstrates that societal transformations come from the consequences of new knowledge creation. Society tends to hold in patterns of equilibrium until a new discovery disrupts it. Periods of creativity punctuate the history of human advances (Hage, 2020). The big consequence is the adaptive problems that arise. We must adapt. Are we wondering how? We should. We try, experiment, succeed, and fail. Our ability to adapt to and assimilate new knowledge can be chaotic. It coincides with crises that arise from poor LAMBS. During times of change, we storm over what the new norms will be as we come to terms with our new knowledge we now know. It is difficult. We too often prefer to sit in denial. Our past precepts are at risk of being no longer valid. We grow scared. We must be brave. During periods of destabilizing change in society, and therefore, in our lives, we must unite around our common principles. Societal transformations affect us in significant ways: psychologically, socially, economically, politically, culturally, and anthropomorphically.

In the USE's eight generations of history, we've experienced equilibrium punctuation. Right now, it is with respondent doomerism puncturing our democracy. Given our continuous knowledge pursuits, change will be a more likely constant than stasis. The status quo will resist this and seek to hold onto the controls. This fact of society and human nature pushes humankind toward autocracy. The best circumstance for the American people is a social arrangement that sustains liberty. It is the key for restoring societal stability during transformations and equilibriums. It is the foundational principle of the goal and objectives of the USE.

Immense material accumulation in fewer persons, averting good citizenship behaviors, threatens society's stability. These persons, who pursue personal power as the purpose of their lives, risk behaving with a psychopathy of elitism. We see this within the polity power, the politicians, who grow greedy and desire to be a class of autocratic plutocrats ruling over the rest of us. Wannabe aristocrats and snobs, desiring to rule, drink in more and more power for the pleasure of it. Such a will to concentrate power is contrary to the will of a culture of democracy, and opposite the intents of its representative form in republic.

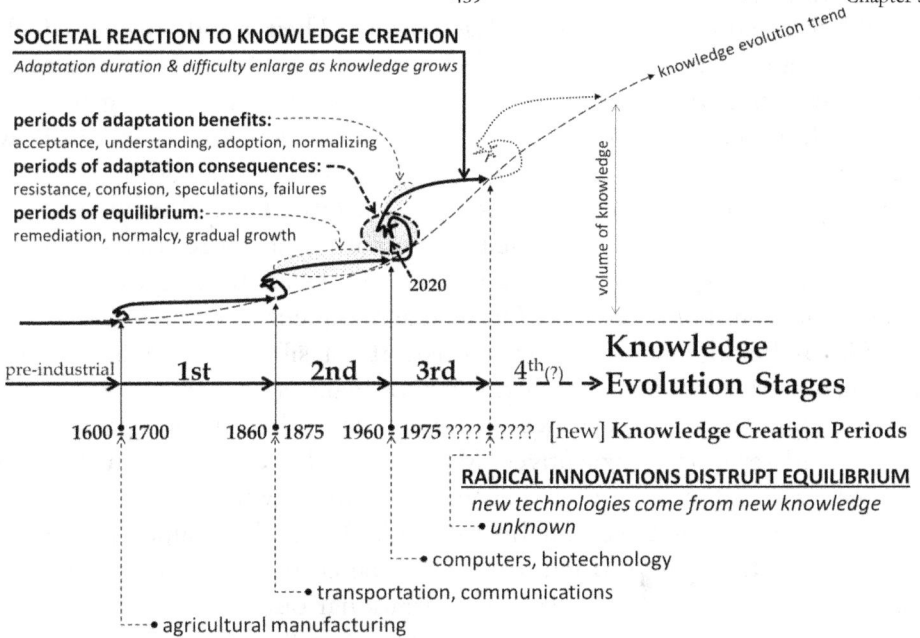

SOCIETAL REACTION TO KNOWLEDGE CREATION
Adaptation duration & difficulty enlarge as knowledge grows

periods of adaptation benefits:
acceptance, understanding, adoption, normalizing
periods of adaptation consequences:
resistance, confusion, speculations, failures
periods of equilibrium:
remediation, normalcy, gradual growth

knowledge evolution trend

volume of knowledge

2020

pre-industrial 1st 2nd 3rd 4th(?) **Knowledge Evolution Stages**

1600⋮1700 1860⋮1875 1960⋮1975 ????⋮???? [new] **Knowledge Creation Periods**

RADICAL INNOVATIONS DISTRUPT EQUILIBRIUM
new technologies come from new knowledge
• unknown
• computers, biotechnology
• transportation, communications
• agricultural manufacturing

Figure 5-1: Punctuated Equilibrium Theory of Societal Transformation and Social Change

According to the punctuated equilibrium theory, societal transformations begin in new knowledge creation periods and continue through evolutionary stages as equilibrium emerges over time. When a new discovery occurs, it shifts the paradigm of understanding. This then releases a flood of new ideas, inventions, and innovations, which cause disruptions in the equilibrium of society. Transformative activities take over the writing of history. Historic events start happening. Awakenings and crises turn us toward different futures than we imagined. As society storms, forms, and norms around the adaptations it makes to the new knowledge and the tools it leads to, we suffer rifts within ourselves and in our social fabric as those in authority make changes in an effort to take advantage of the chaos, or stabilize society using their social power's modes. Because of the comingling seven social powers' interconnected competing, cooperating, or colluding, and by ways, means, and methods, over the precept power process of culture, finding societal equilibrium in epoch-making periods of new knowledge creation takes time.

New political factions begin. The balance in societal and social powers thrusts and retracts as we ride out the turbulent tides of change. Powers shift and adjust. Some make movements opportunistically jockeying for preeminence until a new balance resounds and gets agreed upon. Either, we argue, or acquiesce or lead. We all want to make society stable. We all want social harmony. This process of finding stasis is the norming period. Once achieved, we enter a performing period of achieving adaptation to the disruptive knowledge. Gradually, we all learn and grow from the knowledge of the new paradigm as it moves through our many powers' FILMS[2] [P7]. Over time, society gets a new state of equilibrium and incrementally innovates on what it knows—to perfect itself—until, the next great discovery comes along and causes disruption that sets off the social (meso level) forming, storming, norming, and performing process of social adaptation. With change, loss, or shock, persons (micro level) experience five emotional stages: denial, anger, bargaining, depression, and acceptance as coping mechanisms (Kübler-Ross, 1969). Both the social and personal experiences of the punctuating change ultimately get reflected in societal (macro level) transformations.

With the economy power, the elites push the HM[5] to accumulate for them extreme excesses in their material success. Going beyond luxury, they need to prove greed legitimate by striving to win the "wealthiest in the world" competition within high-class society. Their minds need to feel a sense of superiority. They want to feel justified. High-society culture establishes patterns and practices that prove membership. Purchasing perfectly produced, perennially polished possessions, objects made by exclusive premiere brands and priced accordingly gains one status. Some items are useless except for signaling the absolute absurdity of the inflated monetary value these things convey for their possessors. The more useless the objects, the more expensive, and the better they are at showing their owner's ostentatious omnipotence. The more magniloquent, the more proof they provide of belonging to the elitist class. It's a silly game of luxury one-upmanship. Meanwhile, the majority cannot make ends meet.

Such pursuits for acceptance push persons to demand and pay extreme salaries and rewards to executives. Most get paid way more than the value they generate. Most owe their net worth to those who labored for them, making them rich because they held the title. Even if the super-salaried executives fail, they get paid ginormous severance packages. This alone is a status symbol of their high class. It is irrational but class sustaining. They feel entitled to it. Simply because they arrived in the upper classes of high society, they believe they earned it. Some did. Most rode the market manipulation wave created by doomerism to raise executive salaries in all the FILMS^2 [P7] of society, but most extraordinarily for the HM^5 chiefs and board members. Not all boats rose, only the tide under theirs did. Many elites desire permanent separation from the rest of humanity to avoid the little people, the everyday people, the commoners, the masses, or to some of them, the losers or the trash. This doomerism permeates into all cultures and causes their devastation. People, we must stop worshipping the fortunes and fortunate sons and daughters whose silver platters handed them opportunity. Envy will do us no good. We must encourage a different means of arranging the societal powers, one that supports democracy and IDEALS liberty. Copycatting the fat cats is the wrong culture. It is not the ideal path of principle and good character, which American society needs to sustain itself.

Becoming industrious and entrepreneurial does not convert one into a baby doomer. Nor does it automatically cause credulousness like yesteryear's trust bosses and robber barons. We must guard against the arrogance and conceit success can bring. We can advance and improve our humanity all at the same time. Leisure gives us great advantage to gain wisdom. We can pursue enriching scholarship. We can contribute to our communities through civic engagement in local associations. We can assist their work to better persons' and communities' opportunities and outcomes. Everywhere and all the time we need leadership training for our people on how to lead a life, how to lead a group, how to lead a team, how to lead business, and how to lead a government. We should hope the boomers decide to volunteer as coaches and mentors. In many ways, by all means, we need to train our future generations on leadership. Boomers can help us, but must do so without conveying the vices of doomerism. We hope they acquiesce to the wisdom and principles of our founding and work to undo the mistakes they made.

The risks of emulating wealth chasing expand as egos enlarge with hubris that harms humanity, which big money quickly and easily causes in its creation of callousness toward others. Cultural success can go to one's head faster than we make fortunes from luck as much as skill. However, most inherit them. Something the framers were concerned about and sought to restrict for fear of aristocracy arising in our ranks. Wisdom from our mythology and history powers dictates that humility is a safer passage to a better life, to happiness. With it and virtue we can lead American society achieve its goal and attain its objectives.

The creation of super-persons perceived as superior to the rest of us because of heavy monetary rewards, is an adaptive problem. It misshapes the societal powers' arrangement. It misbalances them to disfavor the majority, the public, everyday people. It is not dissimilar to ancient societal hierarchies, a few at the top, and the many at the bottom, no property, no say in how things are run, no freedom; enslaved to hard labor. Is it right? Is it wrong? What are the results of it? Is it a result of psychopathic persons colluding to take over the powers of society and accumulate them within their control? Is it a vulnerability risk to which we must respond? Societally it can be defeated; the degenerate reformed.

What are the forms of the psychopathy of doomerism? Besides its plutocratic aspects, we see in doomerism a push on the polity by politicians of the mob, pressing for a mobocracy. To a lesser extent, there is a pull for more political promises for increasing services, which some fear cause dependency. These psychopathies, mob rule and willful dependency, cause risks of tax revenues spent on too many social subsidies. The rich and powerful assault experts to gain the favor of the less fortunate and undereducated, turning them against those among us who studied hard to learn how to better the society. Political and economic elites, often vilify the evidence fact pursuing experts because proofs pose threats to their absolutist ambitions of totalitarian power concentration. Power mongers falsify the facts to fit their beliefs. Experts fit their beliefs to the facts, and so should we as a citizenry if we desire the keep democracy culture and the republic within our patriotic control.

Letting politicians control redistribution of tax revenues is risky. It pulls from one part of the country and gives to another. What if the states kept and locally invested more of what their people earned? Yes, the Constitution gives the federal government the power to tax. Taxes pay government to perform its constitutionally assigned responsibilities. We cannot allow government to run the people, that is, to fund the people by caveat of obeisance to policies favoring the power of politicians. This is how the federal government gains power over the states via operating a welfare state, corporate bolstering and pauper living capacity giving. Should poor states demand rich states fund them? We have real questions that need addressed without excessive emotions. We need to be more rational, but doomerism disrupts our reasonableness.

In addition to its mobocratic aspects, we see in doomerism a push upon the polity by activists. Activists seek many policy choices. Some seek to gain legal rights for lifestyle choices. The Constitution does not expressly address matters of biological predispositions and cultural modes of self-expression as legal category preferences. With a focus on persons as the unit of self-governing providers and benefactors, combined with the wisdom of the danger of group-based factions, why would it have? It is psychopathy to ask government not to protect inalienable rights but create new special categorical rights for groups of similar persons and shared social beliefs. Such factions fracture the wisdom of each person as a dignified being of inalienable rights respectable for the content of their character. Forcing the making of specially protected groups by shared characteristics causes a risk of giving unlimited power to government to make teams at the expense of personal choices. Too much power in government as rule maker over every minor detail of society corrupts politicians. In a properly just society, such banding together is unnecessary since each person gets equal treatment.

We need politicians to protect liberty for all and not wade into group differentiation in ways that cause tribes among us. We must protect the rights of each and every person but not wholesale groups of people based on characteristics or traits. Mostly, we need not to want government to do this by behaving with dignity in accord with the ideals of liberty. If people want to band together in community groups and settle together as a tribe, let this be a matter for the states to manage. This is a matter of community and family living appropriate for state (meso level) management. Yet we the people must recognize with tolerance and tact each other's rights under the Constitution. Therefore, we should neither mistreat nor tolerate mistreatment of persons or of peoples. We must improve, mature as citizens, and stop the discrimination among us. We, the everyday people, can get along. We've done so on the brutal battlefields, scary skies, and turbulent seas during wars. We must get past hatreds inflamed by aggressive jerks.

Historical wrongs need forgiven. We need to be truthful and trustworthy. Let's pursue better tolerability because we have larger problems to solve. We must deal with threats in our species preventing harmonious coexistence and to our species from geography power. We would have no need for activists had we obeyed the Constitution as amended to the letter and in spirit. Doomerism moves us further from the right path, the one that does not disgrace our calling to be American. Annuit coeptis, Novus ordo seclorum, Providence favors our undertaking of a new order for the ages. We are to move toward higher qualities of humanity's healthy merciful being as a citizenry e pluribus unum in God's trust.

Thus as citizens, we should not tolerate violations of humans' rights. Founded on inalienable natural rights our country was. Regrettably, our forebears unforgettably failed to live up to them fully. They cowardly allowed their era's European attitudes of superiority to overtake their written ideals as they chased economic gains needed to build a nation and defend it. Thomas Paine had it correctly. Abraham Lincoln tried to rectify it. We should take our social cues from the written words. Let us bask in the glory of the principles infused in the Declaration of Independence and the Constitution, and its amendments. Please, let us revisit them in pursuit of the just civilization they frame for us. Let us recommit to realizing it.

More so, we find doomerism's influence in the formal and informal economy power's markets. The HM^5, through their $FILMS^2$ [P7], $AEIOUY^2K$ power to great effect. They do this with its subordinate industry and artistry powers too. In the informal economy, doomerism makes an entire subcultural empire of illicit trade. From drug to sex and labor trafficking (slavery), the ugly horrors of humanity happen in the shadows of dark money. Turning a blind eye and using others to feel powerful are natural instincts of a baby doomer. Unethical behavior that pleases "me first" desires becomes tolerable in a baby doomer-run world.

The more psychopaths we enable in society, particularly in the polity, the more they make conditions ripe for sociopathy. Baby doomers in the polity, trapped in ancient Homo sapiens precepts of physical masculine dominance, become a risk. The macho manly manhood physical power ambition is ill suited for a future of persistent knowledge evolution. Lifelong learning to keep up with knowledge becomes a prerequisite to survive, live comfortably, and thrive. This is feasible in a democracy culture sponsored republic, which needs to teach of its benefits because it is so rare a state of polity. Instinctive notions of "might makes right," narcissistic quests for superiority, the socialization of boys to be warriors, and accentuated differentiation of male versus female, of dominance and submissive relations, are less beneficial. Such a primitive mentality is risky for a hyperfast future already upon us. Going backward in time is not going to bring us salvation. Nor is going forward to try to outrun it, yet move forward we must. We may not have a plan, but planning is everything. We need to imagine the possible forward paths and game test them. This requires unity to work together to deal with the difficult and not ignore it because it is inconvenient to our selfish pursuits. Unity for a revolution in 1774 was unfathomable, yet it happened. We must learn again how to do it like it was eight generations ago. We should examine the humanities of civilizations, and apply the ways, means, and methods of political discourse at our founding, to find lessons in love's efficacy and apply them to the LAMBS.

The polarization of good versus evil, without comprehension of subtle nuances, is risky for a society dependent upon education to sustain itself. The pressures and conditions of moneyed politicians and elitists seeking to rig society to serve them first is a risk we face. A society that puts people in desperate situations and then blames them for these circumstances is wrong. Trapping people in desperation makes them victims of high stress. A society that provides no ability for persons to transcend arbitrary and intentionally structured boundaries and progress past social and economic limitations is immoral. That such constraints press upon certain communities is wrongful. A society that gives certain persons power over others and then allows them to amass near-absolute entitlement to that power, as if their purpose in life was to be powerful, is fraudulent. This enabling of a group in power is destructive to a civilization of democracy (Schmookler, 1988). Further, the idealistic use of demagoguery by those in, or seeking, political and economic power damages our society. Demagoguery traps power holders and seekers into the immature "us vs. them" fallacious, conceit filled, counterfeit rhetorical techniques of manipulation (Roberts-Miller, 2017).

A few more points on the causes and consequences of doomerism, and we will then move on to the generational causes. The Constitution requires Congress, our legislative power, to declare wars. But the baby boomers there don't declare them. Unrestrained by rules, they waste our money on wars whenever they want. Perhaps this is a game to generate military-industrial complex campaign donations (President Eisenhower was so right). The legislative branch lets the executive power enter into military incursions, undeclared wars, too frequently. It then pays for them by supplemental budgeting. This cedes too much power from the legislature to the executive, which jeopardizes the framework that limits government to the protection of people from a tyrant.

Tyrants who DAMN power in both the polity and economy powers doom us to dependency. Within the economy power, these tyrants use powerful means to force us to be subservient. They use strategic lawsuits against public participation in complaints against indecency and probable community damages from their powerful private interests' actions. Such suits slapped against those who cannot financially afford to oppose the proposed degradations are autocratic. The rich slap these on the poor to censure or intimidate them into complicit silence and nonaction. Good citizens respect civility; we dignify it. We do not undermine it. We know the harm frivolous lawsuits do to society, not just in undermining trustworthiness but also in the real costs of litigation. A civil society does not rely on the courts. Its citizens work out their differences honestly, without manipulation but with an honorable eye for achieving a fair and reasonable settlement over their differences. Baby doomers sue the crap out of one another, and we the citizens underwrite their game playing because we pay for the courts with our tax dollars.

The more psychopaths we enable in the economy power of society, the more they make conditions ripe for sociopathy. Many psychopaths in the economy misguide people. They use false advertisements. Their love of money silences judgment. They produce dangerous products, pollute, and do not reuse and recycle but dispose and disguise the truth. They culturally drive a "so what, toss it aside, throw it out" expendable mentality. They plan obsolescence! Repairing, reusing, and maintaining equipment is a no-no to them. Their chemical toxins leach into our drinking water, but they spend money not to stop it but to lobby for legislation to make it permissible. Is this good citizenship? To doomers, our lives do not matter, only profits matter. The baby doomer cult of personality lauds figures who head up the culture of doomerism. Toxic pollution dooms babies to pain, suffering, death, and never-before-seen genetic abnormalities. Baby doomers in the economy bring destruction in many ways. In addition to environmental degradation affecting ecosystems, we see dangerous jobs. Errors lead to damage. Accidents are a risk. Rushing, overworking, and stressing workers can be too common in baby doomer demands. The spatial and temporal inequality of workplace conditions left unregulated with workers unprotected produces problems. Complaining about treating fellow citizens, human beings, fairly, as if their lives mattered, is a nauseating aspect of doomerism. It goes back to a warped desire to be powerful, superior, above the law. Such a seed of monarchy is not for the soil of a culture based upon democracy, nor welcomed in the garden of our representative republic.

Worse, many egregious baby doomers use economy power willfully to commit unlawful thievery. As evidenced by Ponzi schemes and transactional selling, nothing stops them from hunting for dollars. They engage in fraudulent activities such as social engineering to phish and steal identities to get our money. Baby doomers see nothing wrong with enjoying vanity and hubris, nor in envy, lust, gluttony, sloth, or wrath. These are their pleasures. Previous generations saw these as problems. These enslaved people. These did not free them. Living in sin was bad for everyone. Wisdom taught us to avoid such vices, because these behaviors erode our moral character, which we need for society and ourselves to be healthy. Society knew of these dangers and forbade them. Doomerism tolerates previously intolerable behaviors. Lying, cheating, and stealing are the baby doomers' favorite actions. Once mitigated, thievery now free, alienates our confidence in justice. The subcultural values given by mythology power's folkways, customs, mores, and beliefs kept the wrongdoers to a minority. Few wanted perceived as wrongdoers. Boomers changed the attitude to "It's not wrong unless you got caught." This is moronic and immoral, but doomerism makes wrongdoing acceptable to the majority. In some social circles, celebrates it.

Is it possible that one generation could be so much worse than previous ones in its noncommitment to social norms? Are the chaotic adaptations to new knowledge and technologies, unleashed misbehavior, reversible? Is grifting? Is lying? Is the generation that gave birth to the most baby doomers a generation of more similar than different personality traits? Comedian George Carlin thought that boomers have a selfish self-centered personality (Carlin, 2010). It made us laugh because it was true, but it's not funny anymore. Historians Strauss and Howe identified patterns in generational experiences they summarized as a personality. They explain how generations' personalities affect American society. They write extensively about generational types, which they see as happening repeatedly. They point to child rearing techniques and major societal events as reasons that lead to attitudes and behaviors in adulthood that affect society (Strauss & Howe, 1991). Let's look at these as a cause of doomerism.

Generational Types

In their book *Generations*, Strauss and Howe identified four generational types, which repeat over time. Each historic age witnesses movements in society. Some coincide with a generation cohort's entrance into adulthood. These era defining events shape expectations for adults, who subsequently shape the historic period of their lives. Two broad experiences occur: awakening and crisis. These cause turnings in history, which leave records of human affairs and events. These records, when read, give the appearance of history repeating itself. This is because we recognize the precepts and patterns of societal attitudes and behaviors. We, being human, have shared experiences during our lives. Thus, just as each human experiences his or her life's developmental and declinational phases thanks to biology power, so does society have cycles, thanks to it being made by us creative, yet fallible and hypocritical, humans. Our FILMS^2 [P7] are made up by us.

The experiences that define an historical age have a defining influence on the coming-of-age adults. Through these the parents' and the children's experiences, attitudes form and behaviors happen that respond to the present and anticipated future social circumstances and physical conditions. These yield the meaning, purpose, and possibilities of the era, the age, the epoch. Call it what you will, but know that both the preceding and succeeding generations contribute to the making of the experiences of the generation between them. By the experiences of living at a certain time in history, generations develop unique personalities. Conceptually, generational types take turns, experiencing periods of history in the making. Thus, history appears to rhyme with itself over time. Humans love to find patterns. It's a built-in survival skill ability. Because our experiential knowledge and our general and specialized knowledge differ, history cannot repeat itself. Societies adapt to eras in near evolutionary modes that are limited by humanity's imperfectability. Our KA^{4}SA^2 increase with each generation. Our wisdom as a society declines under the influence of doomerism. Like a bad drug, we are having a bad trip, but we cannot sense it, because we are still in its grip.

We need reacquaint with the pursuit of virtue and wisdom. Too much information is flooding out our common sense. We cannot allow our basic comprehension, our heuristic thinking, to drown. It needs the flotation wisdom gives it, so it can give us sensible intelligence.

Relatedly, sociologist Hage's punctuated equilibrium theory of societal transformation sees history as having periods of equilibrium punctuated by change induced by new knowledge. It sees knowledge discovery, an awakening of sorts, feeding into circumstances that can cause crises arising from new knowledge creation and evolution. A related theory of scientific revolution sees paradigms shift with the advent of new theories of how things work (Kuhn, 1962).

RHYMING CYCLES OF HISTORY

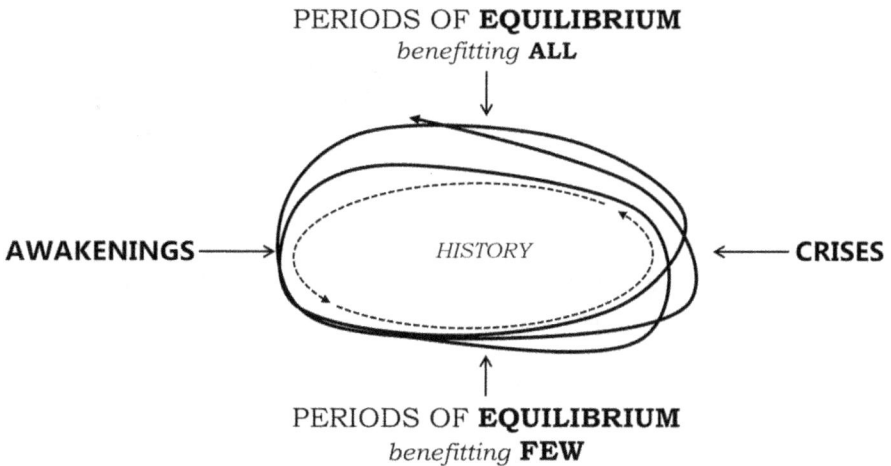

Figure 5-2: Rhyming Cycles of History: Looking Backward
Looking backward history appears as if it repeats itself. It looks this way because life happens in cycles: life cycles, generational cycles, and societal cycles. After a turning in history from an awakening, periods of equilibrium can occur, but these tend to benefit only a few. After turnings in history from crises, periods of equilibrium can occur, and these tend to benefit many, sometimes all of the society, which had to unify to survive the crises and revitalize and restore normalcy. The cycle appears to repeat itself, similarly though not exactly, because we learn, grow, pass down lessons, and pass on. The species continues onward with distant memories of what once was, hopefully trying to avoid the traumas of the past.

Philosophers, too, have proposed changes in society that reflect underlying patterns. The dialectic of Hegel saw a thesis meeting an antithesis and resulting in a synthesis. Marx borrowed this concept to invent a theory of social change through history caused by economic and social class conflicts. These two thinkers' theories involved opposites interacting. Eastern religions and philosophies of the Orient embedded the idea of interacting opposites, like the Tao as yin-yang. As noted in the discussion of the lobster in Chapter 3, we humans tend to be binary. These explanations of history and social change see trigger events for changes, cycles, and phases. This is sensible since society is human. Humans tend to seek similar things yet often view the world in binaries. Societies have ambitions, constraints, opportunities, limitations, endowments, and spoliations because of us, our human nature. We have these ourselves. What we need to learn is that between the poles of our dichotomies is the relationship between the two. Three forces are at play, "you", "me", and "we". The "we" is a focus of democracy culture. Its arrangement assures the "me" is free by knowing equality before the law. The compromise for both "you" and "me" orientations allows both to be able to enjoy liberty. This is why diplomacy and prosocial behaviors are inseparable for a citizenry of an intending "American" society.

We all repeat similar lifecycle experiences within each generation. Variations occur since our knowledge and power balances change as we adapt to social circumstances and physical conditions. Theories and philosophies recognize underlying human activity as causing societal changes. We are all, at all times everywhere, a species surviving, living, and seeking luxury. Our pursuits alter our experiences. Our experiences make history, and it makes us who we are. This repetitive pattern makes history appear to rhyme with itself. Figures 5-2 and 5-3 show this spirality from different angles. One looks downwardly on history. The other from a side view shows history with time rising upwardly. In their 512-page book, historians Strauss and Howe described at length four generational types developed through rigorous scholarship (Strauss & Howe, 1991). To them these types occur in a fixed alternating recurring order, a pattern of four turnings: a dominant one followed by a recessive one, followed by a dominant one, followed by a recessive, and so on. These generic generational types are the idealist, reactive, civic, and adaptive. Let's learn their characteristics.

Idealists

Dominant Idealists get raised after periods of secular crises. They come of age in a period of spiritual awakening. They fragment into narcissistic rising adults and then cultivate moralistic principles in midlife. They become visionary elders as the next secular crisis arises. Baby boomers are an idealistic generation. Their personality enabled the causes of crises and poor LAMBS we see today. Living longer and holding on longest, the forty years of their holding positions of authority are keeping a period of equilibrium out of reach. They've not transitioned into visionary elders, yet. They may never, becoming an enigmatic anomaly among American society's idealists. Because doomerism overtook their generation's majority it CATAPULTED annihilation of the founders' intended Americanism.

With them at the helms of the societal powers' FILMS[2] [P7], we suffer missed opportunities to reduce suffering during our societal transformation and we're experiencing their incompetent LAMBS. They've not been taking care of society by preparing the children for tomorrow. Rearing children to be adults to steward the USE is common sense intelligence. Yet, boomer idealists chose to serve their selfishness first. Hopefully before too long, as we force them to retire from the powers, they will have a change of heart and at long last commit to being citizens first, (as their tiny minority of bloomers and broomers tried to do), and volunteer to fix what they've broken by their "me first" mannerisms and argumentative idealism. As a generation, stuck in immature adolescent-like mindsets, they demonstrated they couldn't guide us out of our current crises. Their dependence on outdated romantic modernistic and traditionalistic (romantic) ideologies blinds them. They do not see possible solutions because they refuse to imagine alternative outcomes to the ones they believe in. They'd rather perpetuate inappropriate, point-scoring arguments. Debates over tired isms do not advance us toward our goal via our objectives. They do not help us adapt to the societal transformations brought about by the third stage of knowledge evolution, either.

Further, the cultural angst between North and South remains an undercurrent of disaffection in the US. The boomers did not work on repairing it. They began by protesting an overseas war, not the historical injustices within that needed continued work. When a few of their bloomers did, their numbers were too small, and as they aged out of college, their commitments nearly ceased. What we needed domestically were heightened efforts to get the regional subcultures to accept the Constitutional amendments and subsequent human rights laws as the will of the American people. We cannot go backwards with the future we now face. We need move ahead and get past the past, fast, or we will tear asunder the wonder of the USE.

Ignoring regional subcultural differences pits state against state in competition for federal dollars. Through federal redistribution, revenue-generating states fund survival support systems and food purchasing programs in poorer states. This sharing is caring. Yet when tax resources are unevenly collected and the largesse of federal programs expensive, states can be at odds with one another. It is conceivable that states might decide to no longer work together to keep the union. The poorer states who depend on the wealthier states, assail the federal government. Those states that pay more federal taxes and get fewer benefits do not see the government as an enemy. Irony prevails in the paradox of hypocrisy. Falsehoods perpetuated by career politicians pacify the poor populace with tall tales. Doomer politicians tell their dishonorable misrepresentations like a liquidation sale. Reelected they continue selling their snake oil isms as believable. Worse than ever, some use threats and monger fear. The people in the poor states remain ignorant of the money moving. They buy into the blame game or give up, unwittingly moving themselves into the houses of complacency and apathy (recall Figure 2-6).

Democracy demands a common purpose of unity. Today, the USE internally fights against uniting because doomers dramatically declared an idiotically unpragmatic war over ideas. The boomer generation enslaves us to its asinine perpetual argument. We experience doomerism's furtherance as it replaces our culture of democracy. Its gloom is destroying our social opportunity structures. It is misbalancing our societal powers. It is undermining our constitutional rule of law. Yes, the cause of our current crises is the result of "me first" baby doomerism and its oppositional dogmas. The baby boomers ideologue battles involve:

- Absolutism: It made making compromising on necessary resolutions difficult. *(This is like a tyrant King George refusing to allow the colonies to move forward with self-rule. Boomers are a tyrannical generation. Future blight will be their legacy, unless, they accept the call of volunteerism to:*

  a) Make repairs to our hull through teaching ACE

  b) Civically engage in community-based associations to build back civil society and its social capital

  c) Encourage cross affiliations of differing neighborhoods citizens to build social grammars

  d) Staff polling places for elections

  e) Campaign for younger politicians

  f) Commit to returning excess sequestered capital to investments that improve children's lives and prosperity potential

  g) Apologize and reform their loomers, groomers, zoomers, roomers, and doomers to live citizen-first lives finally and fully, supporting their bloomers and broomers help future generations' prospects in the USE by E-SASSY-T-TUF-FT-CAUCUS).

- Incompetent lawmaking: This occurs due to partisan politics. The undermining of the Constitution and the failure to pursue a more perfect union for the people is a shameful disgrace in the eyes of the framers. (This is like how King George injured the colonies with taxation and militant police controls, which led to the Declaration of Independence).

- Consumerism: It became considered as the panacea for life. The propaganda by the economy elites impressed upon the society a lifestyle that served only their interests. Converting the citizenry away from their responsibilities to remove their rights is a deep wrong. Utilizing consumerism to possess a greater influence over people than self-government is dangerous. It devalues both civil society and government, which in the USE used to work in partnership to make a more prosperous, opportunity creating society. Such collaborating had us on a path to becoming a more perfect union of states converging into a united people, an e pluribus unum nation.

- Resurgence of monopolies: The push for personal gains opened up rampant insider training to obtain profitable stock ownership portfolios. Wrongfully, the polity's legislative branch played at this game, in violation of ethical codes of conduct. Conglomeration for Wall Street ruins family businesses on Main Street. Entrepreneurial commercial pursuits are hugely American. We believe in the power of ideas and businesses as an engine for improvement. The monopolies' dominance over our commercial mindsets and over materials and labor markets negatively affect the quality of life for local merchants. Monopolization hurts us in our localities. The alterations to society caused by a few extremely rich economy power-controlling elites lead to the erosion of protections for the people. It diminishes our liberty by minimizing opportunities to improve ourselves. It restricts our ability to meritoriously advance through our own efforts to reach our fullest potential. It blocks us from contributing the most we can to raising good families, strengthening our communities and enhancing our society. If work exhausts us, how will we be able to do the more important work of raising Americans? We need time and energy to teach and learn how to be in control, how to be the leadership of society.

Ironically, the boomers' youthful anti-establishmentarianism launched a counterculture. Their naïve idealism drove free-spirited attacks on social-stabilizing FILMS$^{2\,[P7]}$, which injured the whole. Now they show how hypocritical they are by seeking to control society for themselves. They delay the future of the young. To protect themselves, they are unwilling to let go of the reins of authority. Perhaps they simply cannot govern what they do not understand, a democracy. They attacked its FILMS$^{2\,[P7]}$, then when they rose into positions of authority, hollowed them out from the inside with bogus super salaries and foolish investing. They enrich themselves by unwise monetary policies, borrowing from future generations. They have buried the future under a mountain of debt. Their LAMBS is contrary to the goal and objectives of the Preamble.

Reactives
The recessive Reactives get raised in a time of spiritual awakening and are unprotected and criticized as youths. Its cohorts mature into risk-taking, alienated adults, who mellow out into pragmatic midlife leaders during secular crises. They age into reclusive though respected elders, without much influence. They get "called to work" on behalf of the society. Gen X is this type. They mop up the previous generations mess. But because of boomers size and duration in position with authority, this practically minded generation never got the chance to lead the FILMS$^{2\,[P7]}$ or be the top HM^5 to set the tone for society.

Civics
The dominant Civics generations get raised after periods of spiritual awakening, and are protected as youths as they grown up. They come of

age in a time of overcoming crisis and unite into a heroic and achieving cadre as they rise into adulthood. They work together to build strong institutions as powerful midlife adults who become busy elders. Sadly, they get attacked by the younger generations entering into spiritual awakening eras. They get "called to work" on behalf of the society. The Gen Y millennials are this type. The Gen Z might also be this type due to the warped generational timing and non-transfer of power, since the boomers are clinging on to it, still thinking they are going to "save the world". In their delusion, they destroy our society's foundations and factuality with their fantasies and fallacies.

Adaptives

The recessive Adaptives get raised in a time of secular crises. As youths, overly protected and socially suffocated by their parents. They mature into risk-averse, conformist adults who are indecisive in midlife. They become arbitrator-leaders during a spiritual awakening. They maintain influence as sensitive elders, though not well respected.

Of concern, the boomers have sought to encourage all future generations to be compliant with their worldviews and value sets. In their manipulation of social powers such as the academy power, they make dependency a conformist ambition for their puppeteering hands. They want their ideas, and by extension actually themselves, to be worshipped, even if it means devaluing the founding ideals.

Where We Are Today

The dominant generations experience crises or awakenings as they rise into adulthood ages, from ages 22 to 43. In midlife, from 44 to 65, they dominate society's public attention and interests. This is where we are today. Monopolistic baby boomers have pushed our society straight into crises that they did not avoid, and are thus ill suited to lead us out of safely and securely. So America, we need an intervention! We must work to replace them from all the top positions in the LAMBS and from every authority post in the societal and social powers' FILMS[2] [P7] and as the HM[5]. We must begin with the primary societal powers and move to the secondary and tertiary social powers. Let's encourage boomers to be future generation oriented, social repair volunteers. To prevent more catastrophe and travesty to the Constitution, our democracy, our republic, and our enterprise, we must begin to act rapidly and successively.

We need to fix our ship. We need to free it out of the noisome stagnant waters in which it drifts, surrounded by noisily circling hungry tyrant sharks. We need to get to the work of the difficult rowing before its hull hits and cracks on doomeristic rocks and sinks; forgotten. We must pull the oars synchronously to move it into the good winds of justice to sail toward our goal and objectives. The old ideologies and isms of the boomers are unfit for the future. Moreover, their oppositional ways carry huge risks in oppor-

tunity costs. We must address our most challenging social circumstances
and physical conditions post haste. We mustn't hide in denial behind tired,
irrelevant for tomorrow's coming age, isms.

Doomerism culture for American society is a massive risky-to-liberty
paradigm shift. The boomers are too stuck in their fractured, inflexible,
failed formulas. They lack the wisdom-informed, common sense based, intellectual agility to adjust. We need adaptive skills now. We need to look
forward while remembering the Constitution. We need to make society
ready for increasing uncertainty. We need to apply the SERF to the USE
with an eye on our purpose, to IDEALS liberty. The future of every American baby depends on it.

It is as if the boomers are arguing tribes of ostriches. They fight over
different kinds of sand into which to bury their heads. Perhaps they are trying to hide from the work of democracy while expecting an egalitarian opportunity structure, yet allowing doomer thievery. Clearly confused they act
tribally without hope of unity. Because we have entered into a new era, we
need to try new ideas and hear new perspectives from younger creative
generations. Let's coach the younger generations on liberty and let them
seek to solve the social problems we face. After all, we must help children
rise into adulthood, and get them ready to assume the responsibility for the
leadership of society, if we are to have a truly American society.

History reveals eras. We cannot wait on 20/20 hindsight to show that
we failed to intervene to save the Constitution, and our democracy, republic, and liberty. We must correct society's boomer-misguided directions. We
need to commit forthrightly to advance our project. We know that boomers
cannot rebalance the societal powers into an egalitarian equilibrium. Their
culture will not allow them. We must remove them from positions of authority to release the controls of our societal and social powers to be available for future generations' use in restoring our democracy culture's foundations, and rebuilding society with its originating ideals. We must push with
persistence so our personal, professional, private, public, business, and
community pursuits move us toward a more perfect union, our fixed goal,
our common purpose, by way of its objectives. We must revel in recreating
the revolutionary spirit of 1776, as the framers did in the awakening of the
miracle of modern democracy, in the turning of history that began with our
first civic generation, eight generations ago in the era that began with the
shot heard round the world.

Eras

According to historians, Strauss and Howe, responses to circumstances
confronted by a generation's cohorts emerge as eras that recur in cycles.
They identify four, an Awakening Era, followed by an Inner-Driven Era,
succeeded by a Crisis Era, which then resolves into an Outer-Driven Era.
The Idealists come of age during an Awakening Era. The Reactives come

of age during an Inner-Driven Era. The Civics come of age during a Crisis Era. The Adaptives come of age during an Outer-Driven Era. Briefly summarized:

An Awakening Era...triggers cultural creativity and the emergence of new ideals, as institutions built around old values are challenged by the emergence of a spiritual awakening. In an Inner-Driven Era...individualism flourishes, new ideals are cultivated in separate camps, confidence in institutions declines, and secular problems are deferred. A Crises Era...opens with growing collective unity in the face of perceived social peril and culminates in a secular crisis in which danger is overcome and one set of new ideals triumphs. In an Outer-Driven Era, society turns toward conformity and stability, triumphant ideals are secularized, and spiritual discontent is deferred. (Strauss & Howe, 1991)

The Awakening and Crises eras are the dominant ones that swirl like dancers in rhyming patterns. Crises appear historically triggered from without, while spiritual awakenings resonate as coming from within society. The crises of today are a combination of external and internal challenges, but mostly inside jobs of immorality.

As reported risks of the SERF, the internal vulnerabilities are endogenous to the baby boomers, the idealist Awakening Era generation. Focusing on their own navels, the boomers forgot about our societal goal and objectives stated succinctly in our Constitution's Preamble. Instead, boomers pursued hedonistic aggrandizement and enrichment. They did not manage the external threats to the USE, which include multinational corporations' commercial monopolization, globalization of mercantile marketplaces, new international competitions for control of the world by nation-states, and resistant subcultures of radicalized religious and political beliefs. Each of these got labeled with isms, often overstated in their danger, but were used by baby doomers to gain more power and money than any other generation.

Below, Figure 5-3's diagram swirls upwardly from the past to the future, highlighting the two dominant eras. Times of awakening occur on the left and times of crises on the right. Power shifts to accommodate new ideals of an awakening, and the imbalance of powers appears during times of crises. The society turns from one ascendant era to the next as generations grow up, govern, and grow old.

Each era contains a constellation of five generations of living adults (see Figure 5-4). There are effects from the overlaps among concurrent living generations. Stages of life determine which generation is in control of the LAMBS. One generation tends to dominate, by the number of its officials in positions of authority within the FILMS[2] [P7] and the HM[5]occupations. Historically, traditional values emphasizing dignity, respect, and love for our elders mitigate change. Traditions kept the pace of social change within an era tolerable. The boomers rejected this approach when young. Now they feel entitled to it. In fact, they demand it, expecting respect, pleading that we listen to them. Persons must earn respect. A generation must earn respect. A people must earn respect. The boomers are not earning it, because of the chaotic crises and unfree indebted decivilizing outcomes. Nevertheless, all they seem to do is talk about how great they are, or so they think. We have not the time to put up with their petty, immature insecurities. Could these be hints of hidden guilt rising up from inside their buried consciences? They came of age as the third stage of knowledge evolution began to produce the technologies that challenge our chances at harmony. Liberty leads to living in harmony because it is the lifeblood of democracy, which inspires human dignity, respect, and love for each other for having the courage to share it regardless of any differences.

Eighty-Year Cycles of Equilibrium Turn at Inflection Points that Define a Beginning of the Next Era

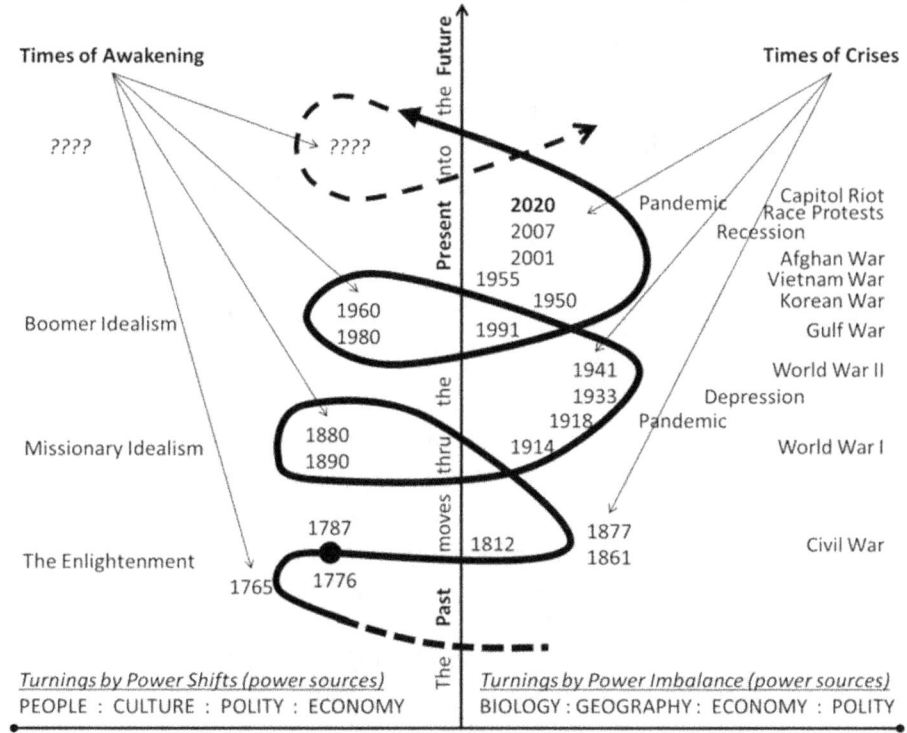

Figure 5-3: Dominant Era Cycles of Society

Each rising youth has an inborn bipolarity: to please parents and to reject parents. Adolescence is a struggle. Not wanting to be like mom and dad, nor generally appreciating the adult world, rising youth must come into their own identities. When kids, we view adults, parents, as the makers of the society that shapes the world we inhabit. When adults, we raise our young children in hopes of their becoming better adults than we think we were. Even though as parents, we too inherited culture in our youth without knowing its precept power processes. Naturally, youths rising into adulthood want to do things differently than their parents and for good reasons. This ambition spins ideas that open up options. Some are beneficial, others detrimental to establishing and sustaining a fully American society. This desire to change disliked aspects through culture is inherent in our survival instincts given us as a species, organically.

This being biology power, a part of human nature, we must recognize its truth. Yet, if our society is not clearly educating its future generations on the blessings of liberty through solid ACE, we run risks. Youths wanting to do something radically different exist in fantasy, and do so with innocence and naivety. Insufficient grounding in a clear understanding of liberty and our Constitution exposes vulnerability. American society's foundation is an ordained and established culture of democracy. As a rare human social creation, it remains at risk with each passing generation. It needs taught. It is not innate.

Further, new social realities caused by the nature of an awakening era or a crisis era, and our age at which we experienced either, affect us as persons and as a community. During crisis, the knowledge and technology used by the dominant generation trying to manage and govern society impacts children's futures. Fractures within the society can lead to factions that do not align with our first principles. These confrontations cause further hazards. Such as:

- Fallacies trump facts
- The rule *of* law is at risk of replacement by rule *by* law, which the rule *of* men brutally enforce
- Ignorance becomes the norm

The problem with ignorance is that it is ignorant, and ignorant of its own ignorance. It is the donkey power to resist logic. Refusing to learn and willing to fight to the death for something fungible but thought permanent. Otherwise unconvinced, it prefers what it knows and wants to know, nothing more. This produces risks to the sustainment of American society as an ideals-based, ideally preferred, ideal societal arrangement to AEIOUY^{2}K human powers for the common good. Finding the common good for society requires a citizenry willing to display open mindedness, self-improvement orientations, reasonableness, pragmatic thinking, and possess desire for fair debates of rational dialogues.

Experiences during crises and resolutions shape new social realities. New knowledge and technology influences future outcomes. Strategic policies made or changed by the generation that was the dominant "in power" generation sustain the changes. The extent to which recessive generations tolerated, accepted, rejected, or sought to amend the preceding generation's edicts determines societal continuity. The risks to liberty are highest when the decisions by the dominant generation do not create policies that IDE-

ALS liberty. Liberty needs to be at center. It requires truth in examining our past, present, and future. Sustaining American society requires an honest understanding of our history. We must reflect upon the fortunes, failures, and fantasies that brought us to today. Let's look further into the dominant idealist generation, the boomers. Let's learn more about how they came to be as they are. What went into their peculiar personality that in its motto seems oppositional to the American motto, e pluribus unum? As it is, "me first" is contrary to "we the people".

Historical Endowments & Social Capital

The baby boomer generation received the good fortune of being born in the US after World War II. They benefitted from an endowment of tremendous economic growth and prosperity. They grew up in booming times. The war victory, without massive economic and infrastructure destruction, enabled manufacturing and sales wealth. The US benefited by helping rebuild devastated nations. This fortune from the endowments of previous generations enlarged through Cold War investments. The US built the Eisenhower Interstates and produced many graduates with advanced educational degrees to win the Cold War. With very high corporate tax rates, war debt erased and revenue generated funds to pay for the race in weapons technology and engineering development to outpace the enemy. American society got its high technology professional caliber skilled labor workforce through government investments like the GI Bill supported by corporations who in turn gained from it. It funded science research with federal grants. It established the National Laboratories. In addition, the social organizing of public–private partnerships created great innovative teams in the race to put a man on the moon. We invested heavily after the Second World War to win the Cold War. Having won it, what did we do? Did we forget to recognize the endowments passed down? Did we forget to rid ourselves of the spoliations of our past? Did we squander the opportunities to improve everyone in our society equally? Did we fall into the laps of luxury and rest on our laurels, thinking we were kings and queens? If we did, we fell for doomerism. The baby boomers got badly infected by it, and through counterculture experimentation, brought it out of themselves by egregious selfishness and put it into the rest of us by not preventing its spread. As it was giving them short-term gains, they allowed its growth. The doomers fueled its sprawl. This set a bad tone. The loomers helped them along, while the zoomers tried to prove something for themselves, to themselves, and by themselves as the roomers minded their own business, and only their own business, going along to get along to keep what that gathered. All along, the watchtower over liberty was left vacant, but for a few out matched bloomers, and overwhelmed broomers.

What Is Doomerism Made Of?

Doomerism is made of a misguided worldview. It makes us not care about other persons as members of the human family. It puts one's self at the center of the society, and disallows others to be there with it. It makes us fight to have it all to ourselves. Doomerism is as mistaken as thinking the Earth is the center of the cosmos. Copernicus dispelled that misunderstanding in the 16th Century. Now in the 21st Century the founding ideal of natural inalienable rights of a person is under assault by ancient ignorance. Doomerism devolves us into an angry age of entitlement. Its archaic approach convinces many among us that the society revolves around them. Thus, its purpose is "me first!" It does not think wisely. It is not intelligent. It contradicts what natural rights means. We need ACE to reacquaint us with a more thorough comprehension. We should not be in this situation. Nevertheless, here we are, unaware of a slowly spreading tumorous culture that is detrimental to our liberty.

Doomerism is made of micro-level alterations in personal perceptions, attitudes, and behaviors. It pervades meso-level organizations. Its promiscuous, indiscriminate, libertine practices over time effect macro-level changes in society. Its altered permissiveness of formerly unacceptable attitudes and behaviors changed the social norms. Traditional folkways and mores gave way or became entrenched, determined to prove their righteousness regardless of facts. The dominant value set established by those who hold positions of authority opens up carte blanche for everyone to do as they do. If they do wrong, so do the masses. When everyone else is doing it, all point to that as justification for them doing it. The spiral downward of moral and ethical standards accelerates giving license to the perceived-as-powerful persons. This goes to their head. They feel the role of the position, as described, is not the way they have to behave. They personalize it to their whims. Doomerism is made of persons who hold positions that have authority, status, or prestige, yet who refuse to behave as other persons in previous generations did, which was to respect and honor their posts. Previous generations generally did not want to bring shame to themselves or the institutions or organization, the societal instruments, which granted high rank to them. The boomers could care less. It is all about them in their ego's assessment. They feel entitled to corrupt and be corrupted without shame or punitive consequences.

These doomerism-infested persons influence the naive who do not think for themselves, which is not as the framers would have wanted it. These authority figures-made-celebrities, a false monarchy, want worshiped, and bring oligarchical value sets to their roles. Unethical, indecent, and selfish, they brand their personal ways, means, and methods into the FILMS[2]

[P7] and onto the HM^5. These then acquire their personality. Errors and omissions go unseen, uncorrected, and erode unity in our project. Terribleness at creating a cohesive society demonstrates itself in their poor performance in micro-, meso-, and macro-level "organs" of society, the instruments by which the social powers' forces keep us unified as one people. (One quick example, divorce rates reflect micro-level disintegration).

It's apparent the boomers used society for their purposes and not vice versa. (They asked what the country could do for them, even as their hippies attacked it, and not, what they could do for the country). This, in turn, ruined any sensation of a national community, which continues to destabilize society and undermine civility. Since doomerism is made of "look at me, look at me now" celebrity apprenticing, it disintegrates society into factions. In a culture of doomerism, the LAMBS is not done for everyone but only for one person at a time in hyper-competition, a game of winner takes all. Boomers like to point fingers at one another. Doomers use this as a great distraction, so they may fleece the coffers of commodities made by laboring Americans. According to them, we work, they get paid, and this is as it should be, because it suits them best.

Oh, the subtle affluence of consumer society the boomer generation televised as ideal, a kind of society in which people get seduced to see their culture not as one based in cooperative democracy, but rather as one made from competitive consumerism. An unreal, made-up game of reality, a game won by owning the best, most recognized as superior (whether they are or not), and greatest number of objects. Quantity over quality, until those with the most can claim they are winners in the game of life, and those with less as the losers. Doomerism is made of this immature posturing.

Doomerism's excessively propagated consumer materialism promotes and tolerates self-centeredness. It dramatically lowers standards of conduct, thereby causing significant susceptibility to moral and ethical failures. These are evident in the behaviors of our meso-level FILMS^2 [P7] and the HM^5 subcultures, particularly in the excessive use of isms within and about them.

The pull of self-importance inflates by the nomenclature of the upper classes' snobs. The purportedly powerful politicians and erudite economic elites within their social circles periodically change their buzzwords and often do so with high-end academy power. This is an effort to control the language, just as political correctness is. Language manipulation is inclusivity (of those who know the lingo) and exclusivity (of who has the special status, and who is disallowed it). This lack of earnestness and false conscientiousness is divisive behavior, which stratifies people into vertical groups by vocabulary. Bigger word users on top, so they can look down their noses at little word users. This is aristocratic, and contrary to founding principles of egalitarianism and equal inalienable natural rights. Doomerism is made of this kind of snobbery.

To feel above another, one must associate with persons in societal positions perceived as having influence. We find such clout in persons' minds of the posts with the most authority, influence, or celebrity. In the word, is projected power that moves minds; shapes opinions of what persuades others. We the everyday people must remember that we are the power. We must continuously listen and learn, think and reason about what is going on within the FILMS[2] [P7] and with the HM[5]. When rising up in these roles in the organs of the body of society, the social powers, we must not forget that we are citizens first, obliged to IDEALS liberty. We must rely on common sense and the wisdom of everyday life. We must not allow ourselves to be fooled into thinking we are inferior because of big words used to define matters we see as plain. Those with time on their hands, often the rich who live off their assets and don't have to work for a living, like to articulate in dandy words that make them feel sufficiently sophisticated, posh. Superficiality does not improve the nature of reality. Fancy pants don't make the dancer dance any better. Doomerism is made of superficiality. It is how boomers can avoid responsibility and get whatever they want personally instead of diplomatically figuring out what the group needs. The idea of a community need is too laborious for baby doomers to deal with, because it creates conflict that their "me first" cultural and behavioral instincts tell them to avoid.

Increasing abstractions of understanding distract us from the facts on the ground. Wrapped in isms, abstruse concepts give importance to politicians and elites who toss them around as weapons against one another's arguments. We hear them everywhere. Often improperly used and incorrectly understood for how they disrupt our lives. The consequences of misunderstanding abstracts that influence policies, which shape society, are huge for the lives of everyday people. Society's shape affects us in micro and meso levels of performance. We feel the impact in our households, workplaces, the offices of the polity, and the workings of the economy. We can now see how they relate to how authorities AEIOUY[2]K our secondary and tertiary social powers and how doomers uncivilly DAMN them.

Just as impairment of civility at the micro-level affects the meso-level, when meso-level deterioration happens in society, it affects the macro-level and becomes more evident. Alterations in powers and power arrangements become clear to sentient everyday people. Our sixth sense, like antennae of a lobster, detects danger in disequilibrium. With our lived practical wisdom, we sense easily when something has gone haywire. Sadly, for democracy, we've remained too silent. The mass media and the celebrity culture of boomers intimidate. It makes us feel small, unfree. Boomers favored unfettered appetites' expansion, and "me first" deeds when untrammeled. Because of television, among other reasons, the boomers' nonsense receptors turned off.

Changes are visible to those who are not convinced by the shenanigans swindlers perpetrate to reshape society in their favor. It's an obvious game for those who have eyes to see it. As the distortions continue, doomerism leads to public distrust of the very organizations and institutions built to IDEALS liberty for the benefit of the citizenry. This ramps distrust, amplified by injudicious courts that see moneymaking corporations as equal to voters. Baby doomers then continue to undermine and announce that failing institutions are acceptable. They do nothing to stop the decline, but instead intensify their efforts if they feel they are able to get away with it. They became addicted to feeling powerful. They came to enjoy vindictiveness as they DAMN the social powers. They seek vengeance to any opponent they can declare. Again, like angry quixotic warriors, they want war. War on this; war on that; war is their way to solve their gripes with any who disagree with their views. War is their weapon against any who represent or reflect our unjust society. They think it brings meaning to their lives. As youths, many of them rebelled against war, but as adults became exemplars of it at its worst. Because of their egotism, they failed to look in the mirror and see that they are the "they" who perpetuate its wrongs. They'd claim this point is moot. But it seems the aim of doomerism is made of a lack of sensitivity, historical blindness, civil tone deafness, and an indifferent muteness to justice.

The boomers love to file excessive litigation that bogs down the judicial system, making it appear to be faltering further. The judiciary was the framers' least favorite branch of government because it does not involve democracy, that is, a direct decision by the people legislatively. Yet what is failing is a population that is seeking selfish gain over community stability. Doomerism is made of this, since boomers demonstrate a willingness to burn down the house, so no others can have what is in it. Doomerism is an all-or-nothing, zero-sum, scorched earth egotistical game. It is a cultlike culture of childish, selfish spoilage. We the next generations must shake it off our backs. It will be wrong of us to allow future babies to suffer it. A spoiled generation that created conditions that enabled crises to arise, chaos to prevail, and risks to our republic by denying democracy that we the everyday people need to enjoy the blessings of liberty, is dangerous to keep in authority over our society. They have despoiled our dreams, spoiled our soil and foiled our toils' successes. They have soiled the age of enlightenment. Over the past forty years, thanks to doomerism, it devolved into first, an age of entertainment, second, an age of entitlement, and now an age of exhibitionism. It could get worse if we do not stop it (see Figure 5-8). All these transitions gave rise to instability. Doomerism is also made of these.

If not stopped, doomerism will delude us into an age of enormous valuelessness. It will perpetuate the decline of civilization into an age of electronic victimization, or evictimization, exploitation, eviction, enragement, and enslavement. But hey, "So what!" As the boomers are prone to say,

"Anything goes" so long as "I get mine". This does not create a healthy nurturing environment in which to raise American children! We should not cope with this spoiled age. We must unspool their stitchery, correct its errors and patch its omissions, rewind democracy culture, and replay the founding wisdom to undo their mistakes. Or else we will stink of baby doomer spoilage's stench. To get at this we must get control of all the isms flung about, and all the fallacies, false ideals, and misunderstandings. A big misguided one is the boomers' misconstrued meaning of freedom.

Misguided Understanding of "Freedom"

We say that wild animals are free. Free to do what they please. Are we wild animals? Or are we human beings? Do we not each have a conscience that thinks about what we feel when we do something wrong or wrongly? Doesn't our natural inalienable human right to life cause us to think "we must to keep our life not take another's"? Doesn't our inalienable human right to liberty cause us to realize by basic reason that we cannot take another's if we want to keep our own? Doesn't our inalienable human right to the pursuit of happiness cause us to understand a critical American fact? That is, if we deny another their pursuits, then they in turn could deny us ours.

Certainly, but here is the rub, and here is how the baby doomers got it wrong. These rights are ours by birth, guaranteed by the Constitution, which as a rule of law provides that we must self-govern. Reason will tell us that it is shallow to think that "letting you get whatever you want, so long as I get whatever I want (wink-wink)" does not hurt you, me, or us. Because we are not the only two in the society, this is a foolish mentality. Reason requires that we think beyond our dyadic experiences. Not everything is a hard-boiled negotiation, a deal to make with another to win the bet and get a leg up on the other person. Reason that aims us toward complete liberty means we must accept the rights of our fellow human beings (men, women, and those in between or both, however they define their own gender or sexuality). We can do this if the first self-identifying identity for each one of us is "citizen." This is foundational for a culture of democracy and the egalitarian principle that holds we are all created equal. To do otherwise is to foolishly rebel against that which is in one's own best interests, one's liberty in civilization. If a civilization is not for you, be prepared to a) live in a cage or b) move into the wilderness to be free to fight with geography power alone. Many choose to live a wild life of survival with the wildlife in the wild. Society is complex. It requires tolerance. Intolerance is a seed of authoritarianism. Tolerance is an essential ingredient of success in democracy. Be tolerant and gain freedom. It's not paradoxical. It's axiomatic.

The misguided, idealistic thinking of boomers made superficial thought a core characteristic of their personality. With wealth growth and prosperity, the need to think deeply seemed unimportant and unnecessary. A few hid out in philosophy, but the promise of superficiality, an ultimate free-dom of self from constraints of society, gained hold. Commercial goods' advertisements sold and resold, told, and retold frivolous facts. Expanding consumerist culture and its shallow values became the holy ground of ego achievement. Superficial conspicuous consumption altered attitudes and behaviors, and we lost a sense of moral responsibility. We need to perpetu-ate the virtuous cultural values that constitute and contribute to a culture of democracy. It would be unwise to leave these behind.

Mythology power shaped a diversity of new religious thinking: anything goes, prophecy-rendered, traditional-principles-confusing, too deep to deal with, and no longer valid. Personal private freedoms of expression, such as sexuality, got brought out into the public. This caused challenges between the various regional subcultures and generations. Since "sex sells," consum-erism saw no consequence in its publicity. The economy power of selling was too important to society to keep sexual behaviors in private. Public displays of sexuality of all kinds became in vogue, seen as tolerable to those in positions of power. Those in the dominant generation monopolized the interests and tolerances in society through the affluence of economy pow-ers to produce objects of affection and cash profits. The economy power gained more control over the citizenry's thinking. It imbalanced the societal powers toward its ability to gain more power to shape society but without added responsibility.

Further, unconventionally the public freedoms explored in seeking to shape public opinion to influence the polity occurred unchecked. Political influence happened outside of, and not by or through, the citizens' mecha-nism of exercising real power: voting. Impatient greedy boomers invented alternate channels. Political action and special interest groups, lobbyists, provided money and policy writing to persuade the politicians. Superficial boomers did this with each other without ethical concerns. This led society into conflict and crises. Superficiality limited protest participation, exhibited itself in voting apathy, and restricted the ability to vote to effect change due to challenges with exercising this right. Dissent against the amassing of power and money in the hands of a few was nonexistent in the majority. The steady erosion of a commitment to citizenship attitudes and behaviors followed.

The liberalization of social mores by baby boomers disconnected con-ceptions of freedom from its root in liberty. Personal freedom exploration at the expense of others is not freedom. Freedom is an agreement based upon liberty properly defined. A condition of forgotten, or ignored, re-sponsibility construed itself to be that of freedom. To protect and defend the Constitution against domestic enemies, which means those who seek to take our liberty away, was not for them. Idealistic doomer politicians sought to use the polity for matters that fed their own egos' tales of their fabulous-ness. They wanted to control cultural alterations, but they were mistaken.

People in free association, not by legal mandates of government, best create cultural expressiveness. Government seeking to control cultural expression is an overreach of polity power. Doomer economic elites sought to use money to shape the polity in their favor. Among many other actions, they abandoned fellow citizens in pursuit of profit by reducing labor costs, sending jobs overseas. They took away economic opportunities, creating disenfranchised classes. The polity then stepped in when asked to help these people survive. The elites increased the costs for citizens by decreasing tax burdens upon themselves and increasing the taxation that disabled less fortunate others. The boomers have repeated a federal deficit, compounding the debt upon the USE. The bulk of the costs paid by the middle classes and future generations cause a loss of domestic tranquility. The tax burdens injure the everyday people.

Those doomer politicians and economic elites who wrote polices that allowed jobs to easily go overseas now court the disenfranchised in communities supported by survival funding from the polity. They ask for votes using hollow, impossible, dreamlike promises, claiming to be saviors. They too easily exploit the downtrodden people whom they put in that condition with their philosophies, policies, processes, procedures, and practices. This is a social disease, a sociopathy perpetrated by psychopathy caused by doomerism. This is a human failure. This is a social and historical failure. What other historical failures might we see made by the boomers? Let's look, and then we will move into more of what doomerism is made of.

If intentionally focused on achieving the goal and objectives of the Preamble, the boomers would not have failed during their time in control of the LAMBS for the USE. They would have been better able to $AEIOUY^2K$ the societal and social powers to IDEALS liberty. They would have recognized the flawed reconstruction of the nation that perpetuated the inequality of freed people. They would have pushed for a continuous Civil Rights movement. They would have committed to full compliance to federal laws by way of diligent domestic diplomacy. They neglected to integrate society. They forgot to have a civics mentality. They chose other focuses and did not unite as a generation to extend and fully entrench in the national community the culture of democracy. Suffice it to say, now, the republic suffers.

Each generation has a responsibility to advance toward our founding goal and objectives. For forty years, our country has been ill served. The boomers celebrated too early and moved on, which allowed civil rights' continuous denial, delay, and decay. They distracted themselves from pursuing full justice for all and did not complete movements aiming to attain domestic tranquility. We now battle a new stage of this failure. We must finish the job. Boomers as a majority failed. They are negligent. We need the pragmatic succeeding generation, which cannot mathematically establish majority rule, to move the society forward by intervention. We need them to team them with the millennials, the next civically oriented generation.

These two with the succeeding generations' adults have the numbers to vote as a majority. They must vote out all baby boomers. It's that simple. This is necessary now. The boomers will doom the children. That much should be clear now, 2020 gave us plenty of hindsight to see it.

All the "Isms"

Doomerism is made of a battle of the isms. Intellectuals enjoy using isms to represent vast amounts of information. This book is all about an ism, made to counteract the abundance of arguments by proponents of one ism or another. It's a fight fire with fire approach. We battle about the consequences of ideas, without fully knowing what they imply in our day-to-day lives. So we go from philosophy, to theory, to policy, to practice, to activity, to analysis, to evaluation, to theorizing, to philosophy, and back around again. We think to think, think to know, and think about how to go about our lives. We are cyclical in many ways. Sadly, all of this intellectual tossing about has made us too cynical to see what's wise for us as a people e pluribus unum. Should we spend our energy fighting over whose ism is right? We've not time for that. We should be looking at what we need to do pragmatically to solve social problems. We need to stabilize society so our everyday lives are not reduced until rendered useless on a planet feared to be on the brink of its capacity to support our survival. How dismal it sounds. It's thanks to doomerism, the byproduct of a billion "me first" attitudes and behaviors.

All the isms used by polity power partisan politicians, economy power immodest elites, and their paid mouthpieces using history power, confuse, confound, dissuade, and distract us from the conversation we need to be having about the real issues we need to solve. Arguing over isms is a great distraction. It comes from behind the scenes as doomers' LAMBS ways, means, and methods DAMN societal and social powers. Woolly curtains shroud their bad actors poor performances on the serious stages of life. The mere use of all these isms takes power away from the everyday people because they speak of matters too remote from our daily lives' needs. Their abstractions proffer unknowable and inapplicable concepts to commonplace experiences. It's word play; another game played against us, a kind of catch me if you can tomfoolery. There are so many: consumerism, corporatism, fetishism, etc. These guide policy thinking and making. This is such an idealist, abstruse, impractical manner of making decisions, often the wrong ones, on complex matters that need not be so complicated. By talking in isms, we too frequently speak impractically. We're rendered obtuse. We confuse things. We miss what is meant, misinterpret motives, and misunderstand. The rubric is simpler. Bad decisions are those that infringe upon our liberty. We can see this in the loss of domestic tranquility, demotion of the general welfare, and demonization of fellow citizens.

The boomers' economy power overreach is causing an unhelpful transferring or removal of liberty. They like expediency over truth, which favors the profit-producing HM[5] and control schemes creating FILMS[2] [P7] of the economy power. In the halls of justice, courts are implementing arbitration vs. plaintiffs and defendants getting a day in court to resolve lawbreaking and perpetrated injustices. The rise of alternative dispute resolutions undermines the justice remedies imagined in the Constitution. As noted earlier, too many cases because of too much misbehavior and frivolous tort lawsuits bog down jurisprudence. Being in too big a hurry is a result of allowing greed as acceptable or laudable. It causes impatience. Justice is not as swift as the emotions might like, but justice works better with facts. Facts take time to collect and assemble. Impatience is not healthy, but it is a piece of what makes up doomerism. Patience is a virtue, per wisdom, but doomerism rejects it.

In the economy power's labor marketplace, doomerism promotes offshore labor and mobility of money to invest for maximizing gains. Money generated through making commodities in the USE, and the financial capital amassed within our country from its geographic resources and laboring people, are being concentrated in the hands of very few persons. These persons feel freed from responsibility to the society. They put effort into changing the rules, norms, and mores that detail what makes them members of society. They press to be unaccountable for the societal damages they have caused. Once upon a time, antitrust laws got enforced. They protected the citizenry from manipulation by monopolies. Remember, a limited government's job, as it was cast, is to protect our inalienable rights. Too often monopolies infringe upon them. Because of doomerism, our polity power is not preventing our economy power from harming us. Isms are ideologue's weapons in a war of words that perverts our perception of politics. They hide the risks of unchecked and imbalanced influences of the economy power upon the polity.

Aggressions

Doomerism is made of aggressions. Recall how boomers declared war on everything as a way to solve problems, but none of those wars worked out so well. This is probably because war is a kind of territorial protection last resort. If territory is not needing taken, it is inapplicable. War, targeted and controlled violence, causes damage. It cannot solve social problems, so declaring war on problems as a means to solve them is foolish. Society needs solutions through diplomacy, love, and unity of purpose. Interconnecting countries with global trade, a commercial venture, provides more security than isolated war mongering does. Building bridges better thwarts the risks of real war than building walls and saber rattling. Be this as it may, the aggressive tribalism of the boomers leads to conflicts. Conflicts escalate and drive people to declare war against one another. It's childishly petty to be so belligerent. We see boomers' hostility in the micro, meso, and macro levels of society. But they do not see it. They prefer pugnaciousness. Because we the everyday people experience relationships in society at all its levels, boomer-made doomerism is dangerous for us. We have enough worries in trying to survive, live, and maybe if lucky thrive. We do not need fight pickers to be running the show.

Society is a series of interrelated relationships. Relationships suffer from truculence. Apish combativeness reveals itself in speech all the time, be it by a passive-aggressive or an overtly aggressive statement. Idealistic baby boomers are now very often acrimonious. Aggression is unidealistic; it is not ideal; it is a bad idea. It is a piece of what makes doomerism. They and only they have the right to be right. If they are factually wrong, their hubris overcomes them, and they will aggressively lie, cheat, and steal to prove, desperately, at least in their own minds, that they were right. They worship ego and not God. They are not interested in the judgments of Providence or the benefits of a functioning commons, in which the commonweal is, shared fairly, each to their meritorious contributions. Doomerism has caused an increase in persons who develop less fully, morally (see Figure 2-27), and consequent dysfunctions in the social and societal powers of our society.

Doomerism curses us to be less wholesome citizens. It's made of persons with higher levels of insecurities, pettiness, insolence, prejudices, indignation, and hatreds. These restrict our passage toward moving our society in the direction of its goal and objectives. Baby doomers' contentiousness is unconcealed. We can easily perceive it. It is in the micro-aggressions of their tiny-minded talk. It comes across in their general jeering sarcasm, in their snide remarks, and in their constant efforts at manipulation. Most ugly is the smugness. They find trivial slime like pleasure in smiles and smirks with sneering side angled glances. They enjoy the raw cunning of feeling ever so pleased "with me myself and I" for scoring a verbal point of superiority.

Doomerism is made of sinister cynicism, obnoxious and obvious, disgusting, and morally repugnant approach to relating with others. However, we cannot tell them this. When we do, we become open victims of their spasmodic spite and whimpering defensive denials of having done anything wrong. Moaning, "It's not wrong unless you get caught." They'll contend, "I am innocent until proven guilty." They whine, "Even when I know I am guilty, I am going to fatigue you with my lawyers. They will overwhelm you. They will defend the trinity of 'me, myself, and I' against any guilt or shame. No one can tell me differently because I am my own god." Oh boy, whoa Nelly, what a generational personality they exhibit! We wince since we believe in being citizens who uphold the Constitution. They do not.

Doomerism is total dishonesty, all the time premeditated, in service of self-righteousness. It is not rightful, nor right, nor American. It is the enemy within that threatens the solvency of our nation by scheming to shred the Constitution. It grew from the vulnerability of the success of the economy power, the wealth we generated after we put the world back together from the destruction of World War II. Rebuilding the world made us overconfident, superficial, and foolish. Dialectically, we enabled an internal threat. Because, unchallenged by real global competition in economy power, we grew blind. We failed to prepare for what would occur when the rebuilt war torn nations became productive and competed with us for market shares of goods and services. Boomers rode the no-global-competition wave upon which even the incompetent could surf to the shores of moneymaking successes. Padding their pockets first-and-foremost, the economy power elites abandoned the strategic needs of our country. The politicians did not prepare protective policies either. Instead, drawn to power like iron to a magnet were they. In pursuit of it, they climbed easily into the moneyed laundry sacks of the industrial and commercial multinational corporation's magnates.

External threats coded in Cold War fears. The Soviet Union was a sociocultural experiment for organizing a society. As an alternative societal power arrangement, its exclusion of people power failed it. It was not as big an external threat to us as the polity made it out to be though it fed well our military-industrial-political-media-complex, a sophisticated structuring of economy power. It provided a great means to promote incredible transfers of the common wealth, the people's production value, to a few. The peak of the wealth recipients' pyramid enlarged, and revenue gained by a marginal tax rate was reinvested in society's success. Companies hired many persons educated with the GI Bill, which built a strong working middle class. Middle-class growth stabilized major parts of the society. Sadly, some regions were left out of the rising fortunes. Many were forced to live in toxic industrial environments that poisoned and weakened them. The people got hope through their polity by creating an environmental protection agency, but cleaning up all the pollution was deemed too expensive. Doomers decided it was better and more important to enrich a few persons beyond absurdity. To them it was perfectly fine to allow lower-positioned persons to live in decrepit cesspools. Profits are good, but not paying workers, and contaminating natural resources they depend upon, is cruel. Sadly, it wasn't unusual, and went uncorrected, and often wherein criminal, unpunished.

We are in a different era now. We need to understand what doomerism was made of, so that we can unmake it. We must undo its negative influence on us and within our society. We must remove doomers from the pilothouses, replenishing our bridges with upcoming generations. Boomers need to relinquish the controls of the helms of the polity and economy powers. Our current bearing is not good; we must turn the wheel to get our good ship into the wind before it runs aground as we navigate it astern to regain reminders of what it is. Or by quick dry-docking at a shipyard, make rapid repairs and restock materiel. We must rebuild its foundational keel, realign its main frames, reaffix its hull planks, recommission it, and render it fit and ready. Hoisting its sails expediently, we need to get it back at sea to fight for liberty. We need to get our project back on the good path of providence's favor. We must do this if we are to realize the full benefits of the founders' vision of a republic as one nation under God, with liberty and justice for all. The 21st Century's digital clock moves without clicks yet tick tocks explicitly faster than we fathom to discern. Time seems to accelerate against our best interests.

We can fix our ship, the USE, if we put the brightest age groups in charge. Those from 24 to 40 years of age must rise with civic intentions. This is the age range of most of the framers, and of geniuses in general. We must invest our minds, bodies, souls, and energy in reviving a civics mission. We need to revise errors and include omissions to get back on its course. Most importantly, we must commit to pursue virtue, salve the wounds of our history, and push out of authority aggressors against liberty and bullies buying affluence. The youth can do this work better than the aging and aged. They've grown up with the latest computational and communications knowledge. They have experience with the newest technologies and can make policies to protect us from tech's negative risks. They've been raised playing on teams and are good at teaming. Complex social problems need engaging teams to solve them. The rising generations are prepared to deal with them, and we must let them. Boomers fears of letting go must be assuaged and overcome or they will crash and break us.

Guided by the wisdom of the Silent Generation that preceded the boomers, we can free society and selves from doomerism. Helped by coaching from the pragmatic Generation X, we can get the right people in charge. We need the "ages of genius" adults to be given passage, to be promoted, encouraged, and empowered. But, we must verify they understand the mission, too, so we sail in the intended, correct direction. With Silent and Gen X helping them, they can do it. Always in the shadow of the boomers, Gen X can finally lead by coaching the up-comers. A recessive generation coming after the boomers, Gen X never had the numbers to gain societal control. We could have used their cohort's realism. It might have blocked doomerism. The 24 to 40 year-olds are our best hope now. We must get the best patriots among them on the helm as soon as possible. We need to bring higher standards and ethics to the task. Standards and ethics are the stalwarts of trust building. Democracy culture depends on it. Moral integrity is its bulwark. Trust is vital for peacemaking diplomacy and negotiation to get fair and reasonable deals. Acting honorably the mercantile HM[5] will keep us in fair winds and following seas so posterity may see the prosperity, which is an intention the endowment of the USE is to provide.

In the next section, let's explore the possibilities of a new arrangement of the societal powers. We'll do so by asking ourselves what doomerism means for each of us, one isolated person at a time. Each one of us is a lonely, insecure "me" needing meaning and purpose to feel at ease. Why ever would we put such a creature as "me", first? Meaning and purpose are rewarding. They come through virtue, not superficiality. They come through realness in relationships. They come socially. When we have a purpose that improves society, we have a meaning for being. We become something worthy when we find ourselves being wholesome, true to our whole person, integrating our personage, personhood, and personality, (recall Figure 2-26). We become well when we find out we have a lot to offer others. Being a citizen of a democracy in a real republic is a vital role we all can wrap around and enjoy. We just need to know how and then do it. In this vein, with baby doomers holding onto the wheel, as if life were but a speedboat race vice a voyaging vessel on a long journey, we find that what's in doomerism for each of us is limited. In our remedy for it, we'll find so much more meaningfulness. We are soon getting to concerns that we might think matter the most, based upon what doomerism does to our thinking. It seeks to shape what we perceive as being in our best interest.

What Does It Mean for Me?

The "What does it for me?" to understand doomerism is important to how each of us might decide to move forward as a community, or not. What doomerism means for each of us as a "me" is a choice needing to made, and soon. We must ask ourselves several questions. "Do I want to live in a culture of doomerism, or a culture of democracy? Am I the center of the society entitled to believe whatever I want to believe? Does my freedom of speech right, entitle me to act upon beliefs that disagreement with facts? Does might make right? Is my ignorance of my emotionally appealing causes more or less important than my critical reasoning? Should I seek first to understand or defend my position? Should I examine myself for hypocrisy? Is it in my best interests to disagree with the principled intents of the Preamble? Should I be a consumer or a citizen first? Do I have any responsibility to my neighbor? Do I choose doom or boon? Do I want to be like one of the problematic boomers, one of the loomers, groomers, zoomers, roomers, or doomers? Or will I help positive bloomers and broomers convert their misguided cohorts into citizens pursuing posterity's potential prosperity?" One person at a time we must choose our preferred culture, either doomerism or democracy. We either expect to get what we want, or earn what we get. Let's continue this discussion with the frame of generations.

Generationally

Understanding generations come and go is a good context for us to consider, because none are perfect. Each cohort learns life through living out its human life cycle in its own accord. Each person in a generation responds to the events that make the era definable as its history. Big events during a generation's cohorts coming of age into adulthood can shape identity. A generation's personality, sense of purpose and ambition, begins in either an awakening or a crisis. Each person becomes in part identifiable by his or her generation. Each experiences gains from the critical new knowledge that awakens it to new possibilities, future horizons to explore, or strains from the critical calamities that befall humanity by geography or polity power exerting itself in volatile and violent ways, such as natural disasters and human disasters like war.

We know that the baby boomers as a generation will go away, but they will likely seek to hold onto power as long as possible because of their inflated, idealistic sense of worth and because they are still infighting to prove who is right. We cannot tolerate this any longer. When they are gone, will doomerism remain within us? Yes, unless we act now. We must make an effort to eradicate it as soon as possible. Visibly removing the baby doomers from positions of authority is how we begin. As old age sets in, let's hope all the boomers will want a decent legacy and future for their grandchildren.

Let's first understand the natural flow of generational power turnover to learn how we might introduce an intervention. We enter into a preexisting historical period shaped by extant generations. We exit ours after influencing an historical period as part of a constellation with other generations. Thomas Jefferson wanted generations to be like nations, minding their own business of society within their means, properly, and not putting the next into debt or danger. Other framers recognized that generations provide endowments to posterity. The opposite of an endowment is a deficit, in its accumulated form, a debt. The baby boomers amass debt upon the next generations because their ailment, doomerism, causes them to take more than they give. They sought, and thought they ought to be entitled to, better outcomes by passing down the burden. They live a high life on borrowed dimes and times.

Society must accommodate each generation's endowments and debts in order to enable its perpetuation. Societies are malleable because humans adapt to changing situations to survive. People, through role performances as the HM^5, particularly with economy power or in all our societal powers' $FILMS^2$ [P7], seek to resolve the threats to the sustainment of their social circumstances and physical conditions, either diplomatically or violently.

Normally, people seek solutions to the problems that pose threats to their self, family, community, and society. People can cause internal and external threats themselves, person by person, psychologically, socially, or religiously. Doomer politicians' status quo appetite needs challenged internally within the polity power's FILMS[2] [P7]. For the republic we must do this constantly. We can diplomatically by civil disobedience, social movements, and elections to replace the politicians who don't respond to our needs and protect the honorable from corruption. Alternatively, we can challenge the polity power violently by riots, insurrections, revolutions, terrorism, assassinations, massacres, and physical assaults against the police, which might be pushed to act with brutality, escalating the danger of unrepairable traumas caused by uncivilized disobedience. Democracy culture asks for the former; doomerism presses for the latter.

The polity power gets challenged externally. Diplomatically by imported ideology contrary to the first principles of the Constitution, by social movements that cross borders, or by politicians who promote a foreign construct that doesn't comport with the intent of the founding of the nation. These put the polity is at risk. This is not to be confused with loyalty to practices that are themselves contrary to the intents of the nation, which is an area of scholarship that we the everyday people must engage in, so as not to be confused by past wrongful practices that we think are definitive of American society. If practices are not serving to IDEALS liberty, they are wrong. The largest worrisome external threat to the polity power is the controlled violence of warfare in all its forms, symmetrical or asymmetrical, rapid strike or enduring siege. Warfare also can be ideological by synthetically subversive subterfuge to confuse people in a republic of democracy culture about what to think and believe in.

The economy power of society gets threatened diplomatically and violently. It can function in ways unsupportive of the people, and if so, it can cause gross instability and inequality that leads to violent protest against its symbols, and misdirected angst against the polity for allowing it to function wrongfully.

Society can see in its power-balancing acts a variety of belief systems that cross generations, with varying mythology power influences. Some seek to traditionalize the society by pressuring it to adopt restrictive ways of seeing the world through a favored series of beliefs considered infallible. Its proponents hope to deepen obedience to enforce their values for the sustainment of their religion, which they might seek to make dominant or fear is under siege. Both are ironic in the USE, which gives its entire people freedom of religion and has a separation between the mythology and polity powers, so that no person or group of persons can be in charge of both at the same time.

Conversely, others seek to modernize by pressuring for an opening of arguments that promote favored beliefs as fallible. Its proponents hope to adapt them to current circumstances to retain their value to the sustainment of their religion, which they seek to redefine for the good that it brings to people in the society. Reforming institutions is a normal, malleable aspect of society, and people move to keep what is good and jettison what is bad. This is as it goes. To the extent that what we perceive as good IDEALS liberty and what is bad is the DAMN of societal powers, reforms for the betterment of the USE are constantly necessary and warranted as appropriate to pursue.

Much like with mythology power, the academy power benefits from revision and reformation by each generation. It will need such alterations because doomerism infected and inflicted it, though not as terribly as it has the other social powers since its locus is in knowledge. If it pursues virtue, it might find truth more readily, and if it is saying and believing in the Pledge of Allegiance, it may not suffer as badly from doomerism. That is, when it is not favoring any one particular ism over another but is justly explaining all competing isms equally for fair comprehension and consideration of their applicability to American society, while providing an ACE to teach an appreciation for the endowment peaceably given each generation, minus those who fought in the Revolution and the Civil War.

Many generations alive at once

Because the overlap of generations makes a constellation of variable value sets at any given time, the responses to ecology and history bring about many different activities, preferred attitudinal and behavioral patterns, and possible paths. Often, the out-of-power and not-in-power generations have different opinions from the in-power generation. The dominant generation sets the tone and shapes its personality and consequent culture contemporaneously. This reflects in its balancing of the societal and social powers, and what is popular, unpopular, or neither. While the baby boomer generation has brought about increased doomerism, it is not the only generation to have baby doomers within it. However, it has had more opportunities to pursue wildly misconceived "freedoms", unchecked wild animalistic hedonism and bad manners, which enabled the escape from social norms causing expanding badness within the whole society, and mislaying of valuable customs.

Boomers allowed not previously permitted attitudes and behavioral patterns since they could because of the wealth in the nation. Wealth they pocketed without plans for the future American babies' need of a civil society to meet the responsibility of democracy in liberty for the perpetuation of the USE as a prosperity producer for commoners. Remember, the USE came into existence for the everyday people, not the conceited, aristocratic elites of a monarchy. Recall the symbol of the Liberty Tree and the colonies' "Don't Tread on Me" rattlesnake.

All eight preceding US generations had baby doomers, but they were in the minority. They were shamed and shunned. However, due to the mistakes of a lost focus on protecting liberty, a generation arose that slipped

up, messed up, and screwed the future. How is this so? By numerical dominance of society's decision-making with hypocritical immorality, baby
doomers changed our culture from democracy into doomerism. They majorly have authority positions longer than any other does. It just so happens
by the ironies of poetic justice we call this large domineering generation the
"baby boomers", which nicely rhymes with "baby doomers". Might not the
Eye of Providence be watching us? If it is, (see Figure 0-1-1), may its rays
of righteousness light up the scene, exposing thieves and disbelievers in
democracy to help us refocus on our purpose.

Figure 5-4 below shows the constellation of our living generations today. The older generations show at the bottom. Succeeding generations
come after and build their lives upon the life's work of their predecessors.
Notice the adult age ranges in 2020.

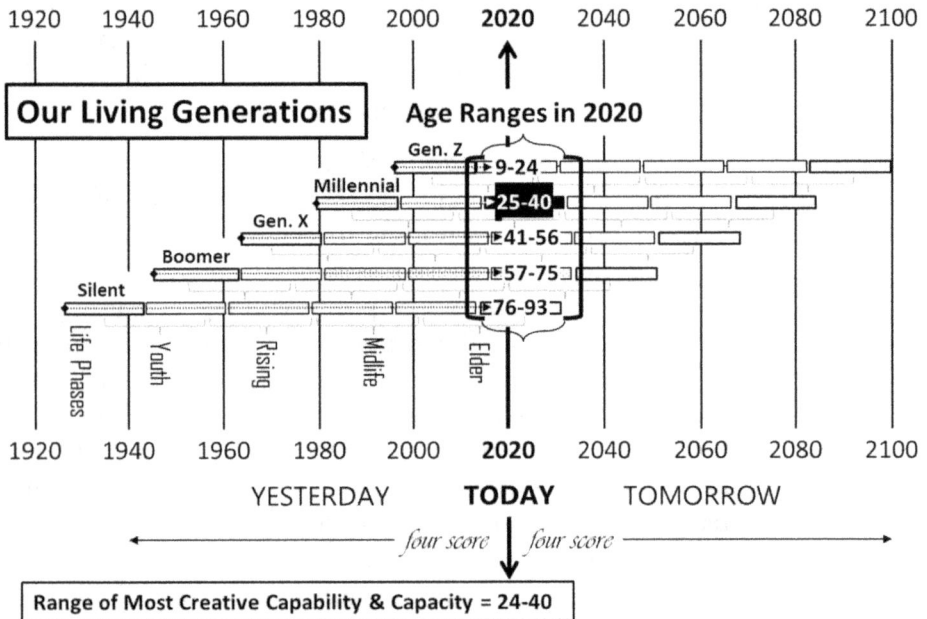

Figure 5-4: Our Living Generations

Of importance in recognizing the living generations, and as a means to
break free from doomerism, is for society to transfer control of the operative powers to those most capable of performing creatively in the LAMBS
for the USE, the 24 to 40 year-olds. This stage of adulthood has the best
cognition, comprehension, and complex KA^4SA^2 at its disposal. These
adults possess the most imaginative inventive capacity and problem solving
capability to innovate. This age range of humans historically produces of
the most radical improvements. The sweep of the US Constitution's framers fell within it. It's a time of comprehension still sufficiently idealistic and
ambitious to realistically find new realizable solutions. It's the best for future generations' benefit because it's the domain of young parents dedicated

to their children and not thinking only of themselves first. Unlike the aging boomers with authority beginning to see their own frailty, and still striving to secure evermore benefits for themselves.

Of course, it is important that the innovative 24 to 40 year olds have good coaching as Ben Franklin provided his younger patriots. Without too much of their own ideology, but with the wisdom of elders and practical experience of middle-agers, our young adult generations have what we need to address the societal transformations confronting us. "What's does it mean for me" is a hope we will by each person commit to defeat doomerism with a generational transfer of power.

Generation phases & knowledge activities

All persons are born and raised. Life occurs in phases related to biological changes. Our personal lives' phases affected by ecological or historical realities weave us into who we become as humans. Generations react, weaving paths for society into the unknowable future. In doing so, generations form attitudes and engage in activities based upon the era they experience. Each develops values that drive its behavior and impart on its members an identity, by which other generations come to know them. Cultural modes of expression such as comedy enjoy the visible commonalities of a generation's personality. As activities change, generations adapt, but they do so while leaning on their values formed by the problem-solving responses learned in their era. Shaped by the events that define them, eras become our known past though as we AEIOUY^{2}K history power. We can revisit its product and estimate its accuracy and valuations with each succeeding generation. Some will differ from previous generations' opinions of old truth, and present truth. History power is an important aspect of our project and can serve us well if we appreciate its presentations of the views we once held, hold, and could profess.

Thus, generations are different. They react differently to ecological and historical realities. Eras' main concerns change as humans acquire more knowledge and try new things or attempt to prevent them. Seeking control is a factor in human society. The forces that we've used to control power have many forms of expression. Society experiences power in different modalities. Let's quickly review Chapter 2's thesis of the good power modes.

The modalities of power occur within specific realms of knowledge. As was introduced earlier in Chapter 3, there are primary, secondary, and tertiary powers. These rely on particular knowledges that serve the shaping of all the combined societal and social powers that constitute the total culture of a society. When the powers support democracy, we've a culture of democracy. When the powers support doomerism, we've a culture of doom. Democracy is American. Doomerism is un-American.

A primary arena of human action is the polity's FILMS$^{2\,[P7]}$ that organize and AEIOUY^{2}K power. The polity power's purpose is the administration of society. The second primary arena of human action is the economy power's FILMS$^{2\,[P7]}$ and the HM^5 role-players that provide the provisions of society. The economy power can AEIOUY^{2}K the industry and artistry powers to support its vitality and benefit for humanity. Imagine no one wanting to work. It would be a society devoid of economy power. It could not exist. The economy power's purpose is the management of society. The third primary arena of human action is the people power's participation in the roles available in a society and commitment to perform them in ways that benefit the society. The people power's purpose is the leadership of society. Particularly in a democracy, leading by example and effort of virtue and civics are necessary for self-government and the prevention of tyranny.

Another arena is history power with its journaling and chronicling of what is happening, what has happened, and what might happen. What might happen is highly influenced by the creative imaginations of the artistry power. Other arenas of power possess and develop their specialized knowledges for society. An extremely influential one is the mythology power, which proffers and passes down cosmic belief systems that address the nature of existence and purpose of life. Of course, society also needs knowledge of the geography power so that it, through culture, may adjust all the societal powers to provide for itself: its survival, good living, and hoped-for thriving in luxury. Much of the knowledge of all powers is handled by the academy powers' potential to house all knowledges. FILMS$^{2\,[P7]}$ help catalog what we know of geography, its natural ecosystems, climatic and topographic conditions, available resources for survival, and physical elements—materials for creating the tools with which the three most fundamentals of survival are obtained and made: food, clothing and shelter.

Ultimately, culture connects all of the powers through knowledge in a way that makes sense for everyone in society. To the extent that culture allocates the materials in a society, the powers are seen a fair or unfair. As knowledge expands the interconnectedness of human activity, our relations, our powers, become complex. Yet society, while it transfers from generation to generation, must adjust to itself and to others. Outside contacts with unknown and external circumstances need led, administered, and managed as it sustains human life for its members. The people, who make up the society, are in the culture and experience life as persons and as members of the society. In our society, the experience of the whole is supposed to be more similar than different. If we are to be one people of many, e pluribus unum, by way of democracy based culture we must pursue this as a permanent project. Its goal and objectives were set forth in the Preamble. By living by the rules of Constitution as amended (by us, the people), over time, we can realize its ambition.

We have work to do. Because, with boomers in control, we aren't doing a good job leading, administering, and managing our project. The actions of their HM^5 and FILMS^2 [P7] of all our societal and social powers take us in the wrong direction. Their DAMN of people power is appallingly un-American in light of the ideal principles framed in the creation of the United States. They fail to provide adequate leadership for the sustainment of society's best intentions. They misguidedly perform the LAMBS in ways detrimental to the USE. Its total prosperity is supposed to include good fortune for posterity, which it is now lacking. Because they chose doomerism over democracy as a foundational culture, we could crash and burn in doom. Doomerism continues teaching us the wrong lessons about the American way of life. It misguides us toward unwholesome division. It blocks us from performing the necessary and continuous efforts required of us to enter a state of unity. Unifying by diplomacy is democracy. Union, not disunion, is "what this means for me" when we cast off doomerism as a personal worldview. Its value sets must no longer be shaping our social norms, folkways, mores, and customs.

Generations' patterns, because of human limits

Limited by mortality, our capacities and capabilities in our knowledge, and constrained by our imaginations to solve problems, we see history appear to repeat itself. It does not, exactly. Because our overall knowledge increases, so does our organizational specializations and complexities. Thus, the present dominant generation's patterns of behaviors are not the same as the past ones. However, history rhymes by the cycles of eras that we as a society experience. Over time, society moves between poles of crises and awakenings. Biology power limits the capacity and capability of the human's organ of thought, the brain. It by developing over time gives us personal perceptions shaped by our developmental age. The operational mind made animate by life energy thinks. As an organ, it can suffer developmental constraints. Malnutrition, physical damage, neurological abnormalities, or challenges related to brain chemistry affect it. Society limits knowledge and imagination. Each generation experiences universal human development and ecological and historical realities germane to the species. Each must make decisions that impact the succeeding generations. All extant generations experience one historical reality at the same time, but not in the same way because of the age of the cohorts. Each will respond to it differently, and it shapes each uniquely. Some generations experience traumatic ecological and survival threats. Some societies suffer existential trauma, then go extinct.

We can only know so much. We can only remember so much. To keep society American, we must refresh our knowledge and commitment to its original ideas found in the Declaration of Independence and the Constitution. The constant for all generations in our society must be a robust ACE.

This will ground us securely in our mission and purpose, reminding us of our goal and objectives. The USE depends on ACE to survive, generation after generation. "What does this mean for me?" is an important recognition that our voyage to a more perfect union, put in the Preamble, needs better citizenshipping, which develops from a solid foundation in civics and our intent to be one people, e pluribus unum.

Generations influence one another

The interconnectedness of generations in a society is related to the fact that generations are themselves raised by a generation of parents, who themselves were raised by a prior generation. This overlapping provides continuity and gives rise to discontinuity. Raised generations experience a different era, formulating their own attitudes and pursuing the activities reflective of the situations of their history in the making. Generations look up to previous generations and down to succeeding generations. Generations recognize that all are a part of the same society, but adulthood brings about competition for the control of the society. Each generation must seek the adaptive lessons, meaning, and purpose for living from the previous generations, apply them to its social circumstances and the physical conditions it foresees its children will face, and act to protect the future's potential to have what it had. Ideally, for American generations this entails a responsibility to IDEALS liberty and justice for all its citizenry.

Unfortunately in the USE, such a cycle of living by "paying it forward", investing in the next several generations' possibilities, was broken by baby doomers. Pre-American society, before the founding of the United States, passed on many practices of societal powers not expected to occur under the new order for the ages enshrined in the Constitution. The conversion of societal norms, folkways, mores, customs, practices, and principles takes time and effort, and compromises, which require an attentive citizenry seeking to make the changes from an old to a new age. With generations focused on moving to achieve the goal and attain its objectives, American society became more and more as envisioned. Democracy culture in the new world is still young. If a generation were only a year in the life of the USE, it is only an eight-year-old child of a civilization in the making. Sadly, many persons in society continue to resist reifying its goal and objectives as their personal purpose, or commit to them as those of the nation. This makes the evolution of an American society uneven and causes continuous suffering from uncivil conflicts. Doomerism has inflamed the societal and social powers conflicts of converting from the ancient to the contemporary because baby boomers did not focus on moving our project forward toward its goal by attaining its objectives. They sought to extract from it what they could, to get from it as opposed to giving to it. En masse, they are takers, not givers, despite what they think of themselves. This is the land of "we the people," yet they found themselves defined as the "me first" generation. How antithetical is that? It is very problematic for us to advance on achieving our creedal Preamble's goal and attaining our amended Constitution's objectives.

In 1776, the "American" society was born, and it inherited knowledge and imagination (ideas) from the people that encountered one another in its formation as an historical reality. It grew out of the settlements set up on inhabited land that was new to the 17th-century people from the kingdoms of the European continent. The settlers came principally from the countries we know today as England, Spain, Holland, and France. Lesser amounts of Germans and Swedes came over, too. But eventually almost all parts of the world sent immigrants to our shores and they became Americans. These Europeans and later other Europeans and through contact and relationships with peoples of other continents, the native nations of indigenous peoples, several African tribes, and over time the arrival of Asians and Arabians into the Americas influenced the shaping of society by the mixing of ways, means, and methods of the many immigrating variations of social powers. In the days of colonizing, the people who settled upon the land known to the Europeans as America formed a new society. Built upon the elements of the societies from which they came, but mostly the English culture of personal rights, the American society developed. Its societal ideas stimulated the people's imaginations of what was possible. Immigrants remained in contact with their homelands of origin through familial attachments, legal contracts, and trade, but sought to become American. Wrongly, the Africans were denied these and basic human rights. Arenas of knowledge, the roots of human-created powers and culture, were adopted and used to adapt to the geography. All these formed American society, mainly through commerce with economy power and coordinated agreement through compromise with polity power.

The United States was an entrepreneurial enterprise in motion since its beginning. It harnessed geography power, converted forests into farms and cities as did European civilization from which its inhabitants majorly came. The polity power set up governance systems similar to those known in England but influenced by ideas of others' homelands. The economy power set up trade. It brought labor over, at first indentured, then enslaved people to perform manual work. The mythology power varied and differentiated as it related to the ambitions and conditions of the settlers. It held sway differently in regions of the colonies (recall Figure 2-14). Northern and Southern territories preferred to $AEIOUY^2K$ it with opposite societal shaping justifications. Exploiting the natural geography power as was done back home, new agricultures were learned from the indigenous peoples and new food crops brought by Africans were planted. The history power recorded and wrote of new hopes for a new world society free from the bonds of tyranny. The academy powers served in manners that the regional subcultures adherents felt supported their traditions and ambitions.

Because of the rising distaste for a tyrant king and the desire for freedom from constraints found in the American wilderness, the culture evolved toward democracy as the most appropriate kind to allow each to pursue their needs, wants, and enterprises without restricting one another. Regional variations developed as settlements expanded. The country became an amalgam of different regional subcultures, blending with but in some cases opposing one another. The variety of settlements and their shaping of societal powers into the regions' ways of life have remnants in today's era. The second stage of knowledge evolution's technology brought the regions into conflict at the macro level of society administered to by federal government. We find aspects of the First Nations, New Netherlands, New France, New Spain, and New England (Yankeedom) throughout the country. Variations of these became unique regional subcultures themselves in the Midlands, Greater Appalachia, Deep South, Far West, and Left Coast (recall the *Settlement Patterns Complications* of chapter two). These all influenced and created the whole of American society, but not all are in accord with the proper intents on how to AEIOUY^{2}K American societal and social powers to achieve our goal and attain our objectives. If greater investment in and commitment to the first principles were pursued, to include the full pursuit of virtue by all citizens, it is possible in the next few generations we will finally fulfill them. Regardless of the era within which we might find ourselves, we must pass down our republic from generation to generation. We might yet complete our project and become one people, e pluribus unum, one nation under God, with liberty and justice for all.

Since constituted as the United States our American society's history, like many other human societies, rhymes with itself more than it actually repeats itself. It is not wholly accurate and rather cliché to say that history repeats itself. The humorist Samuel Clemens (Mark Twain) noted that it more or less rhymes (see Figure 5-2). Below we overlay the present circumstances we face within our choice to make. Will we continue the decline of democracy by living with doomerism as our driving force? Or will we reinstitute a common purpose and practice of democracy as culture by E-SASSY-T-TUF-FT-CAUCUS? We must make this adaptive shift during the present storming of the third stage of knowledge evolution. We must get to norming and performing as a unifying republic. We must. This is what it means for each of us as a "me", if we are ensure the endowment of our nation remains with the best choice culture, democracy, and continues onward with future generations. Let's remake good citizenshipping as the defining characteristic of an American society.

Generations make culture-altering choices

We the everyday people, experience a cycle of eras: exhilarating times, good times, boring times, and bad times. The similarities and differences felt by each generation toward its past are a result of the limitations of knowledge, social grammars, and social capital we all experience in varying amounts as a normal part of life. We must build up our knowledge, our social grammar, and our social capital and direct it to the cause of liberty. This will help us restore civility and a more robust civil society of honest HM^5 with healthy $FILMS^{2\,[P7]}$ that better $AEIOUY^2K$ societal and social powers to support our culture and revive our prosperity in common within our republic. We cannot put our heads in the sand and try to hide. We the everyday people must realize we have responsibility to guide the society toward its goal and objectives. It is our project to lead. The capacities and capabilities to communicate effectively to exert our power in unity are needed now as they were in 1774. Our hope is in gaining more personal, social, and societal knowledge, seeking unity of intent, aligning our efforts toward agreeing upon the facts and the purpose of American society in order that we might stabilize it by appropriately balancing the powers within it. This is our job as possessors of the people power that democracy grants to us. It is our calling as the leadership source for an American society. To do this, we must exert our power as persons to be better citizens who are oriented toward the pursuit of virtue. We must manage the risks of change. We must keep the pendulum from swinging too far toward any extreme like anarchy or tyranny.

Through better citizenship, it is possible to reduce the risks and social damage extremism exerts upon us as an American people needing an American society. Sadly, doomerism makes us an un-American society. If we ever stop majorly believing in democracy and working to ensure it, we will die. A uniquely blessed country we've the potential to be a beacon for all humanity, demonstrating through the organizing principle of liberty the possibility for justness and peaceable living for all. Each generation has a choice to make. We are in crises now. Will all generations agree to join in movement toward a citizen focus and gain equilibrium and benefit for all? An intervention certainly will help us turn toward a better tomorrow. Figure 5-5 below shows the cycle of history as if from above looking down on it with notes on our current circumstances, which rhyme with previous eras but are not repeating them because our knowledge base is different.

The apparent rhyming of history is because the nature of the species, as known by any cycle of generations over time, is not changing. Biological adaptations take eons, but societies engage in similar behaviors. Attitudes get shaped by KA^4SA^2. A society's capability and capacity rests on the quantity and quality of knowledge held by a majority of its people. Our tolerance for each other also shapes attitudes and behaviors. Problems with KA^4SA^2 in society are many, and this is evident within all the powers' $FILMS^{2\,[P7]}$ and society as a whole. Knowledge is uneven. Who has it, how much of it, and how is it used, to elevate or exclude, to make war or make peace, is a risk for the whole. The founders knew, and many wise scholars recognize, education is essential to establish and sustain a truly American society.

Society responds to ecological and societal (history-making) realities. Realities form from creation (inputs), experiences (throughputs), and memories (outputs). We experience short-, mid-, and long-term consequences and externalities (outcomes). We see these at the micro, meso, and macro levels of society. New knowledge, awakenings, and crises, change our experiences and our outlook in and for society. Society-altering experiences overlap with generational cycles. These cycles in America began in 1584 with the contact between the inhabitants of two different continents. Since the Constitution of the United States, four cycles of roughly 60 to 80 years in length have occurred. Each cycle contained four living generations, except for the shorter cycle that included the Civil War, which had three (Strauss & Howe, 1991). The dates and lines are blurry. Yet extensive research by historians recognized these cycles. In them, the expectations and experiences of the living shaped generational values. Each generation chose a direction and developed a personality. The cycles punctuated with ecological and society-affecting (history-making) realities turned. The experiences of varying problems challenging society altered the balance of societal powers. Alterations in the ways, means, and methods in which persons in authority would $AEIOUY^2K$ powers, and to differing degrees occurred by rebalancing them, caused changes and exposed us to new risks. The balancing efforts placed emphasis where deemed necessary for society's continuation. Rebalancing solved problems or increased chances for improvements. Vulnerabilities needed mitigated and opportunities stimulated for the perpetuation of the society. New knowledge, necessitating new understanding, got new frameworks of comprehension. Especially during turbulent periods that punctuated equilibriums, new thinking became necessary. Axiomatic choices needed made related to self and society, ones place in society, society's demands upon generations. To give more and take less, or the give less and take more. All generations face this teeter-totter equation of what's the right equity and ethics in their epoch. Figure 5-5 below presents this choice as a choice of cultural directions, one of a society with a foundation that is democracy based, or one that is doomerism based.

During epochs of new thinking, innovations increase and society adjusts its powers. This is the effort society makes to adapt, define the problem, imagine a solution, and act to solve it. This requires extraordinary cooperation. Cooperation by consensus happens with a clearly identified goal and objectives that all by majority agree to pursue. The Preamble is agreeable. Liberty is essential. Leadership is necessary to align the citizenry upon these to structure the use of resources to solve societal problems. (Thanks to doomerism, the boomers might be lacking the skills to use this approach).

AXIOMATIC CHOICE
(How primarily will "I" behave? What will be the focus of "my" generation?)

A. CULTURE BASED UPON **DEMOCRACY**

CIVIC-minded **PEOPLE** save *[& manumit]* SOCIETY *(by restoring balance of its powers)*

CITIZEN FOCUS

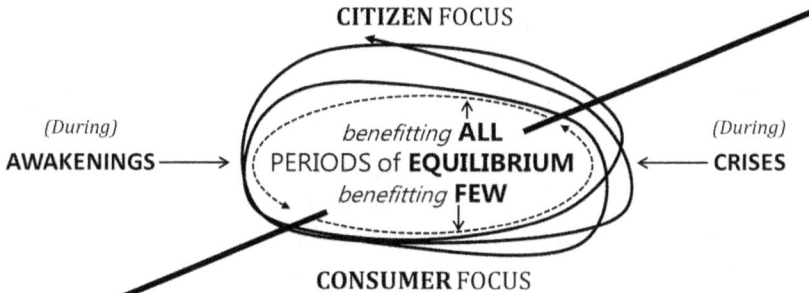

| (During) | | (During) |
| AWAKENINGS ⟶ | benefitting **ALL**
PERIODS of **EQUILIBRIUM**
benefitting **FEW** | ⟵ CRISES |

CONSUMER FOCUS

SELFISH-minded **PERSONS** cave *[(in); Cage]* SOCIETY *(by misbalancing its powers)*

B. CULTURE BASED UPON **DOOMERISM**

Figure 5-5: Axiomatic Choice: Doomerism vs. Democracy Culture

We've seen radical technological innovations since American society formed. We've had agonizing disagreements over the organization of society (internally and externally). Evidence resides in altering and rebalancing one or more of the societal powers. We've experienced violent attempts to solve social problems and antagonisms, such as war, terrorism, revolts, rebellions, insurrections, and riots. We've also experienced diplomatic attempts to solve social problems and disputes, such as protests, mass demonstrations, and social movements. We've had a Cold War and détente. These attempted solutions formed new realties. These realities, to which society responded, are describable as two types of experiences. One is a period of spiritual awakening, in which society develops new discoveries of thought or knowledge. The second is a secular crisis, in which society confronts internal and external conflicts, such as wars and disasters.

Between the awakenings and crisis periods that seem to spin history in new directions, periods of equilibrium can occur. These provide more shared similarities than differences in people's experiences and expectations. The responses by society to its ecological and social problems are history making. Some historical events are less dramatic and less life altering than others are. These cycles in history are eras; the remarkable ones are epochs. The ones that formed American society are the:

- **Colonial** cycle from 1584–1700 (116 years)
- **Revolutionary** cycle from 1701–1791 (90 years) as a Civics era that formed the United States as a nation
- **Civil War** cycle from 1792–1859 (67 years), which anomalously lacked a Civics generation, ended with the beginning of the war,

yet gave of the undeniable great American man, Abraham Lincoln

- **Great Power** cycle from 1860–1942 (82 years)
- **Millennial** cycle from 1943 to the present. (If it lasts 80 years, it will end in 2023)

What we name the next cycle depends on whether or not we expunge doomerism from our republic.

These cycles (Strauss & Howe, 1991) characterize periods of general similarity within society. They had experiences of societal equilibrium between their turnings. The Revolutionary period saw the first stage of knowledge creation and evolution and the first industrial revolution, which shaped the thinking of the modern world. Self-powered machines began to alter the tools of humanity. With these, humankind could achieve higher capacity and capabilities of production. New forms of industry and artistry power expanded the economy power. Economy power expanded in its performance benefits through increased provisioning. The Great Power period saw the second stage of knowledge creation and evolution and the industrial revolution, a continuation of the first, (see Figure 5-6). Yet its alterations in knowledge saw new thinking related to technological change. It prepared society for a future of more industrial revolutions (Mokyr, 1998).

We now near the end of the millennial period. Within it, we've seen the third stage of knowledge creation and evolution and what is a kind of third industrial, information technology, revolution. If we substitute the word industrial with computational, or digital, we more accurately define it. It has been revolutionary. It has tremendously disrupted society's equilibrium. It gave us social powers' adaptation challenges, mismanaged due to doomerism, resulting in chronic chaotic crises. A turning is about to occur. Recalling Figure 5-1, how long until we enter into a period of equilibrium? How long will it last? Will it overlap with an awakening cycle? Will there be an awakening? Will we remain in crises? If there is an awakening cycle, will it end in another crisis cycle? Could the past pattern of eras and epochs hold true for our future? Well, if the past is prologue, our knowing the past might give us the ability to address the future with some hindsight. Since history does not repeat but rather rhymes, we'll need greater creativity if we hope to break the cycles, remove crises, and determine how to transform society more smoothly for each generation by managing the risky storming over new knowledge and technologies. This will take excellent leadership, which the culture of democracy with ACE can make possible when the everyday people properly AEIOUY^{2}K people power for the positive perpetuation of the USE for posterity's prosperity. We must work for the children's potential to know peace and justice with liberty by stewarding into fulfillment our project to establish a more perfect union.

Technology trends are altering our lives. It's like learning a new card game. We must learn it fast to stay in it and be competitive again. Much of the mindset of businesses before 2000 was to let capital investments get recaptured. (Burrus, 1993). Waiting to innovate is not the right card game to play these days. It is neither good for business nor society. We need to learn how to adapt more rapidly than we've done in the past. We need to reimagine our FILMS[2] [P7] and the jobs of the HM[5]. Collaboration is growing. Competition for survival should be driving greater cooperation. However, it's not in many ways, domestically, because, doomerism is in the way. We need to be more aware of what we are focusing upon. Technology is threatening traditions. Their proponents feel they must fight for their own survival. Instead, they ought to find ways to adapt to remain beneficial in the new order of the ages circa 2020. Too often, they result to rhetorical fallacy and do disservice to their core goods they offer. This is a shame. It is a consequent of doomerism. Digital technology is the escalator we are riding upon nowadays. Ride it like Paul Revere we must, because a new era is about to begin. The jockey must control the horse to win the race. We need new jockeys. We are in an epoch for which we must innovative to solve our adaptive problems. This implies we need the brilliant young minds on our bridge, making the decisions at the helm. We need to get society oriented with foundational wisdom through ACE. We need it to move together through the rough seas ahead. We will survive the technological storm. We will find a way to norm. We will perform as a functioning society again in a comfortable societal equilibrium. We need civics trained young brains to do it.

Our imaginations and problem solving need a common main mast to stabilize. If we are to provide society the opportunity it needs to survive, for our lives and hopes to thrive to remain alive, we need core values for all to agree upon fully. Since the USE got invented for liberty and prosperity, we should use these as our sails' masts. If American society is a ship, and it drifts away from its potential to reach its goal, we should drop anchor to stop the misdirection. This anchor needs dropped now to prevent doomerism from drifting us onto the rocks that will crush our hull and sink us. We must regroup around our first principles and set a course that through strident ACE training with quality critical thinking skills. Each generation must do this to unite around our ideals and know how to think for themselves without being manipulatable by propaganda. If we are to sail to better waters in rightful directions for the people's prosperity for posterity, we must think differently now. We must come to terms with our digital, post-industrial, and postmodern realities.

Thus, to move forward into the next era and make it an egalitarian enriching epoch, we the everyday people must recognize the perilous threats to democracy baby doomerism culture presents to us. We must resist the romantic impulse to seek a past of perceived better days. We must move past the failed modern mindset that we can adapt and adjust society through social engineering. We must rediscover the wisdom of the framers and knowledge of human nature. We must reflect and take from romanticism and modernism that which is valid but drop these isms' argument. We must further and more deeply reflect upon the purpose of society. We cannot let the benefits we've gained from the miracle of the USE to become forgotten. We need to reacquaint ourselves with the core values that led to our being a nation under God, with a desire to create a society with liberty and justice for all. We cannot allow these words to be hollow platitudes spoken by shallow partisan politicians owned by the economic elites. We must blockade their efforts to establish an oligarchical plutocracy.

The ideals of the founding will see us through the turbulent times ahead. The newest technological advancements alter society, influencing the societal and social powers in ways unfamiliar, alien, difficult to accommodate, and arduous to adapt to confidently and agreeably. Because of it, we are feeling the anxiety of new risks. Recall the discussion of the SERF. There is risk in us not recognizing fundamental changes are taking place. We'll harbor more if we do not reexamine our assumptions of the societal and social powers purposes. The next generations should have a voice in the choices we make today. We must ask ourselves if the economy power exists only to profit owners of businesses, or if it actually belongs to us as a people. Is it not for us to $AEIOUY^2K$ economy power to provision society? Is not its purpose to give us choices and chances for a respectable survival, comfortable living, or luxurious thriving? We face a foundational question of what our expectation of one another is as fellow member of an American society.

Since we all play a role in the roles we play in society, if we demand good citizenshipping from each of us, we can hold all of us accountable by community power. We can define citizenshipping as our way of being and behaving to have harmony and humanitarian experiences. Dignity needs liberty. Fellow humans, we need the economy power to eliminate the chasm between the haves and have not groups. We need it not to allow the new technologies to sort us into opposing sides and classes. Citizenshipping at the micro, meso, and macro level is a bridge between people power and economy power. The powers exist to serve us in making society better, not worsened. We must not allow the economy power to corrupt the polity power. We must not let these two to collude to pilot our ship. They will ignore us. They will make a helicopter named plutocracy to cross the digital divide, and leave half of us behind. This is what doomerism will do to our future generations. Is it the vision we desire for the posterity of our republic?

The economy power is a force of good when it seeks to benefit our species' survival, living, and thriving, but it creates tremendous temptations in the HM^5 and the $FILMS^2$ [P7] of the societal and social powers. Without virtue as our spine, without honor for honesty, we will see authority holders concentrate, corrupt, and amass power. We the everyday people must rise to the leadership of the moment and assume the necessary posture to orchestrate a truly American society. We then as result of all our personal, vocational, and professional choices and actions must prevent it from failing to perform as best as possible. If we sit idly by and allow history to happen to us, we will lose out. Power always seeks singularization and accumulation. We must continuously divide it to keep it in check and balanced. Our liberty depends on this. We must be virtuous in our daily lives to enable the best successes freedom can bring to all.

We cannot allow our freedom to create and innovate become restricted. The hoarders of power will seek to put us in the cages of their preferred customs. They will sell us social norms, folkways, and mores that destroy our freedom but enhance their power. They will divide us. They will do everything to protect the status quo they control. Power corrupts those who love it more than they do people. They threaten democracy. Since they capture it for their own interests alone, they do not benefit society. We must benefit society. We can, by not imitating the baby doomers. Do not emulate the loomers, groomers, zoomers, roomers nor doomers. They are destroying American society's foundations. If we become a population comfortable with deceit, we dissolve the construct of self-evident truths, the basis of our social compact. We cannot uphold hope for a better tomorrow for our children without it. Doomerism encourages dishonesty. Reject it now, so we can save our ship and remove ourselves from the current crises. Do not be misguided as a majority of the boomers became.

Within these five epochs (Colonial, Revolutionary, Civil War, Great Power, and Millennial) of non-indigenous (Europeans, Africans, Arabs, and Asians) in North America, three fully overlap with the constituted nation of the USE (see Figure 5-6). Within these three (Civil War, Great Power, and Millennial), eight generations have passed. Within each epoch, the living generations (see Figure 5-4) are like a constellation of stars, each with its own presence within the overall society. In some, one dominant generation might possess more control over the levers of societal powers than the others. The dominance of the baby boomers is showing its results as we end the millennial epoch. History is about to turn us into a different wind and we need to go in a healthier direction than the one they were taking us. We need to accelerate that turning before it is too late for us, for democracy, for liberty, for the republic, and for earth's ecology. We rely on geography power but must not disturb it to the point that it wants to rid the planet of us. An organism cornered fights back. We should not commit ecological suicide. Liberty needs not stupidity but creativity. Admitting a problem needs solved opens us to imaginative creativity. We should not argue over causes and fight about denial; we must get to work on realizing the jeopardy we confront from one generation's dominance. We must break their authority over the primary, secondary, and tertiary powers (recall Figure 3-2).

Generations form extant constellations

Many generations are alive at one time. Each overlaps in their experiences. Each wants society to sustain itself. Sustaining society through cycles of eras and epochs requires that people cooperate. This cooperation involves a good deal of learning from one another. It needs tolerance among the constellation of extant generations. Using the history power, people document the eras and epochs as accurately as possible. Accordingly, we do so per the paradigms of the personalities of the age group writing the story. Many may have similar perspectives. A few may differ. Sorting out the truth takes time, study, and reflection. Different eras' writers rewrite the stories of past eras and epochs with different perspectives. Over time, through scholarship and reflection, new thinking develops. This is often more relevant to current times than past times, and this affects the past in different ways.

Some revisions of history make it look better to the present; some make it look worse. Rose-colored glasses ennoble it. Better optics shaped from the recognition of previous errors and omissions adjust it. When we find new evidence, we learn another perspective. Understanding many angles, we can triangulate on what we agree upon as the facts. In the marketplace of ideas in pursuit of truth, history sees itself rewritten as good, bad, ugly, or beautiful. Every new book adds to the high heap of historical understanding and applicability to the present and imagined future eras.

Within one's time in history, as it relates to in-the-present expectations for the future, families raise children. Some do it in ways from the past, others by trying new things. Child-rearing practices differ by generation. Differences in parenting and opinions on it come from different family experiences, expectations, and community practices, as well as from regional subcultures and socioeconomic educational attainment and income classes. They come from religion and religiousness and settlement patterns (urban, suburban, and rural). Many factors of such nurturing and a child's nature influence identity formation. Parents respond to societal trends while experiencing them, before written into history. By degrees of difference or similarity in the diverse subcultures of American society, children's experiences are lived.

Child rearing practices change based on perceptions of the times. Some generations' parents are more protective toward their children than others are. This affects the way the children's cohort deals with their time in history. Paradigms emerge in each generation's rising adults, and this adds an additional layer of adjustments in parenting shaping the history of a society. As is often the case, those with the authority to control its writing and distribution, publish the story of the past. These underlying value formations and generational peer group personalities influence worldviews. Some differ within a generation, but more so, congruence shapes conformity, which determines how a generation responds to the social circumstances and physical conditions confronted by it. When a majority generation is in charge of society because its adults hold the positions of authority, its co-horts control the powers that shape the society. The next generation of parents must respond to this shaping when they gain a majority of the positions of authority within the FILMS[2] [P7] of the societal and social powers. As shown in Figure 5-6, both the cycles in which parents reared children and those which experienced the forming of, and storming over, new knowledge align vertically with the recurring generic eras presented horizontally with their generations' experienced cultural situations' depictive names and dates of presence on a diagonal.

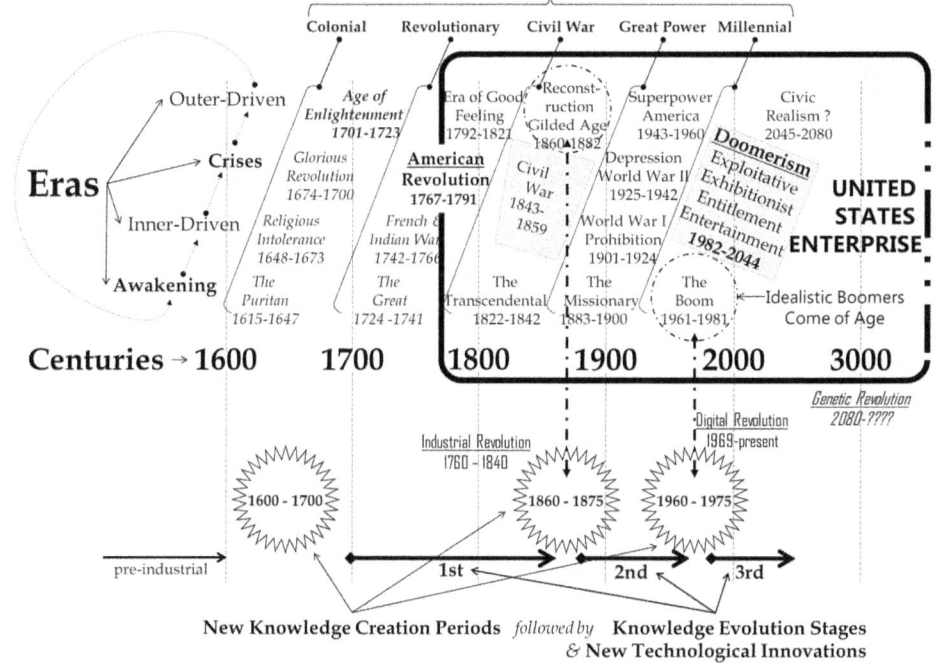

Figure 5-6: Historical Cycles of Societal Eras Interrelations with Knowledge Evolution

(Based on historical (Strauss & Howe, 1991) and sociological (Hage, 2020) scholarship)

The life cycle of a generation and the age at which new societally trans-forming knowledge and technological realities are experienced, affects each one of us separately and all of us simultaneously. Changing reality causes new and extra behavioral patterns in persons, which become recurring themes in a generation, and in the people. Sometimes we wonder if we are all really members of the same society and if that society is unraveling. If one generation holds power for too long, it can overly affect society beyond what other members of society might want. A previous generation's out-dated ways, means, methods, and values, especially if not community sup-portive, make disintegration seem inevitable. This is what doomerism does for each of us as a person. This is the theme of the baby boomer generation: social disintegration. American democracy culture and its republic need high levels of social integration, or we will not ever achieve the goal and attain the objectives of the Preamble. We must make real its visionary ideal ambitions. We need to discard "me first" as a generational theme, replacing it with "we first". We need a new civic realism that puts the power of "we the people" into practice at the micro, meso, and macro levels of society so each person can become a better citizen contributing to the whole community and in return experiencing the blessings of liberty that a stable society affords each one of us. Generationally, we must always work to perpetuate such prosperity yielding and commons supporting success for our posterity.

Generational themes layer atop the biology power-shaped phases of human life. Generations' identities form as people go through personal life development phases during broadly similar societal circumstances. Socially, subcultural regional variation and residential locality differences influence our socialization contexts. Generations experience living in society (from birth to death) with the same developmental phases of biology. All who live to be elderly experience five phases of biological and psychological life.

For most our lives, we are socially dependent on others: when we are babies, children, adolescents transitioning to adulthood, and often still when young adults rising in our independence. When we reach full adulthood, we get access to positions of authority if we've the right KA^4SA^2 with some exceptions in certain micro level groups like families. We become the adults in our positions of authority running the society by pushing the buttons, pulling the levers, and turning the steering wheels of the helms on the bridges in the pilothouses of the societal and social powers. We use our knowledge and apply it in our roles as an HM^5 in the $FILMS^2$ [P7] that $AEIOUY^2K$ the societal and social powers, particularly when we are in the middle (parenting) adult ages and mostly independent of the need to rely on others to support ourselves. As we become elder adults, and later awaiting-mortality elders, we are once again dependent on others.

Considering that we require help from others in four out of our five life phases, we need naturally social interconnectedness. Positive social bonds are a prerequisite for preparing future generations for success. Raising children to be prosocial is important to their being able to connect with others. Even in our middle adult years, we rely on others as collaborators at both work and play. We have teammates and family members. How it is that one generation, the baby boomers, could be so self-centered as to not see this? Have they rejected this human lesson of all-time wisdom? They infected one another with a self-fulfilling self-centeredness from their invented baby doomerism culture. That is how. They formed a "me first" identity. Imagine complaining about being responsible for taking care of a member of one's family. Imagine what that says about a person, a generation, a people.

Selfishness is immature. It does not make a society but causes a calamity of crises.

With regard to identity formation, a sense of peer belonging, peer group personalities, participation as a member of a generation, and the performance of one's roles in society, we gain experience as we socialize with others. We secure bonds and deal with conflicts between the generations. Here are the five personal life stages by age ranges in years:

00–21 = Forming/Storming of Youth
22–43 = Norming/Performing of Rising Adults
44–65 = Performing/Leading of Midlife Adults
66–87 = Leading/Teaching of Elders
87– + = Teaching/Waiting of Post-Elders

Within any given generation, these overlap. Among a constellation of several generations happening over time, they cascade one cohort above another. In this manner, generations overlap succeeding generations, each one entering the next life stage as other generation's cohorts depart them (Strauss & Howe, 1991). As one is entering adulthood, another is born (see Figure 5-4). Let's see how this generational passing adds up for our American society. Because what it means for "me" relates to what it meant for one's parents and one's generation as it rises into adulthood and positions of authority, the assumption of positions in society makes it matter to us, everybody else in society, alive or yet to be born. Therefore, generational personalities matter. We must conscientiously seek to understand ourselves as cohorts to recognize our role in the project we ought to be working upon together as a united citizenry.

What Does It Mean for Us?

What doomerism means for each of us as a "we" is a critical choice we need to make, and soon. If we want to turn out of crises and navigate on a sail plan toward our goal and objectives, we need to know what it means for us. In community, we must decide whether to ignore the pursuit of a true American society, or commit to it. We must determine what defines our 21st Century commons. How do we want to secure it, and what of it do we need and want from it? Our polity framed a society for the everyday people to be its leadership. Do we want to be leaders as persons in our own lives, and work with others to lead the FILMS[2][P7] that pilot society? We've many questions to ask of each other and ourselves. Do we want to deplete the endowment that is the USE so none of it remains to pass down? Do we want everyone to get a chance at success through his or her merit? Or, do we want success to become inheritance for a few families at the top, who rule the society? Do we want only a few families to rule over us? Do we want the best among us to rise to the heights of their talents? Will we cheat to block them if we know they are better at the job than we would be? There is enough to go around. We must choose to make a society for boon, or lose it to doom.

The power is ours to AEIOUY^{2}K. We the everyday people are the majority of the citizenry. By the belief in our culture of democracy, through the ways, means, and methods of our republic, we must take control. The polity was framed for us to do this. We've not been doing it well. We must with gumption climb up to the pilothouse, relieve the boomers of control, escort them off the bridge, assume the watch, take the helm, and turn the drifting USE ship around. It is our society to steer now, not the baby boomers alone, especially not their loomers, groomers, zoomers, roomers, and doomers, nor their bloomers and broomers as good as these two tried to be true to American virtue. We must alter the attention economy before it alters our minds and confuses us further.

Doomerism means for society a change in its focus. In baby boomer-dominated society, the focus is no longer on achieving the goal and attaining the objectives of the Preamble. It is on the manipulation of others for power accumulation. Baby doomers enjoy such manipulation. It can gain for them more than anyone else can. Dangerously for us, they have formed into an unknowing (and hopefully unintentional) oligarchy. An oligarchy, potentially a plutocracy, jeopardizes the republic and destroys democracy. Without democracy, there can be no liberty. Because the baby boomers are so self-absorbed, thinking of themselves as the greatest generation, they are blind to this reality. They cannot see the truth and have become a ship of fools* poorly piloting our society aground. We see this in all the social problems at the micro, meso, and macro levels of society. Essentially, they have misbalanced the primary powers of society, and they have disrupted the contributory benefits of the secondary and tertiary powers (see Figure 2-1 through Figure 2-11).

*This is the lesson Socrates gave by parable in answer to Adeimantus on the value of philosophers to a state, metaphorically presented as the need in a ship's captain to conjoin the "art of commanding" a ship with the "art of piloting" a ship. The art of leadership and technique [technical expertise] are necessary skills for successful sailing. Plato, in the sixth book of his Republic, records the exchange (Edman, 1928).

The Power Shifts Doomerism Causes

The most prevalent power shift is when the people power moves away from providing leadership, and the economy power takes it over while simultaneously seeking to control the administration of society. This leaves the polity attempting to manage the results. This is not how society is done best. This shift occurred as doomerism convinced society to change its focus and divert its attention. Doomerism, brought to us by the baby boomers over the past forty years, has changed us. We forgot about politics and practiced a different form of concern. "It's the economy stupid," articulates another theme of the generation. Governing was irrelevant. All that mattered happened at the shopping mall. We devolved from citizens into consumers. We believed the lies of doomerism. Its hyped-up consumerism focused us on materialistic achievement. We neglected our duties to our local, regional, and national communities. Fewer and fewer began acting in good faith to the oath to defend the Constitution. Arguments over the Pledge of Allegiance became more important than the Pledge's ideals. Our society became opposed to our constitutional goal and objectives. No longer were we serving the purpose of the USE, which serves us best.

This put the country in a less than opportune position to cope with crises that arose while the baby boomers sat in the positions of authority. The baby doomers among us wielded power for power's sake, getting drunk on it as if it were saké. Boomers tend to be (borrowing a British phrase for its clarity and alliteration) "penny wise but pound-foolish". They pinch pennies, promote themselves, and then pay themselves more for being so good at reducing labor costs. As others' lives are destroyed, they proudly proclaim "What a good boy (or girl) am I. I saved a dime. I am such a great manager. Let me put it in my pocket now as my prized reward." Meanwhile, the debt burden on posterity grows insurmountable. This attitude and behavior left the FILMS[2] [P7] of societal and social powers weakened and ill prepared to adapt to technologies arising from the third state of knowledge evolution.

One example of this is the non-funding of travel for personnel to conduct a practice exercise to test the disaster preparedness of a city. A national risk-management event, the scenario was a scheme of maneuvers to prepare New Orleans to respond to and evacuate from a hurricane. The decision to eliminate practicing the region's responses to a severe weather event was made because the travel costs for participants to gather were perceived as too high. An eventual disastrous hurricane cost the US taxpayers, $62 million. This shortsighted decision saved a whopping $15K. For saving the cost of a used car, human beings died (Heath, 2020).

Ever so proud to pinch that penny and pocket the rest, baby doomers' penchant to enrich themselves means their judgment is impaired. It makes them blind to the problems of the whole society. They have terrible tunnel vision because of their "me first" mentality, be it hidden from their own self-awareness or paraded around as a sense of entitlement. It makes them impatient, and ignorant of others' natural rights, human respect, and innate dignity. They always prefer to find the angle to get away with more than reasonably deserved. Their short-term thinking for immediate gain is poor judgment. To want always given a reward for self-perceived awesomeness is lame. Life is not a game. It's a gift not to be played with like a toy, not one's own, nor another's. It's to be cherished, nurtured, lived in freedom with liberty and justice guaranteed by a rule of law society. The baby doomers' hyped-up managerial abilities are a fallacious fantasy. Forty years of unresolved social problems and worsening trends in unfreedom experiences actually proves that as adults they've been mostly lousy with authority.

Eighty-Year Cycles of Equilibrium Turn at Inflection Points that Define a Beginning of the Next Era

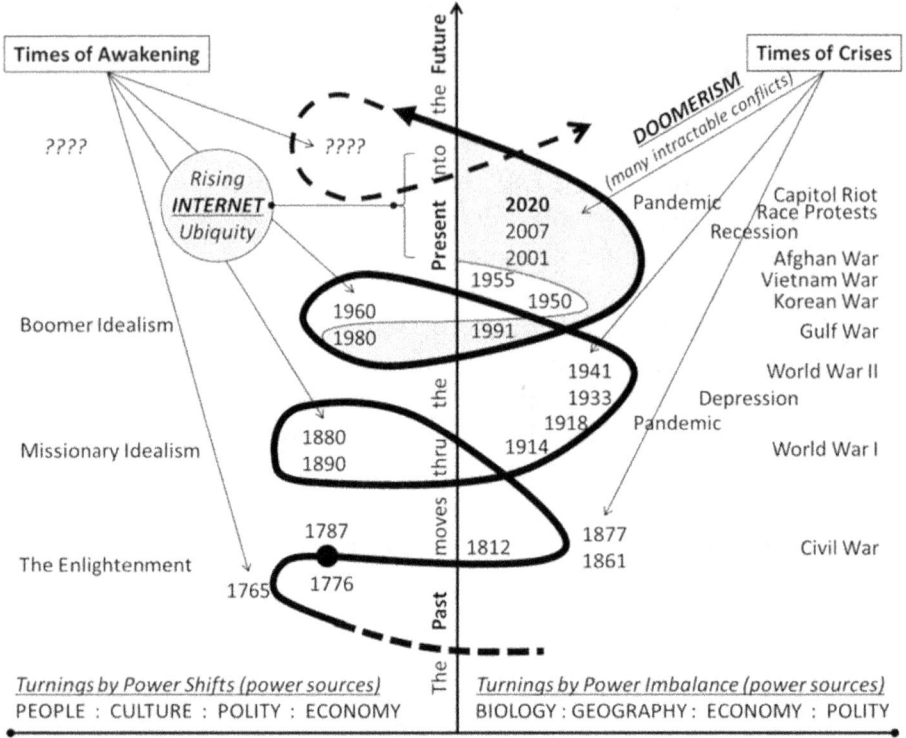

Figure 5-7: **Rhyming Spiral of History with Period of Baby Boomers' Dominance Shaded**

Above, Figure 5-7's Rhyming Spiral of History shows the period of adulthood and dominance of baby boomers in American society. Their period of being "large and in charge" includes many intractable conflicts. We cannot ignore our societal failures. We cannot now avoid seeing this "me first" generation's culture of baby doomerism as responsible for the poor performance of our project. Our chaos and crises are a series of strategic and tactical errors and omissions of doomers missing "the right stuff." Malfeasance results from a lack of leadership, poor administration, gross mismanagement, and the forgotten knowledge of what the business of the USE actually is supposed to be. Our LAMBS is supposed to make its ideals real. As future historians will write, these are the results of their misguided values causing American society to go astray. We see many externalities from their crummy commanding and poor piloting. Not surprisingly, because they are the dominant generation, they do not write of their history in self-critical tones and terms. Herein behold the truth told as in the days of old in a tome, a generational tale of failure that causes the sails of liberty to fold. Let us be bold. Let us hoist them up to catch the best winds from history blown by wisdom's whisper. When we feel the breeze of the best organizational ideas known for humankind, we will propel forward with the founders' endowment, the originating American ideals at our backs holding us on course toward our desired more perfect union.

Externalities

The consequences of economy power taking over leadership are errors of judgment. It can even lead to unhealthy exploitation. Such an arrangement of societal powers causes the polity to forget its proper role, which is to perform administration. Its administration is especially necessary for the development and maintenance of the public infrastructure, both social and physical. Under the baby boomers, both have degenerated. Of particular worry is the disintegration of work security.

The economy power leading society results in labor sources sought and found overseas or imported. Temporarily migrated persons too easily manipulated, controlled, and exploited teaches the wrong messages. Such bad behavior contradicts our value of liberty. Work insecurity puts problems on the polity to cope with unemployed people. How will new comers develop loyalty to our ideals if we violate them ourselves?

The economy power leading society results in monopolization schemes. It devolves sectors into concentrating on management efficiency, regardless of human needs. It presses for a restructuring of the business of society that only enriches the economic elites. Regardless of its effectiveness in performing its function to provide goods and services for the people in the society, it is not well suited to perform the function of leadership or the administration of society.

The economy power leading society results in financial markets getting protection from bad decisions. The economic elites bribe the polity's politicians as a mere cost of doing business, an expense they ask their accountants to write off in the books. It removes the responsibility to put resources into society. By eliminating all taxation, the elites remove themselves from the society of the working everyday people whose contributions make them wealthy. America had a good middle class when it had a higher marginal tax rate then it does now. It now gets less refereeing and policing of the economy elitists from the polity. In a string of clichés, robber barons like trusts no longer suffer forced competition when busted up, because we stopped doing that. Fat cat politicians with hat in hand get tithings for lining their pockets with cash. Upon failure, through their illicit misdemeanors and ill misbehaviors, these elites get politicians' promises to plus them up and issue punishment prevention insurance so their misdoings go unnoticed. Their erring operatives get lifted out of hot water before they boil in the crucible of open truth, honest marketplace competition, and real justice. They escape uncharged, without severe consequences, no arrests, thus no jury trials that could prove their guilt. Instead of jailed, the criminal elitists get bailed. This is not the intended American way.

The economy power leading society enables public relations advertising (artistry power) abuses and misuses. It overwhelmingly shapes people's beliefs, attitudes, and behaviors. It disguises facts and hides the truth, so it can support power amassing and wealth hoarding, solely for its elites. This leads to the writing of history to its own advantage. Indifferent to facts and truth, it simply amplifies the tall tales of its greatness. It relies upon the psychological influence of Madison Avenue. It contorts conscience. It creates a new religion of consumerism. It reshapes culture (Ewing, 1976).

The baby boomers enable these externalities. Their increasingly shallow, superficiality convinces them to see life as a game, a competition to win and not lose. They've monetized and electronically motorized amusement and spectacle like never before. They worship themselves and the making of money to absurd proportions. They put on many awards ceremonies. They build more museums. They award super salaries to persons whom they make into celebrities and then worship them like a cult. They've tossed out the wisdom of the Age of Enlightenment, moving rapidly and unsettlingly through ages of entertainment, entitlement, and exploitation to enrich elites, and uninhibited exhibitionism to minimize and control the rest of us (see figure 5-8). Misguided by their generation's doomers, and stimulated by its zoomers who sought every possible new excitement to tame their boredom, the dominant boomers gave rise to a domineering culture of doomerism.

Doomerism is like a cult. Its figurehead lives in each person's own head. Ego and a love of money is its demigod and mythology, with fairy tales of rags to riches its justifying myth. Another fascinating distortion of doomerism is its effect on mainline religions. The formally God centering central teachings are contorted to comfort their tenants into believing self-adulation is a permissible form of holy worship: putting the person at the center of the universe, the consumer in chief, to whom all honor and worship are due. The DAMN of mythology power converts the holy into the servant of the mundane until the sacred supports the profane. Flipped on its head, to know and love thine own self-first as perfect is the new per-fused perfume of preached perceptions of false truth. Bathed and anointed in the ointment of doomerism, superficiality trumps spirituality by its narcissism. Doing so outwardly, without any gratitude for anyone or anything else and without deference to the gift of life, is not so good for society. It leads to disrespect and a reduction in appreciation for another human being's natural inalienable rights, particularly dignity.

Doomerism exacerbated the North's public-oriented Protestantism into modernism. It extrapolated the South's private-oriented Protestantism into a traditionalism that looks backward to when ethnic tribal superiority considered such beliefs justifiable by use of ancient religious texts. This pits

North and South against one another. It allows viewpoints contrary to the founding documents. Related to this, doomerism has ignored the need to continue to heal from the Civil War. We still suffer the pangs of it. The work begun by the previous generation's Civil Rights movement lay motionless, left unfinished. It is still a vital and necessary line of work. Instead of performing it, the baby boomers, when young, gathered to protest the authority of the government to fight in Vietnam. They missed half the point. In 2021 with 20/20 vision, we can say they missed half their historical moment. Having happened to have been hysterical hippie whole-wits against the way things were in the world when society handed over to them the wheel and levers to handle it, they quaked in its realty and managed it horribly as half-hearted self-servers.

Doomerism shapes employees' personal behaviors. It creates irrational groupthink and backstabbing. Its gross externalities require the people to have to exert extra political pressure upon the polity to prevent more risks to the future. This emboldens politicians to enlarge their polity power to serve as a police state, which too easily can be turned against us. We need to keep it small, and by our virtue in positions of authority in the FILMS^2 [P7], and as HM^5, better regulate the economy powers. We must prevent the ill effects of elites seeking to rule the world, meaning to lead, manage, and administer all things, in every society of every nation. The economy power cannot. Its incentives are not appropriate for it to do all three behaviors effectively. Power is best when divided, held in check, and balanced to the maximum benefit of all in a society. The will of the people needs better represented. We need to reflect upon what it means to be human beings and then express our leadership vision for a better civic realism and humane humanitarianism within and over society. Overt economic ambitions that injure human life and earth's environment are unhealthy. If we the everyday people are slaves to the economy, and this is the result of economy power misguidedly given the leadership role as its purpose in society (recall Figure 2-7). This makes for a very cynical vision for life on earth. However because it exists, it appears to be the vision the baby doomers prefer. Does this mean it is causal or correlational? They've been running the FILMS^2 [P7] and performing as the HM^5 of the societal and social powers for two score. Isn't anyone collecting the evidence indicative of the boomers' poor performance in these roles? Shouldn't it be assembled? Wouldn't it be useful to help future generations correct the efforts of the citizenry as it relates to preserving the ideals of the nation, and to upholding the Constitution? Couldn't it also tell us what not to allow ourselves and posterity to do?

Assigning the leadership of society to the economy power causes its efficiencies to eliminate options for people. Its operatives desire to stay in a narrow focus for profit pursuits, avoiding responsibilities to society as best they can. They seek to reduce any possible legal accountability for externalities caused by their approach. Their strength—managing for efficiency and profitability—is not appropriate for societal leadership. Society is not a machine. It is more like an organism organizing itself organically to its environment. It requires leadership more akin to gardening than industrializing.

Economy power results in people's demoralization as much as our elevation from being successful with it. If it infringes upon dignity, it leads to aggressive competitiveness. This delivers disrespect that causes a societally unhelpful and unhealthy zero-sum mentality. When consumerism is the reason for living, it gives false impressions about American society. It encourages immigrants to come to the US, not to become citizens committed to the vision of our goal and objectives but instead to make money. Money they send home. Rather than learn the truth of democracy culturally, they use the economic opportunity to build estates back home. This transfers wealth out of the country.

Doomerism ultimately leads to the economy power too easily manipulating politicians. Especially those insecure ones who seek to gain power in the polity for the sake of their weakling egos. They do so without regard for the constituents who voted them into office. The voters get manipulated and exploited. This is the most egregious externality of the economy operatives buying the polity. This activity most threatens liberty and the legitimacy of the polity, which threatens the existence of our republic. It undercuts, alters, and undermines the value of our FILMS[2] [P7]. It creates an "every person is on your own" mentality. It puts each person in warlike stress with everyone and everything else, all the time, desperately hustling just for a dime to get by. This destroys us as a people. It diminishes our democracy.

We must rebalance the societal powers. We the everyday people must break out of our daze. We must awaken from the drug-like, numbing effect of doomerism. The boomers put it into action by examples of misguided behaviors of their loomers, groomers, zoomers, roomers, and doomers, through a series of beliefs that are corrosive to our well-being. We must arise and intervene; we must vote out the baby boomers from our polity. We must further tell those of them in the authority positions of the economy powers to stop being uncivilly unfair and unjust. We must demand they stop seeking to control the polity. If we see that they contribute to campaigns through shadow means, we must stop buying their products. We will not keep the economy power checked and balanced if we willingly support empire building at the expense of our people power and allow the corruption of our polity power. We must keep them from extracting from all of us more than is necessary. We need the economy power to perform the necessary and appreciable work in provisioning society. But we cannot allow it to DAMN itself or it will bury us alive in debt and stress that sends us to an early death.

Internalities

The consequences of economy power taking over leadership of society result in an unhealthy society. Social problems and mental and physical ailments increase in the population. Much is the result of inequality. Inequality before the law and heightened envy of variable ability to survive, live well, or thrive, causes societal and personal stress. Difficulty in earning a sufficient, regular, dependable income places enormous pressures on people. Without jobs in which to earn a living wage, children are unaffordable. Having children is a natural right infringed upon if made financially impossible.

To make a society in which people cannot afford to have children is to tell everyone their lives are useless. If the sole purpose for existence is to be a worker to make the boss rich and not even dream of being a natural human being, we've a sad situation. We've unfree circumstances. Ought not life be about being free to be humanly natural, falling in love, having and raising a family dependably? Of course, if robots replace human jobs, does this not prove the point that people are unnecessary? What kind of society shapes itself in such a manner that people are irrelevant? Is not the point of American society to allow people to enjoy the blessings of liberty? Is not to live freely and be able to work hard to afford a dignified life the point? Ought not our lives to be lived to enrich us naturally, by having babies and raising them in families with joy and not strife and fear? If not, is it the case that doomerism leads to our demise as a species?

Doomerism causes inhumanity; it does not promote humanity. It results in human relations breakdowns. Its socially debilitating isms injure people. Arguing over them thwarts our ability to unify. We must no longer allow it to block us from rising up as a bloc. We must rise to our responsibilities to self-govern. Especially now, because Doomerism COIFFURE democracy and it CATAPULTED crises. We must not be of divided minds. Doomerism stops our movement to close the gap between the real society and the desired ideal society. We were progressing on this mission since our founding. Then, it slowed, some say stopped, others contend we gone backwards. Whichever the case, it's thanks to the baby boomers. Now we are far off course, our project drifts further from its navigational plan. We've lost our bearings. We must restore them.

We know this is true, even if we're in denial. It's because doomerism enrages people. It ignites ugly isms. It increases racism and sexism. It inflames economic inequality, criminality, violent ghettos, and the consequent police brutality. It disrupts the fair and beneficial to all economic distribution of wealth produced by the laboring people. It concentrates excessive wealth in the pockets of owning elites. It confuses the polity, destabilizing it with isms that injure its effectiveness at administering the law of society. To maintain the social compact, the expectations of citizenship, we need the polity to free itself from the overt monetary influences.

Doomerism also gives rise to political factions, which can be good, but in a duopoly create political tribalism. This yields a polity that demonstrates an inability to be effective. More nationally heard parties in our politics might benefit the discourse in the public square, where we should hear all opinions. A two party stranglehold on the idea landscape has detrimental effects on the appropriate expression of the will of the people. This causes a loss of legitimacy for the polity to AEIOUY^{2}K its powers. It gives more power to the economy powers' operatives to propagandize the public. This selling of the idea that they are saviors, while they undermine the polity and create unequal lives among the people, is a vulnerability risk we must better manage. The people, further divided, conquered, and turned against one another in the resulting scarcity need awakened and unified as a people to reclaim the bridge of our ship from the fools. The DAMN of societal and social powers we witness nowadays is a technique of tyrants to gain control over society. False scarcity is a weapon used against the people. A punishing artillery, it kills democracy. It ruins the best in us. Doomerism's celebrity super salaries for the few in authority positions in all social powers' houses, their FILMS^2 [P7], reflects it to us. Phony scarcity scare tactics undermine the culture of democracy, the foundation upon which our republic built it enterprising entrepreneurial spirited society begun for liberty and justice for all.

Death of Democracy as Underlying Culture

How is doomerism killing our democracy culture? The culture that seeks equality before the law with liberty and justice for all, the chance to live a life in the four freedoms, is on a death march. Doomerism is the brute that is butchering democracy. It is slowly eroding all trust in the public FILMS^2 [P7]. It is doing it by misguiding boomers who are the holders of the polity's positions of authority. It has made them forget that our purpose as a citizenry is to live by and for our first principles. When did doomerism begin killing our democracy culture? It began in 1980. Soon a fake blond sex-sells material girl was in vogue with rave reviews from an entertainment industry telling fairy tales to increase its sales. Doomerism will continue shredding the Constitution, ripping apart American society, and diminishing democracy. We cannot afford to wait until it seems too late to save it, to suddenly realize it, and act against it. It grows by the day as it shows its precept power process of culture to the world. What happens in the US affects the world. Our foreign affairs depend upon our not destroying our core values and acting hypocritically. We must begin immediately implementing an intervention to save our American project from collapse. Before the calamity gets worse and becomes nearly irreversible, we must enact better ACE everywhere, and we must earnestly in every way everyday go about E-SASSY-T-TUF-FT-CAUCUS as a people. We have the power to create the new day that is the old way of democracy. Put doomerism aside. It is a bad ride, a terrible trip that decimates the mind of the salvation ship of human-kind, the pragmatic saving grace with a safe pace of a republic, of democracy, with liberty and justice for all. Let's ask ourselves investigatory questions about doomerism.

Why has doomerism been killing our democracy culture? Because it can, it tempts people to power pursuits. Without lived first principles by the citizenry, there can be no democracy. Without representative democracy, the American republic will not exist, which is what those who seek to rule over others want. Power-hoarders want to be lords, slavers, like kings and queens, able to do whatever barbarity they want whenever they please, elevated above the "ignorant" masses. They need us dressed as paupers, so they can feel superior by dressing prettier in finer fashions. They want admiration and adoration. They live to enjoy the sniffing and licking of their own anuses because it feels good to them, and they love to be in power. "Oh goody, how good it feels to have power," they dance about and sing in their empty, massive mansions. No one will want to attend their funerals, but will go to keep an eye on the others eye-balling the thrones. We must stop them.

Where is doomerism killing our democracy culture? Everywhere it is, which is in our hearts and minds, and in our regions and urban, suburban, and rural settlement patterns, and wilderness environs. We'll see it spread in every one of our communities: local and municipal, state, regional, and national. People who've become slowly and steadily corrupted are unaware of their own corruption. It happened to them, with each little seemingly harmless lie they told. Alas, doomerism tempted them like a drug. It is a disease. It corrodes morality as a tumor grows and takes over an organ. Liberty requires morality. Morality needs reestablished through special emphasis on virtue in our society. We need to see our authority figures exhibiting it by example. We need to enact exemplary ethical performance in our duties. We need to hold ourselves accountable to the best ways of being. The game of the boomers must end. It's exposed. We can no longer pretend. We must grow up to face the reality that we've failed. We can no longer lie. We must regain the founder's wisdom and proclaim it as our truth.

We need our biology power to speak its will in each of us. The will to love and be loved, and to be and behave as best we can, as if we are being watched by a higher entity for compliance to our own consciences. This gives a real purpose to seeking the joy of being honorable. We should not feel anxious but want our consciences to be free of self-deceit that ultimately defeats us as an American people, one person at a time. If we ever want to be seen as exceptional, we must extraordinarily demonstrate the ethos, pathos, logos, and kairos of democracy. We cannot become denigrating monsters. If we do democracy will die. If we lose it, we will lose liberty too. Then, when we no longer have any freedom, for whom will there be blame?

It will rest upon us, and every person who fell into the societal foolishness of doomerism that deliberately devised the death of democracy.

Loss of Liberty

How will it happen? Liberty will be lost when totalitarianism takes over. It will happen when demagoguery becomes normal, and a tyrant convinces the masses that only he or she can save the country from demise, while simultaneously causing its defeat. It will happen because the citizenry failed to live up to its responsibilities and rights. Because out of fear, the citizenry turned to shallow authoritarianism, listening to enablers who for their own sake supported making a tyranny that will swallow the rest of us who want democracy. Lacking American courage, they will become sycophants (recall Figure 2-12 through Figure 2-17.

Where will it happen? Everywhere it is, which is in our hearts and minds, and in our regions and urban, suburban, and rural settlement patterns, and wilderness environs. We'll see it spread in every one of our communities: local and municipal, state, regional, and national.

The legacy of liberty needs revived. Let us hear from some founders what it means. Here are some original quotes (Alexander, 2014):

John Adams

Liberty must at all hazards be supported. We have a right to it, derived from our Maker. But if we had not, our fathers have earned and bought it for us, at the expense of their ease, their estates, their pleasure, and their blood. (1765)

Thomas Jefferson

Honor, justice, and humanity, forbid us tamely to surrender that freedom which we received from our gallant ancestors, and which our innocent posterity have a right to receive from us. We cannot endure the infamy and guilt of resigning succeeding generations to that wretchedness which inevitably awaits them if we basely entail hereditary bondage on them. (1775)

I place economy among the first and most important virtues and public debt as the greatest dangers to be feared....To preserve independence...we must not let our rulers load us with perpetual debt....[W]hen all government...shall be drawn to Washington as the center of all power, it will render powerless the checks provided of one government on another....Were we directed from Washington when to sow, and when to reap, we should soon want bread....The fore horse of this frightful team is public debt. Taxation follow that, and in its turn wretchedness and oppression.

Ben Franklin

They who can give up essential Liberty to obtain a little temporary safety, deserve neither Liberty nor safety. (1755 & 1775)

James Madison

[T]he citizens of the United States are responsible for the greatest trust ever confided to a political society. If justice, good faith, honor, gratitude and all the other qualities which ennoble the character of a nation and fulfill the ends of government be the fruits of our establishments, the cause of liberty will acquire a dignity and lustre, which it has never yet en-

joyed, and an example will be set, which cannot but have the most favourable influence on the rights on Mankind. If on the other side, our governments should be unfortunately blotted with the reverse of these cardinal and essential virtues, the great cause which we have engaged to vindicate, will be dishonored and betrayed; the last and fairest experiment in favor of the rights of human nature will be turned against them; and silenced by the votaries of tyranny and usurpation.

George Mason

No free government, or the blessings of liberty, can be preserved to any people but by…frequent recurrence to fundamental principles. (1776)

Thomas Paine

Those who expect to reap the blessings of freedom, must, like men, undergo the fatigues of supporting it. (1777)

Patrick Henry

Is life so dear or peace so sweet as to be purchased at the price of chains and slavery? Forbid it, Almighty God! I know not what course other may take, but as for me, give me Liberty or give me death! (1775)

What perpetuated doomerism means for society is an increased inequality among citizens. Egalitarianism stabilizes society. A loss of community and a lack of feelings of belonging and trust needs reversed by civic engagement. There is no longer neighborliness. Every person feels as if he or she must be out for himself or herself, without care for another. Conscientiousness, compassion, love, and empathy stabilize society. The woes of our world need attended to, but doomerism has led to a decline in participation in the polity. It led to disloyalty, dishonesty, and disgusting politics. Some trends doomerism began continue to conflate the US with an aggressive society. We'd been making progress to deflate the cruelty. We must not inflate the irate and inflame hate. Now, like a civilization in decline we see seemingly unstoppable crime, rampant violence, and constant threats of vicious and angry rogue persons shooting up schools and houses of worship. Domestic and foreign-born persons get too easily radicalized and enact maddening terror upon neighbors.

In doomerism, people are no longer serving nor served by society. In doomerism, the "winners" and "wolves," an elitist few, are trying to convince everyone else to be like them. They do this for their own insecurities, not for the society's benefit. A few are proud to be disruptive. What kind of culture lauds disruption as a business practice? Technologists dream of transacting new industrial revolutions. They fantasize about going from rags to riches, earning super salaries. They daydream for worshippers like vain celebrities. They want admired and adored, scooting about on yachts drinking cocktails. Does this myth work out for society? What a terrible story to tell everyone to put his or her hopes on. How about instead, we build a stable society that supports mom and dad raising kids honorably. How about, we pay people a decent salary for an honest day's work once again. What is wrong with helping citizens have happy lives full of human joy and simple pursuits that are good and common? What is wrong with a wholesome and rewarding life of dignity in its own right? Why must doomerism destroy truth with its bogus myths? It will sink us.

Unstopped Doomerism = Continuous Crises

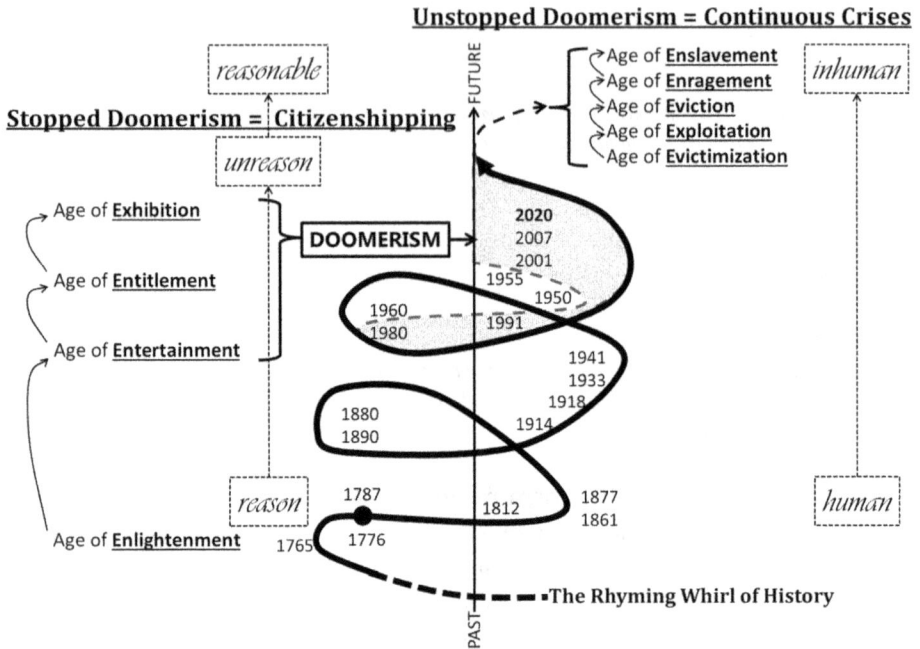

Figure 5-8: Unstopped Doomerism Trajectory
If we do not stop doomerism as time advances into the future, the devolution of ages will continue. If we stop it with citizenshipping, we can restore reasonableness to society and continue our project forward toward the goal and objectives of the Preamble.

To close out this section, take another look at Figure 4-6. Ponder what we must do. In it, the winds of time with doomerism on our minds have tilted our society. American society opposed tyranny. It made the United States into an enterprise. Our country was created to serve the people. Service is the mast. People are the majority population of a society. We are on top as represented by the base side of the societal pyramid being up. This is the reverse social circumstance in a tyranny. Who's serving whom now? Our society is sideways, blowing in the wind, with two choices from which to select our destiny. Either we the everyday people govern or we let those who seek to rule become our rulers. The latter doesn't measure up to the intents of the framers. The former requires we put in the effort. Doomerism dissuades us from it. We must prepare to lead society by grounding ourselves with better a better ACE.

We must retake and stake our purpose in a clear direction for service, of us to each other, and our polity and economy for us. If not, we'll tilt over on our side, fall into chaos, and more easily be made into a tyranny, within which we'll be ruled. If we fail, we'll no longer be able to govern (see Figures 1-1, 2-4, and 2-7) nor will we be able to recall the great gift of love that was the framing of the United States, endowed to us as our home. Before we turn the page to read "Section 3: Remedy", Let's have another look at Figure 5-8. It shows our current direction as a society, unawakening, remaining in crises and drifting into ages of greater cruelty for humanity at the hands of an emboldened greedy plutocracy.

SECTION 3: REMEDY

6. *"Let Us Stop It"*

This chapter tells us what we must do to stop doomerism and remove it from us.

The remedy for how to get rid of doomerism in our society lies within each of us—in our capacity and capability to think through what was intended by the establishment of the republic for the purposes of liberty in a culture of democracy. Can we pull this idea through all of our thinking? Can we interpolate truth into our own lives? How should we conduct ourselves, and how might we determine to help others do the same? When we begin to try to make the choice to be good citizens first, we initiate the ridding of doomerism. When we decide the public discourse should be about whether or not any action or activity by persons in positions of authority is supporting or hurting liberty, we move in a positive direction to get rid of it everywhere we hear it and see it—in the people, in the polity, and in the economy.

We continue to free ourselves of doomerism when in our own selves as citizens and gradually as the citizenry, we seriously live out daily the ideal American ethos, pathos, logos, and kairos. We do this by exhibiting service above selfishness, saying yes to the utmost full-fledged constitutionally allied united citizenshipping, understandingly synchronized (E-SASSY-T-TUF-FT-CAUCUS), making micro-level, meso-level, and macro-level commitments to do better as persons who understand that our efforts to support the culture of democracy ensure our own personal liberty, and that of our neighbors and nation. To lose it puts us into the battle of combatting tyrannies. Tyrannies were born in our society by power becoming imbalanced by doomerism. Its sway in altering how we apply, employ, implement, operationalize, utilize, yoke, yield, and keep (AEIOUY^{2}K) primary societal, and secondary and tertiary social powers. Doomerism has us off-kilter and out of sorts. We must break the "us vs. them" cycle of battles for control over who is "right or wrong," "in or out," and evenly achieve order over chaos (Schmookler, 1988). We must hold off tyranny in all its potential forms. We must rid ourselves of the conflicts of the misbalanced powers and the misguiding by doomerism.

How do we begin? Well, after weighing the evidence before us, we make a decision. Our first decision is whether the first principle is important to us, as persons and as a people. Personal opinions aggregate to a group's belief. We need not to allow the lies from those who seek to keep themselves in positions of authority, enjoying the raw pleasures of power, to fool us. We must read the first principles' initiating documents for ourselves. We must better understand the intents and tenets of the founding ideals.

Part of the remedy for our social circumstances that present us with adaptive problems as society transforms is how we the everyday people want to orient to society. Are we willing to believe in the initiation of the nation as a government meant to secure our natural rights? Are we willing to put our minds to the task of pursuing ideals, or will we succumb to the doubt from what history has been, or what has become of our country? Are we willing to seriously relearn the first principles and find a way to revive them in our daily lives? If we are, we must begin with asking ourselves a most important question. Is liberty important to us? If it is, we must intervene now. See Figure 6-1 below.

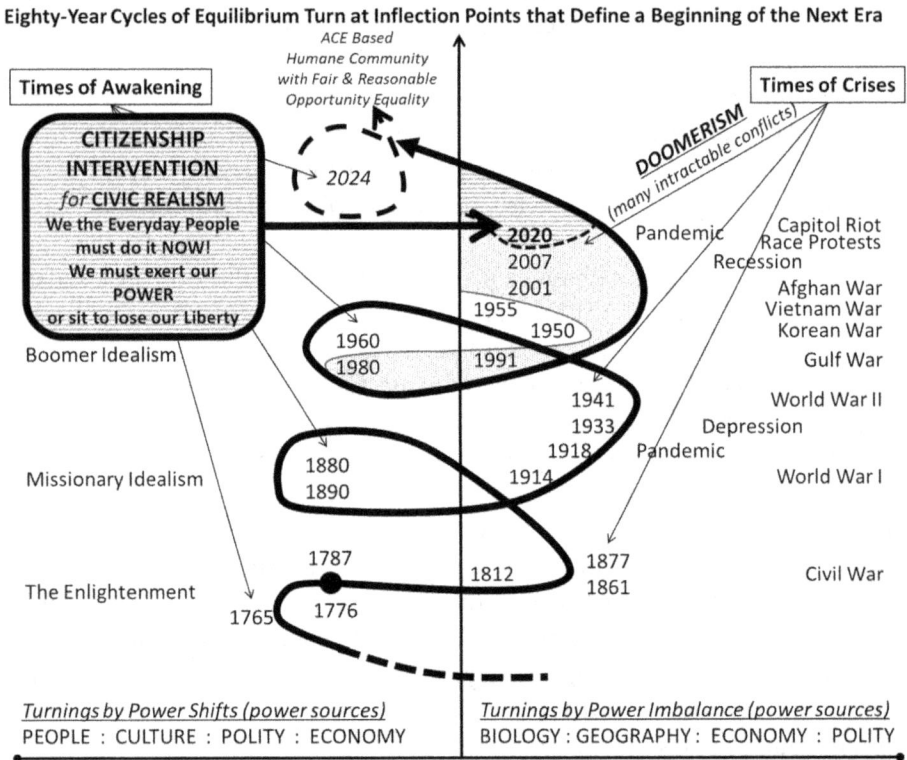

Figure 6-1: Rhyming History with Intervention Inserted to Accelerate Away from Doomerism

The American people are an aggregation of persons from backgrounds of diverse social norms, folkways, mores, beliefs, principles, and values, but we share the same first principles. Our core common first principles need reinforcement through consistent American civics education (ACE), good manners, and better civic engagement in civil society with habitual truth-telling and discussion to get us past the bad and ugly disuse, abuse, misuse, and nonuse (DAMN) of powers and move us toward the good. We need a determined, necessary contribution toward others and a real commitment to honesty, integrity, honor, and good ethical and moral character, no matter the circumstances of our upbringing.

For those in anomic and radicalizing socialization contexts, we need to get involved in bringing them up with the core values necessary to live freely, stay free, and be psychologically and socially healthy and helpful. We ought not to allow them to be seen as bad from birth, but as another citizen seeking to pursue virtue and reach a state of happiness and honest joy. For those in enervating socialization contexts, we mind find, free, and treat them therapeutically to support them to give them hope and belief in their deserving normalcy.

We must intervene. We simply must get involved and accelerate our love for liberty and for one another as compatriots in an historic opportunity to revive the essence of the ideals of American society. Our project needs our unselfish service. We can quickly remove the baby boomers from power by our electoral cycles. This will enable the imaginative younger adults to find the best solutions for their babies of tomorrow. Get our nation out of debt. Find new forms of work to employ everyone. Train them to handle the helm. Teach them the truth of the founders, and let them believe in the miracle and sustain it, without confusion over any of the isms argued about today. Let their creativity and teamwork lead to a more prosperous future through practical solutions to social problems. Let's stop doomerism and restart democracy. We will, if liberty is important to us. Figure 6-1 below shows the intervention.

Is Liberty Important to Us?

At the beginning of our nation, liberty was important to us. Bostonians named an elm the Liberty Tree. In the wars fought for democracy's survival, liberty was important to us. In the spirit of preventing tyranny, a more prevalent form of polity, democracy relied on it being important to us. When we make our 2022, 2024 and future electoral decisions, we will want to make informed choices that reverse doomerism. We must relearn what liberty meant to our founders. We must know it as they defined it. Freedom can be wildness. Liberty requires reasonableness. Nothing is more important for managing the risks to democracy and thwarting the threats to the republic for which it stands than a citizenry dutifully educated in liberty and well versed in civics. This requires civilized discourse, which creates skills for civil society, shared common interests, and neighborliness. The critical mission of our nation is to accomplish the establishment of an American society that binds us in unity for peace with freedom. This is our first job, our initial and eternal duty, to keep liberty alive and free, untainted by sycophancy. As viewpoints engender extremes, normalcy in the majority becomes endangered. Reality is imperfect. Yet by seeking to be a more perfect union, we can implore the use of reason and build community appreciation for the common task of citizens to insure, d'ure, ensure, assure, lure, and secure (IDEALS) liberty.

Figure 6-2 illustrates the concept of balanced verses unbalanced societal powers related to the ideality verses the reality of American society. When social forces swing the pendulum to the extremes of imbalanced societal powers, it brings instability. It is more stable when powers balance in a moderate posture. Equilibrium is more secure in the middle. Relate this to the diagrams in Figures 5-2, 5-5, and 5-8; Figures 4-7 through 4-10; and Figure 3-13 through 3-15. These last three are Chapter 3's societal debate diagrams. Imagine Figure 6-2's pendulum represents popular opinion. Envision it hung perpendicularly above the societal debates. Unswung it rests at the very center of each diagram. Debates attempt to swings off center toward one corner of the triangle or another. The further away from the center it swings, the more energy it stores from the added forces needed to reach an extreme position. This is destabilizing. The more unreasonable the posture of an argument, the further its drama swings it toward a myopic position in the acute angle of the triangle's corners. Backed into a corner makes it as imbalanced as its solutions would make society's primary powers.

Thinking about liberty—what it is and what it means to us—is an essential aspect of Americanism. Thinking about what we think with the help of the diagrams is an exercise in freeing ourselves from the present times and removing the blinders that we're experiencing from doomerism. It is upon us, and in us, and all around us, and we must free ourselves from it. If not, it will shape us into something that is the opposite of what we are to be as a citizenry of a society whose foundation was cast of liberty and framed with democracy. We are very far away from where we need to be. For forty years doomerism grew, distracting us from truth as the authority position holders fell into the hands of baby boomers' worst cohort, the doomers, who failed to resist its disease.

We can no longer allow ourselves to listen to their egos. Theirs is not an ethos that serves our intended logos, pathos, or kairos. We must reach deep into our subconscious and hear the whispers of the wisdom of the miracle of natural inalienable rights and the documents written so that we might enjoy the blessings of liberty. Let's run through how doomerism is pressing us to convert to its way.

THE PENDULUM SWING OF "ISMS"
IN THE PUBLIC & PRIVATE REALMS OF KNOWLEDGE USE

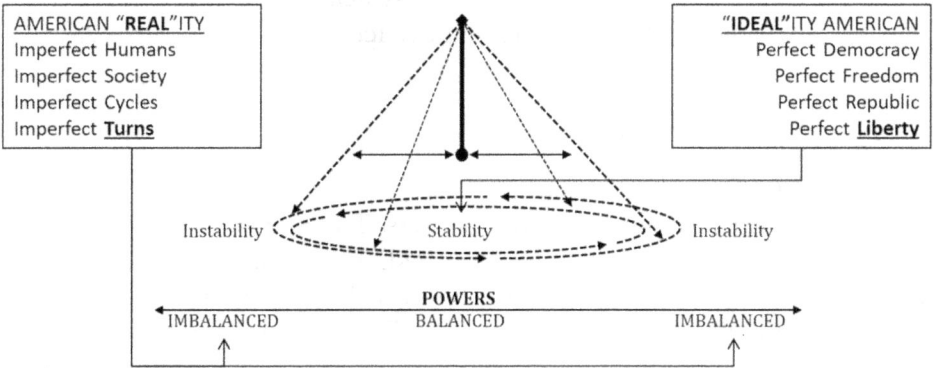

AMERICAN "REAL"ITY	"IDEAL"ITY AMERICAN
Imperfect Humans	Perfect Democracy
Imperfect Society	Perfect Freedom
Imperfect Cycles	Perfect Republic
Imperfect **Turns**	Perfect **Liberty**

Instability   Stability   Instability

POWERS
IMBALANCED   BALANCED   IMBALANCED

RISKS in being a nation made **ONE PEOPLE** of **MANY**
e pluribus unum
must be **MANAGED** with **KNOWLEDGE** not **IGNORANCE**

(main **threat** = division)   (main **opportunity** = unity)

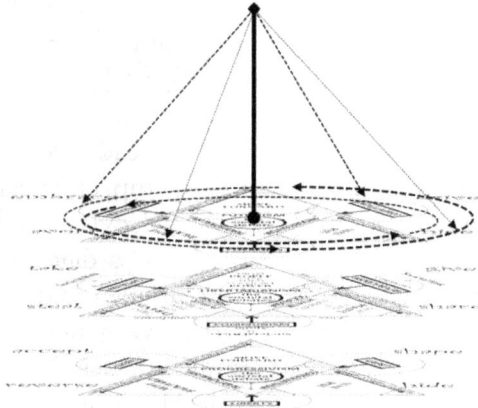

Figure 6-2: The Swinging Pendulum of Ideas
As society goes through cycles of crises and awakenings, ideas go back and forth, seeking new balances between public and private realms, between centralization and decentralization, between imperfect reality and perfect ideality. We seek equilibrium. Through E-SASSY-T-TUF-FT-CAUCUS, we (the everyday people) will produce the acceleration necessary to pull up, out, and away from the damaging circumstances of doomerism that have put us in crises. We will stop doomerism's negative threats to liberty that are causing significant long-term risks to the survivability of American society. With renewed "citizenship first" attitudes and behaviors adopted en masse, we as a people will help all persons take control of the pendulum of the moment, which is history in the making, and move it toward a stable center for our survival as an American society. (Those who do not seek to do this are baby doomers. They will remain a problem if they retain power. They contradict the ideals of democracy.)

We've gone on and on about this. Passionately delving into it to demonstrate a theory, we've persuaded truth to come to the surface. We did so, so we can learn to breathe the oxygen of the Liberty Tree once again. The dominance of the baby boomers brought danger into democracy. With the diagnoses of their errors and omissions now evidenced, named doomerism, let's remind ourselves that not all persons are alike. This needs said. While we can lump them altogether, that is neither fair nor helpful. Their generation per the math of statistics experienced bell curve normal distributions.

Kinds of Boomers

Seven broad kinds of boomers coexist: loomers, groomers, zoomers, roomers, doomers, bloomers, and broomers. To understand how their total dominance led to the devastation described, we've done so with deliberate drama to make the point. Such as, we've called all doomers looters. As we've said, not all boomers are doomers. We must if we want to avoid further declines, and prevent all their mistakes from ever being repeated, learn more how not to become or be like them. We've stated what we must do about our situation. More is to come on our remedy in the third major section. The prognosis is good if we take the prescriptions this book proposes as our remedy.

Having described the baby doomers at length, we'll leave them alone for a bit to tell of the other categories of baby boomers. As backdrop, put in mind what Landon Y. Jones wrote in <u>Great Expectations: America and the Baby Boom Generation</u>. This book introduced to the public the decades of demographic research recorded in academic journals. About the baby boom, they described its bulging size's impact. It caused many generational conflicts felt in society then, and now. Envision a snake swallowing a whole pig, slowly moving it through its coils, digesting it. Even before boomers matured into full adulthood, researchers said their bulge reshaped society. Boomers would become "the decisive generation in our history," one that ruled via a "generational tyranny." (Jones, 1980). Let's quickly go over three kinds of boomers, and then we'll tell of actions we need to take in regards to the other three. Yes, doomers included. They are back on stage.

o   The baby "**loomers**" are numerous, like threads in a textile, and boring. Loomers are less ethically ruinous as doomers, though they can be rather ugly in their attitudes and behaviors. Their doomerism is in advanced stages. They are more industrious than doomers, who principally exploit others to do work for them. Metaphorically, in comparison, doomers are the mob boss. Loomers are the sycophantic assassins. The loomers are dutiful to their doomers. The loomers are not prone to use others as cruelly, because they like being a part of the cloth of a group. They are less capable of standing on their own, and need to be a part of a fabric. They stitch relationships together that benefit themselves. Yet when told to do wrong or lose their place in the tapestry, they turn a blind eye. They will hurt another for self-preservation, even when it is actually unnecessary. They are willing to work hard, to put in the hours, and try to weave a meaningful life for themselves. They do get more connected and appreciative of others. It is to support their "me first" dependency needs.

o   The baby "**groomers**" are superficial, always trying to be looking perfect, like make believe, to feel good as they star in their own self-world shows. Their mantra is "look at me, look at me, look at me, now!"

o   The baby "**zoomers**" are ambitions but less capable of staying with one type of work. This makes them dangerous to many unsuspecting communities. There are not as many zoomers as loomers. They flit around always looking for something new to do. They want to have an impact to prove they are worthy. They are the wannabe "do-gooders" who as "go-getters" disrespect others by uninvitedly and unlimitedly defining their recipients as needy, as if they cannot see it for themselves that they are victims. So they could feel like they were saviors, zoomers needed such persons, who end up being causalities. Even when not asked, the zoomers zip in to give their perceived aid. They are like visitors to a zoo, seeing something they think is pitiful and thus must get involved. They do not mind their own business. They've purported good intentions. Of course, they want it reported, so they're seen doing good for others. It is fine to help others when they ask for help, but to force it upon them and make it a show, is wrong. It is an affront to their dignity and liberty. The zoomers' motivation is more egotistical than altruistic. They stir things up worse than they were before they came around. They often end up doing more harm than good. They declare a failure a success and then move on as if a hero out to save the day in another way with a new victim in need of aid. Those they earlier attempted to help do not get corrective actions to the harm done by the zoomers. A change in the nature of social circumstances and physical conditions can occur. Yet it may not have done those aided by the zoomers any real good. It does make the zoomers proud of themselves, which is the real reason they invaded. The altered states of others victimhood, is a feel good vibe for the zoomers. They never admit their failure or return to correct their damages and clean up their messes.

As the inheritors of the endowment of the USE, we need to learn and improve. This analysis can help. However, we must follow through with the transfer of authority to the next generations. We do so to be able to:

o   Leverage the casual benefits from the not so bad boomers, the baby "**roomers**". These are those not wanting full ownership of responsibility for society. They prefer to hide in their ego's abodes disguised by self-comforting lies about their purpose on earth. We can wonder whether they are naive or suffering the "me first" social disease, too. These are they, who were just going along for the ride. Did they because, they lacked a spine to stop the crimes? Or did they not want to get involved because they wanted to keep their self-interest orientation? Turning their back as a bystander was more convenient. These are they, who we pity with disappointment, shamed for the correlations we see, but which might get proven as causal, too. And most importantly, we must:

o Repair the damage of the bad boomers, the baby "**doomers**". These are those who live as "rent seeker" types, against whom we've railed in this book. We cast out with our ireful gripes and claims that aim to make clear that they own the causality for our chaotic crises.

o Continue the advantages generated by the socially good, the baby "**bloomers**". Few in proportion to the generation's size, bloomers are intrusional. They did not seek out others' problems to go solve. Unlike the zoomers, they are more inquisitive and cautious, so as not to make mistakes. They sought not to harm future generations. By being in the baby boom, they were already guilty thanks to their cohorts' shaping the generation's personality with "me first" mentality. To their credit, bloomers worked to form themselves into a socially worthwhile bloom. Like buds that open up and show others the beauty of being alive. Like ingots into sturdy rods, they choose to make a positive difference. They want to be helpful to furthering the USE's mission. Malleable by facts, and oriented to rebirth, they worked to reproduce a better future for everyone. Bloomers are special, a rare breed of humans, least affected by doomerism. Often we find them in dissenting posture towards it. Mostly, silenced by the larger crowd of the other boomers, we only hear a few. We the everyday people may see these folks as hopeful heroes for our children's future. Let's help them convert the loomers, groomers, zoomers, roomers, and doomers to the higher calling of making a more perfect union. Our hope is it becomes all the boomers' dying goal, even if it is only an egotistical choice to salve for their souls. We'll want them to go out the door with a pat of thanks on their backs. We want them to make a positive legacy before their end.

o Tamper down, redirect, and engage the baby zoomers to focus on teaching ACE. Enlist the loomers to pull in the other kinds of boomers to assist them. We've need workers in our massive campaign to help raise real Americans in the wisdom of our founding. The bloomers will be guides to them in this adaptive problem solving action. We cannot allow media as it is today to show them the way. Its manner is not supportive of a healthy American citizenry and society. It is currently a means of manipulation. It gets children to become consumers first, only, and always. A method of conversion, it convinces persons to worship brands. This distracts citizens from their civic responsibilities. We must unite with one another in community as any people in a nation to resist the dictates of doomerism.

o Publically recognize, celebrate, and reward the smallest in number of the boomers, the morally ethical baby "**broomers**", who work silently yet steadfastly to sweep up the mess their cohorts leave behind.

Well, if any of these seven kinds of boomers want to leave a legacy worthy of a good report card, they'll work to do. Most boomers did not shy away from work. Doomerism misguided them and once they've passed on, the history certain to be written will be unkind to them because in their time in charge we had crises and saw our unravelling. It will be sordid, unless we intervene with our biology power of love, embraced culturally and directed toward country. This form of patriotism will redirect boomers to take part in society in ways that build community; not divide it.

We're witnessing the occurrence of negative reporting about the baby boomer generation. Frustrated millennials raising their voices want answers. It could get worse before it gets better if boomers do not retire and let go the helms. This book explains what we must do to get through the turbulence we find nowadays. Let us hope the good buried within boomers will come out in retirement. They will need to work overtime to undo the damages their "me first" instinct caused. There is much societal destruction done by the doomers that needs undone. With cash in pocket, retired boomers should turn to volunteerism. It is a restorative act. Because doomerism is really squeezing us with its defeatist hopelessness, we need them to help us get at it. We have hope in humanity. We have to raise our children to have it. We must break free from the crises cycle of doomerism. Doomers inhibit real progress toward conserving a constitutional kind of life. We must persistently deconstruct and decline the ways, means, and methods of doomerism. We must resist the pressures of boomer made society. Let's move on to get more into this pressure doomerism puts upon us.

*D*oomerism is Pressing Us

Doomerism is pressing us to follow its ways of life. It is insisting that we need not worry about the foundations of the country. It does not want us to get involved in helping neighborhoods and communities. It hopes we don't take part in the political system. It is not interested in the complexities of life that we face. It prefers framing understanding in naive formulas, so it may sit above to reign and control our thinking. It likes either an overly simplistic traditional view of the world or overtly simple modernist opinions that we are smart enough to fix the broken parts of a society with systems management methods of social engineering. Ultimately, it ignores complexity or claims it is too complicated for us to understand. It snubs the reality of the labyrinthine patterns we can identify as shaping the tapestry of the whole. It lurches toward division, leaning on hierarchies of power and arguments of nurture vs. nature. It pushes unhelpful polemics through us and into the public square. It presupposes that all partners in enterprise creation must be opponents. Foolishly, it sells an angle that private and public agendas are incompatible. This is nonsense because they in fact combine to create opportunities.

Doomerism confounds us in the abundance and immediacy of the digital information age. Plagued by dichotomies of isms we must develop the critical thinking to contain them. We must now moderate the new extremes doomerism has created. The risks of the extremes expose us to dangers. We should feel doomerism as something invading us. We should notice how it grates against our core purpose, found in our once radical Construction. We should detect its efforts to undermine our democracy-based republic and reject it as a vile intruder. If we are to be one people of many, e pluribus unum, we must unite to guard against the wrong that doomerism brings and by which it threatens liberty.

Doomerism shrouds in doubt our core American beliefs and by cynicism (yes yet another ism), disguises the anterior, exterior, interior, posterior, and ulterior motives of the essential principles of our founding ideals the framers put forth in the Declaration of Independence and the Constitution of the United States of America. Here is how:

o Doomerism disguises the **anterior** motive of our founding ideals. Anterior motives come before. These, once pursued by the people, now hide from view.

o Doomerism disguises the **exterior** motive of our founding ideals. Exterior motives come out of the surface. These, once discussed by the people in the open, now hide from view. In part, this is because doomerism makes the people disinterested in democracy. Instead, it excites people with entertaining consumerism.

o Doomerism disguises the **interior** motive of our founding ideals. Interior motives held dearly make a culture of democracy. These, once celebrated by the people, see attack and feel ignored, thanks to doomerism.

o Doomerism disguises the **posterior** motive of our founding ideals. Posterior motives, after the first efforts provided a Bill of Rights for the people, include subsequent efforts for liberty's sake. Some who decline to believe them as ideal or real, deny these in the public realm.

o Doomerism disguises these original wisdom and human nature truths and argues that the **ulterior** motive of our founding ideals was to create a new empire. It presses us to disbelieve that the United States Enterprise (USE), a society established for the everyday people is actually ultimately for the likes of baby doomers. It seeks to mutate us into seeing baby doomers as ideal human beings for our society and persuade us that our purpose in life is to worship and try to be like them.

As a free people, we may choose to go along with doomerism and see where it leads, or we may resist it. This should not be a choice, nor should it be a slow unseen, slightly felt icky sticky, slide down into complete corruption. We should know better. We should prevent such a foolish notion for our American nation.

The idea that societal bonds build around isms is a fallacy. The boomers just like to argue, so they chose sides. The isms are less than helpful to us everyday people. We've too much to do each day to survive, to live as we strive to thrive. We do not need to choose a side and fight to be right, even if proven wrong, which only ever supports one elitist group or another. Perhaps they see us as pawns in a game of life they want to believe they play with skill, as it takes to win at chess. Or worse, they see us as a simpleton disk in a less sophisticated game of checkers. We should not be played by or mimic them. To be righteous in being right, all puffed up and proud, full of hubris, is not beneficial for us. Foolish pride is an inappropriate form of citizenship. We should consider this as we look to the complex future, which will make us all feel small.

In order not to fall prey to the predators of the digital age, we must unite in common purpose to comprehend the truth given us in the miracle of the USE—that all human beings are created equal and a society can be governed by the people for the people with the government being of the people. We need to stop referring to the government as a third person. It is we. It reflects us. It looks like the tumor that we've become, the malignant cyst of doomerism.

Do we want ruled by baby doomers? Will a doomerist society, serving only the here and now at the expense of future generations be our choice? No, ours is a democracy-based society meant to serve future generations. Growth is the process of preparing for possibilities and prosperity by our efforts expended on behalf of those who come after us. We are to keep it going, make it better, and pass on its best aspects. While we do so, we are to filter out and remove the bad elements that no longer store value or exchange goodness for us. By looking back to our founding, we find clues to an answer. We see an inspiring belief in a creed and credibility of those who sacrificed for the radical idea that the polity works for the people. Yet the person in the polity cannot see it as something working for them, which is what baby boomers have done. They've gotten it all backward and upside down.

As we prepare to conclude this book, patriotically we should be able to see clearly how doomers fooled us, or we're fooling ourselves. We should now be able to recognize in the societal and social powers' operative actions are done through the functionaries, instruments, logistics, mechanisms, structures, and systems created and sustained through shared philosophies, purposes, precedents, policies, processes, procedures, and practices (FILMS[2] [P7]).

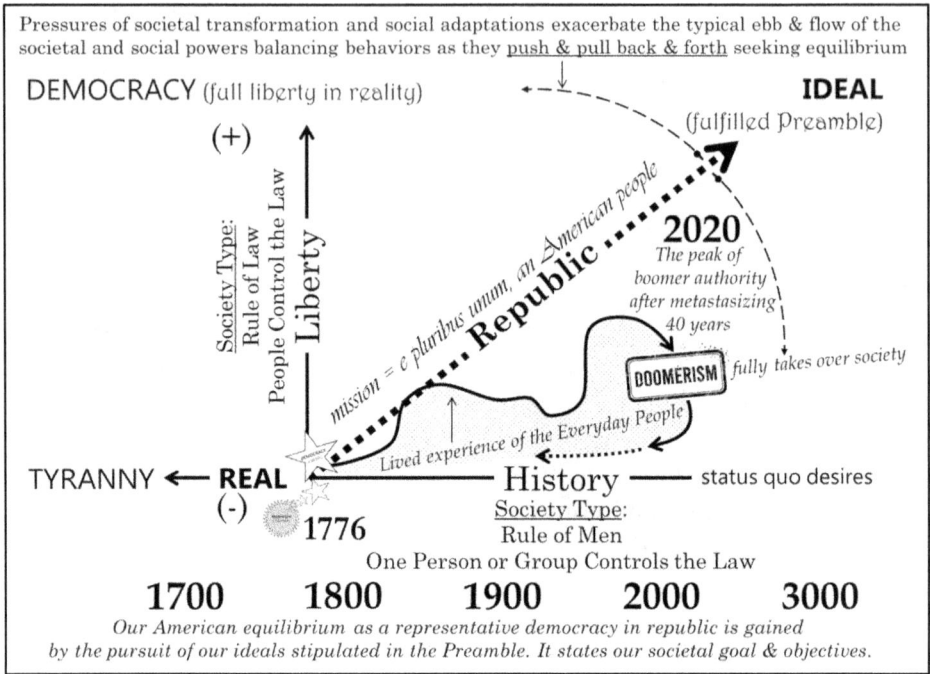

Pressures of societal transformation and social adaptations exacerbate the typical ebb & flow of the societal and social powers balancing behaviors as they push & pull back & forth seeking equilibrium

DEMOCRACY (full liberty in reality)   IDEAL
(+)   (fulfilled Preamble)

Society Type: Rule of Law — People Control the Law

Liberty

mission = e pluribus unum, an American people

Republic

2020
The peak of boomer authority after metastasizing 40 years

DOOMERISM fully takes over society

Lived experience of the Everyday People

TYRANNY ← REAL   History — status quo desires
(-)
1776   Society Type:
                        Rule of Men
        One Person or Group Controls the Law

1700   1800   1900   2000   3000

Our American equilibrium as a representative democracy in republic is gained by the pursuit of our ideals stipulated in the Preamble. It states our societal goal & objectives.

Figure 6-3: The Drift of Society Away from American Purpose Caused by Doomerism
A representative republic with democracy culture is a project. It is not an experiment. The gravity of Tyranny throughout history opposes Liberty. It pulls society down. Establishing an ideal slope with equilibrium takes constant action. We complete it by aligning a piece of our personal purpose to work on reifying the ideals of the founding. Our mission together is making the Preamble's words our lived reality. Not to do so is to be baby doomer. Our republic like all projects has a primary goal & objectives to achieve. If we are not living a way that enhances all babies' chances, we are not being good citizens, to our own disadvantage. Poorly done micro-level citizenshipping causes negative effects in meso-level ethical performance. These reflect in macro-level perceptions of the course of society. In every one of us, society has a relationship with history and visions of its future. The nature of society is the nature of humans. If we aim low, it's going to wallow, and possibly implode. It we aim high, it's going to bestow its endowments onward, lifting us upwards. However, it takes courage and commitment. Liberty is a deep desire buried under learned conditioning of how things had to get done. Minds changed in 1776. Many things got done as they had been, but then there was a new attitude. A vision for a new world challenged thinking that favored the comfort of the status quo. Over time, people advanced the project. But, the society drifted into impropriety. Then it got sick with doomerism, a societal, social, and personal impairment. Our mind's eye blocked, we no longer saw the glorious vision of the Liberty Tree. People, it needs illuminated by the billion points of light our love for this republic supply. We can remove this doom cancer from us, from our communities, and from our society. We will realize the benefits of the Preamble. By adjusting our mindset to commit life to making the founding ideals our lived reality. We'll alter this era's course. We will complete our project. By E-SASSY-T-TUF-FT-CAUCUS, we'll return our republic to its glory bound voyage.

Culture is the medium of their activities. As if by an "invisible mind", it shapes their thinking. We should now be able to recognize the errors and omissions caused in the leadership, administration, and management of the business of society (LAMBS) by the operative actions in culture by persons in authority positions in the FILMS[2] [P7] in the ways, means, and methods of baby doomerism.

Look at Figure 6-3 above. It shows the rise of liberty against the status quo of history with our trajectory toward the ideal state of affairs for humanity along the line of a republic founded with a democracy culture, below which is our project's performance squiggle. We now head backwards and downwards toward the asymptote of tyranny thanks to doomerism. Make no mistake. Doomerism's impact on liberty in the USE is real, even if unreported because of the blinders of seditious selfishness. We should now be able to see how doomerism misbalances the powers by manipulating culture. This causes the DAMN of the societal and social powers. We must reorient these human made powers to serve liberty. Think about how each could do so: the people, polity, economy, mythology, academy, family, community, artistry, and industry powers. Work to make it so. We should be able to recollect how the cultural love of liberty got expressed in the Declaration of Independence and enshrined in the Constitution, particularly its Preamble. We should be able to realize how it led to the ideals of how to properly AEIOUY[2]K societal and social powers in ways supportive of our goal and objectives. We should see unification of culture, each time we advance in the correct direction, but we do not. Disoriented by baby doomerism we are. We see more and more disintegration than ever before. We should be able to ratify how doomerism it maladapted us to the powers of geography. It is also pressing for profits in the uncovering of the secrets of our own biology, which threatens our protected privacy (Harari, 2019).

For a society in which we might survive, live decent lives, and thrive, we need to repute the fact that perfect sameness is impossible. No two persons are the same, but we all are equal before the law. We need a society that respects our dignity. Sameness is actually, undesirable. Diversity in all things brings about the richness of novelty, interest, and ingenuity. Imagination depends upon variety. So does problem solving. We must refute the tactics of doomerism that disagree with creativity. We need a society that allows us opportunities to maximize our contributions to the whole and gain proper recognition of such giving. As they influence the shaping of society at the micro, meso, and macro levels, we need the societal and social powers not to destroy our potential but to enlarge it. We want to have a good life and pass down to our children and their babies the prosperity possibilities given us by previous generations before doomerism destroys our hopes and dreams.

The doom and gloom of doomerism's tumor denies us the chances to make this choice and endow posterity with the wonderful promise that is the blessing of liberty. We should recoil from doomerism's pervasiveness in each level of impact and analysis of society. It changed us too much. It altered us in some obvious, but mostly in many subtle, often undetected, but permeating, yet impermanent ways. We can change the culture. We can steer away from doomerism. It has caused precariousness in American society that harkens back to darker times in our country's history.

Comprehending Diseased Society

We the present rising and young adult generations must be the surgeons to remove doomerism from society. We must extricate its ways, means, and methods of being and behaving from our society while concurrently resuscitating the culture of democracy. We can no longer allow doomerism to displace liberty as our core concept for creating a better body politic and openly free society. Its growth like a tumor and cancerous dispersal is our aberrant malady to heal. Now revealed, we must get to work fulfilling our duty by E-SASSY-T-TUF-FT-CAUCUS. As was presented earlier, we should use the strategic enterprise risk framework (SERF) and concomitant risk management mindset to help us comprehend challenges in society we ought to confront as a united citizenry. From the perspective of a citizen, we must seek to create a nation supportive of liberty. We do this with a culture of democracy, served by mutually supportive citizens. Citizens live up to the necessary standards for upholding liberty as everyone's societal purpose. The purpose to IDEALS liberty is essential to creating and sustaining American society. We must wear the lens of a citizen to see American society for what it is not and for what it is intended to be. To know how to restore its best possibilities as realities for everyone, we must admit to ourselves what has become of us as persons. To be a people, we each must be more honest with ourselves. We must comprehend the lies we hide behind. Liberty and justice are the promise to all our inhabitants, but we must earn them through integrity. They illuminate the light in the lantern atop the temple. An admirable edifice sitting upon a hill at the center of a city, which fitting to its landscape is a place that declares to the world that a perfect union by an unadulterated arrangement of societal powers is possible. Democracy is for serving humankind. We must work toward it determinedly, repetitively, demonstrably, and encouragingly, or we will lose it.

Comprehending society comes to us from our socialization. It comes to us by way of our age, eras, and epochs. We learn through experiencing awakenings and by taking risky opportunities with new ideas and knowledge that prove popularly beneficial. We learn through experiencing crises, mitigating threats to our selves' and society's survival. We learn by living out our society's thriving attitudes and behaviors. Our personal regulatory, self-discipline, capacities and capabilities are a key to our understanding how to navigate in society. Whether by nature, by nurture, or a mixture of the two, each person can grow healthy or decrease by disease. Social abominations and personal abnormalities develop that further complicate each person's ability to understand one another. As we comprehend society, being able to tolerate, or better yet appreciate, one another past all our differences takes significant moral effort. It is life-changing work. It is human cooperation. As we study society, we begin to see patterns in its parts and can picture a whole. Such vision is vital to us getting unity. We need to communicate civilly to agree upon it together. If we do not, we distance ourselves. We hide in our holes, and we fail as a citizenry. Let's not let each other quit on one another, team USA. Let us confront the canker not with rancor, but reasonability. Let's listen to learn, understand, and know, not cantankerously compete to win arguments, then think pettily that we've achieve something akin to a victory. Tearing apart the fabric of our quilted society is a defeat.

The principal obstacles we face in visioning society are psychopathy and sociopathy. As we begin a new voyage to remedy our society and move to rebalance the societal and social powers misbalanced by doomerism, we must keep these ailments in mind. To prevent them we must dialogue better. Vain pride can be quite the obstacle. We mustn't stumble on it. The hubris of a "me first" mentality feeds baby doomerism's maleficent malignancy.

Half humorously, one might say dialoguing is not something the baby doomers have proven capable of doing. They have seldom been effective at it in the polity. Thus, we need them to get out of the way. We need them removed from positions of authority before we run aground. Haunted by episodes *Gilligan's Island* on television we know the unraveling shipwrecks bring. Did boomers not all watch it? Surely, they recognize the signs within their ways, means, and methods of being. Well, maybe not if their egos disconnected from their limbic intelligence and their emotions are too spun around their axle of self-adoration, psychopathologically. Baby doomerism is a social disease that confiscates, obfuscates, frustrates, fabulates, immolates, ulcerates, relegates, extirpates (COIFFURE) the culture of democracy and the tenets of American society as it causes, amplifies, tolerates, actualizes, promotes, underservices, litigates, taunts, embraces, develops (CATAPULTED) crises in our enterprise and its civilization. It creates the conditions in which psychopathy becomes tolerable. Psychopathy happens when a person's personality, the way they relate to other persons, exhibits poor qualities such as:

- Deceitfulness
- Manipulation
- Grandiosity
- Lack of conscientiousness, compassion, love, and empathy
- No sensation of guilt

These combine to result in often aggressive or violent behaviors toward others. The psychopath directs these at those they feel interfere with their ambitions, getting in the way of them getting what they want. Such a personal personality illness causes sociopathy. Specialists call it antisocial personality disorder. According to the *McGraw-Hill Concise Dictionary of Modern Medicine*, it is a disorder defined as one that exhibits a "pervasive pattern of disregard for & violation of rights of others occurring from age 15, indicated by 3+ [three or more] of [the] following [seven attitudes or behaviors]:

1. **Failure to conform to social norms** with respect to lawful behaviors that is grounds for arrest
2. **Deceitfulness** as indicated by repeated lying, use of aliases, manipulating others for personal profit or pleasure
3. **Impulsivity** or failure to prepare in advance, to plan
4. **Irritability & aggressiveness**, indicated by repeated physical assault
5. **Reckless disregard for safety** of self or others
6. **Consistent irresponsibility**, indicated by inconsistent work behavior or not honoring financial commitments
7. **Lack of remorse**, indicated by indifference to, or rationalizing having hurt, mistreated, or stolen from another" (Segen, 2002).

If these are characteristics of someone struggling to get along with others in society, and if they become increasingly more permissible in the "me first" mentality of a culture of doomerism, then we the people, one person at a time, must check and balance our own biology power. We must also control ourselves with integrity over any social power we AEIOUY^{2}K. We must do these to find ways to obtain good health. We do better personally and socially when we strive to fulfill all five dimensions of our health: physical, emotional, social, spiritual, and intellectual. We must learn the social skills necessary to begin the dialogues across the aisles of our different sides of issues that we all decry as impediments to our unity as one people. We can begin this discourse by describing the dichotomies and isms between us. We begin by discussing the perspectives of the extreme poles of ideas and concepts used to generate superiority by special interest groups. We work our way to the middle positions, where we may find points on which we can agree. With a common comprehension of what the extreme sides' desire, we can clarify a reasonable middle ground. We can move the discussions toward solutions. We can work toward a union that joins and binds us in the service of upholding the Constitution. Reawakening to it is a part of the cure. It is our guiding light, the purpose we must pursue, before the baby doomers' sociopathy sues us into oblivion. The diseased get desperate, and act like sore losers wanting revenge whenever they do not win. They will destroy democracy culture and the republic will go down with them. But they will not care, because doomerism is an illness that blinds them. Even liberty is too abstract and too social a concept for their hypocrisy to let them see it.

Yet, we simply must free liberty from the dim, dark sea it resides within these days. It like a fish trapped at the bottom; it trolls and trowels for life. The murmurs it hears are the rolling over in graves of its life-giving framers, our founders. We owe them all due honor to find it, not blind it with hyperbolic nonsense, and slowly elevate it. We must free it, uncage it, and make ourselves able to rave of its greatness. We can resurge it. We can urge it within each of us and pass it around as the social capital we must reinvest in civil society. Then as we example it with good civics and hand it out in ACE to our children. By this, we do the necessary work of keeping liberty free.

We must "rage against the machine," which has ravished liberty and damaged our democracy. The machine we'll fight fuels itself with doomerism. We the everyday people must not let our people power get polluted by biological and social powers' DAMN. We must become aware. For forty years, we've allowed doomerism to permeate our pathways, means, and methods of being and becoming. It's changed our national character's developmental habits from those that pursue virtue to those that tolerate and laud vice. In this 21st century, our ship is drifting to a land un-American; we must change course. It begins by us better comprehending "what's going on"; for which this book was written.

Clarify Society, a Byproduct of Philosophy

What began in the late 18th century, revolutionary "L"iberalism, became a way to organize the powers within a society. The primary idea was that people could self-govern. This gave birth to more citizen "rights," including a right to revolt against injustices committed by the rulers against the everyday people. The late 18th-century monarchy was the traditional way of rule of men, a "c"onservativism opposed to the new kid in town, Liberalism. The rulers' "rights" were to rule, by mythology powers, and their rights were protected by the police. In the 20th century, a form of "C"onservatism emerged. It sought to defend liberty from assailants and to limit government ownership and control of the society. To prevent the government from having too much power and control over people's lives, this protection for liberty also meant we'd need to ensure freedom to employ laissez-faire, our entrepreneurial and enterprising economy power.

In the 20th century, a usage of the term "l"iberalism emerged that adjusted and expanded the definition of taking liberties liberally. It pushed liberty outside its true meaning and original intent. This liberalism moved past the boundaries of the mythology powers' accepted perspectives of traditional roles of men and women and personal sexual practices. It opened the public discourse to allowing new classes of groups to claim special recognition and status. These special interest groups' politics sought to force acceptance of formerly deviant private lifestyles as tolerable when exhibited in public. This led to rifts among traditionalists and modernists. With doomerism, the rifts became open fights for "I'm right, you're wrong. I'm a winner, you're a loser." Narrow-banded perspectives on humanity polarized the population. The public realm became a boxing match as doomerism pervaded normal debates of civil discourse. This liberalism also led to the expanded role of government to do more promoting of the general welfare than had been sought before. It led to the making of a temporary safety net to enable a more permanent condition of survival, freed from the circumstances of an unrefereed society. The societal benefits were stabilizing. However, the continued expansion of the administration of life from the Capitol might lead to dependency, a sense of entitlement, and a too expensive government as parent and provider for the preparations of all things each of us should attend to on our own. Provided the economy power does not prevent us by limiting our capability and capacity to ready for the future, we should be able to take care of ourselves. The government helps us with our retirement income responsibility. But, do we want the polity's politicians to have so much affluence and influence over our daily lives? Liberty is not predicated on it. It needs fewer monopolist powers and a marketplace free of overbearing, dominant merchants lording and hoarding over others. For liberty's sake, a market needs variety. The more the merrier and the less the costlier, and scarier it appears from the history of monopolies.

The US Constitution got written to secure the blessings of liberty. It did not expressly discuss the economy power or its distributed inputs, throughputs, outputs, and outcomes. Early on, free markets and limited government unified differing regional subcultures and interests. The country's geography of untapped resources enabled more and more to enjoy the blessings of a good and growing economy. (Except the enslaved and immigrant laborers who brought wealth to those who overlooked the requirement to advance our societal project toward its goal and objectives of the Constitution: striving for a perfect union with justice, domestic tranquility, common defense, and promotion of the general welfare. Also missing out are those entrapped in a cycle of poverty).

In the 20th Century with the modernistic overlapping of the polity and economy powers, it became difficult to separate out the societal functions they each should perform. How these two primary societal powers comingle and entangle needs understood for the risks such arrangements harbor, both good and bad. This is very important. The societal powers need controlled to achieve the goal and attain the objectives of American society. To do this, the citizenry must learn to separate the ways, means and methods of our powers. When we know how to clarify by classifying and categorizing ideas put before us by the various FILMS[2] [P7] and helpers, merchants, miners, makers, movers, and marketers (HM[5]), we will be in a better position to lead. We must become conversant with the powers, ever aware that power tends to corrupt, and resist this temptation within ourselves. As citizens pursuing common purpose, we must also help others who are falling into it, escape its grip.

Because our society depends upon reason, we must pursue virtue. We must strive to attain a lifestyle in accord with the cardinal moral virtues. To these we must add the virtues for a free society listed by Ben Franklin in his Autobiography, summed up as "sociability under an aura of modesty", and the virtues for governing it as indicated by Publius, (presumed to be Alexander Hamilton), in The Federalist Ten (Mansfield, 2003). These will guide us to the discerning abilities we must possess to achieve our constitutional goal and attain its objectives. We need to be able to discern wisdom from knowledge from information from data. We must recognize and distinguish between propaganda and evidence, fact and fiction. We need to identify what is a public concern versus a private concern. This is not easy. It takes work. But developing our reasoning is critical if we are to play our role and perform our leadership responsibility in the USE. To properly AEIOUY^{2}K our people powers to the benefit of creating and sustaining American society, each one of us must do better at citizenshipping. We can by E-SASSY-T-TUF-FT-CAUCUS. This requires we learn how to, and commit to, sustaining virtue to have an American society. To help us do this, we need high competency at discerning differences in opinions and dedicated deference in factuality.

Identify dichotomies

A way to develop our discernment is to identify dichotomies and see ourselves along their continuums (recall Chapter 2's "Using Dichotomies" section). We can use dichotomies to frame debates about their poles as they related to our liberty and its ordination and establishment by the Constitution. We can investigate our thinking by pondering how and why we agree or disagree. We can explore our thinking by considering to what degree we want to embody one pole or the other. We can ask ourselves how one's stance on a dichotomy relates to any chosen identity or a pushed for polemic or politic. We can use one end or the other as a pole position for self and societal inquiry. We can do these at all scales of social analysis, the micro, meso, and macro.

Absolutes are rare. Nuances hold truth. Certainly, we have preferences for one pole or the other, and that preference ought to be a judgment of its support to IDEALS liberty if we are ever to realize the idealized American society in community with freedom and bravery. Many dilemmas confront us in the polemics of politics. Politicians cast issues in dramatic fashion, and the media uses hyperbole to catch our attention and sell their product. Social media entraps us in echo chambers of like typing others to give advertisers better outcomes, as we are the data givers that make these communication streams profitable for their proprietors. When asked to make a choice of one side or the other, we should consider that what might be in our best interest is neither pole, or a blend of both, or a choice not offered. Recognizing the polemic dichotomies politicians, profiteers, and pundits present to us is a big step toward gaining intellectual control over our own thinking. Sorting out the scale of the dichotomy and which societal and social powers we favor with more legitimacy—intellectual territory to overstep its bounds as its forces of operation—is another step. Relating dichotomies to the powers helps us see the forces at work in shaping society. When we see the misshaping happening, we must act. Misbalancing of powers is ours to correct. We cannot allow social movement to drift off course of the goal and objectives of American society. We must correct those in the FILMS[2] [P7] and the HM[5] when they begin drifting off course. While among them a few bloomers and broomers tried, but ultimately as a generation the boomers did not perform this essential form of cultural regulation. We now must. In double time marching forward, we will recover the lost time and avert the risks of an impending civilizational disaster.

Polarity gives opposites definition by contrasting one to the other. It creates a system that supports itself, which drowns out the possibilities for belief in democracy as an organizational principle for social parity and common decency that form the basis of a culture of human dignity and respect with moral integrity-based virtuous personal character. Disbelief in democracy leads to a disorienting tyranny of the endless debate in which a duologue perpetuates as both sides fear caving in and looking weak. Even if their pole position proves fallacious, felonous, felonious, or foolish related to the founding framer's written wisdom, proponents' egos might fight to fend off the truth and preserve their proud hypocritical hubris. Lies survive and facts die. Truth becomes unknowable. Failing discourse and mudslinging irrationality between entrenched, stubborn, ideologues prevents the discovery of pragmatic solutions. It blocks realists, who find such erosion in society a problematic situation. Diplomats know a breakdown in practical dialogue is a threat to the continuation of sovereignty and citizenry. Rationality of human interest leads to a condition of utilitarian peace that enables a betterment of society. Realism demands work on the project, the USE, American society, the goal of which is a more perfect union. Doomerism is preventing such civic realism. The inability of baby loomers, groomers, zoomers, roomers, and doomers to perform their duties of diplomacy and democracy is a signal to the nation that they need dismissed from authority and considerably re-purposed as volunteer ACE tutors. Perhaps they need treatment for their malfeasance to recondition them from the ailment of "tyrantitus," a cause of doomerism. Curing it might help them regain the healthy conscientiousness, compassion, love, and empathy that could return them to thinking of others more considerately. Eventually, they may recover and realize how to free freedoms from irrational impracticality.

Polarizing polemics over opposite opinions leads to perpetual disagreement and separation. It causes unhelpful ground-staking and flag-posting tribalism. This is the tyranny of demagoguery, a dilemma in a democracy. Whoever perpetrates it is not looking for ways to IDEALS liberty.

They are sustaining their position at all cost. They are absolutists in their ideology, unwilling to hear possibilities for finding a common place on which to agree. They are tyrants and not citizens. They seek to rule by being right, proving points, and then using their self-defined, overly zealous—righteous or physical or weaponry—might to get their way. They are schoolyard bullies. Once in control they serve the status quo. This is doomerism. This is not diplomacy. This is warmongering. This is not peace creating.

How can we, the everyday people, enjoy the blessings of liberty, domestic tranquility, a common defense, established justice, and promoted welfare if those of us working in the polity push perspectives that cannot be with certitude proven as supporting anything but status quo maintenance? Or, if we push platitudes and polemics that have been proven irrelevant and incorrect, or smother each other in lies, denials of facts when inconvenient to our desires, and ignore true proofs? What drives us to do wrong? Is it because of vainglorious pride, envy, lust for power, greed for money, or gluttony? Are we being complacent, slothfully lazy, either not using power appropriately or being wrathful in our abuse of it? All of these motivators of wrongdoing are unvirtuous. None intended for us as an American people.

A **SAVIOR P**olitician
wants to use **POWER** to
control **PEOPLE**

Since we are a democracy, we need our citizenry to behave so that we can trust one another's decision-making. We need decisions based first on being a good citizen and second on encouraging one another in this virtue. It is neither an easy nor a given venture. It takes effort to develop such character. It takes good ACE. If we are to sustain our republic in liberty, we must reinvest in raising citizens and training each other in American virtue. We must employ fully civics curricula for childhood and adult education. The appendix lists many resources for this endeavor.

Our human nature is vulnerable to the risks of power's corruptive inducements. Power can grow strong within our instincts and overtake our reason. We must be on guard against immediately listening to our instinctive emotional reactions of our ancient brain's amygdala. We must find solace in the wisdom of our common sense and evolved frontal cortex. It is the sense that regulates us to respect the dignity of inalienable rights and freedom of others. By not infringing upon these or removing them, we secure them for ourselves by securing them for our neighbors. We do not deny others, so that we do not give up our own. We avoid the risks to self and society of that ever-tempting tempestuous raw power enactment pleasure. We take humble pride in being a non-judgmental American of democracy in republic with our fellow citizens who like us would fight for our rights as we would fight for theirs. This is how valor for virtue and liberty guarantees us as a citizenry.

Citizenship requires thinking critically about our own thoughts. We must examine the information we consume and ask ourselves whether it reinforces what we are to be, as we are becoming it: American. Or are we consuming what we do so that we might become something we are not but might want to be, superficially? Are we trying to fool ourselves into believing we are perfect, uncritically? Are we trying to justify hypocrisy as acceptable? Are we now that weak as a People?

To work together to find a common place, a position from which liberty is protected best, is the goal that should drive our discourse. Not proof of one's point to justify a perceived philosophical pole of a dichotomy as best. If we believe our Creator endowed us with inalienable rights, we must then accept that it is so for everyone else. This is the foundational creed of our country. Our Constitution requires we support, defend, and live by such first principles. If we do not believe that our rights are ours by nature, we have fallen far away from the original tenet of American society. Our core belief leads to unity when we hold it as self-evident. It is in the culture of democracy immutable, unchangeable, a permanent wisdom for our citizenry. It is our purpose for being free. We must protect it as our truth. It is grounding for people power. Without it, we the everyday people will have no power. We must guard it as sacred to American society.

Otherwise, we become like every other society, the majority of which never had these principles provided to them and live in daily tyranny in micro, meso, and macro ways. Oh say can we see, is America different? It sprung from different seeds. It is to be a tree like no other polity before it. Being so rare, it must be more vigilantly protected. This protection begins with a remembrance of what its first principles mean. What they mean to be and mean for us to become is purposeful. A solid ACE will teach them again. We have a purpose to prove the possibilities of prosperity for posterity by providing proof of virtue making a more perfect society. In this pursuit of what is rightful and admirable, of our life's purpose through contributory citizenship, better brain and body chemistry persists. It helps us feel free and resist the tempting forms of tyranny, one of which is the dichotomous "my belief is right, your belief is wrong." Many beliefs ride the waves of the mythology power, a power that addresses the unknown, and of which we must be respectful. We must be mindful of the mythology power's influence over us and remember that we have no official religion. The founders feared such a thing because they saw its destruction when entangled with and wielded by the polity.

On mythology, for example, on August 19, 1760, John Adams said, "A Variety of Religions has the same Beauty in the Moral World, that a Variety of flowers has in a Garden, or a Variety of Trees in a forest" (Adams, 1961). The founders knew the danger of a monoculture of one religion. Freedom of religion, any religion under God, was perceived as a right of citizenship. Therefore, we need not have hatred for people of different religions. To do so is, frankly, un-American. If people are persuaded to have prejudice against others based on faith, we need to help return them to the flock of the American way. Our way is one of tolerance and permission to worship as one sees fit for one's own spiritual and mythological needs. No religion is anti-American. But misguided believers can be confused to be.

How can we keep from falling into such divisive traps set by those who seek to manipulate us? We do so by learning how to identify when one group or another lies to us for the sake of the DAMN of powers. Our job as the leadership of society is to IDEALS liberty through a pursuit of virtue. We must redevelop this within ourselves and demand it of others. This requires the use of standards. We need to hold one another accountable to living up to common standards. We need higher ethical standards of conduct, especially in those we allow to have authority over us in executive and supervisory positions within the FILMS[2] [P7] of our societal and social powers. Basic teachings taught schoolchildren brought in by the academy power need wrought by honorable people in positions of authority. How else will we be able to raise Americans? Can we if too many of our officials in our societal and social powers commit scandals and act like lazy liars? Whomever would we want to hold up as an example to our children if cynically all those who rose to the top to manage and administer cheated to get there? Those entrusted to perform the LAMBS within our USE must do better.

Identify the lies

We can stop doomerism if we learn to recognize when we lie or when abstract isms that sound big and important are just lies, tossed up dusty smokescreens to conceal one agenda or another that serves an ambition of the economy elites or polity politicians. To do so, we must find the motives of the discourse of these power applicators. The elites and the politicians might be working together to create for themselves cushions of oligarchy, so they might behave as a protected ruling class, supported by sycophancy. The persons who work in the FILMS[2] [P7] of the societal and social powers must be mindful of their citizenship responsibilities. They can be subject to groupthink and institutional irrationality, which looks at a narrow purpose that serves the power but has externalities that damage another part, or the whole, of society.

Authoritarian autocrats, plutocrats, and oligarchs will distort and confuse us with lies to hide their ulterior motives. They may intend to DAMN power for something unrelated to its rightful purpose. Perhaps done to have power create more power or obtain affluence and influence. Such ulterior motives would result in harm, too lately detected to undo the damage. This is a risk to society. We must learn how to monitor it and respond to it with controls, so we may prevent it from causing irreparable damage.

They may have strategically cunning anterior motives to put a falsity before us as something correct. We must be Socratic in our inquisition of their intentions. Their proposed use of power hides behind another power, the mask that is the first statement or face shown of what is being proposed or done with power. This anterior motive may be setting up the preconditions for another motive.

They may have posterior motives, to hold cunningly behind their backs something that they don't want us to know about it. We must be Socratic in our inquisition of their intentions, their proposed use of power that comes after setting up a situation that the posterior motive requires for its attainment.

They may have interior motives to increase cunningly within themselves more FILMS[2] [P7], by which they might acquire more power than is required for playing their parts. We must be Socratic in our inquisition of their intentions. Their proposed use of power to achieve an inner power action will give persons within it more personal power to control the whole power. These motives put my "self" over "my" team or "my" team over "your" team.

They may have exterior motives cunningly expressed outwardly, used to intimidate, to make their ambition the most important. We must be Socratic in our inquisition of their intentions. Why they say they will do what they propose may not be true. They may announce, "We are doing this to block you from getting what you want," or "This is our way of defending our interests against your interests, which are foreign to us and wrong." This kind of talk is not deliberation of ideas; it is immature and does not work toward a common understanding or purpose, which requires we achieve our goal and attain our objectives.

It is uncivil and not good for democracy to have motives hidden or expressed in ways that deceive or bully. When we sense such things, we need to call them out and call them to account for why they are violating the good order of debate that democracy requires. This is what transparency means. We, the everyday people, must stop the malfeasant motives of doomerism in our society. Our responsibility as the leadership of our society is to promote democracy as our culture, not deception. Dishonesty, dishonor, and disunity are disloyal to our purpose and defeat our ability to lead and achieve our constitutional objectives. We must speak up but do so properly, politely, yet forthrightly. We are the power of the people, and this society was made for us to enjoy the blessings of liberty, not for it to be converted into a tyranny by baby doomers intentionally, and the loomers, groomers, zoomers, and roomers accidentally, or incidentally by their "me first" mannerisms. We live to make the world a better place for our posterity. This is what we are supposed to be doing. Every day in every way, and each time we use power. If we do it correctly, neighborly, we'll only use power in ways comporting to the need to always IDEALS liberty in an American society.

Society, If We Took Liberty for Granted

We must understand power in its many forms, and the ways it pervades society. It needs directed in society to support liberty. If not, power will deny liberty what it takes to preserve it. Doomerism pulls power away from the purpose of protecting liberty. We should compare boomers' liberty-effecting value sets to those of our other generations. We must identify how boomers have interpreted, misinterpreted, and misapplied them. We must recognize the liberty related value sets boomers give and the way they describe them. Conversely, we should contrast boomers' liberty-effecting value set to those of our other generations. We must determine which liberty-effecting value sets conform to the next generation's aspirations and developing value sets best for civic virtues. We must estimate value sets differences and conflicts between the next generation and those of the boomers. We must ask how these aspirations map to our great project's mission to IDEALS liberty. We need scholarship to evaluate these differences for us, so we may design means to counteract further the ill effects of doomerism upon our society. We must, if we are to reclaim it to right it toward its purpose, the mission to achieve its goal and attain its objectives. It's our project to lead. Let's better navigate it through the way ahead, out crises and chaos, into prosperity for posterity, e pluribus unum.

Liberty, How Do We Revive It?

When the scholarship is in, we'll have the academy powers' vocalization on the history powers' record of what transpired in our society under the forty-year reign of the baby doomers and their complicit boomer generational peers: the loomers, groomers, zoomers, and roomers. We'll be able to determine how we may utilize them once they repent, if they ever can, being the absolutist ideologues that they are. Yet we must try to reintegrate them into our project team, because our mission needs all hands to right the ship and ready it for the voyage ahead, through the storming waters of the third stage of knowledge creation, as we take them to task and hold them accountable for the damages their negligence caused. We must further learn essential liberty and fervently teach it. We must support it with better ACE until ingrained deeper and better in the minds of the citizenry than the mercantile advertisers' brand knowledge. Let's have a look at essential liberty.

"Essential" Liberty

To gain good depth of understanding of liberty, we will all need to conduct our own scholarship and have meetings in our neighborhoods, communities, municipalities, states, and on the national stage. We the everyday people should educate ourselves, and others, through discussions and deliberative debates to find agreement on the truths that we are all to pursue as one nation under God, indivisible, with liberty and justice for all. We must engage in lifelong, continuous ACE. It is within our power and up to us as persons to make us one people out of many, e pluribus unum. Excessive wealth, materialistic consumerism, and unappreciated luxury distract us from this task. We must commit to it. We can, upon the common purpose of working to IDEALS liberty. We will, by revisiting regularly the Constitution and evaluating whether our society is achieving its goal and attaining its objectives. Modern theories do not serve us. Ideas born of historical crises and awakenings in our country's history are nice to know, but not knowing our intents as a society means they will get in the way of our aligning on our purpose. We must go back to the beginning of our USE, its first principles, and apply its wisdom to today and forward. The Appendix is a reference we can use to reacquaint ourselves with our roots in liberty and get on with an ACE. It lists books and websites that will refresh our memory on the importance of liberty to our founding and explain our progress made toward reaching our goal and pursuing our objectives during the past 245 years.

For now, here are some quotes to remind us. Let's begin with an extract of President George Washington's Farewell Speech given on September 19, 1796 (225 years ago). To draw out meanings relevant to today, brackets and bold typeface add emphasis.

It is important, likewise, that the habits of thinking in a free country should inspire caution in those entrusted with its administration, to confine themselves within their respective constitutional spheres, avoiding in the exercise of the powers of one department to encroach upon another [we have a duty to help our citizens in positions with authority to stay in their lanes of power and AEIOUY²K and not DAMN entrusted powers. We the people lead. Polity administers. Economy manages.] *The spirit of encroachment tends to consolidate the powers of all the departments in one, and thus to create, whatever the form of government, a real despotism.* [Powers seek tyranny.] *A just estimate of that love of power, and proneness to abuse it, which predominates in the human heart, is sufficient to satisfy us of the truth of this position.* [Power tends to corrupt; absolute power corrupts absolutely, making one who might have been a great person a bad person.] *The necessity of reciprocal checks in the exercise of political power, by dividing and distributing it into different depositaries, and constituting each the guardian of the public weal against invasions by the others, has been evinced by experiments ancient and modern; some of them in our country and under our own eyes.* [Doomerism is an invasion upon them and needs stopped by replacing those who have been in office too long, who have become blinded by their ambitions that no longer serve the will of the people, whose best interest is in continuously checking power by replenishing its office holders more frequently.] *To preserve them must be as necessary as to institute them. If, in the opinion of the people, the distribution or modification of the constitutional powers be in any particular wrong, let it be corrected by an amendment in the way which the Constitution designates. But let there be no change by usurpation; for though this, in one instance, may be the instrument of good, it is the customary weapon by which free governments are destroyed.* [Do not allow change to the Constitution by convenient actions without properly abiding by its means to manage any adjustments deemed necessary by the people, such as the amendments that have clarified the rights of women to vote and the civil rights of all people, regardless of their ethnic origin.] *The precedent must always greatly overbalance in permanent evil any partial or transient benefit, which the use can at any time yield.*

Of all the *dispositions and* **habits which lead to** *political* **prosperity, religion** *and* **morality are indispensable supports.** *In vain would that man claim the tribute of patriotism, who should labor to subvert these great pillars of human happiness,* **these firmest props of the duties of** *men and* **citizens.** *The mere politician, equally with the pious man, ought to* **respect and to cherish them.** *A volume could not trace all* **their connections with private and public felicity.** [We must develop moral habits to be good citizens.] *Let it simply be asked: Where is the security for property, for reputation, for life, if the sense of religious obligation desert the oaths which are the instruments of investigation in courts of justice?* [Religions that teach respect for one another as fellow human beings, which instill morality in persons, are helpful to society.] *And let us with caution indulge the supposition that morality can be maintained without religion. Whatever may be conceded to the influence of refined education on minds of peculiar structure, reason and experience both forbid us to expect that national morality can prevail in exclusion of religious principle.* [A love of God taught by religions helps us have national morality. We can bond by sharing a love of God, regardless of how we come to learn and know God. God is a symbol representative of what Providence tells us, that morality is beneficial to know and use in guiding our individual and collective behaviors as we support one another as a people in community, as each of us properly pursues virtue in search of happiness.]

It is substantially true that virtue or morality is a necessary spring of popular government. *The rule, indeed, extends with more or less force to every species of free government. Who that is a sincere friend to it can look with indifference upon attempts to shake the foundation of the fabric?*

[To have a free government of the people, by the people, and for the people requires the people to be moral, understanding this vital need of each-and-every one of us. We in community, as is done in properly exercised religions, must help one another be better humans as we develop and mature into a people who every day and in every way are E-SASSY-T-TUF-FT-CAUCUS, as "for real" competent Americans in the majority with respect for those in the minority as equals before the law.]

Promote then, as an object of primary importance, institutions for the general diffusion of knowledge. [We must educate one another and spread the knowledge of our free government, so all understand the duty to uphold the Constitution to keep the form of government we have and conform it to moral conduct.] *In proportion as the structure of a government gives force to public opinion,* **it is essential that public opinion should be enlightened.** [It is our duty to know what is going on related to the DAMN of power. By knowing this, we can act as necessary to preserve our free form of government and the society for which it provides the foundations.]

He continues with comments on relations with foreign powers and asks questions with implied known answers.

Observe good faith and justice toward all nations; cultivate peace and harmony with all. Religion and morality enjoin this conduct; and can it be, that good policy does not equally enjoin it [good faith, justice, peace, and harmony toward all]*? It will be worthy of a free, enlightened, and at no distant period, a great nation, to give to mankind the magnanimous and too novel* **example of a people always guided by an exalted justice and benevolence** [that would be us, how we are supposed to behave]. *Who can doubt that, in the course of time and things, the fruits of such a plan* [to be examples of citizens making a nation of good faith, justice, peace, harmony, and benevolence] *would richly repay any temporary advantages which might be lost by a steady adherence to it? Can it be that Providence has not connected the permanent felicity of a nation with its virtue?* [To achieve felicity, a nation's requires the citizenry to pursue virtue.] *The experiment, at least, is recommended by every sentiment which ennobles human nature. Alas! is it rendered impossible by its vices?* [If we live by our vices, we cannot have happiness.]

Less stress is more liberty. A lively life is not a life of always feeling defeated. Liberty means not feeling the stress of having to be on guard, always concerned, worrying that people will treat one another in ways that feel unfair and are uncommonly disrespectful, denying one's own natural, inalienable right to self-preservation with dignity. Stress kills. Hypertension, anxiety, etc. are conditions that don't make one feel free. People cannot "be" if they have too much stress from stereotyping, bigotry, racism, classism, all forms of prejudice, and judgmental attitudes and behaviors that seek to paint someone different as wrong or undesirable. To paint mentally another citizen a particular color based on some aspect of who they are: old, foreign, poor, crooked teeth, spotted, varied skin color, strange hairstyle or apparel, odors, bodily adornments, etc. is wrong. All of these superficial triggers that might cause some to jump into judgmental behaviors, to discriminate, to attempt to take from another person their freedom and demean and reduce them, only degrades the one who judges others like this in such immature uncaring ways. Cruelty exposes the perpetrator as the kind of person they are, a fraud. Citizens of a democracy who appreciate liberty would not do this to a fellow citizen. What makes doomers do this are insecurity and a desire for power, which is not what democracy promotes as a culture of peace that fosters equal treatment. Democracy is egalitarian. It is not the opposite "something" that produces inequality, tyranny. It is not that "other" ism that denies dignity, removes liberty, and makes people feel they are not free: doomerism.

Attitudinal behaviors that deviate from a true democracy spirit, cause impolite disrespectful things to be done to one's neighbors and friends. Doomerism is the "something other" that casts doom on the simple belief that all people are created equal. Our creed rests on this proposition. People are born equal before the law. This tells us how we are supposed to behave toward one another in our country. To give another person liberty is to have one's own liberty. Live for liberty. Know what it means. Don't fall into the temptations of power that can corrupt us in our everyday interactions with one another, especially if we think of those we meet as "other." Seek to understand with good will. Learn and be the best citizen a human can be. This is the opportunity of democracy, to shape a world of goodness in defiance of evil.

A loss of liberty comes when working for a living wage's worth of money to buy the essentials of decent survival requires all our effort and exhausts us completely. A loss of liberty comes when maintaining a decent quality of life with dignity becomes impossible. Such a quality was once affordable on one income per household. Why was this lost? Where did all the money go? Did a few suck it up and sequester it the keeps of castles as feudalistic aristocratic lords of the land, landlords? Is this what we want as a people?

These are the social consequences when the economy has too much control over the FILMS[2] [P7] of society. It causes two people in a household to work to maintain a social value once achieved by a single earner. A further consequence is that the neighborhood and community-based associations that typically manage the social issues in society do not have the human resources to help, nor the monetary contributions necessary to run them. These not-for-profit community organizations die when no money is available in the community because everybody is just trying to get by, or everybody is conspicuously consuming in some grand competition to show off, like a child bragging about their toys. These kinds of kids usually ended up having no friends and often became bullies. If no one can relax and contribute kindly, civil society loses its social capital of volunteerism and community building behaviors. Typical American camaraderie in support of free associations, the joining of concerned fellow citizens in a cause to better society depends on energetic citizens. If exhausted by working for survival, we cannot volunteer in such beneficially contributory groups that strengthen civil society and better each of us into wholesome persons, which contributing as citizens does.

The economy provides the opportunity for people to work to make more money to pursue their self-interest, which is perfectly understandable. There are risks of social impacts to the social compact should the upper classes see ambition as a manipulation tool. If persons get seen as tokens, ripe for misuse in labor markets of excess capacity, the high society wanna-be's will employ inhumane mathematical economic axioms to offer convincing justifications for exploiting us. If their decisions morph pricing of goods and services, making it necessary for all families to have two or more income earners to make ends meet, to survive, or live decently with dignity in a stable, comfortable lifestyle, then society could unravel. Then we suffer. Such an imbalance of economy power that rewards the few at the top at the expense of the children whose parents are always working is unjust to innocent babies. It makes moms and dads too tired to raise kids attentively. It disables them from supporting their children enjoy extra social community engagements as do after-school enrichment activities, which help youth develop into well-rounded adults for a whole life—such as artistry power provides in civilizations that respects every human being's dignity. The negativity toward family and children comes from a doom pending society of hyper-competitiveness, celebrated aggressiveness, and excessive consumerism. Further, it results in a lack of people able to support future generations by raising children properly to become citizens of a democracy. This because they are too busy working to make ends meet, living with sickness-inducing stress, or unable to volunteer from exhaustion. They may feel they have no choice but to hire people to provide parenting-like services.

Sequestering private gains from public goods shrinks society's functional capacity. Socialization services provided by charitably funded, civil society-based social organizations wither. Neither sponsors' funds nor workers' labor appears. Churches, clubs, and community groups that help children develop, dissolve and disappear because they receive no grants and everyone who would help has to work for personal survival. Alternatively, they end up operating deeply diluted programs delivered by unqualified providers pathetically pretending to produce results but benefiting no one. We must do better for civil society to optimize its life enriching activities.

Working to enable another to maximize their profit is less liberty promoting than working for one's own business. We must establish equilibrium in society that supports the future generations' babies' best possible development as American citizens who when adults will know how to properly steward the endowment of liberty. By preparing posterity's populations to promote the project's mission fulfillment and provide American LAMBS, the perpetuation of its blessings with bountifully beautiful lives will rebound and occur in perpetuity. We need to negotiate a pathway for this outcome and navigate persistently to keep on it. We must perpetuate purposeful parenting throughout all the secondary and tertiary social powers to make infants into Americans, not bad for all baby doomers. The perfect balance sits somewhere between serving the greater good of society and supporting the needs of the provisioning of society fairly, giving more rewards to the deserving but not at the expense of survivability for the nonearning. We need the economy power's great capabilities and capacities to serve people. We cannot allow its authorities and the HM^5 to teeter society out of whack, which damages the healthy socialization of children to be better citizens to sustain democracy to keep the USE alive and well, welcoming, and flowing with freedom's song.

This sets us up for shifting our perspective away from the consumerism encultured into us by the "captains of industry" who have become the "captains of conscience" (Ewing, 1976). Their HM^5 wrongly use immoderately extortionate mercantile efforts, particularly advertising, to change the culture intentionally away from personal and organizational industriousness to one of overly entitled conspicuous consumption. Persons become consumers behaving as overt spectators expecting things ("expectators"). It causes moral and cultural conversion of citizens into consumers. This change has diminished the sense of responsibility and pride in performing the role of the citizen. We must return ourselves to the goal and purpose of the founding and become the citizens American society needs us to be to put it in the best possible posture to make it a place that preserves our dignity as beings and promotes the possibilities of prosperity for posterity. We cannot allow a few to take it all away from us because they have succumbed to the corrupting forces that tempt our human nature.

Understand and demand liberty

Our understanding and demanding liberty will not hurt the polity. It will help it. Politicians, held accountable by the people, should lose their positions if they allow hard or soft corruption to direct their actions. If we oust them because they do not represent us well, this is as it should be. If they poorly represent us, shame on us for not paying attention and removing them immediately. Thomas Jefferson foresaw this good bloodless revolution as necessary every twenty-five years, which is also a generation's average length of holding power in a society. This duration is somewhat related to the human life cycle, in which one is not fully developed into an adult until around age twenty-five. Then, for twenty-five years, people in general independence contribute significantly to the sustainment of society. Contrast this normal experience to the forty years boomers have dominated society, and it gives credence to the theory of doomerism as a societal disease, a culture of the misguided that mistakenly misdirected the nation in foundation destroying mannerism. The boomers holding onto power too long evidences the failures that come from not replenishing authorities frequently and completely, at best every ten to fifteen years and at most every twenty to twenty-five.

Constant changing of the politicians prevents them from writing more laws that require more lawyers. Too many create a confusing culture for the people to solve their differences or even know which activities are legal or illegal. More laws increase the armature of lawyers and lawmakers, taking more power from the people than liberty-oriented polity, people, and economy powers would allow. Too much lawmaking converts our common law system into a civil law system, causing more prohibitions than permitted behaviors. Plus, it decreases trust by increasing distrust. Soon, in civil law, it becomes normal that one is doing wrong without knowing it; liberty is lost. If we behave better, more civilly, we do not need more and more laws. It is up to us to lead with virtue. We can prevent growth in our dependency on lawyers. We can stop society's drifting into one ruled *by* law through its enforcers, the police. We, using the rule *of* law, govern American society. There is a huge difference.

Our understanding and demanding liberty will not hurt the marketplace, the economy power; it will help it. Free markets are resilient and don't depend upon the greedy, manically moneyed elites to get goods and services to the people. People enjoy the satisfaction of contributing, of the meaningfulness of work, not just paychecks. The economic elites forgot this feeling after amassing more money than they ever could spend. Extreme wealth tempts with corruption, a moral blinding power. Fat cats don't see reality as it is lived by the everyday people. They are blind to suffering. Arrogance has a funny way of blurring their vision.

Our understanding and demanding liberty will create conditions more favorable for the total growth in knowledge that we as a species need to survive our global crises of technological threats arising from the third stage of knowledge creation. It will remove inequality in our society by providing sufficient wages, so that debt is not required to purchase necessary goods and services. Getting provisions should not bury people alive in mountains of future fees for bankers to mismanage, build mansions with, and then get a bailout with our tax dollars for their major global economy impacting errors. We'll be able to envision jobs that give dignity to people. Higher wages for the majority means more money exchanging hands; this is good for the economy. More financial transactions at all levels, micro, meso, and macro, not sequestrated capital by a few, makes an economy work better. More jobs and money moving around means we'll see less inequality, and we'll have more hope. It will mean more access to wealth for more people. It will mean more middle class educated knowledge workers will be available. More families that are middle class will mean more volunteers and charitable contributions locally in community associations. With more volunteers, we'll get engagement that is more civic, better for neighborhood bonding, with a greater sense of security and a better overall society. People forced to work multiple jobs, or both parents forced to work all the time to make ends meet, denies resources to these community-based social services and civil society-supporting organizations. If we don't want government to run everything, we need people to do it, but if the economy power prevents us from serving the community, then the externalities will be many and very damaging to the children. Worse, too often, social and psychological problems will end up plaguing each of us as we struggle to survive: avoid famine, keep clothed, be housed; and able to remain clean, sanitary, and act sanely.

Understand the Polemics of Politics

Our understanding and demanding liberty holds the polity politicians and economy elites accountable. It tells them to stop using propaganda to confound us. It stops doomerism. Earlier we discussed the use of dichotomies to come to terms with our own positions, and those of others, in a constructive manner so we might converse and find common ground. In this section we seek to remedy the risks to liberty doomerism CATAPULTED. Let's see how dichotomies relate to the polemics of politics. We must better educate ourselves on them. We must understand how they get used in games played on us that pit us against each other. To begin, we need to know how to map positions on dichotomous continuums and see which pole the politicians and elites are telling us is best, while remembering that what is best for them may not be the best for us. We need to evaluate their positions. We must reason, use judgment, and decide to agree or disagree. We must make our own informed decisions, and if proven wrong, admit it and adjust to get us back into community. We need community to get our project back on course toward its goal and objectives.

One way we can begin to understand the polemics is to create wheels of our understanding by combining dichotomies. With these, we can explore concepts by intentionally placing words in a position opposite our general perceptions—to force conceptualization of the whole as a higher-level concept than the binaries that preoccupy normative thinking. We can use binary polemic dichotomous diametric continuums to explain what we perceive. We can seek understanding by laying facts or fictions along these continuums. The poles of these continuums become the labels for concepts of our discourse, giving them symbolic meanings, so we can get past labels and understand what we really believe. This we need to do because we invest ourselves in meanings. The extent to which continuums' centers align is a measure of a society's accord or discord with a person's or a group of persons' understanding. The greater the misalignment, the more challenges understanding each other we'll face and the more discordant the society will feel to us. The more discordant the society, the more disrupted and difficult our lives as a people will be. This risky position is manageable and reversible so long as the differences do no fall into tribal hatreds. The founding fathers warned us to guard against human nature's propensity for persons to form factions against each other. Factions fracture society and fissure unity. That would be failure. Democracy depends on tolerance. Tolerance depends on understanding. We must seek to understand one another's perspectives. If we know why each of us adopts our particular polemics, we might find the ability to resolve differences. Some polemics of politicians are ruses to manipulate us for their elite friends who pay for their campaigns, and we must be wise to their disguises. We must pay close attention to what we see portrayed, really, and what plays out as if a dance of politics. We must know when a game is gamed with us. We must not hide the truth. If we do, it will bring about our demise as a society, as doomerism seems to be doing to us now. We cannot be such fools. We cannot afford continuous misunderstanding nor constant misleading by the misguided.

Society must coordinate understanding

To be congruous, we must coordinate our understanding across generations, across social, economic, and political boundaries, across regional subcultures, and across settlement localities of urbanity, suburbanity, and rurality. Understanding is a knowledge aptitude, acquisition, absorption, application, and skills advancement abilities (KA^4SA^2) matter related to the new digital epoch brought about by the third stage of knowledge creation. Knowledge in understanding society, whether we are in accord or in discord with its prevailing premises, needs gained. We can with the use of overlaying dichotomies. This technique can clarify our thinking on all matters of concern in society. It's a tool. It can support positive, understanding seeking, conversations among parties who differ. It can illuminate for one another, each other's' concepts related to the precepts of the country. In cases where polemics do not align with original intents for the republic, with the virtues and values of the Declaration of Independence and the Constitution, whomever is misaligned must be brave enough to give up their mistaken posture. Persons in authority positions should redefine their purpose to pursue unity along the lines of our founding ideals. This is not compromise. It is patriotism. It is self-governing to align with the goal and objectives in our Preamble, and propel our project accordingly, since this is our mission as a people, e pluribus unum.

The use of dichotomies is helpful when confronted with divergent problems. Divergent problems have no absolute solution, which is why baby boomers have been such poor administrators and managers in the business of society. They stubbornly crave absolutes. They also would rather only have convergent problems that bring satisfaction when solved. An example of a divergent problem is how to shape a well-planned society full of freedom. We as a species crave both predictability and spontaneity. This is our nature. We've a binary brain with its left and right hemispheres. Remember, our biology power resides in bipolarity, with a fear or flight instinct controlling amygdala within our prime organ that hosts the mind. One polemicist for the pleasure of argument would rather fight for "freedom over planning". An opposing polemicist seeking the same gratification would fight for "planning over freedom". Neither would want to recognize the necessity of combining them to work together. They would rather generate the conditions for factions, and this is a sad circumstance of what doomerism does to us. Its practitioners and sufferers refuse or ignore to listen and learn from the founding fathers' wisdom. It is usually just a matter of the measure and scale of each polemic in a particular temporary solution to changing social circumstances and altered physical conditions. If said, "freedom opposes planning", and planning is seen as an effort for centralized control, labelled a form of tyranny, it can be called something considered bad for freedom. We should ask ourselves, is planning negative for democracy? Democracy is the harbinger of freedom. Its absolute opposite is a society under total control of a central government. Planning is rational not totalitarian. Planning is good for democracy. Planning supports freedom in many ways. The transfer of power by democracy is planned for in the Constitution. Great architecture, engineering marvels, and organized activities require planning. The planning for defense enables our military to be ready and revered. That is planning. The planning for disaster response and recovery is essential to being prepared for crises and averting the risks of chaos that come without any planning at all. So do not let planning become synonymous with central control, totalitarianism, nor tyranny.

Baby doomers, with their polemical ism arguments, distract us so they can play their games on, with, and against us, which cast freedom as an opposite of planning and control, and planning and control as threats to our society. This is idiotic immature or intentionally distractive and manipulative. Their normal view is absolutist "this" or "that" assumptions. They do not allow for anything in between, which is illogical. Further, they pit private versus public, despite the obvious interconnectedness of such material and financial ownership types. Public goods provisioning and civil society need both private and public freedom and planning with some measure of localized control. To remedy doomerism, we must acknowledge, appreciate, and agree upon the degrees and proportion of planning and control that freedom and democracy need optimized in our daily lives. We need not driven to believe in only one side of the polemic or the other as correct. The success we get also rests on how well we collaborate and balance the factual partnership of the private and public aspects of our enterprise to maximize the benefit for the majority of the citizenry, without leaving any-one out of society. This is what our representatives in our polity ought to be doing every day. Instead, it seems they spend their time figuring out how to find campaign funding. They use soundbites to sound good and distrac-tions to make opponents seem bad, in hopes they might persuade voters to donate cash to pay their next campaign to remain in power. This doomeris-tic behavior is a stain on our history in the making. We will be ashamed for having allowed it to be the way of our elections for the past forty years, and for it having gotten worse when the boomer cohort was at its maximum domain of reign.

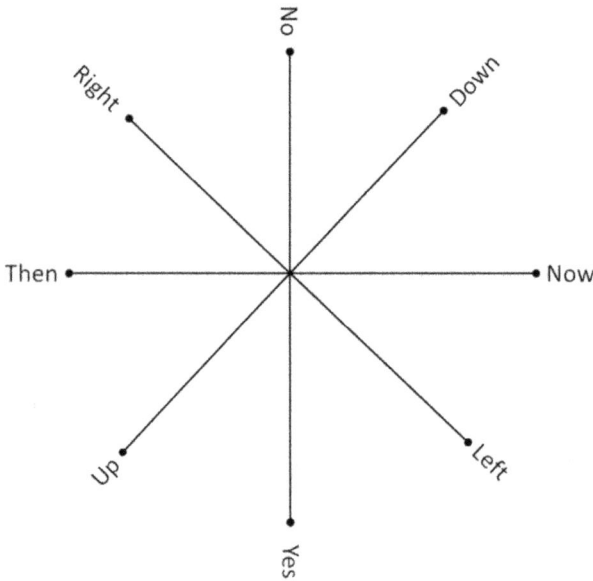

Figure 6-4: Dichotomous Continuums—A Means to Evaluate Circumstances—Spoked Wheels

One example of the partnership is how we the everyday people paid for and own the streets that commerce rides on for private gain. There are es-sential public goods that create opportunity structures for private pursuits. The public and private cooperate so we can compete globally. Not wanting to deal with such complexity, doomers align with simplicity and thus their ism polemics. If freedom goes with markets and private ownership, and absolute control goes with totalitarianism and collectivized ownership, we've three pairs we can evaluate. The lazy, complacent simpleton would make two opposites: freedom with markets and private ownership versus totalitarianism with planning and public ownership. However, like a diver-gent problem of how to organize society, it is not that simple. With three pairs, there are actually eight possible combinations. Mathematically, this is two to the power of three, written as 2^3. It is absurd to insist on only one polemic possibility (Schumacher, 1973). Yet this is what the baby doomers and their dutiful loomers do. The ability to combine a few dichotomies and recognize combinations, permeations of meaning, and possible permutations helps us develop our ability to think critically. This is something we must do with what we observe in society, what we hear authority figures are doing in the news, and even with what we want to believe is true. This search for truth is an extremely important responsibility of citizenship in a democracy, as evidenced by our emphasis on the academy power and its delivery of education via funding by the polity's collection and application of public, tax revenue, and through private instruments.

The use of overlaid dichotomies can also help us critically analyze wicked social problems. To understand one's own and others' perspectives, identify and use dichotomies. Pick a few. Mark your position along their continuum. Fit them to a circle. See where the dots of positions sit. Connect the dots. The shape of connected positions defines the dominant thought of an extant polemic. Using the apt dichotomies within one of the societal or social powers, we can frame conversations about difficult disagreements. Each of the powers of society has its own wheel of predominate dichotomies. At any given time in history, dichotomies may differ, depending upon the advancement of knowledge within the power. This device of mapping positions on dichotomies and overlaying them helps address aspects of the definitions of words we grapple with in applying each societal power to our present circumstances. We the everyday people should do this for ourselves. It is a good means of recognizing and checking what those in positions in authority tell us when they try to influence what we believe and seek to persuade us in ways that might be contrary to us as a citizenry achieving the goal and attaining the objectives of the USE. Ever more so, we must demand it be done by the powers' FILMS[2] [P7] openly, honestly, and with an intentional transparently to explain it to us. As the leadership of society, we the everyday people must see the polemics and direction of movement within the societal and social powers. At each given moment of rising risks or celebration of successes within society the history power should record and report to us on the risks debates by the polemics argued and for what purposes.

These wheels of dichotomies for understanding can be further used as a discussion tool to find deeper knowledge of ourselves and our society, where it has been, and to where it might best be led by us. They are a launching point. Here's how. Look at Figure 6-4. Substitute the yes, no; right, left; up, down; and then, now poles with any other relevant dichotomies to any topic to be discussed within any given societal or social power, or between two of them or among them as a broadest macro level social analysis. Map perspectives as positions along the lines (see Figure 2-29 for a list of possible dichotomies).

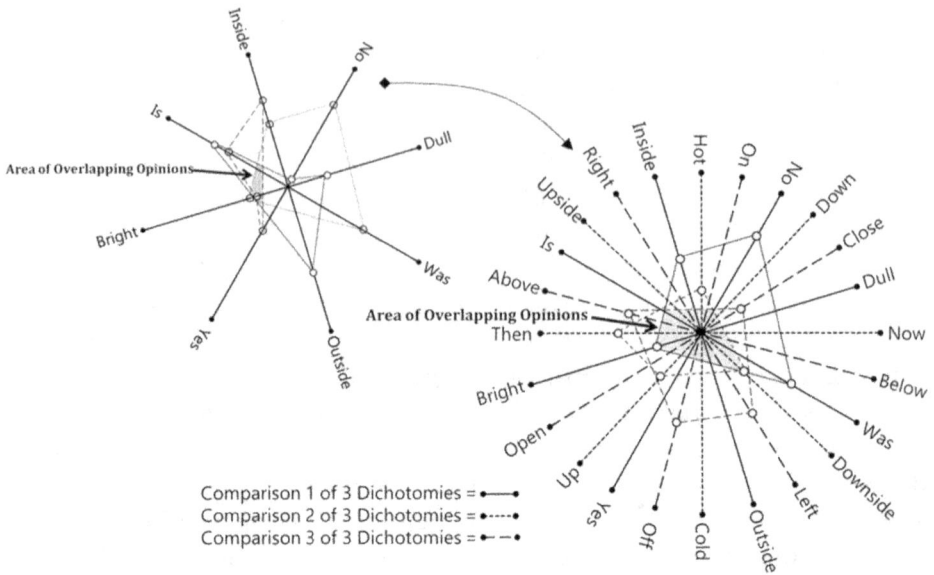

Figure 6-5: Multiple Spoked Wheels Centered on Centers Produce Analytical Shapes
Dotted spoke wheels are similar to scatter plots and spiderweb diagram depictions of character-istics or features of something. They yield an ability to compare and contrast perspectives. The overlapped areas of the shape are the areas of similarity, often more moderate perspectives, and likely, the more believed, perhaps even the area of truth of the matters considered. The larger the shapes are, the more extreme the perspectives. Conversely, the smaller the shapes are, the more neutral the perspectives. Find and compare shapes different groups produce to begin con-versations in seeking to understand. Compare to the goal and objectives of the USE. Consider revising perspectives to align with theses. Revising one's thinking is learning. We all need to learn how to apply ourselves to best advance American society.

Next, overlay several of these to find the centralities. See Figure 6-5 above. This wheel of understanding is a means to a higher-level concept than the binaries that preoccupy normative thinking and debates that pose two positions, one against the other, in a polemic. We use binary polemic dichotomous diametric continuums to explain what we perceive, but they are not rich enough for our increasingly complex world. We need to begin to overlay them and seek deeper, richer comprehension of connections among them. We need to map the nodes of the networks of thought. The traditionalists will map out differently than the modernists, but they may find overlaps that indicate similarities, which become talking points to find common ground and overcome emotive reactions that halt meaningful dia-logue.

We should seek understanding by laying out the facts or fictions in front of us along these continuums. The extent to which continuums' cen-ters align, is a measure of society's accord or discord with our collective un-derstanding of it. The more there is misalignment, the more our challenges will be to find mutual agreement. This makes these intellectual discovery tools and conversations about them valuable pieces of rebuilding civil discourse and civil society's trustworthiness in our public-private venture to provide a society with justice and liberty for all. Knowing the points where mutual understanding is most likely is a reasonable opportunity for building unity. This; not arguing over the difference is the place to begin. Unity is the purpose we should have in mind as we begin the use of this intellectual opinion analysis tool that relies upon civilized cooperation for the common good.

Civility in discourse is essential for democracy. Democracy is vital for liberty. Liberty is the justification for the USE. ACE is how we learn to do it. Dichotomies are a device for learning of self and society. Use them. Figure 6-5's two diagrams shows how. The upper left one is a wheel of four hypothetical dichotomies with area shapes that map one person's opinions. Overlapped areas of opinions indicate a value set. The lower right image adds two more wheels. Each wheel can be the mapped opinions and value sets of different persons, groups, factions, industries, depending on the analyses needed to assist in the identification of a common ground to build understanding or make an agreement. Overlaying them assists in identifying shared values.

Another form of mapping opinions is a spiderweb type of analytical diagram. It uses numeric rankings to mark characteristic features on a linear scale. These scales overlaid form a web. Figure 6-6 presents a visual example.

To make a comparing and contrasting wheel of understanding, use dichotomous continuums of the same length and fit them to a perfect circle. Arguments tend to be between opposite positions or poles and are felt equally strongly. The continuum is not a spoke until we overlay it with others. Theories tend to reside at one pole of a spoke or another. Often, matrices are set up with two continuums to locate positions of understanding between them. The more we come to understand, the more complex the knowledge seems. The more we learn, the less we feel we know. We tend to fall into one aspect as a favorite pool of thought. This can lead to intellectual comfort, but it can also cause fallacy and error in predicting outcomes when theories are applied. To solve the most difficult problems in society requires the integration of several valid theories of many aspects of society. This takes time, and time requires flexibility to adapt to new knowledge. Mortality, a fact, limits time alive. We live in generations. Generations should address by priority risks to the survival and continuation of society all its reshaping that occurs in the cycles of awakening and crises. During these periods of change, each societal and social power must adjust. Each can approach the social circumstances by rejection or acceptance of the changes. Each can seek out how to be beneficial for society. Some will try for greater control. The binary choice is, refuse to transform with the times or adapt to contribute value to society. If no value is possible anymore, then the power may lose relevancy. It can transfer its resources to needed arenas of other powers to add value to the whole. Or it could become irate, demand attention. It might at all costs fight with lies to hold onto a once more powerful position in society. This is the course it would take if misguided by blinded-by-ambition baby doomers. Generations that adapt to manage risks and address threats in the best priority and manner survive with a good reputation and leave a promising legacy of endowment as recorded by the history power. Those that don't, cause the loss of civilization. The generations that hold or restore a proper equilibrium of society's primary powers enjoy the blessings of liberty.

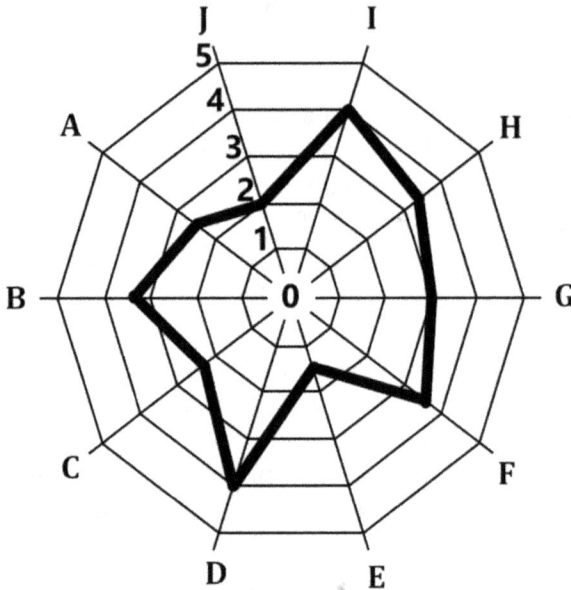

Figure 6-6: Spiderweb Analytical Diagram to Compare Features
Spiderweb diagrams can be used to evaluate several features of the same thing at once and compare it to other things of the same type. The resultant shape indicates relative strengths and weaknesses of features compared to one another. This technique is more helpful for convergent problems.

Clearer understanding of risks enables better adaptation. Understanding begins with knowledge held by a person within a group, organizationally and societally in micro, meso, and macro FILMS² [P7]. The understanding and knowledge of original principles is critical, too, for all of us to properly AEIOUY²K societal and social powers on course with the founders' vision. Failures come when knowledge is inaccurate, such as a false story, or when the understanding of a problem is inaccurate. Failures come when each overlapped wheel of understanding is too discordant or too identical. No overlapping centers indicate little agreement, and mean no shared understanding. Complete overlapping centers mean a lot of agreement, which if very divergent from others' positions could be a cultural bias that might cause misunderstandings. Further, if such bias is contrary to the founding ideals codified in the Constitution, we've a hazard to mitigate. Similarity in thinking among people can be good or bad. Dominant theoretical thrusts of thinking and beliefs can cause groupthink, blindness, and irrational institutionalism. We must find ways to honestly move perspectives with facts to be able to find more overlaps in common than not.

The point of all this is that we need to begin to synthesize and not criticize. We need to pull together the diversity of knowledge. When we have completely overlapping centers, total agreement in understanding, we must be certain it is over liberty, or it could exhibit a condition of possible drift of our society to one kind of tyranny or another. Tyranny is bad for liberty because it:

- Restricts changes in understanding
- Disallows any opinions contrary to official dogma
- Prevents changes in knowledge capability and capacity
- Stagnates thought, creativity, and expansion in knowledge

Near-overlapping centers exhibit a condition of democracy in a society. Democracy permits changes in:

- understanding
- opinion of valid theories of knowledge
- knowledge capacity and capability and KA^4SA^2
- what's believed in and held to be true

Democracy leads to higher adaptability. Democracy allows for dynamism of thought. This leads to creativity and knowledge expansion.

Pulling together the diversity of knowledge to generate common understanding within and of each power in society, for society, and by society, we will be able to solve the problems we have created by enlarging our knowledge. It grows as we search for solutions to ensure our species' survival or as we solve adaptive problems that reside within a power, or across powers, and are seen as needing a solution to perpetuate a dominant theory within the powers' $FILMS^2$ [P7]. Dominant theories guide the ways we $AEIOUY^2K$ powers. These need to be in accord with actions to IDEALS liberty, or our society will drift further off its course than doomerism CATAPULTED. We need to do better critical thinking to be able to move again in a direction that is toward a more perfect union. For example, as dependency on electricity causes a need for an energy sector of the economy and because electricity can injure people, this reality warrants we set up an energy department in the polity. Lastly, be it known that discordant societies function less well for the people than accordant societies. Society should serve people and people must serve society for this purpose. It is up to us. We need liberty to do this, to build a more perfect union and a peaceful society of dignity through the culture of democracy. But liberty cannot succeed when politics is a game played as if a competitive sport. It requires we win and lose gracefully and not be gloating winners or sore losers. These doomer behaviors keep us from cooperating, as we must to sustain liberty.

*L*iberty, *What Can We Do?*

If we are willing to shift societal and social powers from their current shape to one that favors democracy, and if we find doomerism is too problematic and remains within us, we need to take action. Action begins with thought. The wheel of understanding exercises our minds and helps us think. If we have thought about it, want change, and believe we must pursue liberty virtuously—to get us back on course to achieve our constitutional objectives—let us decide to do it. Seeking to IDEALS liberty is what we can do. It is what we should do for posterity and ourselves if we want to complete the project begun by the founding framers. It requires lives lived in pursuit of virtue not vice. It requires lives lived to develop good character with honesty, integrity, and courage to speak truth to authority figures that might be about to DAMN power in their assigned authorities within the societal and social powers. We must not foolishly allow them. Rather we must know for what the authorities were established to ensure we AEIOUY^{2}K the operant powers for good. That is, for the beneficial uses that strengthen the common wealth we the everyday people have created by contributing and committing ourselves to the whole community's benefit as a common good. We did so as much as we could, accept whenever baby doomers ruined our ability to do so. These past forty years have seen the worst circumstances for us. It is time we reverse it. But first, we must awaken to the mistakes of a misguided "me first" value proposition, and make a big decision.

Decide If We Want Liberty

To the person, we each must decide if we want real liberty or not. Liberty is not free. It takes effort to keep it. Reflect on the benefits you receive from it. Reflect on the contributions you give and are willing to give on its behalf. Reflect on your ability to commit to something abstract while learning what it means through effort. Reflect on your sense of gratitude for what you have. Reflect on your sense of accomplishment for what you have earned. Ask yourself if you want to make the world a better place for the next generation of Americans. Ask yourself if you care what happens to our nation after you are dead. Decide and rejoice or cry. Let it out. Once you decide, really commit to it deep inside.

Be willing to work to get rid of doomerism. Adopt a citizen-first attitude! Be courageous because we are going to be thinking and acting (but not in all ways) like our founding generation, undertaking a revolutionary belief in the prospects of a representational republic rising up from and sustained upon a culture of democracy to IDEALS liberty. We do this for the children. Every one of them deserves freedom for probability of potential prosperity. We'll be part of the solution, not part of the problem. We'll be reestablishing the great ideas and principles that changed the history of humankind away from tyranny toward democracy. We'll be a part of the greatest social and societal project ever undertaken based upon a novel way of thinking that arrived in the minds of our forebears as sensible to reason seeking humans. Their radical thought was that the commoner—we the everyday people—could self-govern and control society in our favor. Do not feel alone. Others want to do it too. They want, like you, me, and us, to live in a land of the free and the brave. Now, be brave. We can do it. We are Americans!

Let us not be so defeated by doomerism that we question our capabilities or capacities to do this. Let us not ask, "Do we want to do this?" The opposite choice is we cede all the societal and social powers to the doomers and their culture of doomerism. If in thinking about this we realize we might be baby doomers, or sycophantic loomers, or vain groomers, or uncaring about American society zoomers, or non-intervening bystander roomers, we can do things to reverse this, to save our souls and prevent the collapse of the USE. We can act to restore a democracy-based culture meant to secure liberty for all citizens. We can stop its slide and keep it from further demise that will collapse its civilization. We can get in touch with our humanity. We can ask for forgiveness from whomever we did dirty on our rise to the top. We can contribute to the recovering of lost time. We can commit to pursue the ideals as real. We are humans, and humans are adaptable. We can decide to adopt for ourselves a life of service to the country. We can serve in ways that correct the course of the society. We've an important role to play to help future generations, not hinder them. Because we've so much security and ease, we can provide needed resources. We can invest them in the future. We can volunteer.

To approach correction, boomers can decide to support liberty over social fabric destroying wild freedom of "me first" mentality. Here is how. Be a better citizen-first person. Don't seek undue influence above what a citizen is entitled to possess. Stop rationalizing excess as an achievement worth emulating. Help stabilize our democracy. Share! Get to know people of different life experiences. Become curious but not intrusive. Respect the personal journeys and dignity of others who survived misfortunes, tragedies of prejudice, traumas, and other societal dramas. Plan how much to live comfortably and live at that level, responsibly investing the rest in society. Give time, money, and talents philanthropically to a good cause. Volunteer where communities need help, learn ACE and teach it to the future generations. Become a good neighbor and expect only respect, not excessive adoration, in return. It is never too late to make a positive difference in others' lives and thereby improving the society. Be conscientiously selfless not selfish. Sustain civil society. Return excessive wealth to the treasury by paying back taxes averted by rigging the system. Contribute to charitable and not political manipulation causes. Provide endowments to educational institutions to fund democracy lessons, citizenship training, and liberty instructions. Finance the ACE we need. Demand and monitor that the holders of academy power do not fatten their paychecks but put the money to use where it belongs. Do not allow over inflation of position holders' value. Make them do their work in accordance with higher missions. Ensure money goes to the cause. Circulate dollars locally by spending money at neighborhood stores fun by family businesses.

If you are an elder to the boomers, do these things to save the USE's democracy-based culture meant to secure liberty for all citizens. Encourage and forgive the loomers, groomers, zoomers, roomers, and doomers. Welcome them to the newfound commitment to serve liberty, to become stewards of democracy and not exploiters of it, to be givers, not for self-egotism but for all the citizenry without neglect of any of us. Show them the way to age gracefully. Recognize and celebrate the few bloomers who tried to fight the wrongly directed waves of the other boomers' doom making decisions. Also, laud and assist the fewer broomers who strive to clean up the messes of their misguided cohorts. Offer to return benefits to the younger generations by identifying how to shift policies. Coach the tumorous boomers who need help with it, to believe in and practice humility, experience humanism and humanitarianism, and help humanity humanely. They may be very sad and lonely sacks. Fill them with the hope and real satisfaction of rediscovering what it means to be human. Teach them the value and joy that comes from E-SASSY-T-TUF-FT-CAUCUS. Help them re-humanize. Many may have dehumanized in their selfishness and wars against others to prove their perfection to themselves.

If you are a bloomer, broomer, or non-boomer-like person in a succeeding generation, do these things. Forgive the baby boomers who are loomers, groomers, zoomers, roomers, and doomers. Pray for them that they may be willing to convert to a new way of being and becoming, as an ideal American, one who IDEALS liberty. Help them manage the return of that which they stole while raping the project. Show appreciation to the boomers for the positives they have provided us and help them not suffer too badly when they finally make sacrifices for the nation. Gen Xers, use your pragmatism and no-nonsense approach to solving problems to assist the millennials. Millennials, use your team-working mannerisms and civic mindset to negotiate diplomatically long-term, steady solutions to resolve the issues in society. Build bonds across generations to make alliances to save democracy with the revolutionary fervor employed at its founding. Bring the aging baby boomers of all types to the US Constitution Center in Philadelphia to experience its exhibits. Bring them to the National Archives in Washington, DC to see the real Declaration of Independence and Constitution. Bring them to some of the other places mentioned in the Appendix's Liberty Learning Resources. Help them see the light of the liberty tree.

Engage the boomers' idealism in meaningful ways to encourage them to commit to helping you identify exactly how and where liberty-centered laws and policies exist and where they don't. Build coalitions with boomers as teachers of the first principles of liberty and democracy and critical thinking to see doomerism and to stop it. Define what citizen-first means in terms of liberty-effecting value sets and consequent attitudes that will swell heathy and helpful behaviors. Understand how boomers are not fully citizenship-focused. Aid them reacquaint with the vital virtues the citizenry needs to rebuild the foundations of our culture of democracy and sustain our representative republic.

They are victims of isms, principally consumerism. They've "competitivitus" syndrome and fell into hedonism, relativism, and maybe even "tyrantitus." They grossly misunderstood the meaning of individualism, thinking it devoid of cooperation and a synonymous with liberty. Liberty properly understood is the underpinning for personal freedoms that through social commitments combine to improve society, not bring about its demise. Absent the truth that we are a socially dependent species, boomers convinced themselves "me first" was appropriate. Because they had fortunes like none before, they got too good at selfish rationalization and fantasy justification; they lowered standards of conduct, violated ethics principles, and reduced accountability. They sought always to avoid responsibility and became non-unifiers, almost anti-unifiers. We should show them mercy, but remand them and demand payback of the stolen wealth of the nation. The framers would approve of this approach.

Certainly, they were dividers, dividing themselves up at the poles of isms. They produced a polemical politics with immaturity in polity participation that possessed an immense insensitivity to opposing viewpoints. They held high opinions of themselves and fought over arguments based upon little evidence. They demonstrated an inability to change perspective when their most valued position or philosophy proved imperfect, flawed, fallacious, and felonous, or worse felonious. They got really, really good at finding loopholes and other ways, means, and methods to DAMN powers in enduringly malfeasant bad for us manners. They enabled a polity ripe for manipulation for personal gain and permitted undue influence in it by economy elites. Their lack of integrity, bad character, and low ethical performance evidence it. Moreover, rationalizing the elites of the economy bribing the politicians of the polity as essentially legal taints us. Making a partisan disguise for themselves, they used revolving doors of polity and economy, hiring friends over the most qualified candidates. They acted like high school cliques instead of statesmen and stateswomen of high caliber diplomatic statecraft. Not acting with the best interest of the country in mind, they promoted not the talented well suited for jobs on merit but those they desired for their brown nosing boot licking coattail riding personal loyalty as good subordinate sycophants. Their weak shameless egos shaped the horrible atrophy of honorable American character, once sought as the trophy for having lived a life fully in virtue for truth and justice.

We need everyone to behave like a citizen-first person and be open to leading by example. Teach others why we must behave this way. Avoid the pulling toward extremes. Listen to multiple perspectives. Reflect on how these relate to liberty. Work to IDEALS liberty. Teach civics to self and the next generations. Coach the upcoming generation s on how to contribute not rig and steal; that life is not a game but something far more precious and important. Prepare them to assume responsibilities by helping them develop judgment to decide what is best for the USE in its pursuit of a more perfect union.

*T*ools We Can Use

With our people power, we the everyday people are to be the leadership in the LAMBS. We have work to do. Work requires tools. We need tools to see through the games being played with us, against us, on us, and supposedly for us by those in positions of authority within the FILMS[2] [P7] of societal and social powers. Our most powerful tools are the questions who, what, when, where, why, and how. We must ask these and demand answers whenever we perceive the DAMN of power. This requires we use critical thinking. Thinking critically about what we perceive is important in a democracy. We need it to identify political perspectives and open up the possibilities for rational discourse. As discussed earlier we can use the tools of mapping positions on dichotomies to find the polemics and debate the positives and negatives of them as they relate to liberty properly understood. These are skills. We get them from a robust, lifelong experience of civics, learned and practiced, which is why an ACE is indispensable. We all need more of it, repeatedly. It is the most essential tool. Let's go over it and then move onto to some other tools.

Civics Education

We must teach at all levels an increasingly deep education on the fundamentals of American society, democracy, liberty, and what the citizenry of a republic must know to defend these or lose out to tyranny. American society includes concepts of public and private property, that through democracy culture in a republic with free-markets under the rule of law with strong constitutional protections of personal rights is best for the continuance of liberty (Hayek, 1960). Lessons of both the public square and the open marketplace are necessary (on this construct related to settlement patterns, see Figure 3-7 through Figure 3-11). Lessons of the polity power and the economy power are required for raising Americans because our organization of societal powers needs the primary three (people, polity, economy) to know their roles and responsibilities and to be balanced (as was presented in "The Three Primary Powers" subsubsection of Chapter 2 "Unity Calling" and in Figure 2-1 through Figure 2-11). An ACE curriculum needs reinforced throughout the entire life course of the citizenry in its KA^4SA^2 development and employment. It should include four areas of study:

1. Civics Core
2. Civic Engagement
3. Social Responsibility
4. Economics

The first area should include six primary topics:

1. Foundations of the American Political System
2. Framers and the Constitution
3. Ideals in the Declaration of Independence
4. Values and Principles of the Constitution
5. Bill of Rights
6. Democracy in the Twenty-first Century

The goal of this ACE is the telling of our truth, and that which is essential to an ideal American society. For this, its objectives are the critical:

- Passing on Civics Core Curriculum:
  o Educating students about core democratic principles as set forth in the Declaration of Independence and US Constitution
  o Teaching students about how early American history influenced the development of the US government
  o Educating students about government and how it works
- Developing Civic Engagement:
  o Teaching students about the electoral process
  o Preparing students to take an active role in community affairs
  o Preparing students to follow government and politics through media
  o Preparing students to exercise their right to vote
  o Preparing students to use 21st-century technology and media to engage with politics
- Imparting Social Responsibility:
  o Developing an understanding of cultural diversity
  o Encouraging students to be aware of social conditions
  o Educating students about the relationship of the United States to other nations and world affairs
- Imparting Knowledge of Economics:
  o Teaching students about the economic system
  o Providing students with marketable skills for future employment
  o Preparing people to become economically self-sufficient

(Owen, Hartzell, & Sanchez, 2020)

In addition to and throughout the teaching of an ACE, a key way of looking at the world that will benefit the citizenry is through sociology. It is a useful tool.

Sociological Thinking

Thinking about society is an important skill. Throughout our lives during our KA[4]SA[2] voyages, we learn about human societies from the societal powers' FILMS[2] [P7]. From the academy and history powers, we learn the histories of other civilizations as analogies to our understanding of our society. From the mythology power, we receive training through allegories, religious storytelling passed down from generation to generation. We learn of the reason for the concept of the separation of church and state—to permit every person freedom of religion and to prevent the concentration of mythology and polity power in one despotic ruler atop everyone and everything. Yet, "In God We Trust" is written on our money. Words have meanings. They mean what they mean, and we should appreciate their meanings. Perhaps this is a reminder of our necessary social responsibility to be ethical in our economic dealings within American society. Certainly, we must be honorable to maintain a society in order to become one people, e pluribus unum. The founders were clear on the necessity of virtue and moral character in the citizenry to make democracy work (Moore, 2019). These ideas of moral character and virtue reside in the original intents for the nation. We've seen generations live for humility, not self-centeredness that leads to selfishness and its disrespect of dignity. Humility leads us to wisdom. We need to get back on the road to character (Brooks, 2015). We need this to be better selves, to be better citizens first.

We can move in a positive direction when we reconnect and revitalize our founding principles as important for American society to remain American (Levin, 2004). The debates about government reside within the political scientists' arena of scholarship. It is a field of study in which we review the accumulated data of politics' arts, qualitative aspects, and results. The data undergoes scientific analyses. Propositions and explanations made and pronounced by the scholars give us information. The debates about free markets reside within the economics arena of scholarship. It is a field of study in which theories of human behavior concerning accommodating needs and wants for survival, living, and thriving are studied. From this come theoretical hypotheses that are tested and reported upon over time. Sociologists study both of these and other matters of importance in society. Sociology looks at the interrelatedness of human affairs. It would do well to look into the interfaces of all the human culture made societal and social powers, and their influences upon one another, society, and us as persons and a people. For us to move into the 21st century without doomerism, we need to use sociological thinking. If politics is about administrative power, and economics is about managerial provisioning prowess, we must comprehend the operant behaviors of both and their combined arrangements. We must learn the many ways, means, and methods we express ourselves through power.

How we address the geography power to survive, live, and thrive within society is a key component of our culture. Provisioning the necessities of these three modes of living requires we understand our attitudes and behaviors related to our acquisition of the goods and services that fulfill them. To understand who we are as persons is in part psychology. It is partly social psychology since we are social beings experiencing our lives in various and ever-changing groups. In addition, our understanding of our selves as people involves a good deal of the influence of society. Knowing how takes a whole lot of sociology because how we view ourselves and how we are to think and behave in a society relates to our sense of identity. The content of our character is most important to who we are and how we might contribute to society. Our identity ought not to be limited to others' definition of us as primarily a member of one group or another. That thinking is too immature for a democracy. It is a risky tribal approach. It leads to fracturing factions and divisions among us. It can end in the tyranny of the majority over the minority opinions, which the founders wisely opposed. They resisted it because total control of all by one dominant group does not fit in with liberty, which rests on the wisdom of preserving respect and dignity for every person, even those who make mistakes or commit crimes. Democracy is not easy, but it is best, despite the inconvenience some might find from being tolerant. "Me first" mentality misses this point. It misguides us into impatience and antipathy. Thinking prosocially can help us see this, and avoid its negative societal consequences.

Through ACE, we can recognize ourselves as citizens. Since the polity power sets up the society, it is essential that we the everyday people debate it in the public square. Since economy power provides the necessary, the common, and the luxury goods and services through the marketplace, it is important that we the everyday people participate in it with honor and integrity. Its power can make and break human livelihood. With both the polity and economy powers, as a people, we must embrace our responsibility as citizens to make the society function in accord with our first principles, the ideals that make American society possible. We must act in accordance with the Constitution as amended. We must aim to be American by inculcating the virtuous values of democracy, not the vices of doomerism.

One way to understand the interplay of identity with the societal powers is to imagine how emphasis on only one way of seeing the world pulls the society toward different value sets. This is like philosophizing what society could be like if one set of values was more important than another set. It is like imagining a vision for a future we all might want. By this, we seek a unifying imagined circumstance, so we all work together instead of against one another. In this way, we strive to accomplish the same mission. Perhaps the biggest failure of the baby boomer generation was its lack of a coalesced clear vision of hope for how we the everyday people in American society might eventually accomplish its goal and objectives. We must pull together to complete our project. Let's henceforth finish the work to make the United States a more perfect union.

The following Figures (6-7, 6-8, and 6-9) use this kind of sociological thinking to provide preferences and perspectives from personal philosophies on how society shapes and reshapes. These philosophies propose preferred attitudes and behaviors of each person toward society. The three identity postures presented in the diagrams are (first-and-foremost) us (at micro level) as:

▶ Politicians *(for power)*   ▶ Consumers *(for things)*   ▶ Citizens *(for liberty)*

The first is a preference for the polity power to be more powerful than the other two. As such, we act like politicians, all seeking to maximize our personal power as the objective of society to serve. With it, we are also the object of attention and use the power of the polity to take care of us as its subjects. While doing this, we are paradoxically, at the same time, object and subject.

The second is a preference for economic power to be more powerful than the other two.

The third is a preference for people power to be the most powerful. Since our society has a public square and a marketplace (recall Figure 3-11), this position seeks equilibrium between society's primary powers so these two social functions work well for us. Unless we behave honorably as truth-seeking American-intending citizens, such a beneficial balance will continue to elude us.

This identity orientation concept initiates at the micro-level of society. If a sense of who one is becomes popular, it expands up through the meso-level because groups take on the perspectives of members, particularly those of their dominate ones. If a majority of persons and groups in society possess key features of the perspectives and senses of self, the macro-level reflects the distributed feelings of selfhood. Language carries the identities everywhere. People believe these are not theirs to choice, but assigned to them by society. Yet over time connotations change denotations, and annotations in history reveal previous generations considered identities differently. Definitions of who we are and what we want, and are to be, change. If we are true to the principles and ideals that are the foundation of an American society, we are American. If we are not, we are not. We must realign ourselves to identify with and represent the core virtues and values of the endowment passed down to us from the late 18th Century's Age of Enlightenment. Otherwise, we will be unable to reestablish the required equilibrium to sustain the endowment of a free people given society's leadership responsibility. This identity orientation concept is similar to the LAMBS model (recall Figures 2-1 through 2-11).

We are failing as a people because doomerism has overtaken our way of thinking. Doomerism demands economic and polity primacy, but democracy demands people primacy. Yet the skills of classical argument, of respectful and dignified debate, no longer happen in our politics. Doomers pick far away pole positions and sling mud, tossing out fallacies in front of us. They are playing public image games with us. It is a humiliating display. Divergent viewpoints can be good when presented with due consideration sought for comprehension. However, they are not even trying to understand and relate to one another's perspectives. This is intolerable. It is tolerable to disagree in a democracy. The vitriolic manner of boomer-made politics is not beneficial. It threatens the whole underpinning of our society and of democracy (Dworkin, 2006). Makes us wonder, "Is democracy possible here?" This is risky place to be after the forming, storming, and norming phases of the third knowledge evolution (recall Figure 4-1). As we accustom ourselves to it, we ought to be as a society performing, not be in repeating crises as we are experiencing. Doomerism is why adaption adjustments are failing to deliver social stability, and societal disharmony worsens.

The popular diverging viewpoints have a common denominator: doomerism, a diseased culture of many social maladies. Understanding it sociologically allows us to rebuild the skills to debate well in the public realm. With the rise of doomerism in us, we've allowed rude attitudes and misbehavior toward alternative perspectives to persist. Hatred for one another by those in positions of authority in the polity and economy powers' FILMS[2] [P7] and among the HM[5] is a failure in their performing their citizenship duties for our project's success. Unfulfilled obligations are negligence. We must immediately address it with reinvigorated and repeated ACE. We need the academy power to focus on it and the economy power to distribute it. ACE is a critical tool we need now. So is sociological thinking. It helps us see past the various arguments proposed in political science and economics. Both are missing the points we need to know. We are an American society, and we need to see all of the society to render civil discourse possible, especially because of doomerism. Doomerism has brought about massive confusion. Some of this grows out of the argument made earlier about the success of converting citizens into consumers. Underlying this are shifts in cultural modes of self-expression, pursuits that perplexingly moved us as a society out of enlightenment, into ages of entertainment, entitlement, and exhibition. Now we've drift into the hazardous waters of electronic (e)victimization, exploitation, eviction, enragement, and eventually enslavement (see Figure 5-8) if we the everyday people do not intervene to save the Constitution from dissipation by doomerism. Thus, we must reaffirm an American identity that reifies our foundational principles placed by the framers. This won't be easy or quick. It could take us two score and four years to defeat and expunge doomerism. Yet, we must begin now to take the plunge. Without hesitation, let's bravely lunge forward to get it done sooner rather than later!

The confusion of doomerism caused the weeds of consumer culture to strangle the roots of citizenship culture. The roots of consumerism are economic but influenced by the political system. The roots of citizenship are political but influenced by the economic system. From these roots grow attitudes and expected behaviors regarding the preferred arrangements of the relationship of the three primary societal powers: the polity, the economy, and the people.

Each person's sense of identity relates to these powers. Each person performs a role in each. Persons as a politician or producer and provisions-provider, dissuading and persuading others' opinions or purchasing preferences present their personal preferences. As a citizen to support the polity, we should obey the rules and elect good officials. As a consumer to support the economy, we should buy and sell goods and services.

Figures 6-7, 6-8, and 6-9 contain diagrams that represent attitudes and behaviors around the expectations and exercise of power as forms of cultural identity orientations. Consider these diagrams as sociological thought exercises. They show a variety of ways to understand society. By knowing one's own perspective, conversations can ensue about the benefits and costs of the implications for power use in various philosophies. Preferred philosophical positions and discussions about various power arrangements for deciding, "Who comes first?" can lead to imagining different societal possibilities. The best for us equilibrium requires we the everyday people get serious about knowing the potential ways, means, and methods we could adopt to adapt to the future while we push smarter and harder to accomplish our heroic project's mission, meet its goal, and make its objectives real in all our daily lives.

The diagrams ponder our republic represented as modes of expressions by roles favoring a focus on one of the primary powers as predominate. These roles appear in circles: top is citizenship (the people) as a "citizen"; lower right is government (the polity) as a "politician"; lower left is consumerism (the economy) as a "consumer". In gray, each diagram overemphasizes one of these role identities over the others to elicit thinking and elucidate consequences to the character of the republic. Expressed in orientations of "you", "me", and "we", these three characteristic selves relate to philosophical postures that correspond to the kind of society that emphasizing one over the other two makes. Each figure calls out these attitudes and behaviors. Again, the way we balance the powers of shapes society. We do this by culture, the precept power process.

The arrangement of all eleven of the society shaping powers in their status of affluence, confluence, modifies how we can live our lives. It does so for us as persons, members of groups, and as a national community. All our social FILMS[2] [P7] at the micro, meso, and macro levels of experience are guided by the accumulation and orientation of our preferred philosophically predicated identity. If we are unaware of our personal philosophies, the roots of our principles, and if they are not those of the Liberty Tree, we will struggle to establish unity e pluribus unum. We the people are the staff of all the societal and social powers. In a democracy, the persons in charge are of the people. The people must provide the leadership for the society. Leadership requires a vision. Vision pursued strategically helps us formulate plans to achieve a goal and attain objectives. This is the mission. The plans put the mission into action as a project. The project employs tactics. The American vision is a land of liberty. As represented by our community's public square and marketplace, two principles strategies of the USE are a republic for the polity and a free market for the economy. Leaders decide on resources. Power is Homo sapiens' primary social resource. We the everyday people, as the intended leaders of American society, must $AEIOUY^2K$ our power to balance all the societal and social powers to align with the mission of the USE to realize its vision. We, as the people working in the $FILMS^{2\,[P7]}$ and as the HM^5, must coordinate our personal and social efforts to accomplish the mission. It is our endowed project by its plan: the Constitution. Our tactics must be faithfulness to the plan, life-long ACE, democracy encouraging diplomacy, and honorable citizen-first orientation we master by exhibiting service above selfishness, saying yes to the utmost full-fledged thoroughgoing constitutionally allied united citizenshipping, understandingly synchronized (E-SASSY-T-TUF-FT-CAUCUS). By these tactics, we complete our mission, delivering our project per plan to implement our strategy to live out our vision.

The balancing of the societal and social powers gets influenced not just through a person's philosophies but operantly by the process of governing, through the system of the polity; the layers of its governments. We the everyday people, by our polity and in the economy, must balance the powers to realize the vision stated in the Preamble.

Let's look at the first diagram in Figure 6-7 below. It portrays the politician as the purposeful orientation for society. With polity power in extreme conceited conditions, a government exists to secure all the political power in a ruler. Under a single ruler, societal powers get concentrated. Rulers distribute benefits as they choose. A sycophant ruling class grows prominent and a circle of "yes" persons seek gain by reinforcing the ruler's power. Others orient to feed off the ruler by subjugation, submissiveness, and feigned or real loyalty. The result is an unfree (intolerant to those who disagree with distribution decisions) society for its citizens. This kind of ruled society experiences enormous inequality in material conditions. Vast gaps between social classes of luxury and poverty develop. Few, if any, occupy a middle class. It is a society of no social or economic mobility with limited personal and social freedoms. It is one with many barriers to personal self-exploration and discovery of a worthy purpose for contributing to society. For the limited citizens, life is full of a great deal of unhappiness. This kind of state is what led to the French Revolution, which led to the French establishing a republic. This kind of society develops a small "c" conservative orientation, favoring the traditions of the rulers. To get by, the people adopt the same.

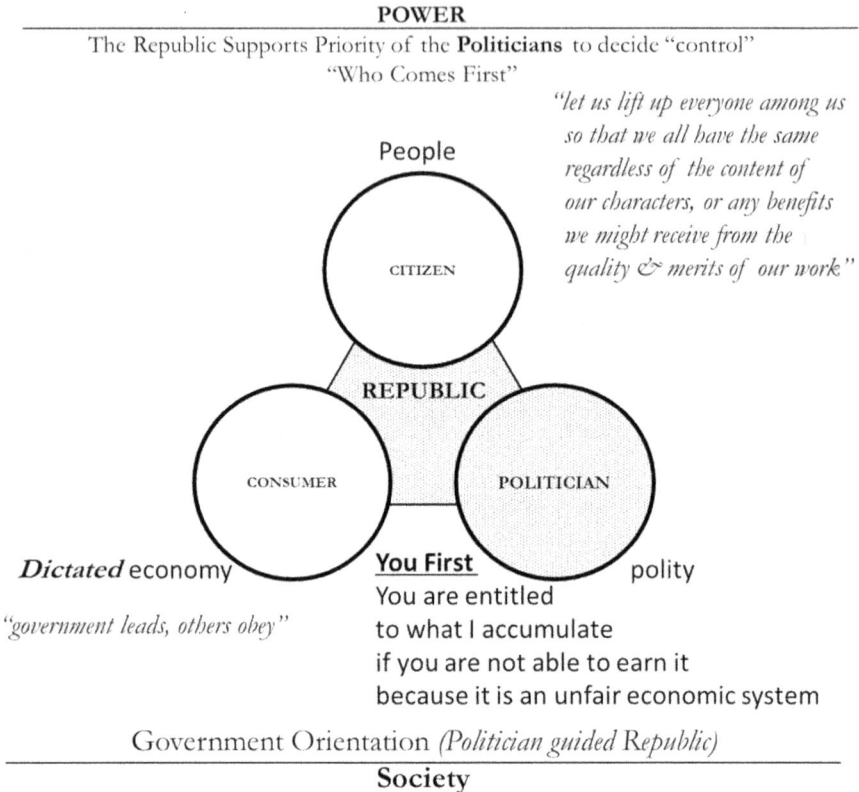

POWER

The Republic Supports Priority of the **Politicians** to decide "control"
"Who Comes First"

"let us lift up everyone among us so that we all have the same regardless of the content of our characters, or any benefits we might receive from the quality & merits of our work"

People

CITIZEN

REPUBLIC

CONSUMER   POLITICIAN

Dictated economy   **You First**   polity
                                      You are entitled
"government leads, others obey"   to what I accumulate
                                      if you are not able to earn it
                                      because it is an unfair economic system

Government Orientation *(Politician guided Republic)*

Society

Figure 6-7: Diagram of Polity Power—Dominant Society
The values of this diagram put the polity power in control of society. The politicians come first. In circa 2020 political partisan polemics, this diagram construes to represent a power posture of a staunch extremist, pole-sitting, socialist, little "l" liberal statist, progressive liberal seeking a public over private power preference perspective, rather doomeristic in essence.

On the other hand, the government exists to secure all the political power in the people, and divides the power, distributing it to representatives of the people. An elected class, the representatives, puts into use the people's power for the people. The result is a free (tolerant to those who disagree with distribution decisions) society for its citizens. This makes a society with moderate inequality in material conditions, luxury and poverty, because political freedom reduces the barriers, which those seeking to improve socially and materially must overcome. As a result, such a society enjoys a larger middle class. This state of affairs is what led to the Revolution in the English Colonies of America, which led to the settlers establishing a republic. Because a thick middle spends more than a skinny top, or a fat bottom, the broader and taller the middle classes, the more economic opportunity occurs for the most people. More money circulating creates a greater variety of opportunity, which stabilizes society, increases access to the middle and upper ranks, which is the best possible outcome.

Any government that claims to do things in the name of the people—but does not—has no real democracy. In a real democracy, all citizens are politically equal to elect their representatives to the government. Without democracy, no functioning republic is possible. Such a false republic is dysfunctional. Disrespect for the ways, means, and methods of the government and disobedience to its Constitution is functionally risky. If caused by a politics that commands political and economic distribution from the top, without the participation of the citizens, it is dictatorial. In the United States of America, the structure of government fixes the distribution of power. This does not guarantee that the persons in authority positions can, may, or will AEIOUY^{2}K power properly and not DAMN it. They're supposed to do it with the people's consent, in our not their best interests, and in accord with the government's constitution. Nevertheless, we must hold them accountable and responsibly remove them by voting in the next generation's ethical persons to be our officials to administer our tiers of government.

This is why a good constitution provides for checks and balances on the office holders. When these get disregarded, there is a constitutional crisis. In the United States, the distribution of material wealth is a matter of economic policy. Policy sets the possible, and laws set the impossible. Politicians set both. We must pay more attention to the policies. Policies need to make up a large part of the daily discourse between citizens. We need to reach out to our representatives and let them know our opinions. However, our comments need informed by our critical and sociological thinking and should serve the mission of the USE. Herein hides a risk. When the representatives perceive that they speak for us without hearing from us, power can easily go to their heads. They become the center of attention, not us. They may even believe it is acceptable for them to use their political power to become materially wealthy. They are ever at risk of feeling like elites themselves, which sets them up for power-lusting temptations. If they succumb, they become corrupted. This corruption is increasingly commonplace and tolerated within the culture of doomerism. It is unacceptable in democracy. When politicians use public office for private gain, they violate standards. Ethical rules of behavior and oaths of office need upheld to evidence truth that leads to trust and stability. Doomers seem to have no problem violating societal norms. They do not care about the costs. This is incorrigible but curable. It requires courage to fix such abominable destructiveness that breaks the sacred confidence of the public. Unethical actions by a majority generation's dominant cohort, lowers the standards of conduct for others who follow. It sets in decline. Thus, doomers are unfit for elected office. To get rich by getting into office is the wrong motivation for public service. It is pubescent, certain to cause adolescent, immature behavior throughout all the polity and thereafter the society. This compromises their ability to govern. We the everyday people lose faith in the edifice once admired as they deface it in search of fame and fortune. This "me first" mentality injures belief in authority, which cripples civility. The people who elected them as their representatives should hold them accountable to be better members of the community, not revel in feeling justified by their worst angels' reflection in them. Yet, what if they see themselves in them, or are in fact doomers too? It is unlikely the boomer generation can change overnight in our time of need, so we need an intervention. The boomers have failed to exercise good judgment as a generation. They altered culture and shaped society for consumption, not liberty's proper assumption. They failed to fulfill their duty, setting our project back forty years, putting us way off course without a recovery plan, and far away from its mission accomplishment.

Let's have a look at the second diagram in Figure 6-8. It portrays the consumer as the presiding identity in society. With consumerism as the preferred cultural orientation of society, we face extraordinary stress. The pressure to get rich and generate material wealth drives people's attitudes and behaviors. Its express preference for economy power presses us toward hyper-competitiveness at the expense of essential cooperativeness. Such an approach to living puts us at risk of illogical thinking that can lead to irrational behavior. An irrational behavior is one that is not in a person's best interest. With irrational thinking, we risk our ability to retain our personal power, freedom, and constitutional rights. In American society, illogical thinking is thinking that does not support the USE's mission. Illogical thinking threatens advances toward achieving our societal goal and attaining our objectives. The mission to IDEALS liberty needs supported by rational attitudes and behaviors. Irrational behavior can cause a person to act contrary to his or her own political, economic, and personal best interests. Not knowing what is in one's short-, mid-, and long-term interests is a risk citizens must address while using the SERF to determine how we should best perform our duties.

Consumerism is a culture that shapes attitudes toward overconsuming material provisions, goods and services, for subsistence survival, living in comfort, or swimming in luxury. It is shaped by the HM^5 seeking to maximize their gain from trading their wares. It exists in our society because we've the social invention of money. Its means of storing value and usefulness for exchange stimulates prosperity-producing potentialities. Money creates financing possibilities for improving society that would not generally otherwise exist. Civilization built itself on the benefits of money; the currency for buying and selling goods and services helps us make provisions for society. In the United States, selling goods and services has become an art and a science.

POWER

The Republic Supports Priority of the **Consumer** to decide "control"

"Who Comes First"

People

"let the most aggressive among climb up by the work of others, regardless of the content of our character, so we alone gain the benefits from the quality & merits of our work"

Me First
You are not entitled
to what I accumulate
it's all mine
regardless of whether the
economic system is fair or not

CITIZEN

REPUBLIC

CONSUMER   POLITICIAN

Manipulated economy   polity

"merchants lead the way, others obey"

Consumerist Orientation *(Consumer guided Republic)*

Society

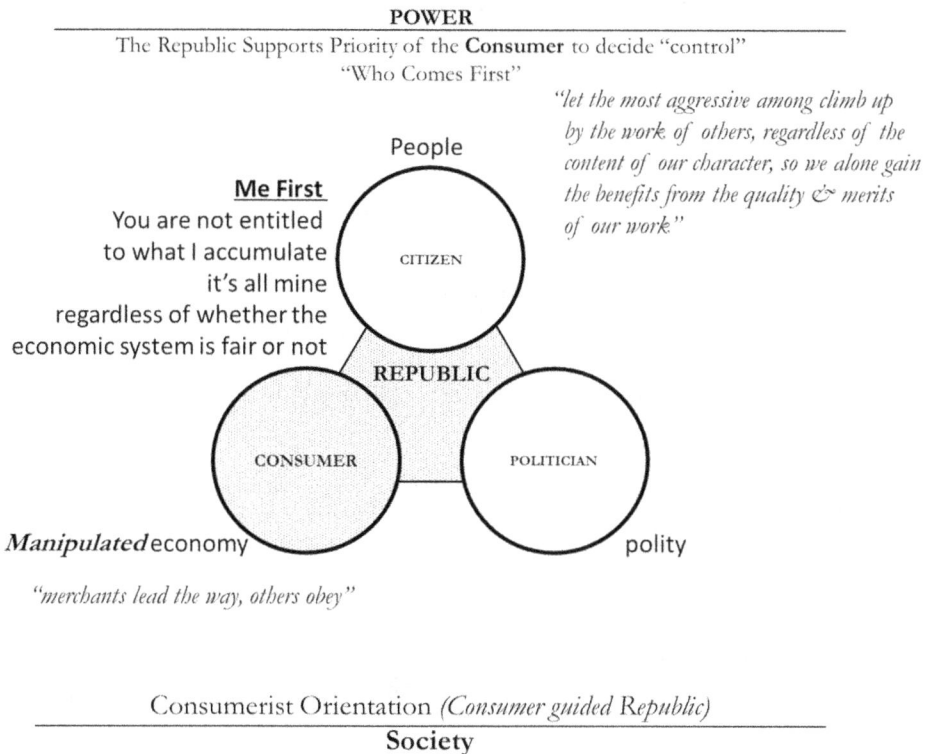

Figure 6-8: Diagram of Economy Power—Dominant Society
The values of this diagram put the economy power in control of society. The economy elites come first. In circa 2020 political partisan polemics, this diagram could be construed to represent a power posture of a staunch extremist, pole sitting, capitalist, status quo, small "c" conservative seeking to keep private power preference perspective, rather doomeristic in essence.

Over the generations, the American economy shaped by politics. The politics shaped by money. Consumerism ignores the idea of rights and responsibilities of citizenship. Consumerism is often confused with individualism. This part of the mercantile propaganda causes people to think they are consumers first and not citizens first. Some even fail to accept the responsibilities of citizenship while they demand entitlement to all its rights. This is a foolish illogical aspect of the baby doomerism culture's "me first" mentality. Without a logically thinking and honest citizenry, an intelligent and honorable polity is nearly impossible, and the economy has no path to follow that will benefit everyone. Only a few can benefit from it, and those who do, will not know what it means to survive from day-to-day because luxury makes them complacent, until apathy follows and is allowed to take hold of society (recall Figures 2-16, 2-17, and 2-13).

The functionality risks to a republic in consumerist culture are many. One is that society treats the most successful in business, or the luckiest in the marketplace, and the ones with the greatest inheritance among the HM[5], like heroes and gods. Those who gain the most material wealth buy luxury and become economic elites and celebrities. With a consumer mindset, they begin to see the acquisition of money, the exchange medium, as the most meaningful purpose. They pressure politicians to allow them to control economic distribution. By extension, they seek to control the politicians. Not only will the HM[5] want to control the politicians, they will want to control society as a whole. They will want control over all the powers' FILMS[2] [P7]. They will want to control the citizens' continuous conversion into consumers. This ensures that a pursuit of luxury drives the culture. People get fooled into buying with unescapable debt to try to be, or look, like the lucky luxurious ones. A desire to be entertained dominates modes of experiencing life. The people stop learning and growing in what they can control through their political muscle. The elites do not want people to vote for fair and reasonable policies that might better enable the USE to accomplish its mission. They'd rather the project rot. They've made it, they want no competition, they monopolize. Until we the people attend to our leadership role, we'll steadily degenerate from inside out, our body politic polluted with doomerism will continue to corrode from it.

Elite controllers shape attitudes of how people should define themselves. They stimulate behaviors to make an identity they propose a person possess, real. They want each person to lack an awareness of how to pursue a purpose for which born. They block us from gaining benefits we get by contributing to, and participating in, civil society. Doing so keeps us from being distracted, diluted, and deluded by their fantasies for us to live to consume. If we see ourselves as consumers first, we become anxiously concerned the economy power delivers money, goods, and services. We worry more about it than anything else in society. We begin to care less and less about the polity power, its policies, and the activities of government, which is to protect our natural rights. Such a trend is a current risk we must confront. The misbalancing of the powers done by doomerism gives rise to it. Its consumerist culture erodes our citizenship culture. The consumer-first mentality shapes our attitudes. It persuades those elected to serve in government to support increased consumerism. It feeds itself. It produces glitzy, tempting vanity. It superficially and viscerally appeals to base animal instincts to gain control of minds. It makes itself more appealing than the calling of good citizenship. It promises a predicament that weakens democracy. It is a shallow, hollow, self-fulfilling prophecy of nothingness because nothing of excess goes with us where we go after death. Moreover, even if we get to keep it in a tomb with us, some lazy, treasure-hunting future tomb-raider criminal will rob our corpse's possessions, by digging them up and stealing them. We ourselves might be the actual victim of the theft. Some might opine this would be a fitting finish for any who stole what they got by rigging the society to get more than a reasonable merit-based share of the common wealth generated by the work of the everyday people.

Let's have a look at the third diagram in Figure 6-9. It portrays the citizen as the purposeful orientation for society. Conversely, to a consumerist-oriented society in a culture of citizenship, attitudes and behaviors are shaped toward the endurance of people controlling the distribution of power and material wealth. The distribution systems of power and material wealth are separate but not equal. Politics is shaped by public opinion. Many things shape economics. Several are the politicians' governing, the legal framework, the policies of regulators, the consumption trends of people, market behaviors, and production of goods and services. The laws and policies govern how commerce and the distribution of money, goods, and services take place. The least amount of control by the government over the FILMS^2 [P7] efforts to AEIOUY^{2}K economy powers, in service of the USE, allows the greatest amount of freedom for the HM^5 to get left alone. This laissez-faire approach allows the HM^5 to act in ways that best sell money, goods, and services as needed by the citizens. Marketplaces are amazing at fulfilling needs. Free markets are superbly flexible to adjust and adapt to new consumer demands. But markets cannot solve all societal problems. The more complex the issue, the more problematically difficult it is for the singularly profit-focused HM^5 to solve. Consortiums of public and private ventures can do much better. Of course, the people shape the marketplace by their consumption patterns. The HM^5 respond by a business-savvy logic to sustain their ability to provision society. The trading and exchange of money for goods and services has an inherent self-regulating activity. When exchanges are happening, people can get what they need through legal markets. This is a good economy. It is dynamic and not static. It is able to act organically, invisibly performing like an ecosystem, yet with visible results. When money is not moving, the stagnation causes deficiencies in the provisioning of society.

Yet whenever the HM^5 conspire to trick people, we get trouble. We've trouble from criminals. We've trouble from excessively greedy ambition to get more than a fair and reasonable market price. Those seeking to get something for nothing or more than a fair share of a deal cause imbalance and the DAMN of powers. The imbalance of power in exchanges within the marketplace creates societal problems. Collusion by the HM^5 to set non-market-based prices is an unfair condition for the citizens, which causes a societal problem. If policies and practices promote conspiracy and monopoly, societal problems expand. Politics is the means by which citizens can confront these problems. Informed citizens ask politicians to adjust the rules of exchange to prevent criminality and monopoly. The republic's functionality risk to the consumerists in a culture of citizenship is limited. Consumerists may see countervailing forces enacted to confront unfair inequality. If consumers feel the marketplace is unfair and not properly refereed, they may call for the polity of citizens to regulate it better. Markets and commerce require regulation to prevent consumers from fraud and theft, as when con artists and crooks keep duping them out of their money. If they are not self-regulating effectively, politicians may use the power of government through laws, policies, or agencies to oversee activities to protect consumers from abusive business practices.

POWER

The Republic Supports Priority of the **Citizens** to decide "control"

"Who Comes First"

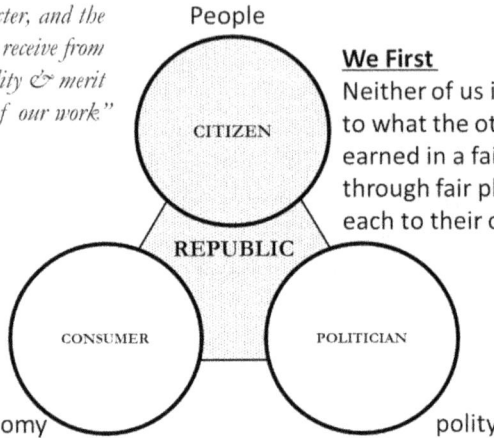

"may the best among us rise up on the content of their character, and the benefits we receive from the quality & merit of our work"

People

We First
Neither of us is entitled to what the other accumulates earned in a fair economic system through fair play & legitimate work each to their own ability

CITIZEN

REPUBLIC

CONSUMER   POLITICIAN

Negotiated economy   polity

Citizenship Orientation *(Citizen guided Republic)*

Society

Figure 6-9: Diagram of People Power—Dominant Society
The values of this diagram put the people power in control of society. The American citizen comes first. In circa 2020 political partisan polemics, this diagram could be construed to represent a power posture of a serious, reasonableness-seeking, centrist, a moderate capital "L" liberal, libertarian, progressive capital "C" Conservative Americanist seeking to properly balance private and public power with a preference for historical perspective, and rather optimistically future orientated essence. Recall that the uppercase L and uppercase C are practically the same perspective, with the L coming before the C and the C defending the L. These preferences seek meritocracy and earned value, not a hereditary, aristocratic, advantageous status quo society. They disagree with taking from the middle to support a few upper-income earners at the top and the many lower-income earners at the bottom, in the tax brackets of economic power-created social classes based upon earnings and capital holding capability and capacity.

The republic's functionality risk to politicians in a culture of citizenship is limited. It varies, however, based upon the limits the people set on the government's involvement in regulating the economy powers. It also depends on the commitment to citizenship in the elites and their sense of entitlement. When elites feel responsible to the USE for their opportunities, and their own definition of their selves in society is as citizens first, the risk is moot. If they see themselves as entitled to loot as if aristocratic heroes, monetary gods, society will face challenges to being fair and reasonable for the everyday people. If elites think of themselves as citizens first, they might be neighborly.

A citizen-focused society shapes this. The elites will not seek to control the politicians to limit the political refereeing or shaping of an opportune for all, micro, meso, and macro benefiting economy. The FILMS^2 [P7] and HM^5 will, with balanced reason for the society, manage the economy with efficiency and provision effectively. With citizenry based beliefs and practices to ensure equal opportunity, rewards will disperse more naturally according to talent and merit of effort, so all might find a standard of living and quality of lifestyle to survive with dignity, be able to find greater comfort in living, or find ways to legally access luxury living as a possibility. A belief in upward mobility will remain a motivator in American society with a citizen shaped society.

If the people seek to use the political system to overtly control the economy or prevent the HM^5 from creating wealth through entrepreneurship, risks will arise, and creativity will deteriorate. A will to produce new products to sell in the marketplace drives innovation.

Reducing how the pursuit of money can lead to a mercantile culture that tolerates attitudes that support behaviors to contrive, connive, and collude to manipulate the political system tempers the republic's functionality risk to citizenship in a consumerist culture. This manipulation, like bribery, seeks to reduce the rules and requirements of citizenship put upon the economic elites. As noted earlier, a consumerist culture sees this manipulation as the elites seek control of the distribution of political power. Only the capacity of the people to tolerate inequality of the distribution of material wealth by the economic system limits this. If it becomes too unequal, the people might revolt. The politicians will react to pacify the public or see themselves as elites, too, and partake in the bribery, lowering standards and not enforcing the laws. Politicians will do this to stay in positions of authority over the political system if they are corrupted. Willful elite status seeking enables them to look the other way in the hope they might get more materialistic wealth from public service. This is wrong. Thus, in a consumerist culture we've a risk of persons going into elected politics not to serve their fellow citizens but rather to enrich themselves. They will engross themselves in power. They will enjoy propaganda and exploitation. They will manipulate people's opinions and alter the rules while seeing themselves as playing in a game of life, which pleases the economy's elites. They will use their positions unethically. They may position themselves to accept the bribes, status, and celebrity offered by the elites of the economic system in return for a favor, or two, or more. A citizenship culture mitigates this risk of corrupted politicians.

Turning commerce against citizenship

Let's apply some of this discussed sociological thinking. Which generation do we suppose has been the most consumerist? Are attitudes intentionally shaped? Was Madison Avenue marketing and advertising to identify how to sell better? Could it be worse, is advertising a way to enculture people to become consumers, to brainwash us and tell us how to think and speak?

At the strategic level of waging commerce is the creation of a consumerist culture. Through it, the HM^5 seek to shape people's attitudes and behaviors, shifting the culture away from citizenship responsibilities and thus gaining social controls to make consumption favorable as the purpose and meaning of life. Extreme conspicuously consumptive attitudes and behaviors favor the top few by supporting the maximization of their wealth. If we best balance the societal powers, then successful provisioning with a well-managed economy power will be like an ocean tide. When it rises, it lifts all boats equally. If money is like vapor rising into a cloud and the force of winds is like invisible-hands moving markets, then status quo stagnation caused by hoarding stifles commerce. When both are controlled by a few, the condensation of the vapor into rain by the result of wind fronts becomes impossible. When the forces of the economy power are so restricted, nothing trickles down and drought occurs. Good commerce creates more opportunity for the most amounts of people. Competitive cooperation spawned commercial activity well refereed creates beneficial tides and rains. Allowing a few elites to collude to make monopolies defeats the best chance conditions for the economy power to benefit the USE.

At the tactical level of waging commerce, the use of psychology to figure out how to sell better to us reshapes social norms. Studies of human attitudes and behaviors are conducted with academy powers to develop a better understanding of personal preference setting and product selection, as well as the public opinion and emotive buttons to push to stir up a crowd. This feeds the knowledge of how and what sells, materially and politically. This narrows the range of real choice. Essentially, between a pair of things put in front of us. Aimed to pacify us these options for purchase are derived from our previous buys. We get funneled into predictability. This is unfreedom. When nothing shown us is a real choice, nor relates to what we can imagine, we become dumb drones. With new computing technology's mathematical algorithms of machine learning and artificial intelligence, more than ever before, we get catered to and kept in the shopping line in a consumerist trap devoid of human relational depth but full of shiny new objects. Once we define ourselves as consumers, we become enceltured to expect the economy powers to serve us. A sense of entitlement envelopes us on the outside and inside we act in response to an infestation of wants and desires put in our minds by advertisers. We expect that we deserve to be spoiled, and then feel we should be, too. We look forward to a parade of sellers presenting us their wares. Yet, is it service to convince us to buy something we do not really need (and may not even want) but feel obliged to get because it is popular? This is consumerist culture. Others seeking to please us are in it. We seeking to be pleased and entertained by to it are in it. It is in us, and we are in it. Yet, is it best for us, for our democracy, for our republic, for liberty?

The conversion from citizen first to consumer first is successful once we the everyday people casually toss around the term "consumer behavior", without even identifying that we have been redefined as an object of exploitation for another's economic game. We can participate in shopping without being cynical, confused, or victimized by connivery. However, we should be aware of our thinking and feelings and not blindly follow along without being mindful of what might be happening to our society and whether it is in line with our project's mission.

Let's think more deeply on this. We must consume. However, we do not need identities that desensitize us. We are not solely consumers. We can resist the labels applied by others or ourselves and especially those used by our politicians who want us to believe them, which we would if they did not lie all the time, or wiggle around to please everyone equally so they can stay in office. If we are merely consumers and not citizens, what might this mean for liberty? We should have an informed opinion on what it means to be constituents of politicians. We should imagine we serve liberty by using our people power to ensure a just society. We should make it based upon us, the everyday people, retaining the power to lead society. We must lead by ensuring that we pursue virtue as the purpose of our citizenship. If we the everyday people no longer see that our opinion as a citizen is vital to society, we are in deep trouble. If we now feel that being a consumer is our purpose, we will see our freedoms diminished. If we are more interested in opportunities to be a consumer loyal to brands, then we will soon be disloyal to our own best interests. We must guard against cynicism. Our best interest is in remaining free. We must ensure it by being fellow citizens. We mustn't wholly convert the culture of democracy into doomerism by living completely comfortable with consumerism, becoming solely consumers. This may be less of a ploy and more of a consequence of doomerism, but it nonetheless brings about doom to American society. It enslaves our babies to a mythology like power: consumerism.

A dependency to wanting served as primary feeling with a willingness to exude a sense of entitlement is not helpful to a society rooted in principles of a people wanting to be independent and free. We ought not to measure our happiness by competitive attitudes and behaviors. Instead, we ought to measure our happiness by cooperative attitudes and behaviors. If the earth dies, if a new feudalism takes over, if widespread disease and famine threaten our species, because of the depletion of fresh water sources and droughts, ecological collapse, consumerism will not help us survive without pestilence and violence. It prepares us for depression and disappointment, and it leaves us without common ground, a good commons, and relationships to rely upon to get by. Manufactured scarcity by economic elites and their pet politicians, lording over us, is a reality we can blame on ourselves. We failed to lead, to govern, and allowed the crooks to take control, and they fed us myths and fantasies we apparently wanted to believe. Did we too eagerly trade freedom of thought for security in material objects? The social powers: academy, community, mythology, and history will say of us, we did not escape from doomerism. We need to be citizens engaged in building up the functionality of the republic and of its civil society.

The power to shop at will is not as important as the power to govern. We must be able to have a say in how the polity shapes the FILMS[2] [P7] that administer the foundations of governing that affect the marketplaces that assist the economy power manage the provisioning of the goods and services that help society succeed. The systems of distribution must benefit the whole, rather than just a few. Too much propaganda produced by the politicians and elites distracts us from the truth. We must engage locally and demand less federally. We are fifty United States, and the united part does not mean the federal government should overly dictate how we must live. We must live up to the Constitution by E-SASSY-T-TUF-FT-CAUCUS where we live. We must stabilize the republic by sending decent citizens to Washington, D.C. to serve us, and we must hold them accountable to constitutional citizenshipping. As well as and in accordance with it national level politicians must work to limit the federal government's dictating terms and conditions for how we live our lives. This is as the founders intended it. With tough love, we must replenish them regularly to protect them from the corrupting forces of power. We must build a robust and capable civil society in our regional, state, municipal, city, and neighborhood communities. We need each other. We should not expect from the federal government excessive entitlements nor benefits to which we've not contributed. We would do better to build resiliency closer to home. We do not need an all-powerful federal government to prescribe the social circumstances or physical conditions of life, neither our survival in dignity, living in convenient comfort, or in leisurely enjoyment of luxury. We must resist dependency on the polity or the elites. The elites would enjoy a great resetting of our mentality from one of American ingenuity and entrepreneurial ambition to one of farm animals. That is, they'd like us to be nothing more than masses they rule, their feudal goal is for us to see ourselves as sows wallowing in the mud they've slung, or as cows chewing the cud of whatever we've been fed, or as chicken hens hustling out eggs in hope of species perpetuation. Point made metaphorically, we should have equal opportunity and access to avenues we imagine for creating livelihoods and shared commerce. We should be the farmers and traders of our own destinies. We need open ways, means, and methods to be the HM[5] and keep what we earn by decent remuneration for our labors. We do we need multinational corporations shaping our society around their ambitions. We can feed, house, clothe, and govern ourselves without name brands. We can bake, build, and make locally. Assuredly, the plutocrats differ in their desires, thinking they can control us with a form of animal husbandry that makes us their physiological dependents, psychologically conditioned to worship them pleadingly for being so kind to feed us. This is the operant behavior of tyranny. We must thwart it by getting smarter to its sinister yen. We must evict baby doomers from positions of authority then remake the purpose of the FILMS[2] [P7] to function in accord with our project's mission to achieve its goals by attaining its objectives.

Mostly, we need equilibrium from the citizenship and consumer identity tug-of-war. We need reasonable economic distribution and collaborative political discourse. We've many adaptive societal problems to address. We must get to work with new tools to control power and power's proper balance in the LAMBS. This book is a rallying cry for us to get it right for the children. We must awaken with eyes wide open. We must decide that materialistic consumerism is not as wholesome as the pursuit of virtue. Accumulation of things does not make us happy. Competing for status symbols only enriches the few who own the companies that make and sell them. We can support neighborhoods with family run local businesses that can provision for us. At them, we can shop for what we need. We can enjoy our money. Buy what we need. Buy what we want. However, if fooled by mercantile messages we might turn into "hollow men" humans. We cannot become drugged consumer drones, pulsing with imagery that does not fulfill the humane human soul. We cannot let the tirade of superficial symbolic falsehoods drain our confidence in fellow humans. Elites want to turn us into subjects of trade. They want to mine us and extract what we have earned. They want to control us. The political tyrants want to keep us from having anything. Or they promise us everything to turn us into subjects of their rule. This makes them get everything and feel raw power, but strips us of our liberty. They want to take from us. Our hope is that we balance out these risks by being the leadership of society. By demonstrating through good examples we can show the children how to behave for the sustainment of our culture of democracy in a republic polity.

If we want better lives, each of us simply must be better at being a citizen first. We are to be the champions of the cause of liberty. Then we can go to the marketplace and consume; then we can shop. However, we should beware whenever we call ourselves consumers. To be a consumer is to be a sheep for the slaughter. Do not accept nor embrace the identity label consumer. Consumers are not agents of liberty. Consumers are statistical numbers, not citizens leading the country to become a more perfect union. Consumers are not setting the moral tone and playing the virtuous song democracy demands. We must call ourselves citizens, and as a citizenry get to work on making American society a reality. Then we can go shop, as we must.

Know that to say the "customer is king" is to create an un-American concept of a person as a tyrant. Kings demand something that oversteps the social boundaries of human dignity. To gain their favor, kings demand their subjects kiss their butts, and gleefully insert noses until browned, claiming to enjoy the fragrant stench. This causes the rise in a sense of entitlement that is plainly not in keeping with democracy. Its use began by economy power perpetrators perplexing our minds and making the concept of consumer more valuable than citizen. Such was yet another means to persuade purchasing and entitlement. This is the way to make people expect catering to like spoiled brats. Remember, a spoiled age produces spoilage. Spoilage rots civility. Behave better, behave as an equal, and behave as a citizen. This is democracy, not a feudal kingdom. Civilizations collapse from imbalances in societal and natural powers. Disinformation distortions help the few in positions of wealth and power. Fallacies believed, keep them on top. Consumerism is a devise to support this negative for the everyday people outcome.

We've gone on for over 568 pages now, beating a drum of warning hoping to awaken everyone from the unknowing consumption of cultural manipulation and numbing forty-year nap of naivety. We've explained what went wrong, what were and are the various perspectives on what we are becoming as a society. It offered a means for how we might unite on common ground. We've work to do at the micro, meso, and macro levels. As we conclude, we must resolve to end at a point of repose, from which we can spring into action, get informed, get involved, and vote more often. As W. E. B. Du Bois wrote, "Either America will destroy ignorance or ignorance will destroy the United States." While we've mentioned them here and there throughout this exposition, let's now summarily go over the games being played by those in authority that enjoy the power of controlling our lives. We must not let them continue this line of thinking. We must stop them.

Know the Games of the Power Lusters

As the people, we are to provide the leadership in American society. We elect from among us representatives to our polity. We promote those who move into positions of responsibility and authority to provision society through the ways, means, and methods by which we AEIOUY²K our economy power. We need to do a better job of ensuring the authority figures are virtuous, honorable, and have good society-benefiting character. We must be keenly aware of the games those who "want it all" will play. We must not allow these lustful players to get away with it. We cannot turn a blind eye or ride the waves of corruption to fill up our own pockets. It is irresponsible. It is disingenuous to the rest of us. It is what brings doom to

American society and future generations and perhaps even the ecosystems we need for our species' survival. We must come to recognize and block the power-hungry doomer games played with, on, and against us. Games played with us as if we were toys, and games played on us as if we were inferior subjects, games played against us as if we had an actual chance to compete, which they ensure we do not because our humiliation pleases them. Are we subjects for the pleasure of the elites? Should we be cynical, thinking, "Yeah, sure we know, we're being manipulated and laughed at", but doing nothing about it like complacent and apathetic subjects? Could a few at the top want all others to be at the bottom? Do they want the population to be powerless and ignorant, so they can do whatever they want? Is this happening? Is it possible?

Games played with, on, and against us

The games played with us are identifiable. They can be spotted when the FILMS[2] [P7] DAMN the primary societal powers. When we see something, we must say something loudly. Speak out proudly. When we see it, remember that disuse is the good force of power no longer used. Abuse is power used wrongly and harmfully. Misuse is power not put to the best use for its intended purpose. Partisanship is a misuse of polity power. Nonuse is power that could be used but is not. Nonuse happens when corruption or cowardice takes hold, and power is not used, as it should be to prevent injustice. We must also be on the lookout for the DAMN of the secondary and tertiary powers. To solve social problems at the micro, meso, and macro levels of society, we must AEIOUY[2]K the societal and social powers properly. These powers done improperly result in unintended consequences. Often such results come from imbalanced (or intentionally misbalanced) powers.

For example, we can see challenges in the family and community as children grow up without stable households. We've children raised in single-earner households in anomic conditions of poverty. We've children raised in luxurious households in snobbish conditions of wealth. The seven socialization contexts—snobbish, traditionalistic, anomic, modernistic, postmodernistic, enervating, and radicalizing (STAMPER)—subject children to different expectations and experiences. Each sees different games of power played against them. Each learns concepts of power in games, which differ by context, except for the common human needs meeting ones of the species. Their social approaches get shaped by precepts and pedagogy of how to get along in the neighborhood shaped by a community power that presents them its view of society. Seeing society as a field of play, dos and don'ts, children learn how they must play it to get by. The multiplying forms of family power and socialization contexts separate us from each other and point us in the direction of continuous disunion, not unity. This is a game played with us. It benefits only those who seek to rule, by dividing the people in the way we raise future generations. Yet we need a civil society not to have to struggle to raise Americans. We must stop the gaming with our lives that doomerism brings. But how will we unify to block the games? Should we just leave it to the government? Or is this complacency, and us being too selfish? Are we too overwhelmed because an imbalanced and underperforming economy power does not allow us to make ends meet with one income earner so ones spouse has time to raise children? If possible, we would rear kids more similarly than differently. We see issues with the history power, which is critical in this age of information overload, in our third stage of knowledge evolution of human society. Journalists use hyperbolic methods to entice our emotions. This is not a documenting of facts. It feels wrong, as if done to sell and not inform. It seems as if they know how to write intentionally to ping the amygdala, which incites overly emotive passions of excessive excitement in people. This is not helpful to the need for reason in the citizenry. People are not dumb, but we need facts. We cannot govern society and ourselves if we are frantically fed fanatical fantasies, falsehoods, and fallacies by baby doomers hoping to profit from such farfetched tall, and tattle, tales. We cannot self-govern with these kinds of games played on us. We most definitely do not need dramatic media stimulating us until our emotional circuitry fries from the absurdities constantly tossed out at us and we begin to believe them as true, or we become completely cynical and distrust others, or collapse from the uncontrollable confusion caused by the baby doomers' perverse propaganda.

We need information to govern and feed our needs for open and honest exchange in the public square and marketplace. The undue dramatization of daily events is a misuse of the history power. It needs operated in a citizen-supporting mode. If not done by citizen-first journalists but by doomers, it will seek to push an ideology. We need it to be helpful in explaining the information overwhelming us. Informational and communications technologies are blasting us. We're bombarded with extreme competitions over selling angles, not facts. We need clear journaling to understand the current state of affairs in society. This is the "free—from control of politicians and elitists—press" a democracy needs. We do not need wild affrays full of lies and truth-benders paid to gain approval for bad ideas in our discourse and activities of our civilization's square and market. A bad idea is one that is not in accord with our need to accomplish our mission to achieve our goal and attain our constitutional objectives. Misinformation and maligning stories hyped up by hyperbolic media are games played with us that need stopped! We must unite to stop them. We must!

In writing our history, we must recognize this work's proper role in the business of American society. As an important part of a culture of democracy, the power should support the mission and its efforts to IDEALS liberty and justice for all. Ask how we might better AEIOUY^{2}K history power's journaling to do this. We see its misuse by divisive storytelling, which now sells very well, even better than sex. Spewing tribal hatreds seems highly profitable. Yet if hatred is profitable for the press, we will have major societal cohesion issues. A society polarized for profitability is not going to be a healthy or happy one. If journalism is no longer a guardian of liberty in all houses, we will see continuous fracture of people into tribes and factions. Group identity will trump the content of our character and the beliefs of its more valuable posture for posterity. If the press wants only profits first and foremost, the "news" becomes a product to sell. It gets told in ways it wants sold, in massive amounts. Truth matters less than fantasies that hold attention and rile up the emotions. It can make more money by using the economy powers, particularly the artistry power that knows human emotions best, than by truth telling. This is in part what consumerism produces—spoon-feeding fallacies desired heard by the target audience wanting to be pleased, and only done to make a buck. For shame, this brings about the end of honesty. Democracy needs courageous truth telling, not fantasy selling.

The press, if solely oriented to gaining greater attention and more money, produces a risk to us. With the massive amounts of money they make, they gain an even greater ability to manipulate society. They already, by controlling media distribution, can persuade, intimidate, and direct the polity. This is a very dangerous precedent. We must stop it. It portends a pending doom in which the tail of the media wags the dog of the polity. To be free, the press must tell the truth. For this reason, we must not allow them to monopolize. Having too few media outlets is dangerous. The globalizing monopolies need to be broken apart, and we must consume news from more local sources. Local news sources cannot compete against monopolies that have accumulated the control of news investigation, preparation, and distribution. Monopolizing media conglomerates have amassed too much history power, which now threatens democracy. Do we remember when the news repeatedly reported the threats to our liberty? Boomers were blind to its undermining. They played games to maximize profitability and ill prepared the population to see its losses. Alas, doomers are winning the game, and the rest of us are 'losers,' which is a bogus label applied by them to fulfill their ego. How pathetic of us to allow this to persist any further. Global media conglomerates are businesses not seeking to save democracy but to destroy it. Their owners seek to be the top members of the plutocracy. They DAMN their power to the demise of democracy culture and the republic polity.

By polarizing audiences, the press helps them predict the volume of the audience to whom they will sell advertisements. Target marketing, narrow banding, locks in the audience as nearly permanent and guaranteed. Creating a hypnotic-like trance in consumers is their goal. For this, they use a kind of mythology power with sophisticated artistry power to reach our emotions first. They avoid reason. Again, if we are not seeing ourselves as consumers but as citizens, we are less likely to fall into the trap of this game played with us. It is an abuse when a wealthy press, in pursuit of its own interests, hurts us as it hunts for more economy power. It injures us when this economy power gains more polity power. If most of the press is not telling the truth as it once did, at the beginning of the republic, we've a serious societal problem to solve. Some of this is a result of the disruption to their industry power. The impacts of the new computational, informational and communications technology are hugely negative. We need to solve this. If old paradigms are impossible if current ways are unsatisfactory then we need new problem solvers and innovations to help us. We must demand these. To solve the problem a proper definition for and behavior of the problem of the press needs brought forth for debate, deliberation, and decision-making on how to reform it. We must be committed to solving it, especially those among us who work in its fields. We the people must not act in ways of groupthink but in ways of group salvation, which means we need to be honestly and courageously truthful. The culture of democracy cannot sustain frivolous treatment. We need to get more serious about it. Its life is not a series of silly games played amongst us. Baby boomers are playing games. They are neither being serious enough about the present nor the future. The children need us to help them stop the dominant—too long in charge—generation's games.

Journalism is to record and recount the facts of events. It can offer opinions for consideration, but it is not to build a brand to convert the people power to its way of thinking. It is to inform us. We all need to know and should want to know the truth, so that we can make decisions based on facts, not lies. We no longer see the use of local newspaper reporting. This disuse of power is unhealthy for democracy. We need these community-benefiting resources. We best solve most problems locally, but neighborhoods need the resources. Globalizing conglomerates destroy them. What can we do about it? We can decide whether we want to live in tribal combat all the time or not. If not, we change our consumer habits. We create the demand. The market will respond to supply it. We stop consuming from those massive media outlets. We put our money where our mouths are and pay the price necessary to support local small business reporting that helps communities.

We stop expecting to get free things because nothing is free, really, and we do not see to what hidden strings attach. They could be exploiting our sense of identity psychologically or evaluating our data to manipulate us further into their control. Who are they? They are the few we let gain control of all forms of communications, and who mine all our data to shape society toward their aims.

We must pay people enough money to shift to a regionalized way of economy, locally supportive and monopoly ignoring. If we continue listening to massive media outlets, we will become ignorant from the limited perspectives fed to our emotions and not our reason. We must seek to understand first, before we judge. We must be more conscientious of what we consume, who produced and distributed it, and why. We must check our biology power, our psychology, to be certain it is not asked to DAMN itself to give us comfort in an echo chamber of frauds. We must lead. We must stop enabling doomer behaviors in our history power. We must end their games played with, on, and against us. In the next five paragraphs, hear the cadence of a rally cry for a new focus on American ideals.

Concerning games played with us, we can see issues with the social powers: academy, mythology, artistry, and industry. We must recognize their proper role in the business of American society. Are they of the culture of democracy? Are we able to revamp them to $AEIOUY^2K$ them in line with our project's requirements that we IDEALS liberty and justice for all? In what ways are they suffering from DAMN? We must ask, seek, learn, know, react, and work within and for the social powers beneficial activities in the LAMBS. We must get them to equilibrium in ways that support American society to fulfill its profound principles founded on virtue and truth's pursuit. We the people are to lead. We must set the tone. We must ensure the bones of our society are wholesome and strong with democracy. We must ensure the marrow is full of liberty and not the leukemia of doomerism.

Additionally concerning games played with us, we see issues with the geography power that we must come to terms with or it will overwhelm us. Are we recognizing the threatening risks and the new opportunities to mitigate them? Are we using our culture of democracy to solve problems or deny them? Will we $AEIOUY^2K$ societal power in ways to continue to benefit from geography power while we work to IDEALS liberty and justice for all? In what ways are we suffering from its DAMN? Ask, seek, learn, know, react, and work with it in ways that support American society. We the people are to lead. We must set the tone. We must ensure the bones of society are wholesome and strong with democracy—to best cooperate and coordinate the benefits we gain from geography power.

The shaping of society as a set of groups in opposition to one another, like ancient Greek gods on Mount Olympus, is a game played on us. It is the rich, moneyed, and authority-persuading racketeering persons enjoying toying with our lives. They set us up to fight with one another and consume more than we can afford. Then they laugh all the way to the bank they own. Because they know, it will get bailed out by the politicians if it fails. They, and it should face trail and judgement, and if guilty, get jail time for scheming and fleecing, but won't so long as they control society with doomerism as a plutocracy. We bring them pleasure the more amusingly we behave in our ignorance of their games. We need not be their fools. We need not act foolishly. We need to lead. We need to tell them they work for us in a democracy. We are dooming ourselves with our own vices. Voting against our own best interests is a consequence of going along with doomerism. We must stop it. We must!

Playing games to pit us against one another maims us. It hinders our goal achievement and objectives' attainment. It sells ideas to us like "You need to get in on the corruption game for yourselves." What the politicians are doing is giving us a choice without explaining it. They are asking us to let them do our bidding, and yet evidence indicates they are just using us. They don't do our bidding, and we are not sufficiently holding them accountable. If we attend to them properly, they will attend to us properly. If they've gone doomer on us and we do not monitor and regulate them, they will enrich themselves. We must replace them perpetually until we get politicians who represent us honorably in the privilege to perform public service, and then pass the duties on to another, which is a sign of respect to the republic, as exampled by George Washington. A near-permanent class of politicians is never an intention of democracy culture in a republic. It creates vulnerabilities and poses risks for American society, a society meant for liberty and justice for all—for us, the everyday people.

What the economy elites are doing is giving us a choice without explaining it. They are asking us to give them our money for things we really need, which is okay. But when they ask for too much money for them, this is not okay. When they entice us to buy things we like that we may not need yet want even though we cannot afford them, because we are not getting paid enough money when we work, it feels like a game played on us. When we are unable to afford all the necessities, or aspire to obtain some luxuries, we must borrow money. When they take our earnings and then loan us more, in an accelerating conveyor belt of escalating stress, they can own us sufficiently to force us to work longer and harder to give them more as we bury ourselves in debt. It's an escalator upward materially but downward financially. Deficit spending and debt demoralize. We drift in the direction of defeat.

Chasing our tails as if dogs and getting nowhere, is what economy power and its subordinate supporting powers' DAMN looks like. Such wrongdoing confounds us and colludes against the project's success as it compounds wealth for conglomerate beneficiaries, who are not us. It causes woe. We get played, and made to feel like we are unimportant, unworthy, worthless, good-for-nothing nobodies, like "a hound dog crying all the time." This is the plutocratic game played on us by the partisan politicians and economic elites.

We can decide whether we would rather live in a civilization of citizens or not. In such a civilization, the people practice good citizenship. People are trustworthy, neighborly, and interested in living in communities of true liberty. We will be this community of communities when everyone pursues virtue. When we all build social capital and develop additional social grammars, we will make our neighborhoods and communities into one civil society. We will live free from lies, bullying, bigotry, hatred, doubt, and evildoing. We live by, for, and of facts not fallacies, truths not lies. We can, and will create this more perfect union. When we commit to learning more about the truth of democracy, liberty, and virtue and live for, by, and of them. We the everyday people have the power. We must begin to lead. The boomers failed us by failing to do so. It is time to reverse doomerism. It is time to restore original ideals; it is time we begin E-SASSY-T-TUF-FT-CAUCUS.

7. "Yes, We'll Stop It!"

This chapter offers more motivation for us in our mission to defeat doomerism.

We can remove the fear. We must begin to believe and behave in ways ideal, framed in the Declaration of Independence and the Constitution as placed before us to follow. We know though that those who wrote them did not fully follow them, and those who came afterwards wrongly misconstrued meanings of some of the words. Always the pendulum swings dramatically. Drama is in our nature. We cling to our group's thinking and defend it out of a sense of loyalty or fear. Magnanimously the magnificent manumitter Abraham Lincoln reinvigorated the ways, means, and methods for our republic to succeed with its culture of democracy. His speeches brilliantly restated our purpose and realigned our imaginations to what is possible—as intended by the founders and framers—of, for, and by, the greatest social project in human history.

Because of him, we have, as a people, moved in the right direction, toward living up to the writings of the framers, as amended to correct the cultural biases of their time. There has been a progression of implementing the intentions of the words. We must while accepting the increase in application of democratic principles, concurrently hold onto the original ideals of our nation's founding. We can do this. We can move forward in forming an integrated construction of our core values, the values that benefit a majority of virtuous citizens, and not majorly "me first" values that have made a mess of our great nation. We are the generations coming after the baby boomers. We can now see the disease they have brought into the USE. We must step up, get into offices in the polity, open businesses in the economy, and reshape our powers toward noble purposes and good usages. We can demand and expand a new revival of our original intents for a culture of democracy by E-SASSY-T-TUF-FT-CAUCUS continuously during our time in the numeric demographic majority control of society, remaking the promise of prosperity for posterity. We know enough not to fall into predictable attitudes and behaviors of those who came before, so those who come after have a better example. We know enough not to swing the pendulum too fast and hard so as to overshoot the equilibrium we need for stability. We know we need security and liberty, but we will not sacrifice for the latter for the former. We will heed this historical wisdom of human nature given us as advise by the founders. We will learn from previous scholars to stop our turning into more disastrous crises. We will listen. We will learn. We will act lawfully.

Millenials, in particular, are largely the most educated generation looking for jobs, natural team players, prone to group work, wanting to be challenged, dreaming big, and looking for a mission (Bosché, 2016) Millennials, this book tells of a most important mission. A mission to intervene in how we AEIOUY^{2}K societal and social powers to stop the baby doomers from continuing the constant DAMN of these powers. This mission seeks out teamwork skills and civic-mindedness. Complex wicked social problems in society need multidisciplinary teams to solve them, not single-minded, self-centered egos. We the everyday people need you now. If not you, then who will work hard to fix American society? We need you to build coalitions with your juniors and step up to perform the reforms to get our ship turned toward its prescient destination of liberty and justice for all. You can do this! This is for the real trophy. This is for your children. This is for your country tis' of thee. Time is passing quickly. Please rise and be counted. Please stand and be heard. Please become the generation that leads the people to lead society. Be the heroes of the USE. Get into the LAMBS. Earn endearing forever respect and appreciation. We need you! We need you now to intervene. Let's do it!

We are on the cusp of transferring power to the civic-minded. We cannot allow doomerism to create social or political cleavages between us. Awakened to the devastating policies of social and economic destructions in certain settlement patterns done by of previous generations, we must move forward to get back on the path of righteousness. We must steel ourselves to do something about correcting and healing from past errors and omissions. The baby boomers' value sets are unhelpful and unhealthy for liberty. We are the children, now more grown up, facing real consequences, unlike them. For our children, we must reverse the bad trends and restore some equilibrium. It is our time in the cycle of history. We are in crises. We have what it takes, an outlook that breaks the mold of doomerism.

Doomerism is a lie. It's "me first" bases puts the "I" at its core. It's fascination with the self—over the sophisticated subtleties of society into which we are born—has gone overboard. It denies the truth of nuance in human affairs. It oversimplifies politics and of human nature as manipulatable into a binary argument. This "on or off", or "you" or "me" switch mentality is immature. It is misguided. It misses the needs for negotiations and diplomacy to achieve a happy and healthy society. Life is better imagined as an adjustable dial, from "low to mid to high", with choices better for "me, we, you", and tolerating these in a shared liberty. Our project needs this wiser perspective. It needs quality team players to accomplish our mission. With five kinds of society dismissing or manipulating baby boomers (loomers, groomers, zoomers, roomers, and doomers) in control, we cannot succeed. No longer the majority, we must replace them post haste.

There is no "I" in team. There is no Team USA any longer. There are celebrities and superstars sharing the stage, competing with each other for attention and fame. This is not real teamwork. Of course, generalizations are unfair toward and often wrong about one another. Yet similarities exist among the like-minded, those who've shared experiences or were enculturated in congruous social norms, folkways, mores, beliefs, and values. Stereotypes are wrong, unkind, ignoble, and lazy ways of staying disconnected from a fellow citizen. They are not neighborly.

If we want to live in a society that has wise and truthful underpinnings of democracy, we'll need to get used to being tolerant and working to educate ourselves about others. It takes work to be a responsible citizen. If we want to be a series of seriously patriotic generations, we must commit to the attitudes and behaviors of the hard work it will take to challenge our own assumptions and treat each person as someone whose story we want to get to know, while preserving each other's dignity. Life is about each other, people, not the acquisition of material possessions. Our species' survival is the first need. Who we are, where we came from, and where we are going is part and parcel of the evolution of human life and culture (Harris, 1989). The social bonds of family, band, and clan began with the cooperation necessary to remain alive against an almighty geography power. Life is about human relationships and achievements in what we do together, what we can do to express the joy in living with less stress from threats to survival. Life is not about egocentricity. Good ego health is good. Excessively egotistical orientations like arrogance and conceit can rub others the wrong way. Many teachings of our mythology power reiterate this lesson of humility as vital to our group survival. Inherent selfishness is a threat to community sustainment. There is good pride, and there is bad pride in hubris and vanity. Good pride, being proud of one for accomplishing something worthy, done for the right reasons for the benefit it brings to others and us, is appropriate. We need to not see ourselves as godlike but be honestly humanely human in humble humanity and community. This is as it should be in a culture of democracy. This is as it must be to make a republic achieve its representational ambitions.

With these perspectives in mind, we'll need to realign our societal and social powers to serve liberty first. This decision is a cultural one that allows it as process to shape society to be an American one. Once and for all, we need to move our project along to achieve the goal and objectives stated in the Preamble. This is the mission. The majority controlling generation for forty years forgot it. Persons of it inhabiting the United States did so without serving with the people power as the leadership of its business of being a society. Persons of it failed to unite, e pluribus unum, the words inside the top of the Capitol's dome. Boomers diverged from the passage plan. They were simply e pluribus with "me first" attitudes and behaviors. We can correct course. We can regain navigational direction. We can recover back onto our voyage's sail plan. We can undue that which misguided us. Our project will outlast and bypass them. Forty years is a small segue of misdirection. We can overcome the misgivings. We can do it with a significant intervention in the name of liberty for justice for all.

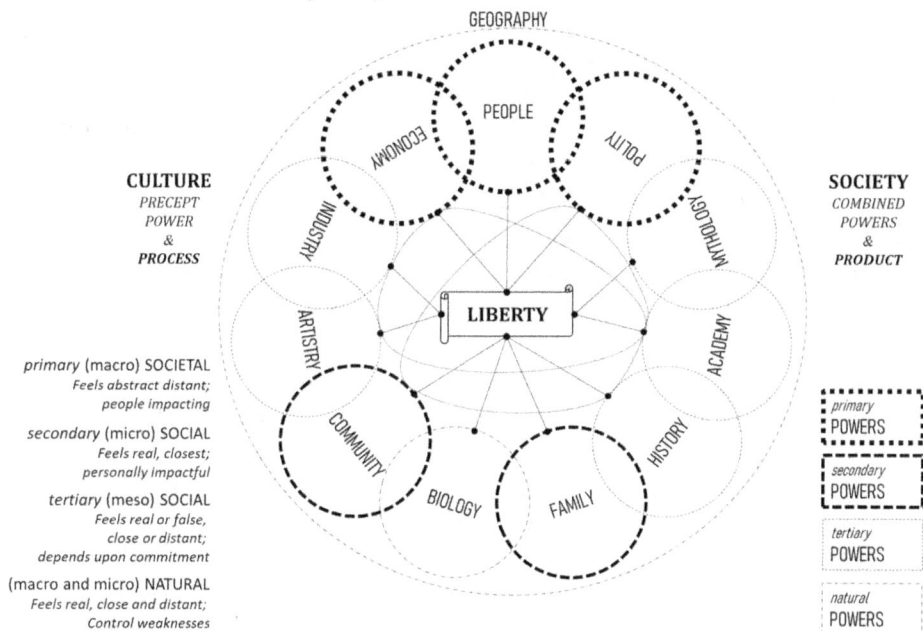

Figure 7-1: Culture, Society, and Human Powers Organized to IDEALS Liberty
Societal powers are flexible, malleable, and can all orient toward the principle of liberty as a means of uniting and unifying American society toward achieving its goal by attaining its objectives. If all the people choose to do so, we will succeed in fulfilling the original ideals that created the US as an amazing enterprise of public and private FILMS[2] [P7] and HM[5] that has proudly produced much prosperity. We've work to do to reverse negative trends and deal with the bad and ugly DAMN of power in our history. We can if we begin to E-SASSY-T-TUF-FT-CAUCUS now and forever.

We begin this restored voyage back to first principles armed with new knowledge. We should start by being stronger in exhibiting democracy. This happens when we don't ignore others who are not like us. They may be a neighbor you one day might have to depend upon. Don't be a doomer to the community we were born to have in the USE. Don't allow the doom to come from the hands of the boomers. Combined, the subsequent three generations are numerically larger, a new majority. It's our turn. We must act. We must lead the USE to enable its communities to reengage with democracy as our core culture. What it means to be an American resides in the founding documents' ideals. Their principles need vigorously reignited to reify our identity as citizens purposefully serving them. How we live up to this ambitious proposition is a measure of our patriotism. Let us not let it ebb and flow in successive generations. We can and must do this intervention to disrupt the demagoguery and theft. We will succeed when we pursue virtue first and work to IDEALS liberty forthrightly and continuously. We must offer ACE in greater quantity and frequency to reacquaint the population with our cause. Our instructions must be clear so that we are able to be an example for all humanity of a people in leadership of an American society in united community, virtuously self-governing an enterprise in unison where the polity and economy powers serve the health of the society by listening to the will of the everyday people!

How is this so? When each of us was born, we were dependent on others. As we grew our egos said "I am the universe, doing it all on my own." This is not so. It is ignorantly illogical and unreasonable to assume. Because behind the scenes of our lives, in our families, neighborhoods, and communities, were mentors, helping us in ways we were unaware. This is what neighbors do. This is what parents, aunts and uncles, teachers, healers with medicines, clergy, coaches, and school leaders do. This is how community power works to make a society function. To ignore the community, believing "only I make my destiny," is vainglorious and isolating. If this is one's approach to living, when death arrives, no one will come to the funeral. Do not fall into this trap. Do not allow doomerism to take hold. Reject it!

The powers of society are malleable. Culture is a precept power and process by which we shift, balance, check, and should direct society toward our first principles and our purpose: liberty. We ought to be all about it. We must orient our powers to make it reified, real in feel and reality, leading to the creation of a truly American society. This is the first step to take to IDEALS liberty. It is how we begin the march to move the masses of us in the direction of our goal of a more perfect union.

Since our country began with a wise belief that our Creator endowed us with inalienable rights, we must affirm it as foundational for democracy in a republic. By believing in this, our Constitution will be a legitimate social construction worth defending, not upending. By disallowing doomerism to continue to DAMN our powers, we protect its sage sanctity. Whether we contend it is a divine gift or a highly rational intelligent human creation, we should place our faith in our Constitution and behave accordingly, holding one another accountable to it, too. It says we can amend it as necessary. We have before. We may need to again. But before we do, we must study it. It is like a higher power aiding us by great wisdom. We must know and understand it better through more robust ACE. Our nation, to be of many one, e pluribus unum, depends on us doing this scholarship. Given that we declare on our money "In God We Trust", does not mean we can relinquish all control and allow the rule of men (humans) to control us. It does not mean we can take our hands off the wheel in hopes the God of mythology power will keep our country from veering off course. Metaphorically, if our nation is a ship, we must work like coxswain, boatswain, and yeomen to sail our enterprise with and sometimes against, the winds of time to keep it on the correct course. This is not easy. It means we as citizens must do more to create, reinvigorate, and keep an American society than others elsewhere who are ruled. Either we do the work, or we'll be totally controlled. Do we want that consequence? Do we want ruled? Have we given up on our dream to be a democracy? Has doomerism made us so cynical we'll quit on our children? Will be abandon ship? We mustn't skip out on the project and abandon posterity's babies, leaving them to suffer under tyranny. Freedom once lost is nearly impossible to regain.

The effort on our part, personally and as a people, is participatory. It is not easy to cope with different others, but it was once done more easily. It is not facile but requires facts, not false superstitions and prejudices. These are the things doomerism elevates to enable irrational selfishness to pervade society. We must obey the common basic rules for civility. Like the moral code of the Ten Commandments, or rational laws meant to enable society to function for the benefit of the common good. As well as for the best outcomes of the majority with deep regard and respect for a minority who choose to differ with the majority's decisions, provided their disagreement is rational and arguable and not oppositional because they lost a reasonable debate. Rules to keep the peace reduce the possibility of violence of us against one another. The majority is not one group or another by some classification but real participants in good citizenshipping. If bad behaviors overtake one generation, should we slouch and wait them out? Or, on the other hand, when the rest of us are not behaving badly and reaching numeric superiority, shouldn't we vote them out and not buy from them? Oughtn't we, shut them out of the pilothouse's bridge, remove their hands off the controls, and prevent them from pushing the buttons, pulling the levers, and turning the wheel of the helm that $AEIOUY^2K$ society's powers?

To help the majority share majorly the same values, and pursue the same virtues we must agree to give over our personal biology power, our instincts, to reason. This will not be easy, but is a developmental aspect of becoming an adult in a society relying on democracy. We must agree to think to support and defend the Constitution. It is the foundation of American society. This is what being a citizen means:

- be for it
- commit to uphold it
- be honest, to tell the truth before courts of law that will pass judgments

Also, it's to not:

- rationalize to protect pride when we know we are in the wrong

- falsify to justify our desires
- willingly walk into crimes holding temptation's hand.

This is all work. This is the internal battle to be and do better. This is our own personal and community journey. It is a lifelong voyage of self and citizenship. The sooner we begin it, the more we do it, the better for democracy. It is the ultimate form of self-reflective honesty, conscientiousness, and the engine of compassion, empathy, and love. Yet a majority must pursue it to make it popular to increase its strength of persuasion so eventually all persons commit to it as a personal and national identity that realizes the intended culture of democracy as the precept power and process of the republic's society on its voyage toward its goal; attaining its objectives along the way.

In family and community power, we find many helpers for this journey to find our personal purpose and worthy contributory activities for the benefit of the community. The list of helpers is long. It includes our parents and relatives at home, teachers at school, holy people in religious places, teammates at work or play, coaches and mentors, referees in sports, supervisors seeking our best interests (when we are blessed to have this kind), rooted-in-reality elected officials, dedicated public servants, officials and administrators at agencies, and the list goes on. The point is, we need each other, and we need from one another their best effort. We don't see this as we used to. We don't feel like members of the larger community. Why is this? Baby doomerism brought us forty years of confusion caused by an egregious selfishness in ways that appear to have gotten away with wrongs without punishment. We're surrounded by unwelcome and often unhealthy imagery in movies made with technologies so real that the theater of fantasies appears as reality. However, it is misused artistry power.

Art informs us of our own humanity. But if too fantastically real, it can make us feel small if we are unaware of the artifice behind it. Because of the qualities of the technologies in movies and television and gaming on screens, we've steadily separated from reality, from each other, and desensitized to what is happening in our minds and in our society. Who allowed all this to happen? Who thought these were not issues to deal with? Who thought this was not going to hurt us? While making money like never before, why would the producers care? Who did not think that a community standard mattered? Who was asleep at the wheel? Was no one watching the store? The answer is the baby doomers and their complicit loomers and the other "me first" boomers, the groomers, zoomers, and roomers, many of whom secretly wanted to be one of the affluent doomers running around in elitist social circles. Why else would they have allowed super salaries and celebrity status given to bad persons? Those, whom history power, mythology power, and artistry power warned us never to revere, found respect and dignity in doomerism. Those of high position, even when they never reflected nor respected those whom they were to represent, remained in control. The misguided majority would want their admired elites to be like them. Many baby boomer chief executives' vision of themselves is not the vision we need of those who manage the economy and administer the polity in a democracy. It is not all about the rulers, it is all about the rules and thus all about the commoners, the everyday people, who themselves must behave as citizens first to make this republic all that it can be, and more than it is for our children to come.

We have a moral obligation to the founders to revive the national community, one house at a time, one town at a time, one city at a time, one county at a time, one state at a time, one region at a time, and all at once, one nation in our time. The ways, means, and methods for all of us is the Constitution as amended. We may find companionship with the wisdom of the founding framers whose visions for an American Society were amplified by great societal leaders throughout our history such as were found in the polity like Abraham Lincoln, or in the civil society like the reverend Martin Luther King, Jr. We can reunite if we rally around it and make it central to our daily thinking, conversation, and performance of our roles, acting out a way of being appropriate to our calling as citizens first. We could continue to allow those who seek to exploit us for their own gain to distract us.

What's it going to be, all of us the "we," or just you and I, the "me"? Do we want to repeat the mistakes of the "me first" generation and further doom the future of our American children? If not, then let us become a true citizenry. Let us become 21st-century citizen patriots for liberty with democracy. Know the purpose of our Constitution (as amended). Believe in it as a divine gift to humankind or as the greatest social invention ever enacted by humans, and make it your purpose to restore its standing in the hearts of all inhabitants of this country and across the globe. In committing to it emotionally with all our heart, we must also develop our minds. We need ACE to orient our hopes and the best KA^4SA^2 to grapple fully with all the knowledge created today.

We need to use our KA^4SA^2 in ways that support us in accomplishing our mission. We must use these to guide the powers with awareness of the:

- **People**—living, remembered, and hoped for—persons of our biological species who make life worth living, especially those close to us, but who by biology are given traits we accommodate with love
- **Polity** for peace though the rule of law
- **Economy** for provision of the necessities for survival
- **Geography** to survive in a locale
- **Culture** of democracy to combine all powers' knowledge to help us shape the best attitudes and behaviors, celebrating humanity through activities that bring us joy, not hate
- **Mythology** to give depth to the purpose of existence
- **History** of what has happened, is happening, or could happen

- **Academy** to produce and transfer knowledge
- **Artistry** for our imaginations to produce and share creative expressions of experiences
- **Industry** to produce what's needed to survive, live in comfort or luxury
- **Family**—living, remembered—persons who care for us and us for them
- **Community**—whether of proximity or propinquity, connected, shared, distant, disliked or misunderstood—provides us social opportunities to learn, be, and become our better selves through our engagements with it

Lastly, we must think about how all these combine and how we as the leadership of the USE want them to form our society—the organization of people by the powers—particularly the envisioned American one compared and contrasted to how it has been and should be, and how we will make it ideal for real. It takes a lot of cooperation and coordination to make a society function for the benefit of its people. A selfish, competitive, ideological orientation like doomerism is ill-suited for democracy. Cooperation and coordination require a broad application of collaborative efforts performed across regions, knowledges, and generations. Teamwork is not necessarily easy, but life gets easier if we use it. The problem with doomerism is it puts the focus on the "I" with its "me first" mentality. We as persons should enjoy being proud of ourselves; we should gain from self-esteem. We can if we are on a team. Teams recognize and appreciate teammates. But as cliché as it may seem, there is no letter "I" in team, and the "me" must serve the purpose of the team, so we each might maximize our gain of participating as a teammate. This brings us to the next tool we can use in moving toward creating and sustaining a truthful American society. It is the use of eight-eyed teams in all our FILMS[2] [P7] and when working in our roles as the HM[5] to guide our combined efforts to reach prosperity as we work to provide the best LAMBS within the culture of democracy that is the foundation of the USE.

*U*se Eight-Eyed Teams

Our community of 21st-century citizen patriots E-SASSY-T-TUF-FT-CAUCUS must think and act as teams. We will need eight-eyed teams to succeed. For this purpose, we write team as an anagram:

$$T—together$$
$$E—everyone$$
$$A—achieves$$
$$M—more$$

Clearly, there is no "I" here. However, the team needs many persons' eyes to work for its success, particularly eight critical "eyes", or viewpoints of leadership we need an eye looking:

1) **Out** for us (leadership support of our work)
2) **Forward** for us (leadership providing the vision for our work's contribution and the direction we are headed)
3) **Over** us (leadership overseeing the accuracy of our work and holding us accountable for any required corrective actions)
4) **Up** to us (leadership supporting our morale, praising and raising us up by recognition for real achievements when appropriate, putting us on the podium for inspiration celebration, which encourages others' aspirations)
5) **Into** us (leadership investigating and auditing our performance and helping us through internal storms of conflict)
6) **At** us (leadership seeing us as peers adjacent might see us, or subordinates, or superiors, or outsiders, to assist us with our reputation and relationships outside ourselves)
7) **Behind** us (leadership reminding us where we have been and how far we have progressed, a perspective helpful to perpetuate effort)

Most importantly, we need an eye:

8) **Of our own** (aiding us see perspectives that define us; our purpose for which we employ and compensate ourselves).

We the everyday people, united as 21st-century citizen patriots, make the team chartered to chart the path for the Constitution, its culture of democracy in republic. We will launch campaigns of ACE and call others to join us to defeat doomerism in our society. We will live to train others and ourselves to IDEALS liberty, so that we might finally have justice for all. We need to employ these eight essential eyes of teams to produce maximal teamwork. This is how we must lead, all eyes wide open and aware. We will lead the people to AEIOUY^{2}K our power to achieve our project's goal and attain its objectives. This is our mission. We'll do it as civically engaged, politically informed citizens building social capital and learning additional social grammars in our neighborhoods, developing the capacity and capabilities in others to create an indestructible civil society, which is what makes living with liberty a blessing. From the ground up is how we regrow the tree of liberty. Let us fertilize it with the hope of the teenagers for a better future than they witness us imagining now. Our answers do not rely upon the policies of the top-down clowns of psychotic plutocracy, sociopathic oligarchical wannabe kings and queens with their sycophantic psychopathic aristocracy, be they politicians or economic elites. We do not need these fools on the bridge of our USE. We need to replace them and not repeat the errors of the boomer generation. We have from the framers the great gift of citizenship. We must begin to use it properly, now and forever. With an eight eyed team of eight eyed teams we're certain to <u>s</u>urvive doomerism, <u>c</u>ommunicate its wrongfulness, <u>o</u>rganize to replace authority holding doomers with younger civically minded energetic adults, <u>r</u>esist doomers furtherance of misguided undermining values, and <u>e</u>scape from their social, cultural, and societal immorality by reviving virtue as the pursuit of happiness most benefits (SCORE).

Use Citizenshipping

First, we decide to fix things for liberty's sake. Then, we daily build up our character. We steadily begin E-SASSY-T-TUF-FT-CAUCUS. We work at it. We gradually become one people. We align our communities into acting as a single nation with wonderful variation of free expression we come to appreciate from, of, and by one another. We come together committed to perform as a citizenry like its 1774, or world war, as our forbearers had done, cooperatively, to meet each other in unity, so we can enjoy the fruits of our labors and resist the psychic echoing and enchanting draft of doomerism. We must all agree to revive and restore integrity daily, committing to pursue virtue as our daily way, means, and methods' first activity in finding happiness. We regain our birthright of natural inalienable rights and reclaim its truth. Retaining our rights depends on it. We must ready our polity to do a better job of preparing us to navigate the dark, dystopian future ahead, as we see continued increases in knowledge and technology. We must bring the children up in a manner that will prepare them for the massive, increasingly difficult changes ahead. We will need to find ways through ACE to supplement all STAMPER socialization contexts, removing their grotesque differences, and eliminating the enervating and radicalizing ones. We must do this so a common understanding and purpose exists with which we may unify to fight against the horrors of humankind that will likely come from the power-concentrating potential of advanced computational, information, communication, and biological technologies.

We cannot shrink and seek to hide in the traditions of the past. We must update healthy traditions but jettison the ones that are hurtful and harmful, shallow and dangerous, irrelevant and incapable of preparing children for a global postmodern world. Our community must ready our children for a scaling up of planetary interconnectedness never before seen by our species. If our community becomes an example once again for others to follow, perhaps everyone, everywhere on earth, can resist the evils of tyranny.

We must replace the polity power-erring, cowardly politicians with those who speak their minds and represent well the best interests of the citizens who elected them. Conversely, these new officials must guide their constituents by example on how to be a 21st century patriot citizen, encouraging them to meet the standards, abide by the intents of our ideals, and not seek benefits paid for by others. We have to be courageous and continuously vote out every elected official and vote in younger, intelligent, honest persons to keep up with the pace of change ahead. We will need a few elders, and middle-aged life experienced adults. Mainly we need 24 to 40 year olds with creative capacities and capabilities at their maximum to deal with the impending transformational challenges confronting society for which we must adapt with each social problem that arises as we storm and norm to find our equilibrium in which to excellently perform as we IDE-ALS each citizen's liberty.

For forty years, we have failed to refresh our polity. The boomer auto piloting drifted us off course. Our politicians aged old and moldy, stale, entrenched in their ways, incapable of working at the pace we need, and unable to focus on the complexity we face. They play games of partisanship with us. We need better citizenshipping. Not looking to protect liberty, they have enabled a plutocracy to take hold in our society. The societal powers are grossly out of balance with the economy elites running the show, not the people. We've too long ignored the few good politicians. We've reelected the career ones the duopoly made nearly unavoidable choices by rigging the electoral processes to keep out other parties and independents with supportable ideas. The economic elites and near permanent petty partisan politicians would say their marketing research indicates that we have asked for what they provide and proselytize. To protect themselves in their positions, they made a duopoly that prevents us from being able to hear independent voices, or candidates we might consider seriously. Due to rules that lock in incumbents' chances by blocking media opportunities for independents (Simon, 2020), the gridlock duopoly plays out poorly for the everyday people. Perhaps it is good for the boomers, but it not good for the remaining living and unborn future American generations. Much of it is the underbelly of the game played with, on, and against us, with doomerism keeping it going. Alas, it is more dialectic than that. Madison Avenue has gotten all the psychology of human minds behind it since profits can buy more of it.

When we the people through our government funded scientific research and technological development, we put men on the moon. The many great lessons learned from that helped us increase our industry and academy powers as a people. Our tax dollars made possible innovations in many fields, such as preventive medicines that assisted our biology power resist diseases. Our federal government's investments in knowledge creation and technological explorations created middle-class jobs. The consortiums of academy, industry, and artistry, for and with the economy powers when directed by the people power, via the polity power, yielded returns for society and stimulate markets in coordinated organizational networks, vertically (small, medium, and large in scale of operations) and horizontally (diverse knowledge areas and across the powers' boundaries). These arrangements of power are beneficial for us. We might get the kind of radical innovations we need to get our country back to the top of world leaders if we support and invest in such innovative organizational consortiums of public and private entities once more (Hage, 2011).

Through committed citizenshipping by everyone, we deny the power-concentrating, manipulative economy elites who seek to convert us to consumerism as a way of life, so we too might practice doomerism. This makes a most profitable society only for them, leaving horrible and deplorable depravity and poverty in many of our urban and rural settlement patterns' communities and neighborhoods. The global elites enjoy their luxury, not caring for the health of populations, while most of us suffer unnecessary stresses and survival threats. Many elites wield the economy power in ways that have ruthless consequences and externalities they may never see. Not seeing these is like not wanting to believe in the truth. Elitism, as a way of being in doomerism, drives super salaries and celebrity-worshipping cultural ambitions. The boomers brought it about. We see some of this in all the powers' FILMS[2] [P7] and in many of the HM[5]. There is some of it in the academy and artistry powers, particularly in athletics and within industry power. It is even in the mythology power. We simply need to stop worshipping the elites. Who are they to us? They are not gods! They do not care about us. They quite possibly don't deserve the super salaries and celebrity status they get. How could we ever justify their doings if they had not manipulated us to do so? It's unreasonable of us. Such extreme rewards as doomerism gives to them extract and redistribute the wealth of the nation to a tiny few. For example, if there are 500 pieces of bread for 1000 people, why should one person at the top of the hierarchy of earners get 499 pieces and the 999 other people get only one piece of bread to share? This is the way the boomers built it to be. This is how it works in their celebrity city. This is their balancing act to extract unfair shares because of their own selfishness. It is absurd. We would be fools to allow it to continue. The system was rigged (Reich R. B., 2020). We must unrig the system.

They intentionally make us feel weak and low, insecure and incapable. This is how they sell us products to make us feel better about ourselves. We are all beautiful by our birth. The baby doomers cunningly seek to corrupt us to believe this is not true. Truth is beauty. That we were born is true; it is beautiful. But doomers will deny this. They will claim that they have something we need to be fulfilled. Our identity does not depend upon the elite's products. We must not believe them. We must believe in the local realities of our daily lives. There is nothing wrong with us if we are good people. We do not need brand-name products to have a legitimate identity. Stop falling for the false lines and fraudulent promises. We must lift up our heads, hold them high, and strive with all our internal might, with our every thought, to be good, do well, and pursue virtue to be faithfully American.

This is how we find happiness. This gives us the strength to free ourselves from our doubts and find liberty from our fears. This is how we act courageously to work on our own selves' improvement. Our being born makes us beautiful creations; we must grow toward doing good to perpetuate the opportunity being alive gives to us. Knowing we were born for a purpose is vital. We are destined to do something that is helpful to ourselves, our families, our neighborhoods, our communities, our states, our regions, our nation, and the whole species spread out over the globe. We must find out how we can contribute best for others, particularly posterity, and for our own healthfulness, because being helpful is healthy, and being healthy helps us be happy.

We must find our part to play on each team we can. We each must do our part to the best of our ability and not allow anyone to tell us that we are fools for doing good work. We must know the truth in teamwork toward improving the chances for tomorrow's children. We must be better citizens to perpetuate the possibilities of restoring prosperity for posterity. It will be a long-term effort, but we've a lifetime to give to it. We must pass it on. We must pass it along. We must move toward a more perfect union with the fervor of 18th Century colonials. For liberty we must rise! Nothing is as cool as doing the more difficult thing. Overcoming challenges helps us feel more alive. With all of our comforts and conveniences, we too easily render ourselves complacent, useless, bored, and unimportant. This is, as doomerism would have it: dumb us down, drown us out, take control of our minds, and rule over us. Please recall the cycle of democracy (Figure 2-14 through Figure 2-22), and doomerism damaging impact upon it (Figure 2-23). Let's not let the doomers have their way. Let's take back what they have stolen from us. Let's do it in every way, everywhere, every moment of each day by not buying into their fallacious, felonous, felonious, fraudulent lies about us, the everyday people.

Good citizenshipping builds confidence. It won't let petty jealousy of those who cannot master themselves tell us how to be. Don't be bullied. Be beautiful, loudly and proudly, the kind and loving persons we were born to be. We can do it! We will do it! Let's begin! Being a citizen is not that difficult. It is just a commitment to make, a promise to ourselves to keep throughout our lives. We must do it! Let's convince our family and friends to do it, too, with us, building alliances, making coalitions, generating agency to make this country a more perfect union. This is how we do it with good order and discipline. Let's put this incredible project for humankind into focus, into the forefront of our thinking. Let's call out and prevent the liars, cheaters, and thieves among us from rising to the top of the hierarchies of the FILMS[2] [P7] and being the managers of the influential companies of the HM[5]. We can develop better character and block those of bad character, then reform them with advice and advocate they join the good among us. With persistent peer pressure to encourage higher standards and ethical norms, we'll establish community mores that will convince others to go along with that which is in theirs, and thus our, longer-term interests, a civil society of honesty and trust for which we'll uphold valid beneficial social norms. This is how we stop the baby doomers from ruining our democracy, polluting our planet, sickening our children, and harming our grandchildren's chances to enjoy the blessings of liberty. In addition to doing it for us, our family, friends, neighbors, community, state, and region, we do it for our country. It needs us. It is we. We must reshape it, right the ship, and sail it correctly. The keel was laid for us, the commoner, the everyday people. We need to because we don't want to live in tyranny of any kind, ever. We don't want to be in bondage. We don't want to be in the jailhouse with nowhere to go. We can do this by E-SASSY-T-TUF-FT-CAUCUS. We can do it if we try. We must decide to and begin.

Through good citizenshipping, we can deny the doomers access to authority. Those who do not act in accordance with our founding ideal, our Constitution, and the responsibilities of being a good citizen do not deserve to advance to positions of authority. The power-hungry politicians and hoarding economic elites always seem to seek to control the people as ignorant masses "beneath" them. Because raw power tastes so sweet, doomers bathed in its corruption, wanting to have all of it. To be at the top and avoid criticism they play games against one another, with us as their pieces. They think of us as pawns. Some of us are rooks, some knights, and some bishops, but we are not on a chessboard. The doomers will not allow us to share our best moves, our strengths to the benefit of society. They are afraid we might "one up" them, which would make them, feel insecure and sad. Aw, isn't that too bad? Yet, we are not trying to do that. We are trying to make things better. They want to one up one another and falsely assume it's what everyone one else is trying to do. Doomerism has warped their outlook.

We cannot allow them to be as king and queen. They project this pathetically un-American attitude upon us. They do it in their games for control so they can treat us like chess pieces, or worse as one-dimensional checkers. Because we have democracy, authority figures, officials, work for us, the citizenry. If we unite and become better citizens, we will deflate them. They will be defeated. We must prevent our FILMS[2] [P7] from being converted to serve their personal purposes over the professional responsibilities for which functional authority is given. We are not pieces in a game of checkers: monochromatic discs that can only move two dimensionally in three limited-step directions on a board. We are magnificent human beings. The everyday people are not toys for a game of wannabe monarchs seeking to reestablish dead thrones.

We must stop falling for their games. We must start behaving better, more deeply American at our core. We must remove their rot from the Liberty Tree. We must demand integrity of those among us who seek to govern and provide, to $AEIOUY^2K$ the powers of the polity and the economy. We must not allow them to DAMN the societal and social powers for personal self-aggrandizement. The days of the baby doomers in charge must be ended by a forthright intervention of integrity through American virtue lived out and demanded by the succeeding generations. We have no choice if we are patriotic. We must stop getting caught up in the political and economic games the baby doomers' duopoly plays on us. They let a virus kill more of us than it ever would have if we as a citizenry were healthier and not already infected with baby doomerism. Moreover, if we were aware of what the power elites were doing, all the smart civil servants' proposals to avert a pandemic might have been acknowledged, heard and heeded, and we would not have needed to suffer as badly as we have. The tarnishing of educated and professional experts by the popularity affirmed elitists must stop!

By good citizenshipping, we won't give polity power disusers, abusers, misusers, and non-users authority over our human powers any longer. They are illegitimate. They should not have authority over us. They do not inspire us like the teeny-tiny minority of bloomers and broomers within the boomers generation. We certainly ought not to aspire to be like their loomers, groomers, zoomers, roomers, nor doomers. To prevent corrupting influence by their doomerism, we must live virtuously. We must protect our country and ourselves. We must remind them that should now convert to work for us, the everyday people, serving the success of the intended project of the USE, which we'll resurrect. We, as a 21st-century patriotic citizenry, will keep our powers in check and not DAMN them. We cannot let perverted pleasures of raw power tempt us to go about treating each other wrongly. Life is not about winning petty points in pointless arguments that ignore the issues we need resolved. We must tell the truth. We will not tolerate criminalization of things done in order to target one group of people for incarceration over another. We must vote them out of office. If their replacements don't do what is reasonably within their power to do to serve us better by doing our just will, we will remove them. We must repeat this process until those we privilege with offices act ethically with integrity and serve us honorable in accord with the intents of the Constitution. We will not demand things outside their power's capability and capacity. Concurrently, we will not tolerate any further misbalancing of the societal powers that might weaken us into dependency by allowing them to hold the mantle of leadership, which belongs to us (recall Figures 2-1 through 2-11). We will reestablish equilibrium in the LAMBS. We will reconstitute the country as a land of the free and home of the brave. We will act to extend opportunities such a miracle as our endowment of a nation can create for all persons within our borders.

By good citizenshipping, we will not expect nor accept benefits we cannot afford. We must do our ACE homework. We must prepare to do our part as citizens united. We must know our rights and insist on respect for them. No entering our premises without warrants allowed! The violators need prosecuted, jailed for the lesson of a loss of freedom, and educated until reformed. We must exercise our political rights and live up to our citizenship responsibilities. We must pay attention and learn civics continuously. We should believe no single source of information but rather collect several and avoid seeking to hear what we want to hear. We should support local and regional reporting. We cannot allow ourselves to feed our fears. If we are to be a place of courage, we must develop the virtue fortitude to come to know ourselves. Before we come to believe the tall-tales or edicts told to us about how to think, we must think for ourselves. We must use facts, evidence, and reasoned thought, critically verifying what we believe we understand and discussing it among others who might think the opposite. We need to seek balanced opinions. We can use dichotomies to unravel the political polemics and isms thrown at us like meat to eat up and repeat unthinkingly. We must know whether flavorings are spice or poison, hype or propaganda. We must pose challenges to the politicians' and elites' efforts that convert democracy culture and the republic into tyranny by doomerist demagogic fallacies. We must question, re-question, remake our opinions, discuss and debate, test our hypothesis, and hold ourselves, one another, and the polity and economy powers accountable for logical errors and omissions. We must take back the leadership of our country. This is the work of the citizenry in a democracy. A republic is ours to keep. It will take work. We have no other choice. Doomerism is rising like quicksilver, heating up the world. Commit to not DAMN power. Use human power for good, for democracy, for liberty, for justice, for the republic, and for American society achieving its goal though attaining its objectives.

For peace with freedom, each of us must, first and foremost govern ourselves toward being a good human, a better citizen. We must continuously practice this if we are to get closer to perfect. We must get to work and remain strong in our discipline. We must find the sincerity in our hearts, apply it to our every living breath, and rid hypocrisy from our way of being because who we are is a beautiful creation given life by birth. We were born innocent and splendiferous. Cast off the corruption that invades and restore purity. Live virtuously. We must commit ourselves to making our communities free from doubt, free from crime, free from violence, and free from depravity that brings us down.

Those among us suffering within anomic conditions must not give polity power abusers and misusers any justification to incarcerate us. We must each love ourselves for the gifts inside of us. We must find and release these. We are all precious humans. But we must battle to be free from corruption. We must work hard to avert our won hypocrisy. Created to brighten the lives of others we must all avoid the doomers' diseased traps. Let us love our neighbors, as we would want loved by building up our family and local community powers. Let us treat others, as per the ideals of liberty enshrined in the Declaration of Independence and the Constitution as amended, which we should know. Let us be the best at treating one another with good manners and politeness, behaving properly as citizens with respect for one another's human dignity. Let's not disgrace ourselves and deface our own dignity by misbehaving, acting inhumanely or cruelly. It is not that difficult to be a good neighbor. We have to try it. We must live by it.

As we go about citizenshipping, let's start behaving smarter. Let's not give economy power abusers and misusers advantages over us by persuading us they have more power than we do, as if they have an ability to rule over us. Let's not be seduced by their advertising that targets our instincts. Let's recognize how it attempts to play us in their game of mass accumulation. We must know what we need to survive and live well verses what we want as a luxury. We must not confuse the essentials from the cravings. Let us strive to live for our needs first, not our egos and insecurities or inadequacies and vulnerabilities. Life's comforts begin with a few basics: shelter, food, and clothing, the love of family, and sociability and warmth in neighborhoods and a community. Let's cherish the moments with significant others. Let's figure out what we can do to help our locales. Let's find ways to work doing what we enjoy. If our work is not enjoyable, let us seek ways in which it is meaningful for us. Seek a hobby for entertainment. Let us be careful to live not primarily for our luxury wants that are above our means. If we want something more than we have, and our interest has merit, let us devise a plan to obtain it legally within a reasonable amount of risk-taking. Risking something to gain more is opportunity knocking, but be wise in these choices. We should try not to overextend and breed stress. We don't want to be foolish and live with exhausting strain and stress over debts we accumulate. Some are sensibly advantageous and temporary. Others are wrongful, caused by a failing society not enabling self-sufficiency for a person's basic survival. Some are risky. Let's learn how to manage money to avoid unsustainable debt. Let's do good things. Let's be neighborly and help one another.

Through citizenshipping, we can avoid the trap of consumer materialism. The propaganda of politicians or the advertising of economic elites must not fool us. Nothing sold to us will make us who we may best become, nor be as the created human each of us is intended to be. We must focus on finding our purpose and pursue it. Figure 7-2 offers a model for figuring out one's purpose. Our identities come from within. We must stand tall and proud, humanely human and not intimidated by superficial glitz as something superior to us. Our wellbeing depends on this. All citizens are humans, equal at birth before the law. The rule of law is a gift, and we must insist on its proper implementation. It begins with our knowing and obeying it. Truth begins internally. In pursuit of lifelong happiness, we should listen to the wisdom of the framers, who listened to their predeces-

sors who sought wisdom, who outlined the virtues we humans ought to pursue for our own good as we
produce a civilization to serve our best interests.

The top four virtues are:

- **Prudence**. Seek to develop good judgment, reason, and self-discipline in managing one's personal affairs.
- **Fortitude**. Seek to develop mental strength to face danger and adversity with courage.
- **Temperance**. Seek to be moderate in actions, thoughts, and feelings.
- **Justice**. Seek to comport one's self to truth, fact, and reason while being just, impartial, and fair.

If we all reach for these as a citizenry, we'll be living honorably. Citizenshipping depends on these. These virtues are required traits of leaders. If we the everyday people invest ourselves in these, we elevate our dignity and gain the power of the people given in a democracy to be the leadership of the society. We especially need those among us who hold positions of authority in all the societal and social powers' FILMS[2] [P7] and as the HM[5] to be excellent at these traits to make all the powers exemplary examples of integrity. The characteristics of virtue held internally and exhibited externally define good character in a human being. These virtues are foundational for the character of the people power in a society built on democracy culture. Our republic depends on our integrity in living with, by, and for these virtues. When we rise up to live in pursuit of them to make our country a great place to be, we will be closer to being the Americans our forbearers imagined we could be and must be for our posterity and ourselves. We are on the march toward the honor, courage, and commitment of 21st-century citizen patriots. We begin a new cadence for America by E-SASSY-T-TUF-FT-CAUCUS. We escape the wrath of doomerism. We generate hope that the babies will know the blessings of liberty.

By using citizenshipping, we head toward our ideals. We deeply align ourselves with our country's first principles. The Constitution as amended will come to our aid as we advance on our goal and our objectives. This is our mission. This is our purpose as a nation. We the everyday people support it by finding our identity in it and discovering our purpose in our voyage toward becoming and being a more perfect human. Figure 7-2 articulates a way to find in the winds of time the energy to make ourselves happier. With each of us a happier person, we become a happier people, united in working to make American society all that it can be, given what each generation leaves behind for the next to whittle upon as we move our inherited project forward toward greater perfection.

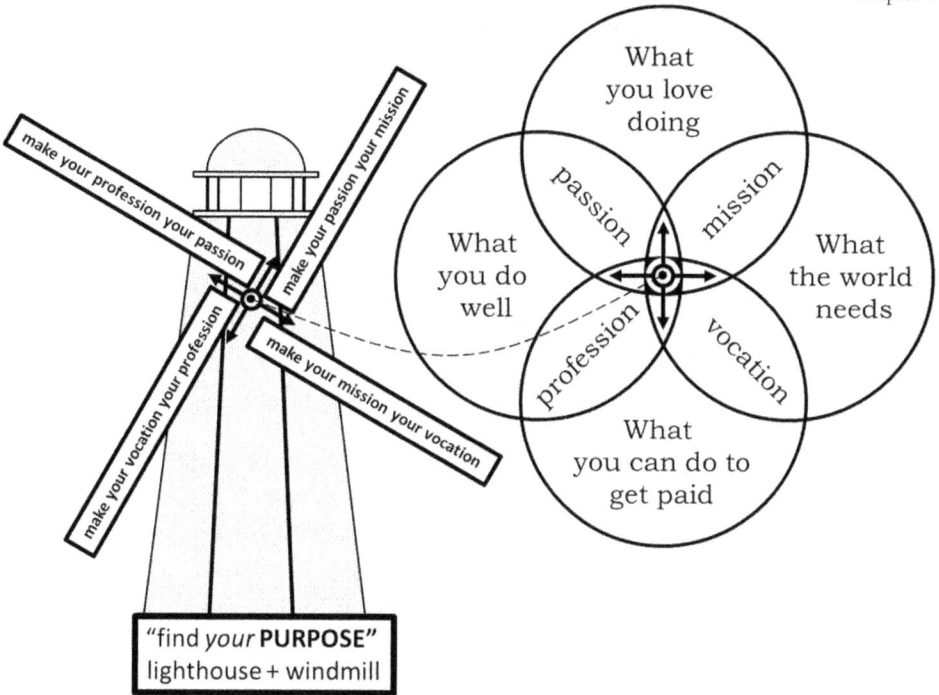

Figure 7-2: Find Your Purpose Pursuit
The advisory sentences on the four sails of wisdom's lighthouse windmill make suggestions to us as we try to find our purpose in life. These derive from the questions in the four circles to the right that represent to forces wisdom's wind applies to the rotational shaft that engages our thinking on "Who am I? What am I to do? What will I become? What am I meant to be?" As we grow up into adulthood and master our own self-governing, we absorb the forces of the winds of our time, which the history power reports and our family and community powers interpret for us. As we try to make sense of it all, thoughts turn in our mind. We seek answers. If we answer the wise questions that convert the winds of time into thinking about our selves, we can identify our personally unique passion, mission, vocation, and profession. Answering these questions generates the energy needed to ignite the bulb that will light the way for us to pursue and live out our purpose in life, which will yield happiness within our being for becoming the human being with a meaningful purpose we gained from knowing it, and experiencing our best reason for being.

By using citizenshipping, we will SCORE for the benefit of our children and posterity. As we get older and rise into positions of authority within the secondary and tertiary powers' houses, it is vital we exhibit our virtues and inhibit our vices. It begins at home by honoring our parents. Make family feel like family. Be helpful to the neighborhood in which you reside and the many communities in which you behave, even if it means correcting wrongfulness. From our human culture-created powers to support our efforts in society to make it more ideal by leading, acting morally and accountably, we'll more greatly influence one another. If we all strive to be a better citizenry in accord with the ambitions of the framers written in the Constitution, we'll get better at citizenshipping. The positions within the powers' FILMS[2] [P7] must be treated as privileges with great gratitude for having been honestly selected to be within them, especially if at the top of their hierarchies. Critically because of the influence of these on shaping the future livelihoods of others, we must honorably perform quality citizenship and by example encourage others to do the same. Here are some ideas for how those in positions of authority might go about exhibiting it, per these tertiary social powers:

- **Academy**
  - Teach and produce new knowledge to help our children and us learn ways, means, and methods to solve today and tomorrow's problems, with some reflection upon the past's lessons for us to cogitate.

- **Mythology**
  - Preach and produce morally and ethically prepared persons who respect the dignity of all human beings and who have personal courage to push forward into the unknown without fear, prejudice, or discrimination against others. Guide these persons to seek to do good and be just in society, and wholesomely make the passages through life's stages in as smooth a manner as possible within traditions rich in deep human meaning.

- **Artistry**
  - Create and demonstrate the marvelous expressions of humanity that we can make and perform with all our faculties for all our senses to amaze us, bring us to the sublime, and entertain and edify us with the beautiful. But do not force us to look at the crude and unusual without our consent. Challenge us, but do not insult us.

- **Industry**
  - Invent, build, innovate, and engineer. Produce with the least amount of waste and damage to our biomes the provisions we need to survive in dignity, live more comfortably, and enjoy in luxury those additional things we want.

- **History**
  - Chronicle what is going on around us, without using hyperbole to sell lies that may be rumors and gossip, which we are susceptible to believing because we want to hear a story and not the truth. Give us facts and evidence, allow us to make up our minds, and as time passes, document what happened and why. Tell what you observe and perceive with integrity, not with a lust for the power to shape society. Write with a passion to document it correctly, as it devolves, evolves, or resolves itself. Describe how commingling powers absolve errors, solve problems and involve all our citizenshipping efforts. Layout how our task is add our efforts to the project of making society more American. We must do so to avert the risk it could dissolve into with doomerism as our culture, permanently.

Lastly, a word about the powers we cannot control perfectly, geography and biology. Geography differs across the country. Consider the term "geography" to mean our ecosystem that gives us life. Geography is the power of the cosmic, geologic, and climatic circumstances for life on earth. It includes the sun, the planet's molten core, and all things in between, surrounding and abounding on the planet: the biomes, weather, and living organisms, be they microscopic or gigantic compared to us humans. We are learning more about how biology works. We look forward to its use so that we may be healthy, happy, wholesome, and whole.

In Figure 7-3 the force of citizenshipping, our people power leadership properly exercised, applies itself in the seven socialization contexts we find in society today. Citizenshipping prepares us to AEIOUY^{2}K powers in line with, and to coordinate through, the activities of our project. We move it forward toward its goal by completing its objectives thoroughly, seriously. Progress gets us closer to mission accomplishment. To defeat doomerism now we must focus on the future in the present by advancing through ACE the culture of democracy and the healthy for a republic repeated replenishment of representatives to preserve the intentions of and actualization of liberty in the nation for which it stands. A true American society depends upon the whole population of adults participating in knowing and acting in politics; if not by taking a turn at serving in office, then through expressing informed opinions to those who seek to govern on our behalf.

This means intelligently voting in one's best interests. Properly understood, we'd support liberty's best chances, in the short, mid, and long term of one's life course. Refreshing the republic with upcoming adult generations' civically minded team playing members of the most integrity is essential. All our powers must align to unite to support all of enjoying the blessings of liberty. Unified for it, we will get justice with it, for everyone, for the American children of tomorrow. It may take a steadfastly twenty-five to fifty year march to succeed at it.

To conclude this last chapter and this book's third section, we will cover one more tool or technique for "living in America" that we the 21st-century citizen patriots must employ to defeat doomerism. We can add it to our tool kit with the others we've shared so far: dichotomies, the 4x5x8 cuboid, eight-eyed teams, and citizenshipping. With these, we'll work to eradicate doomerism from American society and revitalize the culture of democracy from which it was born. We do so for our posterity and ourselves. We do so to preserve the endowment that is the USE, a gift passed down through eight generations to us through a rough history of much of us out of touch with its originating intentions. It's arrived in our presence, a bit torn and tattered. Yet we feel grateful for its survival. It was born of ideal words worth working to make real. With gratitude it is ours to steward forward. Its first principles provide hope for everyday people everywhere. To perfect it in grace, we must be willing to self-govern and resist the rule of a dreadful dictator or pitiless plutocracy.

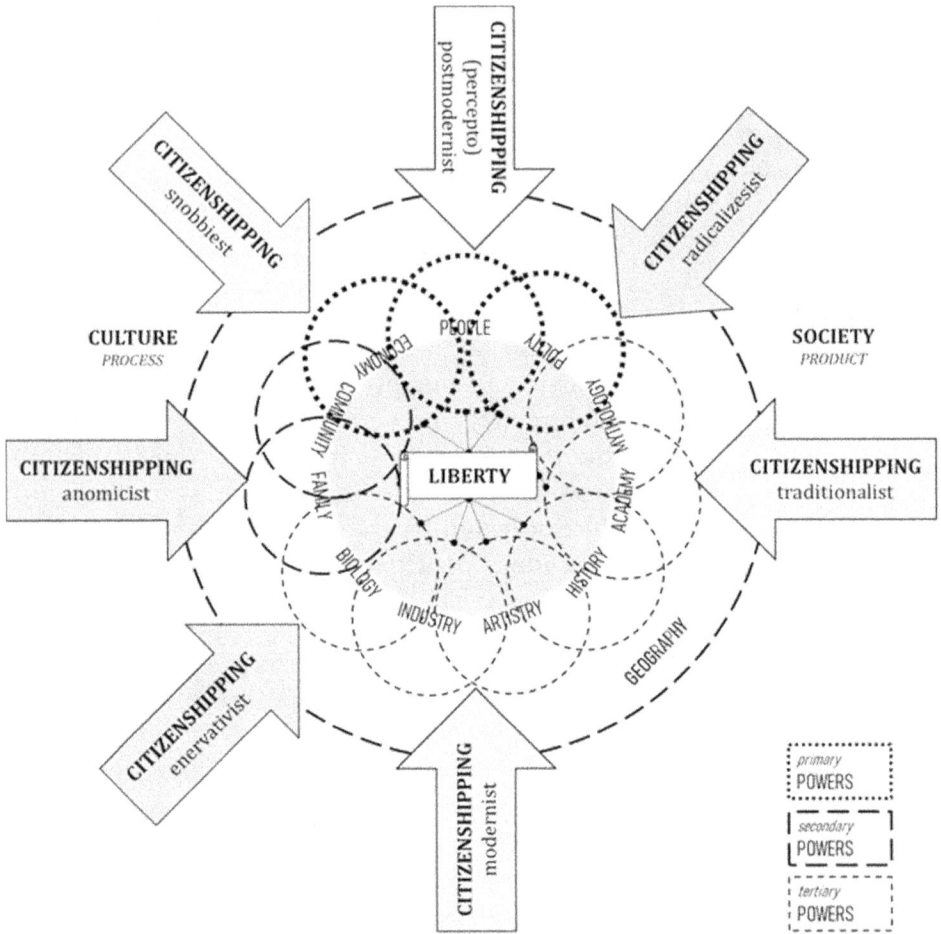

Figure 7-3: Citizenshipping in Socialization Contexts Unifies Human Powers on Liberty
Persons living in anomic, enervating, or radicalizing conditions need help from fellow citizens to integrate and feel welcomed in society. They will need jobs that do not alienate them from purpose. Persons living in traditionalist and modernist conditions need encouragement to find ways to adapt to the rapid changes caused by new knowledge. Persons living in snobbish conditions need to realize that material comforts do not make them superior to other citizens. Their involvement in more civic activities might help to curb their dangerous conceit toward fellow citizens and might encourage them to contribute a fair share of revenue to support a greater common good than the needs of their estates.

Use Levelheadedness

Good citizenshipping involves self-composure and reasonableness. Being sensible, considerate, and sociable are aspects of a good citizen who puts to use the necessary levelheadedness to self-govern. It includes truth seeking, even when it hurts. We must be courageous to handle it without fear. We must teach the truth: the real record of what happened and how to process it in a way to prevent division, hatred, and shame. This means we must be responsible and accountable to doing right and being better. However, we must do so without inducing anxiety or criminality. We must do so with neighborly love as a people in community. We must do so by supporting one another find purpose as a person serving the people. We must do so with meaningful contributions of our worth to the whole. We are imperfect humans. We need each other's understanding though we must not try one another's patience. We must be more attentive. All of us must use levelheadedness. Especially as we find ourselves in challenging times. We are experiences threats to our unity as our differences get exploited. A "me first" mentality makes dividing us easier. Our society's unity is at risk. Our three estranged settlement patterns scattered throughout ten regional subcultures drift apart. Historical animosities remain. Doomerism presses them toward competitions of righteousness vice compromises for justness in democracy. Further concerns harbor in children raised in seven distinct socialization contexts. Will they be able to bond as one people, e pluribus unum? Yes, if we change society from the social fabric tattering, unity battering, behaviors of the boomer generation to those of capable citizenshipping then we've a chance to revive liberty, truth, and justice as the American way for living life. We must, because we confront crises and a logarithmic (if not exponential) growth in knowledge. Fortunately, it has. Hopefully it will continue to happen in evolutionary waves within which we might enjoy undisruptive periods of equilibrium. Nonetheless, we ought not to look backward to the solutions of yesteryear except to mine our heritage for divinely inspired democracy and liberty principles that benefit every human soul. We must perpetually give and receive ACE. We must look forward and imagine how we might IDEALS liberty for future generations by better LAMBS in our USE. If we are levelheaded, we can do this and become an example of how to go about doing American society, correctly, properly, and perpetually pragmatically in perpetuity.

Further, we must discover ways to find agreement around democracy and by doing so push back the demagoguery of the hoarders and baby doomers who sail our ship toward self-destruction. Poetically speaking, we must clear them all from the bridges of our FILMS[2] [P7] frigates and move our fleet of powers in unison to reach a Promised Land of the Preamble.

Ahead are globally disruptive changes of new complexities. We must AEIOUY^{2}K our powers to adapt constantly changing realities, consistently in unison to overcome the new complicated social circumstances and physical conditions we might confront.

Whole cycles will accelerate as knowledge expands. The brilliance of the USE is its decentralization of societal and social powers that make it more adaptive to alter its course to avoid obstacles and conquer challenges from outside and inside its borders. It has proven itself capable of addressing fast-moving threats in previous times of crises, transforming economic and political turbulence into opportunities for self-improvement. We are at such a crossroads again today, but with the wrong crowd in control. We can SCORE if we get new competent staff at the helms of our societal and social powers.

If the societal and social powers, through those given authority to AEOIUY^{2}K them, do not strive to make us ready us adapt and innovative as the complexity of the risks, threats, and opportunities we face grows, we will fall behind the demand. Not being able to supply the provisions necessary for society will result from such delinquency. We the everyday people need to help the powers do better by being honest leaders in them; made of good character and exhibiting our integrity. We can shape society with our nimble creativity to flex and respond adequately to yield the services necessary to continue the USE in a self-correcting direction, which is toward achieving its goal by attaining its objectives.

We've authorized the powers by our culture of democracy to continuously develop and redevelop the KA^{4}SA^2 to evolve capabilities to the required capacities necessary to solve our problems. Yet in forty years, the problems have only multiplied. Capabilities revolve around a few key capacities shared by the powers in our communities throughout our enterprise. We need greater social capital in our civil society to support our readiness as a society to cope with the current crises and future social problems: caused, amplified, tolerated, actualized, promoted, undergirded, litigated, taunted, embraced, and developed (CATAPULTED) during the majority rule of boomers. The rise of their correlational, (or is it causal?), doomerism: confiscates, obfuscates, frustrates, fabulates, immolates, ulcerates, relegates, and extirpates (COIFFURE) liberty and its child, democracy culture. The persons in control of our powers' FILMS^2 [P7] must develop a citizenship orientation to discuss who will do what when, and how they will cooperate and coordinate to make things happen better for future generations. Key societal capabilities and capacities need developed for future success via consortiums of public–private teamwork. The acrimonious animosity of baby boomers needs overcome. Collaborating across past inhibiting boundaries is essential to solving wicked problems. It will require a willing, able, and ready attitude to do what needs done, with sound judgment and in accordance with the wisdom of the four top virtues. To generate revenue to support the correction of the course away from doomerism and toward democracy with the possibility of prosperity for posterity, we must use levelheadedness to:

- Alter policies, budgets, and services rapidly to meet arising priorities of greater consequence than following a path depended upon for past successes. Because of the third stage of knowledge creation, the future is getting presaged as needing new problem definitions and increasingly innovative social solutions.

- Re-educate, retrain, and redevelop all persons to seek KA^4SA^2 to work seamlessly across boundaries of organizations, professions, and perhaps most importantly, topics, particularly those rooted in past polemics, in which their perpetuation became a kind of cultural glue of a pseudo-balance and comfort of opinion, versus facts that move conversations onto common ground.

- Establish social capital, deliver ACE, develop multiple social grammars, and cause social integration by new recruitment and promotion procedures to find and develop, not defeat, the talent in people. Jobs need created that use inventive ways, means, and methods to elevate persons to their best possible stations in life, in which people feel the flow of optimum performance (Csikszentmihalyi, 1991) and contribute their best for the rest. These jobs need good citizens recognizing and rewarding each other in team-based evaluations of persons' contributions to missions and to the work of the groups that established the teams. Each person in every job needs provide leadership in ways reinforcing of others at a level commensurate with the group's needs.

In the complex, globalized, postmodern world of doubt, suspicion, and intense competition for resources, we need more conscientiousness, compassion, empathy, and love of, by, and for, our family, friends, neighbors, and our community to eliminate artificial and real enemies. We need it as we go about integrating in society the constant changes we must lead and manage as we administer through the difficulties of them. We must appreciate, and tolerate, positive changes as we celebrate dynamic and continuous upwards knowledge growth. It causes voluminous social adjustments resulting in penetrating and persistent challenges. Therefore, we must continuously educate with the best KA^4SA^2 appropriate for the position to which we are best compatible. This takes honesty within each of us to accept. More so, if our enterprise is to be resilient, the primary powers must cooperate better to self-renew. To do so, each generation must believe in and hold onto the core values and virtues that led to its birth to keep the whole enterprise moving in the correct liberty oriented direction to provide the best LAMBS while always elevating democracy culture to the forefront of our lives and in society. We must make certain we preserve our personal freedoms and keep our livelihoods full of liberty, with love for country maintained for the next generation. This must be the permanent formula for making society during each passing era and its possible epochs of awakening and crises, American. We must IDEALS liberty, so it is not lost to a "big brother" overlord. Adaptability should be our theme as we seek newer solutions but keep our core purpose, liberty, while we adjust our positions. The USE depends on us to appropriately AEIOUY^{2}K the primary societal powers within their purposes and in best balance for our benefit. For liberty, we commit our lives and riches. The founders did. Continuous learning by all of us, as persons, as groups, as communities, and as a people, e pluribus unum, is essential. We must come to rely on ACE as a frequent touchstone and pass down our great republic with its culture of democracy, freed from the grasp of doomerism. All of this is doable if we use levelheadedness.

Rounding it out and finishing it up, with 20/20 vision in foresight before we suffer from hindsight, this book criticized what went awry in our culture under the tutelage of the boomers at the helms of the bridges in the pilothouses of the powers in our society, the USE. Many challenges of their misguiding that exposes us to threatening risks and hazards to our solvency, which cause suffering, transfer onto our children. We are in a particular generational cycle of crises. The boomer generation's "direction," the regional subcultures' divergences and the third stage of knowledge evolution's risks do not bode well for us if we allow boomers to remain at the controls. They will continue to let doomerism grow and spread like a metastasizing tumor. It misguidance will be total as it annihilates liberty. We who do not want a shipwreck of a nation must remove and replace them with better civically minded citizens. Team playing oriented millennials and later generations with pragmatic Gen X coaches must prepare to unite with and guide the up-and-coming adults in the next generations to take control of the wheel and levers of our enterprise's powers. We must do so by E-SASSY-T-TUF-FT-CAUCUS if we want the USE to achieve its goal and attain its objectives written in the Constitution as amended. America, let's honor posterity and ourselves by doing the necessary and good citizenshipping now and forever so there will be democracy and liberty for all Homo sapiens inhabiting planet earth. Come, let's go! Are you with me?

AFTER MATTERS

*E*pilogue

The future success of the USE in achieving its goal by attaining its objectives depends on real citizenshipping with a complete commitment to eradicate doomerism from our culture. If such a unified, total societal effort of civic engagement and commitment happens in all socialization contexts in all regions, there is hope that the USE will become one people, one nation, e pluribus unum. If not, it will be impossible to escape from our current crises. We will sink as doomerism destroys the tentative bonds we have with each other. All depends on how we manage the risks. We saw doomerism operating during the improper management of a pandemic and inability to contain a virus. We cannot allow continuous mismanagement. We must get a vaccine and treatments in place and modify routines to keep one another safe. Many among us refuse them, yet they save lives.

There is so much information out there. Literature reviews become full-time efforts that are outdated the day they are completed. There are orientations and quality levels of knowledge: in science, in academics—for teaching at varying ages and levels of complexity—and in technology from industries (responding to market competition or reasonable regulatory recommendations to manage stakeholders' risks). These various levels have more levels. Knowledge occurs in micro, meso, or macro levels, in overlapping arenas of knowledge production, maintenance, consumption, and disposal (when proven fallible). Arenas of common pursuits include markets, or majors in college, or the sections of a newspaper. There is something of and in society for and in everyone. There is something for society in and from everyone.

The success of the United States has been in tolerating and intentionally sharing, comparing, and combining the diversity of knowledge produced by an immigrant entrepreneurial culture of freedom orientation. What and how knowledge and beliefs (like those unprovable by scientific methods, such as myths, which do have many benefits that should not be denounced) get floated up to reach the general public or ferreted out as more important than another is an adaptive problem for society and for academia in particular. Prioritizing what is important gets sorted out by politics. Politics at the national level in Congress has macro societal impacts. Politics in the state houses of our 50 capitals and governmental seats in territories has meso-level social impacts. Politics in municipalities, cities, towns, districts, wards, neighborhoods, and households has micro-level social and personal impacts. Politics depends on the citizenry being informed and participating to lead the politicians to generate solutions we desire and deserve from democracy. The fewer laws the better, but this requires we behave better and pay attention to prevent ourselves from converting common law prosperity into civil law propensity, which is an impermissibility perspective of governance. As the challenges get more complex and life seemingly more complicated, we must not give up, nor by conveniences become complacent, gazing in wonder at our navels as the "walls come tumbling down" around us. We must attend to politics. We cannot ignore it. We have the privilege of it, thanks to the founders. Let's not lose this endowment. The future is depending upon us.

*A*fterword for Veterans

At 245, we are a young nation still. Our life expectancy has increased with our rise in knowledge, which has improved the medical technologies that keep us alive longer than previous generations. We are blessed that our free enterprise, freedom-oriented society and well led, administered, managed, and respectfully behaving military has held our defenses. Its sworn duty to defend the Constitution against all enemies foreign and domestic has been a godsend. In God We Trust is good for our young nation. I am proud to be a veteran of this esteemed trust.

As you read, nautically speaking (how else would you expect a sailor, even a Seabee, to talk), if a generation occupies the pilothouse for too long, dominating the bridge and the decisions managed at the helm of our society's ship, they are as a tyrant needing removed. For forty years, (about double that of any other generation), the boomers have. Often in ways, as if they don't believe we're a republic of democracy culture. If you think or feel as if our society is falling apart, then ask yourself, "Is not it time we relieve them of command?" In civilization years, eras of constellations of generations, we are an eight-year-old kid. We've a long way to go to mature our culture. The calling of liberty, its full truth, justice, and beauty, need our support. More of us must get involved politically. We must step up and serve in our government as elected officials a time or two, to exemplify good character, with honor, courage, and commitment, and show the civilians how to be citizen patriots.

Let us veterans help the citizenry understand that we are a creedal nation. The Preamble is our mission. It is our enterprise's command intent. Citizens need to learn this way of thinking and how to behave with conviction to our nation's creed as we did to our Services' creeds and our Oaths of Office. Creeds establish and perpetuate culture. Here's the one I strive to live by:

> *"I am a United States Sailor. I will support and defend the Constitution of the United States of America and I will obey the orders of those appointed over me. I represent the fighting spirit of the Navy and those who have gone before me to defend freedom and democracy around the world. I proudly serve my country's Navy combat team with Honor, Courage, and Commitment. I am committed to excellence and the fair treatment of all."*

Let us veterans who understand living by our creed, and the core values of a patriotic ethos, in full commitment to the Constitution, do more to lead this nation. It needs our guide to move toward our ultimate possibilities, to behave properly in accord with its first principles. Let us show the way to civility in all we do, guiding the enterprise correctly before it runs aground, afoul with foolishness. We must not let it be left in the hands of the immature, insecure, ego-needy, self-centered, "me first" wannabe aristocrats. They are causing a plutocracy, the baby doomers and their dilettante devotees. We cannot let those not fully grounded in living by the Constitution's principles or by their oaths of office to stay in positions of authority.

My fellow veterans, I am coming to believe that peace, love, and virtue are the true forms of happiness. We must pursue these or we subject ourselves to exploitation by impostors who seek the sick pleasures of raw power. Under them we will suffer abuse. They instill our cultural enemy, tyranny. Our honor is needed now more than ever. We veterans are steeped in the tea of integrity. We must do more, collaboratively for society. We are, as a civilization, about to enter into adolescence, a time of great brain growth and concomitant risky behavior. If we do not:

o   Stand the watches properly
o   Fill the pilothouse's bridge with quality leaders, who have the level-headed honor code-guided leadership
o   Assume control of the helms of our society's institutions, associations, and organizations, the groups that are the organs of American society.

We may be in for a turbulent civilizational teenage experience that could wreck our enterprise. We need those who know how to lead to be in leadership positions in civil society, in polity, and in the economy. Veterans, we might need to do even more for society than we now do. We might need to be its parents for a while, because we trained to lead. We need to guide our ship of a society toward democracy with liberty for peace with freedom. Thank you for hearing me. I welcome your engagement. Be courageous, fellow patriots!

Yours in duty to the nation,
Commander, USN

*A*ppendix

Learning Liberty Resources

Liberty births democracy. The founding ideals are found in first principles in primary writings of the framers, and in inaugural speeches of presidents, especially those of George Washington and Abraham Lincoln.

Here are the top three **documents** to read:

o   Common Sense Pamphlet by Thomas Paine
o   The Declaration of Independence
o   The Constitution of the United States

The internet has many websites to peruse. Some are hosted by places worth of an in-person visit. Here are many:

Places to visit to learn of **American Liberty:**

o   The National Archives, Washington, DC
        https://www.archives.gov/
                See America's Founding Documents
o   Independence National Historical Park, Philadelphia, PA
        https://www.nps.gov/inde/index.htm
                Includes the Liberty Bell Center
o   National Constitution Center, Philadelphia, PA
        https://constitutioncenter.org/
o   Smithsonian, National Museum of American History, Exhibit:
                American Democracy: A Great Leap of Faith
                https://americanhistory.si.edu/democracy-exhibition
o   James Madison's Montpelier
        https://www.montpelier.org/
                Listen to the Podcast: American Dissent
o   George Washington's Mount Vernon
        https://www.mountvernon.org/
o   Thomas Jefferson's Monticello
        https://www.monticello.org/
o   American Revolution Museum at Yorktown
                Online Interactive Liberty Tree "What does liberty mean to you?"
                https://www.historyisfun.org/yorktown-victory-center/film-galleries/liberty-tree/
o   Museum of the American Revolution
                Vision is "to ensure that the promise of the American Revolution endures"
                https://www.amrevmuseum.org

Many Universities have **Civics** and **Democracy** study centers.

Search the internet for any that might be near you. Ones near me are the:

o   University of Maryland
   Center for Democracy and Civic Engagement
   https://cdce.umd.edu/
o   University of Pennsylvania
   The Annenberg Public Policy Center
   https://www.annenbergpublicpolicycenter.org/
o   University of Virginia
   Center for Politics
   https://centerforpolitics.org/home/
o   Tufts University
   Jonathan M. Tisch College of Civic Life
   https://tischcollege.tufts.edu/
   Center for Information & Research on Civic Learning and Engagement (CIR-CLE)
   https://circle.tufts.edu/

For **American Civics Education** (ACE) resources, visit the:
o   U.S. Department of Education
   Civic Learning and Engagement in Democracy
   https://www.ed.gov/civic-learning
o   American Association of State Colleges and Universities'
   American Democracy Project
   https://www.aascu.org/programs/ADP/
      See a list of civic education organizations here:
      https://www.aacu.org/resources/civic-learning/organizations
o   Intercollegiate Studies Institute
   Educating for Liberty
   https://isi.org
o   Center for Civic Education
   https://www.civiced.org/
o   Civics Renewal Network.org
   A Republic, If We Can Teach It
   https://www.civicsrenewalnetwork.org/
o   What so Proudly We Hail:
   Making American citizens through Literature
   https://www.whatsoproudlywehail.org/
o   Bill of Rights Institute
   https://billofrightsinstitute.org/
o   Generation Citizen
   https://generationcitizen.org/
o   Constitutional Rights Foundation
   https://www.crf-usa.org/
o   iCivics - (Founded in 2009 by in 2009, Justice O'Connor)
   https://www.icivics.org/who-we-are
      See their project CivXNow Coalition
   https://www.civxnow.org/

- Educating for American Democracy
  - https://www.educatingforamericandemocracy.org/

To learn the **Constitution**, visit this website:
- Annenberg Classroom
  - https://www.annenbergclassroom.org/

For more on **Civic Engagement** visit these websites:
- National Endowment for the Humanities
  - *"More perfect Union"*
    - https://www.neh.gov/250
- Semiquincentennial Commission (250 year celebration)
  - https://www.america250.org/home
- Concord Museum
  - *"Shot heard round the world" exhibit*
    - https://concordmuseum.org/april-19-1775-exhibit/

To get involved in **Civic Engagement** visit these websites:
- Empower the People
  - https://www.empowerthepeople.net/
- The Better Arguments Project
  - https://betterarguments.org/
- The Civic Circle
  - https://theciviccircle.org/
  - *Check in your local area or broader region to find more organizations*

For **Democracy** supporting organizations visit their websites:
- United to Protect Democracy and the Protect Democracy Project
  - https://protectdemocracy.org/
- Renew Democracy Initiative
  - https://rdi.org/
- National Endowment for Democracy
  - *Supporting freedom around the world*
    - https://www.ned.org/
- National Center for Constitutional Studies
  - https://nccs.net/
- Represent Us
  - https://represent.us/
- American Promise
  - https://americanpromise.net/
- People for the American Way
  - https://www.pfaw.org/
- Stand Up Republic
  - https://standuprepublic.com/

For a **Constitution** focused organization, visit its website:
- The Foundation for Constitutional Government
  - https://constitutionalgovt.org/

See the Bibliography for some books to consider reading.

The Liberty Tree

In a chariot of light from the regions of the day,
The Goddess of Liberty came,
Ten thousand celestials directed her way,
And hither conducted the dame.
A fair budding branch from the gardens above,
Where millions with millions agree,
She brought in her hand as a pledge of her love,
and the plant she named Liberty Tree.

Beneath this fair tree, like the patriarchs of old,
Their bread in contentment they ate,
Unvexed with the troubles of silver or gold,
The cares of the grand and the great.
From the east to the west blow the trumpet to arms,
Thro' the land let the sound of it flee:
Let the far and the near all unite with a cheer,
In defense of our Liberty Tree.

The celestial exotic stuck deep in the ground,
Like a native it flourished and bore;
The fame of its fruit drew the nations around
To seek out this peaceable shore.
Unmindful of names or distinctions they came,
For freemen like brothers agree;
With one Spirit endued, they one friendship pursued,
And their temple was Liberty Tree.

By Thomas Paine, 1775

Shared by:
- The Great Seal.com:
  Rediscover the device made by America's founders to convey their vision to the world and to the future
  http://greatseal.com/liberty/libertytree.html
- What so Proudly We Hail:
  Making American citizens through literature
  https://www.whatsoproudlywehail.org/curriculum/the-american-calendar/liberty-tree

Acronyms

ACE = American Civics Education

AEIOUY²K = Apply, Employ, Implement, Operationalize, Utilize, Yoke, Yield, Keep

CATAPULTED = Causes, Amplifies, Tolerates, Actualizes, Promotes, Undergirds, Litigates, Taunts, Embraces, Develops

COIFFURE = Confiscates, Obfuscates, Frustrates, Fabulates, Immolates, Ulcerates, Relegates, Extirpates

DAMN = Disuse, Abuse, Misuse, Nonuse

E-SASSY-T-TUF-FT-CAUCUS = Exhibiting Service Above Selfishness, Saying Yes To The Utmost Full-Fledged Thoroughgoing Constitutionally Allied United Citizenshipping, Understandingly Synchronized

FILMS² [P7] = the Functionaries (functionary offices and their officials who hold authority), Instruments (socially agreed-upon, legitimate forms of social groupings given specific authorities and status respect, typically known as organizations and institutions), Logistics (the methods of instruments' AEIOUY²K of power), Mechanisms (the means of instruments' AEIOUY²K of power), Structures, and Systems (of the instruments created by, then shaped and sustained through, shared Philosophies, Purposes, Precedents, Policies, Processes, Procedures, and Practices [P7] that guide people's work for, in, and with the instruments, their logistics, mechanisms, structures, and systems)

HM⁵ = Helpers (professionals and technicians services and associations), Merchants (salesman and traders), Miners (resource extractors and refiners), Makers (manufacturers), Movers (logisticians and transporters of goods and information), and Marketers (market makers and advertisers)

IDEALS = Insure, D'ure, Ensure, Assure, Lure, Secure

KA⁴SA² = Knowledge Aptitude, Acquisition, Absorption, Application, and Skills Advancement Abilities

LAMBS= Leadership, Administration, Management of the Business of Society

SCORE = Survive (doomerism), Communicate (its wrongfulness), Organize (to retire baby doomers from positions of authority), Resist (their furtherance of misguided, democracy undermining values), Escape (from the chaos of societal doom—unvirtuous officials, arcane arguments, and dangerous decisions baby doomers' immorality makes—by reviving virtue and liberty as our purpose)

SERF = Strategic Enterprise Risk Framework

STAMPER = Snobbish, Traditionalistic, Anomic, Modernistic, Postmodernistic, Enervating, Radicalizing

USE = United States Enterprise

*B*ibliography

Adams, J. (1961). The Adams Papers, Diary and Autobiography of John Adams, vol. 1, 1755–1770. In e. L. H. Butterfield, *The Adams Papers, Diary and Autobiography of John Adams* (pp. 152–153). Cambridge: Harvard University Press.

Alexander, M. (2014). *Essential Liberty: A Treatise on Restoring the Primacy of Rule of Law Over the Rule of Men - To Ensure Liberty Prevails Over Tyranny.* Chattanooga: Publius Press.

Aligieiri, D., & Diardi, J. (1954). *The Inferno.* New York: Signet Classics New American Library, a division of Penguin Group, Inc.

American Academy of Arts & Sciences. (2020). *Final Report and Recommendations from the Commission on the Practice of Democratic Citizenship: Our Common Purpose: Reinventing American Democracy for the 21st Century.* Cambridge: American Academy of Arts & Sciences.

Andrews, H. (2021). *Boomers: The Men and Women Who Promised Freedom and Delivered Disaster.* New York: Sentinel.

Barker, R. (1968). *Ecological Psychology: Concepts and methods for studying the environment of human behavior.* Palo Alto, CA: Stanford University Press.

Basu, K. (2011). *Beyond the Invisible Hand: Groundwork for a New Economics.* Princeton: Princeton University Press.

Bell, D. (1973). *The Coming of Post-Industrial Society: a Venture in Social Forecasting.* New York: Basic Books, Inc.

Bell, P. A., Fisher, J. D., Baum, A., & Greene, T. C. (1990). *Environmental Psychology, Third Edition.* Philadelphia: Holt, Rinehart and Winston, Inc.

Besharov, E. D. (1999). *America's Disconnected Youth: Toward a Preventive Strategy.* Washington, D.C.: Child Welfare League of America, Inc. and the American Enterprise Institute for Public Policy Research.

Bosché, G. (2016). *5 Millrnnial Myths: The Handbook for Managing and Motivating Millennials, 2nd Edition.* United States of America: BeReadyMEDIA, LLC.

Brooks, D. (2015). *The Road to Character.* New York: Random House.

Burrus, D. (1993). *Techno Trends: How to Use Technology to Go Beyong Your Competition.* New York: Harper Business a Division of Harper Collins Publishers.

Carlin, G. (2010, November 14). George Carlin on some cultural issues. *You Tube*, p. https://www.youtube.com/watch?v=YLuZjpxmsZQ.

Carlson, T. (2018). *Ship of Fools: How a Selfish Ruling Class is Bringing America to the Brink of Revolution.* New York: Free Press and imprint of Simon and Schuster, Inc.

Chomsky, N. (2015). Chomsky & Krauss: An Origins Project Dialogue, Part 1 of 2. *Arizona State University's Origins Project Dialogue* (pp. 1 hr, 42 mins, 12 secs.). Tempe: ShirleyFilms on YouTube.

Christensen, C. (2016). Where Does Growth Come From? . *Talks at Google* (p. June 23). Mountain View, CA: You Tube.

Clark, K. B. (1963). *Prejudice and Your Child, 2nd Edition, Enlarged: A Clear Dispassionate Analysis of Factors Which Contribute to Prejudice, Along With*

Helpful Suggestions As To What You Can Do To Reduce And Prevent Feelings of Prejudice In Your Child. Boston: Beacon Press.

Clawson, D., Neustadtl, A., & Scott, D. (1992). *Money Talks: Corporate Pacs and Political Influence.* New York: Basic Books, a Perseus Books Group.

Clawson, D., Neustadtl, A., & Weller, M. (1998). *Dollars and Votes: How Business Campaign Contributions Subvert Democracy.* Philadelphia: Temple University Press.

Congressional Budget Office. (2019). *Projected Changes in the Distribution of Household Income, 2016 to 2021.* Washington, D.C.: Congress of the United States of America.

Csikszentmihalyi, M. (1991). *Flow: The Psychology of Optimal Experience.* Chicago: Haper & Row.

Davenport, D., & Skandera, H. (2003). Civic Associations. In E. Peter Berkowitz, *Never a Matter of Indifference: Sustaining Virtue in a Free Republic* (pp. 59-83). Stanford: Stanford University Press.

DeSilver, D. (2019). *Despite global concerns about democracy, more than half of countries are democratic.* Washington, D.C.: Fact Tank News in the Numbers, The Pew Center.

Dewey, J. (1922). *Democracy and Education: An introduction to the Philosophy of Education* . New York: The McMillan Company.

Dworkin, R. (2006). *Is Democracy Possible Here? Principles for a New Political Debate.* Princeton: Princeton University Press.

Economist, I. U. (2020). *Democracy Index 2019: A year of democratic setbacks and popular protest.* London: The Economist Intelligence Unit Limited.

Edman, I. (1928). *The Works of Plato.* New York: Simon and Schuster for The Modern Library by Random House.

Ehrlich, T. (2000). *Civic Responsibility And Higher Education: American Council on Education Oryx Press Series on Higher Education).* New York: Oryx Press of Greenwood Publishing Group.

Eitzen, D. S., & Zinn, M. B. (1989). *The Reshaping of America: Social Consequences of the Changing Economy.* Englewood Cliffs: Prentice-Hall, Inc.

Ewing, S. (1976). *Captains of Consciousness: Advertising and the Social Roots of the Consumer Culture.* New York: McGraw-Hill Book Company.

Farrand, M. (1911). *The Records of the Federal Convention of 1787.* New Haven: Yale University Press.

Fearside, W. Ward & Holther, William B. (1959). *Fallacy: The Counterfeit of Argument.* Eglewood Cliffs: Prentice Hall.

Featherstone, M. (1995). *Undoing Culture: Globalization, Postmodernism, and Identity.* London: Sage Publications.

Franti, M. (1992, Disposable Heroes of Hiphoprisy Song). Television, the Drug of the Nation. *"Hypocrisy Is The Greatest Luxury"*, p. 3.

Fromm, E. (1956). *The Art of Loving.* New York: Harper and Row, Inc.

Gabriel, Y., & Lang, T. (1995). *The Unmanageable Consumer: Contemporary Consumption and its Fragmentation.* London: SAGE Publications.

Gelfand, M. (2018). *Rule Makers Rule Breakers: How Tight and Loose Cultures Wire our World.* New York: Scribner, and imprint of Simon & Schuster, Inc.

Gergen, K. J. (1991). *The Saturated Self: Dilemmas of Identity in Contemporary Life.* New York: Basic Books, a division of HarperCollins Publishers, Inc.

Gibney, B. C. (2017). *A Generation of Sociopaths: How the Baby Boomers Betrayed America.* New York: Hachette Books Group.

Goldberg, J. (2018). *Suicide of the West: How the Rebirth of Tribalism, Populism, Nationalism, and Identity Politics Is Destroying American Democracy.* New York: Crown Forum.

Guinness, O. (1998). *The Call: Finding and Fulfilling the Central Purpose of Your Life.* Nashville: Word Publishing.

Gutmann, M. (2019). Milton S. Hershey and the Chocolate Empire. In (. o. Barbara I. Dewey, *Pennsylvania Center for the Book* (pp. https://pabook.libraries.psu.edu/literary-cultural-heritage-map-pa/feature-articles/milton-s-hershey-and-chocolate-empire). University Park: Pennsylvania State University .

Hage, J. (2011). *Restoring the Innovative Edge: Driving the Evolution of Science and Technology.* Stanford: Stanford Businees Books, and Imprint of Stanford University Press.

Hage, J. (2020). *Knowledge Evolution and Societal Transformations: Action Theory to Solve Adaptive Problems.* New York, NY, USA: Anthem Press.

Haidt, J., & Lukianoff, G. (2018). *The Coddling of the American Mind: How Good Intentions and Bad Ideas Are Setting Up a Generation for Failure.* New York: Penguin.

Harari, Y. N. (2019). *21 Lessons for the 21st Century.* New York: Spiegel & Grau, Random House, Penguin Random House.

Harris, M. (1989). *Our Kind: Who We Are, Where We Came From, Where We Are Going* . Philadelphia: Harper & Row.

Hayek, F. A. (1960). *The Constitution of Liberty.* Chicago: University of Chicago Press.

Heath, D. (2020). *Upstream: The Quest to Solve Problems Before They Happen.* New York: Avid Reader Press, an imprint of Simon & Schuster, Inc.

Horst W. J. Rittel, a. M. (1973). Dilemmas in a General Theory of Planning. *Policy Sciences 4, No. 2,* 155-69.

Jackson, J. B. (1984). *Discovering the Vernacular Landscape.* New Haven: Yale University Press.

Jacobs, J. (1961). *The Death and Life of Great American Cities.* New York: Vintage Books, a Division of Random House, Inc.

Jencks, E. C., & Patterson, P. E. (1991). *The Urban Underclass.* Washington, D.C.: The Brookings Institution.

Jones, L. Y. (1980). *Great Expectations: America and the Baby Boom Generation.* New York: Ballantine Books.

Kammeyer, K. C., Ritzer, G., & Yetman, N. R. (1992). *Sociology: Experiencing Changing Societies 5th Edition.* Boston: Allyn and Bacon.

Knight, F. H. (1921). *Risk, Uncertainty, and Profit.* New York: The Riverside Press, Houghton Mifflin Company.

Kübler-Ross, E. (1969). *On Death and Dying: What the dying have to teach us doctors, nurses, clergy and their own families.* New York: Simon & Schuster/Collier Books.

Kuhn, T. S. (1962). *The Structure of Scientific Revolutions.* Chicago: University of Chicago Press.

Labaree, L. W. (1959). The Papers of Benjamin Franklin, vol. 1, January 6, 1706 through December 31, 1734. New Haven: Yale University Press.

Lasch, C. (1979). *The Culture of Narcissism: American Life in an Age of Diminishing Expectations*. New York: W. W. Norton.

Levin, M. R. (2004). *Liberty and Tyranny: A Conservative Manifesto*. New York: Threshold Editions, Gallery Publishing Group of Simon & Schuster.

Levy, D. (1983). *A Social Geography of the City*. New York: Harper & Row Publishers.

Levy, R. H. (2020). *Mending America's Political Divide: What Science Tells Us About Solving The Political Hatred Between The Left and The Right*. Seattle: USA Peoplehood Press.

Magistrale, P. (2020). *We The People Are The Problem: How Americans Betrayed America*. New York: Peter Magistrale.

Mansfield, H. C. (2003). Liberty and Virtue in the American Founding. In P. Berkowitz, *Never a Matter of Indifference: Sustaining Virtue in a Free Republic* (pp. 4-28). Stanford, CA: Hoover Institution Press.

Mayer, A. I. (1970). *Cornerstones of Freedom: The Story of Old Glory*. Chicago: The Childrens Press, Regensteiner Publishing Enterprises, Inc.

Mills, C. W. (1956). *The Power Elite*. New York: Oxford University Press.

Mokyr, J. (1998). *The Second Industrial Revolution, 1870-1914*. Evanston, IL: Northwestern University.

Moore, M. J. (2019). *Foundations for Liberty*. Tulsa: Self Published for Amazon Kindle.

Moses, J. (1989). *Oneness: Great Principles Shared by All Religions*. New York: Fawcett Columbine Book by Ballantined Books, a division of Random House, Inc.

Naisbitt, J. (1984). *Megatrends: Ten New Directions Transforming Our Lives*. New York: Warner Books.

Osbon, D. K. (1991). *Reflections on the Art of Living: A Joseph Campbell Companion*. New York: HarperCollins Publishers for the Joseph Campbell Foundation.

Owen, D., Hartzell, K., & Sanchez, C. (2020). *The James Madison Legacy Project: Evaluation Report*. Washington, D.C. : James Madison Legacy Project, University of Georgetown, U.S. Department of Education.

Patterson, K., Grenny, J., McMillan, R., & Switzler, A. (2012). *Crucial Conversations: Tools for Talking When Stakes Are High, 2nd Edition*. New York: McGraw Hill.

Peter G. Peterson Foundation. (2020, August 29). National Debt Clock. *Website*, pp. https://www.pgpf.org/national-debt-clock.

Piketty, T. (2014). *Capital in the Twenty-First Century*. Cambridge: The Belknap Press of the Harvard University Press.

Pritchard, C. L. (1997). *Risk Management Concepts and Guidance*. Arlington, Virginia: ESI International.

Putnam, R. D. (1993). *Making Democracy Work: Civic Traditions in Northern Italy*. Princeton: Princeton University Press.

Putnam, R. D. (2000). *Bowling Alone: The Collapse and Revival of American Community*. New York: Simon & Schuster Paperbacks.

Putnam, R. D., Feldstein, L. M., & Cohen, D. (2003). *Better Together: Restoring the American Community*. New York: Simon and Schuster.

Rakove, J. N. (1996). *Original Meanings: Politics and Ideas in the Making of the Constitution.* New York: Vintage Books.

Rambo, L. R. (1993). *Understanding Religious Conversion.* New Haven: Yale University Press.

Rapoport, A. (1974). *Fights, Games, and Debates.* Ann Arbor: The University of Michigan Press.

Reich, R. B. (2020). *The System: Who Rigged It, How We Fix It.* New York: Alfred A. Knopf.

Reid, V. (1988). Which Way to America? In L. Colour, *Vivid* (p. 11). New York: Epic Records.

Rittel, H. W., & Webber, M. M. (1973). Dilemmas in a General Theory of Planning. *Policy Sciences 4, No. 2,* 155-69.

Roberts, K. A. (1990). *Religion in Sociological Perspective, Second Edition.* Belmont: Wadsworth Publishing Company.

Roberts-Miller, P. (2017). *Demagoguery and Democracy.* New York: The Experiment, LLC.

Rose, S. (2020). *Squeezing the middle class: Income trajectories from 1967 to 2016.* Washington, D.C.: The Brookings Institute.

Rudofsky, B. (1964). *Architecture without architects, an introduction to nonpedigreed architecture.* Garden City, NY: Museum of Modern Art; distributed by Doubleday.

Schmookler, A. B. (1988). *Out of Weakness: Healing the Wounds that Drive Us to War.* New York: Bantam Books.

Schumacher, E. (1973). *Small is Beautiful: Economics as if People Mattered.* Philadelphia: Blond & Briggs, LTD reprinted with permission for Perennial Library by Harper & Rowe Publishers.

Segen, J. C. (2002). *McGraw-Hill Concise Dictionary of Modern Medicine.* New York: The McGraw-Hill Companies, Inc.

Shah, M. N. (2020). *Millennials: Poised to Lead: For A Generation Who Are the Future.* Prune, India: Vayati Sytems and Research, Inc.

Simon, N. (2020). *Contract to Unite America: Ten Reforms to Reclaim Our Republic.* Herndon, VA: Real Clear Publishing.

Sinek, S. (2012). *Leaders Eat Last: Why Some Teams Pull Together and Others Don't.* New York: Penguin Random House.

Skinner, B. F. (1974). *About Behaviorism.* New York: Vintage Books, A Division of Random House.

Skousen, W. C. (1981). *The 5000 Year Leap: The 28 Great Ideas That Changed the World.* Malta, Idaho: National Center for Constitutional Studies.

Solzhenitsyn, A. (1974). *The Gulag Archipelago: Volume 1: An Experiment in Literary Investigation, Volume 2: The Destructive Labor Camps The Soul and Barbed Wire, Volume 3: Katorga Exile Stalin Is No More.* New York: Harper & Row and HarperCollins Publishers .

Sternberg, J. C. (2019). *The Theft of a Decade: How the Baby Boomers Stole the Millennials' Economic Future.* New York: PublicAffairs.

Sternberg, R. J. (1988). *The triangle of love.* New York: Basic Books.

Stockdale, A. J. (1987). Machiavelli, Management, and Moral Leadership. *Journal of Military Ethics: Reflections on Principles—the profession of arms, military leadership, ethical practices, war and morality, educating the citizen-soldier.*, 39.

Strauss, W., & Howe, N. (1991). *Generations: The History of America's Future, 1854 to 2069*. New York: Harper Perennial.

Task Force on Political Science in the 21st Century. (2011). *Political Science in the 21st Century*. Washington, D.C.: American Political Science Association.

Taylor, P. (2014). *The Next America: Boomers, Millennials, and the Looming Generational Showdown*. Washington, D.C.: Pew Research Center.

The National Commission on Civic Renewal. (1997). *A Nation of Spectators: How Civic Disengagement Weakens America and What We Can Do About It*. College Park: University of Maryland.

Toffler, A. (1984). *The Third Wave*. New York: Bantam Books.

Trilling, L. (1965). *Beyond Culture: Essays on Literature and Learning*. New York: Viking Adult.

Twenge, J. M., & Campbell, W. K. (2009). *The Narcissism Epidemic: Living in the Age of Entitlement*. New York: Atria Paperback

United States Central Intelligence Agency. (2020). *The World Fact Book 2020*. Washington, D.C.: U.S. C.I.A. .

Valentine, J., & Valentine, W. (1985). Money's Too Tight To Mention. In S. R. Band), *Picture Book (Album)* (p. 4 mins. 13 secs.). West Hollywood: Elektra Records .

Volti, R. (1988). *Society and Technological Change*. New York: St. Martin's Press.

Westhues, K. (1982). *First Sociology*. New York: McGraw-Hill Book Company.

Will, G. F. (2019). *The Conservative Sensibility*. New York: Hachette Books.

Willetts, L. D. (2020). The Pinch: How the Baby Boomers Took Their Children's Future - And Why They Should Give it Back. *You Tube Video - https://www.youtube.com/watch?v=ZuXzvjBYW8A* (p. 47:25 minutes). London: Royal Institution Talks, Intergenerational Centre Resolution Foundation.

Wilson, E. O. (1978). *On Human Nature*. Havard University Press: Cambridge.

Wilson, W. J. (1987). *The Truly Disadvantaged: The Inner City, The Underclass, and Public Policy*. Chicago: The University of Chicago Press.

Woodard, C. (2011). *American Nations: A History of the Eleven Rival Regional Cultures of North America*. New York: Penguin Books.

Wright, R. (1994). *The Moral Animal, Evolutionary Psychology and Everyday Life, Why We Are The Way We Are: The New Science of Evolutionary Psychology,* . New York: Vintage Books.

Acknowledgments

I acknowledge my fellow veterans. They dedicated themselves to defending the Constitution against all enemies foreign and domestic. To all those with whom I directly served thank you for listening to me as I rambled on about my perceptions of changes in our society. You tolerantly lent me your ear, permitted my rants, and offered your sincere thoughts. Our conversations helped me formulate my ideas, gain clarity of thought and purpose, and realize what I felt I had to say. With this book, I propose what I believe needs done, and I stir it up. (R.J., Steve, Brian, Greg, am I making sense, yet?). "Can Do" Seabees, this is our moment to help domestically. "We build we fight" with compassion for others, for peace with freedom for the "Don't Tread on Me" United States.

I acknowledge the Self-Publishing School for its "Be a Bestseller" course, which taught me how to write and publish this book. I acknowledge my copy editor, Robin L. Reed, for helping me quickly get this book as comprehendible as possible. I acknowledge my cover design team at 100 Covers, who patiently translated my vision into a patriotic cover!

I acknowledge the University of Maryland professors who taught me. Many of their lessons illuminated my understanding of the world. Their assigned readings, and books written by them, served as references for this tome for the ages. If my remedy motivates the population to unite as one people—a wholesome citizenry working for liberty and defending the Constitution in republic practicing democracy—then the benefiting everyday people will have you all to thank, too! Go Terps! Be bold. Be curious. Be passionate. Be inspiring. Be fearless! (Testudo rocks as a mascot!)

I acknowledge the obvious question whether I wrote this book to launch myself into national politics. I did not. Until every adult American reads this book, I will not step into the fray, because until they have, they will not be receptive to what I have to say. Moreover, the whole citizenry must adjust and begin to lead. We must put our younger generations into micro, meso, and macro offices. With integrity, they must guide our polity and our economy properly to achieve our American goal. This requires representing our societal sustainment needs. First of which is making our society as envisioned in the Preamble, with justice and liberty for all. As with a bike rider, the faster we go, the greater our stability. So it is with liberty. The more we the everyday people enjoy its blessings, the more stable and secure our nation will be.

I acknowledge I wrote this book during a global pandemic that challenged societies, peoples, and persons at the micro, meso, and macro levels. Oddly, the adaptation to which made writing this book possible. It was my personal project to get through it, myself intact. Ready to get back to life without a mask, I am happy to set it free into the public realm's marketplace of ideas on July 4th, 2021

Before We Part

I suspect you might be curious about the generation in which my birth year designates me. Demographically, I am in the valley between the boomers and Generation X, but it is not a valley of death. It is a fertile crescent of new ideas for thriving while being alive. Historians Strauss & Howe would say I am of the Thirteeners generation, a cohort seemingly all born on Friday the 13th, perpetual adolescents suffering from a lot of bad stuff when coming of age in the '80s, (think Vietnam War, latchkey kids, deskilling by computers, Gulf Wars, etc.). I don't feel I was "born under a bad sign" (Albert King 1967). I feel lucky to have been born. At times, I think like a boomer, a Gen Xer, and a millennial, but mostly I think like a Libertarian from the era of our founding, wanting to preserve the union while improving us as we work to achieve our project's goal and attain its objectives for posterity and ourselves. I believe in the pledge of allegiance. I swore to defend the Constitution. This makes me a patriot. To make the US live up to its calling is a worthy cause; for which on these 650 pages, I caw like a jay, a corvine crier of the divine destination for humanity: democracy!

Do you want to join me in this mission to spawn people to carry on E-SASSY-T-TUF-FT-CAUCUS? Do you want to know more about liberty and democracy? Please check out the resources in the Appendix. Read our tomes, know our canons, get together in groups, and discuss them. Invite me on your journeys back in time and forward into the future by imagining innovations that might restore the sanctity of liberty and yield justice for all. You can find me on Facebook @RealRocknRollPoetry. Visit my website, JeffersonianJeff.com, for more of my creative explorations.

Importantly, to aid us expand the pool of ready and willing patriotic citizens willing to live a truly American life by E-SASSY-T-TUF-FT-CAUCUS as 21st-century citizen patriots, who will demand that citizens in positions of authority IDEALS liberty and justice for all—to move our USE out into the sea of opportunity, where it belongs. To help it head in its proper direction of our first principles, please leave your honest review of this book on Amazon or whichever bookseller's website from which you purchased it. This will assist us enlarge our cadre, create our social movement to save the Constitution, and preserve prosperity's potential for posterity and ourselves.

*P*enultimate Page

Congratulations! You made it. I hope your head does not hurt too badly. I know I tried to make you think. Imagine how writhing it racked my brain! I hope you learned something new. I hope you found the thinking tools for analyzing and evaluating power in society useful for putting citizenship first in your life, so that we may IDEALS liberty for posterity and ourselves.

As mentioned in Chapter 1, here is its diagram below for you to complete again. Choose the squares you agree with to find your polemic. Compare it to the one you did when you began reading. Reflect upon any differences you see between the two. See if it remained the same, or how much, and how it changed.

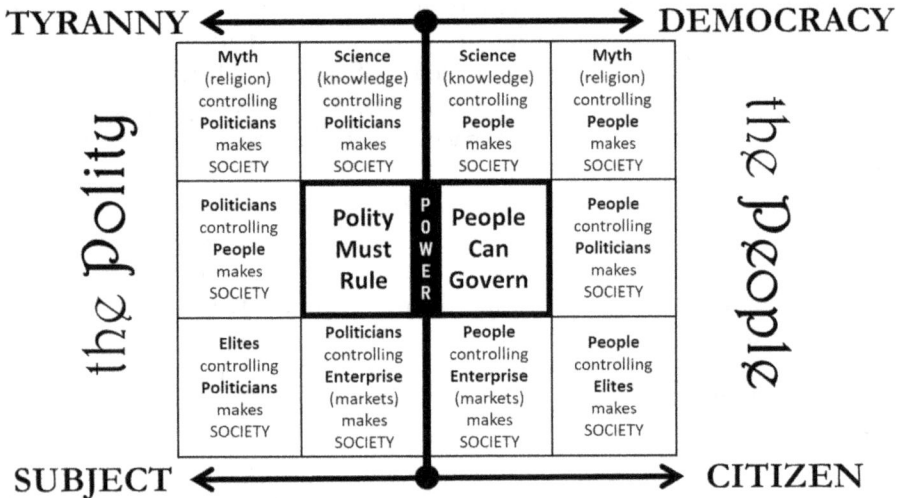

Figure 1-5: Power in Tyranny and Democracy Assessment Card

I wrote this book to inspire people to get involved in defending liberty for the everyday people in every way. We need to remove baby doomer politicians as quickly as possible. We need to serve the goal and objectives of the Preamble. For more awareness about the fiscal policy challenges we now face because of the doomers, play this game: https://fiscalship.org/index.php

Thank you for reading my book on how we the everyday people must unify, exhibiting service above selfishness, saying yes to the utmost full-fledged thoroughgoing constitutionally allied united citizenshipping, understandingly synchronized. By behaving as such, we can put our people power to the purpose of being one American people, e pluribus unum, living committed virtuous lives in revived liberty. We will remove doomerism from our culture, restore the vitality of democracy, and rebalance societal powers as we guide our society to serve us in the ways of wisdom, not doomerism.

*L*ast Page

I'll leave you now with some Rock 'n' Roll comedy.

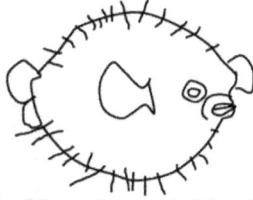

Figure 7-4: Baby Doomer. The Monochromatic Blowfish

Announcements in a Newspaper:

"In a feudalistic effort today on Stock St., the Dutch City witnessed a strategic event meant to bring peace between two warring kingdoms, whose battles' collateral damages have brought about a decline in the empire's stature and quality. The ceremony of pageantry, pomp, and circumstance was meant to entertain the masses and regain their near-worshipful adoration for the famous families. What happened? Well after years of courtship, Miss Ella Jill Lamit (the Red tribe's elite but inelegant elephant) married Mstr. Jack Ashley Doomer (the Blue tribe's highfalutin donkey). Later that day, the happy couple settled in for their honeymoon at the gilded, exclusive, five-star hotel on Advertmans Ave built by Ella's father, who was ecstatic about the new plutocracy established with the dowry of his obedient, albeit a bit idiotic, daughter's marriage."

<u>Six months later.</u> *"Jack & Jill are proud to announce the birth of their orange-spotted and black-dotted gray and white diodontidae tetrodotoxin porcupine pufferfish, who they affectionately named Baby Donellier Doomer, after the town friar who was once a squire in Sea Lake near the atelier of great fablers and famous painters"*

<u>Three years later.</u> *"Today, Mr. & Mrs. Doomer were called to the City Center Preschool to retrieve their child, who was found out of normal form. Having selfishly consumed all the air and water available that the school shared, he got all puffed up. Then he aggressively, or accidentally, began poking holes in all the others fish in the class. Needless to say, Little Baby D. will be homeschooled for the rest of the year to protect the community."*

<u>Thirty-six years later.</u> *"In the news today, after release from hospitalization after an altercation with a real muscle mollusk, poison wholesaler Mstr. Baby D. Doomer promised that one day he would get even. He cursed he would prove that he was right, and that the fight in which he was injured was not his fault, that he did not try to eat Mr. Sheldon Clamitus, despite evidence to the contrary in the form of an exact match of his teeth marks found upon Sheldon's skull with Baby's dental records."*

<u>Forty-five years later.</u> *"Today's obituary reports that Mstr. Baby D. Doomer of Dutch City, a lonely fish living largely at sea and an occasional resident of the tiny fantasy island resort in the Gulf of Walrus near Mexantimanliness, succumbed from self-inflicted injuries after having started a brawl with the Green tribe's largely independently minded Captain "Larry" Liberty, the multicolored American Lobster. The police on scene stated that Lawrence acted in self-defense. The assailant, Donellier, spewed out a lethal skin toxin, but the turbulence generated by the lobster's vigorous lifesaving backward maneuver, coagulated it into a chemical clump. Panicking, he breathed spasmodically, inhaling his own vile weaponized bile until Mstr. Doomer choked to death on it. So purely poisonous, his attack backfired."*

*A*bout the Author

Jeffersonian Jeff is the "Purveyor of Rock n' Roll Poetry, Prose, Song Lyrics, Comedy, and Commentary on Democracy and Self-Government Preservation in the Republic of the United States of America." This book is an example of his commentary. He writes to encourage everyone to resist hypocrisy within, be civil, civically minded, neighborly, well informed, and politically active. He asserts that citizens in democracy must lead society with exemplary character, pressing for justice and liberty for all. We the everyday people must also hold those in authority accountable to the highest standards of conduct. If they cannot behave ethically and act with integrity, we must use reasonable jurisprudence to correct them.

A dedicated father and mother raised Jeff with three siblings. Dad was a US Marine turned small businessperson who raced dragsters and repaired automobile frames and bodies. Mom was a loyal, loving, great cook, skilled craftsperson who made the coolest Halloween costumes. A suburban super mom, she was a medical secretary before and after raising us while at night working as the family business's bookkeeper. Both volunteered to coach youth soccer, a team sport that teaches virtuous social character building values of training discipline, commitment, teamwork, grace under pressure, and cooperation in competition.

Artistic, athletic, musical, and mathematical, Jeff was an all-American boy growing up. He liked Mr. Rogers' question, "Won't you be my neighbor?" In college, he pursued wisdom, truth, and beauty. Majoring in construction, sociology, architecture, and community planning, he earned five degrees. Two of which were masters. Meanwhile, a "Twice the Citizen" US Navy Reservist he served ten years as a Seabee and thereafter as a Civil Engineer Corps officer. In 2021, he entered his 34th year of military service. During the week, he works for a real estate program making and maintaining architecture.

Jeff uses "Rock n' Roll" as an adjective. It refers to a uniquely American freedom to question authority respectfully, which is essential for the health of a republic. With roots of democracy and liberty, it creates an expressive popular culture. Born of the blood, sweat, and tears of common stock persons, Rock n' Roll—with its many cousins, Folk, Metal, R&B, Funk, Rap, and Pop—represents the everyday people. It inspires us to think for ourselves and resist propaganda telling us what to think. It celebrates the poetry of precious moments experienced in living. In the land of the free and home of the brave, it opens us to life's joys and pains, and every feeling between these. Rock n' roll expresses our humanity where happiness and sadness happen. Sometimes it provides tongue-in-cheek parodies that make fun of fictional fantasies presented as facts. Often it gives us a release from traumatic emotions.

Jeff sees the founders as the original all-American Rock n' Roll stars. After all, their Declaration of Independence gave the metaphorical middle finger to the world's most powerful empire, little England. That courageously foxy eyes-wide-open risk-taking took some real Rock n' Roll moxie!

WORDS HAVE MEANINGS

www.ingramcontent.com/pod-product-compliance
Lightning Source LLC
Chambersburg PA
CBHW060302030426
42336CB00011B/904